The Proba.......... ......

Prospects for Bayesian cognitive science

The Probabilistic Mind:
Prospects for Bayesian cognitive science

Edited by

Nick Chater
University College London
UK

and

Mike Oaksford
Birkbeck College London
UK

OXFORD
UNIVERSITY PRESS

OXFORD

UNIVERSITY PRESS

Great Clarendon Street, Oxford OX2 6DP

Oxford University Press is a department of the University of Oxford.
It furthers the University's objective of excellence in research, scholarship,
and education by publishing worldwide in

Oxford New York

Auckland Cape Town Dar es Salaam Hong Kong Karachi
Kuala Lumpur Madrid Melbourne Mexico City Nairobi
New Delhi Shanghai Taipei Toronto

With offices in

Argentina Austria Brazil Chile Czech Republic France Greece
Guatemala Hungary Italy Japan Poland Portugal Singapore
South Korea Switzerland Thailand Turkey Ukraine Vietnam

Oxford is a registered trade mark of Oxford University Press
in the UK and in certain other countries

Published in the United States
by Oxford University Press Inc., New York

© Oxford University Press, 2008

British Library Cataloguing in Publication Data

Data available

Library of Congress Cataloguing in Publication Data

Typeset by Cepha Imaging Private Ltd., Bangalore, India
Printed in Great Britain
on acid-free paper by
Ashford Colour Press Ltd., Gosport, Hampshire

ISBN 978–0–19–921609–3

10 9 8 7 6 5 4 3 2 1

Table of Contents

Contributors

Aaron P. Blaisdell
University of California,
Los Angeles, CA, USA

Henry Brighton
Center for Adaptive Behavior and
Cognition, Max Planck Institute for
Human Development, Berlin, Germany

Kevin R. Canini
University of California, Berkeley,
CA, USA

Nick Chater
University College London,
London, UK

Patricia W. Cheng
University of California,
Los Angeles, CA, USA

Aaron C. Courville
Université de Montréal,
Montreal, QC, Canada

David Danks
Carnegie Mellon University,
Pittsburgh, PA, USA and Institute for
Human and Machine Cognition,
Pensacola, FL, USA

Nathaniel D. Daw
New York University, NY, USA

Peter Dayan
Gatsby Computational Neuroscience
University College London, London, UK

Anat Elhalal
Birkbeck, University of London,
London, UK

Jacob Feldman
Rutgers University,
New Beunswick, USA

Philip M. Fernbach
Brown University, Providence, RI, USA

Klaus Fiedler
Universität Heidelberg, Heidelberg,
Germany

Gerd Gigerenzer
Center for Adaptive Behavior and
Cognition, Max Planck Institute for
Human Development, Berlin, Germany

Noah D. Goodman
Massachusetts Institute of Technology,
Cambridge, MA, USA

Thomas L. Griffiths
University of California,
Berkeley, CA, USA

York Hagmayer
University of Göttingen,
Göttingen, Germany

Ulrike Hahn
Cardiff University, UK

Patrik Hansson
Umeå University, Umeå, Sweden

Ralph Hertwig
University of Basel, Basel, Switzerland

David E. Huber
University of California, San Diego,
CA, USA

Peter Juslin
Uppsala University, Uppsala, Sweden

James L. McClelland
Stanford University, Palo Alto, CA, USA

Craig R. M. McKenzie
University of California,
San Diego, CA, USA

Daniel J. Navarro
University of Adelaide, Adelaide,
SA, Australia

Jonathan D. Nelson
University of California, San Diego, USA

Mike Oaksford
Birkbeck College London, London, UK

Timothy J. Pleskac
Michigan State University,
East Lansing, MI, USA

Adam N. Sanborn
Indiana University, Bloomington,
IN, USA

David R. Shanks
University College London,
London, UK

Shlomi Sher
Princeton University, Princeton,
NJ, USA

Keith Simpson
University of Warwick,
Coventry, UK

Steven Sloman
Brown University, Providence, RI, USA

Maarten Speekenbrink
University College London, London, UK

Neil Stewart
University of Warwick, Coventry, UK

Mark Steyvers
University of California, Irvine, USA

Joshua B. Tenenbaum
Massachusetts Institute of Technology,
Cambridge, MA, USA

Marius Usher
Birkbeck, University of London,
London, UK

Michael R. Waldmann
University of Göttingen, Göttingen,
Germany

Anders Winman
Uppsala University, Uppsala, Sweden

Alan Yuille
University of California, Los Angeles,
CA, USA

Part 1

Foundations

Chapter 1

The probabilistic mind: prospects for a Bayesian cognitive science

Nick Chater

University College London, London, UK

Mike Oaksford

Birkbeck College London, London, UK

From the perspective of human cognition, the world is a highly uncertain place. Our perceptual representations of the environment are inferred from surprisingly sparse sensory input; the consequences of our actions are typically highly unpredictable; and even our scientific proposals concerning the 'laws of nature' are at best conjectures, rather than cold certainties. We are continually surprised by unexpected turns of events; unpredicted sensory data; and the overthrow of apparently solid scientific laws.

This lack of certainty does not seem to lead to cognitive paralysis—indeed, dealing with uncertainty is, we might expect, an everyday challenge for cognitive systems, human, or animal. But dealing with uncertainty successfully presumably requires the application of some kind of *method*—i.e., conforming with, perhaps only approximately, some set of principles. Without some such foundation, the question of *why* the cognitive system copes with uncertainty (well-enough, most of the time) is left unanswered. Any particular instance of uncertain reasoning may, of course, be explained by postulating that the cognitive system follows some special strategy, rather than general inference principles. But the mind is able to deal with a hugely complex and continually changing informational environment, for which special-purpose strategies cannot credibly pre-exist.

One natural place to look for the foundation for successful reasoning about uncertainty is the mathematical theory of probability—and this book is concerned with the question of whether, or when, a probabilistic framework is useful for constructing models of cognition. There are two reasons, independent of specific psychological considerations, which suggest that it is worth considering seriously a probabilistic perspective on human cognition.

The first is normative. It turns out that very mild restrictions on how 'degrees of belief' *should* behave, lead to the conclusion that such degrees of belief can be mapped to the [0,1] interval, and should obey the laws of probability. For example, the celebrated 'Dutch book theorem' shows that, under fairly general conditions, any gambler whose subjective probabilities deviate from the laws of probability, however slightly, can be mercilessly exploited—i.e., the gambler will cheerfully accept a combination of bets such that, whatever happens, he or she is certain to lose money. Moreover, there are many such arguments, starting with different normative assumptions, which converge on the assumption that 'degrees of belief' should be governed by probability. Thus, if we want to explain how it is that people (and, indeed, animals) are able to cope so successfully with their highly uncertain world, the norms of probability provide the beginnings of an answer—to the extent that the mind reasons probabilistically, the normative justifications that imply that this is the 'right' way to reason about uncertainty, and go some way to explaining how it is that the cognitive system deals with uncertainty with a reasonable degree of success.

Alongside these *a priori* normative arguments stands a more practical reason to take probabilistic models of the mind seriously, which arises from artificial intelligence, and related fields such as computer vision and computational linguistics. Understanding any aspect of the biological world is, to some degree, a matter of reverse engineering—of inferring engineering principles from data. Reverse engineering is, though, of course, strongly constrained by the range of options offered by current 'engineering' technologies. There has been something of a probabilistic revolution in the last two decades in proposals concerning engineering solutions to the types of problems solved by the cognitive system. Probabilistic approaches have been increasingly ubiquitous, and widely used, particularly in the light of technical developments that make complex probabilistic models formally and computationally more manageable. From knowledge-bases, to perception, to language and motor control, there has been widespread application of sophisticated probabilistic methods in computational modelling (e.g., Chater *et al.* 2006).

So we have two reasons to take probabilistic models of the mind seriously. Probability is arguably the 'right' way to deal with uncertainty; and it proves practically useful in solving cognitively relevant engineering problems. But how useful does the approach to cognition prove to be in practice? How far does it yield insights into cognition? How far do alternative models provide a better account? In precisely what sense, if any, should the mind be viewed as probabilistic?

In terms of superficial measures of research activity, the signs seem to be positive. The last two decades have seen a steady rise of probabilistic cognitive models, to the degree that the probabilistic viewpoint is now seen as a standard, rather than esoteric, theoretical approach, throughout the cognitive sciences. Useful collections include Blakemore (1990) and Knill & Richards (1996) on perception as probabilistic inference; Manning & Schütze (1999) on the probabilistic viewpoint in computational models of language processing; and Oaksford & Chater (1998a) for a survey of probabilistic cognitive models in high level cognition.

The purpose of this book, and the meeting from which it grew, is to take stock of the state of the growing field of probabilistic cognitive models; to consider what has been achieved; and to ask how probabilistic models should be interpreted, and whether, or in which domains, the field is likely to be productive. In this introductory chapter, we aim to sketch some of the background issues in the field; and to set the scene for the chapters that follow.

The probabilistic approach

The vision of probability as a model of thought is as old as the study of probability itself. Indeed, from the outset of the development of the mathematics of probability, the notion had a dual aspect: serving both as a *normative* calculus dictating how people *should* reason about chance events, such as shipping losses or rolls of a dice, but at the same time interpreted as a *descriptive* theory of how people actually do reason about uncertainty. The very title of Bernouilli's great work, *The art of conjecture* (Bernouilli, 1713), nicely embodies this ambiguity—suggesting that it is both a manual concerning how this art should be practiced, and a description of how the art is actually conducted. This dual perspective was, indeed, not confined merely to probability, but also applied equally well to logic, the calculus of certain reasoning. Thus Boole's (1958/1854) *The Laws of Thought*, which deals with both logical and probabilistic reasoning, also embodies the ambiguity implicit in its title—it aims to be both a description of how thought works; but also views the laws of thought as providing norms to which reason should conform.

In retrospect, the identification, or perhaps conflation, of normative and descriptive programmes seems anomalous. Towards the end of the 19th century, mathematics began to break away from the morass of psychological intuition; and throughout the 20th century, increasingly formal and abstract programmes for the foundations of mathematics developed, seeming ever more distant from psychological notions. Thus, in the context of probability, Kolmogorov provided an axiomatization of probability in terms of σ-algebras, which views probability theory as an abstract formal structure, with no particular linkage to psychological notions concerning degree of belief or plausibility. Indeed, the idea that mathematics should be rooted in psychological notions became increasingly unpopular, and the perspective of *psychologism* became philosophically disreputable. At a practical level, too, the mathematics and psychology of probability became ever more distant. The mathematics became increasingly formally sophisticated, with spectacular results; but most of this work explicitly disavowed the idea that probability was about beliefs at all. The most popular perspective on probability took the view that probabilities should be interpreted, instead, as limiting frequencies over repeatable events. Thus, to say that the probability of a coin falling heads is 1/2 is to say something like: in the limit, if this event is repeated indefinitely, the proportion of times that the coin comes up heads will tend towards 1/2. This frequentist (von Mises, 1957) interpretation of probability aims to separate probability entirely from the beliefs of any particular person observing the coin—the probability is supposed to be a fact about the coin, not about degrees of belief of an observer of the coin.

The premise underlying much of the work in this book is that this divorce was somewhat premature—and that, at minimum, a limited reconciliation should be attempted. In particular, the conjecture is that many aspect of thought can be understood as, at some level of approximation at least, embodying probabilistic calculations.

We mentioned above that, normative considerations aside, one appeal of probabilistic models of cognition is that probability has swept into vogue in fields concerned with engineering solution to information processing problems analogous to those solved by the brain. And this work has overwhelmingly taken the subjectivist rather than the frequentist view of probability, i.e. probabilities are viewed as degrees of belief. One reason for this is that, in many practical applications, the frequentist interpretation of probability simply does not apply—probabilities can only be viewed as degrees of belief (or, more neutrally, degrees of partial information—after all, we may not want to attribute full-blown belief to a simple computational model, or an elementary cognitive process). Thus, in speech recognition or computational vision, each sensory input is enormously complex and will never be encountered again. Hence, there is no meaningful limiting frequency concerning the probability that this particular image on the retina is caused by seeing a dog or a wolf. It definitely is one or the other (the frequencies are 0 or 1 for each category). Similarly, the frequentist interpretation is not appropriate for interpreting uncertainty concerning scientific hypotheses, because, of course, any scientific hypothesis holds, or it does not; and hence limiting frequencies across many trials make no sense. In cases where the goal is to quantify the uncertainty about a state of the world, the uncertainty resides in the computational system (the human or animal brain, the machine learner) attempting to infer the probability. But once we interpret probability as concerning subjective states of belief or information—i.e., once we adopt the *subjective* interpretation of probability—then it is natural to frame the computational challenge of recognizing a word, an animal, an action, or a scientific hypothesis, purely as a matter of probabilistic calculation. Indeed, according to results such as the Dutch book theorem, mentioned above, once we start to assign degrees of uncertainty to states of any kind, it is mandatory that we use the laws of probability to manipulate these uncertainties, on pain of demonstrable irrationality (e.g., being willing to accept combinations of gambles leading to a certain loss).

In perception, as well as in many aspects of learning and reasoning, the primary goal is working out the probability of various possible hypotheses about the state of the world, given a set of data. This is typically done indirectly, by viewing the various hypotheses about the world as implying probabilities concerning the possible sensory data. An elementary identity of probability allows us to relate the probabilities that we are interested in, $Pr(H_i|D)$ (the probability that hypothesis H_i is true, given the observed data, D), in terms of probabilities that are presumed to be implicit in the hypotheses themselves. The elementary identity follows immediately from the definition of conditional probability:

$$Pr(H_i|D)Pr(D) = Pr(H_i,D) = Pr(D|H_i)Pr(H_i)$$

so that we obtain:

$$Pr(H_i|D) = \frac{Pr(D|H_i)Pr(H_i)}{Pr(D)},$$

which is Bayes' theorem. The probability of the data is not, of course, known independently of the hypotheses that might generate that data—so in practice $Pr(D)$ is typically expanded using the probabilistic identity:

$$Pr(D) = \sum_j Pr(D|H_j)Pr(H_j).$$

Thus, taking a subjective approach to probability, where states of the world may be viewed as uncertain, from the point of view of an agent, implies that making inferences about the likely state of the world is a matter of probabilistic calculation; and such calculations typically invoke Bayes' theorem, to invert the relationship between hypothesis and data. The prevalence of Bayes theorem in this type of calculation has led to this approach to statistics (Bernardo & Smith, 1994), machine learning (Mackay, 2003), and scientific reasoning (Howson & Urbach, 1993) to be known as the Bayesian approach—but the point of controversy is not of course the probabilistic identity that is Bayes' theorem; but rather the adoption of the subjective interpretation of probability. Indeed, in cognitive science, given that almost all applications of probability require a subjective interpretation of uncertainty, the probabilistic approach and the Bayesian approach are large synonymous.

Levels of probabilistic explanation

Probability is, we have suggested, potentially relevant to understanding the mind. But it can be applied in a range of different ways, ranging from probabilistic analysis of the neural processes in perception and motor control to normative description of how decision makers should act in economic contexts. But these seem to be explanations at very different levels. It is worth pausing briefly to consider the range of different levels of analysis at which probabilistic ideas may be applied, and hence to clarify the claims that are (and are not) being made in the chapters in this book.

We suggest that the variety of types of explanation can usefully be understood in terms of Marr's (1982) celebrated distinction between three levels of computational explanation: the *computational* level, which specifies the nature of the cognitive problem being solved, the information involved in solving it, and the logic by which it can be solved (this is closely related to the level of rational analysis, see Anderson, 1990, 1991a; Anderson & Milson, 1989; Anderson & Schooler, 1991; Oaksford & Chater, 1994, 1998a); the *algorithmic* level, which specifies the representations and processes by which solutions to the problem are computed; and the *implementational* level, which specifies how these representations and processes are realized in neural terms.

The probabilistic models and methods described in this book have potential relevance at each of these levels. As we have noted, the very fact that much cognitive processing is naturally interpreted as uncertain inference immediately highlights the relevance of probabilistic methods at the computational level. This level of analysis is focused entirely on the nature of the problem being solved—there is no commitment concerning how the cognitive system actually attempts to solve (or approximately to solve) the problem. Thus, a probabilistic viewpoint on the problem of, say, perception or inference, is compatible with the belief that, at the algorithmic level, the relevant cognitive processes operate via a set of heuristic tricks (e.g., Brighton & Gigerenzer, this volume; Gigerenzer & Todd, 1999; Ramachandran, 1994), rather than explicit probabilistic computations.

One drawback of the heuristic approach, though, is that it is not easy to explain the remarkable generality and flexibility of human cognition. Such flexibility seems to suggest that cognitive problems involving uncertainty may, in some cases at least, be solved by the application of probabilistic methods. Thus, we may take models such as stochastic grammars for language or vision, or Bayesian networks, as candidate hypotheses about cognitive representation. Yet, when scaled-up to real-world problems, full Bayesian computations are intractable, an issue that is routinely faced in engineering applications. From this perspective, the fields of machine learning, artificial intelligence, statistics, information theory and control theory can be viewed as rich sources of hypotheses concerning tractable, approximate algorithms that might underlie probabilistic cognition.

Finally, turning to the implementational level, one may ask whether the brain itself should be viewed in probabilistic terms. Intriguingly, many of the sophisticated probabilistic models that have been developed with cognitive processes in mind map naturally onto highly distributed, autonomous, and parallel computational architectures, which seem to capture the qualitative features of neural architecture. Indeed, computational neuroscience (Dayan & Abbott, 2001) has attempted to understand the nervous system as implementing probabilistic calculations; and neurophysiological findings, ranging from spike trains in the blow-fly visual system (Rieke *et al.* 1997), to cells apparently involved in decision making in monkeys (Gold & Shadlen, 2000) have been interpreted as conveying probabilistic information. Nonetheless, large-scale probabilistic calculations over complex internal representations, and reasonably large sets of data, are typically computationally intractable. Thus, typically, the number of possible states of the world grows exponentially with the number of facts that are considered; and calculations over this exponentially large set of world-states are typically viable only in approximation. Thus, the mind cannot credibly be viewed as a 'Laplacian demon,' making complete and accurate probabilistic calculations (Gigerenzer & Goldstein, 1996; Oaksford & Chater, 1998b)—but rather must, at best, be approximating such calculations, perhaps using some very drastic simplifications. How far it is possible to tell an integrated probabilistic story across levels of explanation, or whether the picture is more complex, remains to be determined by future research.

How could probability be so hard for a probabilistic mind?

The question of levels is important in addressing what may appear to be direct evidence against the probabilistic approach—research on how people reason explicitly about probability. Terming probabilities degrees of *belief*, as in the subjectivist interpretation of probability, invites comparison with the folk psychological notion of belief, in which our everyday accounts of each other's behaviour are formed (e.g., Fodor, 1987). This in turn suggests that people might reasonably be expected to introspect about the probabilities associated with their beliefs. In practice, people often appear poor at making such numerical judgements; and poor, too, at numerical probabilistic reasoning problems, where they appear to fall victim to a range of fallacies (e.g., Kahneman *et al.* 1982). The fact that people can appear to be such poor probabilists may seem to conflict with the thesis that many aspects of cognition can fruitfully be modelled in probabilistic terms.

Yet this conflict is only apparent. People struggle not just with probability, but with all branches of mathematics. Yet the fact that, e.g., Fourier analysis is hard to understand does not imply that it, and its generalizations, are not fundamental to audition and vision. The ability to introspect about the operations of the cognitive system are the exception rather than the rule—hence, probabilistic models of cognition do not imply the cognitive naturalness of learning and applying probability theory.

Indeed, probabilistic models may be most applicable to cognitive process that are particularly well-optimized, and which solve the probabilistic problem of interest especially effectively. Thus, vision or motor control may be especially tractable to a probabilistic approach; and our explicit attempts to reason about chance might often, ironically, be poorly modelled by probability theory. Nonetheless, some conscious judgements have proven amenable to probabilistic analyses, such as assessments of covariation or causal efficacy (Cheng, 1997; Griffiths & Tenenbaum, 2005; Waldmann *et al.* this volume), uncertain reasoning over causal models (Sloman & Lagnado, 2005), or predicting the prevalence of everyday events (Griffiths & Tenenbaum, 2006). But unlike textbook probability problems, these are exactly the sorts of critical real-world judgements for which human cognition might be expected to be optimized.

The probabilistic turn in the cognitive and brain sciences

We have suggested that probabilistic analysis may be especially appropriate for highly optimized aspects of cognition—i.e., the domains for which it is credible that the brain has some dedicated computational 'module' or system of modules (e.g., Fodor, 1983; Shallice, 1988). Thus, the probabilistic approach has been widely applied in the areas of perception, motor control, and language, where the performance of dedicated computational modules exceeds the abilities of any artificial computational methods by an enormous margin. Before turning to the main topics of this book, the somewhat ill-defined area of 'central' cognition, we briefly review the much larger and more extensively developed literatures that apply probabilistic methods to these 'modular' domains.

Consider, for example, the problem of inferring the structure of the world, from visual input. There are, notoriously, infinitely many states of the environment that can give rise to any perceptual input (e.g., Freeman, 1994)—this is just an example of the standard observation, in the philosophy of science, that theory is underdetermined by data (Laudan & Leplin, 1991); or, in statistics, that an infinite number of curves can fit any particular set of data points (e.g., Mackay, 1992). A natural objective of the perceptual system, faced with an infinite number of possible interpretations of a stimulus, is to aim to choose the interpretations which are most likely. From this perspective, perception is a problem of probabilistic inference almost by definition.

The idea that the perceptual system seeks the most likely interpretation can be traced to Helmholtz (1910/1962). More recently, it has been embodied in the Bayesian approach to visual perception that has become prominent in psychology and neuroscience. This viewpoint has been backed by direct experimental evidence (e.g., Gregory, 1970; Rock, 1983) for the inferential character of perceptual interpretation; and also by the construction of detailed theories of particular aspects of perceptual processing, from a Bayesian perspective, including low-level image interpretation (Weiss, 1997), shape from shading (Freeman, 1994; Adelson & Pentland, 1996), shape from texture (Blake *et al.* 1996), image segmentation and object recognition (Tu *et al.* 2005), and interpolation of boundaries (Feldman, 2001; Feldman & Singh, 2005). Moreover, the function of neural mechanisms involved in visual perception has also been given a probabilistic interpretation—from lateral inhibition in the retina (e.g., Barlow, 1959), to the activity of single cells in the blow-fly (Snippe *et al.* 2000).

The scope of the probabilistic view of perception may, moreover, be somewhat broader than at might first be thought. Although apparently very different from the likelihood view, the simplicity principle in perception, which proposes that the perceptual system chooses the interpretation of the input which provides the simplest encoding of that input (e.g., Attneave, 1954; Hochberg & McAlister, 1953; Leeuwenberg, 1969, 1971; Leeuwenberg & Boselie, 1988; Mach, 1959/1914; Restle, 1970; Van der Helm & Leewenberg, 1996, though see Olivers *et al.* 2004) turns out to be mathematically equivalent to the likelihood principle (Chater, 1996). Specifically, under mild mathematical restrictions, for any probabilistic analysis of a perceptual inference (using a specific set of prior probabilistic assumptions) there is a corresponding simplicity-based analysis (using a particular coding language, in which the code-length of an encoding of perceptual data in terms of an interpretation provides the measure of complexity), such that the most likely and the simplest interpretations coincide. Thus, theories of perception based on simplicity and coding, and theories of neural function based on decorrelation and information compression (e.g., Barlow, 1959) can be viewed as part of the Bayesian probabilistic approach to perception.

The study of perceptuo-motor control provides a second important area of Bayesian analysis. Sensory feedback, typically integrated across different modalities (e.g., visual and haptic information about the positions of the hand), contributes to estimating the current state of the motor system. Knowing this current state is essential for the brain to be able to plan successful motor movements. The precise way in which movements, such as a grasp, are carried out, is likely to have consequences in terms of 'utility' for the agent. Thus, successfully grasping a glass of orange may presage a pleasant drink; a less successful grasp may result in unnecessary delay, a slight spillage, a broken glass, or a stained sofa. The motor system needs to choose actions which, given the relevant information and utilities, gives the best expected outcome. The machinery of Bayesian decision theory (Berger, 1985) can be recruited to address this problem.

Bayesian decision theory has been widely applied as a theoretical framework for understanding the control of movement (e.g., Körding & Wolpert, 2006). A wide range of experimental evidence has indicated that movement trajectories are indeed accurately predictable in these terms. In a particularly elegant study, Körding and Wolpert (2004) showed that people rely on prior knowledge, rather than evidence from sensory input, depending on the relative precision of each source of information, in a simple repeated motor task. This suggests that the brain learns to model both the distribution of outcomes in prior trials, and the reliability of sensory input. Similar effects arise not just in movement trajectories, but in force estimation (Körding et al. 2004) and sensory motor timing (Miyazaki et al. 2005).

This work can be generalized to consider the on-line planning of motor movements— i.e., the brain must plan trajectories so that its on-line estimation of its own state, and ability to dynamically modify that state, leads to the optimal trajectories. The technical extension of Bayesian methods to problems of this type is the subject of the field of on-line feedback control, and there is experimental evidence that people's movements are well-predicted by these methods (e.g., Knill & Saunders, 2003; Todorov & Jordon, 2002). Overall, the Bayesian framework has proved to be a remarkably productive framework in which to analyze human motor control.

As a final example, consider probabilistic approaches to language processing (see Jurafsky, 2003; Chater & Manning, 2006, for surveys). Traditional approaches to understanding language and language structure have attempted to abstract away from probabilistic aspects of language. A language is viewed as a set of well-formed strings, generated according to formal rules; and these strings are associated with phonological and semantic representations. From this perspective, language understanding requires, among other things, mapping from phonology to semantics; language production requires, among other things, mapping from semantics to phonology. These computational problems seem fully specified without reference to any probabilistic factors. However, probability seems to be crucially involved in language and language processing in a number of ways. First, speech processing, in which the goal is to convert a hugely complex acoustic waveform into a discrete symbolic representation of what has been heard, must necessarily deal with uncertainty—as with any signal processing problem. Not surprisingly, leading methods in this area involve a variety of probabilistic learning methods, including hidden Markov models, and neural networks (Rabiner & Juang, 1993). Probability enters, for similar reasons, where the language processor has to deal with errorful linguistic output—error correction requires a probabilistic model of the language output and the processes by which errors can occur.

Second, because of the ubiquitous ambiguity throughout language, merely enumerating possible interpretations of a sentence is not sufficient—the hearer needs also to figure out which is most likely to be that intended by the speaker. This, too, appears to be a probabilistic inference problem, which is analogous, at an abstract level, to the problem of associating an interpretation with highly ambiguous perceptual inputs, described above. Some theories of parsing assume that the parser does not, nonetheless, use a probabilistic solution—at least in the case of syntactic ambiguity, such theories assume that the ambiguity is resolved purely in accordance with the structure of competing syntactic parses (e.g., Frazier, 1979). Nonetheless, recent research has increasingly viewed the parser as engaged in probabilistic calculations using a range of sources of evidence about which parse is the most probable (MacDonald *et al.* 1994; McRae *et al.* 1998).

Third, there has been increasing interest in the statistical cues that may underpin aspects of the acquisition of aspects of phonology, syntax and semantics. For example, statistical analysis of the contexts in which words occur can be used to classify them into syntactic classes (e.g., Redington *et al.* 1998) or semantic classes (e.g., Landauer & Dumais, 1997). The richness of these statistical cues suggests that they may be able to substantially facilitate language processing and acquisition (e.g., Dennis, 2005; Monaghan et al. in press; Redington & Chater, 1998).

Moreover, very general theoretical results have recently been derived, which cast the general problem of language acquisition in a new light. According to a traditional generative perspective, the problem of language acquisition can be idealized as the problem of picking out the infinite set of well-formed sentences, from a finite sample of 'positive' instances of well-formed sentences that the child encounters (see, Hahn & Oaksford, this volume). Chomsky (1965) influentially argued that the learning problem is unsolvable without strong prior constraints on the language, given the 'poverty' (i.e., partiality and errorfulness) of the linguistic stimulus. Indeed, Chomsky (1981) argued that almost all syntactic structure, aside from a finite number of binary parameters, must be innate. Separate mathematical work by Gold (1967) indicated that, under certain assumptions, learners provably cannot converge on a language even 'in the limit' as the corpus becomes indefinitely large (see Pinker, 1979, for discussion).

A probabilistic standpoint yields more positive learnability results. For example, Horning (1971) proved that phrase structure grammars are learnable (with high probability) to within a statistical tolerance, if sentences are sampled as independent, identically distributed data. Chater and Vitányi (2007) generalized this result substantially to a language which is generated by any computable process (i.e., sentences can be interdependent, and generated by any computable grammar), and showed that prediction, grammaticality, and language production, are learnable, to a statistical tolerance. These results are 'ideal' however—they consider what would be learned, if the learner could find the shortest representation of the linguistic data. In practice, the learner can at best find a short code, not the shortest, and theoretical results are not available for this case.

This raises the question of how well probabilistic learning methods fare in acquiring linguistic structure. Recent results using probabilistic methods have been promising. Thus, Klein and Manning (2002, 2004) have made significant progress in solving the problem of learning to build surface phrase structure trees from corpora of unparsed sentences. This work is a promising demonstration of empirical language learning, but most linguistic theories use richer structures than surface phrase structure trees; and a particularly important objective is finding models that map to meaning representations. Nonetheless, richer grammatical models have been learned from parsed data (Johnson & Riezler, 2002; Toutanova *et al.* 2005), there has been interesting initial work on mapping from linguistic form to meaning representations (Zettlemoyer & Collins, 2005), and on unsupervised learning of a mapping from surface text to semantic role representations (Swier & Stevenson, 2005).

Probability in 'central' cognition

We have described the probabilistic turn in perception, perceptuo-motor control and language. But this book is concerned with the exciting, though less developed, project of applying probabilistic methods to so-called central cognitive processes—i.e., roughly processes that do not appear to be conducted by specialized brain areas or computational machinery, but by more general purpose cognitive mechanisms. Only if central processes have a probabilistic character can we really justify the 'Probabilistic Mind' of our title.

The chapters in this book are divided somewhat arbitrarily into five inter-related sections: *Foundations, Inference and Argument, Judgement and Decision Making, Categorization and Memory* and *Learning about Contingency and Causality*. We see the connections across sections as illustrating one of the strengths of a probabilistic approach to cognition: that it provides a common framework into which a diverse range of traditionally separate issues can be analyzed. Hence, divisions between topics are typically less sharp than in many traditional psychological frameworks. Thus, for example, learning 'associative' contingencies, constructing categories, processes of everyday reasoning, and many more topics may all be viewed in terms of Bayesian updating; and the representational and computational issues arising in such updating may have many common themes. Here, we briefly preview the issues covered in this book, and lightly sketch some background in each area.

The first section of this book, *Foundations*, provides introductory material—namely the present chapter, a technical introduction to Bayesian methods, by Tom Griffiths and Alan Yuille, and an insightful critical reflection on the scope and useful-ness of a 'rational' perspective on the cognitive system, by David Danks.

The second section, *Inference and Argument*, focuses on probability as a framework for understanding how we *reason* about uncertainty. As we discussed above, there has been much discussion of the degree to which people are poor at dealing with explicit probabilistic reasoning problems (Kahneman *et al.* 1982). But it is entirely possible, as we noted, for a person to have a poor grasp of some branch of mathematics, but for that branch of mathematics to, nonetheless, play a fundamental role in their visual, motor or central cognitive processes. Indeed, Oaksford and Chater (1998b, 2007) argue that qualitative patterns of many aspects of reasoning fit surprisingly easily into a probabilistic framework—perhaps all the more surprisingly, because much of the data in the study of human reasoning comes from supposedly 'logical' reasoning tasks. If this is right, then in much of the psychology of reasoning, human rationality has been considerably underplayed, because of comparison with the wrong normative standard. The opening chapter of this section, by Sher and McKenzie, expands on this viewpoint, but showing how the pragmatics of natural language can explain many apparent biases of 'framing' in reasoning. While the formulation of a problem has typically been viewed as irrelevant to its solution, Sher and McKenzie show how the way in which a problem is expressed carries a great deal of information, e.g., about underlying beliefs and values—and that these influence reasoners in systematic ways. Thus, many 'framing effects' may arise, in part, because of the inadequacy of normative models that ignore the crucial informational differences between frames.

The next chapter, by Oaksford and Chater, also focuses on the influence of pragmatic factors on reasoning—focussing on a *prima facie* puzzle for both logical and probabilistic accounts of reasoning: the asymmetry between *modus ponens* (MP) and *modus tollens* (MT) inferences in conditional reasoning. Suppose I know the general rule *if I turn the key, the car starts*. If John says: 'I turned the key' its reasonably natural to infer that the car started (although not necessarily—indeed, John might say 'I turned the key, and nothing happened'). This is MP. But if I hear 'the car didn't start' then it is very bizarre to infer 'the key wasn't turned.' This is because it would be pragmatically pointless to mention that the car didn't start, unless it would have been expected to do so. Thus, MT is often pragmatically inappropriate, which may explain why MT inferences are suppressed in laboratory reasoning tasks. Oaksford and Chater describe an approach to conditionals which trades on such pragmatic factors, in the framework of probability logic (Adams, 1998).

Continuing the theme of enriching the probabilistic picture of inference, Hahn and Oaksford (2007) have applied probabilistic techniques to reconsider the acceptability of different kinds of appealing, but supposedly logically fallacious arguments, arguing, for example, that circular arguments need not always of 'vicious.' Their chapter here reviews recent work on the classic fallacy of the 'argument from ignorance.' This fallacy can be given a formal, Bayesian treatment, which suggests that there is nothing structurally amiss with arguments from ignorance; rather they are differentially strong or weak as a function of their specific content, that is, the specific probabilistic quantities involved. This analysis is then applied to a classic problem of language acquisition involving inference from the absence of certain structures in the data. In the language acquisition literature, such inference has often been taken to be dubious at best. Hahn and Oaksford's chapter re-examines the relative strength of such inferences and seeks to clarify the role of two widely cited mechanisms in language acquisition, pre-emption and entrenchment, from the viewpoint of probabilistic inference.

The next chapter, by Nelson, considers the crucial question of the usefulness of data, with respect to a set of hypotheses under consideration. Some data are clearly irrelevant to the hypotheses of concern; some decisively favour one hypothesis or another. But, in general, data modifies the probability of the hypotheses, but to a modest degree. Only with a measure of the usefulness of data is it possible to formulate a theory of which experiments should be carried out, or which observations should be made. While clearly important in science, this issue is also crucial to understanding how people actively explore their world. Nelson provides a thorough analysis of the strengths and weaknesses of a range of measures of evidential usefulness, drawn from a variety of fields of cognitive science.

The final chapter in this section, by Fiedler, focuses on the complexity and subtlety of inferences from data, and how the cognitive system does not always negotiate these subtleties consistently. Fiedler observes that many important areas of cognitive and social psychology focus on problems in which different levels of analysis can yield different results. He describes the important concept of a pseudocontingency (Fiedler & Freytag, 2004)—a illusory relationship between variables, which is induced by connections with a third variable (a phenomenon closely related to Simpson's Paradox, Simpson, 1951). For example, most people in Class A may be girls; and most people in

Class A may be good at maths; but there may be no relation whatever between gender and mathematical skill (although, given certain independence assumptions, this may be a reasonable default assumption—see, e.g., Chater & Oaksford, 1999). The concept of pseudocontingency is shown to play a crucial role in explaining a wide range of classical psychological phenomena, especially in social cognition.

The third part of this book, *Judgement and Decision Making*, focuses on probability in its role of helping us choose which *actions* to perform. There is, of course, a vast literature indicating that people's decisions do not confirm with the dictates of Bayesian decision theory, and, indeed, that decisions frequently violate apparently basic canons of rationality—e.g., when the way a problem is described affects the decision that is made. As we have noted, McKenzie (e.g., McKenzie, 2004, and see Sher and McKenzie, this volume) notes that some such effects can be viewed as rational from a broader perspective—e.g., where the way in which choice options are described typically carries information about the writer's attitude to those options. But many theoretical approaches have been developed which attempt to weaken rationality assumptions, in some cases drastically. Relatively modest proposals seek to replace calculations of expected utility (required by the 'rational' perspective) with some similar, but in some ways distinct, calculations (e.g., Kahneman & Tversky, 1979; Loomes & Sugden, 1982). More radical approaches seek to jettison expected utility calculations completely, and propose a purely mechanistic approach. Thus, Brandstätter *et al.* (2006) propose that people make choices between risky options by sequentially applying very simple rules—each rule considers only one attribute of the option, and hence there is no trading-off between different features of a choice. Stewart *et al.* (2006) propose instead that 'rational' choices are not made primarily because of computational limitations in the ability to integrate different pieces of information, but because people do not have internal scales in terms of which value, time, probability, quality, and so on, can be represented. Thus, the fundamental cognitive bottleneck is assumed to be representational, rather than concerning processing limitations—we discuss these issues further below, in the next sub-section describing challenges to the probabilistic approach. It is interesting that, while highly non-rational models seem to do well at explaining anomalies when people deal with verbally or numerically stated decision problems, a probabilistic perspective may be more appropriate for understanding highly repetitive decision making. Certainly, probabilistic methods are widely used in studying 'optimal' foraging in animals (Stephens & Krebs, 1986), as well as repetitive decision making in humans (e.g., Trommershäuser *et al.* 2006; Hertwig *et al.*, 2004), and patterns of behaviour appear to be different in experiential, rather than verbally stated, tasks.

The opening chapter of this section, by Brighton and Gigerenzer considers the project of probabilistic rational analysis in relation to a particularly well-studied and simple heuristic, the *Take the Best* algorithm. Brighton and Gigerenzer relate the tension between 'rational' and 'algorithmic' explanations of cognitive phenomena to the bias-variance dilemma in statistics. Roughly, where the cognitive system must make do with little data in relation to the complexity of the problem, they suggest that simple algorithmic models, rather than full-blown probabilistic calculations, may be the cognitive system's best strategy. The next chapter, by Hertwig and Pleskac, also stresses the importance of simplicity, but in a different way—they argue that, where people sample statistical information from experience, they tend to rely on surprisingly small samples (e.g., focussing on a few recent events). They present a formal analysis of possible reasons behind this reliance on small samples. Three key results emerge. First, small samples amplify the difference between the average earnings associated with the payoff distributions, thus rendering choices simpler. Second, they argue that people who use a simple choice heuristic or choose in accordance with prospect theory benefit from this amplification effect, whereas Bayesian updaters do not. Third, they argue that, although not providing a strictly veridical portrayal of the world, small samples can give rise to surprisingly competitive choices.

Hansson, Juslin and Winman's chapter takes a different starting point: it assumes that, roughly, the cognitive system is able to provide a good analysis of the data which it experiences—i.e., cognition can be seen as intuitive statistics (Gigerenzer & Murray, 1987). But, they suggest, the crucial blind-spot in this process is an inability to correct for sampling bias—so that, to the degree that the world is not sampled randomly, the cognitive system is liable to come to misleading conclusions. The mind should be viewed as a *naïve* intuitive statistician (Fiedler & Juslin, 2006). They provide a compelling illustration of their approach, considering the conditions in which people do, and do not, exhibit overconfidence, in relation to sampling and the process of making confidence judgements. In the light of Fiedler's analysis of pseudocontingencies, the naïve intuitive statistician is particularly likely to fall into error.

The final two chapters in this section, by Stewart and Simpson, and by Usher, Elhalal, and McClelland, consider the question of how different pieces of information in judgement are integrated. Stewart and Simpson outline a possible extension of Stewart *et al.*'s (2006) decision by sampling theory, to account for how people integrate probability and value information in considering 'gambles.' The resulting account provides a theory of decision-under-risk that is directly comparable to prospect theory (Kahneman & Tversky, 1979) and its competitors (e.g., Brandstätter *et al.* 2006). Their model correctly predicts the direction of preference for all 16 prospects from the Kahneman and Tversky (1979) data set and produces a high correlation between choice proportions and model predictions.

Usher, Elhalal and McClelland focus on the question of how different pieces of information, of whatever kind, are integrated together into a decision. Their preferred approach, the Leaky Competing Accumulator model, is appealing both because it may have a natural neural implementation, and because it has a close relationship to normative principles in statistics. On the other hand, though, the focus of the chapter is to account for data that appear very non-normative—preference reversals between pairs of items, depending on the values of other 'foil' items. Central both to their approach, and to that of Stewart and Simpson, is the idea that people do not have stable underlying representations of the value of the quantities (whether probability, amount of money, or quality of a consumer good) that enter into the decision. Rather, these values are constructed on the fly, by comparison with the relative merits of a small number of salient items—e.g., other possible choices available in the experiment.

The fourth part of the book, *Categorization and Memory*, takes a probabilistic perspective on questions of how we group items together, how they are represented, and how they are retrieved. Probabilistic approaches to classification and information retrieval are able to build on related work on classification in statistics and machine learning, much of which uses a purely probabilistic approach (although some important recent developments are not wholly probabilistic in spirit, e.g., Support Vector Machines, Christianini & Shawe-Taylor, 2000). Roughly, the goal of categorization is to infer the underlying clustering of a set of items, from a set of (possibly labelled) examples; the goal of information retrieval is to recover the information most likely to 'explain' the retrieval cues that are available. In classification, interesting technical problems are introduced when the items are unlabelled, and when the number of clusters is not known—and indeed might be infinite. One approach to the problem is to have a mechanism for creating new clusters as they are required by the data, an approach pioneered in psychological models of categorization (Anderson, 1991b), but later developed and adapted within the machine learning community (Blei *et al.* 2004; see Pothos & Chater, 2002, for a simplicity-based approach to unsupervised categorization). Tenenbaum and colleagues (Griffiths *et al.* in press; Tenenbaum *et al.* 2006; Xu & Tenenbaum, in press) have been particularly active in showing how rich probabilistic methods, defined over symbolic representations, can capture sophisticated patterns of classification and inference, dramatically broadening the scope of formal models of categorisation.

In comparison with categorization, the psychology of memory might seem a less promising area for probabilistic analysis. Naïvely one might suppose that memories are either present or absent, leaving no room for probability analysis. But probability enters into memory in a number of ways—in theories that assume that memory is organized to make ease of memory retrieval correlate with the probability that an item will be needed (Anderson & Schooler, 1991); theories that consider the integration of different memory cues (Shiffrin & Steyvers, 1998); and how memories can be reconstructed from partial information, based on an underlying probabilistic model of how different pieces of information in memory are inter-related (e.g., Rumelhart *et al.* 1986). Interestingly, the analogous engineering issues concerning the encoding of information (communication theory and related topics, Mackay, 2003) and information retrieval (e.g., Zhai & Laffety, 2001) draw heavily on probabilistic methods.

The first chapter in this part, by Griffiths, Sanborn, Canini and Navarro, applies state of the art techniques from machine learning and statistics to reconceptualize the problem of unsupervised category learning, and to relate it to previous psychologically motivated models, especially Anderson's rational analysis of categorization (Anderson, 1991b). The resulting analysis provides a deeper understanding of the motivations underlying the classic models of category representation, based on prototypes or exemplars, as well as shedding new light on the empirical data. The second chapter in this section, by Steyvers and Griffiths provides a complementary Bayesian analysis of the problem of memory retrieval. A Bayesian model that is able both to classify words into semantically coherent groups, merely from observing their co-occurrence patterns in texts, is used as the basis for understanding aspects not only of how some linguistic categories might be created, but also how *relevant* information can be retrieved, using probabilistic principles. This work can be viewed as a natural follow-on from Anderson and colleagues' pioneering rational analyses of memory (Anderson & Milson, 1989; Anderson & Schooler, 1991).

In contrast to these general analyses, Huber's chapter puts a specific priming effect in memory under the microscope, from a probabilistic point of view. Priming effects in word recognition and memory have typically been viewed as side-effects of the mechanisms of recognition—e.g., as arising from associations between lexical items, which operate automatically. He suggests, instead, however, that many priming phenomena may arise from the structure of the probabilistic reasoning problem that the perceiver faces. The perceiver has a range of pieces of evidence, but has to infer their likely source. When a piece of evidence from one source is attributed to another, priming may be observed. Huber very elegantly demonstrates that experimentally observed priming is sensitive to the rational structure of the 'attribution' problem, rather than to the operation of mere associative mechanisms.

Probabilistic theories of categorization and memory, while having many strengths, are typically viewed as having a key weakness—that, in comparison with methods based on logical systems, they are representationally weak. They may, for example, readily represent correlations between bundles of features, or regions in a multi-dimensional space, but do not so readily capture structural knowledge. To some degree, the contrast here is a false one: probabilistic inference methods may live alongside logical representational formalisms. But demonstrating how richer representations may be probabilistically tractable nonetheless amounts to a huge technical challenge. The chapter by Goodman, Tenenbaum, Griffiths and Feldman, provides a range of conceptual and technical insights into how this project can be attempted— and goes some way to suggesting that probabilistic methods need not be viewed as inevitably unable to capture the richness and complexity of world knowledge. In particular, they argue that structured representations, generated by a formal grammar, can be appropriate units over which probabilistic information can be represented and learned. This topic is likely to be one of the main challenges for probabilistic research in cognitive science and artificial intelligence over the coming decades.

The final part of the book, *Learning about Contingency and Causality*, reconsiders, from a probabilistic standpoint, issues of learning that have typically been viewed from an associative point of view. A probabilistic viewpoint on contingency learning seems, conceptually at least, very natural—such learning can be viewed as a process of inference from data provided by experience. In practice, though, accounts of elementary learning processes, emerging from the behaviourist tradition, have often viewed learning as an associative process, viewed as non-inferential. Recent developments, however, have indicated that this dichotomy may be illusory—instead, associative mechanisms can be viewed as implicitly embodying probabilistic computations. Moreover, different probabilistic assumptions correspond to different associative processes. To the extent that the relevant assumptions hold, at least approximately, for the environment in which the learner operates, the probabilistic analysis is able explain when and why associative principles are practically successful. But the probabilistic approach also provides methods for building more complex associative/mechanistic models of learning that go beyond traditional accounts (Courville *et al.* 2006; Kakade & Dayan, 2002). According to one viewpoint, the learner, whether human or animal, should be viewed as attempting to infer the underlying *causal* structure of its environment (including the causal consequences of its own actions). If this is right, then the basic concept of association is misleading—because the right cognitive goal is to uncover causal, not merely correlational, relations.

Causality may though appear at first sight to be particularly resistant to a probabilistic analysis—traditional probability theory makes no references to causal direction, after all. Nonetheless, probabilistic methods enter in a range of ways—from providing measures of the strength of a causal relationship (based on, e.g., the probability of the effect with or without the cause, Cheng, 1997), to new technical methods, for representing causal dependencies in probabilistic terms (Pearl, 2000). Indeed, these methods concerning how to capture causality and the representations of probabilities of graphical models over which they are defined (see Griffiths & Yuille, this volume), have been used as the basis for building psychological proposals across a range of domains. This development follows the historical tradition of asking how far the latest normative models can be viewed as useful descriptive models of human behaviour (see, e.g., Gigerenzer, 1991). How far this approach will prove to be successful is not yet clear—but early work has been promising (e.g., Gopnik *et al.* 2004; Griffiths & Tenenbaum, 2005).

Speekenbrink and Shanks' opening chapter in this section considers a probabilistic perspective on a classic problem of human contingency learning: finding the relationships between a category or outcome, for which there are several probabilistic cues. They provide their analysis within the framework of Brunswik's (1955) lens model (there are connections between this framework and perspective described in the chapters by Juslin, by Fiedler, and by Brighton and Gigerenzer). Here, the concern is especially with the dynamics of learning, e.g., the rate of learning and how the learner may respond to changing contingencies—which are, presumably, the norm, in many real-world contexts. The chapter by Daw, Courville and Dayan further considers the question of how learning adapts to changing environments, with particular reference to animal studies of operant and classical conditioning. They discuss a variety of probabilistic models, with different assumptions concerning the environment; and contrast this type of model with a model by Kruschke (2006) which carries out local, approximate, Bayesian inference. Daw, Courville and Dayan suggest that it may be too early to incorporate mechanistic limitations into models of conditioning—enriching the understanding of the environment, and working with a 'pure' Bayesian rational analysis for that environment, may, they suggest, provide an alternative, and perhaps theoretically more elegant, way forward.

Waldmann, Cheng, Hagmayer and Blaisdell bring together human and animal studies, with a particular focus on causal learning. Whereas the traditional associative approach to learning views learning contingencies as basic, and the learning of causality (if it is considered at all) to be secondary, they take the goal of the agent to be to infer the 'causal powers' of aspects of the world. Contingencies are primarily of interest to the degree that they provide evidence for such causal relationships. The degree to which the same rational model may be applied to learning, from rat to human, puts a new complexion on the behaviourist's project of building general principles of learning across species. It is possible that such principles may arise not from similarity of underlying associative learning machinery, as was implicit in the behaviourist tradition (although behaviourists did, of course, eschew, on principle, speculation about cognitive mechanism). Such similarities may arise, to some degree at least, from similarities in the probabilistic structure of the learning problems themselves. Faced with such learning problems, it may be that almost any intelligent agent will exhibit similar patterns of behaviour.

The final chapter in this part, by Sloman and Fernbach, provides a skeptical analysis of the technical machinery of causal Bayesian networks. They argue that this machinery provides valuable insights into the *representation* of causality—and, as we noted above, extending the representational power of probabilistic method is of crucial importance. But they suggest that the learning algorithms for such networks do not provide a good model of human causal learning. They argue that human causal learning is rational, to some degree—but also exhibits large and systematic biases. They suggest that models of causality learning that are exclusively based on rational principles are unlikely to be successful.

The book concludes with some brief reflections on the future prospects of the probabilistic approach to the mind. We suspect that probability is 'here to stay' in cognitive science—but that is merely one of many important complementary conceptual frameworks. We consider both challenges, and selected recent technical and conceptual developments, that may play a role in the future development of probabilistic analyses of the mind.

Challenges to the probabilistic approach

The chapters of this book generally treat probabilistic methods as shedding important light on cognitive processes, although in a variety of ways, and at a variety of levels of explanation, as we have seen. Yet these applications of probability can, individually and collectively, be criticized—and the debates between proponents of probabilistic methods, and advocates of alternative viewpoints, have played an important role in the development of the cognitive sciences, and are likely to continue to do so. We briefly here consider some of the many concerns that may be raised against probabilistic approaches.

Probabilistic approaches may be especially vulnerable, as noted above, when considered as models of explicit reasoning. There have been repeated demonstrations that explicit human decision making systematically deviates from Bayesian decision theory (Kahneman *et al.* 1982; Kahneman & Tversky, 2000). Why might deviations occur? Since Simon (1957), computational tractability has been a primary concern—with the conclusion that computationally cheap heuristic methods, which function well in the ecological environment in which the task must be performed, should be viewed as an alternative paradigm. Bounded rationality considerations have gradually become increasingly important in economics (e.g., Rubinstein, 1998)—and hence, economists have increasingly begun to question the usefulness of strong rationality assumptions, such that agents are viewed as implicit probabilists and decision theorists. Gigerenzer (this volume; Gigerenzer *et al.* 1999) has led a particularly influential programme of research, aiming to define an 'ecological' rationality, in which good reasoning is that which works quickly and effectively in the real world, rather than necessarily being justified in terms of normative mathematical foundations. This viewpoint may still see a role for probabilistic analysis—but as providing an explanation of why particular heuristics work in particular environments, rather than as characterizing the calculations that the cognitive system performs.

A very different reason why people may not, in some contexts, be viewed as probabilists or decision theorists, concerns *representation*, rather than processing power. Some researchers (e.g., Laming, 1997) argue that people can only represent sensory magnitudes in relative rather than absolute terms; and that even this relative coding is extremely inaccurate and unstable. Indeed, the radical assumption that, to an approximation, people can make only simple qualitative binary judgements (e.g., 'tone A is louder than tone B'; and 'the difference in loudness between tones A and B is smaller than the difference in loudness between tones B and C') is the basis for a recent model, the Relative Judgement Model (Stewart *et al.* 2005) that provides a simple and comprehensive account of how people can assign sensory magnitudes to discrete categories. If the same principles apply to magnitudes involved in decision making (e.g., time, probability, value, quality and so on), then people may not have a stable cardinal representation of the relevant decision variables, from which probabilistic calculations (of expected utility and the like) can even begin—and hence the issue of computational considerations does not arise. A recent model of decision making, Decision by Sampling (Stewart *et al.* 2006), shows how the assumption that people have no access to internal scales, but rely instead purely in binary judgements, can provide a straightforward account many well-known phenomena concerning decision making. This type of approach is extended to consider how far anomalies of choice in which items have multiple dimensions, which must be traded off, can be explained in this framework (see the chapters by Stewart and Simpson, and by Usher, Elhalal and McClelland).

The concern that people do not have the appropriate representations over which probabilistic calculations can be performed may be most pressing in the context of explicit reasoning—where the underlying computational machinery has not been finely adapted over a long evolutionary history to solve a stable class of problems (e.g., such as perceiving depth, or reaching and grasping) but rather the cognitive system is finding an *ad hoc* solution, as best it can, to each fresh problem. Thus, as noted above, we may accept that explicit reasoning with probability may be poor, while proposing that underlying computational processes of perception, motor control, learning and so on, should be understood in probabilistic terms.

Interestingly, though, related challenges to the Bayesian approach have arisen in perception. For example, Purves and colleagues (e.g., Howe & Purves, 2004, 2005; Long & Purves, 2002; Nundy & Purves, 2002) argue that the perceptual system should not be viewed as attempting to reconstruct the external world using Bayesian methods. Instead, they suggest that the output of the perceptual system should be seen as determined by the ranking of the present input in relation to the statistical distribution of previous inputs. This viewpoint is particularly clearly expressed in the context of lightness perception. The perceived lightness of a patch in the sensory array is determined not merely by the amount of incident energy in that patch, and its spectral composition, but is also a complex function of the properties of the area surrounding that patch. For example, a patch on the sensory array will be perceived as light if it is surrounded by a dark field; and may be perceived as relatively dark, if surrounded by light field.

A natural Bayesian interpretation of this type of phenomena is that the perceptual system is attempting to factor out the properties of the light source, and to represent only the reflectance function of the surface of the patch (i.e., the degree to which that patch absorbs incident light). Thus, the dark surrounding field is viewed as prima facie evidenced that the lighting is dim; and hence the patch itself is viewed as reflective; a bright surrounding field appears to support the opposite inference. This type of analysis can be formulated elegantly in probabilistic terms (Knill & Richards, 1996). Purves and colleagues argue, instead, that the percept should not be viewed as reconstructing an underlying reflectance function—or indeed any other underlying feature of the external world. Instead, they suggest that the background field provides a context in which statistics concerning the amount of incident light is collected; and the lightness of a particular patch, in that context, is determined by its rank in that statistical distribution. Thus, when the surround is dark, patches within that surround tend to be dark (e.g., because both may be explained by the presence of a dim light source); when the surround is light, patches in that surround tend to be light. Hence, the rank position of an identical patch will differ in the two cases, hence leading to contrasting lightness percepts. Nundy and Purves (2002) conduct extensive analysis of the statistical properties of natural images, and argue that the resulting predictions frequently depart from the predictions of the Bayesian analysis; and that the rank-based statistical analysis better fits the psychophysical data.

Various responses from a Bayesian standpoint are possible—including, most naturally, the argument that, where statistical properties of images diverge from the properties of an underlying probabilistic model, this is simply an indication that the probabilistic model is incomplete. Thus, a revised Bayesian approach may account for apparent anomalies, as the model would more accurately capture the statistical properties of images. To some degree, this response may seem unsatisfying, as the ability to choose between the enormous variety of probabilistic image models may seem to give the Bayesian excessive theoretical latitude. On the other hand, the choice of model is actually strongly constrained, precisely because its output can directly be tested, to see how far it reproduces the statistical properties of natural images (Yuille & Kersten, 2006). But the challenge of Purves's approach is that the probabilistic machinery of the Bayesian framework is unnecessary—that there is a much more direct explanation of perceptual experience, which does not involve factoring apart luminance levels and reflectance functions, but which works directly with the amount of incident light in field and surround, and which considers only ordinal properties of relevant statistical distributions. Whether such calculations should best be viewed as departing entirely from the probabilistic approach, or rather as an illustration of how probabilistic calculations can be approximated cheaply, by analogy with heuristic-based approaches to decision making, is not clear.

A more general objection to the probabilistic approach to cognition, which we have touched on already, is the complexity of the approach. In one sense, the probabilistic approach is elegantly simple—we need simply assign prior probabilities, and then remorsely follow the laws of the probability calculus, as further data arises. But in another sense, it is often highly complex—because assigning priors to patterns of beliefs, images, or sentences, may require specifying an extremely complex probabilistic model, from which such information can be generated. Thus, the cognitive modeller may sometimes be accused of putting so much complexity into the model that the ability to capture the relevant data is hardly impressive. The chapters in this book illustrate that the balance between model and data complexity is not necessarily appropriate. Moreover, the contribution of Bayesian models may often be in providing qualitative explanations (e.g., for why there should be a direct relationship between the probability of recurrence of an item, and its retrievability from memory, e.g., Anderson & Milson, 1989; Anderson & Schooler, 1991, Schooler & Anderson, 1997).

Despite this, however, the question of how to constrain probabilistic models as far as possible is an important one. One approach, for example, is to take representation, rather than probability, as the basic construct. According to this approach, the preferred interpretation of a set of data is that which can be used to provide the shortest encoding of that data. Thus, the problem of probabilistic inference is replaced by a problem of finding short codes. It turns out that there are very close relationships between the two approaches, based on both Shannon's theory of communication (Shannon & Weaver, 1949; Mackay, 2003); and the more general concept of algorithmic information, quantified by Kolmogorov complexity theory (Li & Vitányi, 1997). These relationships are used to argue that the two approaches make identical behavioural predictions (Chater, 1996). Roughly, the idea is that representations may be viewed as defining priors, such that, for any object x, with a shortest code of length $c(x)$, the prior $\Pr(x)$ is $2^{-c(x)}$. Conversely, for any prior distribution $Q(x)$ (subject to mild computability constraints that need to detain us here), there will be a corresponding system of representation (i.e., a coding language) c_Q, such that, for any data, x, the most probable representations or hypotheses, H_i, will correspond to those which provide the shortest codes for x in c_Q (as written 2 lines earlier). This means, roughly, that the probabilistic objective of finding the most probable hypothesis can be replaced by the coding objective of finding the hypothesis that supports the shortest code. The equivalence of these frameworks can be viewed as resolving a long-standing dispute between simplicity and likelihood (i.e., probabilistic) views of perceptual organization (e.g., Pomerantz & Kubovy, 1987), as argued by Chater (1996).

Despite these close relationships, taking representation and coding as basic notions has certain advantages. First, the cognitive sciences arguable already have a substantial body of information concerning how different types of information are represented—certainly this has been a central topic of experimental and theoretical concern; but by contrast the project of assessing probabilistic models directly seems more difficult. Second, priors are frequently required for representations which presumably have not been considered by the cognitive system. In a standard Bayesian framework, we typically define a space of hypotheses, and assign priors over that space; but we may also wonder what prior would be assigned to a new hypothesis, *if* it were considered (e.g., if a particular pattern is noticed by the perceptual system; or if a new hypothesis is proposed by the scientist). Assuming that the coding language is universal, then these priors are well-defined, even for an agent that has not considered them—their prior probability of any H is presumed to be $2^{-c(H)}$. Third, rooting priors in a coding language frees the cognitive system from the problem of explicitly having to represent such prior information (though this may be done in a very elegant and compact form, see, e.g., Tenenbaum *et al.* 2006).

Technical developments in coding-based approaches to inference (e.g., Barron *et al.* 1998; Hutter, 2004; Li & Vitányi, 1997; Rissanen, 1987, 1996; Wallace & Freeman, 1987) as well as applications to cognition (e.g., Brent & Cartwright, 1996; Chater & Vitányi, 2007; Dowman, 2000; Feldman, 2000; Goldsmith, 2001; Pothos & Chater, 2002) have been divided concerning whether a coding-based approach to inference should be viewed as a variant of the probabilistic account (i.e., roughly, as using code lengths as a particular way of assigning priors); or whether it should be viewed as an alternative approach. One argument for the former, harmonious, interpretation is that the probabilistic interpretation appears necessary if we consider choice. Thus, for example, maximizing expected utility (or similar) requires computing expectations— i.e., knowing the probability of various outcomes. Thus, rather than viewing simplicity-based approaches as a rival to the probabilistic account of the mind, we instead tentatively conclude that it should be viewed as an alternative, and often useful, perspective on probabilistic inference.

Conclusion

This chapter has introduced the probabilistic approach to cognition; described the different levels of explanation at which it can apply; reviewed past work; previewed some of the content of the rest of this book; and considered potential challenges to the probabilistic approach. The next chapter, by Tom Griffiths and Alan Yuille, introduces the technical machinery of modern Bayesian methods followed by a critical examination of the 'rational' approach to cognitive scientific explanation, of which Bayesian analysis is a part, by David Danks. The four subsequent sections then begin the assessment of the application of probabilistic methods to a wide range of central cognitive processes. Overall, we hope this book provides the opportunity to assess the prospects for a Bayesian cognitive science; its contribution, limitations, and its future direction.

This book developed out of a meeting held on 27–28 June, 2006, held at UCL, in London, entitled *The probabilistic mind: Prospects for rational models of cognition*, organized by Nick Chater and Mike Oaksford, which brought together most of the contributors to this volume. The conference was supported by a grant from the Gatsby Charitable Foundation and by the Gatsby Computational Neuroscience Unit, at UCL. We would like to thank Rachel Howes for so ably providing administrative support for this workshop and Eirini Mitropoulou for her invaluable editorial support in putting this volume together. We also thank Peter Dayan, Director of the Gatsby Computational Neuroscience Unit, for both for the impetus to hold the workshop in the first place and for arranging the venue and administrative support. We further thank the Gatsby Charitable Foundation for fully funding this workshop and supporting the present volume. We finally thank Martin Baum at Oxford University Press for his encouragement and support. Nick Chater would also like to thank the Leverhulme Trust for the Major Research Fellowship that has supported him while working on this book.

This meeting occurred 10 years after a previous meeting (*Rational Models of Cognition*, held at Warwick University in 1996, and organized by Oaksford and Chater). That earlier meeting had led to an early collection on probabilistic models of high level cognition (Oaksford and Chater, 1998a), also published by Oxford University Press, to which the present book is a successor. At the 1996 meeting, there was a sense of large, but relatively unexploited possibilities in the probabilistic approach and a keen interest in the relationship between probabilistic analysis and computational architectures, such as connectionist models and production systems. In the intervening decade, probabilistic models of cognition have flourished and have become more autonomous as a subfield. Moreover, the field has attracted a wave of brilliant young researchers, many of whom are represented in this book, who have considerably extended both the technical possibilities of probabilistic models, and their range of applications in cognitive science. How far the probabilistic approach to the mind progresses over the next decade, and beyond, lies primarily in their hands.

References

Adams, E. W. (1998). *A primer of probability logic*. Stanford, CA: CSLI Publications.

Adelson, E. H., & Pentland, A. P. (1996). The perception of shading and reflectance. In D. Knill, & W. Richards (Eds.), *Perception as Bayesian Inference*, (pp. 409–423). Cambridge University Press.

Anderson, J. R. (1990). *The adaptive character of thought*. Hillsdale, NJ: Erlbaum.

Anderson, J. R. (1991a). Is human cognition adaptive? *Behavioral and Brain Sciences*, **14**, 471–517.

Anderson, J. R. (1991b). The adaptive nature of human categorization. *Psychological Review*, **98**, 409–429.

Anderson, J. R., & Milson, R. (1989). Human memory: an adaptive perspective. *Psychological Review*, **96**, 703–719.

Anderson, J. R., & Schooler, L. J. (1991). Reflections of the environment in memory. *Psychological Science*, **1**, 396–408.

Attneave, F. (1954). Some informational aspects of visual perception. *Psychological Review*, **61**, 183–193.

Barlow, H. B. (1959). Possible principles underlying the transformation of sensory messages. In. W. Rosenblith (Ed.) *Sensory communication* (pp. 217–234). Cambridge, MA: MIT Press.

Barron, A.R., Rissanen, J., & Yu, B. (1998). The minimum description length principle in coding and modeling. *IEEE Transactions on Information Theory*, IT-**44**, 2743–2760.

Bernardo, J. M., & Smith, A. F. M. (1994). *Bayesian Theory*. Chichester: Wiley.

Berger, J. O. (1985). *Statistical decision theory and Bayesian analysis*. Berlin: Springer.

Bernouilli, J. (1713). *Ars conjectandi*. Thurnisiorum: Basel.

Blake, A. Bulthoff, H. H., & Sheinberg, D. (1996). Shape from texture: ideal observers and human psychophysics. In D. Knill, & W. Richards, (Eds.), *Perception as Bayesian inference* (pp. 287–321). Cambridge: Cambridge University Press.

Blakemore, C. (1990). *Vision coding and efficiency*. Cambridge: Cambridge University Press.

Blei, D. M., Griffiths, T. L., Jordan, M. I., & Tenenbaum, J. B. (2004). Hierarchical topic models and the nested Chinese restaurant process. In *Advances in Neural Information Processing Systems 16*. Cambridge, MA: MIT Press.

Boole, G. (1958). *An investigation of the laws of thought*. New York, NY: Dover Publications.

Brandstätter, E., Gigerenzer, G., & Hertwig, R. (2006). The priority heuristic: making choices without trade-offs. *Psychological Review*, **113**, 409–432.

Brent, M. R., & Cartwright, T. A. (1996). Distributional regularity and phonotactic constraints are useful for segmentation. *Cognition*, **61**, 93–126.

Brunswik, E. (1955). Representative design and probabilistic theory in a functional psychology. *Psychological Review*, **62**, 193–217.

Chater, N. (1996). Reconciling simplicity and likelihood principles in perceptual organization, *Psychological Review*, **103**, 566–581.

Chater, N., & Manning, C. (2006). Probabilistic models of language processing and acquisition. *Trends in Cognitive Sciences*, **10**, 335–344.

Chater, N., & Oaksford, M. (1999). The probability heuristics model of syllogistic reasoning. *Cognitive Psychology*, **38**, 191–258.

Chater, N., Tenenbaum, J. B., & Yuille, A. (2006). Special issue on probabilistic models of cognition, *Trends in Cognitive Sciences*, **10**, 287–344.

Chater, N. & Vitányi, P. (2007). 'Ideal learning' of natural language: Positive results about learning from positive evidence. *Journal of Mathematical Psychology*.

Cheng, P. W. (1997). From covariation to causation: A causal power theory. *Psychological Review*, **104**, 367–405.

Chomsky, N. (1965). *Aspects of the theory of syntax*. Cambridge, Massachusetts, MA: MIT Press.

Chomsky, N. (1981) *Lectures on government and binding*. Dordrecht: Foris.

Courville, A. C., Daw, N. D. & Touretzky, D. S. (2006). Bayesian theories of conditioning in a changing world. *Trends in Cognitive Sciences*, **10**, 294–300.

Christianini, N. & Shawe-Taylor, J. (2000). *An introduction to support vector machines*. Cambridge: Cambridge University Press.

Dayan, P. & Abbott, L. F. (2001). *Theoretical neuroscience: computational and mathematical modeling of neural systems*. Cambridge, MA: MIT Press.

Dennis, S. (2005). A memory-based theory of verbal cognition. *Cognitive Science*, **29**, 145–193.

Dowman, M. (2000). Addressing the learnability of verb subcategorizations with Bayesian inference. In L. R. Gleitman, & A. K. Joshi (Eds.), *Proceedings of the Twenty Second Annual Conference of the Cognitive Science Society*. Mahwah, NJ: Erlbaum.

Feldman, J. (2000). Minimization of Boolean complexity in human concept learning. *Nature*, **407**, 630–633

Feldman, J. (2001). Bayesian contour integration. *Perception & Psychophysics*, **63**, 1171–1182.

Feldman, J., & Singh, M. (2005). Information along curves and closed contours. *Psychological Review*, **112**, 243–252.

Fiedler, K., & Freytag, P. (2004). Pseudocontingencies. *Journal of Personality and Social Psychology*, **87**, 453–467.

Fiedler, K., & Juslin, P. (2006). *Information sampling and adaptive cognition*. New York: Cambridge University Press.

Fodor, J. A. (1983). *Modularity of mind*. Cambridge, MA: MIT Press.

Fodor, J. A. (1987). *Psychosemantics*. Cambridge, MA: MIT Press.

Frazier, L. (1979). On comprehending sentences: syntactic parsing strategies. Ph.D. Dissertation, University of Connecticut.

Freeman, W. T. (1994) The generic viewpoint assumption in a framework for visual perception. *Nature*, **368**, 542–545.

Gigerenzer, G. (1991). From tools to theories: a heuristic of discovery in cognitive psychology. *Psychological Review*, **98**, 254–267.

Gigerenzer, G., & Goldstein, D. (1996). Reasoning the fast and frugal way: models of bounded rationality. *Psychological Review*, **103**, 650–669.

Gigerenzer, G., & Murray, D. J. (1987). *Cognition as intuitive statistics*. Hillsdale, NJ: Erlbaum.

Gigerenzer, G., Todd, P., & The ABC Group (Eds.) (1999). *Simple heuristics that make us smart*. Oxford: Oxford University Press.

Gold, E. M. (1967). Language identification in the limit. *Information and Control*, **10**, 447–474.

Gold, J. I. & Shadlen, M. N. (2000). Representation of a perceptual decision in developing oculomotor commands. *Nature*, **404**, 390–394.

Goldsmith, J. (2001). Unsupervised learning of the morphology of a natural language. *Computational Linguistics*, **27**, 153–198.

Gopnik, A., Glymour, C. Sobel, D. M., Schulz, L. E., Kushnir, T., & Danks, D. (2004). A theory of causal learning in children: causal maps and Bayes nets. *Psychological Review*, **111**, 1–31.

Gregory, R. L. (1970). *The intelligent eye*. London: Weidenfeld & Nicolson.

Griffiths, T. L., Steyvers, M., & Tenenbaum, J. B. (in press). *Psychological Review*. Topics in semantic representation.

Griffiths, T. L., & Tenenbaum, J. B. (2005). Structure and strength in causal induction. *Cognitive Psychology*, **51**, 285–386.

Griffiths, T. L., & Tenenbaum, J. B. (2006). Optimal predictions in everyday cognition. *Psychological Science*, **17**, 767–773.

Hahn, U., & Oaksford, M. (2007). The rationality of informal argumentation: A Bayesian approach to reasoning fallacies. *Psychological Review*, **114**.

Helmholtz, H. von (1910/1962). *Treatise on physiological optics*, Vol. 3. In J. P. Southall (Ed. and translation). New York, NY: Dover Publications.

Hertwig, R., Barron, G., Weber, E. U., & Erev, I. (2004). Decisions from experience and the effect of rare events in risky choices. *Psychological Science*, **15**, 534–539.

Hochberg, J. E., & McAlister, E. (1953). A quantitative approach to figural 'goodness.' *Journal of Experimental Psychology,* **46**, 361–364.

Horning, J. (1971). A procedure for grammatical inference. In *Proceedings of the IFIP Congress 71* (pp. 519–523), Amsterdam: North Holland.

Howe C. Q., & Purves D. (2004). Size contrast and assimilation explained by the statistics of natural scene geometry. *Journal of Cognitive Neuroscience*, **16**, 90–102.

Howe, C. Q., & Purves, D. (2005). *Perceiving geometry: geometrical illusions explained by natural scene statistics*. Berlin: Springer.

Howson, C., & Urbach, P. (1993). *Scientific reasoning: The Bayesian approach*. La Salle, IL: Open Court.

Hutter, M. (2004). *Universal artificial intelligence: sequential decisions based on algorithmic probability*. Berlin: Springer.

Johnson, M., & Riezler, S. (2002). Statistical models of language learning and use. *Cognitive Science*, **26**, 239–253.

Jurafsky, Dan. (2003). Probabilistic modeling in psycholinguistics: Linguistic comprehension and production. In Bod, R., Hay, J., & Jannedy, S. (Eds.), *Probabilistic linguistics* (pp. 291–320). Cambridge, MA: MIT Press.

Kahneman, D., Slovic, P., & Tversky, A. (Eds.). (1982). *Judgment under uncertainty: heuristics and biases*. Cambridge: Cambridge University Press.

Kahneman, D., & Tversky, A. (1979). Prospect theory: an analysis of decisions under risk. *Econometrica*, **47**, 313–327.

Kahneman, D., & Tversky, A. (Eds.). (2000). *Choices, values and frames*. New York, NY: Cambridge University Press and the Russell Sage Foundation.

Kakade, S., & Dayan, P. (2002). Acquisition and extinction in autoshaping. *Psychological Review*, **109**, 533–544.

Klein, D., & Manning, C. (2002). A generative constituent-context model for improved grammar induction. In *Proceedings of the 40th Annual Meeting of the ACL*.

Klein, D., &. Manning, C. (2004). Corpus-based induction of syntactic structure: models of sependency and constituency. In *Proceedings of the 42nd Annual Meeting of the ACL*.

Knill, D. C., & Richards, W. A. (Eds.) (1996). *Perception as Bayesian inference*. Cambridge: Cambridge University Press.

Knill, D. C., & Saunders, J. A. (2003) Do humans optimally integrate stereo and texture information for judgments of surface slant? *Vision Research*, **43**, 2539–2558.

Körding, K. P., & Wolpert, D. (2004). Bayesian integration in sensorimotor learning. *Nature*, **427**, 244–247.

Körding, K. P., Ku, S. P., & Wolpert, D. (2004). Bayesian Integration in force estimation. *Journal of Neurophysiology*, **92**, 3161–3165.

Körding, K. P., & Wolpert, D. (2006). Bayesian decision theory in sensory motor control. *Trends in Cognitive Sciences*, **10**, 319–326.

Kruschke, J. K. (2006). Locally Bayesian learning with applications to retrospective revaluation and highlighting. *Psychological Review*, **113**, 677–699.

Laming, D. (1997). *The measurement of sensation*. Oxford: Oxford University Press.

Landauer, T. K., & Dumais, S. T. (1997). A solution to Plato's problem: the Latent Semantic Analysis theory of acquisition, induction and representation of knowledge. *Psychological Review*, **104**, 211–240.

Laudan, L., & Leplin, J. (1991). Empirical equivalence and underdetermination. *Journal of Philosophy*, **88**, 449–472.

Leeuwenberg, E. (1969). Quantitative specification of information in sequential patterns. *Psychological Review*, **76**, 216–220.

Leeuwenberg, E. (1971). A perceptual coding language for perceptual and auditory patterns. *American Journal of Psychology*, **84**, 307–349.

Leeuwenberg, E., & Boselie, E (1988). Against the likelihood principle in visual form perception. *Psychological Review*, **95**, 485–491.

Li, M., & Vitanyi, P. M. B. (1997). *An introduction to Kolmogorov complexity and its applications* (2nd ed.). New York: Springer-Verlag.

Long, F., & Purves, D. (2003). Natural scene statistics as the universal basis for color context effects. *Proceedings of the National Academy of Science*, **100**, 15190–15193.

Loomes, G., & Sugden, R. (1982). Regret theory: An alternative theory of rational choice under uncertainty. *Economic Journal*, **92**, 805–824.

MacDonald, M. C., Pearlmutter, N. J., & Seidenberg, M. S. (1994). The lexical nature of syntactic ambiguity resolution. *Psychological Review*, **101**, 676–703.

Mach, E. (1959). *The analysis of sensations and the relation of the physical to the psychical.* New York: Dover Publications. (Original work published 1914).

Mackay, D. J. C. (1992). Bayesian interpolation. *Neural Computation*, **4**, 415–447.

Mackay, D. J. C. (2003). *Information theory, inference, and learning algorithms.* Cambridge: Cambridge University Press.

Manning, C., & Schütze, H. (1999). *Foundations of statistical natural language processing.* Cambridge, MA: MIT Press.

Marr, D. (1982). *Vision.* San Francisco, CA: Freeman.

McKenzie, C. R. M. (2004). Framing effects in inference tasks—and why they are normatively defensible. *Memory & Cognition*, **32**, 874–885.

McRae, K., Spivey-Knowlton, M. J., & Tanenhaus, M. K. (1998). Modeling the influence of thematic fit (and other constraints) in online sentence comprehension. *Journal of Memory and Language,* **38**, 283–312.

Miyazaki, M., Nozaki, D., & Nakajima, Y. (2005). Testing Bayesian models of human coincidence timing. *Journal of Neurophysiology*, **94**, 395–399.

Monaghan, P., Christiansen, M., & Chater, N. (in press). The Phonological-distributional coherence hypothesis: cross-linguistic evidence in language acquisition. *Cognitive Psychology*.

Nundy, S., & Purves, D. (2002). A probabilistic explanation of brightness scaling. *Proceedings of the National Academy of Sciences*, **99**, 14482–14487.

✳Oaksford, M., & N. Chater (Eds.). (1998a). *Rational models of cognition.* Oxford: Oxford University Press.

Oaksford, M., & Chater, N. (1998b). *Rationality in an uncertain world.* Hove, England: Psychology Press.

Oaksford, M., & Chater, N. (2007). *Bayesian rationality.* Oxford: Oxford University Press.

Olivers, C. L. N., Chater, N., & Watson, D. G. (2004). Holography does not account for goodness: a critique of van der Helm and Leeuwenberg (1996). *Psychological Review*, **111**, 242–260.

Pinker, S. (1979). Formal models of language learning. *Cognition*, **7**, 217–283.

Pomerantz, J. R., & Kubovy, M. (1986). Theoretical approaches to perceptual organization: simplicity and likelihood principles. In: K. R. Boff, L. Kaufnam, & J. P.Thomas (Eds.), *Handbook of perception and human performance, Volume II: Cognitive processes and performance.* (pp. 1–45). New York: Wiley.

Pothos, E., & Chater, N. (2002). A simplicity principle in unsupervised human categorization. *Cognitive Science*, **26**, 303–343.

Rabiner, L., & Juang, L. (1993). *Fundamentals of speech recognition.* New York: Prentice Hall.

Ramachandran, V. S. (1990). The utilitarian theory of perception. In C. Blakemore (Ed.), *Vision: coding and efficiency* (pp. 346–360). Cambridge: Cambridge University Press.

Redington, M., & Chater, N. (1998). Connectionist and statistical approaches to language acquisition: a distributional perspective. *Language and Cognitive Processes*, **13**, 129–191.

Redington, M., Chater, N., & Finch, S. (1998). Distributional information: a powerful cue for acquiring syntactic categories. *Cognitive Science*, **22**, 425–469.

Restle, E. (1970). Theory of serial pattern learning: structural trees. *Psychological Review*, **77**, 481–495.

Rieke, F., De Ruyter Van Steveninck, R., Warland, D., & Bialek, W. (1997). *Spikes: exploring the neural code.* Cambridge, MA: MIT Press.

Rissanen, J. (1987). Stochastic complexity. *Journal of the Royal Statistical Society,* *Series B*, **49**, 223–239.

Rissanen, J. (1996). Fisher information and stochastic complexity. *IEEE Transactions of Information Theory*, **42**, 40–47.

Rock, I. (1983). *The logic of perception*. Cambridge, MA: MIT Press.

Rubinstein, A. (1998). *Models of bounded rationality*. Cambridge, MA: MIT Press.

Rumelhart, D. E., Smolensky, P., McClelland, J. L., & Hinton, G. E. (1986). Schemata and sequential thought processes in PDP models. In J. McClelland, & D. Rumelhart (Eds.) *Parallel distributed processing: explorations in the microstructures of cognition Vol 2: psychological and biological models*. Cambridge, MA: MIT Press.

Saunders, J. A., & Knill, D. C. (2004). Visual feedback control of hand movements. *Journal of Neuroscience*, **24**, 3223-3234.

Schooler, L. J., & Anderson, J. R. (1997). The role of process in the rational analysis of memory. *Cognitive Psychology*, **32**, 219–250.

Shannon, C. E., & Weaver, W. (1949). *The mathematical theory of communication*. Urbana: University of Illinois Press.

Shiffrin, R. M., & Steyvers, M. (1998). The effectiveness of retrieval from memory. In M. Oaksford & N. Chater (Eds.), *Rational models of cognition* (pp. 73–95). Oxford: Oxford University Press.

Simon, H. A. (1957). *Models of man*, New York, NY: Wiley.

Simpson, E. H. (1951). The interpretation of interaction in contingency tables. *Journal of the Royal Statistical Society, Ser, B*, **13**, 238–241.

Sloman, S. A., & Lagnado, D. (2005). Do we 'do'? *Cognitive Science*, **29**, 5–39.

Snippe, H. P., Poot, L., & van Hateren, J. H. (2000). A temporal model for early vision that explains detection thresholds for light pulses on flickering backgrounds. *Visual Neuroscience*, **17**, 449–462.

Stephens, D. W., & Krebs, J. R. (1986). *Foraging theory*. Princeton, NJ: Princeton University Press.

Stewart, N., Brown, G. D. A., & Chater, N. (2005). Absolute identification by relative judgment. *Psychological Review*, **112**, 881–911.

Stewart, N., Chater, N., & Brown, G. D. A. (2006). Decision by sampling. *Cognitive Psychology*, **53**, 1–26.

Swier, R., &. Stevenson, S. (2005). Exploiting a verb lexicon in automatic semantic role labelling. In *Proceedings of the Joint Human Language Technology Conference and Conference on Empirical Methods in Natural Language Processing* (HLT/EMNLP-05).

Tenenbaum, J. B., Griffiths, T. L., & Kemp, C. (2006). Theory-based Bayesian models of inductive learning and reasoning. *Trends in Cognitive Sciences*, **10**, 309–318.

Rubenstein, A. (1998). *Modeling bounded rationality*. Cambridge, MA: MIT Press.

Todorov, E., & Jordon, M. I. (2002). Optimal feedback control as a theory of motor coordination. *Nature Neuroscience*, **5**, 1226–1235.

Toutanova, K., Manning, C. Flickinger, D., & Oepen, S. (2005). Stochastic HPSG parse disambiguation using the Redwoods corpus. *Research on Language and Computation*, **3**, 83–105.

Trommershäuser, J., Landy, M. S., & Maloney, L. T. (2006). Humans rapidly estimate expected gain in movement planning. *Psychological Science*, **11**, 981–988.

Tu, Z., Chen, X., Yuille, A. L., & Zhu, S.-C. (2005). Image parsing: unifying segmentation detection and recognition. *International Journal of Computer Vision*, **2**, 113–140.

van der Helm, P. A., & Leeuwenberg, E. L. J. (1996). Goodness of visual regularities: a nontransformational approach. *Psychological Review*, **103**, 429–456.

von Mises, R. (1957). *Probability, statistics and truth* (Revised English Edition). New York, NY: Macmillan.

Wallace, C. S., & Freeman, P. R. (1987). Estimation and inference by compact coding. *Journal of the Royal Statistical Society, Series B,* **49**, 240–251.

Weiss, Y. (1997). Interpreting images by propagating Bayesian beliefs. In M. C. Mozer, M. I. Jordan, &. T. Petsche (Eds.), *Advances in Neural Information Processing Systems 9* (pp. 908–915). Cambridge MA: MIT Press.

Xu, F. L., & Tenenbaum, J. B. (in press). *Word learning as Bayesian inference. Psychological Review.*

Yuille, A., & Kersten, D. (2006). Vision as Bayesian inference: analysis by synthesis? *Trends in Cognitive Sciences,* **10**, 301–308.

Zettlemoyer, L. S., & Collins, M. (2005). Learning to map sentences to logical form: Structured classification with probabilistic categorical grammars. In *Proceedings of the Twenty First Conference on Uncertainty in Artificial Intelligence* (UAI-05).

Zhai, C., & Lafferty, J. (2001). Document language models, query models, and risk minimization for information retrieval. In W. Croft, D. Harper, D. Kraft, & J. Zobel, (Eds.), *SIGIR conference on research and development in information retrieval* (pp. 111–119). New York, NY: ACM Press.

Chapter 2

A primer on probabilistic inference

Thomas L. Griffiths

Department of Psychology, University of California,
Berkeley, CA, USA

Alan Yuille

Department of Statistics, University of California,
Los Angeles, CA, USA

Probabilistic models aim to explain human cognition by appealing to the principles of probability theory and statistics, which dictate how an agent should act rationally in situations that involve uncertainty. While probability theory was originally developed as a means of analyzing games of chance, it was quickly realized that probabilities could be used to analyze rational actions in a wide range of contexts (e.g., Bayes, 1763/1958; Laplace, 1795/1951). Probabilistic models have come to be used in many disciplines, and are currently the method of choice for an enormous range of applications, including artificial systems for medical inference, bio-informatics, and computer vision. Applying probabilistic models to human cognition thus provides the opportunity to draw upon work in computer science, engineering, mathematics, and statistics, often producing quite surprising connections.

There are two challenges involved in developing probabilistic models of cognition. The first challenge is specifying a suitable model. This requires considering the computational problem faced by an agent, the knowledge available to that agent, and the appropriate way to represent that knowledge. The second challenge is evaluating model predictions. Probabilistic models can capture the structure of extremely complex problems, but as the structure of the model becomes richer, probabilistic inference becomes harder. Being able to compute the relevant probabilities is a practical issue that arises when using probabilistic models, and also raises the question of how intelligent agents might be able to make similar computations.

In this chapter, we introduce some of the tools that can be used to address these challenges. By considering how probabilistic models can be defined and used, we aim to provide some of the background relevant to the other chapters in this volume. The plan of the chapter is as follows. First, we outline the fundamentals of Bayesian inference, which is at the heart of many probabilistic models. We then discuss how to define probabilistic models that use richly structured probability distributions, introducing some of the key ideas behind *graphical models*, which can be used to represent the dependencies among a set of variables. Finally, we discuss two of the main algorithms that are used to evaluate the predictions of probabilistic models—the *Expectation-Maximization* (*EM*) algorithm, and *Markov chain Monte Carlo* (*MCMC*)—and some sophisticated probabilistic models that exploit these algorithms. Several books provide a more detailed discussion of these topics in the context of statistics (e.g., Berger, 1993; Bernardo & Smith, 1994; Gelman, Carlin *et al.*, 1995), machine learning (e.g., Bishop, 2006; Duda *et al.*, 2000; Hastie *et al.*, 2001; Mackay, 2003), and artificial intelligence (e.g., Korb & Nicholson, 2003; Pearl, 1988; Russell & Norvig, 2002). Griffiths *et al.* (in press) provide further information on some of the methods touched on in this chapter, together with examples of applications of these methods in cognitive science.

Fundamentals of Bayesian inference

Probabilistic models of cognition are often referred to as Bayesian models, reflecting the central role that Bayesian inference plays in reasoning under uncertainty. In this section, we will introduce the basic ideas behind Bayesian inference, and discuss how it can be used in different contexts.

Basic Bayes

Bayesian inference is based upon a simple formula known as *Bayes' rule* (Bayes, 1763/1958). When stated in terms of abstract random variables, Bayes' rule is a simple tautology of probability theory. Assume we have two random variables, A and B.[1] One of the principles of probability theory (sometimes called the *chain rule*) allows us to write the *joint probability* of these two variables taking on particular values a and b, $P(a,b)$, as the product of the *conditional probability* that A will take on value a given B takes on value b, $P(a|b)$, and the *marginal probability* that B takes on value b, $P(b)$. Thus, we have

$$P(a,b)=P(a|b)P(b). \tag{1}$$

There was nothing special about the choice of A rather than B in factorizing the joint probability in this way, so we can also write

$$P(a,b)=P(b|a)P(a). \tag{2}$$

It follows from (1) and (2) that $P(a|b)P(b)=P(b|a)P(a)$, which can be rearranged to give

$$P(b \mid a) = \frac{P(a \mid b)P(b)}{P(a)}. \tag{3}$$

This expression is Bayes' rule, which indicates how we can compute the conditional probability of b given a from the conditional probability of a given b.

---

[1] We will use uppercase letters to indicate random variables, and matching lowercase variables to indicate the values those variables take on. When defining probability distributions, the random variables will remain implicit. For example, $P(a)$ refers to the probability that the variable A takes on the value a, which could also be written $P(A=a)$. We will write joint probabilities in the form $P(a,b)$. Other notations for joint probabilities include $P(a\&b)$ and $P(a \cap b)$.

In the form given in (3), Bayes' rule seems relatively innocuous (and perhaps rather uninteresting!). Bayes' rule gets its strength, and its notoriety, by making some assumptions about the variables we are considering and the meaning of probability. Assume that we have an agent who is attempting to infer the process that was responsible for generating some data, d. Let h be a hypothesis about this process, and $P(h)$ indicate the probability that the agent would have ascribed to h being the true generating process, prior to seeing d (known as a *prior probability*). How should that agent go about changing his beliefs in the light of the evidence provided by d? To answer this question, we need a procedure for computing the *posterior probability*, $P(h|d)$.

Bayes' rule provides just such a procedure. If we are willing to consider the hypotheses that agents entertain to be random variables, and allow probabilities to reflect subjective degrees of belief, then Bayes' rule indicates how an agent should update their beliefs in light of evidence. Replacing a with d and b with h in (3) gives

$$P(h \mid d) = \frac{P(d \mid h)P(h)}{P(d)}, \tag{4}$$

which is the form in which Bayes' rule is normally presented. The probability of the data given the hypothesis, $P(d|h)$, is known as the *likelihood*.

Probability theory also allows us to compute the probability distribution associated with a single variable (known as the *marginal probability*) by summing over the other variables in a joint distribution (known as *marginalization*), e.g., $P(b) = \sum_a P(a,b)$. Using this principle, we can rewrite (4) as

$$P(h \mid d) = \frac{P(d \mid h)P(h)}{\sum_{h' \in H} P(d \mid h')P(h')}, \tag{5}$$

where H is the set of all hypotheses considered by the agent, sometimes referred to as the *hypothesis space*. This formulation of Bayes' rule makes it apparent that the posterior probability of h is directly proportional to the product of the prior probability and the likelihood. The sum in the denominator simply ensures that the resulting probabilities are normalized to sum to one.

The use of probabilities to represent degrees of belief is known as *subjectivism*, as opposed to *frequentism*, in which probabilities are viewed as the long-run relative frequencies of the outcomes of non-deterministic experiments. Subjectivism is strongly associated with Bayesian approaches to statistics, and has been a subject of great controversy in foundational discussions on the nature of probability. A number of formal arguments have been used to justify this position (e.g., Cox, 1961; Jaynes, 2003). In the remainder of this section, we will focus on some of the practical applications of Bayes' rule.

Comparing two simple hypotheses

The setting in which Bayes' rule is usually discussed in introductory statistics courses is for the comparison of two simple hypotheses. For example, imagine that you are told that a box contains two coins: one that produces heads 50% of the time, and one that produces heads 90% of the time. You choose a coin, and then flip it ten times, producing the sequence HHHHHHHHHH. Which coin did you pick? What would you think if you had flipped HHTHTHTTHT instead?

To translate this problem into one of Bayesian inference, we need to identify the hypothesis space, H, the prior probability of each hypothesis, $P(h)$, and the probability of the data under each hypothesis, $P(d|h)$. We have two coins, and thus two hypotheses. If we use θ to denote the probability that a coin produces heads, then h_0 is the hypothesis that $\theta=0.5$, and h_1 is the hypothesis that $\theta=0.9$. Since we have no reason to believe that we would be more likely to pick one coin than the other, the prior probabilities are $P(h_0)=P(h_1)=0.5$. The probability of a particular sequence of coin-flips containing N_H heads and N_T tails being generated by a coin which produces heads with probability θ is

$$P(d \mid \theta) = \theta^{N_H} (1 - \theta)^{N_T}.$$

(6)

The likelihoods associated with h_0 and h_1 can thus be obtained by substituting the appropriate value of θ into (6).

We can take the prior and likelihoods defined in the previous paragraph, and plug them directly into (4) to compute the posterior probability of each of our two hypotheses. However, when we have just two hypotheses it is often easier to work with the *posterior odds*, which are just the ratio of the posterior probabilities. If we use Bayes' rule to find the posterior probability of h_0 and h_1, it follows that the posterior odds in favor of h_1 are

$$\frac{P(h_1 \mid d)}{P(h_0 \mid d)} = \frac{P(d \mid h_1) \, P(h_1)}{P(d \mid h_0) \, P(h_0)}$$

(7)

where we have used the fact that the denominator of (4) is constant. The first and second terms on the right hand side are called the *likelihood ratio* and the *prior odds* respectively. Returning to our example, we can use (7) to compute the posterior odds of our two hypotheses for any observed sequence of heads and tails. Using the prior and likelihoods from the previous paragraph gives odds of approximately 357:1 in favor of h_1 for the sequence HHHHHHHHHH and 165:1 in favor of h_0 for the sequence HHTHTHTTHT.

The form of (7) helps to clarify how prior knowledge and new data are combined in Bayesian inference. The two terms on the right hand side each express the influence of one of these factors: the prior odds are determined entirely by the prior beliefs of the agent, while the likelihood ratio expresses how these odds should be modified in light of the data d. This relationship is made even more transparent if we examine the expression for the log posterior odds,

$$\log \frac{P(h_1 \mid d)}{P(h_0 \mid d)} = \log \frac{P(d \mid h_1)}{P(d \mid h_0)} + \log \frac{P(h_1)}{P(h_0)}$$

(8)

in which the extent to which one should favor h_1 over h_0 reduces to an additive combination of a term reflecting prior beliefs (the log prior odds) and a term reflecting the contribution of the data (the log likelihood ratio). Based upon this decomposition, the log likelihood ratio in favor of h_1 is often used as a measure of the evidence that d provides for h_1. The British mathematician Alan Turing, arguably one of the founders of cognitive science, was also one of the first people to apply Bayesian inference in this fashion: he used log likelihood ratios as part of a method for deciphering German naval codes during World War II (Good, 1979).

Comparing infinitely many hypotheses

The analysis outlined above for two simple hypotheses generalizes naturally to any finite set, although posterior odds are less useful when there are multiple alternatives to be considered. However, Bayesian inference can also be applied in contexts where there are (uncountably) infinitely many hypotheses to evaluate—a situation that arises surprisingly often. For example, imagine that rather than choosing between two alternatives for the probability that a coin produces heads, θ, we were willing to consider any value of θ between 0 and 1. What should we infer about the value of θ from a sequence such as HHHHHHHHHH?

In frequentist statistics, from which much of the statistical doctrine used in the analysis of psychology experiments derives, inferring θ is treated a problem of estimating a fixed parameter of a probabilistic model, to which the standard solution is *maximum-likelihood* estimation (see, e.g., Rice, 1995). The maximum-likelihood estimate of θ is the value θ that maximizes the probability of the data, as given in (6). It is straightforward to show that this is $\theta = \dfrac{N_H}{N_H + N_T}$, which gives $\theta=1.0$ for the sequence HHHHHHHHHH.

The case of inferring the bias of a coin can be used to illustrate some properties of maximum-likelihood estimation that can be problematic. First of all, the value of θ that maximizes the probability of the data might not provide the best basis for making predictions about future data. To continue the example above, inferring that $\theta=1.0$ after seeing the sequence HHHHHHHHHH implies that we should predict that the coin would never produce tails. This might seem reasonable, but the same conclusion follows for any sequence consisting entirely of heads. Would you predict that a coin would produce only heads after seeing it produce a head on a single flip?

A second problem with maximum-likelihood estimation is that it does not take into account other knowledge that we might have about θ. This is largely by design: the frequentist approach to statistics was founded on the belief that subjective probabilities are meaningless, and aimed to provide an 'objective' system of statistical inference that did not require prior probabilities. However, while such a goal of objectivity might be desirable in certain scientific contexts, most intelligent agents have access to extensive knowledge that constrains their inferences. For example, many of us might have strong expectations that a coin would produce heads with a probability close to 0.5.

Both of these problems are addressed by the Bayesian approach to this problem, in which inferring θ is treated just like any other Bayesian inference. If we assume that θ is a random variable, then we can apply Bayes' rule to obtain

$$p(\theta \mid d) = \frac{P(d \mid \theta)p(\theta)}{P(d)} \tag{9}$$

where

$$P(d) = \int_0^1 P(d \mid \theta)p(\theta)d\theta.$$

(10)

The key difference from Bayesian inference with finitely many hypotheses is that the posterior distribution is now characterized by a *probability density*, and the sum over hypotheses becomes an integral.

The posterior distribution over θ contains more information than a single point estimate: it indicates not just which values of θ are probable, but also how much uncertainty there is about those values. Collapsing this distribution down to a single number discards information, so Bayesians prefer to maintain distributions wherever possible (this attitude is similar to Marr's (1982, p. 106) 'principle of least commitment'). However, there are two methods that are commonly used to obtain a point estimate from a posterior distribution. The first method is *maximum a posteriori* (*MAP*) estimation: choosing the value of θ that maximizes the posterior probability, as given by (9). The second method is computing the *posterior mean* of the quantity in question. For example, we could compute the posterior mean value of θ, which would be

$$\theta = \int_0^1 \theta p(\theta|d)d\theta.$$

(11)

For the case of coinflipping, the posterior mean also corresponds to the probability of obtaining heads under the *posterior predictive distribution*: the probability with which one should predict the next toss of the coin will produce heads.

The choice of which estimator to use for θ depends on the nature of the problem being solved. Bayesian decision theory (e.g., Berger, 1993) approaches this problem by introducing a loss function $L(\theta,\alpha(d))$ for the cost of making a decision $\alpha(d)$ when the input is d and the true value of the parameter is θ. From this perspective, we should select the decision rule $\alpha^*(\cdot)$ that minimizes the risk, or expected loss:

$$R(\alpha) = \sum_{\theta,d} L(\theta,\alpha(d))p(\theta,d)$$

(12)

where the distribution on θ and d captures both the natural variation in d and the uncertainty of the learner about θ given d, as represented in the posterior distribution. One loss function has the same penalty for all wrong decisions: $L(\theta,\alpha(d))=1$ if $\alpha(d) \neq \theta$ and $L(\theta,\alpha(d))=0$ if $\alpha(d)=\theta$. For this loss function, the best decision rule is the MAP estimator. Alternatively, if the loss function is the square of the error $L(\theta,\alpha(d))= (\theta - \alpha(d))^2$ then the best decision rule is the posterior mean. This approach can be extended to dynamical systems where decisions need to be made over time. This leads to optimal control theory (Bertsekas, 2000) where the goal is to minimize a cost functional to obtain a control law (analogous to the risk and the decision rule respectively). Optimal control theory lays the groundwork for rational models of animal learning and motor control.

Regardless of the estimator being used, different choices of the prior, $p(\theta)$, will lead to different guesses at the value of θ. A first step might be to assume a *uniform* prior over θ, with $p(\theta)$ being equal for all values of θ between 0 and 1. This case was first analyzed by Laplace (1795/1951). Using a little calculus, it is possible to show that the posterior distribution over θ produced by a sequence d with N_H heads and N_T tails is

$$p(\theta \mid d) = \frac{(N_H + N_T + 1)!}{N_H! N_T!} \theta^{N_H} (1 - \theta)^{N_T}.$$
(13)

This is actually a distribution of a well known form, being a beta distribution with parameters $N_H + 1$ and $N_T + 1$, denoted Beta $(N_H + 1, N_T + 1)$ (e.g., Pitman, 1993). Using this prior, the MAP estimate for θ is the same as the maximum-likelihood estimate, being $\frac{N_H}{N_H + N_T}$, but the posterior mean is $\frac{N_H + 1}{N_H + N_T + 2}$. Thus, the posterior mean is sensitive to the fact that we might not want to put as much weight in a single head as a sequence of ten heads in a row: on seeing a single head, we should predict that the next toss will produce a head with probability $\frac{2}{3}$, while a sequence of ten heads should lead us to predict that the next toss will produce a head with probability $\frac{11}{12}$.

Finally, we can also use priors that encode stronger beliefs about the value of θ. For example, we can take a Beta $(V_H + 1, V_T + 1)$ distribution for $p(\theta)$, where V_H and V_T are positive integers. This distribution has a mean at $\frac{V_H + 1}{V_H + V_T + 2}$, and gradually becomes more concentrated around that mean as $V_H + V_T$ becomes large. For instance, taking $V^H = V^T = 1000$ would give a distribution that strongly favors values of θ close to 0.5. Using such a prior, we obtain the posterior distribution

$$p(\theta \mid d) = \frac{(N_H + N_T + V_H + V_T + 1)!}{(N_H + V_H)!(N_T + V_T)!} \theta^{N_H + V_H} (1 - \theta)^{N_T + V_T},$$
(14)

which is Beta $(N_H + V_H + 1, N_T + V_T + 1,)$. Under this posterior distribution, the MAP estimate of θ is $\frac{N_H + V_H}{N_H + N_T + V_H + V_T}$, and the posterior mean is $\frac{N_H + V_H + 1}{N_H + N_T + V_H + V_T + 2}$. Thus, if $V_H = V_T = 1000$, seeing a sequence of ten heads in a row would induce a posterior distribution over θ with a mean of $\frac{1011}{2012} \approx 0.5025$.

Some reflection upon the results in the previous paragraph yields two observations: first, that the prior and posterior are from the same family of distributions (both being beta distributions), and second, that the parameters of the prior, V_H and V_T, act as 'virtual examples' of heads and tails, which are simply combined with the real examples tallied in N_H and N_T to produce the posterior. These two properties are not accidental: they are characteristic of a class of priors called *conjugate priors* (Bernardo & Smith, 1994). The likelihood determines whether a conjugate prior exists for a given problem, and the form that the prior will take. The results we have given in this section exploit the fact that the beta distribution is the conjugate prior for the Bernoulli or binomial likelihood (6)—the uniform distribution on [0,1] is also a beta distribution, being Beta(1,1). Conjugate priors exist for many of the distributions commonly used in probabilistic models, such as Gaussian, Poisson, and multinomial distributions, and greatly simplify many Bayesian calculations.

Using conjugate priors, posterior distributions can be computed analytically, and the interpretation of the prior as contributing virtual examples is intuitive.

The example of tossing a coin serves to illustrate how the posterior distribution forms a compromise between the prior and the information provided by the data, even when we move from a small number of hypotheses to a continuum. This compromise is quite explicit in (14) and the estimators based upon it, where the number of heads and tails exhibited in the data combine directly with the number of heads and tails expected under the prior. Conjugate priors yield this kind of result in many models, but the underlying principle is more general: the posterior distribution will always represent a synthesis of the data, filtered through the likelihood, and the expectations of the learner, as reflected in the prior.

Comparing hypotheses that differ in complexity

Whether there were a finite number or not, the hypotheses that we have considered so far were relatively homogeneous, each offering a single value for the parameter θ characterizing our coin. However, many problems require comparing hypotheses that differ in their complexity. For example, the problem of inferring whether a coin is fair or biased based upon an observed sequence of heads and tails requires comparing a hypothesis that gives a single value for θ—if the coin is fair, then $\theta = 0.5$—with a hypothesis that allows θ to take on any value between 0 and 1.

Using observed data to choose between two probabilistic models that differ in their complexity is often called the problem of *model selection* (Myung & Pitt, 1997; Myung *et al.*, 2000). In frequentist statistics, this problem is addressed via hypothesis testing, a complex and counter-intuitive method that will be familiar to many readers. In contrast, the Bayesian approach to model selection is a seamless application of the methods discussed so far. Hypotheses that differ in their complexity can be compared directly using Bayes' rule, once they are reduced to probability distributions over the observable data (see Kass & Raftery, 1995).

To illustrate this principle, assume that we have two hypotheses: h_0 is the hypothesis that $\theta=0.5$, and h_1 is the hypothesis that θ takes a value drawn from a uniform distribution on $[0,1]$. If we have no a priori reason to favor one hypothesis over the other, we can take $P(h_0) = P(h_1) = 0.5$. The likelihood of the data under h_0 is straightforward to compute, using (6), giving $P(d \mid h_0) = 0.5^{N_H + N_T}$. But how should we compute the likelihood of the data under h_1, which does not make a commitment to a single value of θ?

The solution to this problem is to compute the marginal probability of the data under h_1. As discussed above, given a joint distribution over a set of variables, we can always sum out variables until we obtain a distribution over just the variables that interest us. In this case, we define the joint distribution over d and θ given h_1, and then integrate over θ to obtain

$$P(d \mid h_1) = \int_0^1 P(d \mid \theta, h_1) p(\theta \mid h_1) d\theta \tag{15}$$

where $p(\theta|h_1)$ is the distribution over θ assumed under h_1—in this case, a uniform distribution over $[0,1]$. This does not require any new concepts—it is exactly the same kind of computation as we needed to perform to compute the normalizing constant for the posterior distribution over θ (10). Performing this computation, we obtain

$$P(d \mid h_1) = \frac{N_H! N_T!}{(N_H + N_T + 1)!},$$ where again the fact that we have a conjugate prior on

θ provides us with a neat analytic result. Having computed this likelihood, we can apply Bayes' rule just as we did for two simple hypotheses. Figure 2.2.1(a) shows

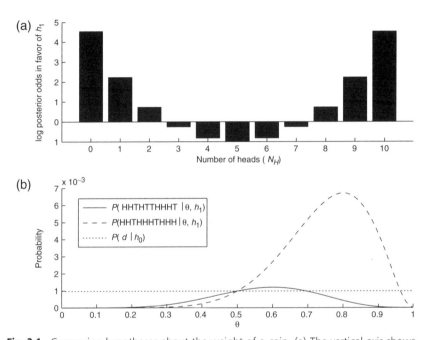

Fig. 2.1. Comparing hypotheses about the weight of a coin. (a) The vertical axis shows log posterior odds in favor of h_1, the hypothesis that the probability of heads (θ) is drawn from a uniform distribution on [0,1], over h_0, the hypothesis that the probability of heads is 0.5. The horizontal axis shows the number of heads, N_H, in a sequence of 10 flips. As N_H deviates from 5, the posterior odds in favor of h_1 increase. (b) The posterior odds shown in (a) are computed by averaging over the values of θ with respect to the prior, $p(\theta)$, which in this case is the uniform distribution on [0,1]. This averaging takes into account the fact that hypotheses with greater flexibility—such as the free-ranging θ parameter in h_1—can produce both better and worse predictions, implementing an automatic 'Bayesian Occam's razor'. The solid line shows the probability of the sequence HHTHTTHHHT for different values of θ, while the dotted line is the probability of any sequence of length 10 under h_0 (equivalent to θ = 0.5). While there are some values of θ that result in a higher probability for the sequence, on average the greater flexibility of h_1 results in lower probabilities. Consequently, h_0 is favored over h_1 (this sequence has $N_H = 6$). In contrast, a wide range of values of θ result in higher probability for the sequence HHTHHHTHHH, as shown by the dashed line. Consequently, h_1 is favored over h_0, (this sequence has $N_H = 8$).

how the log posterior odds in favor of h_1 change as N_H and N_T vary for sequences of length 10.

The ease with which hypotheses differing in complexity can be compared using Bayes' rule conceals the fact that this is actually a very challenging problem. Complex hypotheses have more degrees of freedom that can be adapted to the data, and can thus always be made to fit the data better than simple hypotheses. For example, for any sequence of heads and tails, we can always find a value of θ that would give higher probability to that sequence than the hypothesis that $\theta=0.5$. It seems like a complex hypothesis would thus have a big advantage over a simple hypothesis. The Bayesian solution to the problem of comparing hypotheses that differ in their complexity takes this into account. More degrees of freedom provide the opportunity to find a better fit to the data, but this greater flexibility also makes a worse fit possible. For example, for d consisting of the sequence HHTHTTHHHT, $P(d|\theta,h_1)$ is greater than $P(d|h_0)$ for $\theta \in (0.5, 0.694]$, but is less than $P(d|h_0)$ outside that range. Marginalizing over θ averages these gains and losses: a more complex hypothesis will be favored only if its greater complexity consistently provides a better account of the data. This penalization of more complex models is known as the 'Bayesian Occam's razor' (Jeffreys & Berger, 1992; Mackay, 2003), and is illustrated in Fig. 2.2.1.(b).

Representing structured probability distributions

Probabilistic models go beyond 'hypotheses' and 'data'. More generally, a probabilistic model defines the joint distribution for a set of random variables. For example, imagine that a friend of yours claims to possess psychic powers—in particular, the power of psychokinesis. He proposes to demonstrate these powers by flipping a coin, and influencing the outcome to produce heads. You suggest that a better test might be to see if he can levitate a pencil, since the coin producing heads could also be explained by some kind of sleight of hand, such as substituting a two-headed coin. We can express all possible outcomes of the proposed tests, as well as their causes, using the binary random variables X_1, X_2, X_3, and X_4 to represent (respectively) the truth of the coin being flipped and producing heads, the pencil levitating, your friend having psychic powers, and the use of a two-headed coin. Any set of beliefs about these outcomes can be encoded in a joint probability distribution, $P(x_1, x_2, x_3, x_4)$. For example, the probability that the coin comes up heads ($x_1=1$) should be higher if your friend actually does have psychic powers ($x_3=1$).

Once we have defined a joint distribution on X_1, X_2, X_3, and X_4, we can reason about the implications of events involving these variables. For example, if flipping the coin produces heads ($x_1=1$), then the probability distribution over the remaining variables is

$$P(x_2, x_3, x_4 \,|\, x_1 = 1) = \frac{P(x_1 = 1, x_2, x_3, x_4)}{P(x_1 = 1)}$$

(16)

This equation can be interpreted as an application of Bayes' rule, with X_1 being the data, and X_2, X_3, X_4 being the hypotheses. However, in this setting, as with most probabilistic models, any variable can act as data or hypothesis. In the general case, we use probabilistic inference to compute the probability distribution over a set of *unobserved* variables (here, X_2, X_3, X_4) conditioned on a set of *observed* variables (here, X_1).

While the rules of probability can, in principle, be used to define and reason about probabilistic models involving any number of variables, two factors can make large probabilistic models difficult to use. First, it is hard to simply write down a joint distribution over a set of variables which expresses the assumptions that we want to make in a probabilistic model. Second, the resources required to represent and reason about probability distributions increase exponentially in the number of variables involved. A probability distribution over four binary random variables requires $2^4 - 1 = 15$ numbers to specify, which might seem quite reasonable. If we double the number of random variables to eight, we would need to provide $2^8 - 1 = 255$ numbers to fully specify the joint distribution over those variables, a much more challenging task!

Fortunately, the widespread use of probabilistic models in statistics and computer science has led to the development of a powerful formal language for describing probability distributions which is extremely intuitive, and simplifies both representing and reasoning about those distributions. This is the language of *graphical models*, in which the statistical dependencies that exist among a set of variables are represented graphically. We will discuss two kinds of graphical models: *directed* graphical models, and *undirected* graphical models.

Directed graphical models

Directed graphical models, also known as Bayesian networks or Bayes nets, consist of a set of nodes, representing random variables, together with a set of directed edges from one node to another, which can be used to identify statistical dependencies between variables (e.g., Pearl, 1988). Typically, nodes are drawn as circles, and the existence of a directed edge from one node to another is indicated with an arrow between the corresponding nodes. If an edge exists from node A to node B, then A is referred to as the 'parent' of B, and B is the 'child' of A. This genealogical relation is often extended to identify the 'ancestors' and 'descendants' of a node.

The directed graph used in a Bayes net has one node for each random variable in the associated probability distribution. The edges express the statistical dependencies between the variables in a fashion consistent with the *Markov condition*: conditioned on its parents, each variable is independent of all other variables except its descendants (Pearl, 1988; Spirtes *et al.*, 1993). This has an important implication: a Bayes net specifies a canonical factorization of a probability distribution into the product of the conditional distribution for each variable conditioned on its parents. Thus, for a set of variables $X_1, X_2, \ldots, X_M$, we can write $P\left(x_1, x_2, \ldots, x_M\right) = \prod_i P\left(x_i \mid Pa\left(X_i\right)\right)$ where $Pa(X_i)$ is the set of parents of X_i.

Figure 2.2.2 shows a Bayes net for the example of the friend who claims to have psychic powers. This Bayes net identifies a number of assumptions about the relationship between the variables involved in this situation. For example, X_1 and X_2 are assumed to be independent given X_3, indicating that once it was known whether or not your friend was psychic, the outcomes of the coin flip and the levitation experiments would be completely unrelated. By the Markov condition, we can write

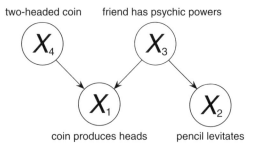

two-headed coin   friend has psychic powers

Fig. 2.2. Directed graphical model (Bayes net) showing the dependencies among variables in the 'psychic friend' example discussed in the text.

coin produces heads   pencil levitates

$P(x_1,x_2,x_3,x_4) = P(x_1|x_3,x_4)P(x_2|x_3)P(x_3)P(x_4)$. This factorization allows us to use fewer numbers in specifying the distribution over these four variables: we only need one number for each variable, conditioned on each set of values taken on by its parents. In this case, this adds up to 8 numbers rather than 15. Furthermore, recognizing the structure in this probability distribution simplifies some of the computations we might want to perform. For example, in order to evaluate (16), we need to compute

$$P(x_1 = 1) = \sum_{x_2}\sum_{x_3}\sum_{x_4} P(x_1 = 1, x_2, x_3, x_4)$$
$$= \sum_{x_2}\sum_{x_3}\sum_{x_4} P(x_1 = 1 | x_3, x_4)P(x_2 | x_3)P(x_3)P(x_4)$$
$$= \sum_{x_3}\sum_{x_4} P(x_1 = 1 | x_3, x_4)P(x_3)P(x_4) \tag{17}$$

where we were able to sum out X_2 directly as a result of its independence from X_1 when conditioned on X_3.

Bayes nets make it easy to define probability distributions, and speed up probabilistic inference. There are a number of specialized algorithms for efficient probabilistic inference in Bayes nets, which make use of the dependencies among variables (see Pearl, 1988; Russell & Norvig, 2002). In particular, if the underlying graph is a tree (i.e. it has no closed loops), dynamic programming algorithms (e.g., Bertsekas, 2000) can be used to exploit this structure. The intuition behind dynamic programming can be illustrated by planning the shortest route for a trip from Los Angeles to Boston. To determine the cost of going via Chicago, you only need to calculate the shortest route from LA to Chicago and then, independently, from Chicago to Boston. Decomposing the route in this way, and taking into account the linear nature of the trip, gives an efficient algorithm with convergence rates which are polynomial in the number of nodes and hence are often feasible for computation. Equation (17) is one illustration for how the dynamic programming can exploit the structure of the problem to simplify the computation. These methods are put to particularly good use in hidden Markov models, which we discuss in further detail later in the chapter.

With a little practice, and a few simple rules (e.g., Schachter, 1998), it is easy to read the dependencies among a set of variables from a Bayes net, and to identify how variables will influence one another. One common pattern of influence is *explaining away*. Imagine that your friend flipped the coin, and it came up heads (x_1=1). The propositions that he has psychic powers (x_3=1) and that it is a two-headed coin (x_4=1) might both become more likely. However, while these two variables were independent before seeing the outcome of the coinflip, they are now dependent: if you were to go on to discover that the coin has two heads, the hypothesis of psychic powers would return to its baseline probability—the evidence for psychic powers was 'explained away' by the presence of the two-headed coin.

Different aspects of directed graphical models are emphasized in their use in the artificial intelligence and statistics communities. In the artificial intelligence community (e.g., Korb & Nicholson, 2003; Pearl, 1988; Russell & Norvig, 2002), the emphasis is on Bayes nets as a form of knowledge representation and an engine for probabilistic reasoning. In statistics, graphical models tend to be used to clarify the dependencies among a set of variables, and to identify the *generative model* assumed by a particular analysis. A generative model is a step-by-step procedure by which a set of variables are assumed to take their values, defining a probability distribution over those variables. Any Bayes net specifies such a procedure: each variable without parents is sampled, then each successive variable is sampled conditioned on the values of its parents. By considering the process by which observable data are generated, it becomes possible to postulate that the structure contained in those data is the result of underlying unobserved variables. The use of such *latent variables* is extremely common in probabilistic models, as we discuss further later in the chapter.

Recently, research has begun to explore the use of graphical models for the representation of causal relationships. Causal graphical models augment standard directed graphical models with a stronger assumption about the relationship indicated by an edge between two nodes: rather than indicating statistical dependency, such an edge is assumed to indicate a direct causal relationship (Pearl, 2000; Spirtes *et al.*, 1993). This assumption allows causal graphical models to represent not just the probabilities of events that one might observe, but also the probabilities of events that one can produce through intervening on a system. The implications of an event can differ strongly, depending on whether it was the result of observation or intervention. For example, *observing* that nothing happened when your friend attempted to levitate a pencil would provide evidence against his claim of having psychic powers; *intervening* to hold the pencil down, and thus guaranteeing that it did not move during his attempted act of levitation, would remove any opportunity for this event to provide such evidence.

In causal graphical models, the consequences of intervening on a particular variable are be assessed by removing all incoming edges to the variable that was intervened on, and performing probabilistic inference in the resulting 'mutilated' model (Pearl, 2000). This procedure produces results that align with our intuitions in the psychic powers example: intervening on X_2 breaks its connection with X_3, rendering the two variables independent. As a consequence, X_2 cannot provide evidence as to the value of X_3. Introductions to causal graphical models that consider applications to human cognition are provided by Glymour (2001) and Sloman (2005). There are also several good resources for more technical discussions of learning the structure of causal graphical models (Glymour & Cooper, 1999; Heckerman, 1998).

Undirected graphical models

Undirected graphical models, also known as Markov Random Fields (MRFs), consist of a set of nodes, representing random variables, and a set of undirected edges, defining neighborhood structure on the graph which indicates the probabilistic dependencies of the variables at the nodes (e.g., Pearl, 1988). Each set of fully-connected neighbors (known as a *clique*) is associated with a *potential* function, which varies as the associated random variables take on different values. When multiplied together, these potential functions give the probability distribution over all the variables. Unlike directed graphical models, there need be no simple relationship between these potentials and the local conditional probability distributions. Moreover, undirected graphical models usually have closed loops (if they do not, then they can be reformulated as directed graphical models (e.g., Pearl, 1988)).

In many unsupervised learning problems, the observable data are believed to reflect some kind of underlying latent structure. For example, in a clustering problem, we might only see the location of each point, but believe that each point was generated from one of a small number of clusters. Associating the observed data with random variables X_i and the latent variables with random variables Y_i, we might want to define a probabilistic model for X_i that explicitly takes into account the latent structure Y_i. Such a model can ultimately be used to make inferences about the latent structure associated with new datapoints, as well as providing a more accurate model of the distribution of X_i. In the following sections we will use X_i to refer to variables whose values can be directed observed and Y_i to refer to latent, or hidden, variables whose values can only be inferred. We will use the vector notation $\mathbf{x}$ and $\mathbf{y}$ to represent the values taken by these random variables, being $x_1, x_2, \ldots$ and $y_1, y_2, \ldots$ respectively.

A standard model used in computer vision is of the form:

$P(\mathbf{x} \mid \mathbf{y}) = \left(\prod_i P(x_i \mid y_i) \right) P(\mathbf{y})$ where the prior distribution on the latent variables is an MRF,

$$P(\mathbf{y}) = \frac{1}{Z} \prod_{i,j,\in \Lambda} \psi_{ij}\left(y_i, y_j\right) \prod_i \psi_i\left(y_i\right)$$

(18)

where Z is a normalizing constant ensuring that the resulting distribution sums to 1 (e.g., Geman & Geman, 1984). Here, $\psi_{ij}(\cdot, \cdot)$ and $\psi_i(\cdot)$ are the potential functions, and the underlying graph is a lattice, with Λ being the set of connected pairs of nodes (see Fig. 2. 2.3). This model has many applications. For example, $\vec{x}$ can be taken to be the observed intensity values of a corrupted image and $\vec{y}$ the true image intensity, with $P(x_i|y_i)$ modeling the corruption of these intensity values. The prior $P(\mathbf{y})$ is used to put prior probabilities on the true intensity, for example that neighboring intensity values are similar (e.g. that the intensity is spatially smooth). A similar model can be used for binocular stereopsis, where the $\mathbf{x}$ correspond to the image intensities in the left and right eyes and $\mathbf{y}$ denotes the depth of the surface in space that generates the two images. The prior on $\mathbf{y}$ can assume that the depth is a spatially smoothly varying function.

Another example of an MRF is the Boltzmann Machine, which has been very influential in the neural network community (Dayan & Abbott, 2001; Mackay, 2003).

In this model the components x_i and y_i of the observed and latent variables $\mathbf{x}$ and $\mathbf{y}$ all take on values 0 or 1. The standard model is

$$P(\mathbf{y},\mathbf{x}\mid\omega) = \frac{1}{Z}\exp\{-E(\mathbf{y},\mathbf{x},\omega)\,/\,T\} \tag{19}$$

where T is a parameter reflecting the 'temperature' of the system, and E depends on unknown parameters ω which are weighted connections ω_{ij}^h between hidden variables y_i,y_j and ω_{ij}^o between observed and hidden variables x_i,y_j,

$$E(\mathbf{y},\mathbf{x},\omega) = \sum_{ij}\omega_{ij}^o x_i y_j + \sum_{ij}\omega_{ij}^h y_i y_j. \tag{20}$$

In this model, the potential functions are of the form $\exp\{-\omega_{ij}^o x_i y_j\}$ and $\exp\{-\omega_{ij}^h y_i y_j\}$, and the underlying graph connects pairs of observed and hidden variables and pairs of hidden variables (see Fig. 2. 2.3). Training the Boltzmann Machine involves identifying the correct potential functions, learning the parameters ω from training examples. Viewing (19) as specifying the likelihood of a statistical model, inferring ω can be formulated as a problem of Bayesian inference of the kind discussed above.

Algorithms for inference

The presence of latent variables in a model poses two challenges: inferring the values of the latent variables, conditioned on observable data (i.e. computing $P(\mathbf{y}|\mathbf{x})$), and learning the probability distribution $P(\mathbf{x},\mathbf{y})$ from training data (e.g., learning the parameters ω of the Boltzmann Machine). In the probabilistic framework, both these forms of inference reduce to inferring the values of unknown variables, conditioned on known variables. This is conceptually straightforward but the computations involved are difficult and can require complex algorithms (unless the problem has a simple graph structure which allows dynamic programming to be used). In this section, we will discuss two algorithms that can be used to solve this problem.

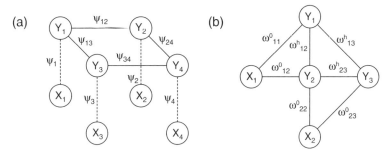

Fig. 2.3. Markov random fields. (a) The undirected graph associated with a Markov random field where $\Lambda=\{(1,2),(2,3),(3,4),(4,1)\}$. (b) The undirected graph associated with a Boltzmann Machine, as discussed in the text.

The Expectation-Maximization algorithm

A standard approach to solving the problem of estimating probability distributions involving latent variables from training data is the Expectation-Maximization (EM) algorithm (Dempster *et al.*, 1977). Imagine we have a model for data **x** that has parameters θ, and latent variables **y**. A mixture model is one example of such a model, in which the distribution of X_i is assumed to be a mixture of several other distributions, each responsible for a cluster of observations. For example, we might believe that our data were generated from two clusters, each associated with a different Gaussian (i.e. normal) distribution. If we let y_i denote the cluster from which the datapoint x_i was generated, and assume that there are K such clusters, then the probability distribution over x_i is

$$P(x_i) = \sum_{K=1}^{K} P(x_i \mid y_i = k) P(y_i = k) \tag{21}$$

where $P(x_i|y_i=k)$ is the distribution associated with cluster k, and $P(y_i=k)$ is the probability that a point would be generated from that cluster. If we can estimate the parameters that characterize these distributions, we can infer the probable cluster membership (y_i) for any datapoint (x_i).

The likelihood for a mixture model is $P(\mathbf{x} \mid \theta) = \sum_{\mathbf{y}} P(\mathbf{x}, \mathbf{y} \mid \theta)$ where the latent variables **y** are unknown. The EM algorithm is a procedure for obtaining a maximum-likelihood (or MAP estimate) for θ, without resorting to generic methods such as differentiating $\log P(\mathbf{x}|\theta)$. The key idea is that if we knew the values of the latent variables **y**, then we could find θ by using the standard methods for estimation discussed above. Even though we might not have perfect knowledge of **y**, we can still assign probabilities to **y** based on **x** and our current guess of θ, $P(\mathbf{y}|\mathbf{x}, \theta)$. The EM algorithm for maximum-likelihood estimation proceeds by repeatedly alternating between two steps: evaluating the expectation of the 'complete log-likelihood' $\log P(\mathbf{x}, \mathbf{y}|\theta)$ with respect to $P(\mathbf{y}|\mathbf{x}, \theta)$ (the E-step), and maximizing the resulting quantity with respect to θ (the M-step). For many commonly used distributions, it is possible to compute the expectation in the E-step without enumerating all possible values for **y**. The EM algorithm is guaranteed to converge to a *local* maximum of $P(\mathbf{x}|\theta)$ (Dempster *et al.*, 1977), and both steps can be interpreted as performing hill-climbing on a single 'free energy' function (Neal & Hinton, 1998). An illustration of EM for a mixture of Gaussians appears in Fig. 2.2.4(a).

Markov chain Monte Carlo

The EM algorithm represents an intuitive solution to the problem of parameter estimation with latent variables, and is effective for a range of applications, but it only provides a solution to one of the inference problems faced in probabilistic models. Indeed, the EM algorithm requires that we be able to solve the other problem— computing $P(\mathbf{y}|\mathbf{x}, \theta)$—in order to be able to perform the E-step (although see Jordan *et al.*, 1999, for methods for dealing with this issue in complex probabilistic models).

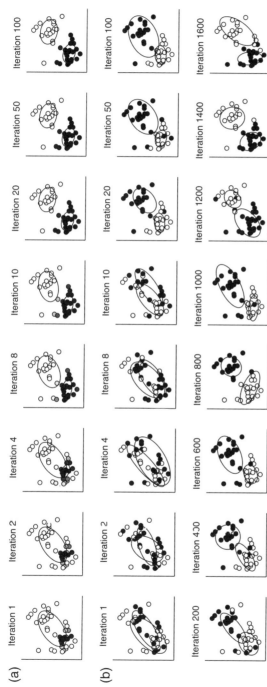

Fig. 2.4. Expectation-Maximization (EM) and Markov chain Monte Carlo (MCMC) algorithms applied to a Gaussian mixture model with two clusters. Colors indicate the assignment of points to clusters (black and white), with intermediate greys representing probabilistic assignments. The ellipses are a single probability contour for the Gaussian distributions reflecting the current parameter values for the two clusters. (a) The EM algorithm assigns datapoints probabilistically to the two clusters, and converges to a single solution that is guaranteed to be a local maximum of the log-likelihood. (b) In contrast, an MCMC algorithm samples cluster assignments, so each datapoint is assigned to a cluster at each iteration, and samples parameter values conditioned on those assignments. This process converges to the posterior distribution over cluster assignments and parameters: more iterations simply result in more samples from this posterior distribution.

Another class of algorithms, Markov chain Monte Carlo (MCMC) methods, provide a means of obtaining samples from complex distributions, which can be used both for inferring the values of latent variables and for identifying the parameters of models.

MCMC algorithms were originally developed to solve problems in statistical physics (Metropolis *et al.*, 1953), and are now widely used both in physics (e.g., Newman & Barkema, 1999) and in statistics (e.g., Gilks *et al.*, 1996; Mackay, 2003; Neal, 1993). As the name suggests, Markov chain Monte Carlo is based upon the theory of Markov chains—sequences of random variables in which each variable is independent of all of its predecessors given the variable that immediately precedes it (e.g., Norris, 1997). The probability that a variable in a Markov chain takes on a particular value conditioned on the value of the preceding variable is determined by the *transition kernel* for that Markov chain. One well known property of Markov chains is their tendency to converge to a *stationary distribution*: as the length of a Markov chain increases, the probability that a variable in that chain takes on a particular value converges to a fixed quantity determined by the transition kernel.

In MCMC, a Markov chain is constructed such that its stationary distribution is the distribution from which we want to generate samples. Since these methods are designed for arbitrary probability distributions, we will stop differentiating between observed and latent variables, and just treat the distribution of interest as $P(\mathbf{x})$. An MCMC algorithm is defined by a transition kernel $K(\mathbf{x}|\mathbf{x}')$ which gives the probability of moving from state $\mathbf{x}$ to state $\mathbf{x}'$. In order for the Markov chain to have the target distribution $P(\mathbf{x})$ as its stationary distribution, the transition kernel must be chosen so that the $P(\mathbf{x})$ is invariant to the kernel. Mathematically this is expressed by the condition $\sum_{\mathbf{x}} P(\mathbf{x}) K(\mathbf{x} \mid \mathbf{x}') = P(\mathbf{x}')$. If this is the case, once the probability that the chain is in a particular state is equal to $P(\mathbf{x})$, it will continue to be equal to $P(\mathbf{x})$— hence the term 'stationary distribution'. A variety of standard methods exist for constructing transition kernels that satisfy this criterion, including *Gibbs sampling* and the *Metropolis-Hastings algorithm* (see Gilks *et al.*, 1996). The algorithm then proceeds by repeatedly sampling from the transition kernel $K(\mathbf{x}|\mathbf{x}')$, starting from any initial configuration $\mathbf{x}$. The theory of Markov chains guarantees that the states of the chain will ultimately be samples from the distribution $P(\mathbf{x})$. These samples enable us to estimate properties of the distribution such as the most probable state or the average state. The results of an MCMC algorithm (in this case, Gibbs sampling) for mixtures of Gaussians are shown in Fig. 2.2.4(b).

Applying MCMC methods to distributions with latent variables, or treating the parameters of a distribution as a random variable in itself (as is standard in Bayesian statistics, as discussed above), makes it possible to solve both of the problems of inference faced by users of probabilistic models. The main problems with MCMC methods are that they can require a long time to converge to the target distribution, and assessing convergence is often difficult. Designing an MCMC algorithm is more of an art than a science. A poorly designed algorithm will take a very long time to converge. There are, however, design principles which often lead to fast MCMC. For example, transition kernels can be carefully constructed to guide the Markov chain so that it explores important parts of the space of possible x.

More complex probabilistic models

The basic ideas outlined in the previous sections can translate into some quite expressive and powerful probabilistic models. In this section, we will illustrate this by briefly reviewing two of these models: hidden Markov models and probabilistic context-free grammars. These models have largely been used in computational linguistics, so we will focus on their application to language, but the underlying principles can be used to define probabilistic models in any domain. A more detailed account of the implications of probabilistic models of language appears in Chater and Manning (2006).

Hidden Markov models

Hidden Markov models (or HMMs) are an important class of graphical models that have been used for problems such as speech and language processing. For example, in speech recognition a hidden Markov model might be used to capture the pattern of speech sounds that make up an individual word. As shown in Fig. 2.2.5(a), the HMM for a word W assumes that there is a sequence of T observations $\{x_t : t = 1,\ldots,T\}$ (taking L values) generated by a set of hidden states $\{y_t : t = 1,\ldots,T\}$ (taking K values). The joint probability distribution is defined by $P(\{y_t\},\{x_t\},W) = P(W)P(y_1 \mid W)$ $\times P(x_1 \mid y_1,W)\prod_{t=2}^{T}P(y_t \mid y_{t-1},W)P(x_t \mid y_t,W)$. The HMM for W is defined by the probability distributions $P(y_1|W)$, the $K{\times}K$ probability transition matrix $P(y_t|y_{t-1},W)$, the $K{\times}L$ observation probability matrix $P(x_t|y_t,W)$, and the prior probability of the word $P(W)$. Using hidden Markov models to recognize words requires solving three related inference tasks. First, we need to learn the models (i.e. $P(x_t|y_t,W)$ and $P(y_t|y_{t-1},W)$ for each word W. Second, we need to evaluate probability $P(\{x_t\},W) = \sum_{\{y_t\}} P(\{y_t\},\{x_t\},W)$ or the observation sequence $\{x_1\}$ for each word W. Third, we must recognize the word by model selection to estimate $W^* = \arg\max_W \sum_{\{y_t\}} P(\{y_t\},W \mid \{x_t\})$. These problems can be solved using probablistic inference algorithms based on dynamic programming and the principles behind the EM algorithm (Rabiner, 1989).

Figure 2.2.5(b) shows a simple example of a hidden Markov model. The representation of the HMM used in this panel is not a graphical model, as in Fig. 2.2.5(a), but a *state transition diagram,* indicating the states of the model, the observations these states generate, and the probabilities of transitioning between states and producing observations. In this model, it is assumed that somebody has two coins, one biased and the other fair, and produces a sequence of heads and tails by flipping these coins, with the coins being switched occasionally. The observable values 0 and 1 indicate whether the coin comes up heads or tails. The hidden states A and B indicate which coin is used on a given flip. There are (unknown) transition probabilities between the hidden states A and B, and (unknown) probabilities for the observations 0,1 conditioned on the hidden states. Given this structure, the learning, or training, task of the HMM is to estimate the probabilities from a sequence of measurements. The HMM can then be used to estimate the hidden states and the probability that the model

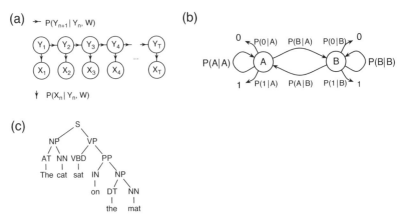

Fig. 2.5. Probabilistic models of language. (a) The graphical model representation for a hidden Markov model (HMM). The Y_i are latent states, and the X_i observations. (b) A state transition diagram representation for an HMM. The circles represent the states of the model, with arrows connecting circles indicating transitions between states. Each state can also produce observations (in this case 0 and 1), with further arcs indicating the possible observations. The probabilities on the arcs represent the parameters of the model. (c) A parse tree from a probabilistic context-free grammar (PCFG).

generated a particular sequence of observations (so that it can be compared to alternative models for classification).

Hidden Markov models were first described by Baum and Petrie (1966). HMMs are widely used for processing text and speech (e.g., Charniak, 1993; Jurafsky & Martin, 2000). One of their most successful applications, other than speech recognition, is part-of-speech tagging (e.g., Charniak *et al.*, 1993), in which the latent states are trained to match the syntactic categories, such as nouns and verbs, that comprise the most basic level of linguistic structure. These analyses are similar to the 'distributional clustering' methods that cognitive scientists have claimed may play a role in the acquisition of syntactic categories by children (e.g., Redington *et al.*, 1998).

Probabilistic context-free grammars

Hidden Markov models are equivalent to probabilistic finite state automata, and consequently are a form of probabilistic regular grammar (e.g., Manning & Shutze, 1999). Generative models can be defined in terms of probabilistic versions of other grammars in Chomsky's (1956) hierarchy of formal languages. In particular, computational linguists have explored probabilistic context-free grammars (PCFGs; Baker, 1979; Charniak, 1993; Jurafsky & Martin, 2000; Manning & Shutze, 1999; Geman & Johnson, 2004). A PCFG can be used to generate sentences and to parse them. The probability of a sentence, or a parse, is defined to be the product of the probabilities of the production rules used to generate the sentence.

For example, we can define a PCFG as follows (see Fig. 2.2.5c). We define non-terminal nodes *S*, *NP*, *VP*, *AT*, *NNS*, *VBD*, *PP*, *IN*, *DT*, *NN* where *S* is a sentence, *VP* is a verb phrase, *VBD* is a verb, *NP* is a noun phrase, *NN* is a noun, and so on (for more details, see Manning & Schütze, 1999). The terminal nodes are words from a dictionary (e.g. 'the', 'cat', 'sat', 'on', 'mat'.) We define production rules which are applied to non-terminal nodes to generate child nodes (e.g. *S*→*NP*, *VP* or *NN*→'cat'). Finally, we specify probabilities for the production rules, so that the probabilities assigned to production rules with the same non-terminal symbol on the left hand side sum to one.

These production rules enable us to generate a sentence starting from the root node *S*. We sample a production rule from the distribution over rules with *S* on the left hand side, and apply it to generate child nodes. We repeat this process on the child nodes and stop when all the nodes are terminal (i.e. all are words). The result is a 'parse tree' of the kind shown in Fig. 2.2.5(c)—a hierarchical representation of the structure of a sentence. As a result of following this procedure for generating parse trees, the probability of obtaining a particular parse tree (with an accompanying sequence of words) is just the product of the probabilities of the rules that produce that parse tree. Multiple parse trees can result in the same sequence of words. To parse an input sentence, we use dynamic programming to compute the most probable way that sequence of words could have been generated by the production rules.

As with hidden Markov models, we can learn the probabilities associated with production rules from a set of observed sentences. This can be done in a supervised fashion, using sentences for which the true parse structure is known, or an unsupervised fashion, working just from the sentences. The supervised learning problem is similar to the problem of estimating the probability with which a coin will produce heads, although on a much larger scale. The unsupervised learning problem involves latent variables—the parse trees—making it an attractive target for methods related to the EM algorithm (Lari & Young, 1990) and Markov chain Monte Carlo (Johnson *et al.*, 2007).

Probabilistic context-free grammars are used throughout computational linguistics, and are the subject of many formal results concerning the tractability of language acquisition (e.g., Horning, 1969; Angluin, 1988). The formalism is also beginning to be used in psycholinguistics, in modeling people's treatment of phenomena such as disambiguation and attachment (e.g., Baldewein & Keller, 2004; Jurafsky, 1996). Recent work in bioinformatics has also begun to exploit the capacity of PCFGs to capture complex dependencies among the elements of sequences (e.g., Ding *et al.*, 2005). However, the strong independent assumptions that underlie PCFGs, as well as their restriction to context-free languages, mean that they are largely a convenient approximation to the structure of human languages, and linguists continue to explore new probabilistic models that remove some of these constraints.

Conclusion

Probabilistic models provide a unique opportunity to develop a rational account of human cognition that combines statistical learning with structured representations. However, specifying and using these models can be challenging. The widespread use of probabilistic models in computer science and statistics has led to the development of valuable tools that address some of these challenges. Graphical models provide a simple and intuitive way of expressing a probability distribution, making clear the assumptions about how a set of variables are related, and can greatly speed up probabilistic inference. The EM algorithm and Markov chain Monte Carlo can be used to estimate the parameters of models that incorporate latent variables, and to work with complicated probability distributions of the kind that often arise in Bayesian inference. These tools make it possible to work with richly structured probabilistic models, such as hidden Markov models and probabilistic context-free grammars. Current work in computer science and statistics is extending the scope of probabilistic models yet further, exploring models in which the number of clusters or features expressed in a dataset is unbounded (e.g., Neal, 1998; Griffiths & Ghahramani, 2005), where hypotheses are defined at multiple levels of abstraction (resulting in 'hierarchical' Bayesian models) allowing information to be generalized across datasets (e.g., Tenenbaum *et al.*, 2006), and where the properties of an object depend probabilistically both on other properties of that object and on properties of related objects (e.g., Friedman *et al.*, 1999; Kemp *et al.*, 2004). One of the great strengths of probabilistic models is this capacity to combine structured representations with statistical methods, providing a set of tools that can be used to explore how structure and statistics are combined. By using these tools and continuing to draw on advances in the many disciplines where probabilistic models are used, it may ultimately become possible to define models that can capture the complexity of human cognition.

Author note

This chapter is an extended version of Griffiths and Yuille (2006), a tutorial on probabilistic inference that appeared as an online supplement to a special issue of *Trends in Cognitive Sciences* on probabilistic models of cognition (Volume 10, Issue 7).

References

Angluin, D. (1988). *Identifying languages from stochastic examples* (Tech. Rep. No. YALEU/DCS/RR-614). Yale University, Department of Computer Science.

Baker, J. (1979). Trainable grammars for speech recognition. In J. J. Wolf & D. H. Klatt (Eds.), *Speech communication papers presented at the 97th meeting of the acoustical society of America* (pp. 547–550). Cambridge, MA: MIT.

Baldewein, U., & Keller, F. (2004). Modeling attachment decisions with a probabilistic parser: The case of head final structures. In *Proceedings of the 26th Annual Conference of the Cognitive Science Society*. Hillsdale, NJ: Erlbaum.

Baum, L. E., & Petrie, T. (1966). Statistical inference for probabilistic functions of finite state Markov chains. *Annals of Mathematical Statistics, 37*, 1554–1563.

Bayes, T. (1763/1958). Studies in the history of probability and statistics: IX. Thomas Bayes's Essay towards solving a problem in the doctrine of chances. *Biometrika, 45*, 296–315.

Berger, J. O. (1993). *Statistical decision theory and Bayesian analysis*. New York: Springer.

Bernardo, J. M., & Smith, A. F. M. (1994). *Bayesian theory*. New York: Wiley.

Bertsekas, D. P. (2000). *Dynamic programming and optimal control*. Nashua, NH: Athena Scientific.

Bishop, C. M. (2006). *Pattern recognition and machine learning*. New York: Springer.

Charniak, E. (1993). *Statistical language learning*. Cambridge, MA: MIT Press.

Charniak, E., Hendrickson, C., Jacobson, N., & Perkowitz, M. (1993). Equations for part-of-speech tagging. In *Proceedings of the tenth national conference on artificial intelligence (AAAI-93)* (pp. 784–789). Washington, DC: AAAI Press.

Chater, N., & Manning, C. D. (2006). Probabilistic models of language processing and acquisition. *Trends in Cognitive Sciences, 10*, 335–344.

Chomsky, N. (1956). Three models for the description of language. *IRE Transactions on Information Theory, 2*, 113–124.

Cox, R. T. (1961). *The algebra of probable inference*. Baltimore, MD: Johns Hopkins University Press.

Dayan, P., & Abbott, L. (2001). *Theoretical neuroscience*. Cambridge, MA: MIT Press.

Dempster, A. P., Laird, N. M., & Rubin, D. B. (1977). Maximum likelihood from incomplete data via the EM algorithm. *Journal of the Royal Statistical Society B, 39*, 1–38.

Ding, Y., Chan, C. Y., & Lawrence, C. E. (2005). RNA secondary structure prediction by centroids in a Boltzmann weighted ensemble. *RNA, 11*, 1157–1166.

Duda, R. O., Hart, P. E., & Stork, D. G. (2000). *Pattern classification*. New York: Wiley.

Friedman, N., Getoor, L., Koller, D., & Pfeffer, A. (1999). Learning probabilistic relational models. In T. Dean (Ed.), *Proceedings of the 16th international joint conference on artificial intelligence (IJCAI)* (pp. 1300–1309). San Francisco, CA: Morgan Kaufmann.

Gelman, A., Carlin, J. B., Stern, H. S., & Rubin, D. B. (1995). *Bayesian data analysis*. New York: Chapman & Hall.

Geman, S., & Geman, D. (1984). Stochastic relaxation, Gibbs distributions, and the Bayesian restoration of images. *IEEE Transactions on Pattern Analysis and Machine Intelligence, 6*, 721–741.

Geman, S., & Johnson, M. (2004). Probability and statistics in computational linguistics, a brief review. In M. Johnson, S. P. Khudanpur, M. Ostendorf, & R. Rosenfeld (Eds.), *Mathematical foundations of speech and language processing* (pp. 1–26). New York: Springer.

Gilks, W., Richardson, S., & Spiegelhalter, D. J. (Eds.). (1996). *Markov chain Monte Carlo in practice*. Suffolk, UK: Chapman and Hall.

Glymour, C. (2001). *The mind's arrows: Bayes nets and graphical causal models in psychology*. Cambridge, MA: MIT Press.

Glymour, C., & Cooper, G. (1999). *Computation, causation, and discovery*. Cambridge, MA: MIT Press.

Good, I. J. (1979). A. M. Turing's statistical work in World War II. *Biometrika, 66*, 393–396.

Griffiths, T. L., & Ghahramani, Z. (2005). *Infinite latent feature models and the Indian buffet process* (Tech. Rep. No. 2005-001). Gatsby Computational Neuroscience Unit.

Griffiths, T. L., Kemp, C., & Tenenbaum, J. B. (in press). Bayesian models of cognition. In R. Sun (Ed.), *Cambridge handbook of computational cognitive modeling*. Cambridge: Cambridge University Press.

Griffiths, T. L., & Yuille, A. (2006). A primer on probabilistic inference. *Trends in Cognitive Sciences, 10*(7), 1–11

Hastie, T., Tibshirani, R., & Friedman, J. (2001). *The elements of statistical learning: Data mining, inference, and prediction*. New York: Springer.

Heckerman, D. (1998). A tutorial on learning with Bayesian networks. In M. I. Jordan (Ed.), *Learning in graphical models* (pp. 301–354). Cambridge, MA: MIT Press.

Horning, J. J. (1969). *A study of grammatical inference*. Unpublished doctoral dissertation, Stanford University.

Jaynes, E. T. (2003). *Probability theory: The logic of science*. Cambridge: Cambridge University Press.

Jeffreys, W. H., & Berger, J. O. (1992). Ockham's razor and Bayesian analysis. *American Scientist*, **80**(1), 64–72.

Johnson, M., Griffiths, T. L., & Goldwater, S. (2007). Bayesian inference for PCFGs via Markov chain Monte Carlo. In *Proceedings of the North American Conference on Computational Linguistics (NAACL'07)*.

Jordan, M. I., Ghahramani, Z., Jaakkola, T., & Saul, L. K. (1999). An introduction to variational methods for graphical models. *Machine Learning*, **37**, 183–233.

Jurafsky, D. (1996). A probabilistic model of lexical and syntactic access and disambiguation. *Cognitive Science*, **20**, 137–194.

Jurafsky, D., & Martin, J. H. (2000). *Speech and language processing*. Upper Saddle River, NJ: Prentice Hall.

Kass, R. E., & Raftery, A. E. (1995). Bayes factors. *Journal of the American Statistical Association*, **90**, 773–795.

Kemp, C., Griffiths, T. L., & Tenenbaum, J. B. (2004). *Discovering latent classes in relational data* (Tech. Rep. No. AI Memo 2004-019). Cambridge, MA: Massachusetts Institute of Technology.

Korb, K., & Nicholson, A. (2003). *Bayesian artificial intelligence*. Boca Raton, FL: Chapman and Hall/CRC.

Laplace, P. S. (1795/1951). *A philosophical essay on probabilities* (F. W. Truscott & F. L. Emory, Trans.). New York: Dover.

Lari, K., & Young, S. (1990). The estimation of Stochastic Context-Free Grammars using the Inside-Outside algorithm. *Computer Speech and Language*, **4**, 35–56.

Mackay, D. J. C. (2003). *Information theory, inference, and learning algorithms*. Cambridge: Cambridge University Press.

Manning, C., & Schütze, H. (1999). *Foundations of statistical natural language processing*. Cambridge, MA: MIT Press.

Marr, D. (1982). *Vision*. San Francisco, CA: W. H. Freeman.

Metropolis, A. W., Rosenbluth, A. W., Rosenbluth, M. N., Teller, A. H., & Teller, E. (1953). Equations of state calculations by fast computing machines. *Journal of Chemical Physics*, **21**, 1087–1092.

Myung, I. J., Forster, M. R., & Browne, M. W. (2000). Model selection [special issue]. *Journal of Mathematical Psychology*, **44**, 1–2

Myung, I. J., & Pitt, M. A. (1997). Applying Occam's razor in modeling cognition: A Bayesian approach. *Psychonomic Bulletin and Review*, **4**, 79–95.

Neal, R. M. (1993). *Probabilistic inference using Markov chain Monte Carlo methods* (Tech. Rep. No. CRG-TR-93-1). University of Toronto.

Neal, R. M. (1998). *Markov chain sampling methods for Dirichlet process mixture models* (Tech. Rep. No. 9815). Department of Statistics, University of Toronto.

Neal, R. M., & Hinton, G. E. (1998). A view EM algorithm that justifies incremental, sparse, and other variants. In M. I. Jordan (Ed.), *Learning in graphical models*. Cambridge, MA: MIT Press.

Newman, M. E. J., & Barkema, G. T. (1999). *Monte carlo methods in statistical physics*. Oxford: Clarendon Press.

Norris, J. R. (1997). *Markov chains*. Cambridge, UK: Cambridge University Press.

Pearl, J. (1988). *Probabilistic reasoning in intelligent systems*. San Francisco, CA: Morgan Kaufmann.

Pearl, J. (2000). *Causality: Models, reasoning and inference*. Cambridge, UK: Cambridge University Press.

Pitman, J. (1993). *Probability*. New York: Springer-Verlag.

Rabiner, L. (1989). A tutorial on hidden Markov models and selected applications in speech recognition. *Proceedings of the IEEE*, **77**, 257–286.

Redington, M., Chater, N., & Finch, S. (1998). Distributional information: A powerful cue for acquiring syntactic categories. *Cognitive Science*, **22**, 425–469.

Rice, J. A. (1995). *Mathematical statistics and data analysis* (2nd ed.). Belmont, CA: Duxbury.

Russell, S. J., & Norvig, P. (2002). *Artificial intelligence: A modern approach* (2nd ed.). Englewood Cliffs, NJ: Prentice Hall.

Schachter, R. (1998). Bayes-ball: The rational pasttime (for determining irrelevance and requisite information in belief networks and influence diagrams. In *Proceedings of the fourteenth annual conference on uncertainty in artificial intelligence (uai 98)*. San Francisco, CA: Morgan Kaufmann.

Sloman, S. (2005). *Causal models: How people think about the world and its alternatives*. Oxford: Oxford University Press.

Spirtes, P., Glymour, C., & Schienes, R. (1993). *Causation prediction and search*. New York: Springer-Verlag.

Tenenbaum, J. B., Griffiths, T. L., & Kemp, C. (2006). Theory-based Bayesian models of inductive learning and reasoning. *Trends in Cognitive Science*, **10**, 309–318.

Chapter 3

Rational analyses, instrumentalism, and implementations

David Danks

Department of Philosophy, Carnegie Mellon University, Carnegie Mellon University, Pittsburgh, PA, USA; Institute for Human & Machine Cognition, Pensacola, FL, USA

Introduction

Rational analyses provide explanatory models of cognition, and I focus here on the nature of that explanation. I argue first that many—and perhaps even most—rational analyses fail to meet the evidential standards required to provide genuine explanations of the sort commonly attributed to them. Put simply, rational analyses (or at least, the actual instances that we usually have) are not as powerful as is normally thought. Second, I argue that there should nonetheless be an expansion of rational analysis to domains that have been thought off-limits. That is, rational analyses can be much more useful than is normally thought. In sum, this chapter argues for a shift in the practice of rational analysis to more widespread application, but with more careful consideration of their actual power. Rational analyses are an important tool that should be used more widely, but with more care about what they actually yield.

A platitude about the sciences is that they are partly (or primarily) in the business of providing explanations. Predictions and data summaries are important and practically useful, but we expect our best scientific theories to tell us something about *why* some phenomenon occurred. The cognitive sciences are no different in this regard: we want an explanation for people's behavior, not just a prediction or retrodiction of it. Rational analyses purport to offer a different type of explanation from that normally found in cognitive science, since the explanation is supposed to be agnostic about underlying cognitive mechanisms. The implication, as I will argue in the second section, is that many current rational analyses are 'simple' instrumentalist theories: they offer data summaries and potentially predictions, but essentially no additional explanatory power.

Instrumentalist theories are not necessarily to be avoided in all cases. I argue in the third section that there are conditions in which instrumentalist theories—and rational analyses in particular—can be valuable, but that we should not be content with such theories. A constant goal (perhaps suspended for a particular project, but still remaining in the background) should be to determine the cognitive mechanisms that underlie particular rational analyses. Understanding this goal requires an understanding of the nature of 'implementation,' and so I turn (in the fourth section) to develop an account of that notion. The proposed model of 'implementation' provides a better understanding of the nature of levels of description, in particular for cognitive mechanisms. I argue that the standard trichotomy of levels of description, due to David Marr, is thus too coarse-grained. More importantly, the present analysis implies that the use of rational analyses is entirely orthogonal to the level of description for a theory. The level of description dictates a particular level of realist commitment to theoretical elements, while rational analysis is a tool by which to develop the theories. No close connection between rational analyses and a particular level of description is warranted, and so rational analyses can (and should) be used much more widely than they currently are.

Rational analyses and explanations

The fundamental idea behind a rational analysis is the intuition that people are behaviorally well-adapted to their environments (Anderson, 1990, 1991a; Chater & Oaksford, 2000; Oaksford & Chater, 1998). More specifically, rational analyses understand 'rational' to be a relation that holds just when there is an appropriate connection between four complicated variables: (i) the relevant environment; (ii) the task or problem to be solved; (iii) the agent's capacities; and (iv) the agent's input and output (typically, but not necessarily, perception and behavior). In particular, 'rational' is taken to mean: 'the agent's input/output are optimal[1] for solving the task in this environment, given the agent's capacities.' A rational analysis consists of specifying any three of these elements, and then deriving the value for the fourth that completes the relation of rationality. In practice, the most common rational analysis specifies the first three elements and then derives the optimal input–output function. That is, one determines the optimal behavior to solve some task given the environment, input, and agent capacities, and then typically aims to confirm that model using various empirical data. Although less common, there are three other species of rational analysis that correspond to specifying a different subset of variables. For example, in order to determine why people exhibit some particular behavior, one might carry out a rational analysis in which the problem is the free variable: that is, one could determine the task for which some given behavior would be optimal (given the environment and agent). The type of rational analysis determines what factor is being explained, and which other three factors must be independently specified (see also Sloman & Fernbach, this volume).

Rational analyses aim to provide explanations for behavior, and they typically make no commitments about the underlying implementing mechanisms. One of the central benefits of a rational analysis is that—when done fully and correctly (see below)—it is capable of supporting a particular type of explanation about behavior: namely,

---

[1] The cost function for evaluating optimality is typically specified as part of element (ii), the problem to be solved.

one that answers questions such as 'why is this behavior optimal?'[2] Optimality-based explanations give a reason for why the world has certain features, rather than simply asserting that those features exist, and are therefore often thought to provide superior, or more 'normative,' explanations than ones that do not appeal to optimality. If we can give an optimality-based explanation for some behavior, then the behavior is not simply an accident, and so, for example, we can infer that it would be likely to arise, even if the world were different in certain ways. Much of the discussion about optimality-based explanations—particularly in the philosophy of biology—has focused on exactly what standards must be met by claims that some behavior results *because* of its optimality (Brandon & Rausher, 1996; Orzack & Sober, 1994, 1996; Seger & Stubblefield, 1996). An optimality-based explanation is typically understood to require the defense of three related claims: (i) behavior X occurs in situation Y; (ii) X is optimal in situation Y; and (iii) people do X because it is optimal. The first and second components are closely connected, as a characterization of the situation is a necessary precursor for demonstration of optimality. The first element is a primarily descriptive task; in a cognitive science context, this corresponds to empirical evidence of a particular behavior pattern. The second part is primarily theoretical/mathematical; the mathematical work of a rational analysis corresponds to the necessary demonstration of optimality.

The third component of an optimality-based explanation is quite different from the other two: it requires one to show that the optimality of X played a causal role— typically, a major causal role—in people's doing X. One must show that X's optimality produced some 'pressure' that pushed people (in some sense) towards behavior X, and so one must specify a mechanism or mechanism-schema by which behavior is shaped and moved towards X, as well as historical evidence that the mechanism was active and relevant. The term 'cognitive mechanism' is notably absent from this description of an optimality-based explanation, since the explanation focuses on changes in the *behavior*, *rather* than in any mechanism for the proximal production of the behavior. One can give an optimality-based explanation without ever appealing to, or even describing, the underlying cognitive mechanism that produces the behavior. Of course, ignorance about the underlying mechanism might make it significantly harder to defend the third claim, but descriptive knowledge of the cognitive mechanism producing X is not a necessary condition of an optimality-based explanation.

There are two standard types of stories that have been provided for the third component. Probably the most common use of optimality-based explanations is to provide explanations of biological traits as evolutionary adaptations. In that domain, the third component comes from a (partial) demonstration that some trait A is widespread in a population because of natural selection on precursors of A in

---

[2] There is (almost) philosophical consensus that all explanations are answers to why-questions, but a long history of debate about exactly what constitutes a satisfactory explanation (Bromberger, 1993; Halonen & Hintikka, 2005; Hempel, 1965; Salmon, 1984, 1989; van Fraassen, 1980). Even for superficially simple why-questions, such as 'why does behavior X occur?', there are many different types of responses that could provide an answer.

previous generations. Selection pressures generally act to increase the proportion of more optimal traits in a population, and decrease the less optimal traits. Thus, if X is optimal (and evolutionarily available), then selection pressures can explain why behavior X emerges (rather than A, B, or …). Evolutionary explanations of X's occurrence in terms of its optimality trace a causal sequence in phylogenetic (i.e., evolutionary) time. The other standard route to providing the third component is through an account in ontogenetic time (i.e., individual development) that shows how the optimal behavior is acquired through learning mechanisms. One can explain behavior X by showing that people learn (perhaps implicitly) that X is the optimal behavior in some domain (and they do X for that reason). In both types of accounts, the primary focus is on the optimality of behavior in 'normal' situations, since those are the ones in which the organism or lineage actually encounters pressure to behave optimally, whether in phylogenetic or ontogenetic time. Optimality-based explanations are thus based principally on ecological norms (Gigerenzer, 2000, 2006; Gigerenzer & Selten, 2001): what matters most is the fit of a behavior with the situation and environment, not some abstract theoretical ideal.

There are tradeoffs between the two routes. For phylogenetic stories, there is no difficulty specifying or establishing the appropriate mechanism providing 'pressure' towards optimality; natural selection requires no defense. One does, however, have to show that natural selection was causally relevant for this trait, and there are significant measurement challenges for such demonstrations, though they can sometimes be overcome (as in, e.g., Gilchrist *et al.* 2000; Losos, 1992; McCracken *et al.* 1999). In contrast, an account in ontogenetic time faces many fewer measurement challenges, since one can track the changes over time in an individual's behavior (or the behavior of a population). That story must, however, show that the behavioral changes were the result of some 'pressure towards optimality,' and it is frequently much harder to demonstrate that *optimality* was the reason for change. These tradeoffs naturally suggest a two-stage account: namely, provide an ontogenetic account for the occurrence of behavior X in the individual's lifetime, and then argue that the necessary 'pressure towards optimality' arises from a learning mechanism that has been optimized in phylogenetic time to find the optimal behavior in any particular situation. Regardless of the details, however, some story must be provided to have a full optimality-based explanation; one cannot simply stop with the assertion that 'behavior X occurs and is optimal,' as it does not follow that optimality was the reason for X's occurrence.

Rational analyses aim to provide optimality-based explanations: 'a rational explanation tells why the mind does what it does' (Anderson, 1991b, p. 410). In practice, however, rational analyses almost always consist solely in optimality analyses that show that a particular behavior is optimal for an environment, agent, and problem, followed by experiments to confirm that the optimal behavior occurs. An optimality analysis alone, though, is insufficient for an optimality-based explanation, as there are many other reasons why X might occur. People might act optimally because of historical accident, or because there are no other options, or a number of other reasons. One can use an optimality argument as a heuristic device to suggest a novel descriptive theory (as suggested by Sloman & Fernbach, this volume), but an optimality-based *explanation* requires more. Rational analyses that fail to provide an account of how the behavior came to be fall short of full optimality-based explanations. There is no principled barrier to providing such explanations; rational analyses just have not typically done so in practice.

Mechanism-based explanations offer a very different type of explanation than optimality-based explanations. They aim roughly to describe the proximal sequence of causes that led to the behavior: they provide an answer to 'how behavior *X*?' It is easiest to think about mechanism-based explanations in terms of an over-simplified picture in which behavior results from cognitive mechanisms proceeding from some initial conditions. This picture is of course highly unrealistic, as it ignores the dynamic nature of cognition, the difficulty of individuating cognitive mechanisms, and so on. However, given this picture of the proximal causes of behavior, we can understand a mechanism-based explanation as one that provides a causal sequence that starts with initial conditions, and then moves through the cognitive mechanisms to a final effect that is the behavior *X*. Mechanism-based explanations are thus entirely descriptive: they point towards cause-effect sequences in the world without an attempt to explain why that particular sequence is the one that occurs. We can offer such explanations to account for both token instances of behavior *X* by a description of specifics of a particular situation, and type-level descriptions of behavior *X* by description of 'standard' conditions and mechanisms. One frequently provides only the initial conditions or mechanism in a mechanism-based explanation for pragmatic reasons: one assumes that the other element is widely known. Most mechanism-based explanations offered in psychological papers, for example, focus on cognitive mechanisms rather than initial conditions, since the latter are usually specified in the description of the experiment.

Rational analyses essentially never offer mechanism-based explanations. Much of the literature on rational analysis is quite explicit with regards to its agnosticism about the underlying cognitive mechanisms (e.g., Anderson, 1990, 1991b; Chater *et al.* 2003; Tenenbaum *et al.* 2007). A nice expression of the attitude is Anderson's (1991a) statement that rational analyses should 'prescribe what the behavior of a system should be rather than how to compute it' (p. 483). This basic attitude is also captured by descriptions of rational analyses as providing 'as-if theories': the agent acts *as if* she were performing the computations of the rational analysis, but need not actually do them. The standard justification for this agnosticism is in terms of the influential framework of levels provided in Marr (1982). Rational analyses offer theories at the *computational level*: the level of description that focuses on goals and problems for an information processor, as well as input–output specifications of solutions.[3]

---

[3] A different view (suggested to me by Josh Tenenbaum) is that Marr's levels provide the scope of applicability: the computational level centers on problems that any agent must solve, the algorithmic level on humans, and the implementation level on neuroscience. Marr-levels in this interpretation do not correspond to 'level of description,' though the computational level will still almost always be focused on input–output, since the underlying mechanism is not directly relevant at that level.

By focusing on high-level characterizations of the problems and processes of an agent, proponents of rational analyses aim to sidestep questions of underlying mechanism or architecture since those are (the argument runs) not directly relevant to questions and concerns at the computational level. Any implementation that computes the particular (optimal, rational) input–output function is acceptable, and so cognitive science can proceed by focusing simply on that level.[4] In practice, of course, rational analyses sometimes have some connection with underlying mechanisms, but the ideal is of strong separation between the rational analysis and implementing mechanism.

Rational analyses and instrumentalism

The strong agnosticism of rational analyses about cognitive mechanisms means that rational analyses are almost always instrumentalist: no commitment is made to the physical or mechanistic reality of the internal structure and computations of the model; they need not correspond to anything in the world. The mathematics is purely a computational device by which one can generate (hopefully) accurate predictions. If placed in an appropriate optimality-based explanation, then a rational analysis can provide more than a simple description, as we can say why the input–output function has the structure it does. The explanation is (when available) only at the level of structure in the <input, output> pairs, but at least it is *some* level of explanation. This observation serves to highlight the importance of the oft-neglected developmental component of an optimality-based explanation. Without it, rational analyses are strongly instrumentalist descriptions of an individual's stimulus-response function, coupled with the observation that the function is optimal (though we do not know if that optimality is the reason for the individual's actions). Instrumentalist theories are also unable, even in principle, to provide mechanism-based explanations, since they avoid any discussion of the underlying cognitive mechanisms.

The lack of anchor in a mechanistic account points towards at least two conditions when one should have much less confidence in the predictions of an instrumentalist theory. The first situation is when one aims to use the instrumentalist theory outside of the domains for which it was originally developed. The claim here is *not* that instrumentalist theories can never be used in novel domains; rather, the concern is that it is much harder to determine for an instrumentalist theory whether it has a sufficiently broad foundation of empirical data to generalize successfully to novel domains. In general, one can transfer theories to novel cases when the underlying causal structures of the two situations are suitably similar. This standard translates in practice

---

[4] Some proponents of rational analyses seem to be motivated by an additional worry: if one can only ever measure behavior (and external situations), then one cannot ever uniquely determine the underlying cognitive mechanisms, and so input–output is the best we can do. For example, Anderson (1990) writes: 'behaviorism was correct … that you cannot infer the mechanisms in the black box from what goes in and what goes out' (p. 26). But although reasoning about unobserved entities and processes is hard, it is certainly not impossible. It is absolutely standard in the natural sciences, and no argument has been provided that cognitive psychology is somehow special in this regard.

into having sufficient coverage in the empirical data to know the approximate causal or correlational structure (as appropriate) in the various conditions. If one has no knowledge of the underlying mechanisms, then there are no natural standards by which to judge whether the confirming empirical data derives from a suitably broad set of conditions. Instead, one simply has to collect data from a wide range of conditions—presumably informed by experiments showing which factors seem to be relevant—and then argue that this set provides sufficient coverage. There are obviously methods to mitigate this problem and ensure suitable generality for one's theory, but the general problem is significantly worse for an instrumentalist theory than for a mechanistic one. Moreover, in the case of rational analyses, we have positive reasons to think that the behavior *will* differ significantly in unusual cases. Rational analyses aim to understand behavior as optimal in 'standard' environments, and if behavior is actually tuned to the environment (as argued by many proponents of rational analyses), then we should expect behavior in unusual cases to be quite *sub*-optimal, and so not conform to a rational analysis that incorporates that situation.[5]

In one particular case, mechanism information is actually necessary for prediction. In cognitive science, we often need to predict or explain an individual's behavior when the system 'breaks' in various ways, whether because of external trauma, various mental deficits, or perhaps even local features of a situation (e.g., extreme time pressure). As the literature on causation repeatedly reminds us (Pearl, 2000; Spirtes *et al.* 1993), predictions about the effects of interventions, manipulations, or changes in the system require knowledge of the underlying causal structure. Instrumentalist theories provide no information about mechanisms, and so no grounds for predictions when the cognitive system breaks. In the particular case of a rational analysis, there is no reason to think that a broken cognitive system will behave optimally, or even close-to-optimally. We cannot just plug the boundary conditions/initial stimuli into the rational analysis to predict the behavior of a broken cognitive system, since we require information about how the system works. As an analogy, if we want to predict what a calculator will do (if anything) if we hit it with a hammer, then knowledge of the input–output functions will not suffice. We need to know how the underlying circuitry works to make accurate predictions.

A more foundational problem is that the very goal of true agnosticism about mechanisms is ultimately a will-o'-the-wisp: even the most diehard proponent of agnostic rational analysis must eventually talk about underlying cognitive mechanisms in various ways. Rational analyses, for example, are supposed to incorporate computational limits, but the nature of those limits depends partly on the underlying cognitive architecture. Putatively instrumentalist rational analyses must have some connection to the underlying mechanisms, or possibility space for the mechanisms. One should not view this dependence as some impurity that should be purged; in general,

---

5 This is another point of agreement between proponents of rational analyses and of ecological rationality: both think that 'failures' by experimental participants are often because the experiment fails to match the structure of the everyday environment along important dimensions.

connections between one's various cognitive theories are clearly a virtue. Some degree of instrumentalism is acceptable and even necessary (see the remainder of this section), but the agnosticism of rational analyses unnecessarily (see Section 4) forces a pervasive instrumentalism that denies the possibility of rational analyses providing mechanistic explanations.

There are positive aspects to treating rational analyses as instrumentalist theories. Instrumentalism frequently has a bad name in the philosophy of science, but all theories—even putatively mechanistic ones—have some degree of instrumentalism, in that certain cognitive operations are left unexplained. For example, associationist models of causal learning (or more generally, stepwise error-correction models) are often characterized as mechanistic theories, but they provide no account of how the prediction is generated, how the error is calculated, and so on. Those theories provide a mathematical account of *what* is calculated (including various intermediate representations, such as associative strengths, error, and so on), but no explanation of *how* those intermediate calculations are carried out.[6] Associationist models—like all theories—have components that are treated instrumentally.

Completely instrumentalist theories can also be appropriate and useful in certain conditions. Instrumentalist theories provide accurate descriptions of the data, as well as some predictions for novel situations. Well-confirmed instrumentalist theories at least have the virtue of descriptive accuracy and predictive power for situations in their purview. Although it is tempting to discount the worth of descriptive adequacy, numerous episodes in the history of science reveal how hard it can be to find a theory that captures the observed data, even if we set aside issues of realism. We should be careful not to downplay the importance of finding a descriptive theory, particularly if it also provides reasonably accurate predictions. These descriptions can sometimes be computationally simpler than mechanistic models of the same data, since the instrumentalist theories are not bound by fidelity to the underlying mechanisms.

Accurate descriptions of input–output functions also enable us to characterize the relevant factors for some cognitive problem, even if we do not know precisely how that factor is used in the cognitive system. For example, rational analyses of causal reasoning highlight the importance of base rate information when one has ambiguous data, and that importance has been experimentally confirmed (e.g., Sobel *et al.* 2004), though we do not know the mechanism by which base rate information is incorporated. Similar stories are available for other domains: rational analyses suggest that certain, previously ignored, environment and task features are cognitively relevant, and subsequent experimental research confirms the importance of those features. Instrumentalist theories are better able to highlight the relevant features of a situation, precisely because they are not committed to a mechanism. Overarching tendencies and generalizations can be straightforwardly expressed in the mathematics of the model.

---

[6] There are of course various neural accounts of associative learning (e.g., Maren, 2001; Menzel & Giurfa, 2001), but those are additional theories.

Complete theories certainly might be the desired end-state, but we need to recognize that much of science occurs in domains that we understand only poorly. Instrumentalist theories are metaphysically less ambitious, and so face a lower standard for confirmation and acceptance. They are more insulated from criticism since they can only be critiqued for failure to match the observed data. As a purely practical matter, one should sometimes pursue an only instrumentalist theory, with the understanding that a mechanistic theory will follow. In particular, if one wants to argue that some previously ignored factor is cognitively relevant, then instrumentalism allows one (by virtue of its metaphysical caution) to focus on that factor, rather than also arguing for a particular account of the underlying cognitive mechanisms. Rational analyses can be particularly helpful in these domains, as the assumptions of optimality provide a defeasible guide to the development of a novel theory. There is at least one descriptive theory—namely, the theory that says people act optimally for this task, environment, etc.—that is salient in the search space. Rather than searching quite broadly through the descriptive theory-space, one can target the optimal and near-optimal models for initial testing.

Rational analyses and implementations

The theses of the previous two sections can be roughly summed up as: rational analyses are almost always instrumentalist (Section 1), and instrumentalist theories are generally undesirable, though they can be useful in some situations (Section 2). One might thus make the natural inference that rational analyses are generally undesirable, but this inference presupposes that the first premise follows from a necessary feature of rational analyses. I claim, however, that the close tie between rational analyses and instrumentalist theories is unwarranted. The instrumentalism of rational analyses derives largely from the connection with the computational level of Marr's trichotomy, and this section argues in two stages that this connection is neither necessary nor desirable. First, I argue that a careful consideration of the notion of 'implementation' shows that (a naïve reading of) Marr's trichotomy of levels is overly coarse, and forces instrumentalism where none is warranted. Second, and more importantly, this account of 'implementation' makes clear that the use of rational analyses is entirely orthogonal to the particular level of description. Proponents of rational analyses have unnecessarily tied themselves to thinking about behavior and cognition at one level of description. Rational analyses can (with appropriate care) have a much wider range of application.

The first question is what it means for some mechanism M to implement a rational analysis R. The standard response in the rational analysis (and related) community seems to be: M implements R whenever the target behavior for which M provides a mechanism-based explanation is the same as the behavior for which R provides an optimality-based explanation. In practice, this means that M implements R whenever the input–output function for mechanism M is approximately the same as the optimal function described by R. The inputs and outputs are assumed to be (something like) stimuli and behavior, respectively; all that matters is same behavior in same situation. This understanding of 'implementation' fits quite nicely with the standard use of rational analysis at the computational level. As just one example, Take-the-Best, combined with the Recognition Heuristic, provides a mechanism explanation of behavior in binary choice problems with limited information (Gigerenzer, 2000; Gigerenzer & Goldstein, 1996; Goldstein & Gigerenzer, 1999). Except in special situations (e.g., non-compensatory cues), Take-the-Best is not a 'rational' algorithm in the sense of being optimal over all cases, as it sometimes ignores information that is potentially useful in decision-making. Nonetheless, Take-the-Best has been described as 'rational' because it produces behavior that closely approximates the optimal behavior in this context (Chater *et al.* 2003; Gigerenzer *et al.* 1999; Martignon & Hoffrage, 1999). That is, the argument runs: Take-the-Best plausibly implements (the model in) a rational analysis because it produces appropriate behavior, and not because of any deeper connection or similarity.

The proposal that 'implementation' means 'input–output function approximation' appeals to the intuition that behavior is ultimately all that really matters; correct behavior is the only means for characterizing a system. This notion does seem to capture an important aspect of implementation: namely, that we can have different implementations of the same high-level algorithm. It also seems too weak to be a full characterization of implementation. For example, we may want to require an implementation of rational decision-making to have separable intermediate representations of utility and probability, but the current definition prohibits us from imposing any such restriction. An implementation (in the input–output sense) of a rational analysis also cannot provide any optimality-based explanation beyond what was already available in the rational analysis (Danks, submitted). This relation of implementation leads to additional understanding of how behavior is generated, but no additional understanding about why (in the optimality sense) the behavior occurs. The intertheoretic relation is so weak that the theories standing in it provide neither constraints nor information for one another.

Philosophical work on intertheoretic relations suggests a different understanding of 'implementation': namely, that the mathematics of the high-level theory is a special or limiting case of the mathematics of the lower-level theory (Batterman, 2002; Nickles, 1973; Rueger, 2001, 2005; Smith, 1998). For example, Newtonian mechanics in a collection of indistinguishable particles is a limiting case implementation of the ideal gas law, since the latter is a limiting case of the relevant statistical mechanics equations in the former. This understanding of implementation can also hold between theories at the same level of description: Newtonian mechanics is a limiting case of relativistic mechanics as $(v/c)^2 \to 0$. This notion of limiting case implementation of a rational analysis is applicable to some psychological theories: for example, Griffiths & Tenenbaum (2005) argue that a mechanistic theory based on the χ^2 statistic is a limiting case implementation of rational causal learning using causal support (though probably not descriptively accurate). Much of the recent philosophical literature has focused on the difficulties that can arise when the limit process yields a singular limit (e.g., Batterman, 2002; Rueger, 2005); those issues have not arisen in the psychological literature.

Implementation *qua* limiting case relation is obviously a much stronger intertheoretic relation than input–output approximation, since it arises when the appropriate mathematical relation holds between the *equations* of the two theories, rather than just the input–output functions. The two notions of implementation are logically independent (Danks, submitted), though in practice, limiting case implementation almost always implies input–output implementation, but not *vice versa*. This additional strength carries with it certain benefits, as numerous theoretical virtues are arguably transferred between theories that stand in this relation (Batterman, 2002; Nickles, 1973; Rueger, 2001). However, limiting case implementation seems to be too strong to use as a general understanding of 'implementation,' since it requires the intertheoretic connection to extend all the way down to the fundamental equations of the theories. This notion does not allow for some steps to be encapsulated in a 'black box.' An appropriate massive look-up table seems like it should count as a type of implementation of addition, even though the algorithm in the look-up table (e.g., a hash code) is not a limiting case of 'real' addition.

I suggest instead that 'implementation' is better understood by thinking about computer programming. In general, we can think about a computer program as a series of function or method calls, where all functions are defined in terms of either (i) a different series of function calls; or (ii) a particular input–output relation. Much of the literature on good programming techniques (e.g., Lakos, 1996; McConnell, 2004) focuses on exactly the question of how to divide up the program into suitable components. I propose then that a program *L* implements a program *U* just when we can transform *L* into *U* by a set of computable transformations, each of which takes (a) some sub-series of function calls in *L* and (b) replaces it with a single function call from *U* with the same input–output relation as the sub-series. That is, if we can 'bundle' sequences of functions in *L* to yield *U*, then we say that *L* implements *U*. I contend that most rational analyses—and more generally, essentially all cognitive theories that make quantitative predictions—can be thought of as programs (broadly construed). This notion of 'implementation' thus transfers straightforwardly to the question of when a mechanistic theory *M* implements a rational analysis *R*.

I do not intend anything particularly fancy by this characterization of 'implementation.' Similar ideas about the nature of implementation and hierarchies of description can be found in box-and-arrow diagrams in cognitive neuropsychology, or in the widespread use of flowcharts or dataflow diagrams to describe cognitive theories. The central difference here is that computer programs—and so my account of 'implementation'—typically require much more specificity about the functions than one finds in standard box-and-arrow diagrams. A dataflow diagram can have a box labeled 'Pragmatic Considerations' without any precise characterization of the input–output function for that box; the same function call in a program or fully specified theory would have to specify those input–output relations.

On this characterization of 'implementation', input–output approximation corresponds to the case in which *U*—the theory being implemented—consists of a single function call that is defined by an input–output relation. Thus, any sequence of other function calls that has the same input–output relation will implement *U*. Limiting-case approximation is roughly the situation where *U* and *L* are nearly identical in terms of close correspondence between both function calls and the internal sequence, but *L* is slightly more specific, or uses a slightly different input vector. If the two programs are identical except that L uses a slightly different—and usually more general—method at a particular place in the computation, or L uses slightly more information, then L is a limiting case implementation (given a few technical constraints). Both types of implementation are therefore special cases of this characterization of 'implementation.' In general, the granularity of specification in U sets an upper bound for all implementing theories: L cannot implement U unless its sequence of function calls is more specific.

This notion of 'implementation' appropriately captures the earlier observation that all theories are partially instrumentalist, and none are completely instrumentalist. The ubiquity of instrumentalism arises from the fact that all cognitive theories have some 'basic' (relative to the theory) operations or functions for which no mechanism is provided, just as all computer programs have function calls (e.g., addition) that are specified only by input–output relations. One cannot specify every function call in terms of other function calls without regress. At the same time, all computer programs must be sensitive to the function calls that are available in the architecture, and so must be aware of characteristics of the system on which the program is running. One cannot write or run a computer program in *complete* ignorance of the underlying hardware system,[7] and even the most agnostic rational analysis assumes that certain functions can somehow be computed.

Most importantly, this characterization of 'implementation' leads to a more refined understanding of levels of description. This notion implies that 'level of description for a theory' really means something like 'granularity of the realist commitments of a theory.' By expressing a theory as a computer program, one must clearly identify which components of the theory should be interpreted realistically (i.e., the ordered sequence, and the function calls), and which only instrumentally (i.e., the internal computations in function calls specified only by input–output relations). One is committed only to realism about the stated function calls in the 'cognitive computer program,' and not to any particular way of generating that input–output relation. There is no ambiguity about what theories could implement this particular cognitive model. The complexity of interesting cognitive theories also suggests that there will very rarely be only three levels of description. One will typically be able to continue to 'push downwards' to find even finer grains of description, and so there is no reason to accept Marr's trichotomy of levels (or at least, a naïve understanding of it).[8] There will typically be (almost) infinitely many levels of description, corresponding to the different ways that the function calls can be instantiated in sequences of other function calls, and so there is no sharp line distinguishing the computational, algorithmic, and implementation levels. Instead, there are many different degrees of realist commitments corresponding to the different granularities of specification of the cognitive

---

[7] Even for putatively cross-platform languages such as Java, important hardware constraints can periodically trickles up. Spolsky (2004, ch. 26) gives this phenomenon the wonderful title of The Law of Leaky Abstractions.

[8] The observation that Marr's levels are too coarse is certainly not novel to me. For example, Anderson (1990, p. 17) argues that we should use four levels.

program, ranging from a single function call at the most abstract, downward in a series of increasingly precise expressions of the program.

The current view in cognitive science that there is a special computational level is reinforced by the persistent identification of that level (i.e., a single function call) with rational analyses. The preceding discussion shows that the use of rational analyses *qua* optimality analyses is entirely orthogonal to the level of description. A rational analysis viewed through the present lens simply aims to find the optimal sequence of function calls for some task and environment *given some set of basic functions*. Most rational analyses use a set of basic function calls corresponding to (roughly) all computable functions and so have no need to consider sequences of function calls, but one can ask about the optimal sequence even when we substantially restrict the basic functions. The problem is made even more interesting if one imposes time constraints on the overall problem and time costs for each of the function calls.[9] In general, the optimality of a program is determined by its performance relative to its competitors; the level of description is irrelevant, except when the level is used to define the possibility space. Rational analyses thus actually have a much wider range of application that one typically finds. One can ask about the optimality of a particular mechanistic theory relative to other potential mechanistic theories. One can even determine the optimality of a theory relative to ones that have exactly the same overall input–output relation. The current agnosticism about mechanisms that one finds in rational analyses is unnecessary: a rational analysis can focus directly on the optimal mechanism for a particular problem, and not just the optimal input–output function. Rational analyses focus on a property of a theory (relative to its competitors) that does not depend on the level of description.

There is a pro-computational level argument that I have not yet considered. An optimality analysis aims to identify the highest-performing (by some metric) function from the search space. The explanatory power of the optimality analysis is arguably positively correlated with the size of the search space: if the optimal function is determined more by the lack of serious competitors than by high performance, then the *optimality* of the function seems to provide little explanatory power. The lack of competition seems to be explaining the occurrence of the behavior. Thus, a rational analysis is thought to be more powerful if the observed behavior is optimal relative to a large set of competitors, and the relatively unrestricted computational level provides the largest such set.

This argument is superficially appealing, but I think that it makes a major mistake. Consider the general claim about the correlation between the explanatory power of an optimality analysis and the size of the search space. The claim of a correlation is plausible: if the search space is small, then it is (arguably) less likely that the optimality of the function is the reason for the individual having that function, and so it is correspondingly less likely that there is any optimality-based explanation available for the behavior. (Recall that an optimality-based explanation requires an account of the

---

[9] Without such a restriction, the space of programs (i.e., series of function calls) will typically cover all or almost all computable functions, even for quite restricted basis functions.

development of the function in which the optimality of the function plays an important causal role.) But we are not interested simply in optimality analyses; we want optimality analyses—and optimality-based explanations—that are actually true of the world. A demonstration that some function is optimal relative to a large search space is mathematically interesting, but it is not clear how it is relevant from a cognitive science point-of-view unless that optimality, relative to *that* set of competitors, played some role in the development or maintenance of the behavior. To establish this latter point, the search space for the optimality analysis needs to be approximately the same as the search space for the developmental story. One needs to use the *actual* possibility space, and not one that that would have provided more explanatory power, if only it had been the actual possibility space.

There is one final, practical argument in favor of research at the computational level. Search for the optimal function can be quite difficult, and is arguably made even more challenging if the possibility space is 'complex' in various ways. The computational level—i.e., descriptions in terms of a single input–output function call—using all computable functions is a large search space with relatively simple structure. Thus (the argument continues), one should do optimality analyses at the computational level for practical reasons. Of course, to the extent that one subsequently learns more about the underlying physical and architectural constraints, one could amend the optimality analysis. But (the argument concludes) given our current (relative) ignorance about underlying cognitive architectures and implementations, one should do rational analyses at the highest level of description (unless one has substantial additional knowledge as in, e.g., Lee & Mumford, 2003).

This practical argument suffers from the same flaw as the previous argument: our rational analyses only can figure in optimality-based explanations if they use approximately the actual space of competitors. Mathematical tractability may be an important pragmatic reason for working at the computational level at first, but it does not justify an exclusive focus on that level. Moreover, it is not even obvious that the search space of single input–output function calls is dramatically simpler once one actually has some knowledge of the possibility space of underlying mechanisms. It is often much easier to specify the space of possible functions in terms of the intermediate steps, rather than remaining at solely the input–output level. Any particular *program* will be described more simply by a single function call, but the *space* of possible programs will not necessarily be described more simply in those terms. It just is not the case that the description of the function possibility space at the level of single input–output function calls is always simpler than a description in terms of intermediate function calls. Thus, the claim that optimality analyses at the level of single input–output function calls will always be more mathematically tractable falls apart. Much depends on how much information one has about the underlying architectures or possible implementations.[10]

---

[10] Of course, my reply assumes that human cognition is not arbitrarily plastic (in the relevant sense). If people can actually implement almost any computable function, then the restriction to the broadest search space at the computational level is probably justifiable.

Conclusion

Rational analyses have, without a doubt, been a useful tool in finding novel descriptive theories, previously unknown causally relevant task and environment variables, and have provided powerful frameworks for modeling complex cognition. I have nonetheless argued that their current use is not quite right. Extant rational analyses almost never provide full optimality-based explanations, as they almost never provide a developmental story—either phylogenetic or ontogenetic—that shows how the optimality played a major causal role in the establishment or maintenance of the behavior. By focusing on Marr's computational level, proponents of rational analyses have turned their attention away from theories of underlying cognitive mechanism, and the result has been rational analyses that provide essentially no explanations at all; they are just instrumentalist accounts. But as I have tried to argue in the last section, this tie to the computational level is entirely unnecessary: conditional on a set of competitors, the level of description of a theory is irrelevant to its optimality. The level of description might shape the possibility space in certain ways, but that does not imply that rational analyses can only be carried out at the highest levels of description. Rational analyses can and should be performed at all levels of description, depending on the particular knowledge one has about the underlying cognitive mechanisms at that level.

Acknowledgements

Early versions of these ideas were presented in talks at 'The Probabilistic Mind: Prospects for Rational Models of Cognition' workshop held at the Gatsby Computational Neuroscience Unit (University College, London), and at the Center for the Philosophy of Science (University of Pittsburgh). Thanks to audiences there, and to Nick Chater, Clark Glymour, Tom Griffiths, Edouard Machery, Josh Tenenbaum, and Annika Wallin for helpful discussions.

References

Anderson, J. R. (1990). *The adaptive character of thought*. Hillsdale, NJ: Erlbaum.

Anderson, J. R. (1991a). Is human cognition adaptive? *Behavioral and Brain Sciences*, **14**, 471–484.

Anderson, J. R. (1991b). The adaptive nature of human categorization. *Psychological Review*, **98**, 409–429.

Batterman, R. W. (2002). *The devil in the details: asymptotic reasoning in explanation, reduction, and emergence*. Oxford: Oxford University Press.

Brandon, R. N., & Rausher, M. D. (1996). Testing adaptationism: a comment on Orzack and Sober. *American Naturalist*, **148**, 189–201.

Bromberger, S. (1993). *On what we know we don't know: explanation, theory, linguistics, and how questions shape them*. Chicago: University of Chicago Press.

Chater, N., & Oaksford, M. (2000). The rational analysis of mind and behavior. *Synthese*, **122**, 93–131.

Chater, N., Oaksford, M., Nakisa, R., & Redington, M. (2003). Fast, frugal, and rational: How rational norms explain behavior. *Organizational Behavior and Human Decision Processes*, **90**, 63–86.

Danks, D. (submitted). Explanatory power, input–output approximation, and the case of rational analysis. *Philosophy of Science*.

Gigerenzer, G. (2000). *Adaptive thinking: rationality in the real world*. New York: Oxford University Press.

Gigerenzer, G. (2006). Bounded and rational. In R. J. Stainton (Ed.), *Contemporary debates in cognitive science* (pp. 115–133). Oxford: Blackwell.

Gigerenzer, G., Czerlinski, J., & Martignon, L. (1999). How good are fast and frugal heuristics? In J. Shanteau, B. Mellers, & D. Schum (Eds.), *Decision research from Bayesian approaches to normative systems* (pp. 81–103). Norwell, MA: Kluwer.

Gigerenzer, G., & Goldstein, D. G. (1996). Reasoning the fast and frugal way: models of bounded rationality. *Psychological Review, 103*, 650–669.

Gigerenzer, G., & Selten, R. (Eds.). (2001). *Bounded rationality: the adaptive toolbox*. Cambridge, MA: The MIT Press.

Gilchrist, A. S., Azevedo, R. B. R., Partridge, L., & O'Higgins, P. (2000). Adaptation and constraint in the evolution of *Drosophila melanogaster* wing shape. *Evolution & Development, 2*, 114–124.

Goldstein, D. G., & Gigerenzer, G. (1999). The recognition heuristic: How ignorance makes us smart. In G. Gigerenzer, & P. M. Todd (Eds.), *Simple heuristics that make us smart* (pp. 37–58). New York: Oxford University Press.

Griffiths, T. L., & Tenenbaum, J. B. (2005). Structure and strength in causal induction. *Cognitive Psychology, 51*, 334–384.

Halonen, I., & Hintikka, J. (2005). Toward a theory of the process of explanation. *Synthese, 143*, 5–61.

Hempel, C. (1965). *Aspects of scientific explanation*. New York: Free Press.

Lakos, J. (1996). *Large-scale C++ software design*: Addison-Wesley Professional.

Lee, T. S., & Mumford, D. (2003). Hierarchical Bayesian inference in the visual cortex. *Journal of the Optical Society of America A, 20*, 1434–1448.

Losos, J. B. (1992). The evolution of convergent structure in caribbean Anolis communities. *Systematic Biology, 41*, 403–420.

Maren, S. (2001). Neurobiology of Pavlovian fear conditioning. *Annual Review of Neuroscience, 24*, 897–931.

Marr, D. (1982). *Vision*. San Francisco: W.H. Freeman.

Martignon, L., & Hoffrage, U. (1999). Where and why is 'take the best' fast, frugal and fit? In G. Gigerenzer, & P. M. Todd (Eds.), *Simple heuristics that make us smart* (pp. 119–140). Oxford: Oxford University Press.

McConnell, S. C. (2004). *Code complete* (2nd ed.). Redmond, WA: Microsoft Press.

McCracken, K. G., Harshman, J., McClellan, D. A., & Afton, A. D. (1999). Data set incongruence and correlated character evolution: an example of functional convergence in the hind-limbs of stifftail diving ducks. *Systematic Biology, 48*, 683–714.

Menzel, R., & Giurfa, M. (2001). Cognitive architecture of a mini-brain: The honeybee. *Trends in Cognitive Sciences, 5*, 62–71.

Nickles, T. (1973). Two concepts of intertheoretic reduction. *The Journal of Philosophy, 70*, 181–201.

Oaksford, M., & Chater, N. (1998). *Rational models of cognition*. New York: Oxford University Press.

Orzack, S. H., & Sober, E. (1994). Optimality models and the test of adaptationism. *American Naturalist, 143*, 361–380.

Orzack, S. H., & Sober, E. (1996). How to formulate and test adaptationism. *American Naturalist*, **148**, 202–210.

Pearl, J. (2000). *Causality: Models, reasoning, and inference.* Cambridge: Cambridge University Press.

Rueger, A. (2001). Explanations at multiple levels. *Minds and Machines*, **11**, 503–520.

Rueger, A. (2005). Perspectival models and theory unification. *British Journal for the Philosophy of Science*, **56**, 579–594.

Salmon, W. C. (1984). *Scientific explanation and the causal structure of the world.* Princeton, NJ: Princeton University Press.

Salmon, W. C. (1989). *Four decades of scientific explanation.* Minneapolis, MN: University of Minnesota Press.

Seger, J., & Stubblefield, J. W. (1996). Optimization and adaptation. In M. R. Rose, & G. V. Lauder (Eds.), *Adaptation* (pp. 93–123). San Diego: Academic Press.

Sloman, S., & Fernbach, P. M. (this volume). The value of rational analysis: an assessment of causal reasoning and learning. In N. Chater, & M. Oaksford (Eds.), *The probabilistic mind: prospects for rational models of cognition.* Oxford: Oxford University Press.

Smith, P. (1998). Approximate truth and dynamical theories. *British Journal for the Philosophy of Science, 49*, 253–277.

Sobel, D. M., Tenenbaum, J. B., & Gopnik, A. (2004). Children's causal inferences from indirect evidence: backwards blocking and Bayesian reasoning in preschoolers. *Cognitive Science*, **28**, 303–333.

Spirtes, P., Glymour, C., & Scheines, R. (1993). *Causation, prediction, and search.* Berlin: Springer-Verlag.

Spolsky, J. (2004). *Joel on software: and on diverse and occasionally related matters that will prove of interest to software developers, designers, and managers, and to those who, whether by good fortune or ill luck, work with them in some capacity.* New York: Springer-Verlag.

Strevens, M. (2003). *Bigger than chaos: understanding complexity through probability.* Cambridge, MA: Harvard University Press.

Tenenbaum, J. B., Griffiths, T. L., & Niyogi, S. (2007). Intuitive theories as grammars for causal inference. In A. Gopnik, & L. E. Schulz (Eds.), *Causal learning: psychology, philosophy, and computation* (pp. 301–322). Oxford: Oxford University Press.

van Fraassen, B. C. (1980). *The scientific image.* Oxford: Oxford University Press.

Part 2

Inference and Argument

Chapter 4

Framing effects and rationality

Shlomi Sher

Princeton University, Princeton, NJ, USA

Craig R. M. McKenzie

University of California, San Diego, CA, USA

Preamble: problems of normative complexity

Most research in experimental psychology aims to construct good models of human cognitive faculties. Some important work, however, is not principally invested in the search for descriptive models of cognition. This research aims instead to test the empirical fit of a special class of cognitive and behavioral models, deemed interesting in their own right—the so-called 'rational actor' or 'rational choice' models (Shafir & LeBoeuf, 2002). Even if psychologists unanimously rejected these models on empirical grounds (as most do), many would still seek to study their patterns of empirical divergence and fit. This is because of the apparent practical and philosophical significance of rational actor models, as well as their undeniable prominence in the social sciences.

A further strand of research, amply documented in the present volume, attempts to fuse empirical and normative studies, modeling rational actors and human actors interactively. This tradition is not interested in the classical rational actor models *per se*; it supposes, instead, that better normative models can be developed by looking closely at human behavior, and that a deeper understanding of human behavior can be achieved with the aid of suitable normative models. Some investigators in this third tradition make explicit working assumptions about the optimality of human psychological processes. Others (the present authors among them) share the basic intuition that normative and empirical analyses commonly shed valuable light on one another, albeit in sometimes subtle ways.

Still, the simple question of the empirical fit of the classical rational actor models is the central concern in several research areas in experimental psychology. This chapter examines one such area: the study of framing effects in judgment and choice.

Empirical tests of rational models run into two classes of problems. The first class is the common frustration of all experimental research in psychology: it is necessary, though often maddeningly difficult, to keep a thorough accounting of the information that is available to the subject. If the characterization of experimental inputs is incomplete, the observed outputs can severely mislead the analyst. Human cognition seems, at first blush, a strange brew of the remarkably crude and the exquisitely subtle. For example, in studies of (explicit) visual recognition, people can be oblivious to changes even in gross details of the visual scene (Rensink *et al.*, 1997); while in studies of (implicit) visual priming, people can be highly sensitive to subtle unattended features of the visual stimulus, sometimes for weeks after a single viewing (Treisman & DeSchepper, 1996). For this reason, the ramifications of subtle information seeping unintended through an experimental design are usually difficult to prejudge. In empirical tests of all kinds—whether of rational actor models or explicitly cognitive models—the researcher must take pains to ensure that all of the information available to the subject has been accounted for.

The second class of problems is more specific to the empirical study of normative models. This research requires, not just accounting for all the information that is *available* to the subject, but also for all the information that is *relevant* to the normative model. As we will see, the latter accounting is not always easy to make.

Researchers naturally try to circumvent this second problem by examining specially contrived situations in which the normative analysis seems clear-cut—that is, in which a favored rational actor model generates clear prescriptions for normative action. One such area is framing research, an area of central importance in the psychology of judgment and decision-making. Framing researchers study situations in which apparently equivalent descriptions of choice options—for example, ground beef described as '75% lean' or '25% fat' (Levin & Gaeth, 1998)—lead to markedly divergent preferences. Normative predictions here seem particularly stark and compelling, and violations of these predictions are easy to come by. However, it turns out that, even in the simplified situations experimenters have specially contrived, the normative model used in their analysis has been inadequate. Even in this simple case, the experimental situation makes subtle information available which should matter to the normative analysis, but which has not been considered in the interpretation of experiments.

The framing literature thus affords a case study in the pitfalls of normative analysis. We do not think it is an isolated case; indeed, we will argue that closely similar problems arise in areas outside of the traditional framing literature. Such cases indicate that, in the interpretation of natural and experimental situations, adequate normative models are often as elusive as adequate empirical ones. This fact does not invalidate the empirical study of rational models, but it does highlight a basic background condition that should inform such studies. Human cognitive goals are complex. Because the function of rational norms is to guide us through our cognitive environments towards our cognitive goals, it should not surprise us if the rational norms themselves ultimately turn out to be similarly complex.

The problems and results described in this chapter illustrate this problem of normative complexity in a particularly simple empirical setting: framing effects in judgment and choice.

Framing effects: a brief review

A 'framing effect' is usually said to occur when *equivalent descriptions lead to different decisions*. Though this definition will require some amendment in what follows, some examples will suffice to illustrate the sorts of situations that framing researchers seek to understand:

Example 1: Evaluating a Medical Treatment. Participants are told to imagine that they have a terrible disease and must decide whether to accept a specific treatment option. Some participants are told that the treatment has 'a 20% mortality rate within 5 years' while other participants are told that the treatment has 'an 80% survival rate after 5 years'. The robust experimental finding is that participants are more likely to accept the treatment option when it is described in the 'survival' frame than when it is described in the 'mortality' frame (Marteau, 1989; McNeil *et al.*, 1982; Wilson *et al.*, 1987).

Example 2: The Asian Disease Problem (Tversky & Kahneman, 1981). Participants read the following background blurb:

> Imagine that the U.S. is preparing for the outbreak of an unusual Asian disease, which is expected to kill 600 people. One possible program to combat the disease has been proposed. Assume that the exact scientific estimate of the consequences of this program is as follows:

Some of the participants are then presented with the following two options:

> A: If this program is adopted, 200 people will be saved.

> B: If this program is adopted, there is a one-third probability that 600 people will be saved and a two-thirds probability that no people will be saved.

The other participants instead read:

> C: If this program is adopted, 400 people will die.

> D: If this program is adopted, there is a one-third probability that nobody will die and a two-thirds probability that 600 people will die.

The robust empirical finding is that most participants in the first condition prefer A to B, while most participants in the second condition prefer D to C.

Note that, in Example 1, the different descriptions of the medical treatment are *logically* equivalent, in that the truth of either description necessarily entails the truth of the other: 20% of patients die within 5 years if and only if 80% of patients survive after 5 years. Similarly, an inspection of Example 2 will reveal that A is logically equivalent to C, and B is logically equivalent to D (but see Jou *et al.*, 1996; Kühberger, 1995).

Levin, Schneider, and Gaeth (1998) taxonomized framing effects into three major categories. Example 1 above is an instance of what they called *attribute framing*: the value a single object (here, a medical treatment) assumes on a single bounded dimension (here, patient outcome after 5 years) can be described in terms of either of two logically equivalent proportions (here, '% survival' or '% mortality'). When the frames are valenced (one good, one bad), the standard finding is a *valence-consistent shift*: Preferences and evaluations shift in the direction of increasing valence. Thus treatment options described in terms of 'survival' rates are rated more highly than options described in terms of logically equivalent 'mortality' rates, '75% lean' beef is preferred to '25% fat' beef, etc (Levin & Gaeth, 1988).

Example 2, the so-called 'Asian Disease Problem' is the most well-known and widely studied instance of *risky choice framing*. In framing problems in this category, participants face two options rather than only one, and these options are gambles which can be described in terms of probabilities and proportions of gain or of loss. Usually, one option is a *sure thing* (in which an intermediate outcome is specified as certain, as in A and C above) while the other is a *gamble* (in which extreme positive and negative outcomes are both assigned non-zero probabilities, as in B and D above). The sure thing and the gamble are usually equated in expected value, making it possible to interpret observed patterns of preference in terms of participants' risk seeking or risk aversion. If we adopt this rubric of interpretation, participants encountering the Asian Disease Problem appear to be risk-averse for gains and risk-seeking for losses, a central tenet of prospect theory (Kahneman & Tversky, 1979).

Attribute and risky choice framing are widely studied[1]—the former because of its simplicity of experimental manipulation and its ubiquity in social settings (especially in persuasion situations); the latter because of its usefulness in experimentally testing classical expected utility theory and other quantitative choice models, including prospect theory.

Though risky choice framing problems are used in testing empirically oriented models, their implications for the empirical adequacy of rational actor models have been a lightning rod for debate. Attribute framing effects are of almost exclusively normative and practical interest. 'Framing effects,' Kahneman (2000, p. xv) has noted, 'are less significant for their contribution to psychology than for their importance in the real world … and for the challenge they raise to the foundations of a rational model of decision making.'

It is important, then, to be precise about just what challenge framing effects may raise to rational actor models. According to Tversky and Kahneman (1986, p. S253), *description invariance*—the condition that equivalent descriptions must lead to identical decisions—forms '[a]n essential condition for a theory of choice that claims normative status … so basic that it is tacitly assumed in the characterization of options rather than explicitly stated as a testable axiom'. Description invariance strikes most people as a *prima facie* reasonable normative condition, and for decades it has been generally accepted as such by psychologists.

However, there is imprecision at the heart of this formulation of the description invariance principle—*equivalent* descriptions must lead to identical decisions. What does it mean for a pair of descriptions to be 'equivalent'? While the sense of equivalence at issue is often left unspecified, the most common specification is *logical equivalence*. In this case the principle of description invariance becomes: logically equivalent descriptions must lead to identical decisions. As a theoretical criterion, logical equivalence has the virtue of transparency. Logical equivalence is well-defined (a pair of statements is logically equivalent if the truth of each entails the truth of the other); and, though disputes of application sometimes arise, they are relatively rare and, in most cases, easily circumvented.

---

[1] Levin *et al.*'s (1998) third category, *goal framing* (Meyerowitz & Chaiken, 1987), figures less prominently in the literature, and will not be considered here.

There is, however, one problem. As we show below, there is no general normative problem with logically equivalent descriptions leading to different decisions.

A hole in the normative model: information leakage

Every meaningful statement has infinitely many logically equivalent variants. Imagine a cup of water on the table before you. The statements 'The cup is 1/4-full' , 'The cup is 3/4-empty' , 'The cup is 25%-full' , 'The cup is twice as full as a 1/8-full cup' are constrained to covary in truth value. Though heterogeneous in style and emphasis, the statements share a common core of logical content. The normative model which forms the backdrop for all framing research insists that the decision maker must respond identically to all of these statements.

However, the decision maker must receive the statement from a speaker of some kind, and a speaker who wishes to convey this logical content will not select a statement at random. Various factors will influence the speaker's selection, these factors varying in degree of intentionality and conscious accessibility. In general, the speaker's selection will vary as a function of the information that is available to the speaker, as well as the speaker's attitudes about the thing being described. But if the speaker's choice of frame varies as a function of the speaker's beliefs and attitudes, then it also potentially conveys information about those beliefs and attitudes. Surely rational actors would not be expected to artificially ignore such information, should it prove relevant to the choice at hand.

That is, the normatively relevant equivalence between frames is not *logical equivalence*, but *information equivalence*—can any choice-relevant inferences be drawn, not only from the logical content conveyed, but also from the speaker's choice among logically equivalent statements? The normative analysis of framing effects cannot be neatly separated from the phenomena of *pragmatics*—i.e., the ways in which speakers typically select utterances and convey meaning in human conversational environments.

The condition of information equivalence can easily be formalized. For simplicity, suppose that the speaker is selecting among two frames, 'A' and 'B' , and that there is some choice-relevant background condition C with the property that the speaker is more likely to select 'A' when C holds than when C fails. That is, $P(\text{'}A\text{'}|C) > P(\text{'}A\text{'}|$ not-$C)$. A simple Bayesian argument establishes that $P(C|\text{'}A\text{'}) > P(C|\text{'}B\text{'})$. (There is nothing special about the two-frame case. the argument immediately generalizes to multiple frames.) Therefore, a listener, aware of the regularity that relates the background condition C to the speaker's choice of frame, may rationally infer a higher probability of C when the speaker says 'A' than when the speaker says 'B'. If C is choice-relevant, we should expect a rational actor to use this information, and therefore potentially to respond differently depending on the speaker's choice of frame. When no choice-relevant background condition C meeting the above description exists, two frames are *information equivalent*. Otherwise, they are *information non-equivalent*, and we say that the speaker's choice of frame leaks choice-relevant information (Sher & McKenzie, 2006).

For framing effects to raise normative concerns, they must violate a revised principle of description invariance, which states that *information equivalent* descriptions must lead to identical decisions. The principle that logically equivalent descriptions must lead to identical decisions has no standing as a normative principle.

The formal argument that establishes the potential information content of a speaker's choice among logically equivalent frames is an elementary one. Considering the size and significance of the framing literature, this raises a natural question: why has an inadequate standard of equivalence been used so widely for so long?

There is a misleading argument that logically equivalent utterances should be treated equivalently in reasoning: if '*A*' and '*B*' are logically equivalent, there is no inference that can be drawn from knowledge that *A* that cannot be drawn from knowledge that *B*. This observation is correct, because logical implication is transitive— indeed, it is transitive with respect to forms of intuitive or probabilistic implication, which themselves may not be strictly transitive. If one knows that *A*, one knows necessarily and certainly that *B*; therefore, whatever can be inferred, logically or intuitively, from *B* can also be inferred from *A*. So *A* and *B*, when logically equivalent, must support precisely the same set of inferences, and hence, it seems, should have precisely the same effects on decision.

This normative argument would apply to framing research if it were possible for experimenters to somehow *magically endow* their subjects with knowledge that A, or alternatively with knowledge that *B*—but this is not possible. In the typical framing experiment, the participant knows that A, assuming the participant trusts the speaker, only because the participant knows that the speaker has said '*A*' . *The speaker said 'A'* is a fact which is logically equivalent neither to *A* nor to *B*. It is certainly not logically equivalent to *The speaker said 'B'* . It is true, as the above argument notes, that no inferences can be drawn from *A* which cannot be drawn from *B*. But it is false that no inferences can be drawn from the fact that the speaker said '*A*' which cannot be drawn from the fact that the speaker said '*B*' .

Because it is not possible to surgically implant statements of interest into participants' heads, the normative model we apply in experimental situations must account for the participant's knowledge that the speaker selected this statement and no other. One possible explanation for the persistence of the inadequate logical equivalence standard in framing research, then, is that experimenters may have had an idealized conception of their experimental manipulations, viewing them as implanted bits of knowledge rather than as a speaker's verbal communication (Hilton, 1995; Schwarz, 1996).

A different possible explanation for the widespread and longstanding use of a theoretically inadequate normative model in framing research is that the model is adequate for all practical purposes. Perhaps, within the linguistic domains studied by framing researchers, logical equivalence and information equivalence effectively coincide. Presumably *some* information is leaked in any speaker's selection among logically equivalent frames—but such information may be irrelevant to the listener's decision problem, or too minor to explain substantial shifts in preference. On this view, logical equivalence may not be the appropriate theoretical standard, but it is nonetheless a safe proxy standard in experimental design.

The next section will show that this optimistic view is untenable. In one major segment of the framing literature—attribute framing—there is strong empirical evidence for the systematic leakage of information which (a) is choice-relevant and (b) qualitatively justifies the sorts of framing effects that are commonly observed empirically. Whether information leakage is an important normative or explanatory factor in risky choice framing is less clear—this issue is tentatively explored in a subsequent section. Finally, the information leakage framework can be extended to psychological research areas falling outside of the traditional framing literature. The normative models employed in these areas, too, employ normative standards of equivalence which fail to take heed of the way information is presented to participants. Information equivalence is the needed normative standard in these areas as well, and a re-examination of classical results in the light of information leakage argues for the moderation of some classical normative verdicts.

Information leakage in attribute framing

Recall that attribute framing effects involve logically equivalent descriptions of a single proportion. When one of these descriptions has positive valence ('% survival', '% lean', '% successes') and the other has negative valence ('% mortality', '% fat', '% failures'), the standard finding is a valence-consistent shift. Participants rate the option more highly, and are more likely to select it, when it is framed with the positive description.

But are logically equivalent descriptions of proportion really information equivalent? The parable of the half-empty cup ('is the cup half-empty or half-full?') suggests otherwise, and experimental studies confirm that logically equivalent attribute frames leak information that, in typical framing experiments, is choice-relevant.

To understand what information is leaked, we need to step back from valenced frames, and consider logically equivalent descriptions of proportion more generally. Consider, for $0 < p < 1$, domains D in which *the proportion of D which is X1 is p* if and only if *the proportion of D which is X2 is $1 - p$*. For example, if D is a sequence of coin tosses, the proportion of tosses which come up heads ($X1$) is p if and only if the proportion of tosses which come up tails ($X2$) is $1 - p$.

Reference Points in Attribute Framing. The reference point hypothesis (McKenzie & Nelson, 2003; Sher & McKenzie, 2006) concerns situations in which some reference point level of $X1$ is salient to the speaker. This may be the initial, expected, or standard value of $X1$. Thus, in a sequence of coin tosses, a natural reference point value for the percentage of tosses coming up heads would be 50%. According to the reference point hypothesis,

(1) Speakers are more likely to describe D in terms of '$X1$' when $X1$ is above the reference point.

(2) Listeners are sensitive to this regularity—they are more likely to (implicitly or explicitly) infer that $X1$ is above, and $X2$ below, a salient reference point when the speaker describes D in terms of '$X1$'.

For fixed observed frequencies of $X1$ and $X2$, speakers are more likely to coin '$X1$' descriptions when the $X1$ frequency is above the reference point than when it is below the reference point. For example, Sher and McKenzie (2006) had participants roll a six-sided die six times. For some participants, five sides of the die were black and the remaining side was white. For other participants, five sides were white and one was black. Thus, for the first group of participants, the natural reference point for the number of black outcomes out of six rolls would be five, while for the second group it would be one. Participants were not informed that the dice were weighted. For some participants, the die was weighted to fall most often on the minority color side (e.g., white in a die with five black sides). For other participants, the die was weighted to fall most often on a majority color side (e.g., black in a die with five black sides). After rolling the die six times, the participants had to describe the outcome. The reference point hypothesis predicts that, when black comes up between one and five times out of six, participants should be more likely to describe the outcome in terms of the 'black' proportion when black is the minority color on the die (and hence the black proportion is at or above reference point) than when black is the majority color on the die (and hence the black proportion is at or below reference point). This is exactly what we found. For example, when black came up three times and white came up three times, 83% of participants chose to describe the outcome as 'the die came up black three out of six times' when black was the minority color on the die, whereas only 36% did so when black was the majority color. Thus the reference point systematically influences the speaker's choice of frame.

Are listeners sensitive to such regularities in speakers' frame selection? In another series of experiments, Sher and McKenzie (2006) presented participants with two glasses of water, one full and one empty. Some participants were asked, 'just to get things started', to pour water from one glass to the other and place 'a half-full cup' in a square marked on the table. Other participants were asked instead for 'a half-empty cup.' In other experiments, different proportions were used: '1/4-full'/'3/4-empty' and '3/4-full'/'1/4-empty'.

Assuming that, for each cup, its initial state gives its reference point level, the initially empty cup, after pouring, ends up above reference point, and the initially full cup ends up below reference point. Thus the reference point hypothesis predicts that the initially full cup should be furnished more often when 'a p-empty cup' is requested than when 'a $(1 - p)$-full cup' is requested. This was in fact the case, for all proportions tested. Furthermore, follow-up questionnaires revealed that the purpose of the experiment was opaque to participants—that is, they were not aware that we were testing their interpretations of proportion frames. Therefore, it is reasonable to suppose that proportion frames convey reference point information even when participants are not focused on extracting it.

These studies affirmed and extended results obtained by McKenzie and Nelson (2003) in paper-and-pencil studies. In these studies, for both cups of water and medical treatments, 'speakers' were more likely to choose an attribute frame ('% empty', '% mortality') when that attribute was above the reference point level than when it was below. Furthermore, 'listeners' were able to accurately infer the reference point from the speaker's choice of frame.

Therefore, a *rational listener* in a natural conversational environment who is uncertain about typical medical treatment outcomes *will assign* a higher probability to a treatment's mortality rate being atypically high when the medical treatment is described in terms of its 'mortality rate' than when it is described in terms of the corresponding 'survival rate'. In general, the choice of a negatively valenced attribute frame is in fact evidence that the negative attribute is present to a greater extent than is typical. In other words, when there is uncertainty about the reference level of a choice-relevant variable, *rational actors will exhibit a valence-consistent shift*.

Implicit Recommendations in Attribute Framing. The reference point hypothesis implies that choice-relevant information is leaked in most attribute framing experiments, and that rational actors participating in such experiments would exhibit a valence-consistent shift. The empirical evidence summarized above strongly indicates that the reference point hypothesis is true. But why is it true? That is, why would speakers tend to describe objects in terms of relatively abundant attributes?

It seems likely that the speaker's choice of frame is a function, more broadly, of psycholinguistic salience, and the reference point hypothesis holds because relative abundance is one determinant of salience: more abundant attributes tend to be more salient in the speaker's psycholinguistic representations of the thing being described. But this perspective suggests that the reference point hypothesis may be profitably generalized. Reverting to the above formal terminology:

(1) A speaker is more likely to describe D in terms of '$X1$' when $X1$ is salient in the speaker's psycholinguistic representation of D.

(2) Listeners are sensitive to this regularity—they are more likely to (implicitly or explicitly) infer that $X1$ is salient in the speaker's representation of D when the speaker describes D in terms of '$X1$'.

To be sure, this generalized hypothesis is not an entirely satisfying one, because in addition to being more general than the reference point hypothesis, it is also vaguer. What psycholinguistic representations are at issue? What does it mean for an attribute to be salient in these representations? And what are the determinants of salience? However, though incomplete as a substantive hypothesis, (1)–(2) provide a valuable compass for research on information leakage in attribute framing. They set out two paths that researchers can profitably follow.

First, absent a general theory of psycholinguistic salience, one can still plausibly identify well-defined variables which are likely, all else being equal, to monotonically affect salience. Once such a variable V is identified, a corresponding pair of well-defined information leakage hypotheses is generated:

(1) Speakers are more likely to describe D in terms of '$X1$' when V assumes a higher value for $X1$.

(2) Listeners are sensitive to this regularity—when a speaker describes D in terms of '$X1$', they are more likely to (implicitly or explicitly) infer that V assumes a high value for $X1$.

The reference point hypothesis is the special case of (1)–(2) in which the variable V is *relative abundance*, one plausible determinant of salience. But many other determinants of salience could be substituted for V. For example, attributes which are more representative of the thing being described, more intrinsically notable, or more pragmatically consequential are likely to be more salient in the speaker's psycholinguistic representations. For example, a football team with unusually dramatic and interesting victories and run-of-the-mill losses is, we suspect, more likely to be described in terms of its win rate than a team with ordinary victories and spectacular defeats. A range of such variables could be specified and the corresponding information leakage hypotheses tested. If there are exceptions to the rule—if some plausible determinants of salience fail to influence frame selection—these may particularly reward further investigation. Insofar as the rule holds up well, frame selection probability in suitably designed experiments could be employed as a measure of psycholinguistic salience in relevant areas outside of traditional framing research.

A second strategy is to employ strong and clear salience manipulations whose interpretation does not hinge on subtleties of psycholinguistic theory. Sher and McKenzie (2006) adopted this strategy in an experiment in which participants described the accomplishments of a research and development (R&D) team in a hypothetical high-tech firm. This study was the frame selection complement of a specific framing effect from the literature (Duchon *et al.*, 1989), in which an R&D team was evaluated more favorably when described in terms of its 'successful' project rate than when described in terms of its corresponding 'unsuccessful' project rate. In our experiment, participants first read a background blurb about an R&D team. For half of the participants, the blurb described an extremely impressive R&D team: the researchers were leaders in their fields, the team took on very difficult projects, the successes were revolutionary and the failures valiant, and the team was widely admired in the research community. The other participants read a blurb describing an utterly incompetent R&D team. The success/failure rate was the same for both teams, and there was no clear reference point manipulation (because the impressive team was highly skilled but also took on highly challenging projects). Participants then described the team to a hypothetical supervisor by circling words and filling in blanks. One of the three incomplete sentences forced participants to describe the team in terms of its 'success' rate or its logically equivalent 'failure' rate. As predicted, participants were much more likely to describe the impressive team than the terrible team in terms of its 'success' rate. In this experiment, there were no clear reference points, but various other factors conspired to make the successes more salient in participants' likely representations of the impressive team. This team's successes were more spectacular, more noted by the R&D community, and more representative of the team's overall high caliber.

In this way, the speaker's choice of valenced frame conveys a kind of *implicit recommendation* to the listener. That is, a rational listener can infer, from the speaker's selection of a positively valenced frame, that the favorable attribute is more likely to be salient in the speaker's representation of the thing being described—whether because the favorable attribute is relatively abundant, more representative, or otherwise notable. Hence attribute frames leak choice-relevant information about attribute salience, and this information, absorbed by listeners, justifies the ubiquitous valence-consistent shift.

Information leakage in risky choice framing

Information equivalence, rather than logical equivalence, is the needed normative standard in the analysis both of attribute and of risky choice framing experiments.

The foregoing evidence suggests that the frames studied in typical attribute framing experiments are not information equivalent, and that the leaked information is sufficient to justify the qualitative patterns of shifting preferences observed in those studies. Does information leakage have similarly strong implications for the normative analysis of risky choice effects? (Readers new to the framing literature may wish to revisit the description of the Asian Disease Problem—Example 2 above—as it will be frequently referenced in what follows.)

Risky choice framing experiments present certain challenges to an information leakage analysis. First, the descriptions communicated to participants have more moving parts: there are two options rather than just one, and various probabilities and proportions are framed conjointly. Second, the models (e.g., prospect theory) which are put forward to explain these effects are also advanced as explanations for other phenomena. Because of the relative complexity of risky choice framing problems, information leakage predictions are harder to derive. Because of the logical relationships of risky choice framing problems to other models and phenomena, these models and phenomena must ultimately be considered in any serious analysis of these problems.

However, despite their architectural and theoretical complexity, there is some reason to hope that an information leakage analysis might shed some light on risky choice framing. After all, every risky choice framing problem can be viewed as a patchwork of attribute frames (i.e., of proportions and probabilities framed in terms of gains and losses). More generally, robust implicit recommendations like those considered above may not be specific to the simple framing situations considered above.

Is there important information leakage in risky choice framing problems? The short answer is: we do not know. The available evidence is too sparse and fragmentary to undertake a serious analysis at this point. We could not hope, in particular, to do justice to the full range of evidence which argues for a prospect-theoretic interpretation of these effects. We were, however, curious to see how far the explanatory constructs developed for the simple attribute case can be extended to the more complex setting of risky choice framing. The preliminary experiments presented here are offered, not as conclusive evidence, but in the hopes of stimulating further research in this direction.

A first question is whether speakers with preferences or persuasive goals can effectively anticipate listeners' likely reactions to the different frames. That is, do speakers select frames for risky choice problems which make listeners more likely to choose the speaker's own preferred option? We have conducted a number of unpublished experiments to begin to address this question. In all of them, participants read about the sure thing and gamble in the Asian Disease Problem, but the options are *fully described* rather than selectively framed (e.g., 'If Program A is adopted, 200 people will be saved and 400 people will die'). In one experiment, participants were explicitly assigned a persuasive goal—e.g., some were to persuade a listener to choose the sure thing—and asked to pick a joint 'saved' or 'die' framing for both programs. Consistent with an information leakage account, participants indeed were more likely to pick the 'saved' framing when persuading the listener to select the sure thing than when persuading the listener to select the gamble. However, this heavy-handed manipulation may be too artificial—e.g., speakers may deliberately simulate listener reactions to the different frames in this contrived experimental setting, but select frames quite differently in natural conversational environments. We want to understand information leakage in those environments.

To better simulate a natural conversational environment, participants in another experiment were not assigned a preference or a persuasive goal. Instead, they read the fully described options (i.e., not framed) of the Asian Disease Problem, and then indicated which program they preferred and rated their strength of preference. In this way, we were able to determine participants' personal preferences independent of framing. The participants were then presented with the following task:

Imagine that your job is to describe the situation, and the programs which have been proposed, to a committee who will then decide which program, A or B, to use. Please complete the sentences below as if you were describing the programs to the committee.

> be saved
>
> If Program A is adopted, _____ people will   .
>   (write #)   die
>   (circle one)
>
> If Program B is adopted,
>
>   be saved
>
> there is _____ probability that _____ people will   ,
>   (write #)   (write #)   die
>   (circle one)
>   be saved
>
> and _____ probability that _____ people will   .
>   (write #)   (write #)   die
>   (circle one)

Notice that, in contrast with the previous experiment, participants could independently frame the sure thing and the gamble. Regardless of prior preference (sure thing versus gamble), participants tended to frame the gamble in the same way ('1/3 probability that 600 people will be saved and 2/3 probability that 600 people will die'). However, we found a strong effect of prior preference on the framing of the sure thing. Among those who preferred the sure thing, 81% framed the sure thing in terms of lives 'saved', whereas, among those who preferred the gamble, only 48% did so. Furthermore, participants preferring the sure thing were more likely to select the 'saved' label when they rated their preference as stronger. (Those preferring the gamble were equally likely to choose the 'die' label regardless of strength of preference, indicating a possible ceiling effect for 'die' descriptions.)

This result indicates that, when given full flexibility in framing the two options, the attribute framing of the sure thing leaks choice-relevant information about the speaker's preferences. However, one limitation of this result is that participants tended to give the gamble a mixed framing throughout. To fully understand what information is leaked in standard risky choice framing problems—in which the sure thing and gamble are jointly framed—it will be important to examine reasonably naturalistic situations in which participants nonetheless tend to choose a pure joint framing for both the sure thing and the gamble. This is because the information leaked in joint framing need not be a simple additive sum of the information leaked in the separate framing of each option.

Though preliminary, these results suggest that a deeper investigation of information leakage in risky choice framing may prove fruitful. When assigned an explicit persuasive goal, participants select the frame that would be most effective in persuading the listener. In a less constrained setting, the framing of the sure thing, at least, can leak choice-relevant information about the speaker's spontaneous preference. Further work will be needed to fully characterize the information that may be leaked in speakers' selection of joint frames in natural conversational environments.

Framing and information equivalence: new directions

Framing experiments are typically designed to scrutinize the coherence of human beliefs and decisions. However, in the analysis of these experiments, framing researchers have not sufficiently considered the relation between evidence and belief. They have generally viewed framing manipulations as implanted bits of knowledge rather than as informative utterances issued in a communicative situation. A less idealized conception of the experimental manipulations requires that we adopt a subtler normative model, subjecting frames to the standard of information equivalence rather than logical equivalence. At least in the case of attribute framing, factoring in the relation between evidence and belief undermines otherwise compelling conclusions about the coherence of beliefs and preferences. However, this problematic idealization is not unique to normative models of choice, and its problems are not unique to the experimental study of traditional framing effects.

Consider, for example, the experimental literature on hypothesis testing. In hypothesis-testing tasks, participants are commonly asked to test hypotheses of the form, 'If $X1$, then $Y1$,' where variables X and Y each have two levels ($X1$ and $X2$, $Y1$ and $Y2$). A robust finding is that participants consider an $X1\&Y1$ observation to be more supportive than an $X2\&Y2$ observation, even though both observations support the hypothesis. In other words, confirming observations that are mentioned in the hypothesis are deemed more informative than confirming observations that are not mentioned in the hypothesis (Klayman, 1995; Klayman & Ha, 1987; McKenzie, 2004b; Nickerson, 1998; Oaksford & Chater, 1994).

This tendency to consider mentioned observations maximally informative can lead to a framing effect in hypothesis testing. McKenzie and Mikkelsen (2000) had participants imagine that they were researchers investigating a possible relation between genetics and personality type. They were told that everyone has either genotype A or genotype B, and either personality type X or personality type Y. Some participants tested the following hypothesis: 'if a person has personality type Y, then he/she has genotype B' (i.e. '$Y \rightarrow B$'). Of the first two people observed, one had genotype A and personality type X ($A\&X$) and one had genotype B and personality type Y ($B\&Y$). Both observations support the hypothesis, but when asked which provided stronger support, most participants selected the mentioned *B&Y* observation. Other participants were asked to test the hypothesis 'If a person has genotype *A*, then he/she has personality type *X*' (i.e., '*A → X*'). Most of these participants selected the mentioned *A&X* observation as most supportive.

Note that the two hypotheses are logically equivalent (one is the contrapositive of the other), and therefore whichever observation supports one hypothesis most strongly must also support the other hypothesis most strongly. Nonetheless, participants selected different observations as most supportive depending on which logically equivalent hypothesis was presented to them. In other words, the framing of the hypothesis impacts the evaluation of evidence.

But are the logically equivalent framings of the hypothesis information equivalent? If, when testing $X1 → Y1$, participants assume that $X1$ and $Y1$ (the mentioned events) are rare relative to $X2$ and $Y2$ (the unmentioned events), then the two logically equivalent framings are *not* information equivalent. And indeed, there is evidence that people do phrase conditional hypotheses in terms of rare events (McKenzie *et al.*, 2001).

If mentioned events tend to be rare, then, from a Bayesian perspective, the mentioned observation would be *normatively* more informative than the unmentioned observation. To see this, imagine testing the hypothesis that dwarfism leads to polydactyly (having more than 10 fingers). Because most people are not dwarfs and most people do not have more than 10 fingers, it would not be unusual to observe a 10-fingered non-dwarf regardless of whether dwarfism and polydactyly are related. However, although observing an 11-fingered dwarf would be unusual even if the two variables were related, it would be *very* unusual to observe such a person if there were no relation. Thus, observing an 11-fingered dwarf provides stronger support for the hypothesis than observing a 10-fingered non-dwarf, because the former is rare and the latter is common. (For formal details on why rarity matters, see McKenzie & Amin, 2002; McKenzie & Mikkelsen, 2000, 2007; McKenzie, 2004a; see also Anderson, 1990; Oaksford & Chater, 1994.)

In other words, treating mentioned observations as most informative is normatively justifiable because hypotheses tend to be phrased in terms of rare events. This provides a rational explanation of the fact that 'listeners' consider different data most supportive when hypotheses are rephrased in logically equivalent ways: the speakers' phrasing of a conditional hypothesis leaks normatively relevant information about event rarity.

Furthermore, the framing effect is reduced when it is clear to participants which events are rare. When this is the case, participants no longer need to rely on how hypotheses are phrased to infer event rarity. For example, the framing effect was reduced when participants were told that few people have a particular personality type and genotype. The reduction of the framing effect was especially marked when concrete hypotheses (regarding psychosis and being HIV+) were used, allowing participants to tap into real-world knowledge about rarity. Indeed, when participants were presented with concrete hypotheses and 'reminded' which events were rare, the framing effect virtually disappeared: participants were likely to select the rare observation as most informative regardless of whether it was mentioned in the hypothesis.

Thus, the application of the information equivalence standard to the normative analysis of conditional hypothesis testing helps us to understand why framing effects occur in hypothesis testing—the phrasing of conditional hypotheses leaks normatively relevant information about event rarity—and why they disappear—when event rarity is known, listeners no longer need to infer event rarity from the phrasing of the hypothesis.

McKenzie and Mikkelsen (2007) have recently made similar arguments in a discussion of human covariation assessment (for reviews, see Allan, 1993; McKenzie, 1994). In covariation assessment tasks, participants judge the strength of the relationship between two variables, each of which assumes values of presence and absence. Because people tend to give the most weight to joint presence observations, logically equivalent presentations of data can lead participants to report different judgments of covariation—a framing effect. However, because the presence of named variables tends to be rare and their absence common—e.g., there are fewer red things than non-red things, fewer accountants than non-accountants—joint presence is normatively more informative than joint absence from a Bayesian point of view. Furthermore, as with hypothesis testing, framing effects in covariation assessment virtually disappear when participants know which events are rare and which are common.

The standard normative models of covariation assessment and hypothesis testing consider only the logical content of a conditional hypothesis or data array. While these models may be well-suited to an analysis of the manipulation of idealized bits of knowledge, they are not adequate to an analysis of judgments based on specific utterances received in a complex linguistic environment. For typical abstract covariation assessment and hypothesis testing scenarios, these utterances often turn out to be information non-equivalent, leaking information about event rarity which qualitatively supports the positive conjunction strategies which are commonly observed. Determining just how far the information leakage account can go in explaining detailed results from the covariation assessment and hypothesis testing literatures would require a fuller treatment than we can provide here. However, in evaluating any given experiment in those literatures, the question of the existence and significance of information leakage from data formatting or conditional phrasing should be addressed.

Other ostensibly counter-normative phenomena, in which data or options which seem logically equivalent are treated non-equivalently, may benefit from a similar approach. McKenzie et al. (2006) took this approach to default effects in public policy, in which an alternative, often of considerable practical or moral significance, is more likely to be selected when it is designated as the default option—i.e., the option that will take effect barring an explicit decision to the contrary. For example, nations in which organ donation is the legal default have much higher rates of organ donation than nations in which citizens have to explicitly declare themselves donors (Johnson & Goldstein, 2003). Such 'default effects' are theoretically interesting because the options are the same in either case (e.g., 'Should I be an organ donor or not?'). While various interpretations of this phenomenon are available, information leakage may be one significant factor: the default option may serve as a kind of implicit recommendation from the policy maker to the individual, an implicit endorsement of a course of action. McKenzie et al. (2006) presented evidence that people draw such inferences from the designated default. For example, they found that participants were more likely to infer that the policy makers probably thought that people ought to be organ donors when being an organ donor was the default compared to when not being an organ donor was the default. The authors also found that participants view the default to either be enrolled or not enrolled in a retirement plan as implicit financial advice. Because our normative models commonly abstract away from the way in which information is presented to decision makers—and hence they abstract from potentially important information that may leak through the speaker's choice of presentation mode—it is plausible that further examples of seemingly counter-normative behavior shine light on deficiencies, not in our everyday decisions, but in the simple normative models we use to evaluate them.

Conclusion

Experimentalists continually worry about information leaks in their research designs—they need to understand exactly what information is available to the participant if they are to understand how the participant makes use of this information. But experimentalists testing the empirical fit of normative models must worry about another kind of information leakage—they must specify exactly what subset of the available information is relevant to the proper normative model of the experimental situation. We have argued that, in the traditional framing literature, as well as in the literatures on covariation assessment, hypothesis testing, and default effects, researchers have employed normative models which are insufficiently sensitive to subtle information leaked in experimental environments. Some important results from these areas are qualitatively consistent with the hypothesis that participants are simply more sensitive to this leaked information than the idealized normative models which researchers use to evaluate their behavior.

This paper has focused on the *complexity of information* available even in simple experimental situations. Another important factor, not considered here, is the *complexity of human cognitive goals*. For instance, in normative analyses of our epistemic interactions with the world, consistency is often regarded as an end in itself. Even consistency, however, should ultimately be viewed as a means to a more sophisticated epistemic end. This is made plain in the so-called 'preface paradox': I reasonably believe that some of my beliefs are false, even though this belief renders my total class of beliefs inconsistent. Logical consistency of beliefs is a simple and compelling cognitive norm, highly useful if applied locally and with normal discretion, but it is ultimately too simple. Even if our only cognitive goals are goals of understanding, both the complexity of goals and the complexity of information situations raise formidable hurdles to the formulation of prescriptively adequate normative models.

These problems, while formidable, should not deter researchers from critically examining the rationality of human thought and action. Many phenomena of pressing social importance seem difficult to understand without some kind of irrationality assumption, and these phenomena are too significant not to try to understand. Nonetheless, in attempting to study irrationality phenomena with the aid of simple normative models in contrived experimental situations, we should proceed with caution.

Human communicative situations are commonly awash in subtle cues. Despite our obstinate confusions and our crudeness of understanding, we are often more sensitive to such subtle information than we realize.

References

Allan, L. G. (1993). Human contingency judgments: rule based or associative? *Psychological Bulletin*, **114**, 325–448.

Anderson, J. R. (1990). *The adaptive character of tought*. Hillsdale, NJ: Erlbaum.

Duchon, D., Dunegan, K. J., & Barton, S. L. (1989). Framing the problem and making decisions: the facts are not enough. *IEEE Transactions on Engineering Management*, February, 25–27.

Hilton, D. J. (1995). The social context of reasoning: conversational inference and rational judgment. *Psychological Bulletin*, **118**, 248–271.

Johnson, E. J., & Goldstein, D. (2003). Do defaults save lives? *Science*, **302**, 1338–1339.

Johnson-Laird, P. N., & Shafir, E. (1993). The interaction between reasoning and decision making: an introduction. *Cognition*, **49**, 2, 1–9.

Jou, J., Shanteau, J., & Harris, R. J. (1996). An information processing view of framing effects: the role of causal schemas in decision making. *Memory & Cognition*, **24**, 1–15.

Kahneman, D. (2000). Preface. In D. Kahneman, & A. Tversky (Eds.), *Choices, values, and frames*. Cambridge: Cambridge University Press.

Kahneman, D., & Tversky, A. (1979). Prospect theory: an analysis of decision under risk. *Econometrica*, **47**, 263–291.

Klayman, J. (1995). Varieties of confirmation bias. *Psychology of Learning and Motivation*, **32**, 385–418.

Klayman, J., & Ha, Y.-W. (1987). Confirmation, disconfirmation, and information in hypothesis testing. *Psychological Review*, **94**, 211–228.

Kühberger, A. (1995). The framing of decisions: a new look at old problems. *Organizational Behavior and Human Decision Processes*, **62**, 230–240.

Kühberger, A. (1998). The influence of framing on risky decisions: a meta-analysis. *Organizational Behavior and Human Decision Processes*, **75**, 23–55.

Levin, I. P., & Gaeth, G. J. (1988). How consumers are affected by the framing of attribute information before and after consuming the product. *Journal of Consumer Research*, **15**, 374–378.

Levin, I. P., Schneider, S. L., & Gaeth, G. J. (1998). All frames are not created equal: a typology and critical analysis of framing effects. *Organizational Behavior and Human Decision Processes*, **76**, 149–188.

Marteau, T. M. (1989). Framing of information: its influence upon decisions ot doctors and patients. *British Journal of Social Psychology*, **28**, 89–94.

McKenzie, C. R. M. (1994). The accuracy of intuitive judgment strategies: Covariation assessment and Bayesian inference. *Cognitive Psychology*, **26**, 209–239.

McKenzie, C. R. M. (2004a). Framing effects in inference tasks—and why they are normatively defensible. *Memory & Cognition*, **32**, 874–885.

McKenzie, C. R. M. (2004b). Hypothesis testing and evaluation. In D. J. Koehler, & N. Harvey (Eds.), *Blackwell handbook of judgment and decision making* (pp. 200–219). Oxford: Blackwell.

McKenzie, C. R. M., & Amin, M. B. (2002). When wrong predictions provide more support than right ones. *Psychonomic Bulletin and Review*, **9**, 821–828.

McKenzie, C. R. M., Ferreira, V. S., Mikkelsen, L. A., McDermott, K. J., & Skrable, R. P. (2001). Do conditional hypotheses target rare events? *Organizational Behavior and Human Decision Processes*, **85**, 291–309.

McKenzie, C. R. M., Liersch, M. J., & Finkelstein, S. R. (2006). Recommendations implicit in policy defaults. *Psychological Science*, **17**, 414–420.

McKenzie, C. R. M., & Mikkelsen, L. A. (2000). The psychological side of Hempel's paradox of confirmation. *Psychonomic Bulletin and Review*, **7**, 360–366.

McKenzie, C. R. M., & Mikkelsen, L. A. (2007). A Bayesian view of covariation assessment. *Cognitive Psychology*, **54**, 33–61.

McKenzie, C. R. M., & Nelson, J. D. (2003). What a speaker's choice of frame reveals: reference points, frame selection, and framing effects. *Psychonomic Bulletin and Review*, **10**, 596–602.

McNeil, B. J., Pauker, S. G., Sox, H. C., Jr., & Tversky, A. (1982). On the elicitation of preferences for alternative therapies. *New England Journal of Medicine*, **306**, 1259–1262.

Meyerowitz, B. E., & Chaiken, S. (1987). The effect of message framing on breast self-examination attitudes, intentions, and behavior. *Journal of Personality and Social Psychology*, **52**, 500–510.

Nickerson, R. S. (1998). Confirmation bias: a ubiquitous phenomenon in many guises. *Review of General Psychology*, **2**, 175–220.

Oaksford, M., & Chater, N. (1994). A rational analysis of the selection task as optimal data selection. *Psychological Review*, **101**, 608–631.

Oaksford, M., & Chater, N. (2003). Optimal data selection: revision, review, and re-evaluation. *Psychonomic Bulletin and Review*, **10**, 289–319.

Rensink, R.A., O'Regan, J. K., and Clark, J. J. (1997). To see or not to see: the need for attention to perceive changes in scenes. *Psychological Science*, **8**, 368–373.

Schwarz, N. (1996). *Cognition and communication: judgmental biases, research methods, and the logic of conversation*. Mahwah, NJ: Erlbaum.

Shafir, E., & LeBoeuf, R. A. (2002). Rationality. *Annual Review of Psychology*, **53**, 491–517.

Sher, S., & McKenzie, C. R. M. (2006). Information leakage from logically equivalent frames. *Cognition*, **101**, 467–494.

Treisman, A. & DeSchepper, B. (1996). Object tokens, attention, and visual memory. In T. Inui, & J. McClelland (Eds.), *Attention and performance XVI: information integration in perception and communication* (pp. 15–46). Cambridge, MA: MIT Press.

Tversky, A., & Kahneman, D. (1981). The framing of decisions and the psychology of choice. *Science*, **211**, 453–458.

Tversky, A., & Kahneman, D. (1986). Rational choice and the framing of decisions. *Journal of Business*, **59**, S251–S278.

Wilson, D. K., Kaplan, R. M., & Schneidermann, L. J. (1987). Framing of decisions and selections of alternatives in health care. *Social Behaviour*, **2**, 51–59.

Chapter 5

Probability logic and the *Modus Ponens–Modus Tollens* asymmetry in conditional inference

Mike Oaksford

Birkbeck College London, London, UK

Nick Chater

University College London, London, UK

The conditional, *if … then*, is the most important single phrase in natural language for understanding human reasoning. The conditional is used to express rules, regulations, laws of nature, promises, legal obligations, among many other uses. For many aspects of human thought and behaviour it is important to know how conditionals work: i.e., what inferences can be drawn from accepting the conditionals expressing these relationships. Only then can it be determined what it is to break a regulation; what happens next or explains what has just happened; what it is to break a promise or renege on an obligation and so on. It is therefore not surprising that perhaps the majority of research in the psychology of reasoning has focused on the conditional (see, for example, the introductory chapters on reasoning in Eysenck and Keane [2000] and Braisby and Gellatly [2005]).

The starting point for the psychology of conditional inference has been the formal analysis of the conditional provided by standard logic. According to standard logic, a conditional *if p then q* is true, and so can be accepted, and, if and only if either the *antecedent* (p) is false or the *consequent* (q) is true. This semantics for the conditional licenses two formal rules of inference called *modus ponens* (MP) and *modus tollens* (MT):

$$\text{MP} \quad \frac{p \to q, p}{\therefore q} \qquad \text{MT} \quad \frac{p \to q, \neg q}{\therefore \neg p} \qquad (1)$$

These inference schemata read that if the propositions above the line are true, then it can be inferred that the propositions below the line are true. For example, for MP, if it is true that *if John has a runny nose* (p), *he has a cold* (q) and that *John has a runny nose*, then it is true that *Johnny has a cold*. According to standard logic both MP and MT inferences are *valid*. Consequently, if people are logical then they should endorse both inferences and reject the inferential fallacies of *denying the antecedent* (DA) and *affirming the consequent* (AC):

$$\text{DA} \quad \frac{p \to q, \neg p}{\therefore \neg q} \qquad\qquad \text{AC} \quad \frac{p \to q, q}{\therefore p} \qquad\qquad (2)$$

However, rather than exhibiting the predicted symmetry between MP and MT, participants tend to endorse MP far more than MT. For example, in a recent meta-analysis involving 65 conditional inference experiments and 2774 participants, 97% (SD = 3.6%) on average draw the MP inference but only 72% (SD = 13.5%) the MT inference (Schroyens & Schaeken, 2003; see also Oaksford & Chater, 2003a). Over the 65 studies, this result represents a highly significant asymmetry, $t(64) = 15.44$, $p < 0.0001$, between MP and MT. Moreover, participants also endorse DA and AC. According to most theories (see below), this is because some participants interpret *if p then q* as *implicating* (Levinson, 2000) its converse, *if q then p.*, i.e., the conditional is interpreted as a *bi-conditional*: *if and only if p, then q*. Drawing the valid MP and MT inferences on the converse is like committing the fallacies of AC and DA respectively on the original rule.

The MP–MT asymmetry is illustrated in Panel A of Figure 5.1. The line marked 'data' (filled diamonds with a full line) shows the results of Schroyens and Schaeken's (2003) meta-analysis with 95% confidence intervals. The line marked 'model' (open squares with a dashed line) shows the best fit to these data that can be obtained by standard logic allowing for errors (Oaksford & Chater, 2003a). If people interpret the task rule as a conditional they should accept just MP and MT; if they interpret it as a bi-conditional they should accept all four inferences.

Not surprisingly, explaining the MP–MT asymmetry has become the first hurdle that any psychological account of human conditional inference must clear. In *mental logic* theories (Braine & O'Brien, 1998; Rips, 1994), people are hypothesized to draw inferences by applying mental inference schemata rather like in (1). However, in Rips (1994) version of this account, people do not possess the MT schemata and must therefore draw this inference using a more complex inference form. Figure 5.1 also reveals that there is a significant AC—DA asymmetry, $t(64) = 5.47$, $p < 0.0001$, which should not occur according to standard logic. Mental logic explains this asymmetry as another instance of the MP—MT asymmetry but this time on the converse of the original rule, i.e., on *if q then p*.

In *mental models* theory (Johnson-Laird & Byrne, 1991, 2002), people reason over pictorial representations of what those sentences *mean*, i.e., the states of affairs in which they are true. These representations concern the different *possibilities* that a logical expression may allow. For a conditional, *if p then q*, each possibility depends on whether *p* and *q* are true or false, which leads to four possibilities. If *if p then q* is true then the possibility where *p* is true and *q* is false is excluded leaving three other possibilities. People have a preferred initial possibility, where *p* and *q* are both true, which they represent in working memory as,

$$[p] \quad q \qquad\qquad (3)$$

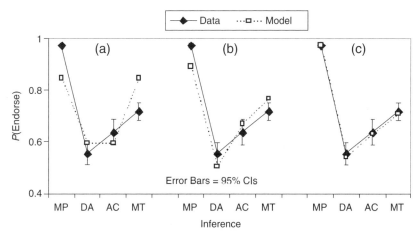

Fig. 5.1. The probability that each inference is endorsed showing the fits of standard logic (Panel A), the conditional probability model (Panel B), the revised probability model (Panel C) to the data from Schroyens and Schaeken's (2003) meta-analysis.

The ellipsis indicates that there might be other conditions that can 'flesh out' this representation and the square brackets indicate that p is exhausted and is not paired with anything else. Given the premise p, the representation in (3) shows that the conclusion q is licensed because it indicates that all the objects (given by []) that are p are also q. Consequently, people are happy to draw the MP inference.

However, nothing can be inferred given the MT premise, $\neg q$, as it does not match anything in working memory. MT can only be drawn when this representation is 'fleshed out' with the remaining two possibilities that make the rule true:

$$
\begin{array}{cc}
p & q \\
\neg p & q \\
\neg p & \neg q
\end{array}
\tag{4}
$$

From this representation it can be seen that $\neg q$ can only be paired with $\neg p$, so the MT inference can be made. Mental models adopt a very similar explanatory tactic as mental logic to explain the AC–DA asymmetry, i.e., some people adopt the bi-conditional interpretation for which the initial model is

$$
[p] \quad [q]
\tag{5}
$$

which licenses the MP and AC inference. When fleshed out as in (6)

$$
\begin{array}{cc}
p & q \\
\neg p & \neg q
\end{array}
\tag{6}
$$

all the four inference can be made.

In both mental models theory and in mental logic theory, the MP–MT asymmetry is explained at the algorithmic level (Marr, 1982). That is, the reason for the asymmetry is located in the mental representations and processes that implement deductive reasoning in the human mind. However, recently there have been attempts to explain the MP–MT asymmetry at the computational level (Marr, 1982). That is, there may be a normative theory that provides a descriptively adequate account of this asymmetry. A different computational level theory of what function the mind is trying to compute in conditional inference may well entail a different algorithmic level account.

The probabilistic approach (Oaksford & Chater, 2001; Oaksford *et al.*, 2000) proposes that people draw, for example, MP in proportion to their assessment of the conditional probability of *q* given *p*, $P(q|p)$. A similar approach has been endorsed by others (Anderson, 1995; Chan & Chua, 1994, George, 1997; Liu, 2003; Liu *et al.*, 1996; Politzer, 2005; Stevenson & Over, 1995). Moreover, it has recently been discovered that people treat the probability of a conditional, $P(if\ p\ then\ q)$, to be $P(q|p)$ (Evans *et al.*, 2003; Oberauer & Wilhelm, 2003). This result is at least consistent with the probabilistic approach (see below). Appropriate conditional probabilities can also be derived for MT ($P(\neg p|\neg q)$) and the fallacies, DA ($P(\neg q|\neg p)$) and AC ($P(p|q)$) on the assumption that people have prior knowledge of $P(p)$ and $P(q)$ (Oaksford *et al.*, 2000). According to this account as long as $P(q|p) < 1$, then some asymmetry can result between MP and MT. The precise nature of the asymmetry will depend on the values of $P(q|p)$, $P(p)$ and $P(q)$. This is no different from the mental logic and mental models theories. These accounts can only explain the precise nature of the asymmetry by appeal to different proportions of participants adopting different interpretations of the conditional, as we have seen. However, the probabilistic account, originally proposed by Oaksford *et al.* (2000; see also Oaksford & Chater, 2003a–d), may not go far enough in explaining the MP–MT asymmetry (Evans & Over, 2004; Schroyens & Schaeken, 2003). The details of the probabilistic account are discussed in more detail below. However, for now it is sufficient to consider Panel B in Figure 5.1, where the fit of the probabilistic model to the data is shown. Panel B shows that probability theory does a better job than logic in explaining these data, explaining a further 29% of the variance (Oaksford & Chater, 2003a). It moreover captures the MP–MT and AC–DA asymmetries. However, the probabilistic account *underestimates* the magnitude of the MP–MT asymmetry (Schroyens & Schaeken, 2003): it underestimates endorsement of MP and overestimates endorsement of MT. Moreover, in both cases the predicted probability of endorsing these inferences falls outside the 95% confidence interval for those data points. Panel B also shows that the probabilistic account *overestimates* the magnitude of the AC–DA asymmetry.

Despite the existence of converging evidence (Evans *et al.*, 2003; Oberauer & Wilhelm, 2003) highly consistent with Oaksford *et al.*'s (2000) probabilistic approach to inference, it has still met some resistance primarily because of the empirical results on the magnitude of the MP–MT asymmetry (Evans & Over, 2004; Schroyens & Schaeken, 2003). In this paper, it is suggested that adopting a probabilistic interpretation of the conditional, such that $P(if\ p\ then\ q) = P(q|p)$, commits one to an account of conditional inference that must be formally very close to that proposed by Oaksford *et al.* (2000, and Oaksford & Chater, 2003a–d). Moreover, within the context of the normative probabilistic approach to the conditional provided by *probability logic* (Adams, 1998), it is argued that a more extreme form of the MP–MT asymmetry may be *normatively defensible* (McKenzie, 2004).

The chapter begins with the account of the conditional developed in Adams (1998) probability logic. It is shown that when applied to conditional inference, recent research in the normative literature (Sober, 2002; Sobel, 2004; Wagner, 2004) is consistent with the account presented by Oaksford *et al.* (2000). Moreover, these normative accounts introduce an important condition on *probabilized* MP and MT, called the *rigidity condition* (Wagner, 2004) which may explain the MP–MT asymmetry. It is then argued that by exploiting this condition far better fits to the data on conditional inference can be obtained. Finally, some loose ends are tidied up and some proposals for further work made before concluding.

Probability logic and the conditional

The core of probability logic for the conditional is what Edgington (1995) refers to as *The Equation*, which equates the probability of an everyday indicative conditional ('$\rightarrow$') with the conditional probability:

$$P(p \rightarrow q) = P(q \mid p), \text{ where } P(p) > 0 \qquad (7)$$

Where $P(q|p)$ is given by the *Ratio formula* (Bennett [2003] proposed this name; '$\wedge$' is the logical symbol for *and*):

$$P(q \mid p) = \frac{P(p \wedge q)}{P(p)} \rightarrow \qquad (8)$$

The Ratio formula is not to be interpreted as a definition of conditional probability, which is regarded as more primitive. Our understanding of $P(q|p)$ is given by the subjective interpretation provided by the *Ramsey Test*. As Bennett (2003, p. 53) says:

> The best definition we have [of conditional probability] is the one provided by the Ramsey test: your conditional probability for q given p is the probability for q that results from adding $P(p) = 1$ to your belief system and conservatively adjusting to make room for it.

The Ratio formula indicates that in calculating the probability of the everyday conditional all that matters are the probabilities of the true antecedent cases, i.e., $P(p \wedge q)$ and $P(p \wedge \neg q)[P(p) = P(p \wedge q) + P(p \wedge \neg q)]$. This contrasts immediately with standard logic where the probability of a conditional is given by probability of the cases that make it true, i.e., $P(p \rightarrow q) = P(\neg p) + P(p,q)$. Evans *et al.* (2003) and Oberauer and Wilhelm (2003) have confirmed that people interpret the probability of the conditional as the conditional probability and not the probability suggested by standard logic. The Equation means that everyday indicative conditionals are *zero-intolerant* (Bennett, 2003). That is, they are not acceptable when $P(p) = 0$, because you should 'believe $p \rightarrow q$ to the extent that you think that $p \wedge q$ is nearly as likely as p' (Edgington, 1991, p. 189). So when $P(p) = 0$, you should not accept $p \rightarrow q$.

The Equation has some important consequences. First, the *probability conditional*, as Adams (1998) refers to it, is not truth functional and it is not truth conditional either, i.e., conditionals are not propositions that can have a truth value. If they were propositions, then asking about their probability, $P(p \rightarrow q)$, would be equivalent to asking about the probability that $p \rightarrow q$ is *true*. But from the Equation $P(p \rightarrow q) = P(q|p)$ and so the question being asked appears to be: what is the probability that $q|p$ is true. However, '$q|p$' is not a claim about the world, i.e., it doesn't make sense to ask whether this is true or false. According to the Ramsey test, this expression relates to a mental process, not a fact about the world that could be true or false. This is because the conditional probability $P(q|p)$ is the probability of q given that p holds; it is not the probability of some mysterious proposition $q|p$.

The Equation also means that conditionals can not be embedded in truth functional compounds. If the conditional $p \rightarrow q$ does not assert a proposition (or the probability that a proposition holds), then $\neg(p \rightarrow q)$ is also not defined; and similarly for conjunction and disjunction of conditionals. Accordingly, *its not the case that if you turn the key the car will start*, cannot be glossed as having the form $\neg(p \rightarrow q)$; but must rather be glossed as *if you turn the key the car will not start*, with the well-defined structure $p \rightarrow \neg q$. In standard logic $p \rightarrow q$ and $p \rightarrow \neg q$ are consistent with one another, one is not the denial of the other (and both will be true of p is false). For the probability conditional, in contrast, they are *probabilistic contraries*. This is because $P(q \mid p) + P(\neg q \mid p) = 1$, so asserting that $p \rightarrow \neg q$ has a high probability simultaneously means that $p \rightarrow q$ has a low probability. Similar moves can be made in relation to the conjunction and disjunction. Thus, there need not necessarily be a lack of expressiveness by moving to the probability conditional (Adams, 1975; Bennett, 2003).

The probability conditional and inference

If indicative conditionals do not have truth values, then from a standard logical viewpoint, it would seem impossible to define any valid inferences that follow from them. An inference is classically valid if the *truth* of the premises guarantees the *truth* of the conclusion. However, while classical validity is inapplicable for arguments involving conditionals they may possess another virtue, *probabilistic validity* or *p-validity*. Adams (1975) observed that all classically valid arguments also possess a property that can best be formulated using the concept of *uncertainty*. The uncertainty of a proposition p, $U(p)$, is simply $1 - P(p)$. The property he discovered was that, '*in a classically valid argument the uncertainty of the conclusion cannot exceed the sum of the uncertainties of the premises*' (Bennett, 2003, p. 131). That is,

$$\text{If } p_1 \quad p_n \text{ entail } q, \text{ then } U(q) \leq \sum_{i=1}^{n} U(p_i) \tag{9}$$

An argument fulfilling this condition, Adams (1975) calls *p-valid*. Arguments containing indicative conditionals, while not candidates for classical validity may be *p*-valid and so can be evaluated on that basis.

Many inferences that are classically valid but counterintuitive, in standard logic turn out not to be *p*-valid. For example, in standard logic, *the moon is made of cheese* implies that *if the Moon is made of cheese, then grass is blue* is true, because any conditional with a false consequent is true. This inference, known as one of the 'paradoxes' of material implication, does not arise for the probabilistic conditional. Indeed, the probability of the conditional is not even well-defined when the antecedent is false, e.g., $P(the\ moon\ is\ made\ of\ cheese) = 0$. In Equation (8), attempting to evaluate the conditional probability would yield 0/0, which is undefined.

Another important inference that is classically valid for the material conditional but turns out not to be *p*-valid for the probability conditional is *strengthening the antecedent*:

$$\text{Strengthening the antecedent: } \frac{p \to q}{\therefore (p \wedge r) \to q} \tag{10}$$

Although it makes sense to assign a high probability to *if Tweety is a bird, then Tweety can fly*, because most birds fly, anyone would assign a very low probability, i.e., 0, to *if Tweety is a bird and Tweety is one second old, then Tweety can fly* (how old Tweety is can be adjusted to produce probabilities for the conclusion that are greater than 0). Thus the uncertainty of the conclusion, i.e., 1, is greater than the uncertainty of the premise. Failure of strengthening the antecedent is the *sine qua non* of *non-monotonic* or *defeasible* reasoning systems. Oaksford and Chater (1991, 1993, 1995, 1998, 2001) have argued that it is a significant challenge to psychological accounts of human reasoning to capture the defeasibility of everyday reasoning (see also, Bonnefon [2004] for a more recent assessment, in the context of mental models theory). But the probability conditional is defeasible at its very foundation.

Probabilized MP and the rigidity condition

In probability logic, both MP and MT are *p*-valid. However, this simple statement covers over a range of important issues. For Adams (1975, 1998) the whole point of the indicative conditional is to perform MP inferences. That is, conditionals are *inference tickets*—an idea that goes back to Ryle (1949)—that allow people to update their beliefs given new information. So if a high probability is assigned to *if x is a bird, x flys*, then on acquiring the new information that *Tweety is a bird*, one's degree of belief in *Tweety flies* should be revised to one's degree of belief in *Tweety flies given Tweety is a bird*, i.e., my degree of belief in the conditional. So using P_0 to indicate *prior* degree of belief and P_1 to indicate *posterior* degree of belief, then:

$$P_1(q) = P_0(q \mid p), \text{ when } P_1(p) = 1 \tag{11}$$

This result can be generalized (Hailperin, 1996; Sober, 2002) to the case when the new information is not that $P_1(p) = 1$, but that $P_1(p)$ equals some probability b, then assuming $P_0(q \mid p) = a$, and no further assumptions, the bounds on $P_1(q)$ are:

$$ab \leq P_1(q) \leq ab + 1 - b. \tag{12}$$

These bounds arise from allowing the posterior probability of q given $\neg p$, $P_1(q \mid \neg p)$, to vary between 0 and 1.

Jeffrey conditionalization (Jeffrey, 1983) assumes that the conditional probabilities $P_1(q \mid \neg p)$ and $P_1(q \mid p)$ remained the same as their prior values. This is called the *rigidity* condition:

$$\text{Rigidity Condition: } P_1(q \mid p) = P_0(q \mid p) \qquad (13)$$

In terms of our example, this means that learning that *Tweety is a bird* does not alter your degree of belief in the conditional *if x is a bird, x flies*. Although MP is *p*-valid it is only valid in a restricted sense because *strengthening of the antecedent* is not valid. Consequently, if you then discover that *Tweety is a penguin*, you would have to assign an uncertainty of 1 to the conclusion of the original MP inference, i.e., *p*-validity would be violated. So the context in which it is learned that *Tweety is a bird* ($P_1(p) = 1$) must not be one in which this fact gives grounds to alter one's degree of belief in the conditional, e.g., it must not give grounds to accept *Tweety is a penguin*.

Contexts like this are not unimaginable. For example, on being told that an islander's pet, Tweety, is a bird, an ornithologist on Penguin Island might refrain from using his normal inference ticket to infer Tweety can fly because Tweety is most likely a penguin. A more subtle example derives from the nature of the Ramsey test. There is an important distinction, recently emphasized in the psychology of reasoning by Evans and Over (2004), between *supposing* and *believing*. Supposing *A* to be true is not the same as actually believing *A* to be true. Using Bennett's (2003) example, an atheist presumably thinks that the proposition that God exists is false, and may not revise that opinion on *supposing* that she has a terminal illness. The Ramsey test for assessing conditional probabilities relies only on *supposing* the antecedent to be true. Thus our atheist's assessment of the conditional probability that God exists (q) given she has a terminal illness (q) may not vary from her initial low probability that God exists, i.e., $P_0(q|p) \approx 0$. However, on actually being told that she has a terminal illness, she may nonetheless come to believe that God exists. That is, on coming to *believe* she has a terminal illness, the relevant conditional probability changes to a much higher value, i.e., $P_1(q|p) \approx 1$, in violation of the rigidity condition. Rigidity sets a limit on when MP is *p*-valid but it seems in practice a reasonable assumption that rigidity holds. For example, the strength of the initial conviction of atheists who relinquished their beliefs under extreme circumstances could be questioned.[1]

Oaksford *et al.* (2000) and probabilized MT, AC, and DA

The implications of The Equation have been extensively explored in the psychological literature (particularly in Evans & Over, 2004; Evans *et al.*, 2003; Oberauer & Wilhelm, 2003). However, there has been very little discussion of the account of inference that arises from the probability conditional and how this relates to current proposals like those made by Oaksford *et al.* (2000). In this section this situation is redressed.

----

[1] *Defeasibility* and the *rigidity condition* are clearly closely related. However, as these examples show, rigidity can be violated for other reasons and not just as a consequence of the possibility that a particular everyday inference may be defeated.

Oaksford *et al.* (2000) argued that people endorse, for example, the conclusion of MP in proportion to the conditional probability of the conclusion given the categorical premise, i.e., $P_0(q|p)$. This amounts to exactly the same prescription as probabilized MP. People derive an estimate for $P_0(q|p)$, i.e., the probability of the conditional premise $(p \rightarrow q)$, via the Ramsey test. The categorical premise, p provides the information that $P_1(p) = 1$, so $P_0(q|p)$ can now be conditionalized upon to provide the best estimate of $P_1(q)$, which—assuming *rigidity*—is $P_0(q|p)$. From (12) we also know that this account can be readily generalized to the case where $P_1(p) < 1$. In this case, $P_1(q) \geq P_0(q|p)P_1(p)$, or by Jeffrey conditionalization, $P_1(q) = P_0(q|p)P_1(p) + P_0(q|\neg p)P_1(\neg p)$. What of the remaining inferences?

Probabilized MT, AC, and DA

Sober (2002) has argued that a *probabilistic MT* would have to be invalid. Sober's arguments primarily concern how evidence e impacts on a hypothesis, H. He assumes that the given conditional probability is the likelihood of the evidence given the hypothesis, $P_0(e|H)$, and that you now receive evidence that $\neg e$, i.e., $P_1(\neg e) = 1$. The MT inference involves updating your probability for $\neg H$ by conditionalizing on $\neg e$ to reach the conclusion that $P_1(\neg H)$ is high. However, as Sober (2002) observes, this updating requires $P_0(\neg H|\neg e)$ for $\neg e$ to conditionalize on, but the premises indicating that $P_0(e|H)$ is high and $P_1(\neg e) = 1$ do not entail a value for $P(\neg H|\neg e)$. The same applies to AC and DA, i.e., the premises of these inferences do not entail a specific value for the relevant conditional probabilities for the categorical premises to conditionalize on, i.e., $P_0(p|q)$ and $P_0(\neg p|\neg q)$, respectively.

Recently, Wagner (2004) has proposed a probabilistic version of MT which indicates the following bounds on the probability of the conclusion of this inference, i.e., $P(\neg p)$. Letting $P(q|p) = a$ and $P(\neg q) = b$:

$$\max\left[\frac{1-a-b}{1-a}, \frac{a+b-1}{a}\right] \leq P(\neg p) < 1, \quad \text{when } 0 < a, b < 1 \qquad (14)$$

$$1 - b \leq P(\neg p) < 1, \qquad\qquad \text{when } a = 0 \text{ and } 0 < b \leq 1 \qquad (15)$$

$$b \leq P(\neg p) < 1, \qquad\qquad \text{when } a = 1 \text{ and } 0 \leq b < 1 \qquad (16)$$

Wagner (2004) shows that under the conditions in (14) – (16) (i.e., the *when* clauses) these bounds arise it $P(\neg q)$, $P(q|p)$ und $P(p)$ are used to derive expressions for the joint probabilities, $P(p \wedge q)$, $P(p \wedge \neg q)$, $P(\neg p \wedge q)$, $P(\neg p \wedge \neg q)$. Letting $P(p) = c$, these probabilities can be shown in a standard contingency table:

	q	$\neg q$
p	ac	$(1-a)c$
$\neg p$	$1 - b - ac$	$b - (1-a)c$

(17)

The bounds in (14)–(16) arise because c must be subject to the restrictions of a probability model, i.e., that the joint probabilities are greater than or equal to zero and must sum to 1.

In the terminology of belief updating, Wagner (2004) assumes that people have a prior estimate of $P_0(q|p) = a$. Wagner considers the constraints that the probability model in (17) places on $P_1(\neg p) = 1 - c$, given that $P_1(\neg q) = b$. Oaksford *et al.*'s (2000) approach was similar and can be characterized as follows. Assuming that people have prior estimates of $P_0(p) = c$, $P_0(q) = 1 - b$, and $P_0(q|p) = a$, what constraints does the probability model in (17) place on the conditional probabilities relevant in assessing AC, DA, and MT. Notational differences aside, Wagner's (2004) contingency table in (17) is the same as that presented in Oaksford *et al.* (2000, Table 1). The relevant conditional probabilities can be calculated as follows:[2]

$$MP \quad P_1(q) = P_0(q \mid p) = a \tag{18}$$

$$DA \quad P_1(\neg q) = P_0(\neg q \mid \neg p) = \frac{b - (1 - a)c}{1 - c} \tag{19}$$

$$AC \quad P_1(p) = P_0(p \mid q) = \frac{ac}{1 - b} \tag{20}$$

$$MT \quad P_1(\neg p) = P_0(\neg p \mid \neg q) = \frac{b - (1 - a)c}{b} \tag{21}$$

(18)–(21) are equivalent to (1)–(4) in Oaksford *et al.* (2000, p. 884). So, by assuming that people also have prior beliefs about the marginal probabilities of the antecedent, $P_0(p)$, and the consequent, $P_0(q)$, appropriate conditional probabilities can be derived for the categorical premises of DA, AC, and MT to conditionalize upon. This approach has the advantage that people are attempting to do exactly the same thing for each inference, i.e., update their beliefs about the conclusion by using the categorical premise to conditionalize on the relevant conditional probability. Figure 5.2 shows the behaviour of this model of conditional inference.

In (18)–(21), it is assumed that the categorical premise is known for sure, i.e., has a probability of 1. However, as discussed in relation to (11) and (12), this assumption can be relaxed. Jeffrey conditionalization (Jeffrey, 1983), which assumes rigidity, MP, for example, becomes:

$$MP \quad P_1(q) = P_0(q \mid p)P_1(p) + P_0(q \mid \neg p)P_1(\neg p) \tag{22}$$

Other than the posterior $P_1(p)$, (22) can be expressed purely in terms of the parameters, a, b, and c and so does not introduce any additional complexity. It also shows clearly why the bounds in (12) rely on varying $P_0(q \mid \neg p)$ between 0 and 1. For almost all the data we look at later on, the generalization in (22) is not needed because for these data, experimental participants are invariably told that the categorical premise holds with certainty, e.g., for MP, $P_1(p) = 1$ and so $P_1(\neg p) = 0$.

---

[2] In Oaksford *et al.* (2000) the contingency table in (17) was parameterized in terms of $P_0(p)$, $P_0(q)$, and the conditional uncertainty $1 - P_0(q|p)$, which was referred to as the 'exceptions parameter.'

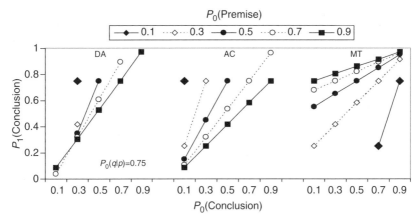

Fig. 5.2. How the probability that a conclusion should be drawn varies as a function of the prior probabilities of the categorical premise and conclusion for DA, for AC and for MT.

This analysis shows that accepting The Equation leads quite naturally to an account of conditional inference like that proposed by Oaksford *et al.* (2000). Equations (18)–(21) also indicate why somewhat different behaviour might be expected for MP than for MT and the fallacies. Our understanding of conditional probability in this account is given by the Ramsey test. Equation (18) shows that MP is particularly simple. People only have to consider the conditional premise and conduct the appropriate Ramsey test. However, DA, AC, and MT are more complex. People have to take more information into consideration. They must derive estimates of $P_0(p)$, $P_0(q)$, and $P_0(q|p)$, which must act as sources of constraint on the Ramsey test used to derive $P_0(\neg q|\neg p)$, $P_0(p|q)$, and $P_0(\neg p|\neg q)$. It is now suggested that the additional complexity might lead to violations of the rigidity condition, with potentially interesting inferential consequences. These considerations will provide the grounds for an adjustment to the model in (18)–(21). This adjustment suggests that a more extreme version of the MP–MT asymmetry than apparently licensed by these equations may not only be consistent with the data, but may also be normatively defensible (McKenzie, 2004).

Rigidity and probabilized MT

Sober (2002) points out that a probabilized version of MT seems to have some odd consequences:

> It is easy to find counterexamples to this principle. You draw from a deck of cards. You know that if the deck is normal and the draw occurs at random, then the probability is only 1/52 that you'll obtain the seven of hearts. Suppose you *do* draw this card. You can't then conclude just from this that it is improbable that the deck is normal and the draw was at random.

However, Sobel (2004) observes that this probabilized version of MT is subject to *rigidity* restrictions just as for MP. The probability that you would *not* draw the seven of hearts before drawing a card, given the deck is normal and the draw random is 51/52, i.e., $P(\neg 7$ of hearts$|$RandomNormal$) = 51/52$. But if you are sure you drew the seven of hearts then the probability you did not, $P(\neg 7$ of hearts$)$, is zero, consequently the probability that you do not draw the seven of hearts, given the deck is normal and the draw random is now zero, i.e., $P(\neg 7$ of hearts$|$RandomNormal$) = 0$. This is a very large change in the relevant likelihood and a clear violation of the rigidity condition. Sobel (2004) observes that most counterexamples to probabilized MT violate rigidity in this way. However, he also points out that,

> In striking contrast (to probabilized MP) it is very difficult to assemble cases in which there are reasons to think that the likelihood for a person 'beforehand' of some likely evidence on a theory is not perturbed when this person learns that this evidence has failed to materialize.

That is, it is difficult to arrive at conditions whereby probabilized MT would be appropriate because of the high likelihood that the rigidity condition is not met. What this shows is that although MP and MT are *p*-valid, they are valid only in the restricted sense given by the rigidity condition. Moreover, because satisfying this condition is likely to be rarer for MT, there is an asymmetry between MP and MT.

The possible effects of the failure of rigidity can be illustrated using a concrete example, i.e., what happens if you believe that *if you turn the key* (*p*) *the car starts* (*q*) and that on this occasion *the car did not start*. There would seem be little reason to expect the car to start unless one was reasonably confident that the key had been turned. Put another way, from a pragmatic point of view, the assertion of the categorical premise of MT only seems to be informative against a background where the car was expected to start.[3] So this seems to be a case where rigidity might be violated, i.e., it is a counterexample, and so $P_0(q|p)$ needs to be adjusted. Oaksford and Chater (2007) discuss how the possible existence of a single counterexample might affect the value of $P_0(q|p)$ used to evaluate the relevant conditional probabilities for the inferences DA, AC, and MT. We referred to this revised probability as ' $P_0^R(q \mid p)$ ' and it was derived by Bayesian revision based on comparing a dependence model with an independence model as in Oaksford and Chater's (1994, 1996, 2003e) account of data selection in the Wason selection task. Oaksford and Chater (2007) found that $P_0^R(q \mid p)$ based on a single counterexample provided better fits to the data on conditional inference than Oaksford *et al.*'s (2000) original model.

Oaksford and Chater's (2007) account treats the probabilities involved as concerning repeated rather than single events, and interprets them as relative frequencies rather than as subjective probabilities. However, conditional inference can involve specific conditionals that can not sensibly be interpreted as relating to repeated events.

----

[3] This is an instance of a pre-suppositional use of negation, i.e., the assertion of the categorical premise denies the presupposition that the car should have started (Wason, 1965) presumably because it is highly likely that the key was turned.

For example, suppose that John promises that *if it is sunny tomorrow, then I will play tennis.* This need not be an instance of one of John's general behavioural traits but can simply relate to a specific dated case. Under these circumstances, it is nonsensical to suggest that the truth of this claim could be assessed by looking at the relative frequencies of whether John plays or does not play tennis when it is sunny on, say the 14th February 2007 (tomorrows date as we write). Rather we must look to other sorts of evidence that bear on this claim derived from world knowledge. For example, is John generally reliable when making promises, what is the chance that something will prevent him from playing tennis even if it is sunny? Similarly, conditional promises tend to implicate their converses, *if John played tennis, then it was sunny.* Possibilities to be considered here relate to the possibility of John playing tennis although the weather was not sunny, e.g., indoor facilities were available, an old friend arrives in town unexpectedly who wants to play tennis, etc.

These classes of evidence affect peoples estimates of $P_0(p, \neg q)$ and $P_0(\neg p, q)$, which in turn will affect $P_0(q|p)$. However, the probabilities of these cases only tend to be considered for DA, AC, and MT. It is only for these inferences that participants must combine their knowledge of the marginals with $P_0(q|p)$ to derive conditional probabilities on the which the categorical premise of these arguments can conditionalize. The classes of evidence we have identified can not be regarded as individual pieces of evidence that can be used to update $P_0(q|p)$ to $P_0^R(q \mid p)$ by Bayesian revision as proposed by Oaksford and Chater (2007). Rather they must directly influence $P_0(p, \neg q)$ and $P_0(\neg p, q)$, while the marginals remained fixed. The latter condition holds because although these factors may affect whether John manages to keep his promise tomorrow, there is no reason to expect them to affect the probability that it is sunny tomorrow or the probability that John plays tennis (at least by much). Under these conditions, similar upward revisions of $P_0(p, \neg q)$ for MT or $P_0(\neg p, q)$ for DA and AC would lead to similar values of $P_0^R(q \mid p)$. Figure 5.3 shows the revision procedure.

In sum, (18)–(21) reveal an asymmetry between MP and the remaining inferences. Only in MP are people provided with the appropriate conditional premise to conditionalize on. In the conditional inference task participants are asked to accept this premise, and so for MP they only need to conduct the appropriate Ramsey test to determine their revised degree of belief in the conclusion. For the remaining inferences, the conditional premise only provides a source of constraint, along with $P_0(p)$ and $P_0(q)$, on the Ramsey test required to compute the relevant conditional probability. However, according to standard pragmatics, encountering the other categorical premises typically yields implicatures that suggest possible violations of rigidity. This possibility leads to lower estimates of $P_0(q|p)$ because rigidity violations suggest higher values of $P_0(p, \neg q)$ or $P_0(\neg p, q)$.

We now address two possible concerns with this approach. First, it could be argued that there is a distinction between revision of $P_0(q|p)$ because of rigidity violations as in the example of MT and similar revision because of the need to compute the relevant conditional probability for the other inferences, i.e., $P_0(\neg q|\neg p)$ for DA, $P_0(p|q)$ for AC. The critical difference relates to considering the possibility of a counterexample to *if p then q*, which seems clear for the car starting example for MT—the car not starting only seems pragmatically relevant given the key has been turned otherwise, it

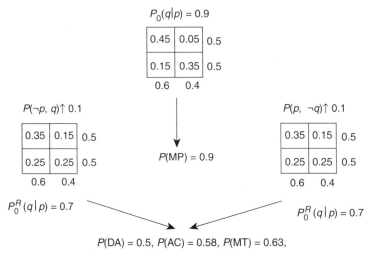

Fig. 5.3 Revising $P_0(q|p)$ to $P_0^R(q|p)$ in the conditional probability model.

would be a communicatively pointless statement to make. But it seems equally clear that this will happen for DA and AC. Consider DA. One is asked to consider whether the car does not start given the key was not turned. To assess this probability, i.e., $P_0(\neg q|\neg p)$, one has to immediately consider the possibility of the car starting even though the key has not been turned; otherwise, again, the minor premise is pragmatically bizarre. Both mathematically and intuitively this just *is* the process of assessing this probability. This contrasts with MP, where the *assertion* of the conditional *means* $P_0(q|p)$ is to be regarded as high. However, the relevant conditionals are *not* asserted for DA, AC, or MT (i.e., the converse, inverse, and obverse, respectively).

A second issue relates to our claim that taking rigidity violations in to account provides a better *normative* account of conditional inference. This claim could be questioned because one might argue that rigidity failures are a matter of pragmatic implicature *rather than* part of a normative theory of inference. Of course, once one gives up the notion that there is monolithic normative theory of inference that applies in every domain then pragmatics is always required to determine what is the appropriate normative theory to apply? We are talking about the conditionals of everyday discourse rather than, say, mathematics, where the material conditional is typically viewed as normatively correct (except by intuitionists, Brouwer, 1951/1981; Dummett, 1977). Nothing in standard logic or probability theory tells you whether you are doing mathematical or everyday reasoning. Moreover, as we pointed out in the last paragraph, calculating $P(q|p)$ normatively entails considering $P(p, q)$ and $P(p, \neg q)$. Thus rigidity failures for DA, AC, and MT can not simply be dismissed as 'mere' pragmatic implicatures. Rather, in the context of understanding how people make probabilistic inferences using verbal materials, understanding the pragmatic inferences that can be drawn from what is said is of fundamental importance (and are subject to strong, highly conventionalized regularities, Levinson, 2000). Thus, in the absence of an assertion of the appropriate conditional probability, they arise as a normative consequence of determining this probability.

An everyday counterexample that has been suggested to us, as demonstrating that the probability conditional should not be taken as normative in the context of everyday conditionals is, 'if a person is guilty then they were at the scene of the crime.' The claim is that any sensible theory of inference should reach the conclusion that a person is not guilty given they were not at the scene of the crime and one should certainly not broach the conclusion that this might be a counterexample. But this surely begs the question against the probabilistic view. The argument is supposed to establish that a logical interpretation is necessary and yet this interpretation is presupposed – this inference only goes through if the conditional is assumed to be true *simpliciter*, i.e., without exceptions. On a probabilistic interpretation, this may be regarded as a strong argument for someone's innocence but not as definitive. Moreover, in the legal context, surely one *should* interpret this conditional probabilistically and so consider whether the accused could be guilty even though they were not at the scene of the crime. Did the accused pay an accomplice, or aid and abet the crime by other means? In sum, it seems to us that the probability conditional captures what people *should* infer in this example better than logic. One thing the reasoner most certainly should not do is reject this conditional as false if it were found that the defendant did pay an accomplice as logic would recommend, as this would mean this very useful probability conditional would not be available to guide future decision making.

Modelling the MP–MT asymmetry revisited

We now turn to modelling the MP–MT asymmetry given our analysis that perceived violations of the rigidity condition (Sobel, 2004) reduces $P_0(q|p)$ for DA, AC, and MT. To account for the data, Oaksford and Chater (2007) proposed that Oaksford *et al.*'s (2000) model needed to be adjusted to take account of the fact that people are likely to treat $P_0(q|p)$ as higher for MP than for the remaining inferences. One way to achieve this is to allow the model to always capture the MP inference and then fit the model for just for DA, AC, and MT. Oaksford and Chater (2007) modelled the data in this way, setting $P_0(p)$ equal to 0.5 for all 65 studies in meta-analysis conducted by Schroyens and Schaeken's (2003)—otherwise the model would have been saturated. They were able to show that with this adjustment, the conditional probability model accounted for the data significantly better than the original Oaksford *et al.* (2000) model and as well as Schroyens and Schaeken's (2003) revised mental models theory.

In this paper, we address the results of Schroyens and Schaeken's (2003) meta-analysis in a slightly different way than Oaksford and Chater (2007). They had fitted the data with $P_0(p)$ set to 0.5. This was partly in response to the point emphasized by Evans and Over (2004) that $P_0(p)$ should be high in conditional inference where p is asserted in the categorical premise. The pragmatic effect of assertion is to implicate the truth of what is asserted. However, on our dynamic account of inference as belief revision the probability that needs to be high is *the posterior probability of the categorical premise*, i.e., for MP this is $P_1(p)$, $P_0(p)$ is set by prior world knowledge. In general, in most of the modelling we have done, the posterior probability of the categorical premise is assumed to be 1, i.e., as high as it can be. So our models implicitly capture the constraint that the assertion of the categorical premise means it has a high probability. Consequently, in remodelling Schroyens and Schaeken's (2003) data we allowed $P_0(p)$ to vary and we set $P_0^R(q|p)$ to 0.85.

We also noted that for some studies in Schroyens and Schaeken's (2003) data, DA was selected more than AC. As we will discuss in much more detail when we discuss Oberauer's (2006) recent modelling work, this can happen in the probabilistic model but only when $P_0(p)$, $P_0(q)$ and $P_0^R(q|p)$ are all low, i.e., around 0.5. There were 12 studies where DA selections exceeded AC and for these we set $P_0^R(q|p)$ to 0.5. As in Oaksford and Chater (2007), 5 conditions from Evans, Handley, and Buck (1998) were excluded. We then sought the best fitting values of $P_0(p)$ and $P_0(q)$. The revised model fitted the data very well. The average R^2 was 0.97 (SD = 0.05). The best fit value for $P_0(p)$ was 0.49 (SD = 0.12) and for $P_0(q)$ it was 0.64 (SD = 0.11). To provide fits such that DA was selected more than AC, one would expect $P_0(p)$ and $P_0(q)$ to be lower when $P_0^R(q|p) = 0.5$ and this was the case: for $P_0(p)$, $t(58) = 2.61$ ($P_0^R(q|p) = 0.5$: mean = 0.41 [SD = 0.10]; $P_0^R(q|p) = 0.85$: mean = 0.50 [SD = 0.11]), and for $P_0(q)$, $t(58) = 4.88$ ($P_0^R(q|p) = 0.5$: mean = 0.52 [SD = 0.09]; $P_0^R(q|p) = 0.85$: mean = 0.66 [SD = 0.09]). The model provided a much better fit than in Oaksford and Chater (2007). Moreover, in contrast to Oaksford and Chater (2007), it provided a significantly better fit to the data than the version of the mental model theory evaluated by Schroyens and Schaeken (2003), $t(59) = 2.76$, $p < 0.005$ (Mental Model: mean R^2 was 0.92 [SD = 0.10]). Because the distributions of R^2 showed high negative skew (being bounded on the 0–1 interval), we also assessed this difference non-parametrically, $Z = 2.56$, $p < 0.005$.

The revision to the probability model suggested by a consideration of possible violations of rigidity for inferences with the probability conditional have suggested an account of the MP–MT and DA–AC asymmetries that provides a much better account of the data. These fits have been obtained for the existing data from Schroyens and Schaeken's (2006) meta-analysis. However, it is clear that these data sets are inadequate for assessing more complex models of human conditional reasoning. Data on the conditional syllogisms only yields four data points, one for each inference.[4] Consequently even relatively simple models are close to being saturated when tested against this data. Recently this issue has been addressed by Oberauer (2006), who looked at configural responses (see, below), and we conclude this chapter by discussing Oberauer's approach and how our revised model relates to his conclusions.

Modelling configural responses in conditional inference

Oberauer (2006) modelled participants' *configural* responses rather than the overall frequencies of MP, DA, AC, and MT. That is, the models were fitted to the frequencies of

---

[4] Although Oaksford *et al.* (2000) used high and low probability antecedents and included converse inferences where the negation of the conclusions of MP, DA, AC, and MT were also presented on the assumption that they would be endorsed in inverse proportion (see also, Marcus & Rips, 1978).

the 16 possible combinations of drawing or not drawing these four inferences that each participant can produce. The overall frequencies of MP, DA, AC, and MT are normally aggregated over these possible configurations. Klauer (1999) and Perham and Oaksford (2005) used a similar approach to fitting models to data from Wason's (1968) selection task. This is an important change because from the same experiment, 16 rather than 4 data points are made available to allow the testing of more complex models.

Oberauer (2006) compared a variety of models of conditional reasoning. This involved using a processing tree implementation of all these models with the exception of the conditional probability model. A processing tree model is a way of assigning values to the probabilities that the mental processes invoked by a theory will be used. So, for example, in Schroyens and Schaeken's (2003) version of the mental models account, all reasoners are assumed to represent p, q (see, (5) above) initially but only a certain proportion then add the representation of $\neg p$, $\neg q$ (see (6) above). Consequently, the model only makes predictions for actual data if these proportions are fixed. Model fitting works in reverse: it asks the question what must this proportion be to explain the data?

To allow the conditional probability model to make configural predictions, Oberauer (2006) made several assumptions. The standard assumption in modelling the overall frequencies of MP, DA, AC, and MT is that this aggregate data reflects the probabilities an individual would assign to each inference. And in experiments where participants are asked to do this, this assumption seems to be confirmed (Evans & Over, 2004). Consequently, it makes sense to fit a single set of parameters to these data, as if modelling a single participant. This does not make sense with configural data because each participant is not presented with 16 possible options to choose between. Oberauer (2006), therefore, used a distributional approach. Each parameter of the model was treated as the mean of a dummy normally distributed variable which was transformed into the 0—1 interval via a logistic function. The standard deviations of each parameter were assumed to be equal. The model fitting therefore recovered the best fitting means of each of the three normal distributions, one each for $P_0(p)$, $P_0(q)$, and $P_0(q|p)$, together with their best fitting common standard deviation. Predicted values of the frequency of each configuration were calculated by integrating over all possible values of the dummy variables.

The result of this exercise was that the pure probability model originally presented in Oaksford *et al.* (2000), faired worst and other models based either on an extension of mental models theory (Schroyens & Schacken, 2003) or incorporating mental models at one level of processing (Verschueren *et al.*, 2005) faired best.

We make three comments on Oberauer's (2006) impressive attempt to distinguish quantitatively between virtually all the various models that are currently vying for acceptance in the psychology of conditional reasoning. First, we question some of the assumptions of the implementation of the conditional probability model. Second, we point out that the revised model—presented here and in Oaksford and Chater (2007)—address the most fundamental problems revealed by Oberauer's implementation. Third, we observe that there are configurations of inferences that make perfect probabilistic sense but which can not be predicted by non-probabilistic approaches. Moreover, there would appear to be some evidence for these configurations, assuming—as these non-probabilistic approaches do—that people are doing something very similar in the Wason (1968) selection task.

Distributions and sampling

Our first comment on Oberauer's implementation is that the samples on which people base their estimates of the parameters of the conditional probability model are likely to be small and biased (Fiedler & Juslin, 2006). For example, corpus analysis underlying the *Decision by Sampling* model (Stewart *et al.* [2006]) revealed that it is not the case that all probability values are mentioned with equal frequency. Instead, probabilities near 0 and 1 are strongly overrepresented. They argue that this suggests that there are more cognitively relevant events with small and large probabilities than with mid-range probabilities—most events we are interested in are either likely to happen or unlikely to happen. One consequence may be that it can not be assumed that people's estimates of the parameters of the conditional probability model will be normally distributed.[5] Moreover, we may avoid the need to transform a dummy variable if we used a prior distribution in modelling that is bounded on the 0—1 interval. The Beta-distribution is appropriate (Lee, 2004). Moreover, variation in the two parameters of this distribution, *a* and *b*, can reflect Stewart *et al.*'s observation above, e.g., with *a* and *b* both greater than 0 but less than 1, the pdf of the Beta distribution is U-shaped over the probability interval.

We have yet to explicitly model Oberauer's (2006) data. However, we have used this data to examine the possible distributions of the parameters of the conditional probability model. For all 16 response configurations we asked whether there were possible values of the model that would yield that configuration assuming a threshold probability above which people would select that card and below which they would not. We set the threshold to 0.58 which was the best fit value found by Oberauer (2006) in Version 2 of his probability model. We used *Mathematica's* FindInstance function to determine if there were values of the parameters that would satisfy the relevant inequalities with respect to the threshold to produce a particular configuration. We then used the frequencies of each configuration in Oberauer (2006, Table 4, Basic/TS) to estimate a mean and standard deviation for each parameter from which we computed the parameters of the corresponding Beta-distribution. For $P_0(p)$, $a = 0.72$ and $b = 0.85$; for $P_0(q)$, $a = 4.87$ and $b = 1.25$; for $P_0(q|p)$, $a = 3.80$, $b = 1.28$. These values suggest that $P_0(p)$ has the U-shaped distribution discussed above, whereas $P_0(q)$ and $P_0(q|p)$ are both negatively skewed, i.e., toward the high end of the 0–1 interval.

These values seem reasonable, because $P_0(p)$ is the only really unconstrained parameter that might be expected to follow the empirical distributions described by Stewart *et al.* The constraints of the conditional inference paradigm suggest that $P_0(q|p)$ is generally high; and probability theory tells us that $P_0(q)$ must be greater than $P_0(p)P_0(q|p)$. This analysis suggests that using Beta distributions for the relevant parameters may

---

[5] We assume that the distribution in the population of participants will mirror the distribution of individuals' estimates of these probabilities by sampling exemplars from memory as in decision by sampling.

provide better fits for the original Oaksford *et al.* (2000) model. Moreover, the shape of these distributions may be independently motivated (Stewart *et al.*, 2006).

The revised conditional probability model

Our diagnosis of the cause of the MP–MT asymmetry as relating to rigidity violations that lead to a revision of $P_0(q|p)$ to $P_0^R(q \mid p)$, can account for many of the problems Oberauer (2006) identifies for the conditional probability model when modelling configural data.

An interesting problem arises, however. Using the threshold to find values of the parameters for different configurations revealed that no possible set of values could predict the MP, DA nor the AC, MT configural responses. The MP, DA configuration is selected sufficiently often to make this failure a concern. In the original model, this failure arises because for $P_0(q|p)$ to be sufficiently high to draw MP and DA, MT will also be above threshold. Similarly, for $P_0(q|p)$ to be sufficiently high to draw AC and MT, MP will also be above threshold. This is why, as Oberauer (2006) observes, the model overpredicts the MP, AC, MT and MP, DA, MT configurations, while under-predicting the MP only response. In the revised model, the probability of drawing MP, i.e., $P_0(q|p)$, can be much higher than $P_0^R(q \mid p)$, which means that the MP and DA response is possible. And it does occur much more frequently than AC and MT in Oberauer's (2006) data.[6]

The problems identified above occur mainly for arbitrary material, e.g., alphanumeric stimuli. For more contentful material, Oberauer found that the conditional probability model generally underpredicted the most frequently occurring configurations, which include MP, and overpredicted the least frequently occurring configurations, which do not include MP. This tendency arises again because of the original model's tendency to underpredict MP, which should not arise for the revised model. However, to fully establish these claims would require remodelling Oberauer's (2006) configural data using the revised model and a distributional approach which is beyond the scope of the current chapter.

Unpredicted configurations

An intriguing aspect of Oberauer's (2006) modelling is that many configural responses can only be 'predicted' by the non-probabilistic models by guessing. That is, the actual theories can not predict these configurations of inferences will be drawn on the basis of the representations and processes they propose to explain human reasoning. We concentrate on one such configuration, DA, MT.

In Oberauer's (2006) experimental data, there were few examples of this configuration. However, it is easy to create a probabilistic context in which it would be an

---

6 This difference is a general manifestation of the fact that the revised model, where $P_0(q|p) > P_0^R(q \mid p)$, can account for the finding that for the standard abstract data very few configurations occur where MP is not drawn. However, for more naturalistic real world material—that would be expected to directly activate relevant world knowledge—far more configurations occur where this happens.

appropriate response. For example, take the conditional *if a bird is a swan then it is white*. Suppose someone is trying to infer a bird's colour on learning that it is not a swan. If few birds are swans or white, then it is highly probable that this bird is not white. Moreover, assuming equal numbers of black southern hemisphere and white northern hemisphere swans, the DA inference can be much more probable than MP (a similar argument applies for AC and MT). To make this more concrete, let us assume that $P(\text{swan}) = P(\text{white}) = 0.2$ and $P_0(\text{white}|\text{swan}) = 0.5$, then $P(\text{MP}) = P(\text{AC}) = 0.5$ (below threshold), whereas $P(\text{DA}) = P(\text{MT}) = 0.875$ (above threshold). Increasing $P_0(\text{white}|\text{swan})$ rapidly leads to MP and AC going above threshold, decreasing $P_0(\text{white}|\text{swan})$ sharply accentuates the difference between DA, MT and AC, MP. So the original conditional probability model can predict the DA, MT configuration. Notice also that for this configuration to occur, DA must be above threshold and AC below. We exploited the conditions under which this happens in modelling Schroyens and Schaeken's (2003) meta-analysis.

Is there any evidence for this configuration? Not, as far was we are aware, in the conditional inference paradigm. However, advocates of the mental models and mental logic approach (Feeney & Handlely, 2000; Klauer, Stahl, & Erdfelder, 2006; Rips, 1994) assume that people are drawing the same conditional inferences in the Wason (1968) selection task. In one condition of Oaksford and Wakefield's (2003) experiment on the selection task, the most probable responses were those corresponding to DA and MT (significantly more probable than those corresponding to MP and AC). If people are drawing conditional inferences in this task, then this result would not appear to be predictable by the non-probabilistic approaches assessed in Oberauer (2006).[7] However, Oaksford and Wakefield (2003) did not present configural data. Could the configural responses predicted by non-probabilistic accounts aggregate in a way that could produce this result? The problem with this proposal is that all these accounts predict that MT should only occur when MP does, although MP can occur on its own. So MT could never occur more than MP when the configural responses are aggregated. Consequently, non-probabilistic approaches are on the horns of a dilemma. Either Oaksford and Wakefield's (2003) data shows that people don't draw conditional inferences in the selection task or, if people do draw conditional inferences in this task, then Oaksford and Wakefield's (2003) data seems to show that non-probabilistic accounts of the conditional can not predict the observed behaviour.

We do not believe that people are drawing conditional inferences in the selection task (Oaksford & Chater, 1994, 2003e). Nonetheless, the original conditional probability

---

[7] The condition in Oaksford and Wakefield (2003) that yields this result is actually the high $P_0(p)$ and $P_0(q)$ condition (probabilities were manipulated). This is because on the probabilistic approach (Oaksford & Chater, 2007) people are doing very different things in these two tasks, i.e., people are *not* drawing conditional inference in the selection task. However, the conditional probability model can predict a DA and MT response in the conditional inference paradigm, which other approaches can not.

model can predict the DA, MT configuration exactly as in the swans example. It could be argued that the revised model can only do so at the cost of failing to capture the original MP–MT asymmetry. In the revised model, we have argued that MP, and so $P_0(q|p)$, can be much higher than $P_0^R(q \mid p)$ to account for the fact that MP is usually endorsed. However, to predict the DA, MT configuration, MP, and so $P_0(q|p)$, must be low. We believe that for real world material people may not necessarily assume that $P_0(q|p)$ is as high as they do when asked to assess conditionals using only abstract alphanumeric stimuli. This is because once real world content is available the possibility of counterexamples may be apparent even for MP. For example, people endorse the MP inference more for a conditional such as, *if the apple is ripe, then it fell from the tree*, than for the conditional, *if John studies hard, then he will do well in the test* (Cummins, 1995). There are many new pieces of information we may subsequently learn about John that might lead us to withdraw the conclusion that he will do well even though he studies hard, e.g., he is depressed, he has a low IQ ... etc. There are far fewer pieces of information that we may subsequently learn about apples that might lead us to withdraw the conclusion that the apple will fall when it is ripe. Our guess is that with real world content, such as the swans example, the DA, MT configuration would predominate, in line with both intuition, and as the predictions of the conditional probability model.

In summary, the move to configural responses is an important innovation. However, there are reasons to doubt the assumption underlying Oberauer's implementation of the conditional probability model; the revised model presented here and in Oaksford and Chater (2007) addresses most of the concerns raised by this implementation; and, moreover, there would appear to be configurations of inferences that make sense probabilistically but which can not be predicted by non-probabilistic approaches.

Conclusion

The MP–MT asymmetry is the first hurdle any psychological account of conditional inference must get over. In this chapter, it has been shown that recent normative developments in probability logic suggest an account of conditional inference as belief revision by conditionalization, which is consistent with Oaksford *et al.*'s (2000) original conditional probability model. This model reveals a potential asymmetry between MP and the remaining inferences due to the need to calculate the relevant conditional probabilities for the remaining inferences and the consequent possibility of violations of the rigidity condition. Failures of the rigidity condition are more likely for MT, AC, and DA, which may result in lower values of $P_0(q|p)$ than for MP, which can explain the MP–MT asymmetry. On this account, this asymmetry is not a result of systematically biased logical processing but a result of rationally taking into consideration the factors dictated by a probabilistic theory of conditional inference. Consequently, it would appear that there are good normative reasons to expect an MP–MT asymmetry like that observed in the data, i.e., this behaviour is *normatively defensible* (McKenzie, 2004).

References

Adams, E. W. (1975). *The logic of conditionals*. Dordrecht: Reidel.

Adams, E. W. (1998). *A primer of probability logic*. Stanford, CA: CSLI Publications.

Anderson, J. R. (1990). *The adaptive character of thought*. Hillsdale, NJ: LEA.

Anderson, J. R. (1995). *Cognitive psychology and it implications*. New York: W. H. Freeman and Company.

Bach, K., & Harnish, R. M. (1979). *Linguistic communication and speech acts*. Cambridge: MIT Press.

Bennettt, J. (2003). *A philosophical guide to conditionals*. Oxford: Oxford University Press.

Bonnefon, J.-F. (2004). Reinstatement, floating conclusions, and the credulity of mental model reasoning. *Cognitive Science*, **28**, 621–631.

Braine, M. D. S., & O'Brien, D. P. (1998). *Mental logic*. London: Lawrence Erlbaum.

Braisby, N., & Gellatly, A. (Eds.) (2004). *Cognitive psychology*. Oxford: Oxford University Press.

Brouwer, L. E. J. (1981). *Brouwer's Cambridge lectures on intuitionism*, D. van Dalen (Ed.). Cambridge: Cambridge University Press. (Originally, 1946–1951).

Chan, D., & Chua, F. (1994). Suppression of valid inferences: syntactic views, mental models, and relative salience. *Cognition*, **53**, 217–238.

Cummins, D. D. (1995). Naïve theories and causal deduction. *Memory & Cognition*, **23**, 646–658.

Dummett, M. A. E. (1977). *Elements of intuitionism*. Cambridge: Cambridge University Press.

Edgington, D. (1991). The matter of the missing matter of fact. *Proceedings of the Aristotelian Society*, **65**(Suppl.), 185–209.

Edgington, D. (1995). On conditionals. *Mind*, **104**, 235–329.

Evans, J. St.B. T., & Over, D. E. (1996). Rationality in the selection task: epistemic utility versus uncertainty reduction. *Psychological Review*, **103**, 356–363.

Evans, J. St.B. T., & Over, D. E. (2004). *If*. Oxford: Oxford University Press.

Evans, J. St.B. T., Handley, S., & Buck, E. (1998). Order effects in conditional reasoning. *British Journal of Psychology*, **89**, 383–403.

Evans, J. St.B. T., Handley, S. J., & Over, D. E. (2003). Conditionals and conditional probability. *Journal of Experimental Psychology: Learning, Memory, & Cognition*, **29**, 321–335.

Eysenck, M. W., & Keane, M. (2000). *Cognitive psychology*. Hove, Sussex, UK: Psychology Press.

Feeney, A., & Handley, S. J. (2000). The suppression of q card selections: Evidence for deductive inference in Wason's selection task. *Quarterly Journal of Experimental Psychology*, **53**, 1224–1242.

Fiedler, K., & Juslin, P. (Eds.) (2006). *Information sampling and adaptive cognition*. Cambridge: Cambridge University Press.

George, C. (1997). Reasoning from uncertain premises. *Thinking and Reasoning*, **3**, 161–190.

Hailperin, T. (1996). *Sentential probability logic: Origins, development, current status, and technical applications*. Bethlehem: Lehigh University Press.

Johnson-Laird, P. N., & Byrne, R. M. J. (1991). *Deduction*. Hove, Sussex: Lawrence Erlbaum.

Johnson-Laird, P. N., & Byrne, R. M. J. (2002). Conditionals: a theory of meaning, pragmatics, and inference. *Psychological Review*, **109**, 646–678.

Klauer, K. C., Stahl, C., & Eredfelder, E. (2006). The abstract selection task: an almost comprehensive model. Unpublished manuscript. Alberts-Ludwigs-Universität Freiburg.

Lee, P. M. (2004). *Bayesian statistics*. London: Hodder Arnold.

Levinson, S. (2000). *Presumptive meanings*. Cambridge, MA: MIT Press.

Liu, I. M. (2003). Conditional reasoning and conditionalisation. *Journal of Experimental Psychology: Learning, Memory & Cognition*, **29**, 694–709.

Liu, I. M., Lo, K., & Wu, J. (1996). A probabilistic interpretation of 'If-then.' *Quarterly Journal of Experimental Psychology*, **49A**, 828–844.

Marr, D. (1982). *Vision*. San Fransisco, CA: W. H. Freeman & Co.

McClelland, J. L. (1998). Connectionist models and Bayesian inference. In M. Oaksford, & N. Chater (Eds.), *Rational models of cognition* (pp. 21–53). Oxford: Oxford University Press.

McKenzie, C. R. M. (2004). Framing effects in inference tasks–and why they are normatively defensible. *Memory and Cognition*, **32**, 874–855.

Oaksford, M. (2004). *Conditional inference and constraint satisfaction: reconciling probabilistic and mental models approaches?* Paper presented at the 5th International Conference on Thinking, University of Leuven, Leuven, Belgium.

Oaksford, M., & Chater, N. (1991). Against logicist cognitive science. *Mind & Language*, **6**, 1–38.

Oaksford, M., & Chater, N. (1993). Reasoning theories and bounded rationality. In K. I. Manktelow, & D. E. Over (Eds.), *Rationality* (pp. 31–60). London: Routledge.

Oaksford, M., & Chater, N. (1994). A rational analysis of the selection task as optimal data selection. *Psychological Review*, **101**, 608–631.

Oaksford, M., & Chater, N. (1995). Theories of reasoning and the computational explanation of everyday inference. *Thinking and Reasoning*, **1**, 121–152.

Oaksford, M., & Chater, N. (1996). Rational explanation of the selection task. *Psychological Review*, **103**, 381–391.

Oaksford, M., & Chater, N. (1998). *Rationality in an uncertain world: essays on the cognitive science of human reasoning*. Hove, Sussex: Psychology Press.

Oaksford, M., & Chater, N. (2001). The probabilistic approach to human reasoning. *Trends in Cognitive Sciences*, **5**, 349–357.

Oaksford, M., & Chater, N. (2003a). Computational levels and conditional reasoning: Reply to Schroyens and Schaeken (2003). *Journal of Experimental Psychology: Learning, Memory & Cognition*, **29**, 150–156.

Oaksford, M., & Chater, N. (2003b). Conditional probability and the cognitive science of conditional reasoning. *Mind & Language*, **18**, 359–379.

Oaksford, M., & Chater, N. (2003c). Modeling probabilistic effects in conditional inference: Validating search or conditional probability? *Revista Psychologica*, **32**, 217–242.

Oaksford, M., & Chater, N. (2003d). Probabilities and pragmatics in conditional inference: suppression and order effects. In D. Hardman, & L. Macchi (Eds.), *Thinking: psychological perspectives on reasoning, judgment and decision making* (pp. 95–122). Chichester, UK: John Wiley & Sons Ltd.

Oaksford, M., & Chater, N. (2003e). Optimal data selection: revision, review and re-evaluation. *Psychonomic Bulletin & Review*, **10**, 289–318.

Oaksford, M., & Chater, N. (2007). *Bayesian rationality: the probabilistic approach to human reasoning*. Oxford: Oxford University Press.

Oaksford, M., Chater, N., & Larkin, J. (2000). Probabilities and polarity biases in conditional inference. *Journal of Experimental Psychology: Learning, Memory & Cognition*, **26**, 883–899.

Oaksford, M., & Wakefield, M. (2003). Data selection and natural sampling: Probabilities do matter. *Memory & Cognition*, **31**, 143–154.

Oberauer, K. (2006). Reasoning with conditionals: a test of formal models of four theories. *Cognitive Psychology*, **53**, 238–283.

Oberauer, K., & Wilhelm, O. (2003). The meaning of conditionals: conditional probabilities, mental models, and personal utilities. *Journal of Experimental Psychology: Learning, Memory, & Cognition*, **29**, 321–335.

Philips, L. D., & Edwards, W. (1966). Conservatism in a simple probability inference task. *Journal of Experimental Psychology*, **72**, 346–354.

Politzer, G. (2005). Uncertainty and the suppression of inferences. *Thinking and Reasoning*, **11**, 5–34.

Rips, L. J. (1994). *The psychology of proof*. Cambridge, MA: MIT Press.

Rumelhart, D. E., Smolensky, P., McClelland, J. L. & Hinton, G. E. (1986). Schemata and sequential thought processes in PDP models. In J. L. McClelland, & D. E. Rumelhart (Eds.), *Parallel distributed processing: explorations in the microstructure of cognition, Vol 2: Psychological and biological processes*, Chapter 14 (pp. 7–57). Cambridge, MA: MIT Press.

Ryle, G. (1949). *The concept of mind*. London: Hutchinson.

Schroyens, W., & Schaeken, W. (2003). A critique of Oaksford, Chater, and Larkin's (2000) conditional probability model of conditional reasoning. *Journal of Experimental Psychology: Learning, Memory & Cognition*, **29**, 140–149.

Sobel, J. H. (2004). *Probable modus ponens and modus tollens, and updating on uncertain evidence*. Unpublished Manuscript, Department of Philosophy, University of Toronto at Scarborough. (www.scar.toronto.ca/~sobel/ConfDisconf.pdf)

Sober, E. (2002). Intelligent design and probability reasoning. *International Journal for Philosophy of Religion*, **52**, 65–80.

Stevenson, R. J., & Over, D. E. (1995). Deduction from uncertain premises. *Quarterly Journal of Experimental Psychology*, **48A**, 613–643.

Stewart, N., Chater, N., & Brown, G. D. A. (2006). Decision by sampling. *Cognitive Psychology*, **53**, 1–26.

Verschueren, N., Schaeken, W., & d'Ydewalle, G. (2005). A dual-process specification of causal conditional reasoning. *Thinking and Reasoning*, **11**, 278–293.

Wagner, C. G. (2004). Modus tollens probabilized. *British Journal for Philosophy of Science*, **55**, 747–753.

Wason, P. C. (1965). The contexts of plausible denial. *Journal of Verbal Learning and Verbal Behavior*, **4**, 7–11.

Wason, P. C. (1966). Reasoning. In B. Foss (Ed.), *New horizons in psychology* (pp. 135–151). Harmondsworth, Middlesex: Penguin.

Wason, P. C. (1968). Reasoning about a rule. *Quarterly Journal of Experimental Psychology*, **20**, 273–281.

Chapter 6

Inference from absence in language and thought

Ulrike Hahn

Cardiff University, Cardiff, UK

Mike Oaksford

Birkbeck College London, London, UK

Abstract

In this chapter we review recent work on the classic fallacy of the 'argument from ignorance' or 'argumentum ad ignorantiam'. This fallacy has been given a formal, Bayesian treatment, which suggests that there is nothing structurally amiss with arguments from ignorance; rather they are differentially strong or weak as a function of their specific content, that is, the specific probabilistic quantities involved. This analysis is then applied to a classic problem of language acquisition involving inference from the absence of certain structures in the data. Such inference has often been taken to be dubious at best. We re-examine the relative strength of such inferences and seek to clarify the role of two widely cited mechanisms, pre-emption and entrenchment, in this context.

Introduction

In this chapter, our goal is to show how our recent normative, Bayesian approach to argumentation (Hahn & Oaksford, 2006, 2007) can be applied to a problem in language acquisition. Specifically, we will show how our account of the argument from ignorance (Hahn & Oaksford, 2006, 2007; Oaksford & Hahn, 2004) can be used to address the problem of the absence of explicit negative evidence in acquiring grammar. We first present our Bayesian account of the argument from ignorance focussing on what is called the *epistemic closure* argument from ignorance. We then relate the argument from ignorance to language acquisition.

Bayes, argumentation and fallacies

Argumentation is a verbal and social activity of reason aimed at increasing (or decreasing) the acceptability of a controversial standpoint for a listener or reader, by putting forward a constellation of propositions intended to justify (or refute) the standpoint before a 'rational judge' (van Eemeren, Grootendorst, and Snoeck Henkemans, 1996, p. 5).

The study of argumentation has suffered from the lack of a normative theory that can distinguish between good and bad arguments. This is a pressing problem because many of the argument forms that feature in everyday argumentation would appear to be fallacious according to logical standards. There is, in fact, a canon of over twenty odd argument fallacies, many of which were first identified by Aristotle (see e.g., Woods, Irvine & Walton, 2004). These so-called fallacies or arguments that philosophers and logicians have viewed as potentially psychologically persuasive, even though they should not be (Copi & Burgess-Jackson, 1996) are prevalent in day to day discourse.

It is a recent realisation (Hamblin, 1970) that many of these 'fallacies' seem to have perfectly acceptable instantiations. For example, the following are two versions of the classic fallacy of an argument from ignorance (*argumentum ad ignorantiam*) first discussed by Locke in *An essay concerning human understanding* (1690) (cited e.g., in Hamblin [1970]).

(1) Ghosts exist because no one has proved that they do not.

(2) This drug is safe because we have no evidence that it is not.

In an argument from ignorance, the absence of a proof or evidence to contradict a proposition is taken as establishing that the proposition is true. (1) seems unacceptable. In contrast, given that all legitimate attempts to find side effects of the drug have failed, (2) seems perfectly fine. As there was no current theory of argumentation that seemed capable of articulating formally what underpins this difference, we developed a Bayesian interpretation of argumentation in general which was first applied to the argument from ignorance (2006, 2007; see also Oaksford & Hahn, 2004).

According to this view, individual arguments such as (1) and (2) are composed of a conclusion and evidence for that conclusion. So for (1), the conclusion is that *Ghosts exist* and this argument provides as evidence the proposition that *no one proved that Ghosts do not exist*. For (2), the conclusion is that *this drug is safe* and this argument provides as evidence the proposition that *there is no evidence this it is not safe*. Both conclusion and evidence have associated probabilities that are viewed as expressions of subjective degrees of belief. Bayes' theorem allows the calculation of the *posterior* probability of the conclusion after receiving some evidence, $P_1(C)$, from various prior probabilities (subscripted '0'):

$$(3) \qquad P_1(C) = P_0(C \mid e) = \frac{P_0(e \mid C)P_0(C)}{P_0(e \mid C)P_0(C) + P_0(e \mid \neg C)P_0(\neg C)}$$

it provides an update rule for the degree of belief associated with the conclusion, C, in light of the evidence, e. Argument strength, then, on this account is a function of the degree of prior conviction, $P_0(C)$ and the relationship between the conclusion and the evidence, in particular how much more likely the evidence would be if the conclusion were true, $P_0(e|C)$ (we will omit subscripts in the following where there is no danger of confusion).

The strength of the argument from ignorance is given by the conditional probability that the conclusion is false given negative evidence, $\neg e$, is found, $P(\neg C|\neg e)$. This probability is referred to as *negative test validity*. The strength of the corresponding positive argument is called *positive test validity*. These probabilities can be calculated from *sensitivity* ($P(e|C)$) and *specificity* ($P(\neg e|\neg C)$) and the prior belief that C is true ($P(C)$). This is illustrated for positive test validity in (3) and for negative test validity, or the argument from ignorance in (4):

$$(4) \qquad P\big(\neg C \mid \neg e\big) = \frac{P(\neg e \mid \neg C)(1 - P(C))}{P(\neg e \mid \neg C)(1 - P(C)) + (1 - P(\neg e \mid C))P(C)}$$

Sensitivity corresponds to the 'hit rate' of the test and 1 minus specificity corresponds to the 'false positive rate.'

In a variety of experiments, we have shown that people's assessments of the argument from ignorance are sensitive to variations in the factors a Bayesian account would predict. For example, we have shown that the argument from ignorance (4) can be regarded as a good argument but weaker than its positive counterpart (3) because of people's experience whereby specificity is usually higher than sensitivity (Hahn & Oaksford, 2007; Oaksford & Hahn, 2004). Varying the amount of evidence in a negative evidence version increases the perceived strength of an argument from ignorance (Oaksford & Hahn, 2004) as does increasing sensitivity via a source reliability manipulation (Hahn & Oaksford, 2007). Moreover, the higher the prior, the stronger the argument is considered to be (Hahn & Oaksford, 2007; Oaksford & Hahn, 2004).

There are different versions of the argument from ignorance (Walton, 1996). Oaksford and Hahn (2004) concentrated on the *negative evidence* case exemplified by the argument in (2). However, more recently Hahn and Oaksford (2007) have extended their Bayesian analysis to the *epistemic closure* version of the argument from ignorance, which we now describe. This type of argument from ignorance is knowledge based and relies on the concept of *epistemic closure* (De Cornulier, 1988; Walton, 1992) or the *closed world assumption* (Reiter, 1980, 1985). The concept of epistemic closure refers to the extent to which a data base or set of records is complete. If one has confidence that a database is exhaustive, that is, is epistemically closed, then the failure to find a piece of information within it is informative. This underlies the negation-as-failure procedure (Clark, 1978) in Artificial Intelligence whereby one argues that a proposition is false—so its negation is true—because it can not be proved from the contents of the data base. Walton (1992) provides an everyday example of a railway timetable. Suppose the point at issue is whether the 13:00 train from London, King's Cross to Newcastle stops at Hatfield. If the timetable is consulted and it is found that Hatfield is not mentioned as one of the stops, then it can be inferred that the train does not stop there. That is, it is assumed that the timetable is epistemically closed such that if there were further stops they would have been included. Such arguments may fail because, in the real world, the closed world assumption is rarely justified.

These arguments can be integrated formally into a Bayesian account by considering that what is being asserted is that there is not a record in the data base saying that the train stops at Hatfield. This could be because there is a record saying that it does not stop at Hatfield or because their data base says nothing about whether it does or does not stop there. So there are three options: either the data base explicitly says the train stops at Hatfield, it explicitly says it does not stop there or it says nothing about the topic. This third category, 'says nothing', can readily be incorporated into the Bayesian account: The data base can say that the claim, C, is true, represented by 'C', it can say it is false, represented by '$\neg C$', or it can say nothing, represented as n. Sensitivity is then $P('C'|C)$ and specificity is $P('\neg C'|\neg C)$. The probability corresponding to the strength of the affirmative argument is $P(C|'C')$, but the probability corresponding the strength of the argument from ignorance is $P(\neg C|\neg'C')$. Without the n category the probability of not asserting the truth of the claim $P(\neg'C')$ and the probability of asserting that the claim is false, $P('\neg C')$, are the same. With the introduction of the additional category this is no longer the case.

The analysis of the epistemic closure case highlights an important distinction between types of the argument from ignorance not previously noted (Hahn & Oaksford, 2007). Textbook example like (1), differ from the cases we have considered so far. The argument for ghosts not only involves negative evidence, but also a flip in polarity between evidence and conclusion: negative evidence is provided to support the *positive* existence of something. In other words the inference is of the form:

(5)   *not* proven (*not* exist) → exist

as opposed to merely:

(6)   *not* proven (exist) → *not* exist

The examples we have considered so far arguably have the structure in (6) not the structure in (5). But it may be the *opposite polarity* case (5) that constitutes the true fallacy of the argument from ignorance. The strength of this opposite polarity argument from ignorance (5) is related to $P(C|\neg'\neg C')$, i.e., the probability that the claim is true given the data base does not say it is false. This contrasts with the strength of (6), which we refer to as the *same polarity* argument from ignorance (S), which is related to $P(\neg C|\neg'C')$, i.e., the probability that the claim is false given the data base does not say it is true.

However, even for the opposite polarity argument from ignorance (O) compelling examples can readily be found: Imagine your colleagues at work are gathering for a staff picnic. You ask the person organizing the picnic whether your colleague Smith is coming, to which you receive the reply that 'Smith hasn't said that he's not coming'. Should this allow you to infer that he is in fact coming, or has he simply failed to send the required reply by e-mail? Your confidence that Smith will be attending depends on the number of people that have replied. If you are told that no one has replied so far, assuming Smith's attendance seems premature; if by contrast you are told that everyone has replied, you would be assured of his presence. More precisely, you would be as confident of Smith's presence as you are on any occasion when he says he will do something, that he will, in fact, then do it. In between these two extremes your degree of confidence will be scaled: the more people that have replied the more confident you will be. In other words, the epistemic closure of the database in question (the e-mail inbox of the organizer) can vary from no closure whatsoever to complete closure, giving rise to corresponding changes in the probability that *not says* (*not p*) does in fact suggest that *p*.

The relationship between O and S varies most dramatically with the likelihood ratio $P(n|C)/P(n|\neg C)$ (LR_n) and the prior, $P(C)$. O and S have the same strength when $LR_n = 1$ and $P(C) = 0.5$ (as long as the other likelihoods are equal). Increases in LR_n or $P(C)$ from these values can lead to the probability of the conclusion of O to be greater than the probability of the conclusion of S. That is, according to a Bayesian account, the opposite polarity argument from ignorance can also be a good argument. Hahn and Oaksford (2007) report the results of experiments showing that under the right circumstances O can indeed be perceived as a stronger argument than S. Hahn *et al.* (2005) used four argument forms, which we will use later on, where *C* is the contested conclusion:

(A) (Database says: *C*) → *C* (Affirmative)
(O) (*not* (Database says: *not C*)) → *C* (Opposite)
(N) (Database says: *not C*) → *not C* (Negative)
(S) (*not* (Database says: *C*)) → *not C* (Same)

Each argument form was used with four different contents which varied in the degree of epistemic closure of the relevant data base, e.g., an electronic library catalogue (high closure) and a newspaper archive (low closure). For the high closure case, O was regarded as a stronger argument than S, as predicted.

Having outlined our approach to the argument from ignorance we now introduce the problem of language acquisition and show how our Bayesian account of the argument from ignorance can shed some light on how language acquisition is possible despite the poverty of the stimulus.

Arguments from ignorance and language acquisition

So-called 'poverty of stimulus arguments' form a cornerstone of generative linguistics, that is, the approach to language and language learning that attributes much of our linguistic knowledge to innate structures (Chomsky, 1957, 1980, 1986). Poverty of stimulus arguments make, in one way or another, the claim that the linguistic input to the learner is insufficient to give rise to the kinds of knowledge that governs our adult use of language. This in turn means that this knowledge cannot have been acquired through experiential learning, lending support to the notion that the knowledge in question is innate.

The concept of the poverty of stimulus, which also goes under the header of 'the underdetermination problem', 'Plato's problem', the 'logical problem of language acquisition', the 'deductive gap' and 'Baker's paradox', has a history that now spans several decades of linguistic research (for an overview see Thomas, 2002), and now encompasses several interrelated claims: (i) the input to the child is deficient or impoverished because it contains 'errors' such as fragments, false starts, and slips of the tongue (ii) it contains no evidence for ungrammaticality, and (iii) it is finite, but nevertheless enables us to produce an indefinite number of new utterances (e.g, Hornstein & Lightfoot, 1981; Thomas, 2002, for summaries; for most recent debate see the special issue on poverty of stimulus, volume 19 of the journal Linguistic Review; MacWhinney, 2004, and Pinker, 2004). The last point (if indeed true), points more to the nature of our linguistic knowledge than a particular acquisition problem in that it indicates that our knowledge of language must consist of more than a simple enumeration of previously encountered utterances, and contains some mechanism for creating new sentences. Grammars are a standard way of conceiving of such knowledge, and even very simple grammars that allow basic forms of embedding can give rise to an infinite number of sentences, given only a finite vocabulary ('Mary stroked the dog biting the cat that was chasing the bird which was ...'). The real issue for acquisition is whether knowledge of sufficient complexity can be learned from the data. The existence of 'errors' in the input can be assumed to make any such learning more difficult. This has, however, typically not been construed as the most devastating problem for the learner. Rather it is the complete absence of certain kinds of evidence from the input as highlighted by (2) above, that has been seen by many as most devastating: the input to the learner typically contains no, or very little, information about what constructions are *not* part of the language, that is what sentences are ungrammatical (see recently, e.g., Lasnik & Uriagereka, 2002).

The consequences of this are underpinned by formal results. Gold (1967) provided analyses to suggest that induction of anything but the simplest grammar is not possible given only information about which sentences *are* in the language, but no information about those which are *not*. The crucial problem for the learner is that of ruling out overly general, or permissive hypotheses; without explicit feedback on ungrammatical sentences, the learner cannot decide whether a particular construction licensed by his or her overly general grammar is indeed ungrammatical (and that grammar consequently not the right one) or whether that construction has simply not been encountered yet.

Though Gold's results are widely cited in the context of language acquisition (see e.g., Atkinson, 1992), his results need not be viewed as devastating by those wishing to develop learning based accounts of acquisition. This is because the formal framework within which Gold's result is set can be questioned in its applicability to the goals of human language learning in more than one way.[1] In particular, if the criterion of

---

[1] Namely, as identification in the limit of a grammar in a semantics free concept learning task. One might question whether a grammar, as opposed to routines for comprehension and production is the goal of acquisition: learning a mapping function from sound to meanings given a sequence of phonetic–semantic representation pairs as input is considerably easier than stringset identification, see e.g., Scholz & Pullum, 2002; for excellent discussion on other limitations of Gold's framework also see Rohde & Plaut, (1999), and Pullum (2003). Moreover, Shinohara (1994) shows how languages definable by so-called length bounded Elementary Formal Systems with at most *n* axioms can be learned from positive data alone. This class of languages coincides with the class of context sensitive languages in the Chomsky hierarchy, within which human languages can be assumed (at worst) to fall. For demonstrations of how probabilistic sequence prediction might rely on positive evidence alone see Chater and Vitanyi (in press).

success is relaxed from correct identification of the target grammar to approximately correct, Gold's result no longer holds (Wharton, 1974; see also, Pinker, 1979).

Nevertheless, Gold's work does highlight that the problem of how to rule out ungrammatical constructions needs to be taken seriously. This is all the more so, because it is uncontested that children do not receive systematic feedback about what is not allowed, even with regards to their own ungrammatical utterances. Corrective feedback is noisy and incomplete at best (Marcus, 1993), even though it might be somewhat wider than assumed if indirect forms of correction such as recasting the child's utterance in different words is taken into account (from the ongoing debate on recasts see e.g., Morgan *et al.*, 1995; Saxton, 1997; Saxton *et al.*, 1998; Chouinard & Clark, 2003).

Crucial to the issue of what learning is possible in this context is the extent to which the absence of particular constructions from the input can be taken to be informative. If the learner has little or no explicit feedback on ungrammatical sentences, agrammaticality can only be *inferred*. Seemingly, all the learner is left with is an argument from ignorance of the form

(7) This sentence/construction is agrammatical because it has not been seen in the input.

This is clearly an inductive inference, and as such necessarily uncertain: it is always possible that the sentence/construction simply has not been encountered *yet*. Consequently the possibility of such an inference has often been dismissed. But, in principle, it is in no way different from other arguments from ignorance as we discussed them in the Introduction above. As we saw there, such arguments vary in strength given the nature of the exact probabilities involved. The question then is what these probabilities suggest in the context of language acquisition. With regards to the general weight of poverty of stimulus arguments such analysis is crucial. If such inferences as (7) are inherently weak then, indeed, the acquisition of the construction in question must proceed via a path other than learning.

However, the question of inferential strength from such negative evidence is also of relevance for aspects of language for which it is widely assumed that they *are* learned.

In particular, it has bearing on the acquisition of so-called lexical rules. Lexical rules (or 'lexical redundancy rules') are assumed to relate our mental representations, in the mental lexicon, of related words such as 'tie' and 'untie', or 'pack' and 'unpack' (Jackendorf, 1975) but also verbs that systematically appear in different constructions, referred to as alternations.

Dative alternation, for example, refers to a simple pattern between related constructions. For a whole range of verbs involving two objects and an action, speakers can choose between two constructions that are seemingly equivalent in meaning:

(8) John gave the book to Mary.

(9) John gave Mary the book.

and,

(10) John passed the salt to Mary.

(11) John passed Mary the salt.

Other examples include passive constructions,

(12) John hit the dog.

(13) The dog was hit by John.

And so-called subject raising,

(14) George expects that Liverpool will win.

(15) George expects Liverpool to win.

However, there are then semantically closely related verbs for which only one of these constructions is possible

(16) John donated the money to the charity.

(17) John donated the charity the money.*

and

(18) Pinker's book costs twenty five dollars.

(19) Twenty five dollars is cost by Pinker's book.*

where (17) and (19) are marked with an asterisk(*) to indicate that they are generally perceived to be ungrammatical.

These 'exceptions' pose a problem to the learner that has been of interest to theorists from a wide range of theoretical frameworks (see Pinker, 1984, for an initial overview). How do speakers come to know that this construction is not part of the language also?

One strategy is to assume that there simply are no rules or generalizations being extracted, so that the problem of exceptions does not conceptually arise (Baker, 1979). In other words, if the speaker adopts for their lexicon only those constructions for a particular verb that they have actually encountered, then they will never be prone to overgeneralization. However, this approach conflicts with the finding that patterns are treated as productive by both children and adults, that is, applied to verbs that have not been encountered in that specific construction before (Bowerman, 1988; Pinker, 1984) even if recent evidence suggests that children are *initially* conservative (see Tomasello, 2000, for a review of the evidence on this point).

Solutions have primarily focussed on recasting the problem as one of inference from *positive evidence*. Specifically, researchers have sought to identify phonological (sound) and semantic (meaning) based factors that influence whether or not a particular construction is possible.

In the case of dative alternations, for example, it has been noted that verbs with Germanic roots, such as 'give' (8 above) allow the alternation whereas one's of Latinate origin, such as 'donate' (15 above) typically do not (Pinker, 1984). Similar analyses identifying a range of contributing semantic factors have been conducted for the passive (Granger, 1983)

In other words, there may be a host of cues that determine whether or not a particular construction is likely to occur or not. One caveat, here, is that these analyses have been linguistic, i.e., they involve the determination of cues in the external language. What is less clear, and can only be experimentally ascertained, is whether learners and adult speakers actually show any sensitivity to these cues (for some experimental evidence see Ambridge *et al.*, in press; Brooks & Zizak, 2002). Moreover, there has been little attempt to examine in quantitative terms the strength and utility of these cues.

Finally, these cues are not categorical, but seem graded and hence probabilistically associated with the possibility of a particular constructions. This means that *other* constraining information would continue to be useful (see also MacWhinney, 2004).

What then of *implicit* or *indirect* negative evidence? Pinker (1984, p. 321) who has dealt in great detail with the acquisition problem notes that:

> Chomsky (1981) and others have conjectured that the child might somehow exploit 'indirect negative evidence': if a certain form never appears in the input, he or she might assume that it is ungrammatical, without requiring overt corrections, disapproval, evidence of comprehension failure, and so on ….

He notes further that given the infinite and creative nature of language, any given sample is bound to lack evidence of a particular, *grammatical* construction. Hence, he concludes the child would have to do one of two things:

> If he or she could predict from the context that a particular form would *have* to be uttered by the adult if the language would only permit it, the absence of such a form would indicate that the form was ungrammatical. Or if children were capable of calculating that if a given form was grammatical its probability of *not* occurring in an input sample of a given size was close to zero, then the absence of such a form in a sufficiently large sample would indicate that it was indeed ungrammatical.

However he also goes on to note that no worked out proposal of this kind exists.

One response to the problem has been modelling work, in particular making use of connectionist models, that seeks to demonstrate that a particular system can learn using positive examples alone (Elman, 1993; Rohde & Plaut, 1999). Such models have embodied the key assumption that the learner makes use of implicit negative evidence through the formation and evaluation of implicit, online predictions, where predictions are assumed to be an inherent part of language processing (see e.g., Rohde & Plaut, 1999, for detailed discussion, but also Fodor & Crain, 1987 for criticism of this idea). Such work is essential, in particular to the development of mechanistic accounts of language acquisition. However, it is less useful for a transparent characterization of the circumstances under which inference from absence is justified, along with the factors that might contribute to the inference's strength. In particular, the convincingness of such demonstrations as general arguments is determined directly by how convincing and representative of the acquisition problem one finds the system's overall learning success to be.

Another response has been to identify further, general constraints on the generalization process that could help to rule out overly general constructions. The key proposals here are 'pre-emption' and 'entrenchment (Bates & MacWhinney, 1989; Braine & Brooks, 1995; Clark, 1987; Goldberg, 1995; Tomasello, 2000):

> **Usage Entrenchment**: The more often a child hears a verb used in a particular construction, the less likely they will be to extend it to a novel construction in which they have not heard it.

> **Pre-emption**: If a child hears a verb in a construction that serves the same communicative function as some possible generalization, they can infer that that latter putative generalization is not actually available.

Slightly differing variants of these definitions, in particular with regards to pre-emption, exist and there has also been a range of opinions regarding their utility in helping children avoid syntactic overgeneralization (see e.g., Bowerman 1988; Bowerman & Croft, 2007). However, they seem intuitively informative at least to some extent, and there is some experimental evidence to support the usage of both pre-emption and entrenchment by children (Brooks & Tomasello, 1999; Brooks & Zizak, 2002; Brooks et al., 1999; Theakston, 2004; Ambridge et al, in press). This makes a further investigation of their inferential utility desirable.

It is clear then that a range of (often conflicting) intuitions regarding inference from so-called indirect negative evidence exist. Given this, it seems desirable to provide a formal treatment of the inference that allows one to examine the question of when and where—if ever—such an inference would be rationally justified on the part of the learner. To this end, we next provide a Bayesian analysis of the learner's position.

Formal analysis

In dealing with language acquisition, explicit, corrective feedback, whether positive or negative has to be distinguished clearly from the absence of evidence which might be used as 'indirect or 'implicit' negative evidence. Even if corrective feedback is rare, it is possible. Consequently, three possibilities in the input to the learner have to be distinguished: positive evidence, explicit negative evidence and no evidence on the particular question at hand. This means that we are dealing with a multi-valued hypothesis as outlined in the section on epistemic closure above. Specifically, we need to distinguish a total of six possible cases that the learner is faced with regarding a particular construction: that construction could be grammatical or ungrammatical, and in each case, the learner could receive positive evidence, explicit negative evidence or no evidence at all. These possibilities are enumerated in Table 6.1

Table 6.1

	Says 'c'	Says 'not c'	Says nothing
C grammatical	$P('c'\|C)$	$P('\neg c'\|C)$	$P(n\|C)$
C ungrammatical	$P('c'\|\neg C)$	$P('\neg c'\|\neg C)$	$P(n\|\neg C)$

where 'c' refers to an occurrence of construction C, '$\neg C$' refers to explicit information that C is ungrammatical, and 'n' means 'nothing' regarding c occurs in the input.

Given probabilities for each of these cells, one can calculate the corresponding posterior degrees of belief in C, given a unit of each kind of evidence, for the four possible arguments we introduced above:

(A) construction in input: Construction grammatical   (Affirmative)
(O) *no* explicit evidence that ungrammatical: (Opposite)
       Construction grammatical
(N) explicit evidence ungrammatical: Construction   (Negative)
       ungrammatical
(S) *no* construction in input: Construction ungrammatical   (Same)

or, formally:

Affirmative:	$P(C|'c') = P('c'|C).P(C)/P('c')$
Opposite:	$P(C|\neg'\neg c') = P(\neg'\neg c'|C).P(C)/P(\neg'\neg c')$
Negative:	$P(\neg C|'\neg c') = ('\neg c'|\neg C).P(\neg C)/P('\neg c')$
Same:	$P(\neg C|\neg'c') = (\neg'c'|\neg C).P(\neg C)/P(\neg'c')$

A first observation is that the inference (O) is possible and needs to be considered. This inference has been neglected in the language acquisition literature, but, as we saw above, in cases of high epistemic closure it can be plausible.

The relative strength of all four inferences is determined by the exact probabilities assigned to each of the cells of Table 6.1. In language acquisition there are several strong constraints on the values these probabilities can take:

1. Explicit negative feedback is fairly rare, i.e., $P('\neg c'|\neg C)$ is low.

2. Even rarer, however, is explicit negative feedback that is *false*, i.e., the ratio $P('\neg c'|\neg C)/ P('\neg c'|C)$ is considerably larger than 1. In fact, correct explicit negative feedback might outweigh incorrect feedback by orders of magnitude.

3. There is some evidence for degenerate, agrammatical input to the child, i.e. $P('c'|\neg C)$ is not zero, but it is considerably less frequent than grammatical input, i.e., the ratio $P('c'| C)/ P('c'|\neg C)$ is also greater than 1.

4. Similarly, though there is degenerate, agrammatical input, most of the input is grammatical. Given that explicit negative feedback is rare, this means that it is most likely that an ungrammatical construction will simply never be mentioned at all, either positively or negatively, i.e., $P(n|\neg C)$ is very high, and the ratio $P(n|\neg C)/P('c'|\neg C)$ is very high.

5. The probability of a given construction occurring in the input can be low where that construction is rare, i.e., $P(n|C)$ can be high. However, this probability of non-occurrence must still be lower than the corresponding probability for an ungrammatical construction, i.e., the ratio $P(n|C)/ P(n|\neg C)$ is *less* than 1.

These constraints have several immediate consequences: because $P('\neg c'|C)$ is extremely low (see constraints 1. and 2.), $P('c'|C)$ and $P(n|C)$ are almost complementary, i.e., $P('c'|C) \approx 1—P(n|C)$. That is, any change in the expected probability of a construction, given that it is grammatical, immediately and directly impacts on its chance of non-occurrence as well. Moreover, these constraints suffice to specify a reasonable range of values.

To explore the different inferences in more detail we assigned initial values as in Table 6.2.

We then let $P(n|C)$, and with that $P('c'|C)$, vary. This is because these probabilities cannot be assumed to be constant in the input. This is the case because a particular verb will not have a constant probability of appearance given the constraints provided by its meaning: when talking about swimming, the word 'donate' is less likely to appear than when talking about charities. Strictly speaking the probability of explicit negative feedback $P('\neg c')$ will also vary, given that such feedback occurs only in response to an actual utterance. However, we are assuming simply a plausible upper

Table 6.2

	'says_c'	**'says_not_c'**	**says nothing**
C grammatical	$P('c'\mid C)$	$P('\neg c'\mid C)$	$P(n\mid C)$
		LOWER !! (≈ 0)	
C ungrammatical	$P('c'\mid \neg C)$	$P('\neg c'\mid \neg C)$	$P(n\mid \neg C)$
	PRETTY LOW!	*LOW*	**VERY HIGH**

	'says_c'	**'says_not_c'**	**says nothing**
C grammatical	$P('c'\mid C)$	$P('\neg c'\mid C)$	$P(n\mid C)$
		$=0.00008$	
C ungrammatical	$P('c'\mid \neg C)$	$P('\neg c'\mid \neg C)$	$P(n\mid \neg C)$
	$=0.02$	$=0.0008$	$=0.9792$

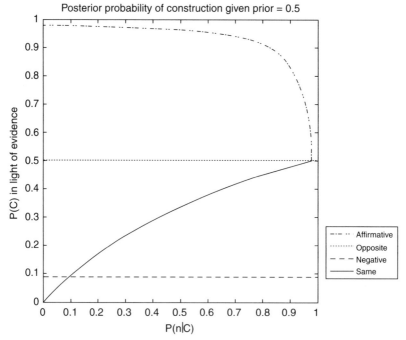

Fig. 6.1. The figure graphs posterior degrees of belief in the grammaticality of the construction under consideration as a function of possible values of $P(n\mid C)$ (and thereby also for $P(c\mid C)$). The assumed prior degree of belief is 0.5, the other probabilities are fixed, with the values given in Table 6.2. The graph is constrained to the region where grammatical error does not exceed correct production of the construction. For ease of comparison, we show the impact of all four arguments on the posterior $P(C)$, that is, for the 'negative' arguments 'Negative', N, and 'Same', S, we have graphed $1 - N$ and $1 - S$, as opposed to the posterior probability of $P(\neg C)$.

bound on this probability in those cases, and neglecting the fact that it might drop even further on many occasions as this leaves all main results unaltered.

Results, then, based on a prior degree of belief in the existence of the construction of $P(C) = 0.5$, reflecting ignorance, are shown in Figure 6.1. Displayed is the impact of varying $P(n|C)$ on the posterior degree of belief in C. We might also want to consider how this pattern is affected by changes in prior to reflect, for example, the impact of previous learning, or a higher prior degree of belief in the existence of the construction on the basis of analogy to other verbs, see MacWhinney (2004), or Tomasello (2000), or conversely a lower prior stemming from inherent conservatism on the part of the learner. As can be seen from Figures 6.2 and 6.3, changing the value of this prior simply moves the lines up and down the probability scale, without altering their basic relationship.

Several aspects of these graphs are worth note:

1. The Opposite argument ('construction exists, because nobody has told me it doesn't') is worthless in these circumstances. Because $P(`\neg c')$ is so low, $P(\neg'\neg c')$ is too high to allow any discernable impact of this inference on posterior degree of beliefs in C. The posterior basically equals the prior.

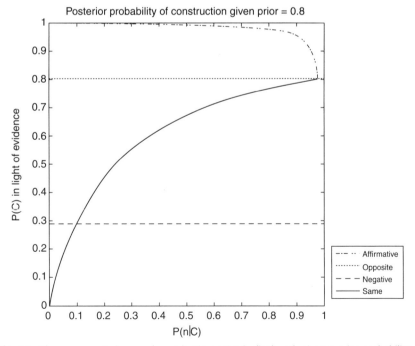

Fig. 6.2. The same posteriors as shown in Figure 6.1 is displayed, given a prior probability of 0.8. All other factors remain unchanged.

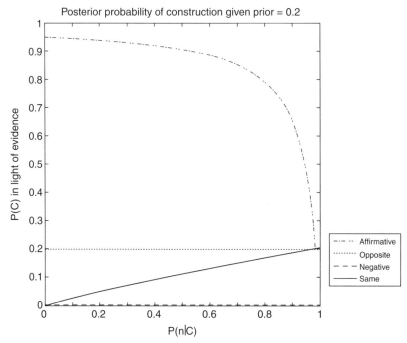

Fig. 6.3. Effect of starting from a prior of 0.2, that is, scepticism towards the grammaticality of the construction is shown. All else is unchanged.

2. Though the probability of explicit feedback $(P(`\neg c'))$ is low, it nevertheless has a considerable impact when it occurs. This is because it is the ratio $P(`\neg c'|\neg C)/P(`\neg c'|C)$ that determines the strength of this inference, not the absolute values. Because incorrect negative feedback is even rarer than correct negative feedback, feedback, when present, is extremely diagnostic. Note that these calculations *presume* that feedback has been recognized as such, something that anecdotal evidence suggests is not always straightforward for the child (Marcus, 1993). Where corrective feedback is not even recognized as such, these calculations cannot, of course, apply.

3. Only the positive argument, A, and the argument from absence, S, are influenced by the value of $P(n|C)$. This follows directly from the defining equations above. What is notable, however, given the values assumed here, is how little the Affirmative argument is affected; the posterior remains high virtually throughout the range of possible values of $P(n|C)$. This is because the probability of ungrammatical input, $P(`c'|\neg C)$, is fairly low.

4. As expected, the argument from absence S ('this construction is ungrammatical because I have never encountered it before'), varies from useless (when $P(n|C)$ is maximal), that is, without noticeable impact on posterior degrees of belief to very strong, when $P(n|C)$ is low—and potentially as strong as a positive, affirmative inference.

We consider this final point in more detail. The intuitive inference made by the learner in the case of a 'Same' argument from absence is of the form

I have not encountered this construction

(I would have expected to encounter it, if it existed)

Therefore, this construction does not exist

As for all arguments from ignorance, the plausibility of the bracketed assumption governs the strength of the inference: the higher the expectation of encountering the construction, the stronger the inference from its absence.

This is where pre-emption and entrenchment can come into their own. Both affect the plausibility of $P(n|C)$. In the case of pre-emption, having heard a semantically similar construction marks out the preceding context as one whose meaning context gives the disputed construction a high probability of occurring. In the case of entrenchment, the fact that the verb in question has occurred, again, marks out the context as one in which that verb is fitting, suggesting that its other forms could also have been expected to occur.

Both pre-emption and entrenchment, then, can be viewed as useful, easy to track indicators that $P(n|C)$ was lowered in a given context.

Of course, they are not the only information that is potentially relevant or available in order to estimate the plausibility of occurrence, and consequently are not *necessary* for the inference: any semantic, syntactic or real-world knowledge can be informative. Identifying, for example, simply that a verb is part of the semantic field of the current discourse should raise estimates of its chance of occurrence and hence the potential informativeness of its absence.

Crucial to the probabilistic nature of the inference is that it is *graded* in strength. Even where $P(n|C)$ is high, there is still *some* evidential impact of absence, and weak evidence of this kind, could, in principle, accumulate over time. Vis a vis Pinker's (1984) comments above, then, inference from indirect negative evidence is easier than his comments suggest, in that the probabilities involved do not have to be 'close to zero' for the inference to be justified.

But the difficulties inherent in inference involving 'indirect negative evidence' have also been over-estimated by linguists from outside the generative framework. MacWhinney (2004) considers indirect negative evidence to be one of several sources or strategies that can be used in conjunction to overcome the inductive problems faced by the learner. The computation he assumes to be involved in this is as follows:

> This computation can be illustrated with the error '*goed'. To construct indirect negative evidence in this case, children need to track the frequency of all verbs and the frequency of the past tense as marked by the regular '-ed'. Then they need to track the frequency of the verb 'go' in all of its uses and the frequency of '*goed'. To gain a bit more certainty, they should also calculate the frequency of a verb like 'jump' and the frequency of 'jumped'. With these ratios in hand, the child can then compare the ratio for 'go' with those for 'jump' or verbs in general and conclude that the attested cases of '*goed' are fewer than would be expected on the basis of the evidence from verbs like 'jump'. They can then conclude that '*goed' is ungrammatical. (p. 908).

The Bayesian analysis makes clear that there is no need for this. The inference can be made on the basis of the individual construction alone. Its strength, of course, depends on the probability of $P(n|C)$, but this quantity can be estimated on the basis of *any* information that is available and relevant, including, as discussed above, semantic information. If one has information to suggest that the construction in question had a good chance of occurring, then—normatively—one should draw negative conclusions from its absence.

Finally, the Bayesian analysis is informative with regards to the power of inference from lack of evidence in different kinds of circumstances. Baker (1979) distinguished between exceptions that were 'benign' and involved errors that could in principle be corrected without corrective feedback, and ones that were 'embarassing', because they seemed to require evidence that children do not receive. Examples of the former are overregularization errors such as 'goed' or 'foots'. The assumption by researchers here has been that 'consistent exposure' to the irregular forms 'went' and 'feet' is enough, in principle, to inform the child that the overregularized form is wrong (Bowerman, 1988; Pinker, 1984; MacWhinney, 2004). Baker's 'embarrassing exceptions', by contrast, are ones for which there is no exact counterpart that could come to block the overgeneralization. This has been viewed as problematic, because it has been assumed that pre-emption requires a single, consistent alternative in the adult input (see to this effect for example, Bowerman, 1988). That is, for many authors (Pinker, 1984), pre-emption has involved a single, contrastive form, coupled with an assumption on the part of the child that unique meanings have unique forms (and conversely, different forms are contrastive, see also Clark, 1987). It should be clear from the above analyses that this restriction is not necessary. A single alternative, well matched in meaning, will make the absence of the expected form seem particularly pronounced, but inference is not limited to these cases. Absence is informative, wherever the form was expected but failed to occur. This expectation in turn, can be more or less pronounced. Weaker forms of pre-emption are consequently entirely possible. In fact Goldberg (1995) has expressed the intuition that pre-emption can be particularly informative where a construction that is in some ways 'less optimal' than the disputed construction is encountered. The very fact that it is perceived to be 'less optimal' is indicative of the perception that it is in some ways less probable in that context than the expected, but absent construction, implying conversely that the subjective probability associated with the latter is even higher.

To conclude, it seems important to clarify the nature of our analyses. Bayesian inference can be viewed as a normative framework for the revision of beliefs in light of new evidence (see, e.g., Hahn & Oaksford, 2006b; for discussion; Howson & Urbach, 1989). This means we are seeking to demonstrate the conditions under which inference from absence is *rationally justified*, given plausible assumptions about the relevant statistics of feedback and error in the linguistic input. This is not to be confused with the empirical claim that the child is making such inferences, or that the child is Bayesian. Nor are we proposing here a process or mechanism account. However, the fact that such inference can be justified, does suggest it is worth considering as part of a computational level explanation of actual learners' behaviour. Here, one need not assume even that the learner has accurate knowledge of the probabilistic quantities assumed. Our results are robust, in the sense that nothing hinges on the exact numerical values we have assumed. This is demonstrated in Figures 6.4 to 6.6, which show

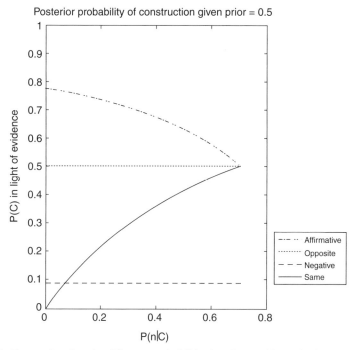

Fig. 6.4. The results given by different probabilities less favourable to the learner in that the probability of ungrammatical input, $P('c'|\neg C)$, has been increased to 0.29; $P(n|\neg C)$ is set to 0.7, $P('\neg c'|\neg C)$ is 0.01, $P('\neg c'|C) = 0.001$ are shown. The prior is set to 0.5. The graph is restricted to the range where grammatical input exceeds ungrammatical input to the child.

corresponding plots based on different values. Even assuming, for example a level of ungrammatical input of almost 30%, still gives rise to the same basic relationships documented above; and these hold as long as the probability of correct inputs exceeds that of incorrect input.

What the exact rates of ungrammatical input are in the real world will vary somewhat according to construction, however, it is clear that they cannot exceed some upper bound without the grammatical status itself being affected: 30% seems generous here, in that a form that was produced on one out of three occasions though 'wrong', is unlikely to still be widely perceived as 'ungrammatical'. The rate of incorrect feedback, too, can substantially be increased without altering the fundamental relationships. This suggests that even a learning system with quite different estimates of the probabilities involved will draw the same kinds of inference, diverging only in their exact strength. This is the case as long as basic ordinal constraints hold whereby correct input exceeds incorrect input, both in the case of production and feedback, even if the input were *much* noisier to the child than can plausibly be assumed.

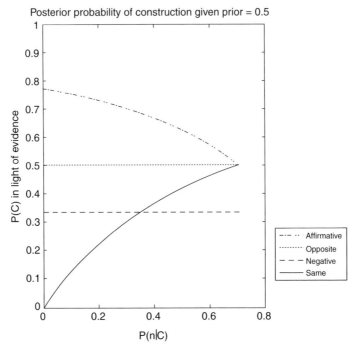

Fig. 6.5. A situation even less favourable to the learner is shown. Ungrammatical input is still at 0.29, but the probability of correction is now down to 1 in 10,000, and is itself more noisy in that erroneous corrections now occur at half (as opposed to 0ne-tenth) of that rate. As can be seen, this impacts only the strength of the *N* argument, that is, inference from explicit correction.

Conclusions

In conclusion, inference from absence in the context of language does not seem as inherently problematic as has widely been assumed. This is revealed by a high-level Bayesian analysis that allows the linguistic case to be compared with other day to day versions of such inference. Such an analysis suggests that the linguistic case is less special than has been assumed (see also Sampson, 2002).

What has seemed a particular stumbling block in the case of language is that the linguistic input is clearly *not* epistemically closed—language is typically assumed to be infinite. However, the range of available constructions is limited, even if the actual sentences in which they could occur are not. Moreover, incomplete closure can still allow a probabilistic inference and such inference need not depend on a brute force search. The strength of the inference depends on where you have looked—you do not have to have looked everywhere. If I am trying to ascertain whether or not I still have the other green sock, I can be almost as confident that I have lost it after looking in the washing machine, the sock drawer and under the bed, than as if I had searched the

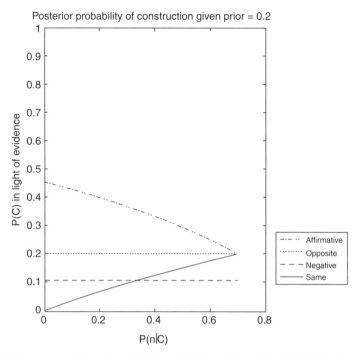

Fig 6.6. The same result as shown in Figure 6.5, but with a prior of 0.2. All other factors remain unchanged.

whole house; conversely, the impact of a thorough search of the refrigerator on my degree of belief will be negligible.

Exactly the same is true of language acquisition, and pre-emption and entrenchment reflect situations in which it is relevant to look. Likewise, the non-appearance of sentences which are merely semantically odd will *not* be informative: 'colourless green ideas sleep furiously' will not be ruled out by its mere failure to occur, because there is no expectation that this sentence will occur in the first place (cf. Chomsky, 1957).

Indirect negative evidence in the form of inference from absence seems a genuinely useful tool in constraining language learning, last but not least, because the kind of inference presented here can, in principle, be conducted at arbitrary levels of generality, that is, involving not just individual verbs, but also classes of verbs, and general constructions.[2] The harder part of understanding language acquisition is understanding where generalization comes from in the first place, not how incorrect generalizations might subsequently be pruned.

---

[2] Though the amount of work required to estimate probabilities of classes of verbs, or abstract constructions defined over abstract syntactic categories is correspondingly larger.

References

Ambridge, B., Pine, J. M., Rowland, C. F., & Young, C. R. (in press). The effect of verb semantic class and verb frequency (entrenchment) on children's and adults' graded judgements of argument structure overgeneralization errors. *Cognition*.

Atkinson, M. (1992). *Children's syntax: an introduction to principles and parameters theory.* Blackwell.

Baker, C. L. (1979). Syntactic theory and the projection problem. *Linguistic Inquiry*, **10**, 233–280.

Bates, E., & MacWhinney, B. (1989). Functionalism and the competition model. In B. MacWhinney, & E. Bates (Eds.), *The crosslinguistic study of sentence processing*. Cambridge: Cambridge University Press.

Bowerman, M. (1982). Reorganizational processes in lexical and syntactic development. In E. Wanner, & L. R. Gleitman (Eds.), *Language acquisition: the state of the art*. New York: Cambridge University Press.

Bowerman, M. (1988). The 'no negative evidence' problem: how do children avoid constructing an overly general grammar? In J. A. Hawkins (Ed.), *Explaining language universals*. Oxford: Blackwell.

Bowerman, M., & Croft, W. (2007). The acquisition of the English causative alternation. In M. Bowerman, & P. Brown (Eds.) *Crosslinguistic perspectives on argument structure: implications for learnability*. Hillsdale, NJ: Lawrence Erlbaum.

Braine, M. D. S. (1971). On two types of models of the internalization of grammars. In D. I. Slobin (Ed.), *The ontogenesis of grammar*. New York: Academic Press.

Braine, M. D. S., & Brooks, P. J. (1995). Verb argument structure and the problem of avoiding an overgeneral grammar. In M. Tomasello, & W. E. Merriman (Eds.), *Beyond names for things: young children's acquisition of verbs* (pp. 353–376). Hillsdale NJ: Erlbaum.

Brooks, P. J., & Tomasello, M. (1999). How children constrain their argument structure constructions. *Language*, **75**, 720–738.

Brooks, P. J., & Zizak, O. (2002). Does pre-emption help children learn verb transitivity. *Journal of Child Language*, **29**, 759–781.

Brooks, P. J., Tomasello, M., Dodson, K., & Lewis, L. B. (1999). Young children's overgeneralizations with fixed transitivity verbs. *Child Development*, **70**, 1325–1337.

Chater, N., & Vitanyi, P. (in press) 'Ideal learning' of natural language: positive results about learning from positive evidence. *Journal of Mathematical Psychology*.

Chomsky, N. (1957). *Syntactic structures*. The Hague: Mouton.

Chomsky, N. (1980). *Rules and representations*. Oxford: Oxford University Press.

Chomsky, N. (1986). *Knowledge of language: its nature, origin and use*. New York: Praeger.

Chouinard, M. M., & Clark, E. V. (2003). Adult reformulations of child errors as negative evidence. *Journal of Child Language*, **30**, 637–669.

Clark, E. (1987). The principle of contrast: a constraint on language acquisition. In B. MacWhinney (Ed.), *Mechanisms of language acquisition*. Hillsdale, NJ: Erlbaum.

Clark, K. L. (1978). Negation as failure. In H. Gallaire, & J. Minker (Eds.), *Logic and databases* (pp. 293–322). New York: Plenum Press.

Copi I. M., & Burgess-Jackson, K. (1996). *Informal logic*. Upper Saddle River: Prentice-Hall.

Crain, S. (1991). Language acquisition in the absence of experience. *Behavioral and Brain Sciences*, **14**, 597–650.

De Cornulier, B. (1988). Knowing whether, knowing who, and epistemic closure. In M. Meyer (Ed.), *Questions and questioning* (pp. 182–192). Berlin: Walter de Gruyter.

Eemeren, F. H. van, Grootendorst, R., & Snoeck Henkemans, F. (1996). *Fundamentals of argumentation theory*. Mahwah, NJ: Lawrence Erblaum.

Elman, J. L. (1993). Learning and development in neural networks: the importance of starting small. *Cognition*, **48**, 71–99.

Fodor, J. D., & Crain, S. (1987). Simplicity and generality of rules in language acquisition. In: MacWhinney, B. (Ed.) *Mechanisms of language acquisition* (pp. 35– 63). Hillsdale, NJ: Lawrence Erlbaum Associates.

Gold, E. (1967). Language identification in the limit. *Information and Control*, **16**, 447–474.

Goldberg, A. (1995). *Constructions: a construction grammar approach to argument structure*. University of Chicago Press.

Granger, S. (1983) *The be+past participle construction in spoken English—with special emphasis on the passive*. North Holland.

Hahn, U., & Oaksford, M. (2006). A Bayesian approach to informal argument fallacies. *Synthese*, **152**, 207–236.

Hahn, U., & Oaksford, M. (2006b) A normative theory of argument strength. *Informal Logic*, **26**, 1–24.

Hahn, U., & Oaksford, M. (2007). The rationality of informal argumentation: a Bayesian approach to reasoning fallacies. *Psychological Review*, **114**, 704–732.

Hahn, U., Oaksford, M., & Bayindir, H. (2005). How convinced should we be by negative evidence? In B. Bara, L. Barsalou, & M. Bucciarelli (Eds.), *Proceedings of the 27th Annual Conference of the Cognitive Science Society* (pp. 887–892). Mahwah, NJ: Lawrence Erlbaum Associates.

Hamblin, C. L. (1970). *Fallacies*. London: Methuen.

Hornstein, N., & Lightfoot, D. (Eds.) (1981). *Explanation in linguistics: the logical problem of language acquisition*. London: Longman.

Jackendorff, R. S. (1975). Morphological and semantic regularities in the lexicon. *Language*, **51**, 639–671.

Lasnik, H., & Uriagereka, J. (2002). On the poverty of the challenge. *The Linguistic Review*, **19**, 147–150.

MacWhinney, B. (2004). A multiple process solution to the logical problem of language acquisition. *Journal of Child Language*, **31**, 883–914.

Marcus, G. F. (1993). Negative evidence in language acquisition. *Cognition*, **46**, 53–85.

Morgan, J. L., Bonamo, K. M., & Travis, L. L. (1995). Negative evidence on negative evidence. *Developmental Psychology*, **31**, 180–197.

Oaksford, M., & Hahn, U. (2004). A Bayesian approach to the argument from ignorance. *Canadian Journal of Experimental Psychology*, **58**, 75–85.

Pinker, S. (1979) Formal models of language learning. *Cognition*, 7, 217–?83.

Pinker, S. (1984). *Language learnability and language development*. Cambridge, MA: Harvard University Press.

Pinker, S. (2004). Clarifying the logical problem of language acquisition. *Journal of Child Language*, **31**, 949–953.

Pullum, G. K. (2003) Learnability. In *Oxford International Encyclopedia of Linguistics*, (2nd Edn.) (pp. 24–26). Oxford: Oxford University Press.

Reiter, R. (1980). A logic for default reasoning. *Artificial Intelligence*, **13**, 81–132.

Reiter, R. (1985). On reasoning by default. In R. Brachman, & H. Levesque (Eds.), *Readings in knowledge representation* (pp. 401–410). Los Altos, CA: Morgan Kaufman.

Rohde, D. L. T., & Plaut, D. C. (1999). Language acquisition in the absence of explicit negative evidence: How important is starting small? *Cognition*, **72**, 67–109.

Sampson, G. (2002). Exploring the richness of the stimulus. *The Linguistic Review*, **19**, 73–104.

Saxton, M. (1997). The contrast theory of negative input. *Journal of Child Language*, **24**, 139–161.

Saxton, M., Kulcsar, B., Marshall, G., & Rupra, M. (1998). Longer-term effects of corrective input: an experimental approach. *Journal of Child Language*, **25**, 701–721.

Scholz, B. C., & Pullum, G. K. (2002). Searching for arguments to support linguistic nativism. *The Linguistic Review*, **19**, 185–223.

Shinohara, T. (1994). Rich classes inferable from positive data: length bounded elementary formal systems. *Information and Computation*, **108**, 175–186.

Theakston, A. L. (2004). The role of entrenchment in children's and adults performance on grammaticality judgment tasks. *Cognitive Development*, **19**, 15–34.

Thomas, M. (2002). Development of the concept of 'the poverty of the stimulus'. *The Linguistic Review*, **19**, 51–71.

Tomasello, M. (2000) Do young children have adult syntactic competence? *Cognition*, **74**, 209–253.

Walton, D. N. (1992). Nonfallacious arguments from ignorance. *American Philosophical Quarterly*, **29**, 381–387.

Wharton, R. (1974). Approximate language identification. *Information and Control*, **26**, 236–255.

Woods, J., Irvine, A., & Walton, D. N. (2004). *Argument: Critical thinking, logic and the fallacies* (Revised Edn). Toronto: Prentice Hall.

Chapter 7

Towards a rational theory of human information acquisition

Jonathan D. Nelson

Computational Neurobiology Lab, Salk Institute,
and Computer Science and Engineering Department,
University of California, San Diego, CA, USA

Introduction

Many situations require judiciously choosing particular pieces of information to acquire before otherwise acting. Consider the case of a scientist studying gravity. Dropping an apple from a bridge, to see whether it will fall, is a possible experiment. But it does not appear to be a useful experiment, perhaps because all plausible theories predict the apple will fall. In a Bayesian optimal experimental design (OED) framework, simply testing predictions of various theories does not constitute good science. Rather, possible experiments are judged useful to the extent that plausible competing theories make contradictory predictions about the results.

Beginning roughly 1980, psychologists began to use OED theories of the value of information as normative (theoretically optimal) or descriptive models of human queries and intuitions about the value of information (Table 7.10). Examples of scenarios studied include people's intuitions about what medical tests are most useful (Baron *et al.*, 1988), about what features would be most helpful to categorize objects (Skov & Sherman, 1986; Slowiaczek *et al.*, 1992), and about what cards are most useful on Wason's selection task (Klayman & Ha, 1987; Oaksford & Chater, 1994); human eye movements for learning an object's shape (Walker-Renninger *et al.*, 2005), for finding an object hidden in noise (Najemnik & Geisler, 2005), or for categorization (Nelson & Cottrell, 2007); and monkeys' eye movements to query the location of a hidden target (Nakamura, 2006).

In life, of course, information gathering is frequently also coupled with other goals (Baron *et al.* 1988; Box & Hill, 1967; Chater *et al.* 1998; Chater & Oaksford, 1999; Lindley, 1956). For instance, a foraging animal may wish to learn the geographical distribution of a food source, while simultaneously maximizing immediate energy intake. Similarly, a physician diagnosing an illness would want to balance the expected informational value of diagnostic tests with their monetary cost and possible harm to the patient. (An expensive test that deposits large quantities of radiation on the patient, such as a CT scan, should be avoided if an inexpensive blood test provides equivalent information.) It would be inappropriate to build mathematical models of these situations based solely on information gathering; the other goals must also be incorporated. There is evidence that in some situations people can optimize fairly arbitrary utility functions (Trommershäuser *et al.*, 2003) and that in other situations, people have difficulty doing so (Baron & Hershey, 1988). In this chapter, however, our focus is on situations in which information gathering is the only goal. A unified theory of information gathering might be possible in these situations, depending on the consistency of intuitions across people and across tasks. Whether or not a unified theory is plausible will be discussed further on.

The issue of how to assess potential experiments' usefulness is complicated by the fact that an experiment's outcome is not known until the experiment is conducted. But in some cases, people have strong intuitions about which experiments (or questions, or queries) are most useful. The planet Vuma scenario (Fig. 7.1), introduced by Skov and Sherman (1986), illustrates this. The experimental subject imagines that they are on the planet Vuma, which is inhabited by two species of creatures, gloms and fizos. Because of the blinding light and blowing sand, the creatures are effectively invisible. The task is to categorize a randomly chosen creature as a glom or a fizo, by asking either whether it wears a hula hoop or whether it drinks iced tea. As in scientific inference, the hypotheses of interest (species of creature) cannot be queried directly, but probabilistic predictions of the hypotheses (presence or absence of features) can be tested. Suppose that $P(glom) = P(fizo) = 0.50$, $P(hula \mid glom) = 0.90$, $P(hula \mid fizo) = 0.50$, $P(drink \mid glom) = 0.28$, and $P(drink \mid fizo) = 0.32$. Which feature would be the most useful to query, based on the probabilities involved?

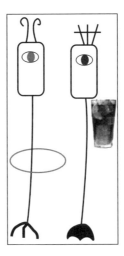

Fig. 7.1. Planet Vuma.

Most everyone thinks the hula feature is more useful. Why? Note that its usefulness depends on whether the feature is present or absent. Absence of the hula feature provides strong evidence for fizo: using Bayes' (1763) theorem, we can calculate that P($fizo$ | ~$hula$) = 0.88. Presence of the hula feature provides moderate evidence for glom: P($glom$ | $hula$) = 0.64. To assess the usefulness of the hula question, however, we need precise methods to:

(1) quantify the usefulness of each possible *answer* (presence or absence of the feature), and

(2) weight each possible answer's usefulness, to quantify the usefulness of the *question*.

Several mathematical ideas for doing this have been proposed, in a Bayesian optimal experimental design (OED) framework. (Optimal data selection, a term used by Oaksford & Chater, 1994, 2003, and optimal experimental design are equivalent terms.) Note that environmental probabilities, and posterior probabilities of fizo or glom, given presence or absence of a feature, do not depend on what feature is queried. Suppose, for sake of illustration, that we were to use probability gain (Baron 1981, as cited in Baron, 1985, pp. 130–167) to calculate the usefulness of obtained answers. Probability gain defines an answer's usefulness as the extent to which the answer improves the probability of correct guess (or reduces probability of error). If probability gain is used to calculate the utility (usefulness) of each answer (query result), absence of the hula hoop is worth 0.33 utility units, and presence of the hula hoop is worth 0.14 utility units. But how do we calculate the usefulness of the hula *question*? We could average the usefulness of the two answers, e.g. (0.33 + 0.14)/2 = 0.24. However, the hula hoop is present 70% of the time, so it would not make sense to weight presence and absence equally. Savage (1954, chap. 6) suggested weighting the usefulness (utility) of each answer according to its probability of occurrence. If we use probability gain to measure utility, then the expected utility of the hula question:

$$\text{eu}(Hula) = P(hula)\, \text{u}(hula) + P(\sim hula)\, \text{u}(\sim hula)$$
$$= 0.70\, \text{u}(hula) + 0.30\, \text{u}(\sim hula)$$
$$= 0.20 \text{ utility units.}$$

Note that here and throughout the chapter, we use capitals for random variables, such as the hula question (*Hula*), and lowercase for specific values taken by random variables, such as the answers that a hula hoop is worn (*hula*) or is not worn (~*hula*).

We can think of calculating the expected utility of the question as a balancing game (Fig. 7.2), in which we represent particular answers' utilities with weights on the right side of a fulcrum, and find what weight will balance the fulcrum on the left side. Balancing the fulcrum, as described below, is mathematically equivalent to calculating the expected usefulness of a question's possible answers. The more frequent an answer, the farther from the center of the fulcrum. Suppose we let 0.01 utility unit = 1 gram, and 1% probability of occurrence = 1 cm. We would then weight the hula absent answer at 33 grams, and put it 30 cm right of the fulcrum; and the hula present answer at 14 grams, and put it 70 cm right of the fulcrum. To find out what the hula

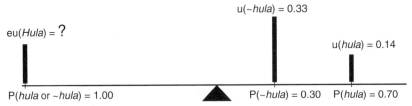

Fig. 7.2. Fulcrum diagram to illustrate expected a question's expected utility (at left) as a function of the utility and probability of its possible answers (at right).

question is worth, we check how much weight needs to be placed 100 cm to the left of the fulcrum to balance it: in this case, 20 grams. The *expected utility* of the hula hoop question is therefore 0.20 utility units, if probability gain is used to measure utility. (We could similarly calculate that the drink question is worth only 0.02 utility units.)

We would like to know whether human information acquisition is optimal (rational, in the sense of Anderson, 1990). But, as mentioned above, in this chapter we are dealing with situations where no extrinsic utility (cost) function is given. Several different optimal experimental design (OED) theories of the value of information have been proposed, in most cases by statisticians considering how to calculate the usefulness of possible experiments. It would therefore be unreasonable to arbitrarily pick a particular measure of the value of information, against which to test people's intuitions. However, it would be remarkable if people's intuitions approximate any of these theories. But the data will push us to conclude something even stronger. We will find (1) that among the OED models, some are better motivated than others as normative models of the value of information, and (2) that among the OED models, the better-motivated models also provide better description of human intuition and behavior!

Optimal experimental design theories of the usefulness of information

Each theory that we will consider follows Savage's (1954, chap. 6) suggestion to define a question Q's usefulness as the expected usefulness, given current knowledge, of the possible answers q_j:

$$eu(Q)=\sum_{q_j}P\left(q_j\right)u\left(q_j\right)$$

The six OED theories of the value (utility or usefulness) of information that we will consider are Bayesian diagnosticity, log diagnosticity, information gain (uncertainty reduction), Kullback-Liebler (KL) distance, impact (absolute difference), and probability gain (error reduction). Table 7.1 gives how each theory calculates the usefulness of a particular answer q. Individual c_i are particular categories, on a categorization task. (Mathematically, we will treat possible categories c_i as hypotheses to test.) The inquirer's (or learner's) goal in each case is to identify which category (or hypothesis)

Table 7.1. OED theories for the value of information on categorization tasks

OED theory	usefulness of obtained answer q, $u(q)$
probability gain	$\max\limits_{c_i} P(c_i \mid q) - \max\limits_{c_i} P(c_i)$
information gain	$\sum\limits_{c_i} P(c_i)\log\dfrac{1}{P(c_i)} - \sum\limits_{c_i} P(c_i \mid q)\log\dfrac{1}{P(c_i \mid q)}$
KL distance	$\sum\limits_{c_i} P(c_i \mid q)\log\dfrac{P(c_i \mid q)}{P(c_i)}$
impact	$0.5\sum\limits_{c_i} abs\big(P(c_i \mid q) - P(c_i)\big)$
Bayesian diagnosticity	$\max\left(\dfrac{P(q \mid c_1)}{P(q \mid c_2)}, \dfrac{P(q \mid c_2)}{P(q \mid c_{1.})}\right)$
log diagnosticity	$\log\max\left(\dfrac{P(q \mid c_1)}{P(q \mid c_2)}, \dfrac{P(q \mid c_2)}{P(q \mid c_{1.})}\right)$

is correct. Nelson (2005, pp. 996–997) gives example calculations of each theory. Here are some very brief highlights of each OED theory:

— Probability gain (Baron, 1981, as cited in Baron, 1985) quantifies the value of an answer as the extent to which that answer improves probability of correct guess of the true category. Maximizing probability gain corresponds to maximizing probability correct, as well as to minimizing probability of error. In this chapter we assume an optimal response strategy (rather than probability matching or other suboptimal strategies) when calculating probability gain.

— Information gain (Lindley, 1956; Box & Hill, 1967; Fedorov, 1972) is based on the idea that an answer that reduces uncertainty (Shannon, 1948, entropy) about the true category is useful. Oaksford and Chater (1994, 2003) used expected information gain (mutual information) in their probabilistic models of Wason's selection task as optimal data selection.

— Kullback-Liebler (KL) distance defines an answer's usefulness as the distance from prior to posterior beliefs about the categories (Kullback & Liebler, 1951; Cover & Thomas, 1991). The expected KL distance of a query and the expected information gain of a query are identical (Oaksford & Chater, 1996), although KL distance and information gain sometimes give different ratings of the usefulness of individual answers.

— Impact measures the usefulness of information as the absolute change from prior to posterior beliefs. Impact appears to have been independently proposed on three separate occasions (by Wells & Lindsay, 1980; Klayman & Ha, 1987, pp. 219–220; Nickerson, 1996). It was initially defined for situations with two categories; Nelson (2005) generalized it to situations with two or more discrete categories. It has been slightly reformulated here, in a way functionally equivalent to Nelson (2005), but so that the presence or absence of very-low-probability categories does not change its scale. Impact and probability gain are equivalent if prior probabilities of the categories are equal.

— Bayesian diagnosticity (Good, 1950, 1975, 1983) and log diagnosticity are based on the likelihood ratio of the answer obtained. (Note that despite their names, these measures are in no way more Bayesian than any others; nor does being Bayesian compel the use of these or other measures.) The idea is that answers are useful if they are more probable given one category than given the other category. However, both of these diagnosticity measures have serious flaws (Nelson, 2005). One flaw is that Bayesian diagnosticity and log diagnosticity are unbounded, and consider a question to be infinitely useful if there is any probability that its answer will rule-out one hypothesis, even if the probability of that answer is very low.[1] Another is that in some cases they are independent of priors. Another limitation is that they are only defined for cases with exactly two categories, c_1 and c_2, whereas the other theories are defined for two or more categories c_i. In some cases, both diagnosticity measures make strange claims; in others, only one of the measures does. For instance, Nelson describes how log diagnosticity has bizarre nonmonotonicities in some situations in which diagnosticity is monotonic.

What does each OED theory of the usefulness of information say about our example scenario? As we would hope, these six OED theories agree that the hula question is far more useful than the drink question (Table 7.2).

In the remainder of this chapter we will consider a number of issues important for a rational theory of human information acquisition. How do various OED theories differ from each other? Which are best motivated? Which best describe human intuitions? Do people follow suboptimal heuristic strategies when picking queries? Do monkeys, people, and other animals have similar intuitions about the value of information? Finally, can OED principles be used to design the most informative experiments for addressing these issues?

Nonnegativity, additivity, and sequential questions

Before making statements about whether human information acquisition is rational, it would be helpful to know what theoretical OED models best capture the value of information. This is difficult in the situations we are considering, because there

---

[1] Suppose there were a gender discrimination task, in which you could choose one feature to look at, to tell whether a person is male or female. Suppose further that one man in the world had a distinctive tattoo on his left arm. The diagnosticity measures consider looking for that tattoo to be an infinitely useful query.

Table 7.2. Usefulness of particular answers, and expected usefulness of questions, in example scenario.

OED theory	eu(*Hula*)	u(*hula*)	u(*~hula*)	eu(*Drink*)	u(*drink*)	u(*~drink*)
probability gain	0.2000	0.1429	0.3333	0.0200	0.0333	0.0143
information gain (bits)	0.1468	0.0597	0.3500	0.0014	0.0032	0.0006
KL distance (bits)	0.1468	0.0597	0.3500	0.0014	0.0032	0.0006
impact	0.2000	0.1429	0.3333	0.0200	0.0333	0.0143
Bayesian diagnosticity	2.7600	1.8000	5.0000	1.0840	1.1429	1.0588
$\log_{10}$ diagnosticity	0.3884	0.2553	0.6990	0.0348	0.0580	0.0248

Note. In this example, $P(glom) = P(fizo) = 0.50$, $P(hula \mid glom) = 0.90$, $P(hula \mid fizo) = 0.50$, $P(drinks \mid glom) = 0.28$, and $P(drinks \mid fizo) = 0.32$. Therefore, $P(hula) = 0.70$, and $P(\sim hula) = 0.30$. The expected utility of the hula hoop question is given by eu(*Hula*). The utility of the answers that the hula hoop is (or is not) worn are given by u(*hula*) and u(*~hula*), respectively.

are no (at least no obvious) unique externally-imposed utility functions. Despite some statements in the literature (Good, 1975, pp. 52–53, said Bayesian diagnosticity 'was central to my first book and occurred also in at least 32 other publications.... What I say thirty-three times is true'), we will refrain from calling any particular utility optimal by definition. Two people could both be perfectly calibrated to the same environment, completely Bayesian in how they update their beliefs as new information is obtained, and yet choose to use different utility functions to evaluate potential queries' usefulness.

One issue in the literature is whether it is better to have a measure of information that is always positive if beliefs change (nonnegativity), such as impact or KL distance; or a measure of information in which two questions' sum utility, if the questions are answered sequentially, is the same as the utility if both questions are answered at once (additivity), such as probability gain or information gain. As a very rough analogy, we can think of current beliefs as a location on a journey to the desired destination, where a single category will have probability one, and the other categories will have probability zero. In this analogy, the various OED models of the utility of information are different metrics of distance traveled (the nonnegative measures), or of the distance remaining toward the destination (the additive measures). Distance traveled may or may not correspond to getting closer to the destination (as lost travelers can attest). It is hopefully intuitive that one could not have a measure that is guaranteed to be positive if beliefs change (e.g. an odometer), and also guaranteed to be additive (because driving in circles is possible, and beliefs sometimes do fluctuate in ways that do not bring the goal closer).

To make this more explicit, suppose a physician determines that a particular patient has Disease A with 76% probability, and Disease B, C, or D each with 8% probability.

Suppose further that a diagnostic test, Test 1, provides evidence against Disease A, such that after seeing the test results the physician determines that each disease has 25% probability. Information gain and probability gain treat these results of Test 1 as having negative utility, whereas the other measures value the change in beliefs. Now suppose that Test 2 provides such strong evidence for Disease A that beliefs once again become 76% Disease A, and 8% for each of the other diseases. Any measure of the value of information that positively values changes in beliefs would regard results of both Test 1 and Test 2 (obtained after Test 1) as useful. KL distance, impact, Bayesian diagnosticity, and log diagnosticity are examples of such measures. By contrast, measures of the value of information that are additive (probability gain and information gain) view results of Test 1 as having negative utility, but results of Test 2 (obtained after Test 1) as having equal and opposite positive utility.

Evans and Over (1996) stated that the possible negativity of information gain was counterintuitive and theoretically problematic. (This criticism would apply equally to probability gain.) Evans and Over were also concerned that the probability of a category might fluctuate, sometimes above 50% and sometimes below 50%, indefinitely, as new information came in. The following section uses an example Planet Vuma scenario which was designed so that it is possible for beliefs about the probability of a category go from 75% to 25%, and back to 75%. The scenario illustrates (1) that indefinite fluctuation of beliefs of this sort is implausible, and (2) that nonnegativity itself can cause counterintuitive results. For instance, Bayesian diagnosticity values both Test 1 and Test 2 in the above medical diagnosis example, if the test results are obtained sequentially. However, if those test results are obtained simultaneously, such that beliefs about the probability of the diseases do not change, then Bayesian diagnosticity does not value them at all, despite the fact that the same information is obtained, and resulting beliefs are identical.

In the discussion below, *F1* refers to the question, whose answer is unknown, about whether or not feature 1 is present, and *f1* and *~f1* are the specific answers that feature 1 is present or not. eu(*F1*) is the expected utility (usefulness) of querying whether or not feature 1 is present; u(*f1*) and u(*~f1*) are the utility of learning that feature 1 is or is not present, respectively. Suppose that $P(glom) = 0.75$, $P(fizo) = 0.25$; $P(f1 \mid glom) = 0.11$, $P(f1 \mid fizo) = 0.99$; $P(f2 \mid glom) = 0.99$, and $P(f2 \mid fizo) = 0.11$. The features are conditionally independent, given the species (there are no symmetries).

Consider two learners, who encounter the same creature, as follows:

— the *sequential learner* first asks about feature 1, learning whether or not it is present, and then asks about feature 2, and learns whether it is present or not;

— the *all-at-once learner* asks about features 1 and 2 in a single question, and learns in one fell swoop whether each feature is present or not.

Both learners have perfect knowledge of environmental statistics and are optimal Bayesians in updating their beliefs. This means that irrespective of what creature they encounter, both learners come to identical posterior beliefs (Table 7.3). Yet if the learners use certain OED models to compute the utility of information, they may disagree about the information's usefulness! Two examples will illustrate.

Table 7.3. Possible feature values and posterior beliefs in example scenario.

Feature values	$f1, f2$	$f1, {\sim}f2$	${\sim}f1, f2$	${\sim}f1, {\sim}f2$
Probability of these feature values	0.1089	0.2211	0.6611	0.0089
P($glom$ | these feature values)	0.7500	0.0037	0.9996	0.7500
P($fizo$ | these feature values)	0.2500	0.9963	0.0004	0.2500

Note: P($glom$)=0.75, P($fizo$) = 0.25, P($f1$ \| $glom$) = 0.11, P($f1$ \| $fizo$) = 0.99, P($f2$ \| $glom$) = 0.99, and P($f2$ \| $fizo$) = 0.11. Features are class-conditionally independent. Probability of these combinations of feature values, and posterior probabilities of the categories, are the same for both the sequential and all-at-once learners.

Both features present case. The vast majority of the time, exactly one feature is present, such that the learner becomes almost certain of the true category once the presence or absence of each feature is known (Table 7.3). (This argues against the assertion that beliefs could fluctuate indefinitely.) About 11% of the time, however, both features are present. For the sequential learner, this causes beliefs about the probability of glom to change from 75% to 25%, after feature 1 is observed, and then back to 75% after feature 2 is observed. For the all-at-once learner, beliefs do not change at all, because P($glom \mid f1, f2$) = 0.75, and P($fizo \mid f1, f2$) = 0.25. Note, again, that both learners had the same prior beliefs, obtained the same information, and have the same posterior beliefs. How does each learner value this information (Table 7.4)? The all-at-once learner considers this information to be useless, irrespective of which OED utility they use to measure the value of information. Sequential learners who use information gain or probability gain to measure the value of information also consider the information to be useless. However, sequential learners who use KL distance, impact,

Table 7.4. How the sequential and all-at-once learners value queries if both features are present, in example scenario.

OED model	Sequential learner: $u(f1) + u(f2 \mid f1)$	All-at-once learner: $u(f1, f2)$
probability gain	0.0000	0.0000
information gain	0.0000	0.0000
KL distance	1.5850	0.0000
Impact	1.0000	0.0000
Bayesian diagnosticity	18.0000	1.0000
$\log_{10}$ diagnosticity	1.9085	0.0000

Note: The two learners have the same posterior beliefs: P($glom \mid f1, f2$) = 0.75, and P($fizo \mid f1, f2$) = 0.25; these beliefs are equal to the prior beliefs. However, if KL distance, impact, Bayesian diagnosticity, or log diagnosticity are used to measure queries' usefulness, the learners disagree about whether the obtained information is useful.

Table 7.5. Sequential learner. Expected usefulness of *F1* question, eu(*F1*). Usefulness of each possible answer to *F1* question, right two columns.

OED model	eu(*F1*)	u(*f1*)	u(~*f1*)
probability gain	0.1650	0.0000	0.2463
information gain	0.5198	0.0000	0.7758
KL distance	0.5198	0.7925	0.3855
impact	0.3300	0.5000	0.2463
Bayesian diagnosticity	62.6000	9.0000	89.0000
log$_{10}$ diagnosticity	1.6210	0.9542	1.9494

Note: P(*f1*) = 0.33, P(~*f1*) = 0.67, eu(*F1*) = 0.33· u(*f1*) + 0.67· u(~*f1*).

Bayesian diagnosticity or log diagnosticity regard each obtained answer as informative, despite the fact that beliefs (in the end) did not change at all!

Expected utility, averaging over all possible answers. Would the two learners agree, even on average, about the usefulness of the obtained information in our example scenario? The sequential learner first experiences the usefulness of the first question (*F1*, about whether feature 1 is present), and then experiences the usefulness of the second question (*F2*), given what they already learned about the first feature. For the sequential learner, then, we need to calculate the expected usefulness of the first question, eu(*F1*) (Table 7.5), plus the expected usefulness of the second question given the first question, eu(*F2* | *F1*) (Table 7.6). For the all-at-once learner, who learns the presence or absence of both features simultaneously, we only need to compute eu(*F1*, *F2*) (Table 7.7). Do the two learners, who obtain the same information and have the same posterior beliefs, equally value that information (Table 7.8)? If the learners use KL distance, probability gain, or information gain, then on average, they equally value the

Table 7.6. Sequential learner. Expected usefulness of *F2* question, given *F1* question, eu(*F1* | *F2*). Usefulness of each possible answer to *F2* question, given each possible answer to *F1* question, in four right columns.

OED model	eu(*F1* | *F2*)	u(*f2* | *f1*)	u(~*f2* | *f1*)	u(*f2* | ~*f1*)	u(~*f2* | ~*f1*)
probability gain	0.0544	0.0000	0.2463	0.0033	−0.2463
information gain	0.1846	0.0000	0.7758	0.0302	−0.7758
KL distance	0.1846	0.7925	0.3855	0.0035	1.2093
impact	0.1133	0.5000	0.2463	0.0033	0.2463
Bayesian diagnosticity	27.4000	9.0000	89.0000	9.0000	89.0000
log$_{10}$ diagnosticity	1.1831	0.9542	1.9494	0.9542	1.9494

Note: See Table 7.3 for the probability of each combination of feature values.

Table 7.7. All-at-once learner. Expected usefulness of $F2$ and $F1$ questions, answered simultaneously, eu($F1$, $F2$). Usefulness of each possible set of answers to $F1$ and $F2$ questions, in four right columns.

OED model	eu(F1, F2)	u(f1, f2)	u(f1, ~f2)	u(~f1, f2)	u(~f1, ~f2)
probability gain	0.2194	0.0000	0.2463	0.2496	0.0000
information gain	0.7044	0.0000	0.7758	0.8060	0.0000
KL distance	0.7044	0.0000	1.9586	0.4104	0.0000
impact	0.3300	0.0000	0.7463	0.2496	0.0000
Bayesian diagnosticity	706.7600	1.0000	801.0000	801.0000	1.0000
$\log_{10}$ diagnosticity	2.5616	0.0000	2.9036	2.9036	0.0000

Note: See Table 7.3 for the probability of each combination of feature values.

obtained information. If the learners use impact, Bayesian diagnosticity, or log diagnosticity, they do not equally value that information, even on average. Suppose the learners were to use Bayesian diagnosticity. For the sequential learner, the total expected diagnosticity is 90 (eu($F1$) = 62.6; eu($F2 \mid F1$) = 27.4). Yet the all-at-once learner values the same information as having expected diagnosticity of 706.76! Which property is more important:

1. additivity, where eu($f1$) + eu($f2 \mid f1$) = eu($f1, f2$); or

2. nonnegativity in cases where beliefs change?

It seems that with respect to these properties, we can have additivity (probability gain, information gain) or nonnegativity (KL distance, impact, Bayesian diagnosticity, log diagnosticity), but not both. The above example shows how lacking additivity can lead to strange contradictions between sequential and all-at-once learners. Is nonnegativity also a critical property? Actually, neuroeconomic theories (e.g. Schultz, 1998) suggest

Table 7.8. Expected usefulness, calculated sequentially (sum of two questions) vs. all at once.

OED model	Sequential learner: eu(F1) + eu(F2 | F1)	All-at-once learner: eu(F1, F2)
probability gain	0.2194	0.2194
information gain	0.7044	0.7044
KL distance	0.7044	0.7044
impact	0.4433	0.3300
Bayesian diagnosticity	90.0000	706.7600
$\log_{10}$ diagnosticity	2.8041	2.5616

Note: learners who use impact, Bayesian diagnosticity, or log diagnosticity will on average experience different sum utility if querying the features sequentially, vs. simultaneously, despite having the same prior and posterior beliefs.

that having negative utility is critical for learning. Savage's (1954, chap. 6) account of information acquisition also allows for zero or negative utility. It is ultimately an empirical question whether people experience some information as having zero or negative utility. Physiological measures such as recording from individual neurons (Nakamura, 2006), or EEG, MEG, fMRI, and galvanic skin response, as well as behavioral experiments, could potentially address this.

Would it ever make sense to use the diagnosticity measures?

Nelson (2005) argued that Bayesian diagnosticity and log diagnosticity are poor theoretical models of the utility of information, and are not needed to explain empirical data. Perhaps because those measures highly (even infinitely) value high certainty, several people have subsequently inquired whether the diagnosticity measures *should* be used in situations that require high certainty. The short answer is no. If a learner wishes to maximize a particular goal, they should directly compute the utility of candidate queries with respect to achieving that goal (Savage, 1954), without use of any OED theories of the value of information. However, we can still ask whether the diagnosticity measures might approximate the learner's goals in situations that require high certainty. This section illustrates that even in situations where high certainty is required, relying on the diagnosticity measures can be counterproductive (Table 7.9). In each situation here:

- querying feature 2 leads to higher probability of achieving the learner's goal;
- KL distance, information gain, impact, and probability gain prefer feature 2;
- Bayesian diagnosticity and log diagnosticity either prefer feature 1 or are indifferent between the features.

Scenario 1. Suppose that the learner must become 99% sure of the true category for the information to be useful, and therefore wishes to maximize the probability that their posterior beliefs will be at least 99% in favor of one category or the other. Would they then want to use Bayesian diagnosticity to choose what question to ask?

Table 7.9. Evidence-acquisition scenarios with more specific goals than information acquisition alone

Scenario	P($glom$)	P($f1$ | $glom$), P($f1$ | $fizo$)	P($f2$ | $glom$), P($f2$ | $fizo$)	Goal considered
1	0.50	0.000, 0.100	0.010, 0.990	achieve 99% probability of either hypothesis
2	0.70	0.000, 0.200	0.000, 0.800	falsify working hypothesis
3	0.70	0.600, 0.001	0.001, 0.800	almost eliminate working hypothesis
4	0.70	0.200, 0.000	0.800, 0.000	eliminate alternate hypothesis

Note: Where P($glom$) = 0.70, glom is the working hypothesis, and fizo is the alternate hypothesis.

Feature 2 offers 100% chance of being useful; feature 1 offers 5% chance of being useful. Yet the Bayesian diagnosticity (and log diagnosticity) of feature 1 is infinitely greater than that of feature 2.

Scenario 2. Suppose the learner needs to falsify their working hypothesis (glom) with 100% confidence for the information to be useful. This goal implements Popper's (1959) suggestion that scientists should do the experiment with the best hope of falsifying their current best hypothesis. Feature 2 falsifies the working hypothesis 24% of the time, whereas feature 1 falsifies the working hypothesis only 6% of the time. Yet Bayesian diagnosticity is indifferent between the features, as both features have infinite diagnosticity.

Scenario 3. Suppose the learner wishes to almost eliminate their working hypothesis (glom), by reducing its probability to no more than 1%. If feature 2 is present, this goal is achieved: $P(glom \mid f2) = 0.0029$; feature 2 is present about 24% of the time. Feature 1 *never* achieves this criterion, yet the diagnosticity measures prefer it.

Scenario 4. Suppose the learner wishes to have the highest probability of eliminating their *alternate* hypothesis (or, equivalently, achieving 100% confidence in their working hypothesis). If either feature is present, the alternate hypothesis is ruled-out. Feature 2 is present four times as often as feature 1 (56% versus 14% of the time). Yet the diagnosticity measures are indifferent between the features.

Research to date. Which OED model best explains human intuitions?

Several articles (Table 7.10), involving a diverse set of tasks, have examined whether human (or monkey) information acquisition follows OED principles. Some recent work has even explored whether eye movements could also be modeled in an OED framework, where each eye movement is modeled as a query of the visual scene that returns high-resolution information from the center of gaze and lower-resolution information from the periphery.

Which OED model best approximates human intuitions about the value of information, and choices of questions to ask? Most articles use only a single OED theory of information. Thus, it is entirely possible that different theories would disagree about which queries are most informative, and about whether human information acquisition is rational. To address this possibility, Nelson (2005) re-analyzed the tasks in several articles (Skov & Sherman, 1986; Baron *et al.*, 1988; Slowiaczek *et al.*, 1992; Oaksford & Chater, 2003; McKenzie & Mikkelsen, 2007) to identify the predictions of each of six OED models of the value of information, on each task. There was high agreement between models on which questions were most (and least) useful.[2]

---

[2] An important caveat is that small changes in the hypotheses and prior probabilities in a model can have strong implications on the apparent usefulness of subjects' queries (Nelson, 2005; Nelson *et al.*, 2001). How can researchers know what hypotheses and prior probabilities most accurately model subjects' beliefs? The complexity of various hypotheses (Feldman 2000, 2003, 2006; Nelson & Cottrell, 2007), meta-hypotheses about the types of hypothesis spaces that are feasible (Kemp *et al.*, 2006), generalization ratings (Tenenbaum, 1999, 2000; Tenenbaum & Griffiths, 2001), and error data can provide guidance. Use of natural sampling

Table 7.10. Value of information tasks that have been modeled in an OED framework

Task	References
Medical diagnosis	Good & Card (1971); Card & Good (1974); Baron, Beattie, & Hershey (1988)
Personality characteristics	Trope & Bassok (1982, 1983); Bassok & Trope (1983–1984)
Planet Vuma	Skov & Sherman (1986); Slowiaczek et al. (1992); Garcia-Marques et al. (2001); Nelson (2005); McKenzie (2006)
Selection task, Reduced array selection task	Oaksford & Chater (1994, 1996, 1998, 2003); Laming (1996); Over & Jessop (1998); Oaksford et al. (1997, 1999); Klauer (1999); Hattori (2002); Oaksford & Wakefield (2003)
Covariation assessment	McKenzie & Mikkelsen (2006)
Hypothesis testing	Klayman & Ha (1987); Klayman (1987)
2-4-6 task, active number concept task	Baron (1985); Ginzburg & Sejnowski (1996); Nelson & Movellan (2001); Nelson et al. (2001)
Alien mind reading (inferring causal structure)	Steyvers et al. (2003)
Urns and poker chips	Baron (1985)
Eyewitness identification	Wells & Lindsay (1980); Wells & Olson (2002)
Social contingency detection	Movellan (2005)
Eye movement tasks:	
Free viewing	Lee & Yu (2000); Itti & Baldi (2006); Bruce & Tsotsos (2006)
Reading	Legge et al. (1997, 2002); Legge et al. (2002)
Visual search	Najemnik & Geisler (2005); Zhang & Cottrell (submitted)
Shape learning	Renninger et al. (2005, 2007)
Contrast entropy reduction	Raj et al. (2005)
Target detection	Nakamura (2006)
Concept learning	Nelson & Cottrell (2007)

Note: Most of the articles here concerned experimental data with human subjects; some were purely theoretical. Pseudodiagnosticity articles (e.g. Doherty et al., 1996) address similar issues. Some eye movement models are 'bottom-up,' driven by image properties in a task-blind manner, in an OED

....

to convey environmental statistics to subjects (Knowlton et al., 1994; Oaksford & Wakefield, 2003) may help ensure that subjects assimilate the hypothesized probabilities better than via reading words and numbers alone. People seem well calibrated to statistics of visual scenes (Knill & Richards, 1996; Kersten et al., 2004; Yuille et al., 2004; Knill, 2006). Given this, eye movement tasks, in which each eye movement is modeled as a query of a visual scene, can also be helpful. Irrespective of how subjects learn prior probabilities, it is helpful to show (1) that subjects' beliefs are accurately described by a particular probability model, or (2) that the ordering of the usefulness of various queries does not depend on which plausible model best describes subjects' beliefs.

This result supported the feasibility of a rational (Anderson, 1990) theory of information acquisition, suggesting that irrespective of which OED model is the best motivated theoretically, human behavior closely agrees with it. However, this result left unclear which theoretical model best matches human intuitions.

Is it possible to differentiate which OED models best describe human intuitions? Nelson (2005) used computer optimization to find a limiting scenario in which the various OED models strongly disagree about which features are most useful, and then tested that scenario (Table 7.11) with human subjects. Subjects were asked to rank order the features from most to least useful, if they could just ask about one feature to classify a creature as a glom or fizo. Most OED models predict that the harmonica feature will be ranked as most useful, and the hula feature as least useful. Bayesian diagnosticity and log diagnosticity, however, hold that the hula feature is infinitely useful, because it sometimes (with probability 1 in 200) leads to certainty of the true species.

What did the 148 subjects think? Responses were strongly positively correlated with most OED models (Spearman rank correlations of 0.69–0.78), yet negatively correlated with Bayesian diagnosticity (correlation = -0.41) and with log diagnosticity (correlation = -0.22). A majority of the subjects gave a rank order that exactly matched information gain, KL distance, impact, or probability gain. No subjects gave a rank order that matched either Bayesian diagnosticity or log diagnosticity. This result suggests that the diagnosticity measures do not provide the most accurate approximation of human intuitions about the value of information.

Results from Nelson's (2005) experiment do not distinguish among probability gain, impact, information gain, and KL distance, because the predictions of those models were highly (or perfectly) correlated. Nelson did describe situations in which the remaining theories make moderately contradictory predictions. However, these situations include unequal prior probabilities of the categories (glom and fizo), which could not be effectively conveyed to subjects with a words-and-numbers-based experiment. If the desired environmental probabilities could be effectively conveyed to subjects, it could prove feasible to discriminate which of the remaining OED models best describes human intuitions.

Table 7.11. Features used in Nelson's (2005) behavioral experiment

	Drink	Harmonica	Gurgle	Hula
P(*feature* | *glom*)	0.0001	0.01	0.30	0.99
P(*feature* | *fizo*)	0.30	0.99	0.70	1.00

Note: Prior P(*glom*) = P(*fizo*) = 0.50. From Table 10 in Nelson (2005), copyright American Psychological Association; adapted with permission.

Suboptimal heuristics vs. OED models

The research discussed in the chapter suggests that OED theories provide a good approximation to human intuition about the usefulness of information. But do OED theories provide the best descriptive account? Perhaps people rely on heuristic strategies that only partly approximate optimal models. How could we tell? Here we briefly consider three heuristic strategies that have been reported in the literature. (Many others, including fast and frugal heuristics, e.g. Chase *et al.*, 1998, could be considered as well.)

Feature difference heuristic. Skov and Sherman (1986), and Slowiaczek *et al.* (1992) noted that many subjects query features with the highest absolute difference in feature probabilities, e.g. the feature with maximal abs($P(f \mid h_1)$—$P(f \mid h_2)$). Those authors called this strategy heuristic, implying that it is suboptimal. However, Nelson (2005), who also observed this heuristic empirically, proved that the feature difference heuristic exactly implements the impact OED model. This is true in all situations where there are two categories of objects and binary features, irrespective of the prior probabilities of the categories and the specific feature probabilities. Because the feature difference heuristic exactly implements an optimal model, its use does not support claims of suboptimality in human information acquisition.

Information bias. Baron *et al.* (1988) reported that even when a feature (a medical test, in their experiment) had zero probability gain, subjects judged it as useful if it would change beliefs. Baron *et al.* called this phenomenon information bias. This phenomenon may be a bias if probability gain, which Baron *et al.* used as their normative benchmark, is uniquely applicable as a normative model. However, information gain, KL distance, and impact also value queries that lead to changed beliefs but not improvement in probability of correct guess. In other words, whether or not information bias is in fact a bias depends on what normative model one applies to the situation.

Hypothesis confirmation. Skov and Sherman (1986), in a planet Vuma scenario, defined hypothesis-confirming queries as testing features for which $P(f \mid h_1) > P(f \mid h_2)$, where h_1 is the focal hypothesis. (As Klayman, 1995, noted, if Bayes' theorem is used to update beliefs, no question can introduce bias, although some questions can be more informative than others. Skov and Sherman's definition of hypothesis confirmation, which we adopt here, implies that a feature's presence favors h_1, and its absence favors h_2.) The questions available to subjects in Skov and Sherman's experiment included a variety of high, medium, and low usefulness features. Most subjects were in conditions where glom or fizo was marked as the working hypothesis, such that features could also be classified as confirmatory or disconfirmatory. Subjects were very sensitive to usefulness: about 74% of choices of questions were to high usefulness features, 21% to medium usefulness features, and 4% to low usefulness features (chance would be 33% each). Were subjects also influenced by hypothesis confirmation? Despite Skov and Sherman's statement (p. 93, echoed later in reviews by Klayman, 1995, Nickerson, 1998) that subjects showed a 'strong and consistent tendency to ask hypothesis-confirming questions,' the evidence was comparatively weak. About 60% of choices were to hypothesis-confirming features (chance would be 50%). This result is consistent with 80% of subjects being indifferent to whether a feature is hypothesis-confirming or not, and just 20% of subjects preferring hypothesis-confirming features.

But because there was no tradeoff between usefulness and hypothesis confirmation, the results do not show whether *any* subject would give up *any* information to test a hypothesis-confirming feature.

Optimal experimental design as a way to implement strong inference

By and large, research to date suggests that human information acquisition is in good accord with rational (Bayesian optimal experimental design) principles, on a wide variety of tasks. In situations where some OED theories are better motivated than others, the better-motivated theories tend to better describe human intuitions and queries. Yet the tasks studied to date barely scratch the surface of the theoretical issues that are important in information acquisition. For instance, planning several steps ahead is more efficient than just planning the next query, but little research has studied sequential queries. Similarly, whether human information acquisition is sensitive to class-conditional feature dependencies (such as bilateral symmetries in vertebrates) is not known. Some research suggests that monkey eye movements (Nakamura, 2006) may follow OED principles. It would be helpful to also study other cases of perceptual information acquisition, such as bat echolocation and rat whisking. Can OED principles be used to design the most informative experiments for addressing these issues?

Platt (1964), inspired by a tradition of scientific thought, suggested that science progresses most quickly when scientists enumerate alternate hypotheses to explain a phenomenon, devise experiments in which those hypotheses make strongly contradictory predictions, and then conduct those experiments. A limit in some research is that the stimuli were not designed to maximally differentiate between competing theoretical models. In some cases the theoretical account reduces to 'theory X claims query 1 is more useful than query 2; subjects agree; therefore subjects follow theory X.' The problem is that if every theory holds that query 1 is more useful than query 2, it is neither surprising nor interesting that people agree. A challenge in future work is to find and test cases in which candidate theories most strongly disagree about which queries people will conduct. If people have strong intuitions and consistent behavior in those cases, the results will of course contribute to theory of human information acquisition. But equally importantly, those scenarios may enhance our own developing concepts (Baron 2002, 2004) of what utilities are best suited to quantify the value of information in scientific inference and in other tasks.

Author note

I thank Nick Chater, Ulrike Hahn, and Mike Oaksford both for ideas towards the research discussed here, and for helpful feedback on a draft manuscript; Flavia Filimon, Craig McKenzie, Javier Movellan, Jon Baron, Terry Sejnowski, and Gary Cottrell for research ideas; Craig Fox for suggesting certain scenarios in the 'Would it ever make sense to use the diagnosticity measures' section; Tim Marks for suggesting the 'blinding light and blowing sand' interpretation of planet Vuma; and NIH T32 MH020002–04 to T. Sejnowski. Any corrections will be posted at http://www.jonathandnelson.com/.

References

Anderson, J. R. (1990). *The adaptive character of thought*. Hillsdale, NJ: Erlbaum.

Baron, J. (1985). *Rationality and intelligence*. Cambridge, England: Cambridge University Press.

Baron, J. (2002). *Value trade-offs and the nature of utility: Bias, inconsistency, protected values, and other problems*. Paper for conference on behavioral economics. American Institute for Economic Research, Great Barrington, MA, July, 2002.

Baron, J. (2004). Normative models of judgment and decision making. In D. J. Koehler & N. Harvey (Eds.), *Blackwell handbook of judgment and decision making* (pp. 19–36). London: Blackwell.

Baron, J., Beattie, J., & Hershey, J. C. (1988). Heuristics and biases in diagnostic reasoning: II. Congruence, information, and certainty. *Organizational Behavior and Human Decision Processes*, **42**, 88–110.

Baron, J., & Hershey, J. C. (1988). Heuristics and biases in diagnostic reasoning: I. Priors, error costs, and test accuracy. *Organizational Behavior and Human Decision Processes*, **41**, 259–279.

Bassok, M., & Trope, Y. (1983–1984). People's strategies for testing hypotheses about another's personality: Confirmatory or diagnostic? *Social Cognition*, **2**, 199–216.

Bayes, T. (1763). An essay towards solving a problem in the doctrine of chances. *Philosophical Transactions of the Royal Society of London*, **53**, 370–418.

Box, G., & Hill, W. (1967). Discrimination among mechanistic models. *Technometrics*, **9**, 57–71.

Bruce, N., & Tsotsos, J. K. (2006). Saliency Based on Information Maximization. In Y Weiss, B Sch&oumlaut;lkopf, & J Platt (Eds.), *Advances in neural information processing systems* (Vol. 18, pp. 155–162). Cambridge, MA: MIT Press.

Card, W. I., & Good, I. J. (1974). A logical analysis of medicine. In R. Passmore & J. S. Robson (Eds.), *A companion to medical studies* (Vol. 3, pp. 60.1–60.23). Oxford, England: Blackwell.

Chase, V. M., Hertwig, R., & Gigerenzer, G. (1998) Visions of rationality. *Trends in Cognitive Science*, **2**(6), 206–214.

Chater, N., Crocker, M., & Pickering, M. (1998). The rational analysis of inquiry: The case for parsing. In N. Chater & M. Oaksford (Eds.), *Rational models of cognition* (pp. 441–468). Oxford, England: Oxford University Press.

Chater, N., & Oaksford, M. (1999). The probability heuristics model of syllogistic reasoning. *Cognitive Psychology*, **38**, 191–258.

Cover, T. M., & Thomas, J. A. (1991). *Elements of information theory*. New York: Wiley.

Doherty, M. E., Chadwick, R., Garavan, H., Barr, D., & Mynatt, C. R. (1996). On people's understanding of the diagnostic implications of probabilistic data. *Memory & Cognition*, **24**, 644–654.

Evans, J. St. B. T., & Over, D. E. (1996). Rationality in the selection task: Epistemic utility versus uncertainty reduction. *Psychological Review*, **103**, 356–363.

Fedorov, V. V. (1972). *Theory of optimal experiments*. New York: Academic Press.

Feldman, J. (2000). Minimization of Boolean complexity in human concept learning. *Nature*, **407**, 630–633.

Feldman, J. (2003). The simplicity principle in human concept learning. *Current Directions in Psychological Science*, **6**, 227–232.

Feldman, J. (2006). An algebra of human concept learning. *Journal of Mathematical Psychology*, **50**, 339–368.

Garcia-Marques, L., Sherman, S. J., & Palma-Oliveira. J. M. (2001). Hypothesis testing and the perception of diagnosticity. *Journal of Experimental Social Psychology*, **37**, 183–200.

Good, I. J. (1950). *Probability and the weighing of evidence*. New York: Griffin.

Good, I. J. (1975). Explicativity, corroboration, and the relative odds of hypotheses. *Synthese*, **30**, 39–73.

Good, I. J. (1983). *Good thinking*. Minneapolis: University of Minnesota.

Good, I. J., & Card, W. I. (1971). The diagnostic process with special reference to errors. *Methods of Information in Medicine*, **10**, 176–188.

Itti, L., & Baldi, P. (2006). Bayesian surprise attracts human attention. In Y. Weiss, B. Scholköpf, & J. Platt (Eds.), *Advances in neural information processing systems* (Vol. 18, pp. 547–554). Cambridge, MA: MIT Press.

Kemp, C., Perfors, A., & Tenenbaum, J. B. (2006). Learning overhypotheses. In *Proceedings of the Twenty-Eighth Annual Conference of the Cognitive Science Society* (pp. 417–422).

Kersten, D., Mamassian, P., & Yuille, A. (2004). Object perception as Bayesian inference. *Annual Review of Psychology*, **55**, 271–304. doi:10.1146/annurev.psych.55.090902.142005

Klauer, K. C. (1999). On the normative justification for information gain in Wason's selection task. *Psychological Review*, **106**, 215–222.

Klayman, J. (1987). An information theory analysis of the value of information in hypothesis testing. Retrieved May 23, 2005, from http://www.chicagocdr.org/cdrpubs/

Klayman, J. (1995). Varieties of confirmation bias. In J. R. Busemeyer, R. Hastie, & D. L. Medin (Eds.), *Decision making from a cognitive perspective*. New York: Academic Press.

Klayman, J., & Ha, Y.-W. (1987). Confirmation, disconfirmation, and information. *Psychological Review*, **94**, 211–228.

Knill, D. C. (2006). Learning Bayesian priors for depth perception [Abstract]. *Journal of Vision*, **6**(6), 412, 412a, http://journalofvision.org/6/6/412/, doi:10.1167/6.6.412.

Knill, D. C., & Richards, W. (Eds.). (1996). *Perception as Bayesian inference*. Cambridge, UK: Cambridge University Press.

Knowlton, B. J., Squire, L. R., & Gluck, M. A. (1994). Probabilistic classification learning in amnesia. *Learning and Memory*, **1**, 106–120.

Kullback, S., & Liebler, R. A. (1951). Information and sufficiency. *Annals of Mathematical Statistics*, **22**, 79–86.

Laming, D. (1996). On the analysis of irrational data selection: A critique of Oaksford and Chater (1994). *Psychological Review*, **103**, 364–373.

Lee, T. S., & Yu, S. X. (2000). An information-theoretic framework for understanding saccadic eye movements. In S. A. Solla, T. K. Leen, & K.-R. Müller (Eds.), *Advances in neural information processing systems* (Vol. 12, pp. 834–840). Cambridge, MA: MIT Press.

Legge, G. E.; Hooven, T. A.; Klitz, T. S.; Mansfield, J. S., & Tjan, B. S. (2002). Mr. Chips 2002: New insights from an ideal-observer model of reading. *Vision Research*, **42**, 2219–2234.

Legge, G. E.; Klitz, T. S., & Tjan, B. S. (1997). Mr. Chips: An ideal observer model of reading. *Psychological Review*, **104**, 524–553.

Lindley, D. V. (1956). On a measure of the information provided by an experiment. *Annals of Mathematical Statistics*, **27**, 986–1005.

McKenzie, C. R. M. (2006). Increased sensitivity to differentially diagnostic answers using familiar materials: Implications for confirmation bias. *Memory and Cognition*, **23**(3), 577–588.

McKenzie, C. R. M., & Mikkelsen, L. A. (2006). A Bayesian view of covariation assessment. *Cognitive Psychology*, **54**(1), 33–61. doi:10.1016/j.cogpsych.2006.04.004

Movellan, J. R. (2005). An infomax controller for real time detection of contingency. In *Proceedings of the International Conference on Development and Learning*, Osaka, Japan, July, 2005.

Najemnik, J., & Geisler, W. S. (2005, March 17). Optimal eye movement strategies in visual search. *Nature*, **434**, 387–391.

Nakamura, K. (2006). Neural representation of information measure in the primate premotor cortex. *Journal of Neurophysiology*, **96**, 478–485.

Nelson, J. D. (2005). Finding useful questions: On Bayesian diagnosticity, probability, impact, and information gain. *Psychological Review*, **112**(4), 979–999.

Nelson, J. D., & Cottrell, G. W. (2007). A probabilistic model of eye movements in concept formation. *Neurocomputing*. doi:10.1016/j.neucom.2006.02.026

Nelson, J. D., & Movellan, J. R. (2001). Active inference in concept learning. *Advances in Neural Information Processing Systems*, **13**, 45–51.

Nelson, J. D., Tenenbaum, J. B., & Movellan, J. R. (2001). Active inference in concept learning. In J. D. Moore, & K. Stenning (Eds.), In *Proceedings of the 23rd Conference of the Cognitive Science Society* (pp. 692–697). Mahwah, NJ: Erlbaum.

Nickerson, R. S. (1996). Hempel's paradox and Wason's selection task: Logical and psychological puzzles of confirmation. *Thinking and Reasoning*, **2**, 1–32.

Nickerson, R. S. (1998). Confirmation bias: A ubiquitous phenomenon in many guises. *Review of General Psychology*, **2**(2), 175–220.

Oaksford, M., & Chater, N. (1994). A rational analysis of the selection task as optimal data selection. *Psychological Review*, **101**, 608–631.

Oaksford, M., & Chater, N. (1996). Rational explanation of the selection task. *Psychological Review*, **103**, 381–391.

Oaksford, M., & Chater, N. (1998). A revised rational analysis of the selection task: Exceptions and sequential sampling. In M. Oaksford & N. Chater (Eds.), *Rational models of cognition* (pp. 372–393). Oxford, England: Oxford University Press.

Oaksford, M., & Chater, N. (2003). Optimal data selection: Revision, review, and reevaluation. *Psychonomic Bulletin & Review*, **10**, 289–318.

Oaksford, M., & Wakefield, M. (2003). Data selection and natural sampling: Probabilities do matter. *Memory & Cognition*, **31**(1), 143–154.

Oaksford, M., Chater, N., & Grainger, B. (1999). Probabilistic effects in data selection. *Thinking and Reasoning*, **5**, 193–243.

Oaksford, M., Chater, N., Grainger, B., & Larkin, J. (1997). Optimal data selection in the reduced array selection task (RAST). *Journal of Experimental Psychology: Learning, Memory, and Cognition*, **23**, 441–458.

Over, D., & Jessop, A. (1998). Rational analysis of causal conditionals and the selection task. In M. Oaksford & N. Chater (Eds.), *Rational models of cognition* (pp. 399–414). Oxford, England: Oxford University Press.

Platt, J. R. (1964). Strong inference. *Science*, **146**(3642), 347–353.

Popper, K. R. (1959). *The logic of scientific discovery*. London: Hutchinson.

Raj, R., Geisler, W. S., Frazor, R. A., & Bovik, A. C. (2005). Contrast statistics for foveated visual systems: Fixation selection by minimizing contrast entropy. *Journal of the Optical Society of America, A: Optics, Image Science, and Vision*, **22**(10), 2039–2049.

Renninger, L. W., Coughlan, J., Verghese, P., & Malik, J. (2005). An information maximization model of eye movements. In L. K. Saul, Y. Weiss, & L. Bottou (Eds.), *Advances in neural information processing systems* (Vol. 17, pp. 1121–1128). Cambrdige, MA: MIT Press.

Renninger, L. W., Verghese, P., & Coughlan, J. (2007). Where to look next? Eye movements reduce local uncertainty. *Journal of Vision*, 7(3), 6, 1–17, http://journalofvision.org/7/3/6/, doi:10.1167/7.3.6.

Savage, L. J. (1954). *The foundations of statistics*. New York: Wiley.

Schultz, W. (1998). Predictive reward signal of dopamine neurons. *Journal of Neurophysiology*, **80**, 1–27.

Shannon, C. E. (1948). A mathematical theory of communication. *The Bell System Technical Journal*, **27**, 379–423, 623–656.

Skov, R. B., & Sherman, S. J. (1986). Information-gathering processes: Diagnosticity, hypothesis-confirmatory strategies, and perceived hypothesis confirmation. *Journal of Experimental Social Psychology*, **22**, 93–121.

Slowiaczek, L. M., Klayman, J., Sherman, S. J., & Skov, R. B. (1992). Information selection and use in hypothesis testing: What is a good question, and what is a good answer? *Memory & Cognition*, **20**, 392–405.

Steyvers, M., Tenenbaum, J. B., Wagenmakers, E.-J., & Blum, B. (2003). Inferring causal networks from observations and interventions. *Cognitive Science*, **27**, 453–489.

Tenenbaum, J. B. (1999). *A Bayesian framework for concept learning*. Ph.D. Thesis, MIT.

Tenenbaum, J. B. (2000). Rules and similarity in concept learning. In S. A. Solla, T. K. Leen, & K.-R. Müller (Eds.), *Advances in neural information processing systems* (Vol. 12, pp. 59–65). Cambridge, MA: MIT Press.

Tenenbaum, J. B., & Griffiths, T. L. (2001). Generalization, similarity, and Bayesian inference. *Behavioral and Brain Sciences*, **24**(4), 629–640.

Trommershäuser, J., Maloney, L. T., & Landy, M. S. (2003). Statistical decision theory and trade-offs in the control of motor response. *Spatial Vision*, **16**(3–4), 255–275.

Trope, Y., & Bassok, M. (1982). Confirmatory and diagnosing strategies in social information gathering. *Journal of Personality and Social Psychology*, **43**, 22–34.

Trope, Y., & Bassok, M. (1983). Information-gathering strategies in hypothesis testing. *Journal of Experimental and Social Psychology*, **19**, 560–576.

Wells, G. L., & Lindsay, R. C. L. (1980). On estimating the diagnosticity of eyewitness nonidentifications. *Psychological Bulletin*, **88**, 776–784.

Wells, G. L., & Olson, E. A. (2002). Eyewitness identification: Information gain from incriminating and exonerating behaviors. *Journal of Experimental Psychology: Applied*, **8**, 155–167.

Yuille, A. L., Fang, F., Schrater, P., & Kersten, D. (2004). Human and ideal observers for detecting image curves. In S. Thrun; L. Saul & B. Schoelkopf (Eds.), *Advances in neural information processing systems* (Vol. 16). Cambridge, MA: MIT Press.

Zhang, L., & Cottrell, G. W. (submitted). Probabilistic search 1.0: a new theory of visual search.

Chapter 8

Pseudocontingencies—A key paradigm for understanding adaptive cognition

Klaus Fiedler

Universität Heidelberg, Heidelberg, Germany

The probabilistic mind has to mirror the structure of the probabilistic world. Because the mind reflects the environment, the topic of the present volume should not be misunderstood as referring only to intrapsychic processes within individual organisms' brains or minds. Rather, the 'probabilistic mind' refers to the adaptive match between cognitive functions and environmental tasks and affordances. Studying the probabilistic mind calls for a cognitive-ecological approach that relates mental functions to environmental structures, rather than a purely cognitive approach that relates individual mental functions to micro-level intrapsychic processes, such as neuronal processes. In this respect, the cognitive-ecological perspective that guides the present article, and most other articles in the present book, may be conceived as complementary to a neuro-scientific approach to the human mind. The cognitive illusion that is in the focus of the present chapter—called pseudocontingencies—highlights the need to study the top-down constraints imposed by the environment on cognitive behavior, which are quite distinct from the bottom-up constraints of internal neuronal processes.

The nature of the probabilistic world

Before I can explain and illustrate the key concept of pseudocontingencies, a moment of reflection is in order about the nature of the probabilistic world. What renders nature so uncertain and so difficult to handle? A most common answer suggests, like the title of this book, that difficulty arises because the world is probabilistic, rather than deterministic. Real correlations are hardly ever perfect. Although there is no question that imperfect, probabilistic correlations are more difficult to represent in memory than deterministic relations, I believe that this idea provides only an impoverished picture of the actual vicissitudes of the complex world. Imperfect, merely probabilistic relations between environmental variables need not in and of themselves be taxing and complicating. They can be quite plausible, natural, and they can create optimism. That the relationship between socio-economic status and income is less than perfect creates hope and chances in those belonging to the lower social class. Any optimism presupposes that the future world is not totally determined. Thus, probabilistic relations are desired properties in a world that should be predictable on one hand while leaving latitude for change and improvement on the other hand.

What is really bothersome and a permanent source of conflict and erroneous decisions, though, is the fact that the 'true' relationship that actually holds between any two variables is often ambiguous, or indeterminate, because there is more than one correct or best solution. To illustrate this ultimate source of uncertainty, which pervades virtually all normative models of rational behavior, let us look for the common denominator underlying the following paradigms of psychological research:

(a) A *delay of gratification* task (Metcalf & Mischel, 1999) involves a forced choice between one option leading to a relative short-term advantage (e.g., shorter education → earlier job with a reasonable income) and another option leading to a relative long-term advantage (longer education → qualification for greater variety of jobs). Determining the 'best' option involves a trade-off between short-term and long-term utilities, and a decision for the most appropriate time frame to assess the utility. There is no *a priori* principle saying that a long-term frame is more 'real' or 'more rational' than a short-term frame.

(b) A *dilemma* task is by definition a task that involves a conflict between two strategies, to defect or to cooperate. The pay-off of defecting is higher at the level of individual trials. However, averaging across many trials of a dilemma game, cooperation is the more successful strategy, because extended defection evokes negative payoffs or sanctions from the environment that override the seeming advantage. What strategy is optimal cannot be determined absolutely. It depends on the level of analysis, as evident in economists' differential treatment of single-shot games and games repeated over multiple trials.

(c) Many *optimizing* problems call for a choice between two options. An animal whose major adaptive task is to find and collect food may experience that the average amount of food is higher in location A than in location B. At the level of the individual animal, then, it is rational to move to A. However, when aggregating over many individuals of the same species, this implies that other animals will move to A as well, causing a hard and dangerous competition for resources and a virtual decrease in the actual amount of food provided well below the average amount that could be expected from the less prominent location B.

(d) Conversely, *Simpson's (1951) paradox* typically starts with an overall correlation showing that, say, more female than male applicants for graduate studies are rejected. However, as this aggregate relationship is broken down to a lower level of analysis, the apparent correlation turns out to be spurious. Within both of two graduate programs, females are more successful than males. The apparent disadvantage of females in the overall analysis merely reflects the fact that most females apply to the more difficult graduate program with a greatly enhanced rejection rate. In other words, when the impact of the unequal graduate programs is partialled out (i.e., when changing from an overall to a more specific level of analysis), the sign of the observed correlation is reversed. Again, there is no *a priori* basis for considering the partial correlation more correct than the zero-order correlation. To be sure, it is possible that a true female advantage is only visible when the impact of specific programs is controlled for. However, it is also possible that the higher rejection rate of the seemingly more difficult program merely reflects a higher rate of female applicants.

(e) When it comes to *correlations over time*, spectral analysis or time series analysis tells us that the correlation that holds between two variables over time depends on the frequency or periodic unit. Sometimes, correlations emerge strongly when considering time segments of seconds or milliseconds (e.g., EEG data) but disappear when aggregating measures over larger time units. Other trends of correlations can only be assessed at the level of long-term moving averages (e.g., the global warming effect and its correlates). In still other domains (e.g., the stock market), correlations (e.g., between share values and unemployment rates) may be positive in the short run and negative in the long run. In general, time-series analyses highlight the fact that different frequency filters render different phenomena visible.

(f) Last but not least, to add a prominent example from social psychology, the *hidden-profile* paradigm in group decision making (Mojzisch & Schulz-Hardt, 2006; Stasser & Titus, 1985) involves divergent decision preferences at the levels of the entire group and its individual members. One option excels in the information available to individual decision makers; applying an 'optimal' majority or Condorcet rule (Hastie & Kameda, 2005) will lead the group to choose this very option. However, when all information distributed over all group members is shared by communication, another option may be superior. Although the common premise in this paradigm is that the group-level information is the validity criterion, there is no rational basis for this assumption. It is very possible that the quality of the totally shared information is worse than the individual-level information. In any case, correlations and preference structures can change and even reverse when information is aggregated over individuals or group members—a huge challenge for all democratic societies. Thomas Schelling's (1978) book on micromotives and macrobehavior anticipated these intriguing insights three decades ago.

Ecological correlations provide a statistical model

All these paradigms share, as a common denominator, the disillusioning insight that globally correct solutions for these puzzles and pitfalls of the probabilistic world may not exist. What is correct, rational, or beneficial can only be determined locally, that is, conditional on pragmatic assumptions that specify a specific perspective, aggregation level, or units of analysis. Standard normative models, such as correlation statistics or Bayesian calculus, only afford a locally rational solution, once a specific perspective and level of analysis has been chosen. They offer no way of dealing with the trade-off between the solutions pertinent to different aggregation levels.

For a statistical model of the generic structure underlying these multi-level problems, let us refer back to the old notion of ecological correlations, which provides a starting point for our recent research on pseudocontingencies, the focus of the present chapter. As indicated by Robinson (1950) and explained statistically by Hammond (1973), the correlation between race and illiteracy can be close to zero when computed across individuals. However, when computed at the level of districts or larger ecologies, the correlation between the average rate of Black people and the average illiteracy rate can rise to over +0.90. In a similar vein, the correlation between price and quality can vary greatly when computed over either individual consumer products or markets or providers. Or, the relation between socio-economic status and academic performance can be quite different when considering either individual students, or entire classes, or school systems.

One must not discard these examples as simply reflecting reliability artefacts (i.e., the enhanced reliability of aggregate units of measurement). Indeed, it is easy to find correlations that are stronger at individual than at aggregate levels. The actual reason for divergent correlations is that different causal factors can be operating at different levels. Consider the following example, which provides a generative model to understand and simulate the degree of divergence between aggregation levels that is possible. Imagine there are 50 towns in a country, differing in the tourist ratio (relative to the total population of a town) and the average consumption rate (i.e., the amount of money spent by an average person on a day). Across all towns, the correlation between tourism and consumption is probably very high, because nice towns attract both tourists and rich people whereas nasty towns will remain for poor people and have few tourists. In contrast, assuming that all residents of the country have a clearly higher income than tourists from other countries (if the focal country is, say, Switzerland), the individual correlation between tourism and consumption (within towns) may be negative. That is, the higher the rate of tourists (with markedly lower income) in any town, the lower the consumption. Thus, a causal parameter of towns (i.e., attractiveness) can account for a high positive correlation, while a causal parameter for individuals (i.e., income) can account for the co-existing negative correlation. No artifact is involved. The two correlations are equally correct. They just reflect a genuine divergence between aggregation levels. Using this problem for recent simulations and decision experiments, it was easily possible to create co-existing correlations as positive as +0.76 at town level and, yet, as negative as −0.48 at individual level.[1]

Problems like these are neither artifactual nor far-fetched. In many real-world domains, they appear to be the rule rather than the exception. In psychological research, for instance—to put the finger on a nearby-ecology—researchers use to employ group data to make inferences about genuinely individual processes (such as memory or emotions). There is no guarantee, however, even in experimental research, that group aggregates reflect the same relationships that exist within individuals and that

---

[1] To simulate n individuals' consumption, one only has to use a (e.g., normally distributed) random variable of inter-individual consumption differences and add a salary parameters for residents (rather than tourists) and to add an attractiveness parameter a for all people (residents as well as tourists) in attractive towns. Depending on the value of a and s, relative to the variance between individuals, the resulting correlations can differ markedly.

are often the focus of theoretical interest.[2] Researchers who commit the category mistake to base inferences about individual processes on group averages come very close to the pseudocontingency illusion to be introduced next.

The pseudocontingency illusion—a cognitive analog of ecological bias

For a more vivid illustration of this cognitive illusion, which can be understood as a cognitive analog of Robinson's (1950) ecological bias, consider a teacher who is confronted with the task of evaluating and grading the performance of boys and girls in a physics class (cf. Fig. 8.1). Imagine a teacher who, at the beginning of a new school year, enters a class that has a high baserate of boys (75%) and a high baserate of high achievement (75% correct responses). In another class, then, the teacher encounters a low baserate of boys (25%) jointly with a low baserate of good achievement (25%). Empathizing with the teacher, we understand that at this point she will already assume a positive correlation between male gender and achievement in physics. This conviction will increase to certainty when there are two other classes, again one with high baserates and one with low baserates of both attributes. However, a glance at individual students' performance shows that within all four classes, the good-achievement rate is lower for boys than for girls (see Fig. 8.1). Pooling across all four classes, the correlation turns out to be zero. A teacher who—like the empathic reader of this paragraph—believes to have experienced an advantage of boys although boys are in fact not superior, or even inferior, to girls, has fallen prey to the pseudocontingency (PC) illusion.[3]

Definition of the PC illusion

How can the PC illusion be defined and explicated more precisely?—To introduce the concept, consider the elementary case of a relation between two variables, X and Y, in a two-dimensional space. (A more general definition extends to an n-dimensional relation in n-dimensional space.) To keep within the preceding example, let X and Y be two dichotomous variables, student gender and achievement. The genuine contingency between these two variables is determined by the 2×2 joint frequencies of a contingency table (cf. Fig. 8.2). Virtually all previous research assumes that the cognitive process of contingency assessment is a function of the four stimulus frequencies, a, b, c, d, in accordance with standard statistical correlation models (Allan, 1993; Alloy & Tabachnik, 1984; Fiedler, 2000a; McKenzie, 1994). Errors and biases in correlation

---

[2] Although experimental designs based on randomized groups attempt to eliminate the systematic variance between groups, the problem may still persist in more subtle ways, for instance, when experimental treatments (e.g., emotion treatments) applied to groups do not guarantee the same influence on every individual.

[3] Note that the term 'illusion' does not imply the violation of an incontestable norm of rationality. PC illusions can be functional or dysfunctional, depending on what level of aggregation is adequate, just as the functionality of other illusions, like overconfidence, depends on the learning environment (cf. Haselton & Funder, 2006; Hoffrage *et al.*, 2000).

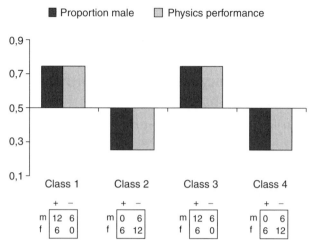

Fig. 8.1. Illustration of divergent contingencies between student gender (m = male, f = female) and achievement (+ = high, – = low). At the level of classes, average performance is perfectly correlated with male proportion. However, within all classes, females outperform males.

assessment are attributed to unequal attention and differential weights given to these four cells, due to prior expectancies, the salience of variable levels, or the asymmetry of present versus absent information. In any case, it is presupposed that human (like animal) contingency assessment is based on a cognitive function that uses the joint frequencies, or cell entries, as its argument.

In contrast, a pseudocontingency (PC) is an inference rule that uses the marginals of the contingency table, rather than the cell entries (Freytag, 2003; Fiedler & Freytag,

	a+c= 100	b+d= 50	Marginal baserate distributions	Contingency
I	a=60	b=40	100 = a+b	$r = -0.20$
	c=40	d=10	50 = c+d	
II	a=67	b=33	100 = a+b	$r \sim 0.00$
	c=33	d=17	50 = c+d	
III	a=75	b=25	100 = a+b	$r = +0.25$
	c=25	d=25	50 = c+d	

Fig. 8.2. Setting pseudocontingencies apart from genuine contingencies. All three distributions imply positive pseudocontingencies, because the marginal distributions for rows and columns are skewed in the same direction, however, the contingency varies from negative (a) to zero (b) to positive (c).

2004; Fiedler *et al.*, 2007b). In other words, the PC algorithm (mis)takes two skewed baserate distributions for a contingency. When the marginals or baserate distributions are skewed in the same direction (i.e., mostly male students and mostly good achievement), the inferred contingency between male gender and achievement is positive. When the marginals or baserate distributions are skewed in opposite directions (i.e., mostly male students but rarely good achievement), the inferred contingency is negative. As vividly shown in Fig. 8.2, inferring a contingency from the alignment of two baserate distributions is not justified, because the same baserates allow for positive, zero, and negative correlations. Confusing baserates with contingencies is like confusing two main effects (i.e., a row difference and a column difference) with an interaction (changing column differences as a function of rows). However, judges and decision makers— or more generally: organisms—commit this category mistake in many different task contexts, as evident from a good deal of empirical evidence reviewed in the next section.

In fact, the PC illusion is not as stupid as it may appear at first sight. Like Robinson's (1950) ecological bias and the other multi-level problems depicted at the outset, the PC illusion produces an error at one level but a sound inference at another, aggregate level. After all, at the level of classes, the rates of boys and of good achievement are jointly elevated, in comparison to some normative standard that usually holds for other classes. Indeed, by exposing the teacher to a contrast class with a low baserate of boys and a low baserate of good achievement (regardless of the within-class correlation across students), the teacher's PC illusion could be amplified. However, such an explicit ecological correlation between the proportions of boys and higher achievers across two or more classes or ecologies is not strictly necessary for the PC effect to occur. Even if there is but one class or ecology, the teacher can use her prior knowledge of normal classes to infer the covariation of baserates across ecologies, whether explicitly observed or implicitly memorized.

Thus, to complete the definition, PCs result when the correlation of category baserates is (mis)taken for inferring the correlation of individual measures. The term PC refers to illusions arising from this inference rule; it does not refer to the erroneous outcome of an illusory correlation inference, which can reflect many other processes (cf. Fiedler, 2000a). The PC illusion occurs under many conditions that render the efficient assessment and encoding of aggregate-level information (i.e., baserates) more likely than individuating information (i.e., joint frequencies). By analogy, a generalized definition of PCs in n-dimensional space says that inferences on complex contingencies involving n dimensions are often based on observations gathered in an aggregate space of lower dimensionality (resulting from aggregation over some dimensions). Thus, with reference to the above PC example, cognitive inferences about a three-dimensional data array, involving student performance × gender groups × students within gender groups, are based on a two-dimensional array involving aggregate scores for performance × gender groups.[4]

---

4 More generally, PC-like inferences occur whenever a higher-dimensional problem design (e.g., a 4-dimensional design involving factors A × B × C × D) is 'studied,' either in people's mind or in science, through one or more sub-designs (e.g., design A × B; design C × D; design A × D, etc.), which aggregate over the levels of the omitted factors.

Empirical evidence

A cursory review of empirical evidence for experimentally controlled PC effects will further help to illustrate the various manifestations of the illusion. Note that, psychologically, PCs suggest a tendency for higher-order, aggregate correlations to dominate and overshadow lower-order, individuating correlations. A recent series of experiments conducted within a simulated classroom paradigm (Fiedler *et al.*, 2007) speaks to the very example that was used here to introduce the phenomenon, namely the correlation between student gender and achievement.

In this paradigm, participants are asked to take the role of a teacher who has to observe the performance of a class of 16 students, 8 boys and 8 girls, represented graphically on the computer screen. Each lesson is devoted to a particular subject matter, such as maths, physics, English, or German. Over an extended period of time, the teacher can select a knowledge question from a pull-down menu of questions representing the subject matter. Once a question is announced, a subset of all students raises their hand, and the teacher selects one student who then provides either a correct or a wrong answer. Across many question–answer cycles of this kind, the teacher can assess the achievement of all 16 students in the class. As each student's true ability parameter (i.e., his or her probability of providing a correct response) and motivation parameter (i.e., his or her probability of raising hand) are controlled by the computer program that drives the simulated classroom, both the accuracy and the potential biases in the teachers' assessment can be studied systematically.

In one experiment, teachers were asked to test the hypothesis that boys are good in science (maths and physics) whereas girls are good in language, corresponding to common gender stereotypes. This led most participants to engage in positive testing (Klayman & Ha, 1987; Oaksford & Chater, 1994), that is, to ask more questions to boys in science and to girls in language lessons. Consequently, the gender baserate distributions were skewed in opposite directions for science and language lessons; there were clearly more answers from boys in science but clearly more answers from girls in language. Distinct PC effects were induced when these skewed gender baserates were aligned with the skewed correctness baserates of smart students (with a correctness rate of 80%). For smart students in science, the coincidence of mostly male responses and mostly correct responses led teachers to judge the ability of smart boys higher than the ability of smart girls (with the same objective ability parameter). For language lessons in contrast, mostly female responses and mostly correct responses led teachers to judge smart girls higher than (objectively equivalent) smart boys. Closer analyses revealed that this finding was confined to those teachers who actually engaged in positive testing (i.e., who actually produced skewed gender distributions).

That the PC bias reflects the alignment of skewed baserates, rather than expectancies based on gender stereotypes, was demonstrated by the reverse task instruction, namely, to test the hypothesis that (in this particular class) girls tend to be good in science but boys tend to be good in language. Positive testing now led teachers to mainly focus on girls in science and on boys in language, thus producing an opposite skew in the gender baserates. As a consequence, mostly female and mostly correct responses led teachers to judge smart girls higher than smart boys in science. In language, in contrast, mostly male responses together with mostly correct responses led smart boys appear superior to smart girls. Again, the biases were confined to those teachers who actually engaged in positive testing, the precondition of skewed gender baserates.

In another experiment from the same series, a PC effect accounts for the impact of the class context on the evaluation of individual students' performance. In one class, the ability of all students was set to a constant correctness baserate of 70%. In another class, the correctness baserate was constantly low, 30%. Within both ecologies, the individual students' motivation parameters varied from 20% to 50% and 80%. Thus, the true correlation between students' motivation and their ability was by definition zero, because individual ability was invariant and the correctness of responses to specific questions depended on the computer's random generator, which is independent of whether a student had raised his or her hand or not.

Nevertheless, distinct PC effects reflected subjectively inferred correlations between motivation and ability. In a high-ability class environment, with a high correctness baserate, the motivation baserates for highly motivated students was skewed in the same direction, suggesting a positive PC, which led teachers to judge the ability of high-motivation students higher than low-motivation students. In contrast, in a low-ability environment, the low correctness baserates were skewed in a direction opposite to the high hand-raising baserates of highly motivated students. The resulting negative PC suggested a negative relation between motivation and ability, leading teachers to judge the ability of high-motivation students lower than the ability of low-motivation students (whose low motivation baserates were well aligned with the low correctness baserates).

In still other experiments, PC effects demonstrated the impact of group aggregates on judgments of individual students. The class was divided into two subgroups of eight students supposed to come from different former classes or teachers. In one subgroup, there were mostly high-ability students and high-motivation students, whereas the other subgroup consisted of mostly low-ability and low-motivation students. However, crucially, the correlation between ability and motivation at the level of students was zero, as the ratio of high- to low-ability students was the same among both high- and low-motivation students. Nevertheless, when teachers rated the individual students' ability and motivation at the end of the session, the resulting sets of 16 ratings were correlated, reflecting a typical PC effect. The coincidence of high baserates of both attributes in one subgroup and low baserates of both attributes in the other subgroup—that is, the existing correlation between ability and motivation baserates at the level of subgroups—misled teachers to infer a corresponding correlation at the level of individual students.

An analogous finding was obtained in still another experiment between individual students' positions on two political attitude topics, as uttered in a civics lesson. Although the correlation between the 16 students' pro and con positions on one attitude were completely uncorrelated with their pro and con stands on the other attitude, the teachers believed to have seen a correlation because one subgroup of students held mostly pro attitudes on both topics, whereas another subgroup held mostly con attitudes on both topics. The sign of the PC illusion was reversed, that is, teachers believed that pro positions on one attitude came along with con positions on the other attitude, when the baserates of pros and cons in the two subgroups were skewed in opposite directions.

Convergent evidence for PC illusions that reflect the same theoretical principle (alignment of skewed baserates) comes from a whole variety of task settings and content domains. Conceptual replications include PCs between individual scores on different personality tests, when respondents belong to different groups with different baserates of test scores (Fiedler & Freytag, 2003); PCs between dieting and symptoms of patients in two wards of a hospital (Fiedler & Freytag, 2004); PCs between a couple's responses to the items of a partner questionnaire when several subtests yield different baserates of yes and no responses (Freytag *et al.*, 2008); between the occurrence of a virus and a disease in different geographical areas (Fiedler & Graf, 1990); or between the desirability of behavior and the belongingness to one of two social groups with different towns serving as ecologies (Meiser, 2006; Meiser & Hewstone, 2004).

In more recent studies, we were even able to demonstrate PC effects in sequential learning and speeded classification tasks such as evaluative priming with different baserates of positive and negative primes and targets (Fiedler *et al.*, 2007a), in the Implicit Association Test (IAT) with different baserates of target attributes and valence attributes (Blümke & Fiedler, 2007), and in Goodie and Fantino's (1996) probability-learning paradigm (Kutzner *et al.*, 2007).

Of particular interest is the analysis of the specific task conditions that give rise to PC illusions. An overview of the available evidence suggests, first of all, that the phenomenon generalizes over a variety of conditions. PC effects have been shown to result from the alignment of skewed baserate distributions in a single group, in two groups, or in four groups or categories. PCs occur whether the groups or ecologies can be assumed to reflect a common cause of the skewed baserates (i.e., preceding therapy in one group as a cause of skewed test baserates) or a common effect (i.e., therapy as a consequence of observed test values).

Setting PCs apart from genuine contingencies

Most importantly, the illusion generalizes over different presentation modes, called successive versus simultaneous. In the successive presentation mode, participants are first presented information about individuals' high versus low values on one variable (e.g., test X) in one run, before they are later presented information about a second variable (test Y) in another run. In other words, they are not fed with genuine contingency information about the joint occurrence of X and Y in the same persons. Rather, they merely receive information about the uni-variate distribution of each variable within the group. It is this condition that clearly sets PCs apart from the usual contingency assessment paradigm, in which the stimuli are always bi-variate observations of both variables shown at the same time. Thus, in the successive mode, participants have no chance to solicit the contingency proper; the only remarkable finding is that participants readily infer subjective contingencies from two separate series of uni-variate observations.

In the simultaneous presentation mode, in contrast, joint observations for both variables (e.g., test X and Y) are presented simultaneously, linked to the same person, thus providing all information that is necessary to assess the genuine contingency. PCs are pitted against contingencies (cf. Fig. 8.2a); that is, skewed marginal distributions suggest a PC opposite to the contingencies given by the cell entries of the contingency table. It is remarkable that even in this 'home domain' of contingency assessment, PCs often override contingencies proper. In other words, even though the joint frequencies or cell entries are available, participants utilize the baserates or marginals for contingency inferences. This intrusion of PC illusions into the contingency domain suggests the challenging idea that many previous findings on illusory correlations may, to an unknown degree, reflect hidden PC effects.

Learning environments fostering the evolution of PC illusions

Why should evolution have allowed homo-sapiens to develop such a serious category mistake, given the great adaptive value of accurate contingency assessment? Why should an organism exposed to the contingency in Fig. 8.2 1, which is negative ($r = -0.20$), make predictions from individual X to Y scores as if the relation were positive, as suggested from the alignment of skewed distributions (mostly high values on both X and Y)?

Upon some reflection, there are indeed several good reasons for PCs. An analysis of the learning environments in which organisms typically have to assess contingencies shows that PC-based inferences are not at all stupid or irrational. First of all, it has to be kept in mind that PCs are not simply wrong or fully detached from reality; rather, they correctly reflect ecological correlations that hold at an aggregate level of groups or higher-order categories. The question then becomes why and under what conditions is homo-sapiens inclined to assess ecological correlations at aggregate level rather than individuating correlations at more specific levels, even when a decision problem calls for individuating information?

Nasty environment for contingency assessment

A simple and striking answer to this crucial question can be found if one considers the structure of the probabilistic world surrounding the probabilistic mind. To illustrate this point, let us return to the teacher who is to learn correlates of student achievement. There are many potential correlates in the information environment: student motivation, personality of teacher, instruction style, socio-economic status, TV consumption, variation between subject matters, and so forth (cf. Fig. 8.3). As the teacher gathers data about student achievement, she does not know which particular correlate will be the focus of a judgment problem at some future time. To be prepared for any problem (i.e., relating achievement to any of these correlates), the teacher would have to assess the full multivariate contingency table. Here, however, she encounters a number of insurmountable problems. First, the environment rarely provides us with complete multivariate data points. At the very time when a student's achievement is observed, the corresponding data for many other variables (SES, former teacher's method, parents' style) may not be available. Second, even if it were available, the teacher's attention focus (on achievement) would typically prevent her from effectively assessing all the other variables at the same time. Third, even when multivariate information is available and the teacher is able to jointly attend to and encode the multivariate contingency data, memory restrictions would prevent

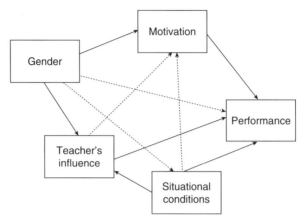

Fig. 8.3. Variety of factors bearing contingencies with student performance.

her from remembering the full multi-dimensional distribution. Fourth, the time and patience needed to fill such a monstrous array with data would paralyze the teacher. Before the rarest cells of the giant design are filled with observations, the school year would be over.

Thus, closer analysis of the information input from which correlations have to be inferred reveals that the notion of multivariate observations, which is so familiar from statistics courses, may be far away from the real empirical world. Exactly because extensional information about joint frequencies is often not available, several authors have emphasized that causal inferences and contingency judgments have to rely on intensional information and spatial-temporal contiguity (Chater & Oaksford, 2006; Fiedler, 2000a).

PC inferences afford a viable alternative

However, the PC illusion suggests an alternative. Even when joint frequencies of the full Cartesian product of all event combinations cannot be used, statistical information may still be used at a realistic level. Just like animals can naturally learn statistical proportions, such as the reinforcement rate associated with specific ecologies, or the baserate of a signal or conditional stimulus, the teacher can be assumed to be quite effective at learning the baserates of observations for many attributes of interest: a student's baserate of correct responses as an indicator of achievement; the student's rate of raising hands as an indicator of motivation; the relative number of TV-related remarks from that student, etc. To be sure, these learned proportions or baserates cannot be interpreted on an absolute scale; they only provide ordinal information about the relative prevalence of an attribute across different ecologies. A particular student is characterized by a high baserate of correct responses (high achievement) and, observed on a different occasion, a high baserate of raising hands (motivation), or by a relatively low proportion of TV comments (low TV consumption). There is no evidence that individual responses are more correct when the same student raised her hand or on particular days following high TV consumption. Rather, at a higher level of aggregation, the teacher combines a high-achievement baserate with a high-motivation baserate, or a low TV baserate, in a PC-type inference. Similarly, at the level of classes, when the achievement baserate is high and the motivation baserate is also high, the co-occurrence of two baserates is used for inferring a positive contingency between motivation and achievement.

PC inferences in empirical research

From this sketch, it is but a small step to realizing that our teacher basically applies the same rationale that empirical scientists use in a probabilistic world that calls for analyses of group data to filter out noise and unreliability. For example, researchers compare student groups with different baserates of TV consumption and conclude from differential aggression baserates in both groups that TV enhances aggression. However, the PC inference is not only common in correlational research but even extends to empirical research. In a typical experimental setting, a manipulation (e.g., films to induce good mood) is administered to an experimental group but not to a control group. A manipulation check is then used to ensure that a majority of participants in the experimental group shows the intended change on an independent variable (mood). If a majority of participants in the experimental group exhibits an effect in the dependent variable (e.g., increased top–down inferences; Fiedler, 2001), researchers assume to have demonstrated an individual-level causal influence of mood on cognition: positive mood causes top–down thinking. However, the ecological correlation between mood and cognition baserates at group level does not logically imply that mood and cognition are related within individuals (e.g., watching the film may have caused good mood in most participants, and the same film may have also caused a procedural priming of top–down thinking, but independently of the mood effect). Whatever the real impact of the group treatment was, it may have affected mood and cognition independently, inducing the same tendency toward top–down thinking in both subsets of good-mood and bad-mood participants. To repeat, two baserates do not make up a contingency proper.

PC-like thinking is also common when scientists engage in theoretical reasoning. Theoretical models often involve more variables than can be controlled in singular experiments. Facing this situation, empirical tests of a theory linking a dependent variable Y to, say, four independent variables U, V, W, X, are based on different experiments, each of which includes a different subset of, say, two independent variables: U,V; U,W; U,X; and so forth. Researchers then combine the findings obtained in two-factorial designs to inferences about a four-factorial theory. Logically, this inference from two-factorial relations to a four-factorial relation reflects the same category mistake as the elementary PC inference from two main effects (baserate tendencies) to an interaction (contingency).

Thus, when everyday judges and decision makers fall prey to PC effects, they seem to adapt to hard constraints of the information ecology, which also force scientists to resort to the same inference scheme. Just because in reality complete multivariate data arrays are either not available, or because the assessment and memorization of such highly demanding data is not feasible, a plausible and economical heuristic is to resort to sizeable contingencies at aggregate level. Rather than assessing the contingency of student achievement and TV consumption (in addition to SES, motivation, parent's profession, etc.) over individual students, the teacher analyzes the relation between baserates of all these variables in different ecologies (e.g., groups, categories, time aggregates). Likewise, researchers take the correlation of group baserates as evidence for intra-individual processes. All this may be considered a normal manifestation of bounded rationality (Simon, 1956)—a rationality that is bounded by the accessibility constraints of the environment and by the cognitive-capacity constraints of the human mind.

Functional value of PCs

As already pointed out, there is often no alternative to using aggregate data as a proxy for individuating processes, that is, to making inferences from categories to individual cases. However, the crucial question is whether the PC proxy is functional, informing correct predictions, and decisions. The above allusion to the analogy between PCs and scientific inference already suggests that the proxy cannot be that irrational. Prudent theorists (e.g., Huttenlocher *et al.*, 2000) have made a strong point arguing that reliance on category knowledge may often inform rational inferences. However, explicating the functionality of PC illusions is not that easy. The utility (i.e., the benefits and costs) of judges' reliance on group baserates or averages depends on several considerations.

First of all, there is no *a priori* ground to assume that any particular aggregation level is the ultimately true or most useful level. PC illusions shift attention toward contingencies that hold at higher rather than at lower levels of aggregation. But what can be said about the functionality of such a shift?—One asset, already pointed out, is that higher levels of aggregation make assessment possible at all. Another obvious asset of aggregation is to increase the reliability of observations in a fallible, noisy world. Sill another, related advantage is that regularities observed at a higher level are more general and less restricted to the peculiarities of higher-order interactions and particular cases. However, aside from these apparent assets, it is worth while speculating about the systematic influence that a bias toward higher aggregate levels can have in the long run.

Crucial to adaptive cognition is the prediction and control of the origins of positive and negative payoffs. A cognitive module that supports the formation of higher aggregates (e.g., averages over longer time segments) forces the organism to attend more to long-term, global payoffs than to short-term, local payoffs. This can be of considerable value in overcoming delay-of-gratification problems, which is a precondition for long-term adaptive behavior.

In a similar vein, causal influences may be induced more effectively and interventions may often be more feasible at the aggregate level of ecologies than at the level of particular individuals. Just as experimental treatments do not warrant the same influence on every individual but only an average influence on a randomized group, many everyday interventions may be more easily applied to ecologies than to individuals. The teacher can make her lesson more interesting or change her teaching style for the whole class. Purchasing a TV set changes the ecology rather than a specific student. Similarly, for an animal to survive, it is typically more feasible to avoid certain ecologies than to try to change an individual predator. Or, for a consumer to reduce the consumption costs, she should search for a less expensive market rather than trying to negotiate the price of individual products. Anyway, to arrive at an informed analysis of the adaptive value of PC illusions, one has to engage in a systematic analysis of the payoff structure of the environment—which is a demanding theoretical task.

As usual, the various benefits of aggregate-level assessment come along with distinct costs. To the extent that ecological class differences intrude into the teacher's evaluation of individual students' performance, of course, evaluation becomes unfair and biased. After all, what has to be evaluated is individual students' performance, independent of the class. In this regard, it cannot be denied that PCs, like all cognitive illusions, turn out to produce erroneous results when carried over to new task settings, for which they are not functional. Nevertheless, from a more distant perspective, interpreting individual students' achievement in the context of their class environment is not that irrational, for the causes of achievement may be found at class level (teacher, group behavior, subject matter) and appropriate interventions may also lie at class level. What is good and effective from a systemic or evolutionary point of view may not always appear 'fair' or 'just' at individual level.

Failures to aggregate: factors that counteract PC illusions

If an analysis of the learning context of contingency assessment renders the PC illusion plausible, then by the same token the learning environment may also explain those conditions that counteract PC illusions. Recall that the overview of tricky paradigms at the outset included several phenomena that run opposite to the PC effect, reflecting failures to consider aggregate information. For instance, suboptimal choices in dilemma games originate in the failure to understand that cooperation is of great advantage across many trials, although defection is clearly the optimal strategy at the level of individual trials. A similar failure to aggregate over longer time frames is apparent in various delay-of-gratification problems (Metcalf & Mischel, 1999). In group decision making, too, performance suffers from the fact that the information that is distributed over group members is not combined effectively (Mojzisch & Schulz-Hardt, 2006). Thus, the PC bias toward higher aggregation levels is not universal but restricted to certain task conditions. But what are the boundary conditions that trigger either PC-like biases toward higher aggregation levels or reverse biases toward low-aggregate, individuating information in different task settings?

Encoding and reinforcement structure of the task

There is little direct empirical evidence at the moment to provide an informed answer, but two crucial boundary conditions suggest themselves, the encoding structure and the reinforcement structure of the task. For a general rule, PC illusions can be expected to occur under conditions that facilitate aggregate-level encoding and aggregate-level reinforcement. In contrast, when the task environment emphasizes individual events or outcomes and prevents the decision maker from aggregate-level encoding and reinforcement, then an opposite bias can be expected to occur.

To illustrate this crucial point, consider the hypothetical dilemma game depicted in Fig. 8.4. Given nature plays cooperatively, the participant wins 10 from cooperation but 20 from defecting on every trial. Given nature defects, the participant wins nothing (0) from cooperation but 2 from defecting. Thus, at trial level, one ought to defect. However, it is well known that multi-trial dilemmas create reciprocal behavior, that is, on aggregate, across trials, nature tends to match one's own strategy, playing tit for tat. Let us assume nature cooperates 75% of the time when participant also cooperates on 75% of the trials, and that nature's cooperation rate is 25% when the participant's cooperation rate is 25%. As Fig. 8.4 shows, when aggregating over many trials, the expected payoff is clearly higher (i.e., 5.625 vs. 1.874) when the cooperation baserate is high (75%) rather than low (25%). The question then is whether participants have a real chance to encode this aggregate-level contingency and to vividly experience the reinforcement associated with aggregate-level strategies.

In a typical dilemma game environment, participants have to make a decision on every single trial, and they are immediately reinforced with a feedback about the outcome of that trial. Such immediate reinforcement forces the participant not to forgo any profit at trial level and prevents her from costly long-term explorations at aggregate level. In order to experience and encode the aggregate-level contingency in favor of cooperation, it would be necessary that (a) the participant refrains from maximal payoffs over an extended time period; (b) that nature reciprocates and also converts to cooperation; (c) that the participant must somehow anticipate reciprocal cooperation; and (d) that learning and memory of the contingency between one's own cooperation baserate and nature's reciprocation baserate has to be successful. No doubt, these conditions are very unlikely to be met simultaneously.

Conversely, a slightly modified version of the very same dilemma task may indeed produce a PC-effect, facilitating the insight that cooperation is worth while. Let us assume the participant is not an actor in a dilemma task who is reinforced on every trial but, rather, an observer who witnesses an actor's cooperation rate and reward rate over a longer time period, postponing a judgment to the end of the entire sequence.

	Nature cooperates	Nature defects	
Player cooperates	10	0	Payoff matrix at the level of individual trials
Player Defects	20	2	

Player cooperates	5.625	Expected value in a "friendly" environment. Nature cooperates 75% of the time. 25% defection
Player Defects	1.874	

Fig. 8.4. Dilemma game as a multi-level problem. Although payoffs at the level of individual trials are higher when the player defects (upper panel), the aggregate value of cooperation is higher over many trials.

From such a remote perspective, the participant should easily recognize that a high baserate of cooperation comes along with a high payoff rate, especially when other strategies (e.g., high-defection baserates observed in other players or in different time periods) are met with low payoffs or losses.

To continue this thought experiment, moreover, closer analyses may reveal that the wise observer uses the PC algorithm rather than a contingency algorithm proper. That is, it may be sufficient to recognize that both cooperation baserates, for the player and for nature, are skewed in the same direction, regardless of whether the player's and nature's cooperation actually correlate over trials. To test this assumption one might let observers witness a sequential dilemma game in which both the player and nature cooperate at a high (75%) or both at a low (25%) baserate. However, in one experimental condition, nature cooperates clearly more when the player cooperates. In another condition, nature cooperates at the same (constantly high or low) rate regardless of whether the player cooperates or not. If the observer's belief that payoff increases with cooperation is the same in both conditions, this would be cogent evidence for PC inferences rather than contingencies proper.

Further analyses of other multi-level problems corroborate the assumption that the spontaneously chosen aggregation level reflects the encoding and reinforcement structure of the task. In group decision making, what is most likely to be encoded and communicated in group discussion is the individual decision maker's personal preferences. In contrast, the group-level information and the group-level preference is unlikely to be encoded, discussed and assessed effectively (Mojzisch & Schulz-Hardt, 2006). With respect to reinforcement, or payoffs, although the modal individual preferences may diverge from the aggregate group preferences, decisions based on simple majority rules, such as the Condorcet principle,[5] have been shown to provide close to optimal solutions most of the time (Hastie & Kameda, 2005). Moreover, the unreflected premise in group decision making research that group-level information is more valid than a majority rule applied to individual-level information is an open empirical question, rather than an *a priori* truth. In any case, it is no surprise that group decisions do not exhibit PC illusions (i.e., no bias toward aggregate-level information), simply because the encoding structure of the task setting does not support aggregate-level encoding.

The crucial point to be conveyed here—that the encoding and payoff structure of the task determines the aggregation level of the decision process—is nicely illustrated in recent research on Simpson's paradox. In a typical experiment (Fiedler *et al.*, 2003; Schaller, 1992; Waldmann & Hagmayer, 1995), participants observe, as already depicted above, that more female applicants for graduate programs than male applicants are rejected. However, the seeming disadvantage of females turns out to reflect an ecological correlation; that is, what renders females less successful is the higher rejection rate of those universities to which females apply predominantly. When the unequal rejection rate of different universities (ecologies) is partialled out, the rejection

---

[5] According to the Condorcet rule, a choice option or candidate is chosen if it receives more than half of the individual votes in group decision making.

rate of female individuals within universities actually turns out to be lower than the male rejection rate. Thus, Simpson's paradox is a special case of a multi-level problem that entails a spurious correlation.

Participants who have to judge and compare males and females on such complex tasks have to make a choice between two representations: (a) they can either encode the female disadvantage across universities (noting that rejection rate in some universities are high because there are too many female applicants), or (b) encode the female advantage within universities (noting that the apparent male superiority merely reflects the unequal rejection rates of different universities). What level is rational, or normatively correct, depends on one's causal model. If the cause lies in the universities' unequal difficulty level, it is rational to compare individual males and females within universities. If the cause lies in the universities' unequal gender composition, it is rational to focus on the ecological correlation between gender rates and rejection rates across universities.

What cognitive representation is chosen in judgment experiments using Simpson's paradox depends on the encoding and reinforcement structure. On one hand, with regard to encoding, when the temporal order in which the stimulus observations are provided supports interpretation (a), presenting applicant's gender before the university name to highlight the primacy of applicant gender as an antecedent of university rejection rates, then they tend to see a female disadvantage. If, however, the presentation order facilitates interpretation (b), indicating the university prior to the applicant's gender to highlight the antecedent role of university standards, they tend to recognize the female superiority (Fiedler et al., 2002, 2003).

On the other hand, with regard to reinforcement, when feminist motives are solicited or when participants hold feminist attitudes, they tend to prefer interpretation (b) over (a) because the former interpretation is more reinforcing from a feminist perspective (Schaller, 1992).—Needless to repeat that the 'true' solution to the problem is unknown, or at least it cannot be determined on the basis of statistical contingencies alone.

Higher-order memory codes

PC-like biases toward higher aggregation levels are most pronounced when complex information calls for higher-order categorical encoding. Participants in a study by Fiedler and Graf (1990) first learned whether a virus was observed or not in 24 different countries. Then, in a second run, they were informed about the occurrence of a disease in the same countries. To be sure, memorizing the precise distribution of virus and disease across as many as 24 countries is hardly possible. However, given that all countries could be categorized into six geographical clusters (Scandinavian; Mediterranean; South American, etc.), the memory load reduced to learning the relative occurrence rate of virus and disease in only six geographical clusters. These were spontaneously used as highly effective and economical encoding units, as often demonstrated in memory experiments with categorized lists (Cohen, 1969; Shuell, 1969). Thus, holding the contingency between virus and disease constant (i.e., the number of matching pairs, or countries in which virus and disease were jointly present or absent), participants came up with pronounced contingency estimates only when matching pairs consistently came from the same clusters (i.e., virus and disease jointly present in all countries of some clusters and jointly absent in others), but not when the same number of matches was evenly distributed across all clusters. In the former case, a marked ecological correlation helped participants to encode the coincidence of virus and disease at the level of higher-order memory units.

Summary and conclusions

The present chapter started with the contention that the complex and difficult problems of the environment that the probabilistic mind has to deal with do not primarily reflect the probabilistic nature of the empirical reality. That the world is not strictly deterministic not only creates uncertainty and sometimes stress but also entails optimism and the potential for progress and control. Rather, what renders the world difficult and conflict-prone is that it looks different from different perspectives. This important insight is at the heart of several research paradigms that have enhanced our understanding of the probabilistic mind. The conditional reasoning paradigm highlights the fact that inferences from X to Y may diverge drastically from reverse inferences from Y to X (Fiedler, 2000b; Koriat et al., 2006). Construal-level theory is concerned with the changing appearance of the world as a function of temporal, spatial and social distance (Trope & Liberman, 2003). The pseudocontingency (PC) illusion that was the focus of the present chapter adds another way in which the world is subject to perspectival changes and relativity (see also Stewart et al., 2003). As a matter of principle, environmental correlations vary in size and even in sign when considered at different aggregation levels. The PC illusion reflects a cognitive bias toward assessing contingencies at high rather than low levels of aggregation. The contingencies that hold between group or category baserates are (mis)taken as a proxy for the contingency that holds between individuating people or events within categories.

The PC illusion was only recently discovered, but it was then found to generalize across many task conditions, content areas, and decision problems. Like all illusions, the impact of PC biases can be quite massive and hard to believe. However, just like other perceptual and cognitive illusions, PCs can be understood as plausible and functional when their learning environment is taken into account. Like any illusion, PCs can be characterized as overgeneralizations of heuristics that function well in many task contexts while producing errors and distortions when carried over to other contexts.

In any case, PCs constitute a fascinating topic in the study of the probabilistic mind, the topic of higher-order contingency problems. A closer examination of other examples of such higher-order contingencies—such as Simpson's paradox, dilemma games, or group decision making—suggests that PC biases to attend to high aggregation levels may be reduced, eliminated, or even reversed when the encoding and reinforcement structure of the task facilitates an attention shift from high levels to low levels of aggregation.

Research on higher-order contingency problems is only beginning to grow (Fiedler & Plessner, in press; Spellman, 1996). However, in spite of the paucity of systematic research conducted so far, there can be no doubt that such problems provide a major challenge for the probabilistic mind as it has to cope with the pitfalls of utility assessment, risky choice, causal inference, and prediction and—last but not least—with the pitfalls of scientific inference.

Author note

Thanks are due to Nick Chater, Peter Freytag, Ralph Hertwig, Florian Kutzner, Mike Oaksford, and Tobias Vogel for their thoughtful and constructive comments on an earlier draft of this chapter.

References

Allan, L. G. (1993). Human contingency judgments: Rule based or associative? *Psychological Bulletin*, **114**, 435–448.

Alloy, L. B., & Tabachnik, N. (1984). Assessment of covariation by humans and animals: the joint influence of prior expectations and current situational information. *Psychological Review*, **91**, 112–149.

Blümke, M., & Fiedler, K. (2007). *Base rate effects in the IAT*. Manuscript submitted for publication.

Chater, N., & Oaksford, M. (2006). Mental mechanisms: Speculations on human causal learning and reasoning. In K. Fiedler & P. Juslin (Eds.), *Sampling and adaptive cognition* (pp. 210–236). New York: Cambridge University Press.

Cohen, B. H. (1966). Some-or-none characteristics of coding behavior. *Journal of Verbal Learning and Verbal Behavior*, **5**, 182–187.

Fiedler, K. (2000a). Illusory correlations: A simple associative algorithm provides a convergent account of seemingly divergent paradigms. *Review of General Psychology*, **4**, 25–58.

Fiedler, K. (2000b). Beware of samples! A cognitive-ecological sampling approach to judgment biases. *Psychological Review*, **107**, 659–676.

Fiedler, K. (2001). Affective states trigger processes of assimilation and accommodation. In L. L. Martin & G. L. Clore (Eds.), *Theories of mood and cognition: A user's guidebook.* (pp. 85–98). Mahwah, NJ: Lawrence Erlbaum Associates.

Fiedler, K., Blümke, M., & Unkelbach, C. (2007a). *Impact of valence baserates on evaluative priming.* Unpublished Research, University of Heidelberg.

Fiedler, K., & Freytag, P. (2003). Social judgments based on pseudocontingencies: A forgotten phenomenon. In J. P. Forgas, K. D. Williams, & W. von Hippel (Eds.), *Social judgments: Implicit and explicit processes* (pp. 162–179). New York: Cambridge University Press.

Fiedler, K., & Freytag, P. (2004). Pseudocontingencies. *Journal of Personality and Social Psychology*, **87**, 453–467.

Fiedler, K., Freytag, P., & Unkelbach, C. (2007c). Pseudocontingencies in a simulated classroom. *Journal of Personality and Social Psychology*, **92**, 665–667.

Fiedler, K., & Graf, R. (1990). Grouping and categorization in judgments of contingency. In J.-P. Caverni & J.-M. Fabre (Eds.), *Cognitive biases* (pp. 47–57). Oxford: North-Holland.

Fiedler, K., & Plessner, H. (in press). Induction: From simple categorization to higher-order inference problems. In F. Strack & J. Förster (Eds.), *Social cognition—The basis of human interaction*. New York: Psychology Press.

Fiedler, K., Walther, E., Freytag, P., & Nickel, S. (2003). Inductive reasoning and judgment interference: Experiments on Simpson's paradox. *Personality and Social Psychology Bulletin*, **29**, 14–27.

Fiedler, K., Walther, E., Freytag, P., & Stryczek, E. (2002). Playing mating games in foreign cultures: A conceptual framework and an experimental paradigm for trivariate statistical inference. *Journal of Experimental Social Psychology*, **38**, 14–30.

Freytag, P. (2003). *Contextually determined typicality*. Berlin: Logos.

Freytag, P., Vogel, T., Kutzner, F., & Fiedler, K. (2008). *Pseudocontingencies due to baserate reproduction*. Unpublished research, University of Heidelberg.

Goodie, A. S., & Fantino, E. (1996). Learning to commit or avoid the base-rate error. *Nature*, **380**, 247–249.

Hammond, J. L. (1973). Two sources of error in ecological correlations. *American Sociological Review*, **38**, 764–777.

Haselton, M. G., & Funder, D. C. (2006). The evolution of accuracy and bias in social judgment. In M. Schaller, J. A. Simpson, & D. T. Kenrick (Eds.), *Evolution and social psychology*, (pp. 15–37). Madison , CI: Psychosocial Press.

Hastie, R., & Kameda, T. (2005). The robust beauty of majority rules in group decisions. *Psychological Review*, **112**, 494–508.

Hoffrage, U., Hertwig, R., & Gigerenzer, G. (2000). Hindsight bias: A by-product of knowledge updating? *Journal of Experimental Psychology: Learning, Memory, and Cognition*, **26**, 566–581.

Huttenlocher, J., Hedges, L., & Vevea, J. L. (2000). Why do categories affect stimulus judgement? *Journal of Experimental Psychology: General*, **129**, 220–241.

Klayman, J., & Ha, Y. (1987). Confirmation, disconfirmation, and information in hypothesis testing. *Psychological Review*, **94**, 211–228.

Koriat, A., Fiedler, K., & Bjork, R. A. (2006). Inflation of conditional predictions. *Journal of Experimental Psychology: General*, **135**, 429–447.

Kutzner, F., Freytag, P., Vogel, T., & Fiedler, K. (2007). *Base-rate neglect based on base-rates in experience-based contingency learning*. Manuscript submitted for publication.

McKenzie, C. R. M. (1994). The accuracy of intuitive judgment strategies: Covariation assessment and Bayesian inference. *Cognitive Psychology*, **26**, 209–239.

Meiser, T. (2006). Contingency learning and biased group impressions. In K. Fiedler & P. Juslin (Eds.), *Sampling and adaptive cognition* (pp. 183–209). New York: Cambridge University Press.

Meiser, T., & Hewstone, M. (2004). Cognitive processes in stereotype formation: The role of correct contingency learning for biased group judgments. *Journal of Personality and Social Psychology*, **87**, 599–614.

Metcalfe, J., & Mischel, W. (1999). A hot-cool analysis of the delay of gratification: The dynamics of willpower. *Psychological Reiew*, **106**, 3–19.

Mojzisch, A., & Schulz-Hardt, S. (2006). Information sampling in group decision making. In K. Fiedler & P. Juslin (Eds.), *Sampling and adaptive cognition* (pp. 299–326). New York: Cambridge University Press.

Oaksford, M., & Chater, N. (1994). A rational analysis of the selection task as optimal data selection. *Psychological Review*, **101**, 608–631.

Robinson, W. S. (1950). Ecological correlations and the behavior of individuals. *American Sociological Review*, **15**, 351–357.

Schaller, M. (1992). In-group favoritism and statistical reasoning in social inference: Implications for formation and maintenance of group stereotypes. *Journal of Personality and Social Psychology*, **63**, 61–74.

Schelling, T. C. (1978). *Micromotives and macrobehavior*. New York: Norton.

Shuell, T. J. (1969). Clustering and organization in free recall. *Psychological Bulletin*, **72**, 353–374.

Simon, H. A. (1956). Rational choice and the structure of environments. *Psychological Review*, **63**, 129–138.

Simpson, E. H. (1951). The interpretation of interaction in contingency tables. *Journal of the Royal Statistical Society, Series B*, **13**, 238–241.

Spellman, B. A. (1996). Acting as intuitive scientists: Contingency judgments are made while controlling for alternative potential causes. *Psychological Science*, **7**, 337–342.

Stasser, G., & Titus, W. (1985). Pooling of unshared information in group decision making: Biased information sampling in group discussion. *Journal of Personality and Social Psychology*, **48**, 1467–1478.

Stewart, N., Chater, N., Stott, H. P., & Reimers, S. (2003). Prospect relativity: How choice options influence decision under risk. *Journal of Experimental Psychology: General*, **132**, 23–46.

Trope, Y., & Liberman, N. (2003). Temporal construal. *Psychological Review*, **110**, 403–421.

Waldmann, M., & Hagmayer (1995). Causal paradox: When a cause simultaneously produces and prevent an effect. In *Proceedings of the Seventeenth Annual Conference of the Cognitive Science Society*. Hillsdale, NJ: Erlbaum.

Part 3

Judgement and Decision-Making

Chapter 9

Bayesian brains and cognitive mechanisms: harmony or dissonance?

Henry Brighton and Gerd Gigerenzer

Center for Adaptive Behavior and Cognition, Max Planck Institute for Human Development, Berlin, Germany

Introduction

The complexity of the cognitive system makes powerful metaphors such as the probabilistic mind and the Bayesian brain appealing on the one hand, but limited on the other. The trick is to not only harness their productivity, but also recognize their limits. One problem confronting the notion of the probabilistic mind and the accompanying 'quiet probabilistic revolution' is the apparent intractability of rational probabilistic calculation (Chater *et al.*, 2006b, p. 293). Rational probabilistic models, however, are not typically interpreted as algorithmic or mechanistic theories but functional level theories used to establish connections between observed behavior, a rational principle of inductive inference, and the structure of the environment. These correspondences tell us when the cognitive system is performing well and, to varying degrees, are used to suggest that human behavior is consistent with rational principles of inductive inference. From an algorithmic standpoint, how should these empirical findings be interpreted?

The distinction between functional and algorithmic level theories has its roots in what is now termed the rational analysis of cognition, an adaptationist program which aims to understand the structure and function of the cognition system as an adaptive response to the challenges posed by the environment (Marr, 1982; Shepard, 1987; Anderson, 1990; Oaksford & Chater, 1998). While working on a purely functional level, the tractability problem is in one sense irrelevant given that no commitment is made to a mechanistic level interpretation, but in another sense, unsatisfactory. Indeed, a principle objective of the rational analysis of cognition is to narrow down candidate algorithmic level theories by establishing empirically determined performance criteria. If the grand prize in cognitive science is uncovering both why minds do what they do and how they do it, then the productivity and scope of the metaphor would ideally extend to the process level.

Can the notion of the probabilistic mind be seamlessly extended to the algorithmic level, or there exist unmovable barriers to reconciling rational probabilistic models with plausible mechanisms of mind? We will examine these questions by considering the metaphor of the probabilistic mind from an alternative adaptationist perspective, and one that views much of human inductive inference as relying on an adaptive toolbox of simple heuristics (Gigerenzer *et al.*, 1999; Gigerenzer & Selten, 2001). Unlike the notion of the probabilistic mind, the metaphor of the adaptive toolbox is rooted to an algorithmic level hypothesis, which proposes that adaptive behavior, and inductive inference in particular, is in large part the result of an interaction between processing simplicity and ecological context. This view leads to the notion of ecological rationality. Here, the cognitive system is viewed as adapted to the relevant aspects of its environment to the extent that it achieves good enough solutions using the limited resources it has available, rather than attempting to find optimal ones. On this view, organisms do not optimize but satisfy (Simon, 1996), which makes the notion of adaptive success for the organism—its ecological rationality—inseparably tied to an algorithmic level analysis.

What barriers, if any, stand between a synthesis of the study of ecological rationality and functional level probabilistic models? First, we consider the role of rationality and optimality in framing the study of cognition, and examine how these concepts represent key points of divergence between the study of ecological rationality and rational analysis. Second, we examine the consequences of the intractability of optimal probabilistic calculation, and propose that the statistical problem known as the bias/variance dilemma arises as a consequence, and represents a significant and often overlooked dimension of the functional problem facing the cognitive system (Geman *et al.*, 1992). The bias/variance dilemma brings into focus a connection between estimation error, ecological context, and the properties of learning algorithms. Therefore, in addition, it has the potential to bridge functional level models, simple heuristics, and the notion of ecological rationality. Ultimately, the adaptationist perspective should encompass both functional and algorithmic level analyses. Our guiding concern will be the understanding how these two levels of analysis can be aligned.

The rational and the psychological

We will focus on the problem of inductive inference. Given some sequence of observations, an organism makes a successful inductive inference to the extent that it selects a hypothesis, which is *probable* (Tenenbaum & Griffiths, 2001a), *predictive* of future observations (Anderson, 1991b, p. 479), or one which leads to a *succinct recoding* of past observations (Chater & Vitányi, 2003). Thus, prediction, probability, and coding length are fundamentally related concepts which point to the essence of the rational problem of inductive inference (Li & Vitányi, 1997). Although the formal instantiation of these concepts can lead to slight inconsistencies, we will not consider these inconsistencies here (Vitányi & Li, 2000; Grünwald, 2005). Next, it is worth setting out what role rational principles can play when used to examine, evaluate, and ultimately frame the problem of inductive inference facing biological organisms.

Functional and algorithmic level explanations

Rational principles can be used to construct functional level models of cognition. When used in this way the objective is to understand to what extent human behavior coincides with rational expectation, and to what extent rational principles 'point to deep functional reasons why our minds work the way that they do' (Tenenbaum & Griffiths, 2001b, p. 776). This level of abstraction dispenses with the need to specify how, in mechanistic terms, data are processed to yield behavior. Viewing the organism as a black box, 'the structure of such a theory is concerned with the outside world rather than what is inside the head' (Anderson, 1991a, p. 410). In contrast, an algorithmic level model aims to provide a mechanistic account of how the organism processes data in order to address the task. Such a model is algorithmic in the sense that it describes the steps required to transform inputs to outputs such that these steps could plausibly be implemented on some form of computing machinery.

In part, the rational analysis of cognition seeks functional level models in order to alleviate some of the problems in arriving at mechanistic accounts: 'If we know that behavior is optimized to the structure of the environment and we also know what the optimal relationship is, then a constraint on mental mechanisms is that they must implement that optimal relationship' (Anderson, 1991b, p. 471). The idea is that mechanistic theorizing does not typically center on adaptationist assumptions, but rather aims to fit 'the facts at hand', those potentially second order effects which may arise as a consequence of the deeper and more concisely articulated problem of being adapted to the structure of the environment.

We will critically examine rational principles of inductive inference as appropriate concepts with which to explain adaptive cognition. Probabilistic notions of rationality and optimization, as analytic tools, should be uncontroversial. They are theory neutral. But as concepts used to characterize and explain cognition we question their validity. Without doubt, a range of opinion exists on the extent to which the metaphor of the probabilistic mind refers to a purely functional theory concerned with a behavioral perspective on cognition, a normative theory implying that deviation from rational expectation reflects irrationality or maladaptation, or to a deeper property impacting on how, in mechanistic terms, the cognitive system actually processes data. To examine these perspectives, it will prove useful to distinguish between the notion of the probabilistic mind in the broad sense and in the narrow sense.

The probabilistic mind in the broad sense

What we will refer to as the broad sense of the metaphor is the familiar one from rational analysis, where a strict separation between function and process is maintained. Here, a functional model, beyond setting behavioral constraints on candidate mechanisms, remains mute on how these outcomes are arrived at. This perspective is broad given that it leaves the door open to a wide range of possible mechanisms capable of producing the observed behavior. For example, when Tenenbaum and Griffiths (2001b) state that 'we do not assert that any of our statistical calculations are directly implemented, either consciously or unconsciously, in humans minds, but merely that they provide reasons why minds compute what they do' (p. 776), they are clearly adopting a strict analytic separation between functional level and process level explanations. The strength of this approach rests on the range of settings in which a close fit between a model of the environment, the rational principle, and the behavioral findings are established. These findings catalog instances of the cognitive system performing well, sometimes to the degree that the observed behavior is interpreted as optimal (Griffiths & Tenenbaum, 2006a).

When used in this way, a rational principle, such as Bayesian statistics, 'provides a principled framework for understanding human inductive successes and failures, by specifying exactly what a learner is and is not justified in concluding given certain assumptions about the environment' (Tenenbaum & Griffiths, 2001b, p. 776). Correspondences such as these, where human behavior coincides with rational expectation, represent important empirical findings because they indicate that the cognitive system has performed extremely well, under the assumption that the rational principle provides an appropriate notion of success. A tentative conclusion might then be that, to one degree or another, the mind behaves as if it were Bayesian. Knill and Pouget (2004), for instance, remark on the 'myriad ways in which human observers act as optimal Bayesian observers' (p. 712). The strength of this viewpoint—the implied ability of the cognitive system to 'act Bayesian'—rests on the range of settings in which this finding holds, and the degree to which they imply that the cognitive system is maladaptive, or irrational, in the cases when it fails.

The issues of failure and maladaptation are problematic. After all, poor rational performance in one context could reflect an extremely well measured trade off for good performance in another. For the organism, the most effective deployment of limited processing resources for addressing the problems posed by the environment may well result in such a trade off being made. Clearly, the separation of the functional problem from the processing problem involves an idealization. Although idealizations can be productive, the come at a price. After all, if a Bayesian rational analysis is interpreted as 'specifying exactly what a learner is and is not justified in concluding' (Tenenbaum & Griffiths, 2001b, p. 776), and human behavior deviates from what is justified as result of a processing trade off, should this response be considered as irrational, reflecting a maladaptation? For instance, if a slightly less probable hypothesis is chosen over a more probable one, to what extent would this reflect a failure if such a choice can be arrived at far quicker and by using significantly fewer processing resources?

From a strictly functional level perspective, this argument makes little sense since the notions of adaptation and rationality are typically separated from issues of processing, and hence resource usage. Although Anderson's original formulation of the rational analysis of cognition considered the role of processing limitations in constraining the optimal response function, and productive examples of such considerations exist in, for example, the rational analysis of memory (Schooler & Anderson, 1997; Schooler, 1998), the role of processing limitations are often neglected. For the problem of inductive inference the impact of processing limitations are arguably harder to integrate, and what Anderson (1991b) referred to as the 'true Achilles heel of the rationalist enterprise' (p. 473) has been largely sidestepped in recent work. In the discussion to come we will discuss how constraints on processing change the functional problem quite significantly. This is why, from our perspective, an appropriate notion of adaptive success and rationality for biological organisms should take into account the contributors to function other than mere outcomes, they should also consider how these outcomes are achieved, and therefore extend to the algorithmic level (Simon, 1996; Todd & Gigerenzer, 2003).

The probabilistic mind in the narrow sense

What we will refer to as the narrow sense of the metaphor of the probabilistic mind are those interpretations which, to varying degrees, make a projection from the functional level description to an algorithmic level explanation. Ranging from speculative proposals, which consider the 'in principle' possibility, to full theoretical projection, this stronger interpretation considers probabilistic calculation as a potentially valid algorithmic level concept. Current opinion varies on if and when such an extension is justified. Certain forms of low level perception are viewed as the kinds of information processing problems for which this extension is likely to be valid, giving rise to proposals such as the 'Bayesian coding hypothesis', the idea that probability distributions may be neurally coded and rationally processed (Knill & Pouget, 2004). For other forms of cognition, and especially higher-level cognitive tasks such as decision making, the question is treated as an open one in need of exploration (Chater *et al.*, 2006a). The fly in the ointment for the probabilistic mind in the narrow sense is the fact that rational calculation—the direct use of rational principles as processing principles—tends to be computationally intractable for anything but trivial problems. We will tackle this issue at greater length in the coming discussion, but in the interests of completeness, it is worth pointing out that the boundary between functional level and algorithmic level theories is, for us at least, not always clear.

For instance, when considering the role of compression, an interpretation of the rational principle of induction by minimum description length (MDL), Feldman (2003) argues that 'the neglect of complexity in concept learning has stemmed from the ascendancy of exemplar theories' (p. 227) and 'human learning involves a critical element of compression or complexity minimization that is not present in exemplar models' (p. 230). Such an argument contrasts exemplar models (an algorithmic level theory) with the minimization of coding length (a functional level rational principle), and casts doubt on the former as a result of not conducting the explicit rational calculation implied by the latter. In a given setting, the inferences made by the exemplar model could in principle be consistent with those suggested by the rational principle but, obviously, arrived at without any form of explicit complexity minimization. Unless one views the minimization of coding length as a valid processing principle, such a comparison appears questionable. Fass and Feldman (2003), in a similar vein, consider that 'while it is premature to conclude that humans construct anything like the two part code [...], it seems likely that they employ some closely related complexity minimization principle'. Such a view implies that, to one degree or another, the cognitive system is itself applying the rational principle (the two part code interpretation of MDL, or something close to it). At the very least, there appears to be an implicit belief that organisms have the ability to perform something approaching rational calculation as if 'the machinery of probability and information theory' existed (Movellan & Nelson, 2001, p. 691).

Summary: from tools to metaphors

Our distinction between the metaphor of the probabilistic mind in the broad sense and in the narrow sense is an attempt to mark out degrees of projection of the analytic tools of probability and information theory to theories of the cognitive system itself (Gigerenzer, 1991). We accept that such a coarse grained distinction will miss some subtleties, but the distinction remains an important one. The broad sense of the metaphor is in large part an issue of degrees of idealization, and the theoretical price one is willing to pay for abstracting from the algorithmic level. The narrow sense of the metaphor is more of a technical issue, which we consider next by contrasting our own view of an adaptive toolbox with some of the specific features of the rational analysis of cognition.

The optimal and the psychological

An essential step in the rational analysis of cognition is to find the optimal response function. But to what degree does the goal of understanding the cognitive system as being adapted to problems presented by the environment require the notion of optimality? Is optimality merely an analytic tool for setting a performance benchmark, or a processing assumption made in order to support the metaphor of the probabilistic mind? For the broad sense of the metaphor, 'the optimal behavior function is an explanatory tool, not part of an agent's cognitive equipment' (Chater *et al.*, 2003, p. 70). For the narrow sense of the metaphor the role of optimality is problematic, as optimization as a cognitive processing principle is questionable from a tractability perspective. Until now, we have separated the issues of rationality and optimality because rational principles can be used without invoking the notion of optimality during the analytic process, as a feature of metaphor, or as an assumed property of the organism.

Adaptationism without optimality

Rational principles are required in order to say anything of substance about the success of the organism, or any model of the organism. After all, some normatively justified metric is required in order to inform the task of gauging success. Gauging success, on the other hand, does not require knowledge of the optimal solution. Furthermore, using a rational principle to inform an adaptationist analysis does not mean that optimality or rationality, when used in a broader sense, will necessarily be productive concepts with which explain the function and internal workings of the organism. To illustrate the point, two uses of a rational principle need to be distinguished. Functional models in rational analyses define an optimal benchmark against which behavior is judged, and something to be approached to varying degrees of approximation by the organism. Here, the rational principle is used as an *absolute* measure of function. Although the principle itself may well be interpreted as an approximate measure of function, it nevertheless sets a benchmark, and is absolute in this sense. Rational principles can also be used as model selection criteria, where competing processes are evaluated on their ability to perform the task adequately. Here, the rational principle is used as a *relative* measure of function. The optimal solution does not need to be known when a rational principle is used in this way.

For example, it is standard practice in machine learning to use Bayesian statistics, the MDL principle, or cross validation to assess the functional performance of learning algorithms in the absence of knowledge of the optimal response (Hastie *et al.*, 2001). Our analysis of simple heuristics, and how they perform in comparison to models carrying out more intensive forms of processing, relies on the use of rational principles as model selection criteria. Processes are viewed as performing better or worse than each other, rather than optimally or sub-optimally. On finding that a simple heuristic outperforms several intensive forms of processing model in a given ecological context, we examine the degree to which the simple heuristic is ecologically rational, and view it as a potentially interesting instance of how processing simplicity can be used to exploit the structure of the environment. Because we view cognitive processes as satisficing processes, which seek good enough inferences rather than optimal ones, there is no need to invoke the notion of optimality in order to assess this hypothesis (see also Vicente & Wang, 1998 for a similar perspective). We have no objection to using knowledge of the optimal solution to inform this process, but for many problems that we consider determining the optimal response is infeasible (Martignon & Laskey, 1999).

Comparing this approach to the practices of rational analysis, Chater and Oaksford (1999, p. 59) view our approach as being 'at least in the spirit of an optimality approach'. To clarify this issue, we view knowledge of the optimal response—when it can be reliably identified—as potentially useful knowledge, but not necessarily a useful concept with which to characterize cognitive processing, and certainly not a requirement for carrying out an adaptationist analysis. Indeed, often the significant difficulties in deriving the optimal response can restrict the problems one considers to 'toy world' settings lacking the complexity of the natural contexts faced by the organism. Thus, the methodological priority of identifying the optimal response can be a hindrance, particularly as it presupposes full and certain knowledge of the problem being considered.

In contrast, Chater and Oaksford (1999), argue that 'the need to explain the success of cognition means that, even if they are currently unavailable, deriving optimal solutions will remain a desideratum. Using Marr's analogy, ignoring this step of a rational analysis would be like trying to understand why birds can fly without a theory of aerodynamics.' (p. 59). Trying to understand the cognitive system from an adaptationist perspective without some normatively justified metric of success informing the analytic process, we agree, is likely to obscure the question. In this respect, rational principles should inform the analytic process to the extent that they provide a convincing model of functional success. But the same cannot be said for the role of optimality in adaptationism, both in our approach and, as others have argued, in Marr's (Gilman, 1996).

Optimizing processes and the problem of computational intractability

If the objective is to describe the behavior of an organism by comparing it to an optimal benchmark, then optimality is used as analytic tool only, with no commitment to the possibility or likelihood of optimal processing being a viable proposition. In the absence of an algorithmic level theory an optimal benchmark will often be the only non-arbitrary reference point available. However, if adherence to the optimal solution is taken to reflect or imply an optimizing process, then one must seriously consider if such a process provides a psychologically plausible and computationally tractable solution to the problem. This is why we view theories that consider optimization as a viable process level concept as often involving questionable idealizations that are likely to obscure the essence of the problem. Yet, on the other hand, all processes are optimal given a sufficiently contrived and narrow processing context.

The study of algorithms is often the study of approximating methods. Artificial intelligence, for example, usually concerns itself with the study of problems for which the optimal solution is either intractable or uncomputable (Simon, 1956; Reddy, 1988; Russell & Norvig, 1995). For the problem of inductive inference, ideal forms of rational calculation are uncomputable (Solomonoff, 1964; Li & Vitányi, 1997; Hutter, 2005). In more restricted and realistic settings, inductive inference using Bayesian belief networks can quickly become intractable even when one relaxes the objective to approximate Bayesian reasoning (Cooper, 1990; Roth, 1995; Dagum & Luby, 1993). Statistical machine learning, which provides a significant source of insight and motivation for those examining probabilistic cognition, is chiefly the study of approximation and, as Bishop (2006) points out, 'for many models of practical interest, it will be infeasible to evaluate the posterior distribution or indeed compute expectations with respect to this distribution' (p. 461) and 'in such situations, we need to resort to approximation schemes' (p. 462). Thus, even when the inference problem is reduced to quite restricted settings, tractable algorithms capable of yielding optimal rational outcomes remain illusive. Identifying the optimal solution for a specific problem by analytic means is often beyond reach, a task, which is significantly less tricky than specifying a tractable algorithm capable of arriving at the optimal solution for such problems in general.

Dealing with error: the bias/variance dilemma

How can a functional model suggest certain kinds of mechanisms and not others? In order to help the induction problem—the problem of identifying process level theories which can explain the adaptive success of the cognitive system—assumptions about the algorithmic level are required. In order to provide traction on the induction problem, how theory-specific do these assumptions have to be? Rather than making specific assumptions about the algorithmic layer, the issue we turn to now points to how quite a general formalization of the processing problem can be used to narrow down the kinds of process capable of approaching the significant performance requirements set by rational analyses of cognition.

The assumptions we start with are very general ones concerning the anatomy of inductive processes, and how they can be viewed as performing search over a model class. In this setting, the statistical problem of the bias/variance dilemma can then be used to narrow down the kinds of search procedures and model classes that will be successful in certain contexts (Geman *et al.*, 1992). Ultimately, we will argue that the contexts of interest in cognition, where good performance from sparse data appears to be a hallmark, point to the reduction of variance, or equivalently, the objective of imposing stability on the learning map, as fundamental problems to be overcome by cognitive processes. Simple heuristics, the processing model on which our research program is based, will ultimately be shown to address this objective. By framing the problem in terms of the bias/variance dilemma, bounded rationality can be given a statistical interpretation and justification, which has previously been lacking (Brighton, 2007).

The anatomy of an inductive process

All inductive processes can be formalized as maps from sequences of observations to hypotheses drawn from a hypothesis space. An observation is a pair composed of an input and an output. A particular environment can be thought as a joint probability distribution on an observation space, such that the combination of the two determine how likely each observation will be. We will sometimes refer to this environmental setting in terms of a *target function*, where the target function defines the form of relationship between inputs and outputs occurring in the environment. The task of the learning algorithm is to process sequences of observations in order to induce a hypothesis. The hypothesis space of the algorithm can also be viewed as a model class. A model is simply a parameterized family of hypotheses, were each hypothesis is a fully specified conditional probability distribution. A model class represents the set of models that the algorithm induces over.

Function and the bias/variance dilemma

Organisms process sequences of observations, samples of the target functions governing the environment. Inductive inference is the task of identifying the systems of regularity that govern this environment, given only these samples. An organism well adapted to this task should not be judged solely on its ability to perform well on a single sample. For example, the Bayes optimal classifier—as a process—is optimal only in the sense that it optimal on average. Other processes will outperform it if the sampling assumptions are violated. When estimating the mean predictive accuracy over many samples of the target function, the mean error of the algorithm can always be decomposed into three terms:

$$\text{Error} = \text{Irreducible Error} + \text{Bias} + \text{Variance.} \quad {}^* (1)$$

Irreducible error is noise, and sets an upper bound on the achievable predictive accuracy. The remaining error can be decomposed and controlled through the design of the learning algorithm. This decomposition results in two terms, *bias* and *variance* (see Geman *et al.*, 1992, Bishop, 1995, and Hastie *et al.*, 2001 for derivations and further discussion). Across samples, bias is the difference between the mean predictions of the algorithm and the target function. Variance is the expected squared deviation about this mean, and arises because different hypotheses are likely to be induced for different samples of the target function.

The bias/variance dilemma.

The potential for an algorithm to achieve low bias will depend on how well it can approximate the underlying target function. General purpose processing methods, such as the nearest neighbor classifier and decision tree inductive algorithms, excel at achieving low bias by inducing over model classes with little, if any, restrictions on the functional form of the models. Consequently, a serious problem stands in the way of these methods, and nonparametric[1] methods in general, as being adequate process models of inductive inference. When the training sample is small, in the sense that it provides sparse coverage of the observation space, there is likely to be a potentially significant variance component to the error. Generally speaking, the smaller the size of the training sample, the higher the variance.

To combat the problem of high variance, restrictions on the model class are needed in order to impose stability on the learning map. But clearly, by restricting the model class the method will then suffer from high bias for certain classes of target function. To achieve accurate predictions across samples requires that a process must strike a good balance between reducing bias and reducing variance. Whether or not a process achieves a good balance depends entirely on context. Without stating the class of target functions likely to be encountered, practically nothing can be said about how well a process will achieve this balance when data are limited. This problem is known as the bias/variance dilemma (Geman et al., 1992). All inductive processes can be thought of as making a bet, not only on what kinds of target function the environment will present, but also the likely degree of exposure to these target functions.

Sparse exposure and the context of induction

When functioning in a natural environment, the bias/variance dilemma will pose a significant problem for the organism: complete exposure to the systems of regularity occurring in the environment is typically not possible, observations are limited and often costly, and inductive inference is most pressing when there is a need to generalize to unseen cases. Indeed, the remarkable effectiveness of the cognitive system is seen as remarkable precisely because good inferences appear to be made despite sparse exposure to the underlying regularities (Tenenbaum et al., 2006; Griffiths & Tenenbaum, 2006b, p. 130).

Importantly, the notion of the bias/variance dilemma was originally motivated by the need to account for these phenomena, and align mechanistic accounts with studies of cognition which propose that 'the brain is a proof of existence of near-optimal methods that do not require prohibitively large training samples' (Geman et al., 1992, p. 46). The chief conclusion arising from this work is that, from a processing perspective, 'off the shelf' nonparametric methods such as feed-forward neural networks, nearest neighbor methods, and decision tree induction algorithms, fail as adequate responses to the bias/variance dilemma when data are limited. Without customization, they induce over ostensibly unrestricted model classes, a perspective which 'teaches us all too little about how to solve difficult practical problems' and 'does not

---

[1] Nonparametric methods are those which make minimal assumptions about the functional form of the data generating model (Geman et al., 1992; Bishop, 2006).

help us out of the bias/variance dilemma for finite-size training sets.' (Geman *et al.*, 1992, p. 45).

The bias/variance dilemma implies that general purpose learning, in natural contexts of sparse exposure, is unachievable in any meaningful sense because tractable processes will suffer from error, and the degree of error is likely to vary significantly depending on the content and size of the training sample. Furthermore, it narrows down the kinds of processing strategies capable of meeting levels of performance suggested by rational analyses, and stresses the need to understand the context of induction. More generally, as soon as an organism makes inferences from impoverished data, the variance component of error becomes critical, and one must, to one degree or another, abandon the objective of nonparametric inference. The substantive question now is how this can be done.

Ecologically rational processing

A decomposition of the inference task, and the cognitive system more generally, is often viewed as necessary on grounds of computational tractability (Barrett & Kurzban, 2006; Samuels, 2005) and biological plausibility (Gallistel, 2000). For instance, skepticism toward the tractability of global Bayesian updating can be partially alleviated by updating on a within module basis, leading to the idea that one can 'jettison the goal of being globally Bayesian and instead assume only that each module is Bayesian itself' (Kruschke, 2006, p. 681). But once the black box is opened, on what basis should its contents be organized? For the problem of inductive inference, the bias/variance dilemma suggests that processes induce over constrained model classes in order to impose stability on the learning map, and hence reduce variance. Therefore, decomposition is not merely driven by issues of tractability, but is perhaps more fundamentally driven by issues of function.

We now attempt to tie together the general form of the relationship between functional level analyses, simple heuristics, and the bias/variance dilemma in order to say something about an alignment between ecological focus and processing simplicity. Our hypothesis is that constraints on cognitive processing can align a process with the structure of the environment. An extreme, but nevertheless entirely plausible consequence of this hypothesis is that conducting less processing is just as likely to reduce variance than conducting more processing. This explains why heuristics 'work', adding a statistical interpretation for why the mind might 'operate via a set of heuristic tricks, rather than explicit probabilistic computations' (Chater *et al.*, 2006a, p. 290). Our objective now is to say something about how the retreat from the objective of general purpose nonparametric inference can proceed and be given cognitive-ecological guidance.

Simple heuristics for the bias/variance dilemma

To flesh out our argument we will briefly examine the simple heuristic Take The Best (Gigerenzer & Goldstein, 1996) but frame it in different terms than previously used (see Brighton, 2007, for details). Take The Best is a cognitive process model for making inductive inference on the paired comparison task, where the problem is to rank two objects on their unobserved criterion values. This is a specific form of supervised concept learning. Training observations are pairs of objects, along with feedback on which object scores higher on the criterion. In an induction phase, Take The Best orders the cues by their validity. In the decision phase, it searches for the first cue in the order that discriminates between the two objects, and uses this cue alone to make a prediction. Validity is naïve measurement of a single cue, and simply captures the accuracy of the inferences made by this cue alone when inferring the rank of objects. By referring to Take The Best as simple, we are referring to the fact that it ignores conditional dependencies between cues when selecting a hypothesis, and does not weigh and add cues when making inferences.

The performance and analysis of take the best.

Take The Best often outperforms linear regression models and other simple heuristics over a wide range of environmental contexts (Czerlinski *et al.*, 1999). Using a more reliable model selection criterion than that used by Chater *et al.* (2003), Brighton (2007) shows, contrary to their findings, that Take The Best frequently outperforms a range of neural network, decision tree induction, and exemplar models. In short, Take The Best provides a good illustration of how performing less processing can lead to improved performance in natural environments. Understanding the environmental conditions under which Take The Best, and other simple heuristics, can outperform more computationally intensive methods is the next question.

When viewed in terms of bias/variance dilemma previous work focusing on this question can be seen as identifying conditions for low bias. Conditions for low bias tell us when an algorithm has the ability to closely approximate the target function given a large enough training sample. For example, the non-compensatory environments, those which have rapid decay in cue validities, point to the cases when Take The Best will perform as well as a linear model (Martignon & Hoffrage, 1999, 2002; Katsikopoulos & Martignon, 2006). But matching the performance of another linear model under these conditions is only guaranteed when there is a sufficiently large training sample to saturate the observation space and, crucially, such arguments offer no explanation for the fact that Take The Best can *outperform* a number of linear and nonlinear models. In short, previous analyses of when and why simple heuristics perform well do not consider the very statistical property which confers the performance advantage (Brighton, 2007).

Context sensitive induction.

To frame the performance of Take The Best in terms of the bias/variance dilemma, we will consider two further processing models, and two environments which will elicit drastically different relative performance between the models. The first (natural) environment is the often-studied German city environment (Gigerenzer & Goldstein, 1996; Chater *et al.*, 2003). The second (synthetic) environment is an instance of the more general class of non-compensatory environments, where cue validities decrease rapidly as a function of their rank (Martignon & Hoffrage, 1999, 2002). The two further models we consider are the well known decision tree induction algorithm CART (Breiman, Friedman, Olshen, & Stone, 1994), and a variant of Take The Best (labeled here as *TTB.CV*) which carries out the additional computations required to assess conditional dependencies between cues, and then ranks cues by conditional validity (Martignon & Hoffrage, 1999).

These two methods reflect two useful points for comparison. First, the model class of Take The Best is nested with respect to the model class of CART, since Take The Best is itself a decision tree induction algorithm, inducing trees with restricted function form. Second, the model class of Take The Best is identical to that of TTB.CV. The two methods differ only in how they perform search in order to select the cue order. Now, Figure 9.1(a) plots the predictive accuracy of Take The Best and these two models as a function of sample size for the German city population environment.

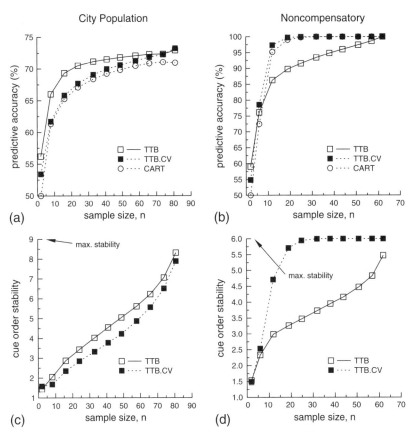

Fig. 9.1. A model comparison of Take The Best (labeled TTB), CART, and a variant of Take The Best which orders cues by conditional validity (labeled TTB.CV). Plot (a) compares the predictive accuracy of the models as function of sample size for the German city population task. Plot (b) compares the models in a synthetic non-compensatory environment. Plots (c) and (d) shows the average Levenschtein distance between induced cue orders as a function of sample size. Cue order stability predicts predictive accuracy very closely.

Predictive accuracy is estimated using cross-validation. Take The Best significantly outperforms both methods across the majority of sample sizes. Second, Figure 9.1(b) shows the same comparison for the non-compensatory environment. Now the other methods outperform Take The Best across the majority of sample sizes. These two environments illustrate how the performance of the process is determined not only by the environment, but also the size of the learning sample. Why is this?

Using search to control variance and stability.

When considering the contribution of bias and variance, Take The Best will tend to outperform a model with a richer models class, such as CART, as a result of reducing variance, since any function Take The Best can approximate, CART can too. But Take The Best is also able to outperform TTB.CV, which has an identical model class. This point illustrates that controlling variance is not simply a matter of placing restrictions on the model class, but can also arise as a consequence of restricting search (Mitchell, 1982; Domingos, 1999). To illustrate the point, the structural stability of the cue orders induced by Take The Best and TTB.CV can be measured directly, and their dependence on sample size and connection to accuracy clarified. For the German city population environment, Figure 9.1(c) shows how the structural stability of the cues orders—here measured as the mean Levenshtein (1966) distance[2] between induced cue orders—predicts almost exactly the relative difference in predictive accuracy of Take The Best and TTB.CV. Notice how CART and TTB.CV perform almost identically.

Figure 9.1(d) shows the same comparison for the non-compensatory environment. Again, stability reflects predictive accuracy: Take The Best performs well to the extent that it imposes stability on the learning map, and hence reduces variance (Turney, 1995; Poggio *et al.*, 2004). One way of thinking about the sensitivity of a cognitive process to the contents of particular samples of the environment is to view this instability as reflecting a failure to ignore accidental, unsystematic, and therefore unpredictive regularities. If a process ignores these accidental regularities and truly focuses on systematic ones, then differences in the content of samples of the target function should not matter too much. Crucially, the determining factor in imposing stability is not the model class itself, but how search is conducted over the model class. By performing less processing and ignoring conditional dependencies between cues, the ecological focus on the ability to achieve stability can be shifted from the synthetic non-compensatory environment (where TTB.CV excels) to the natural German city population environment (where Take The Best excels).

The implications of the bias/variance dilemma for processes and priors

When the variance component of error is the major source of error, the relationship between the properties of the process and the environment is not so clear. In this

---

[2] Levenshtein distance is the minimum number of additions, deletions, and substitutions required to transform one string into another. By interpreting cue indices as symbols, Levenshtein distance provides a distance measure between any two cue orders.

situation, assumptions made on the part of the process and their relationship to the structure of the environment can have a strong positive impact on performance, despite a clear mismatch between the two. For instance, many years of sustained interest in the naïve Bayes classifier is due to the fact that it can perform surprisingly well despite the assumptions made during processing being explicitly violated by the underlying target function (Domingos & Pazzani, 1997; Friedman, 1997; Kuncheva, 2006). With respect to a given process, findings such as these indicate that environmental conditions for low bias can be orthogonal to the conditions for low variance.

From a probabilistic perspective, given full knowledge of the regularities and probabilities governing the environment, and therefore a good model of the hypothesis space and the prior, Bayes optimal inference defines the rational outcome. On accepting that a tractable mechanistic instantiation of this process will be approximate, the variance component of error enters the picture and must be controlled in order to approach rational outcomes. Or, from an MDL perspective, the model in the model class, which reduces the stochastic complexity of the observed data to the greatest extent is the rational choice (Rissanen, 1997; Grünwald, 2005). Given that an exhaustive search through the model class will be infeasible, the use of heuristic search in order to approximate this choice is required. Again, a tractable mechanistic instantiation of the rational process will lead to variance when the performance of the process is measured for different samples of the target function (e.g., the mean compression rate).

For the organism, variance about this mean is important. It reflects the sensitivity of the inductive process to the particular contents of the samples. As soon as approximation is the name of the game, the bias/variance dilemma has to be tackled. The greater the sparsity of exposure to the environment, the more critical this problem becomes. And, this is clearly a statistical problem contributing to the functional success of the organism, since the inductive performance of the organism should not be highly sensitive to different potential encounters (different samples) of the environment. Given that processes are approximate, and not optimal, a significant part of the essence of inductive inference arises due to the realities of resource bounded computation (Simon, 1996). On this view, the issue of cognitive limitations, and how they may serve a functional role by helping to reduce variance, becomes a significant source of further questions. If the rational analysis of cognition and the associated development of the probabilistic view on cognition are to be reconciled with mechanistic accounts, then these issues need to be confronted.

For example, does the bias/variance dilemma imply that for different likely degrees of exposure to the environment, different hypothesis spaces and priors are required to control variance? Thus, on asking where the priors come from, does the bias/variance dilemma play a role? Furthermore, if an analysis of the structure of the environment can only be loosely connected to the assumptions required on the part of the process, does this represent a barrier to reconciling Bayesian analyses with process level accounts? More generally, machine learning and artificial intelligence are often viewed as a rich source of ideas for furthering the probabilistic view on cognition, but to what extent do these disciplines focus on problems with an essentially different character? Large samples, a focus on nonparametric inference, and little concern for cognitive plausibility may represent a counterproductive source of inspiration (Geman et al., 1992). These are some of the questions that need to be addressed.

Summary and conclusion

The notion of probabilistic mind and the study on functional level rational models has been described as the 'the most exciting and revolutionary paradigm to hit cognitive science since connectionism' (Movellan & Nelson, 2001, p. 691). The benefits of this approach are often presented relative to the common practices of cognitive science, which suggest 'a ragbag of arbitrary mechanisms, with arbitrary performance limitations' (Chater & Oaksford, 1999, p. 63). It points to a dichotomy between purposive and mechanistic explanation, with the implication that one faces a choice between an adaptationist perspective relying on rational models abstracted from the algorithmic level, or a mechanistic one with limited prospects of informing purposive explanation (Anderson, 1991b; Chater & Oaksford, 1999). Although this dichotomy is to a certain extent an accurate reflection of current practices, is such an explicit distinction beneficial?

The study of ecological rationality and the adaptive use of simple heuristics is an adaptationist program, which in contrast to the proposed dichotomy, is rooted to an algorithmic level hypothesis. Rather than using the concepts of rationality and optimization to theorize about how the cognitive system might be adapted to its environment, the notion of ecological rationality addresses how good enough solutions can be found with limited processing resources. Here, the basis on which the cognitive system is judged to be adapted to its environment takes into account the specifics of processing, and how the limited resources available to the cognitive system are harnessed to achieve adaptive cognition. In this way, the objective of understanding adaptive cognition need not sacrifice our understanding of the realities of processing. Can these two orientations, which clearly share deep commonalities, be aligned? We have taken work on functional level analyses as providing a valuable insight: They indicate that human level performance and current approaches to cognitive processing and artificial intelligence do not match, in the sense that human performance sets an extremely high standard yet to be achieved reliably by computational models. Something beyond minor repair to existing processing metaphors may be required in order to bring them closer.

The bias/variance dilemma is all about the inevitabilities of error, and points to a fundamental connection between performance and ecological context. It suggests that cognitive mechanisms must effectively reduce variance in order to address the kind of inductive inference problems of interest to cognitive science, which typically involve considerable degrees of accuracy despite sparse exposure to the environment. We showed how the simple heuristic Take The Best confers function by exploiting the connection between processing simplicity, the structure of the environment, and variance reduction. In this sense, we have sought a connection between the rational probabilistic models of cognition and simple heuristics: simple heuristics offer a form of processing model that the cognitive system could rely on in order to reduce the variance component of error. Variance will inevitably arise given the extreme implausibility of optimal rational calculation and the need to generalize despite sparse exposure to the environment. Machine learning tends to address this problem by performing more processing (Schapire, 1990; Breiman, 1996). We suspect that the cognitive system does not have this option, and instead tackles the problem by performing less processing.

From an algorithmic perspective the mind achieves adaptive behavior to varying degrees depending on ecological context. Rational principles are to a certain extent required to substantiate this view, but as the centerpiece to a metaphor, or the guiding principle of a paradigm, we believe they obscure something of the essence of cognition. As with all metaphors, one pays some kind of a price. The price one pays clearly depends on the problem, and the kind of answers one is looking for. For us, the *why* question—why the cognitive system behaves as it does, and the *how* question—how it does it—should not be separated. Indeed, we would find it deeply surprising to find that evolution had overlooked the use of simple processing solutions as way of adapting the organism to the environment using limited resources. Examining the cognitive system using principles divorced from the impact of processing may, on this view, be a heavy price to pay.

Acknowledgments

We would like to thank Nick Chater, Lael Schooler, Henrik Olsson, Peter Juslin, and Nathan Berg for insightful discussion, criticism, and comments.

References

Anderson, J. R. (1990). *The adaptive character of thought*. Hillsdale, New Jersey: Lawrence Erlbaum.

Anderson, J. R. (1991a). The adaptive nature of human categorization. *Psychological Review*, **98**(3), 409–429.

Anderson, J. R. (1991b). Is human cognition adaptive? *Behavioral and Brain Sciences*, **14**, 471–517.

Barrett, H. C., & Kurzban, R. (2006). Modularity in cognition: framing the debate. *Psychological Review*, **113**(3), 628–647.

Bishop, C. M. (1995). *Neural networks for pattern recognition*. Oxford: Oxford University Press.

Bishop, C. M. (2006). *Pattern recognition and machine learning*. New York: Springer.

Breiman, L. (1996). Bagging predictors. *Machine Learning*, **24**(2), 123–140.

Breiman, L., Friedman, J. H., Olshen, R. A., & Stone, P. J. (1994). *Classification and regression trees*. Belmont, CA: Wadsworth International Group.

Brighton, H. (2007). *Ecological rationality and the bias/variance dilemma*. (Manuscript under review)

Chater, N., & Oaksford, M. (1999). Ten years of the rational analysis of cognition. *Trends in Cognitive Sciences*, **3**(2), 57–65.

Chater, N., Oaksford, M., Nakisa, R., & Redington, M. (2003). Fast, frugal, and rational: How rational norms explain behavior. *Organizational Behavior and Human Decision Processes*, **90**, 63–86.

Chater, N., Tenenbaum, J. B., & Yuille, A. (2006a). Probabilistic models of cognition: conceptual foundations. *Trends in Cognitive Sciences*, **10**(7), 287–291.

Chater, N., Tenenbaum, J. B., & Yuille, A. (2006b). Probabilistic models of cognition: Where next? *Trends in Cognitive Sciences*, **10**(7), 292–293.

Chater, N., & Vitányi, P. M. B. (2003). Simplicity: a unifying principle in cognitive science? *Trends in Cognitive Sciences*, **7**(1), 19–22.

Cooper, G. F. (1990). The computational complexity of probabilistic inference using Bayesian belief networks. *Artificial Intelligence*, **42**, 393–405.

Czerlinski, J., Gigerenzer, G., & Goldstein, D. G. (1999). How good are simple heuristics? In G. Gigerenzer, P. M. Todd, & The ABC Research Group (Eds.), *Simple heuristics that make us smart* (pp. 119–140). Oxford: Oxford University Press.

Dagum, P., & Luby, M. (1993). Approximating probabilistic inference in Bayesian belief networks is NP-hard. *Artificial Intelligence*, **60**, 141–153.

Domingos, P. (1999). The role of Occam's razor in knowledge discovery. *Data Mining and Knowledge Discovery*, **3**, 409–425.

Domingos, P., & Pazzani, M. (1997). On the optimality of the simple Bayesian classifier under zero-one loss. *Machine Learning*, **29**, 103–130.

Fass, D., & Feldman, J. (2003). Categorization under complexity: A unified MDL account of human learning of regular and irregular categories. In S. Becker, S. Thrun, & K. Obermayer (Eds.), *Advances in neural information processing systems 15* (pp. 35–34). Cambridge, MA: MIT Press.

Feldman, J. (2003). The simplicity principle in human concept learning. *Current Directions in Psychological Science*, **12**(6), 227–232.

Friedman, J. H. (1997). On bias. variance, 0/1-loss, and the curse-of-dimensionality. *Data Mining and Knowledge Discovery*, **1**, 55–77.

Gallistel, C. R. (2000). The replacement of general-purpose learning models with adaptively specialized learning modules. In M. S. Gazzaniga (Ed.), *The cognitive neurosciences* (pp. 1179–1191). Cambridge, MA: MIT Press.

Geman, S., Bienenstock, E., & Doursat, R. (1992). Neural networks and the bias/variance dilemma. *Neural Computation*, **4**, 1–58.

Gigerenzer, G. (1991). From tools to theories: a heuristic of discovery in cognitive psychology. *Psychological Review*, **98**, 254–267.

Gigerenzer, G., & Goldstein, D. G. (1996). Reasoning the fast and frugal way: models of bounded rationality. *Psychological Review*, **103**(4), 650–669.

Gigerenzer, G., & Selten, R. (2001). *Bounded rationality: the adaptive toolbox*. Cambridge, MA: MIT Press.

Gigerenzer, G., Todd, P. M., & The ABC Research Group. (1999). *Simple heuristics that make us smart*. Oxford: Oxford University Press.

Gilman, D. (1996). Optimization and simplicity: computational vision and biological explanation. *Synthese*, **107**, 293–323.

Griffiths, T. L., & Tenenbaum, J. (2006b). Statistics and the Bayesian mind. *Significance*, **3**(3), 130–133.

Griffiths, T. L., & Tenenbaum, J. B. (2006a). Optimal predictions in everyday cognition. *Psychological Science*, **17**(9), 767–773.

Grünwald, P. (2005). Minimum description length tutorial. In P. Grünwald, I. J. Myung, & M. A. Pitt (Eds.), *Advances in minimum description length* (pp. 23–79). Cambridge: MIT Press.

Hastie, T., Tibshirani, R., & Friedman, J. (2001). *The elements of statistical learning: Data mining, inference, and prediction*. New York: Springer.

Hutter, M. (2005). *Universal artificial intelligence*. Berlin: Springer-Verlag.

Katsikopoulos, K. V., & Martignon, L. (2006). Naïve heuristics for paired comparison: Some results on their relative accuracy. *Journal of Mathematical Psychology*, **50**, 488–494.

Knill, D. C., & Pouget, A. (2004). The Bayesian brain: The role of uncertainty in neural coding and computation. *Trends in Neurosciences*, **27**(12), 712–719.

Kruschke, J. K. (2006). Locally Bayesian learning with applications to retrospectve revaluation and highlighting. *Psychological Review*, **113**(4), 677–699.

Kuncheva, L. I. (2006). On the optimality of Naïve Bayes with dependent binary features. *Pattern Recognition Letters*, **27**, 830–837.

Levenshtein, V. I. (1966). Binary codes capable of detecting deletions, insertions and reversals. *Russian Physics Doklady*, **10**(8), 707–710.

Li, M., & Vitányi, P. M. B. (1997). *An introduction to Kolmogorov complexity and its applications*. New York: Springer-Verlag.

Marr, D. (1982). *Vision*. San Francisco, CA: Freeman.

Martignon, L., & Hoffrage, U. (1999). Why does one-reason decision making work? A case study in ecological rationality. In G. Gigerenzer, P. M. Todd, & The ABC Research Group (Eds.), *Simple heuristics that make us smart* (pp. 119–140). Oxford: Oxford University Press.

Martignon, L., & Hoffrage, U. (2002). Fast, frugal, and fit: Simple heuristics for paired comparisons. *Theory and Decision*, **52**, 29–71.

Martignon, L., & Laskey, K. B. (1999). Bayesian benchmarks for fast and frugal heuristics. In G. Gigerenzer, P. M. Todd, & The ABC Research Group (Eds.), *Simple heuristics that make us smart* (pp. 169–188). Oxford: Oxford University Press.

Mitchell, T. M. (1982). Generalization as search. *Artificial Intelligence*, **18**, 203–226.

Movellan, J. R., & Nelson, J. D. (2001). Probabilsitic functionalism: A unifying paradigm for the cognitive sciences. *Behavioral and Brain Science*, **24**(4), 690–692.

Oaksford, M., & Chater, N. (1998). *Rational models of cognition*. Oxford: Oxford University Press.

Poggio, T., Rifkin, R., Mukherjee, S., & Niyogi, P. (2004). General conditions for predictivity in learning theory. *Nature*, **428**, 419–422.

Reddy, R. (1988). AAAI presidential address: foundations and grand challenges of artificial intelligence. *AI Magazine*, **Winter 1988**, 9–21.

Rissanen, J. (1997). Stochastic complexity in learning. *Journal of Computer and Systems Sciences*, **55**, 89–95.

Roth, D. (1995). On the hardness of appproximate reasoning. *Artificial Intelligence*, **82**, 273–302.

Russell, S., & Norvig, P. (1995). *Artificial intelligence: a modern approach*. Englewood Cliffs, NJ: Prentice Hall.

Samuels, R. (2005). The complexity of cognition: tractibility arguments for massive modularity. In P. Carruthers, S. Laurence, & S. Stich (Eds.), *The innate mind: structure and contents* (pp. 107–121). Oxford: Oxford University Press.

Schapire, R. E. (1990). The strength of weak learnability. *Machine Learning*, **5**(2), 197–227.

Schooler, L. J. (1998). Sorting out core memory processes. In M. Oaksford & N. Chater (Eds.), *Rational models of cognition* (pp. 128–155). Oxford: Oxford University Press.

Schooler, L. J., & Anderson, J. R. (1997). The role of process in the rational analysis of memory. *Cognitive Psychology*, **32**, 219–250.

Shepard, R. N. (1987). Towards a universal law of generalization for psychological science. *Science*, **237**, 1317–1323.

Simon, H. A. (1956). Rational choice and the structure of the environment. *Psychological Review*, **63**, 129–138.

Simon, H. A. (1996). *The sciences of the artificial* (3rd ed.). Cambridge, MA: MIT Press.

Solomonoff, R. J. (1964). A formal theory of inductive inference, part 1 and part 2. *Information and Control*, **7**, 1–22, 224–254.

Tenenbaum, J. B., & Griffiths, T. L. (2001a). Generalization, similarity, and Bayesian inference. *Behavioral and Brain Sciences*, **24**, 629–640.

Tenenbaum, J. B., & Griffiths, T. L. (2001b). Some specifics about generalization. *Behavioral and Brain Sciences*, **24**, 762–778.

Tenenbaum, J. B., Griffiths, T. L., & Kemp, C. (2006). Theory-based Bayesian models of inductive learning and reasoning. *Trends in Cognitive Sciences*, **10**(7), 309–318.

Todd, P. M., & Gigerenzer, G. (2003). Bounding rationality to the world. *Journal of Econonmic Psychology*, **24**, 143–165.

Turney, P. (1995). Bias and the quantification of stability. *Machine Learning*, **20**, 23–33.

Vicente, K. J., & Wang, J. H. (1998). An ecological theory of expertise effects in memory recall. *Psychological Review*, **105**(1), 33–57.

Vitányi, P. M. B., & Li, M. (2000). Minimum description length induction, Bayesianism, and Kolmogorov complexity. *IEEE Transactions on Information Theory*, **46**(2), 446–464.

Chapter 10

The game of life: how small samples render choice simpler

Ralph Hertwig

University of Basel, Basel, Switzerland

Timothy J. Pleskac

Michigan State University, East Lansing, MI, USA

Life is a gamble at terrible odds. If it was a bet you wouldn't take it.

> Tom Stoppard (1967), 'Rosencrantz and Guildenstern are dead' (p. 115)

Bet your shirt on a horse, your retirement on GE, your premiums on disaster, your tuition on a college ... your energy on a book. Birth is just anteing up; every action thereafter is a bet.

> Michael and Ellen Kaplan (2006) 'Chances are ...' (p. 82)

In the interest of fairness, the CPS [Chicago Public School system] resorted to a lottery. .... Imagine two students, statistically identical, each of whom wants to attend a new, better school. Thanks to how the ball bounces in the hopper, one goes to the new school and the other stays behind.

> Steven Levitt & Stephen Dubner, (2005), 'Freakonomics' (p. 158)

Arguably one of the most successful metaphors guiding psychological theorizing is not so much a metaphor of the mind, but of how the world presents itself to us. As Goldstein and Weber (1997) pointed out the *life as a gamble* metaphor that enters psychology via the work of von Neumann and Morgenstern (1947) and Savage (1954) has roots dating back to Jacob Bernoulli's (originally published 1713) *Ars Conjectandi*. Relying strongly on monetary gambles, he pursued probability as 'a general theory of rational decisions under uncertainty'—a theory that would apply to 'choices about witness (or creed) to believe, which venture to invest in, which candidate to elect, what insurance premium to charge, which scientific theory to endorse' (Daston, 1988, pp. 40, 50). Savage proposed that virtually all alternative courses of actions have risky, not perfectly predictable consequences, and that therefore everyday choices could be seen as choices between monetary gambles. By making this analogy, Savage sanctioned the future ubiquitous use of a very simple and convenient experimental tool in economists' and psychologists' laboratories, namely, the investigation of choices between monetary gambles.

Choice between monetary gambles is the topic of this chapter. We will distinguish between two different choice contexts, one in which a person can persue convenient descriptions of gambles' outcomes and probabilities, and one in which a person can sequentially sample outcomes thus being able to form an impression of the gambles' stakes and their probabilities. The former choice context gives rise to *decisions from descriptions*, the latter to *decisions from experience*. We will be concerned with decisions from experience, and offer a simple explanation as to why people appear to be content with small samples of experiences before they render their choice. First, however, we illustrate both choice contexts.

Decisions from description and decisions from experience

If the Wason selection task is, as psychologists' wisdom has it, indeed the most studied 'fruit fly' in cognitive psychology, then choice between monetary gambles must be a close runner up. This particular *Drosophila melanogaster* can be studied in many different strands. One involves representations in which people are provided with convenient descriptions of possible alternatives, the possible consequences associated with each alternative, and their respective likelihoods. Faced with such descriptions, we can afford making what Knight (1921) called *decisions under risk*. Decisions under risk are almost exclusively studied via *decisions from description* (Hertwig *et al.*, 2004), namely, situations in which individuals are fully informed about the possible outcomes of each option and their probabilities, in either a visual or a numerical format.[i]

Take Maurice Allais' (1953/1979) famous article on 'The foundations of a positive theory of choice involving risk' for illustration. Herein he described a person who tenders successive choices between four independent prospects, which are described as follows (p. 41):

$$(P_0)\begin{cases} \frac{1}{2} \ \$100 \\ \frac{1}{2} \ \ 0 \end{cases} \quad (P'_0)\begin{cases} 1 \ \$100 \end{cases} \quad (P_1)\begin{cases} \frac{1}{2} \ \$1000 \\ \frac{1}{2} \ \ 0 \end{cases} \quad (P'_1)\begin{cases} 1 \ \$300 \end{cases}$$

That is, the person encounters four prospects, each one involving explicitly stated outcomes and likelihoods. There are real world analogies to these comprehensively described choices in information sources such as weather forecasts, actuarial tables, and mutual-fund brochures. But all the same, compare such fully described prospects with those that we *typically* encounter once we step outside the confines of the experimental laboratory. An admittedly drastic example is that of a patient who considers participating in clinical trials on which basis the Food and Drug Administration decides whether or not to approve an experimental drug. The development and test of new drugs is a fiscal gamble of colossal proportions. By the time a drug reaches the market the manufacturer is estimated to have spent nearly a billion dollars on its

----

[i] In a recent meta-analysis of all studies involving decisions between a two-outcome risky prospect and a sure thing (with equal expected value), Weber *et al.* (2004) found that all 226 choice situations called for decisions from description.

development, and nearly nine out of ten experimental drugs that enter the first stage of a three-stage regime of clinical trials are eventually abandoned (Groopman, 2006). For the drug manufacturers, the gamble of developing a drug is just about money, albeit enormous amounts of money, and guesses of the likelihoods of success can be garnered from the past.

For a patient, in contrast, entering a clinical trial can be a life-or-death wager, and one in which the likelihoods remain unknown. For illustration, consider *Torcetrapib*, an experimental cholesterol drug developed by Pfizer, the world's largest drug maker. Hailed as the company's most promising experimental drug and—should it work— potentially the 'largest-selling pharmaceutical in history' (Groopman, 2006), all Torcetrapib trials were halted in December 2006 after it was found that it actually caused an increase in deaths and heart problems. Eighty-two people had died so far in a Stage III trial, versus 51 people in the same trial who had not taken it (Berenson, 2006). Partaking in the experimental trial is a gamble, but one in which, unlike in Allais' choice prospects, patients cannot simply consult a list of outcomes and precisely specified likelihoods. Being unaware of the outcomes' probabilities, their decision was thus—in Knight's (1921) terms—a *decision under uncertainty*. Uncertainty is a defining property of human existence, and unfortunately, more often than not there is no reliable probability and outcome information (see also Knight, 1921; Lopes, 1983).

In the twilight of uncertainty, there are at least two strategies to fill the void of knowledge. One is to turn to previous experience—experience that was gathered by us, or others, when facing similar decisions—to thus simulate and anticipate the future (e.g., Dudai & Carruthers, 2005). This ubiquitous strategy is used, for instance, when we remember previous meetings to anticipate what might happen during tomorrow's big meeting. Or take one of the most uncertain of all businesses: predicting the intentions of one's enemy. The political scientist Alexander George (1959) described in his book *Propaganda Analysis* how small groups of intelligence analysts from the Allies successfully applied this strategy, reliance on past experience, during World War II to uncover German secrets.

Cut off from normal sources of information about events in enemy territory, the analysts' task was to monitor everything that came over the radio waves from Nazi Germany. In domestic broadcasts in 1943, Nazi propaganda boasted that the German military had developed a secret 'super weapon.' Were those claims to be believed? The analysts predicated their analysis on their past experience that 'German propaganda never deliberately misled the German people in questions involving an increase of German power' (George, 1959, p. 143). The likely reason was that propaganda was supposed to boost morale. If the propagandists' claims had been bluffs, their attempts at manipulation would have swiftly become ineffective. So, if they broadcast that Germany had a secret super weapon it meant, quite likely, that indeed they had one. Starting from that premise, the intelligence analysts mined other German public pronouncements for more insight, and as George described thus arrived at a surprisingly accurate sequence of inferences about the super weapon. It turned out to be Nazi's fabled V-1 rocket.

Resorting to past experience to anticipate the future, however, only works if there is a past. Sometimes there is none. Contemplate, for instance, the analysts' work at the beginning of the war when they had no experience with the German propaganda machine.

In other cases, the current problem is truly unique making the past a poor model for the present or the future. In such cases, another strategy that, given its feasibility, enables a person to deal with uncertainty is to garner novel experience before making a decision. Novel experience can be collected through sampling information from the payoff distributions under consideration. As Bernstein (1996) pointed out, many critical decisions would be impossible without sampling. And it is a fact of life's limitations (time, resources) that sampling needs to be limited as well. On basis of samples we can make an educated guess as to which option is preferable (see also Gladwell, 2005). For instance, one sip of wine, perhaps even as little as a sniff or a look, determines whether the contents of the bottle are drinkable. Enjoying a two-week free trial of a daily newspaper tells us whether it is to our political taste. A quick look on the online traffic cams tells us which route to choose for the morning commute. Glancing at the plates of the other guests helps us to determine which dish to choose from a restaurant's menu. Polling friends about which of two new movies they enjoyed renders our night at the movies more pleasurable.

Hertwig *et al.* (2004) referred to decisions based on thus sampled experience as *decisions from experience*. A number of studies have demonstrated that decisions from experience are distinct from decisions from description (e.g., Hau *et al.*, in press; Hertwig *et al.*, 2004; Gottlieb *et al.*, 2007; Weber *et al.*, 2004), but see Fox and Hadar (2006). Hertwig *et al.* argued that the key to their difference is people's sampling behavior—especially their tendency to rely on relatively small samples of information. Next, we describe the context in which people rely on small samples of experience.

Decisions from experience: heeding small samples' call

What do we know about the psychology of decisions from experience? Relatively little. As mentioned earlier, this is because studies of human risky choice have almost exclusively examined decisions from description. This situation, however, has been changing rapidly. Recently, a number of studies have turned to environments in which people are confronted with choices between initially unknown payoff distributions where they must overcome their ignorance by sampling from these distributions (e.g., Barron & Erev, 2003; Busemeyer, 1985; Denrell, 2007; Hertwig *et al.*, 2004; March, 1996; Weber *et al.*, 2004). By sampling they can form an impression of the distributions' respective attractiveness.

In decisions from experience the environment and its structure play a substantial role as opposed to the minimal role they play in decisions from description. As a result, models of decisions from experience must adopt more of an ecological approach (Anderson, 1991; Brunswik, 1943; Simon, 1956). To that end we must distinguish between two ecologies when people sample from both distributions. One is characterized by an inherent trade-off between exploiting and exploring options (see Berry & Fristedt, 1985; Daw *et al.*, 2006; Erev & Barron, 2005; March, 1996), and one in which the agent's only objective initially is exploration for information (Hertwig *et al.*, 2004; Weber *et al.*, 2004). In the former ecology, the sampled outcomes simultaneously provide information and payoffs to the agent. He thus has to strike a balance between exploring alternatives and exploiting them. This trade-off adds a different dynamic to decision making, and makes such choices distinct from decisions from description. Specifically, a risk-neutral person may come to prefer a certain alternative to an uncertain one with identical expected values, thus exhibiting risk aversion (see Denrell, 2007; March, 1996). In addition, properties of the decision maker—such as the tendency to probability match, memory constraints, and loss aversion—are likely to shape such choices (Erev & Barron, 2005).

In this chapter we focus on the second information ecology, in which, much like perusing the Gault-Millau or the Michelin Guide to select a restaurant, the sampled outcomes only provide information. Exploitation of the options—dining at one of the acclaimed two- or three-star gastronomic temples—only comes after the agent has terminated search for information. Therefore, people can afford—disregarding opportunity costs for the moment—to further explore a distribution even if the previously sampled outcomes were anything other than attractive. Sampling is thus like testing the water without footing the bill: the sampled outcomes educate about the possible payoffs but do not yet constitute actual earnings. This sampling dynamic in turn makes decisions from experience different from decisions from description.

For illustration consider a study by Hertwig et al. (2004) where participants were presented with several choices between two gambles. Not being told anything about the gambles, they were afforded the opportunity to sample information about them. Each respondent saw two boxes on a computer screen, with each box representing a payoff distribution. Clicking on a given box triggered a random draw (with replacement) of an outcome from its distribution. Respondents could sample outcomes in whatever order and as often as they desired. They were encouraged to sample until they felt confident enough to decide from which of the two boxes ('decks') they would like to make one final draw with monetary consequences. After they had stopped sampling they indicated this preference. On this choice and this choice only, respondents received the monetary payoffs identified by their draw.

Hertwig et al. (2004) compared the choices found when a group of participants made decisions from experience for six problems with those of a second group who, although responding to the same problems, made decisions from description. Although respondents in the *experience* and *description* groups faced structurally identical problems their choices were drastically different. For instance, respondents faced Problem 1:

> *Deck A*: 4 with probability 0.8, 0 otherwise,
> or
> *Deck B*: 3 with certainty.

In this case, a large majority of respondents (88%) in the experience group selected *A*, whereas only about a third of respondents in the description group did so. Choices in the description group were consistent with prospect theory's postulate that people choose as if small-probability events (here $0 with probability 0.2 in option *A*) receive more weight than they deserve according to their objective probabilities of occurrence (Kahneman & Tversky, 1979; Tversky & Kahneman, 1992). In contrast, in decisions from experience rare (small-probability) events appear to have less impact than they deserve according to their objective probabilities.

Hertwig et al. (2004) argued that rare events are not duly appreciated in experience-based decisions because decision makers tend to rely on small samples to make their choices. Two recent studies of decisions from experience have documented this tendency. Hertwig *et al.* found that the typical number of draws respondents made—with the outcome of each draw appearing immediately—was approximately 7 from each deck (and 15 across both decks). In a similar study, Weber *et al.* (2004) reported a median size of 17 total draws, collapsed across both decks. Reliance on *genuinely* small samples proved to be complemented by reliance on *functionally* small samples due to recency. In Hertwig *et al.*'s study, the most recently experienced outcomes tended to shape the final choice more than previously sampled ones (for more evidence for this *recency* effect see Barron & Erev, 2003; Busemeyer & Stout, 2002; Erev & Barron, 2005; Hertwig *et al.*, 2006; Yechiam & Busemeyer, 2005).

Such small samples interact with the environment in interesting ways. Events in the typical decisions from experience design (as described above) are binomially distributed, where n is the number of draws from a particular gamble or deck, and p is the probability of the maximum outcome in the gamble. When n is small (i.e., few draws) and p—or by implication, $1-p$—is small (i.e., the event is rare) the binomial distribution is skewed for the number of times this rare outcome will be observed in n independent trials. This, in turn, increases the probability that a frugal searcher will not come across the distribution's rare event, keeping her ignorant of its existence. But even if she encounters the rare event in her small sample, she will tend to observe it less frequently than expected (given its objective probability; see Hertwig *et al.*, 2004, for the detailed argument).

The Hindu fable of the elephant and the six blind men is famous precisely because each one took a tiny sample of the entire animal (e.g., the tusk, the trunk, the ear) and arrived at rather erroneous conclusions (e.g., the elephant was very much like a spear, a snake, or a fan). By analogy, if small samples tend to give rise to inaccurate mental models of events—for instance, by raising the risk of overlooking rare events—why then do people rely on such small samples? Next, we put forth an explanation. It complements but does not rule out other possible reasons such as memory constraints, opportunity costs, and lack of motivation (see also Hau *et al.*, in press). However, rather than looking into people's minds to explain their frugal sampling, we suggest that their behavior is a reflection of how gambles present themselves to the player through the windows of small samples.

Gambling in Smallville: why intuitive sampling may be destined to be frugal[ii]

In many domains, sampling in itself is a form of risk-taking. How representative are the samples from which we draw inferences? When are the samples large enough to render possible a good guess? When does further sampling just becomes a waste of time? In Hertwig *et al.* (2004) and Weber *et al.*'s (2004) studies, respondents could have sampled for as long as they wanted without penalty, and each draw required merely a few seconds. By sampling more they could have markedly enhanced their chances of identifying the distribution with the higher expected value. For example,

---

[ii] The following exposition of the argument is an adapted extension of the analysis reported by Hertwig and Pleskac (2007).

in Problem 1 if respondents had calculated the observed sample mean for each deck and deterministically chosen the gamble with the larger mean, the median sample size of seven draws from each deck would have offered a meek chance of 58% to select the higher expected value deck.[iii] Can small samples nevertheless be beneficial on some other dimension? Not denying its cost, reliance on small samples can indeed have benefits too. One is that they make it easier to choose. Moreover, to foreshadow a later result, the risk of selecting the inferior gamble in a representative environment is by no means as pronounced as one might fear, based on the analysis of Problem 1.

To appreciate the argument that small samples render choice simpler let us first turn to a distinction discussed by Griffin and Tversky (1992), namely, that between the strength and the weight of evidence. To illustrate both concepts, they used the following example that also involves a decision from experience:

> [s]uppose we wish to evaluate the evidence for the hypothesis that a coin is biased in favor of heads rather than tails. In this case, the proportion of heads in a sample reflects the strength of evidence for the hypothesis in question, and the size of the sample reflects the credence of these data. The distinction between the strength of evidence and its weight is closely related to the distinction between the size of an effect (e.g., the difference between two means) and its reliability (e.g., the standard error of the difference). (Griffin & Tversky, 1992, p. 412)

Griffin and Tversky also suggested that 'people focus on the strength of the evidence—at least, as they perceive it—and then make some adjustment in response to its weight' (p. 413). Typically, this adjustment is insufficient and therefore 'the strength of the evidence tends to dominate its weight in comparison to an appropriate statistical model' (p. 413).

In choosing between two gambles about which one needs to sample information, we also suggest that people focus primarily (but not exclusively) on the size of the effect or the strength of the evidence.

As we will show the size of the effect is larger with smaller samples, thus rendering choice easier. Before explaining this relationship, let us first propose a simple choice rule that rests on the strength of evidence, measured in terms of the difference between means. The *natural mean heuristic* consists of two steps:

> Step 1. Calculate the sample mean for each deck, SM_A and SM_B by summing all the experienced (sampled) outcomes in the respective decks, and dividing by respective sample sizes n_A and n_B, respectively. [iv]

> Step 2. Choose the deck with the strictly larger sample mean; otherwise guess.

This choice strategy accounts well for people's choices between payoff distributions (henceforth *decks*). It predicted a total of 77% of people's choices in Hertwig *et al.* (2004), relative to 67% for cumulative prospect theory (Fox & Hadar, 2006). For a set *n*, the strategy even maximizes expected earnings *given* the knowledge of the person.

[iii] The sample mean equals the decks' expected value as calculated on the basis of the sampled outcomes and likelihoods.

[iv] If the sample sizes for each deck are equal, then the rule only requires computing the sum of the outcomes per deck.

In addition, with increasingly larger *n*s, the rule grows more likely to select the gamble with the highest objective expected value. With smaller samples, in contrast, the heuristic runs the risk of selecting the inferior gamble. But resting one's choice on the sample means renders choice easier with small samples. To appreciate this, consider a user of the natural mean heuristic who draws seven observations from deck *A* that offers $32 with probability 0.1, $0 otherwise, and seven from deck *B* that offers $3 for sure. She may encounter seven times a '0' from deck *A*, and a '3' each time from deck *B*, amounting to a sample mean of 0 and 3, respectively. The *experienced difference* is thus 15 times as large as the *description difference* (i.e., the objective difference between the gambles' expected values), 3 versus 0.2. That is, the experienced difference is *amplified*, relative to the description difference.

Amplification was the rule rather than the exception in Hertwig *et al.*'s (2004) study. In a reanalysis of their data, we found that in 121 (81%) of the total of 150 choices the experienced differences were greater than those based on the gambles' descriptions. In merely 12 cases (8%), they were identical, and in 17 choices (11%) the experienced difference was less than the description difference. On average, the experienced difference was 10.8 times larger than the description difference. This amplification is not a coincidence but, as the following formal proof shows, a necessity. Before we turn to the proof, however, one clarification is in order. We do not conjecture that people *exclusively* attend to the strength of evidence and terminate sampling when the experienced difference is largest, thus completely ignoring the reliability of the difference. Rather, we suggest that if—as Griffin and Tversky (1992) proposed—the strength of the evidence tends to dominate its weight, strength can eclipse weight even more by means of the amplification effect. As a consequence, early termination of search is fostered.

The amplification effect: a simple proof

If we assume two options, *A* and *B*, of which *A*'s expected value is greater than *B*'s, then the *absolute* expected difference between the sample means (or strength of evidence), SM_A and SM_B, will always be as large or larger than the expected or description difference, $EV_A - EV_B$. To arrive at this finding, we take the following steps: Setting $Y = SM_A - SM_B$, the expected value of Y, $E(Y)$, can be calculated as follows:

$$E(Y) = P(Y \geq 0)E(Y \mid Y \geq 0) + P(Y < 0)E(Y \mid Y < 0) = EV_A - EV_B. \quad (1)$$

The expected *absolute* difference of $E(|Y|)$ can be found because using the absolute values is tantamount to moving the area below '0,' representing all 'erroneous' differences (i.e., suggesting *B*'s expected value to exceed *A*'s) in the distribution of differences onto the positive reals. Consequently, the expected absolute difference $E(|Y|)$ can be stated:

$$E(|Y|) = P(Y \geq 0)E(Y \mid Y \geq 0) - P(Y < 0)E(Y \mid Y < 0). \quad (2)$$

Because $E(Y \mid Y < 0)$ is by definition negative (the expected value of Y given that Y is smaller than 0), the second term in (2) becomes positive. Therefore, $E(|Y|)$ is at least as large as $E(Y)$. Put differently, the experienced difference is, on average, larger than the objective or description difference.

This proof also suggests what factors are moderating the amplification effect. Specifically, anything reducing $P(Y<0)$ will result in $E(|Y|)$ approaching $E(Y)$. Three factors that do this are (a) increasing sample size n; (b) increasing the difference between the expected values of the two options; and (c) reducing the pooled variance across the two options. This simple proof, however, leaves several key questions unanswered: What is the magnitude of the amplification effect in a given uncertain environment? How robust is it across different choice rules that people may use? What price does the amplification effect and, by extension, the benefit of easier choice exact? To find answers, we turned to a simulated environment of gambles.

The amplification effect: an analysis based on simulation

We assume that a person chooses between simple two-outcome payoff distributions of the type 'a probability p to win amount x; a probability $(1 - p)$ to win amount y' $(x, p; y)$, using the natural mean heuristic. We analyzed a total of 12 different sample sizes, consisting of 1, 2, 3, 4, 5, 6, 7, 8, 9, 10, 15, and 25 draws from either deck. For each of these sizes, we calculated several statistics including the expected absolute value and median absolute value of the experienced difference. For illustration, consider choosing between the following two randomly generated decks (Problem 2):

> A: 26 with probability 0.76, 0 otherwise,
>
> or
>
> B: 48 with probability 0.55, 0 otherwise.

Deck A has an expected value of 19.76, whereas B's value is 26.4. With a difference of 6.64 points between the gambles' expected values, choosing between them appears fairly easy—especially if the choice comes in the form of a decision from description. But how hard is the choice on the basis of a sample of, say, five draws from either deck? In such a sample, a person could encounter $k = 0, 1, 2, 3, 4,$ or 5 occurrences of the maximum gain (26 and 48, respectively), and $n - k$ observations of the minimum gain (i.e., 0 in each gamble). The binomial distribution provides the probability of obtaining each k (and $n - k$, respectively). Table 10.1 lists the probability of each k, and the resulting sample mean. For instance, the probability of the A's maximum gain (26) occurring twice in a sample of five draws equals 0.08. The sample mean for this particular sample would be 10.4. Note that the likelihood of this mean mirrors the likelihood of $k = 2$ in five draws.

In the second step of the analysis, we determined all differences between all possible sample means a person might experience. Table 10.2 lists for Problem 2 all possible absolute experienced differences (assuming sample size of five), and the likelihood with which they occur (values in parentheses). For example, the probability of experiencing a (absolute) difference of 1.6 equals 0.11. The latter value results from multiplying the probability of observing a sample mean of 20.8 in deck A, namely, $p(SM_A = 20.8) = 0.40$, with the probability of observing a sample mean of 19.2 in option B,

Table 10.1. The probability of encountering the maximum outcome exactly k times out of *five draws* and the resulting empirical means in samples of two payoff distributions: Deck A (26 with probability 0.76, 0 otherwise) and deck B (48 with probability 0.55, 0 otherwise), respectively. The values are rounded.

Frequency of maximum outcome k	Deck A		Deck B	
	Probability of k	Sample Mean ($n = 5$)	Probability of k	Sample ($n = 5$)
0	0.00	0.00	0.02	0.00
1	0.01	5.20	0.11	9.60
2	0.08	10.40	0.28	19.20
3	0.25	15.60	0.34	28.80
4	0.40	20.80	0.21	38.40
5	0.25	26.00	0.05	48.00

namely, $p(SM_B = 19.2) = 0.28$. By collapsing across the probabilities of observing each absolute difference, one can determine the expected absolute value of the experienced difference between two decks for a given sample size. In a sample of size 5, for instance, this value is 10.98, 1.7 times larger than the description difference of 6.64. The median absolute value of the experienced difference, 7.92, also exceeds the description difference. Indeed, for 70% of the possible observations in our example the experienced difference is greater than the description difference. Note that for the purpose of analyzing the magnitude of the amplification effect we focus on the absolute difference and ignore the direction of the amplification. Respondents who sample outcomes from the two decks of cards, of course, experience a difference that points toward one or the other. Moreover, we will shortly address how often the difference points toward the objectively better gamble.

To examine the degree to which this amplification effect generalizes to other gambles it is necessary to establish an environment of gambles. To that end 1,000 pairs of

Table 10.2. The absolute values of all possible sample differences (assuming sample size of five), and the likelihood with which they occur (values in parentheses) for Problem 2.

SM_A/SM_B	0	9.6	19.2	28.8	38.4	48
0	0 (0.00)	9.6 (0.00)	19.2 (0.00)	28.8 (0.00)	38.4 (0.00)	48 (0.00)
5.2	5.2 (0.00)	4.4 (0.00)	14 (0.00)	23.6 (0.00)	33.2 (0.00)	42.8 (0.00)
10.4	10.4 (0.00)	0.8 (0.01)	8.8 (0.02)	18.4 (0.03)	28 (0.02)	37.6 (0.00)
15.6	15.6 (0.00)	6 (0.03)	3.6 (0.07)	13.2 (0.09)	22.8 (0.05)	32.4 (0.01)
20.8	20.8 (0.01)	11.2 (0.05)	1.6 (0.11)	8 (0.13)	17.6 (0.08)	27.2 (0.02)
26	26 (0.00)	16.4 (0.03)	6.8 (0.07)	2.8 (0.09)	12.4 (0.05)	22 (0.01)

randomly generated two-outcome gambles were created (e.g., Problem 2). For each gamble the probability values were randomly sampled from a uniform distribution between 0 and 1. One payoff value was set to 0 whereas the other payoff value was drawn from a uniform distribution between 0 and 100. None of the gamble pairs were allowed to have stochastically dominating options.

How robust is the amplification effect?

As a function of increasing sample sizes, Fig. 10.1 plots the expected absolute values of the experienced differences for the natural mean heuristic, across all gambles. The straight line represents the average description difference (15.2). Assuming the natural mean heuristic, small samples substantially *amplify* the difference between gambles. For instance, with two draws from each deck, the average expected experienced difference is 23.1, 1.5 times larger than the description difference. Not surprisingly, as sample sizes increase the expected experienced differences converge to the description difference. With 10 draws the expected experienced difference (17.2) is merely 1.1 times larger than the description difference, and with 50 draws, they are nearly the same. Figure 10.2 shows the same finding for the median experienced difference, except that the amplification effect is smaller relative to Fig.10.1.

The basis for the amplification effect, as the formal proof above illustrates, is the positive skew of the distribution of possible experienced differences. The top panel in

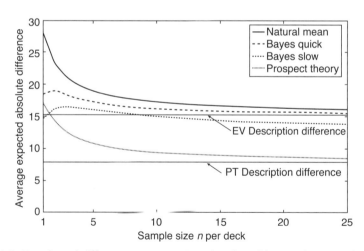

Fig. 10.1. Experienced differences across 1,000 pairs of gambles as a function of sample size (per deck). The four curves represent the mean of the expected absolute difference for the natural mean heuristic, two Bayesian updating strategies (slow versus quick updating), and cumulative prospect theory, respectively. The upper straight horizontal line represents the average description difference based on expected value (15.2). The lower straight horizontal line represents the average description difference after values and probabilities have been transformed according to prospect theory's value and weighting function (7.8).

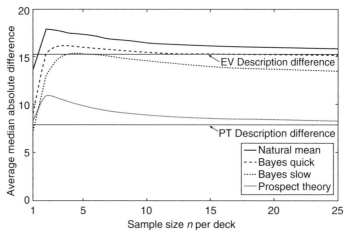

Fig. 10.2. Experienced differences across 1,000 pairs of gambles as a function of sample size (per deck). The four curves represent the median of the experienced absolute difference for the natural mean heuristic, two Bayesian updating strategies (slow versus quick updating), and cumulative prospect theory, respectively. The upper straight horizontal line represents the average description difference based on expected value (15.2). The lower straight horizontal line represents the average description difference after values and probabilities have been transformed according to prospect theory's value and weighting function (7.8).

Fig. 10.3 illustrates this skew for Problem 2 (*A*: 26 with probability 0.76, 0 otherwise, or *B*: 48 with probability 0.55, 0 otherwise) when *n* = 5 samples are drawn from *A* and *B*, respectively. As the figure shows, the expected absolute value of the experienced difference is markedly larger than the description difference. Moreover, the range of possible differences is bounded at zero (i.e., the smallest experienced difference is zero), whereas the largest experienced difference is over seven times larger than the description difference.

The primary reason for the change in the amplification effect as sample size increases, as our proof suggested, is that as sample size increases a larger proportion of the distribution's mass gathers around the description difference, decreasing the distribution's positive skew. Figure 10.3 shows this reduction in the skew for Problem 2. Comparing the bottom panel to the top panel shows that the skew systematically decreases as sample size increases. The other two factors that determine the amplification effect, namely the magnitude of the difference between the expected values of the two gambles and the pooled variance across the two options, can help explain how changes in our environment of gambles would influence the amplification effect. For example, what would happen if the gambles in each problem of our environment had two non-zero outcomes rather than having one zero outcome and one non-zero outcome? If both outcomes are equally likely to fall between 0 and 100 then each of the gambles on average would have less variance in the experienced differences. This is tantamount to decreasing the skew in the distribution of experienced differences.

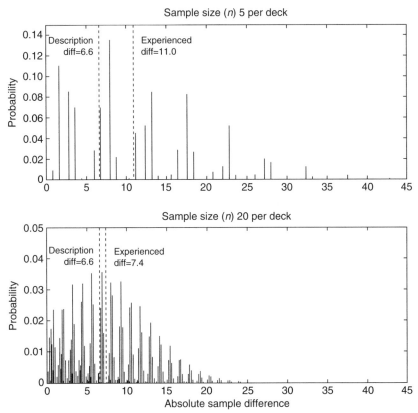

Fig. 10.3. The distribution of all possible experienced differences for Problem 2 (*A*: 26 with probability 0.76, 0 otherwise, or *B*: 48 with probability 0.55, 0 otherwise) when *n* = 5 samples are drawn from *A* and *B*, respectively (see upper panel). The distribution has a positive skew causing the expected and median (absolute) value of the experienced difference to be markedly larger than the description difference. Over 70% of the possible experienced differences are larger than the description difference. The bottom panel is the distribution for Problem 2 for *n* = 20 samples drawn from each deck. The larger sample size decreases the skew of the distribution.

As a result there would be a smaller amplification effect. Our own analysis shows this decreases the amplification effect from, for instance, 1.3 to 1.1 times the description difference at *n* = 5. A similar result holds for mixed gambles with the same range of possible outcomes.

How does more processing affect the amplification effect?

The natural mean heuristic bets on the observed sample and nothing else. Alternatively, a person may aim to combine prior beliefs about the environment in which she finds herself with the newly sampled evidence. Or, alternatively, rather than taking the sample at face value the sample's parameters (i.e., outcomes and probabilities) may be interpreted through prospect theory's value and weighting function. In what follows, we examine both of these computationally taxing alternatives to the natural mean heuristic. We first turn to the possibility that a person combines new data and existing beliefs through use of Bayes' theorem.

Bayesian probability updating: will the amplification effect persist?

To address this question we assumed that searchers started with the initial assumption that in each deck there are two possible outcomes, a minimum and maximum. Believing that there were two outcomes but having no *a priori* reason to believe that one outcome was more likely than another, people could use Laplace's principle of indifference and treat the likelihoods for either payoff in both decks as equally likely. To model this we worked with the probability of the maximum outcome for deck A and B, $\hat{P}_A$ and $\hat{P}_B$.

Specifically, we modeled the person's belief in $\hat{P}_A$ with a beta distribution—often used in Bayesian statistics because it is conjugate to the binomial distribution (see Gelman *et al.*, 2003)—that had a uniform distribution on the interval [0, 1]. Beta distributions are described with two parameters α and β and setting them equal to 1 reproduces this assumption for each deck. We used the mean of the beta distributions as the person's best estimate of $\hat{P}_A$ and $\hat{P}_B$. For deck A, for instance, the estimate is

$$E(\hat{p}_A) = \frac{\alpha}{\alpha + \beta} = 0.5, \tag{3}$$

and the chances of the minimum outcomes are then $1 - E(\hat{p}_A)\,0.5$ and $1 - E(\hat{p}_B) = 0.5$, respectively. Note that this is only an approximation of a Bayesian learner. In decisions from experience decision makers are also ignorant of the payoffs. To bypass this problem we stipulated that until they experienced the payoffs they assumed them to be zero. More precise models would also account for the decision maker's uncertainty in the payoffs.

Under this model, two things occur when people draw a sample of size n from each deck and observe k_A draws of the maximum outcome from deck A and k_B from deck B, respectively. First, they learn about the value of the maximum outcome. Second, they use their sampling experience to update their prior opinions according to Bayes' theorem. Because the beta distribution is conjugate to the binomial distribution, the updated beliefs for both decks can be expressed as a function of the prior distributions and the experienced sample. In light of her sampled experience, an individual's updated estimate $\hat{p}_A$ about deck A is

$$E(\hat{p}_A \mid k_A, n) = \frac{\alpha + k_A}{\alpha + \beta + n}. \tag{4}$$

The same procedure takes place for deck B using the number of draws of the maximum outcome from it, k_B. The chances of the minimum outcomes are then $1 - E(\hat{p}_A \mid k_A, n)$ and $1 - E(\hat{p}_B \mid k_B, n)$. Using their updated estimates people then determine the expected value for both decks, SEV_A and SEV_B, and choose the deck with the (strictly) higher expected value (otherwise they guess).

Figures 10.1 and 10.2 show the experienced differences for two Bayesian updaters, a slow and a quick updater. The quick updater represents a Bayesian with $\alpha = \beta = 1$. With such low values the person would be very sensitive to the observed data and quickly update her beliefs in light of new evidence. By and large the experienced difference quickly tracks the description difference (see the horizontal line), the reason being that the Laplacian assumption counteracts the possible extreme observations seen in small samples by initially anchoring the decision maker at 50/50. We can also assess how different levels of confidence in one's prior beliefs might impact the amplification effect. By setting $\alpha = \beta = 10$, the variance of the beta distribution decreases and becomes more peaked around the values of $p_A = p_B = 0.5$. In other words, the individual is now more confident in her beliefs, and changes her beliefs at a slower rate than the less confident Bayesian ($\alpha = \beta = 1$). Consequently, the slow updaters lean more heavily toward their prior beliefs. As the slow updater lines in Figs. 10.1 and 10.2 show, the prior beliefs of the slow updater remove the amplification effect and in some cases reverse it, making it harder for him to distinguish between the two decks. It takes him over 100 observations to counteract his dulled discrimination.

Weighting of outcomes and probabilities: will the amplification effect persist?

Cumulative prospect theory (Kahneman & Tversky, 1979; Tversky & Kahneman, 1992) is a Neo-Bernoullian theory. It retains the original expected utility scaffolding, that is, the assumption that human choice can or should be modeled in the same terms that Daniel Bernoulli (1738/1954) postulated: that people behave as if they multiplied some function of probability and utility, and then maximized. Resting on this core assumption, cumulative prospect theory assumes that the impact of probabilities on choice is nonlinear such that small probabilities are overweighted and moderate and large probabilities are underweighted. It also posits that the value (or utility) function is S-shaped, and that the function is steeper for losses than for gains, thereby yielding 'loss aversion' (i.e., the fact that a loss of size k has greater impact than does a gain of size k). Cumulative prospect theory was developed to model decisions from description, that is, risky choices involving stated probabilities. By entering the sample probabilities and outcomes that Hertwig *et al.*'s (2004) respondents encountered into cumulative prospect theory's weighting and value function, Fox and Hadar (2006) showed that this two-stage model (Tversky & Fox, 1995) could also be applied to decisions from experience. In doing so, one can predict 67% of people's choices (compared with 77% by assuming the natural mean heuristic; see Hau *et al.*, in press).

Does the amplification effect continue to exist even if the sampled experience is fed into cumulative prospect theory's value and decision weighting functions? To investigate this issue, we turned to all 1,000 pairs of gambles investigated earlier. As a function of increasing sample size, we used the observed relative frequencies of minimum and maximum outcomes, respectively, as a proxy for people's subjective beliefs. In addition, we calculated prospect theory's value for each gamble (and given sample size), assuming Tversky and Kahneman's (1992) median estimates for the three parameters describing the value function and the two parameters describing the decision weighting function. Across all pairs of gambles, we then calculated the expected experienced difference and the median experienced difference, respectively. Because the value and weighting function are transformations on the original values the amplification effect remains and in fact approximates the one seen for the natural mean heuristic (Figs. 10.1 and 10.2). However, all the values are shifted down for both the experienced differences and the description differences. This is a result of the value and weighting functions mitigating the impact of extreme payoffs and probabilities.

Our concern in this section was whether the amplification effect continues to exist even if people process the sampled information in a cognitively more taxing way. We found two results. First, if respondents update their beliefs starting with a Laplacian assumption, then the amplification effect will disappear. Consequently, Bayesian updaters will forego the 'benefit' of having more dissimilar alternatives. Second, if respondents behave as though they weighted outcomes and probabilities according to prospect theory, then the amplification will continue to exist.

Fine: small-sample choices are easier, but how competitive are they?

The old adage of economists goes, 'There's no such thing as a free lunch.' In line with this wisdom, searchers do not get to enjoy for free the simultaneous advantages of small search costs, small opportunity costs, and amplified differences. The price comes in terms of unreliable representations of the gambles' parameters, and less than optimal choices. As Fig. 10.1 shows, the larger the sample, the more veridically the experienced difference reflects the objective difference between the gambles. Therefore, searchers who sample extensively—say, 25 draws per deck—could thus maximize their earnings by being able to consistently select the gamble with the larger objective payoff. To find out how good or, perhaps, how bad choices based on small samples are, we calculated, using the aforementioned framework, per sample size and across all 1,000 pairs of gambles the proportion of times a respondent would choose the deck with the objectively larger expected value.

Figure 10.4 depicts the results of this analysis. Several striking results emerge. First, choices derived from small samples are clearly not *optimal*, but they are also far from being disastrous. With a sample as tiny as *one* draw from each deck a person has an approximate chance of 60% of selecting the higher-expected value gamble. Second, the information value garnered from each draw is subject to a diminishing return. Using the natural mean heuristic a person can, for instance, reap an 18-percentage point performance increase from 60% to 78% by increasing the sample from 1 to 5. By doubling the sample size from 5 to 10 draws, one achieves another 6-percentage point performance boost to 84%. By again doubling the sample size from 10 to 20 draws, accuracy increases by a mere 4 percentage points. If a person drew 100 rather than 20 observations from each deck, the expected accuracy would amount to

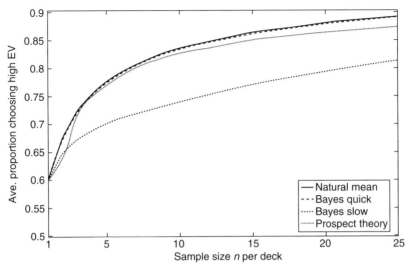

Fig. 10.4. Choice proportions across 1,000 pairs of gambles of the deck with the higher expected value as a function of sample size (per deck) for the four choice rules analyzed here. In the long run, the natural mean heuristic and the Bayesian strategies will choose the better gamble 100% of the time, relative to prospect theory's long run accuracy of 92%.

95% (compared to 81% at $n = 7$). Although accuracy continues to increase with each further draw, it increases at a diminishing rate.

Third, as Fig. 10.4 also shows, with small samples a person who does without complex calculations and bets on the sample means to choose between the decks either exceeds (slow updating) or equals (quick updating or cumulative prospect theory) the level of accuracy reached by a Bayesian updater. After a large number of draws from each deck the Bayesian and the natural mean strategies converge. This occurs for the two Bayesian strategies and the natural mean heuristic at around 100 draws from each deck where all three have an expected accuracy of approximately 95%. In the limit these strategies would choose the higher expected value gamble 100% of the time. Interestingly, people who perceive values through the lenses of prospect theory and draw larger and larger samples do not converge to this accuracy. Instead, they make systematic mistakes in the gambling environment and converge at 92% accuracy in the long run, the proportion of times the higher expected value gamble is chosen in decisions from description.

To conclude, betting on small samples exacts costs. At worst, small samples can give rise to mental representations in which the higher-value gamble appears inferior, and the lower-value gamble superior. In our environment of randomly selected gambles, however, small samples—even as small as one draw per deck—resulted in markedly more accurate than inaccurate choices. Drawing as few as seven times from each deck secured an 86% chance to select the gamble with the higher expected value. To avoid misunderstandings: We do not conjecture that reliance on small samples is the optimal strategy—and in fact, it is not clear to us how to compute the optimal solution for decisions from experience. Yet, as our analysis has shown, relatively small samples afford a surprisingly high probability of choosing the gamble with the higher expected value.

If life is a gamble, then it is not one but many

At any given time, our ancestors played a myriad of gambles. They had to wager on what they could eat, what they could capture, what could capture them, and whom they could trust, to name just a few (see Buss, 2005, for many others gambles). In light of the many dicey choices that our ancestors faced, and, by the same token, we face every day, a key issue emerges: How much information should we forage in each of the choices? And, when does the cost of more choice outweigh the benefits? There is no simple answer because any answer depends on multiple factors such as the costs of wrong decisions, and the cost of search. Without the pretension of having an answer to these questions, our analytical frame enables us to take a first, simple step toward an answer.

Let us assume the following simplified world. People encounter in the course of their lives a total of 100 pairs of payoff distributions, each pair representing one of life's gambles. Before making a decision, they can sample from the distributions (about which they initially are ignorant) as many times as they wish before deciding which one they prefer to play once for real money. In realistic models, search must be limited because real people have only a finite amount of time, knowledge, attention, or money to spend on a particular decision. In our microworld, limited search is represented in terms of a finite budget of draws that each person can afford to sample across all gambles. How should people employ the budget across decisions?

There is no simple answer. Because the parameter of the payoff distributions can be estimated better the larger the number of draws, people stand to increase their expected payoffs *per decision* with more observations. However, the increase in expected payoffs diminishes with larger sample sizes. In addition, the strategy of maximizing accuracy per decision may ultimately decrease average earnings across many decisions, simply because once the budget of draws is used up one cannot help but to choose randomly.

To investigate this trade-off between maximizing accuracy per decision and across decisions, we investigated the expected earnings of players who used the natural mean heuristic in 100 pairs of gambles in the gain domain with a zero-outcome as a second payoff in both gambles. In addition, we let the players set different aspiration levels for identifying the gamble with the highest expected value ranging from 50% to 95% accuracy. The aspiration levels determined the sample size agents took based on the analysis presented in Fig. 10.4. So, for instance, recall that with $n \approx 100$ participants can expect 95% accuracy and setting $n = 0$ they can expect 50% accuracy. We also assumed that once the budget of draws is exhausted players resort to choosing randomly between the options. This budget was varied and ranged from $R = 100$, 200, ..., to 1,000 draws per decks A and B, respectively.

Table 10.3 summarizes the average earnings as a function of the aspiration level (and corresponding sample size), and the available number of draws per deck.[v] To interpret the results let us first point out that if respondents chose to learn nothing about the gambles and guessed they would, on average, earn 2,390 points. If instead, they had access to the gamble descriptions and chose according to expected value, they would, on average, earn 3,164 points. Three results deserve to be highlighted.

First, the analysis gives new meaning to the phrase, 'Jack of all trades, master of none, though ofttimes better than master of one.' That is in our analysis agents do best—regardless of how tight or generous their resources are—by distributing the draws equally among the gambles and being content with limited knowledge rather than allocating resources to just a few selected gambles. This conclusion is supported by the values in the diagonal: They represent the highest average earnings within a given budget, and they coincide with a strictly equal distribution of draws across decks. Take, for instance, the value 2,929. It corresponds to making three draws per deck for each of the 100 A and B decks, respectively. Any other strategy that aims to invest more resources in some gambles (thus striving for a high level of accuracy) and, as a consequence, fewer in others is outperformed by an equal-sampling policy (compare 2,929 to all other values in the '300' row). Second, the results again demonstrate that the increase in information value across sample size is subject to diminishing return. Whereas the average earnings increase by 6 percentage points when increasing the budget from 100 to 200 draws for decks A and B, respectively, this increase shrinks to 0.3 percentage points when increasing the budget from 900 to 1,000 draws. Third, the average earnings, assuming seven draws per deck (and a corresponding accuracy of identifying the higher-expected value option of about 80%), amount to 96% of the maximum earning, 3,039 versus 3,164 points, respectively.

Our implementation of the life-as-a-gamble metaphor suggests that relying on a small sample proves to be a competitive strategy in the long run. One reason for this result in our microworld of gambles, and, perhaps, by extension in life's gambles, is that players are faced with the problem of flat maximum (Winterfeldt & Edwards, 1986). The problems in which decision makers stand to gain the most via more observations are also the ones in which sampling produces the least marginal gain. The reason is that these problems involve gambles that are close in their expected values. In some cases, two gambles might be so close together that one might just as well flip a coin to decide. In contrast, the natural mean heuristic only needs a small

---

[v] The expected earnings for each problem can be calculated in the following manner. For each problem we can calculate the probability of choosing the higher expected value gamble, $C(n)$, for a player who uses the natural mean after drawing a sample size n from each gamble. With some level of resources, R, the player can sample from R/n of the 100 gambles, where $n \leq R/100$. In the long run this means that for each problem there is a probability of $r = R/(100n)$ of using natural mean with sample size n to make a choice, and a probability of $(1-r)$ to guess. The expected earnings for all 100 gambles is then $[C(n)r + 0.5(1-r)]EV_A + [(1-C(n))r + 0.5(1-r)]EV_B$, where EV_A and EV_B are the expected values of the two gambles. Gamble A is assumed to have a higher expected value then B.

Table 10.3. The average earnings in our life-is-a-gamble simulation, assuming budget of draws ranging between 100 and 1,000 draws for decks A and B, respectively, and confidence level ranging between 0.5 and 0.95 (corresponding to sample sizes of 0–134 per deck). The confidence level denotes the chances of selecting the gamble with the higher-expected value. The values in the diagonal represent the highest average earning with a given budget size.

Sample size per deck (aspiration level)

Global budget per deck	1 (0.60)	2 (0.67)	3 (0.73)	4 (0.76)	5 (0.77)	6 (0.79)	7 (0.81)	8 (0.82)	9 (0.83)	10 (0.83)	31 (0.90)	134 (0.95)
100	2,666	2,614	2,573	2,541	2,518	2,504	2,487	2,483	2,471	2,465	2,419	2,405
200	—	2,830	2,753	2,685	2,639	2,604	2,583	2,561	2,544	2,532	2,441	2,405
300	—	—	2,929	2,829	2,760	2,710	2,673	2,647	2,617	2,599	2,471	2,412
400	—	—	—	2,973	2,881	2,817	2,763	2,726	2,691	2,667	2,493	2,420
500	—	—	—	—	3,002	2,917	2,853	2,811	2,771	2,734	2,515	2,428
600	—	—	—	—	—	3,023	2,949	2,890	2,844	2,801	2,537	2,428
700	—	—	—	—	—	—	3,039	2,975	2,917	2,869	2,566	2,435
800	—	—	—	—	—	—	—	3,054	2,991	2,936	2,588	2,443
900	—	—	—	—	—	—	—	—	3,064	3004	2,610	2,450
1000	—	—	—	—	—	—	—	—	—	3,071	2,632	2,450

number of observations to choose relatively accurately between gambles when the difference between their expected values is large.

Some potential benefits of small samples

Why do people rely on small samples? Standard accounts implicate (cognitive and economic) costs such as those involved in internal and external search, opportunity costs, lack of appreciation for the empirical law of large numbers, or they attribute frugal search to limits in our cognitive architecture. It is only recently that cognitive psychologists and cognitive ecologists have begun to explain frugal information search in terms of potential benefits of small samples. Some of these benefits are less disputed than others. One advantage is, for instance, the enhanced ability to detect environmental change. An organism remembering only a small number of recent events—tantamount to drawing small samples from memory rather than from the environment—is better equipped to detect a change in its environment than it would be if it remembered all of its history (e.g., Heinrich, 1979; McNamara & Houston, 1985, 1987; Shafir & Roughgarden, 1998). The optimal number of items to be remembered depends on the rate of the changes in the environment, but perfect memory appears to be a liability rather than an advantage in a world that continues to change.

Real (1992) investigated the foraging behavior of bees across different floral reward distributions, and concluded that 'bees frame their decisions on the basis of only a few visits' (p. 133). He then argued that calculating reward probabilities based on small frame lengths could prove advantageous under several scenarios, one of which takes the structure of bees' natural habitat into account:

> Short-term estimation may be adaptive when there is a high degree of spatial autocorrelation in the distribution of floral rewards. In most field situations, there is intense local competition among pollinators for floral resources. When 'hot' and 'cold' spots in fields of flowers are created through pollinator activity, then such activity will generate a high degree of spatial autocorrelation in nectar rewards. If information about individual flowers is pooled, then the spatial structure of reward distributions will be lost, and foraging over the entire field will be less efficient. In spatially autocorrelated environments ('rugged landscapes'), averaging obscures the true nature of the environment (p. 135).

In psychology, Kareev (1995, 2000) advanced the argument that the cognitive system—more precisely, working memory—may have evolved so as to increase the chance for early detection of covariation. In Kareev (2000), he argued that the experienced sample size most conducive to the detection of *useful* binary correlations (i.e., value ≥ 0.5) is close to Miller's (1956) estimate of the limited capacity of working memory. This conjecture of the evolutionary advantage of small samples (or, more precisely, a limited working memory) has fueled a controversial debate (Anderson *et al.*, 2005; Juslin *et al.*, 2006; Juslin & Olsson, 2005; Kareev, 2005; and see also Fiedler & Kareev, 2006). Among other issues, it focuses on the question of what elements should enter the payoff function in determining the benefits or lack thereof of small samples (e.g., false alarms).

We do not conjecture that small samples provide a more veridical picture of the gambles in our environment. They do not (see Fig. 10.4). Our key points are: (a) Drawing small samples from payoff distributions leads to experienced differences of sample means that are larger than the objective difference; (b) such biased differences may make the choice between payoff distributions simpler, and may thus explain the frugal sampling behavior observed in decisions from experience investigated by Hertwig *et al.* (2004) and Weber *et al.* (2004); (c) sampling larger samples, *ceteris paribus*, gives rise to more accurate knowledge of the objective parameters of the payoff distributions; (d) more accurate knowledge derived from larger samples, however, yields surprisingly modest gains in terms of the probability of selecting the higher-value distribution (diminishing return of the value of information); and (e) choices based on small samples although not optimal are surprisingly competitive. Last but not least, our analysis, although conducted in the domain of monetary gambles, generalizes to other realms of life that can be modeled in terms of the binomial distribution.

Sample size and choice difficulty: empirical evidence

Small samples amplify the difference between the options' average rewards, thus, we suggest, easing the difficulty of choosing between them. This thesis gives rise to several testable predictions. One is that if people sample large samples before they choose, the options will appear more similar and choice will be more difficult. One indicator of more difficult choices is if choice proportions are closer to 50%. In another study (Hau *et al.*, in press) we conducted two experiments where people used larger samples to make a choice. In the first experiment, as in Hertwig *et al.* (2004), participants decided when to stop sampling and make a choice. Choice accuracy, however, was stressed with two procedural changes from Hertwig *et al.* Stakes were ten times higher and people were required to explicitly estimate the relative frequencies of outcomes. People drew a median sample of 33 draws (relative to 15 draws in Hertwig *et al.*) from both decks. In the second experiment, participants were required to make 100 draws from both decks. Both experiments used the same six problems as Hertwig *et al.* Consistent with the prediction that larger samples render choice more difficult, in 10 out of 12 problems choice proportions were—relative to Hertwig *et al.*—closer to 50% in Hau *et al.* Pr(10 or more by chance) < 0.02. Choice proportions were 12 percentage points (median) closer.

The present account also sheds new light on research regarding people's proclivity to reason statistically in everyday problems. Fong *et al.* (1986) asked respondents to consider everyday problems to which the law of large numbers could be brought to bear. In one problem, people were asked to decide which of two car manufacturers, Volvo or Saab, was more likely to produce cars free of troublesome repairs. Respondents could resort to two pieces of information, namely, (a) objective information in terms of the consensus of *Consumer Reports'* experts and readers, and (b) personal experience of three friends who owned one of the cars. Fong *et al.* found that most people did not spontaneously reason statistically, thus being guided more by personal experience rather than the aggregate consensus. The amplification effect offers one possible explanation as to why. The large sample, represented by the aggregate consensus in *Consumer Reports*, suggests that 'both cars were very sound mechanically, although the Volvo felt to be *slightly* superior on some dimensions'

(p. 285, emphasis added). The small sample, represented by the friends' experience, in contrast, reports a huge difference between both cars: 'Both Saab owners reported having had a few mechanical problems but nothing major. The Volvo owner exploded when asked how he liked his car. 'First that fancy fuel injection computer thing went out: $250 bucks. […]. I finally sold it after 3 years for junk'. (p. 285). One way to interpret the lure of personal experience is that the small sample amplifies the difference between the two options, whereas the large sample reports only a slight difference. The small sample thus renders the choice easier, albeit pointing to the option that is likely to be inferior.

The generality of our analysis

One challenge to the generality of the current analysis is that it is predicated on the assumption that people derive their choice from differences in the samples' average rewards. There are, however, numerous choice strategies that do not exploit this dimension. Take, for instance, the minimax heuristic according to which the decision maker selects the payoff distribution with the highest minimum payoff, irrespective of any probability information. This heuristic was originally suggested for choice under ignorance (see Luce & Raiffa, 1957), that is, for choice when probabilities are unknown. In decisions from experience, probabilities are indeed initially unknown and small samples can result in substantial estimation biases. Therefore resorting to a strategy that ignores probabilities may be a justifiable strategy. Although the minimax heuristic may not be unreasonable, people do not employ it, or many other strategies for that matter in decisions from experience (Hau et al., in press).

As our analysis has revealed the amplification effect, however, is not restricted to samples' average rewards. It also occurs when the experienced outcomes and probabilities per sample are entered into cumulative prospect theory's value and weighting function (Fig. 10.4). This is not surprising because a sample's natural mean is quantitatively (though not computationally) identical to the sample's expected value (assuming the experienced probabilities and outcomes). Any choice theory that retains the Bernoullian framework scaffolding (see Brandstätter et al., 2006)— namely, the assumption that people behave as if they multiplied some function of probability and value, and then maximized—will entail some kind of the amplification effect. In other words, all contemporary models that Selten (2001) subsumed under the label 'repair' program—that is, models that introduce psychological variables such as emotions, reference points, decision weights to rescue the original multiplication scaffolding—imply amplification effects. Examples of such models include disappointment theory (Bell, 1985; Loomes & Sugden, 1986), regret theory (Bell, 1982; Loomes & Sugden, 1982), the transfer-of-attention exchange model (Birnbaum & Chavez, 1997), decision affect theory (Mellers, 2000)—to name a few.

The amplification effect also generalizes to another class of descriptive choice models, namely, experiential-learning models (e.g., Busemeyer & Stout, 2002; March, 1996). They conceptualize human choice not in terms of a calculated expected utility, but as a response gauged from experience. On this assumption people choose one deck over the other on the basis of the experienced outcomes, which are integrated through an averaging operation and in which recent outcomes can have more weight than previous ones. Due to this recency weighting (for example see Hertwig *et al.*, 2006), experiential-learning models would yield amplified differences in the gambles' values regardless of the actual number of observations drawn. To conclude, the occurrence of the amplification effect can be expected to occur across a wide range of descriptive choice models, ranging from Neo-Bernoullian modifications of expected utility theory to experiential-learning models.

Admittedly, the difference in the samples' average reward is not the only dimension from which people can derive their decision. Alternatively, they can encode the frequency of occurrence of different outcomes in each payoff distribution, and rest their decision on those. Indeed, the human mind is often conceptualized as acutely sensitive to frequency information (e.g., Zacks & Hasher, 2002). Of course, with event frequencies, differences between them will, on average, increase as the sample grows larger. In other words, here large rather than small samples would amplify differences. Event frequencies, however, can hardly be the sole basis for the decision between two payoff distributions for at least two reasons. One is that in payoff distributions with more than one outcome (and each of our gambles had two outcomes), frequency information may be inconclusive: For instance, one of gamble *a*'s two outcomes may be more frequent and one less frequent than both of gamble *b*'s two outcomes. So, which gamble is better? Second, a very frequent outcome may be small in say monetary value, and a rare outcome's value may be vast, thus ignoring outcome information altogether can paint a quite misleading image of a gamble's value. Sample means, in contrast, integrate both value and frequency information into one dimension. In addition, a person can arrive at sample means without the cognitively demanding operation of weighing outcomes by the likelihood but merely by summing and dividing by the sample size; if sample sizes are identical, then just summing suffices.

Conclusion

The life-is-a-gamble metaphor suggests that life's decisions have the same structure as games of chance. If they indeed do, investigating how people play those games promises insight into how they play the game of life. Hundreds of studies in decisions under risk have provided people with convenient descriptions of games of chance, that is, their monetary outcomes and probabilities, thus giving rise to *decisions from description*. Life's decisions, however, do not often come nicely packaged. Investigating how people make decisions in the absence of complete knowledge of the gambles' properties, that is, *decisions from experience*, turns out novel questions and revives old unanswered ones. Understanding the psychology of decisions from experience requires an ecological approach to cognition (see Anderson, 1991; Brunswik, 1943; Simon, 1956), encompassing models of both the cognitive processes and their interaction with the statistical structures of the environment. Early termination of information search and the tendency to rely on small samples in decisions from experience can at least partly be understood in terms of the statistical structures of the world.

Authors' note

We are grateful to Nick Chater, Klaus Fiedler, Robin Hau, and Robin Hogarth for their helpful comments. We also thank Laura Wiles for editing the manuscript, and the Swiss National Science Foundation for a grant to the first author (100013-107741/1).

References

Allais, M. (1979). The foundations of a positive theory of choice involving risk and a criticism of the postulates and axioms of the American School. In M. Allais & O. Hagen (Eds.), *Expected utility hypotheses and the Allais paradox*. Dordrecht, The Netherlands: Reidel (originally published in 1953).

Anderson, J. R. (1991). Is human cognition adaptive? *Behavioral and Brain Sciences*, **14**, 471–517.

Anderson, R. B., Doherty, M. E., Berg, N. D., & Friedrich, J. C. (2005). Sample size and the detection of correlation—a signal detection account: Comment on Kareev (2000) and Juslin and Olsson (2005). *Psychological Review*, **112**, 268–279.

Barron, G., & Erev, I. (2003). Small feedback-based decisions and their limited correspondence to description-based decisions. *Journal of Behavioral Decision Making*, **16**, 215–233.

Bell, D. E. (1982). Regret in decision making under uncertainty. *Operations Research*, **30**, 961–981.

Bell, D. E. (1985). Disappointment in decision making under uncertainty. *Operations Research*, **33**, 1–27.

Berenson, A. (2006, December 4). End of drug trial is a big loss for Pfizer and heart patients [electronic version]. *The New York Times*. Retrieved 2007 May 31 from: http://www.nytimes.com/2006/12/04/health/04pfizer.html

Bernoulli, D. (1954). Exposition of a new theory on the measurement of risk. *Econometrica*, **22**, 23–36 (Original work published 1738).

Bernoulli, J. (1969–1975). *Ars conjectandi*. In *Die Werke von Jacob Bernoulli* (Vol. 3, pp. 107–259). Basel, Switzerland: Basel Naturforschende Gesellschaft. (Original work published 1713.)

Bernstein, B. L. (1996). *Against the gods: The remarkable story of risk*. New York: Wiley & Sons.

Berry, D., & Fristedt, B. (1985). *Bandit problems*. London: Chapman and Hall.

Birnbaum, M., & Chavez, A. (1997). Tests of theories of decision making: Violations of branch independence and distribution independence. *Organizational Behavior and Human Decision Processes*, **71**, 161–194.

Brandstätter, E., Gigerenzer, G., & Hertwig, R. (2006). The priority heuristic: Making choices without trade-offs. *Psychological Review*, **113**, 409–432.

Brunswik, E. (1943). Organismic achievement and environmental probability. *Psychological Review*, **50**, 255–272.

Busemeyer, J. R. (1985). Decision making under uncertainty: A comparison of simple scalability, fixed-sample, and sequential-sampling models. *Journal of Experimental Psychology: Learning, Memory, and Cognition*, **11**, 538–564.

Busemeyer, J. R., & Stout, J. C. (2002). A contribution of cognitive decision models to clinical assessment: Decomposing performance on the bechara gambling task. *Psychological Assessment*, **14**, 253–262.

Buss, D. M. (Ed.). (2005). *The handbook of evolutionary psychology*. New York: Wiley.

Daston, L. (1988). *Classical probability in the enlightenment*. Princeton, NJ: Princeton University Press.

Daw, N. D., O'Doherty, J. P., Dayan, P., Seymour, B., & Dolan, R. J. (2006). Cortical substrates for exploratory decisions in humans. *Nature*, **441**, 876–879.

Denrell, J. (2007). Adaptive learning and risk taking. *Psychological Review*, **114**, 177–187.

Dudai, Y., & Carruthers, M. (2005). The janus face of Mnemosyne. *Nature*, **434**, 567.

Erev, I., & Barron, G. (2005). On adaptation, maximization, and reinforcement learning among cognitive strategies. *Psychological Review*, **112**, 912–931.

Fiedler, K., & Kareev, Y. (2006). Does decision quality (always) increase with the size of information samples? Some vicissitudes in applying the law of large numbers. *Journal of Experimental Psychology: Learning, Memory & Cognition*, **32**, 883–903.

Fong, T. G., Krantz, D. H., & Nisbett, R. E. (1986). The effects of statistical training on thinking about everyday problems. *Cognitive Psychology*, **18**, 253–292.

Fox, C. R., & Hadar, L. (2006). 'Decisions from experience' = sampling error + prospect theory: Reconsidering Hertwig, Barron, Weber & Erev (2004). *Judgment and Decision Making*, **1**, 159–161.

George, A. L. (1959). *Propaganda analysis: A study of inferences made from Nazi propaganda in World War II*. Evanston, IL.: Row, Peterson and Co.

Gladwell, M. (2005). *Blink: The power of thinking without thinking*. New York: Little, Brown and Company.

Goldstein, W. M., & Weber, E. U. (1997). Content and discontent: Indications and implications of domain specificity in preferential decision making. In W. M. Goldsmith & R. M. Hogarth (Eds.), *Research on judgment and decision making: Currents, connections and controversies* (pp. 566–617). Cambridge, England: Cambridge University Press.

Gottlieb, D. A., Weiss, T., & Chapman, G. B. (2007). The format in which uncertainty information is presented affects decision biases. *Psychological Science*, **18**, 240–246.

Griffin, D., & Tversky, A. (1992). The weighting of evidence and the determinants of confidence. *Cognitive Psychology*, **24**, 411–435.

Groopman, J. (2006, December 18). The right to a trial. *The New Yorker*, p. 41.

Hau, R., Pleskac, T., Kiefer, J., & Hertwig, R. (2007, in press). The description–experience gap in risky choice: The role of sample size and experienced probabilities. *Journal of Behavioral Decision Making*.

Heinrich, B. (1979). 'Majoring' and 'minoring' by foraging bumblebees, *Bombus vagans:* An experimental analysis. *Ecology*, **60**, 245–255.

Hertwig, R., Barron, G., Weber, E. U., & Erev, I. (2004). Decisions from experience and the effect of rare events in risky choice. *Psychological Science*, **15**, 534–539.

Hertwig, R., Barron, G., Weber, E. U., & Erev, I. (2006). The role of information sampling in risky choice. In K. Fiedler & P. Juslin (Eds.), *Information sampling and adaptive cognition* (pp. 72–91). New York: Cambridge University Press.

Hertwig, R., & Pleskac, T. (2007). *Decisions from experience: Small samples and the perception of differences*. Manuscript submitted for publication.

Juslin, P., Fiedler, K., & Chater, N. (2006). *Less is more in covariation detection—or is it?* New York: Cambridge University Press.

Juslin, P., & Olsson, H. (2005). Capacity limitations and the detection of correlations: Comment on Kareev (2000). *Psychological Review*, **112**, 256–267.

Kahneman, D., & Tversky, A. (1979). Prospect theory: An analysis of decision under risk. *Econometrica*, **47**, 263–291.

Kaplan, M., & Kaplan, E. (2006). *Chances are … Adventures in probability*. New York: Viking.

Kareev, Y. (1995). Through a narrow window—working-memory capacity and the detection of covariation. *Cognition*, **56**, 263–269.

Kareev, Y. (2000). Seven (indeed, plus or minus two) and the detection of correlations. *Psychological Review*, **107**, 397–402.

Kareev, Y. (2005). And yet the small-sample effect does hold: Reply to Juslin and Olsson (2005) and Anderson, Doherty, Berg, and Friedrich (2005). *Psychological Review*, **112**, 280–285.

Knight, F. H. (1921). *Risk, uncertainty, and profit*. New York: Sentry Press.

Levitt, D. S., & Dubner, S. J. (2005). *Freakonomics: A rogue economist explores the hidden side of everything*. New York: Harper Collins.

Loomes, G., & Sugden, R. (1982). Regret theory: An alternative theory of rational choice under uncertainty. *The Economic Journal*, **92**, 805–824.

Loomes, G., & Sugden, R. (1986). Disappointment and dynamic consistency in choice under uncertainty. *Review of Economic Studies*, **53**, 271–282.

Lopes, L. L. (1983). Some thoughts on the psychological concept of risk. *Journal of Experimental Psychology: Human Perception and Performance*, **9**, 137–144.

Luce, R. D., & Raiffa, H. (1957). *Games and decisions*. New York: John Wiley & Son.

March, J. G. (1996). Learning to be risk averse. *Psychological Review*, **103**, 309–319.

McNamara, J. M., & Houston, A. I. (1985). Optimal foraging and learning. *Journal of Theoretical Biology*, **117**, 231–249.

McNamara, J. M., & Houston, A. I. (1987). Memory and the efficient use of information. *Journal of Theoretical Biology*, **125**, 385–395.

Mellers, B. A. (2000). Choice and the relative pleasure of consequences. *Psychological Bulletin*, **126**, 910–924.

Miller, G. A. (1956). The magical number 7, plus or minus 2—some limits on our capacity for processing information. *Psychological Review*, **63**, 81–97.

Real, L. A. (1992). Information processing and the evolutionary ecology of cognitive architecture. *American Naturalist*, **140**, 108–145.

Savage, L. J. (1954). *The foundations of statistics*. New York: John Wiley & Sons.

Selten, R. (2001). What is bounded rationality? In G. Gigerenzer & R. Selten (Eds.), *Bounded rationality: The adaptive toolbox* (pp. 13–36). Cambridge, MA: MIT Press.

Shafir, S., & Roughgarden, J. (1998). Testing predictions of foraging theory for a sit-and-wait forager, *anolis gingivinus*. *Behavioral Ecology*, **9**, 74–84

Simon, H. A. (1956). Rational choice and the structure of the environment. *Psychological Review*, **63**, 129–138.

Stoppard, T. (1967). *Rosencrantz & Guildenstern are dead*. New York: Grove Press Books.

Tversky, A., & Fox, C. R. (1995). Weighting risk and uncertainty. *Psychological Review*, **95**, 269–283.

Tversky, A., & Kahneman, D. (1992). Advances in prospect theory: Cumulative representation of uncertainty. *Journal of Risk and Uncertainty*, **5**, 297–323.

von Neumann, J., & Morgenstern, O. (1947). *Theory of games and economic behavior*. Princeton, NJ: Princeton University Press (1980).

Weber, E. U., Shafir, S., & Blais, A. R. (2004). Predicting risk sensitivity in humans and lower animals: Risk as variance or coefficient of variation. *Psychological Review*, **111**, 430–445.

Winterfeldt, D. von., & Edwards, W. (1986). *Decision analysis and behavioral research*. Cambridge, England: Cambridge University Press.

Yechiam, E., & Busemeyer, J. R. (2005). Comparison of basic assumptions embedded in learning models for experience-based decision making. *Psychonomic Bulletin and Review*, **12**, 387–402.

Zacks, R. T., & Hasher, L. (2002). Frequency processing: A twenty-five year perspective. In P. Sedlmeier & T. Betsch (Eds.), *Ect.: frequency processing and cognition* (pp. 21–36). Oxford: Oxford University Press.

Chapter 11

The *naïve* intuitive statistician: organism—environment relations from yet another angle

Patrik Hansson

Umeå University, Umeå, Sweden

Peter Juslin

Uppsala University, Uppsala, Sweden

Anders Winman

Uppsala University, Uppsala, Sweden

Throughout the years the need to (seriously) consider the structure of people's real, everyday environments surface again and again in cognitive science. Especially influential and prominent examples in the history of this discipline are perhaps provided by the work of Brunswik (1955; see also Hammond & Stewart, 2001) and Gibson (1979). In more recent years this list has been amended by the research program of *rational analysis* proposed by Anderson (1990; see also Oaksford & Chater, 1996). As in economics and behavioral ecology it is proposed that important properties of behavior can be inferred from the assumption that behavior is a rational adaptation to the natural environment.

Yet these more or less 'ecological' approaches to cognition differ in how the assumption of rationality enters into the analysis. In Brunswik's probabilistic functionalism *investigation* of the rationality (achievement) of the behavior is the main agenda of cognitive science. The degree to which the responses by an organism accurately achieve relevant distal properties of its natural environment is, as such, an open question, although it is emphasized that the question can only be addressed with a representative sample of the environment. In Gibsonian psychology, the existence of information (invariants) in natural environments is an empirical possibility taken seriously, and whether humans have developed the means to exploit this information is investigated (e.g., Runeson *et al.*, 2000).

More specifically, rational analysis differs from these 'older' ecological traditions in at least two important respects: First, whereas Brunswikian and Gibsonian psychology has emphasized *correspondence criteria* of rationality (Hammond, 1996), the actual agreement between beliefs or actions and relevant properties of the environment, rational analysis has been addressed in terms of *Bayesian optimization* (Anderson, 1990). Second: in contrast to in these earlier approaches, with rational analysis rationality is not the subject of empirical investigation, but is entered as an *assumption* of optimized behavior, serving as a theoretical tool to predict behavior and to constrain theorizing about cognitive mechanisms.

The last years has seen the birth of yet another approach to ecological psychology, emphasizing the distinction between the *proximal sample* of information that is available to the organism or judge and the *distal variable* that is the target of achievement (Fiedler, 2000; Fiedler & Juslin, 2006a). This approach is based on a correspondence criterion of rationality and assumptions of rationality are entered in a more limited way, implying that, in general, people accurately describe the proximal information they have available. The rationality of the *behavior* depends, in each situation, on the specific relationship between the proximal information and the relevant distal property. The explanatory focus is thereby shifted from the processing of the proximal sample, often presumed to be plagued by the negative effects of simplifying heuristics (Gilovich *et al.*, 2002) and motivational biases, to the relationship between the proximal samples and distal environmental properties. This approach accordingly puts the *interface* between mind and environment under scrutiny.

In this chapter we will outline this approach to cognition, which we refer to as the metaphor of *the naïve intuitive statistician* (Fiedler & Juslin, 2006b). First, we discuss and motivate its main assumptions and provide some illustrative examples. Thereafter, we provide an in-depth illustration of its application by showing how the metaphor can help us to understand and cure one of the more perplexing cognitive illusions in the judgment literature, the extreme overconfidence bias with intuitive confidence intervals. Finally, we discuss how this approach can complement other probabilistic approaches to cognition.

Approaches to judgment research

Cognitive research on judgment is often portrayed as a sequence of partially incompatible paradigms or metaphors. Early research that compared human judgments to normative principles from probability theory and statistics suggested that the mind operates like an *intuitive statistician* (Peterson & Beach, 1967). People quickly learn probabilities and other distributional properties from trial-by-trial experience in laboratory tasks. Although some discrepancies from probability theory were reported, for example, that people were conservative updaters as compared to Bayes' theorem (Edwards, 1982), by large they were responsive to the factors implied by normative models (e.g., sample size). On the basis of peoples' often remarkable memory for frequencies in controlled laboratory settings memory researchers likewise proposed that frequency is encoded automatically (Hasher & Zacks, 1979; Zacks & Hasher, 2002). The perspective of the 'intuitive statistician' emphasized our ability to learn frequencies in well-defined laboratory learning tasks and suggests that the cognitive algorithms of the mind are in basic agreement with normative principles.

By contrast, the heuristics and biases perspective introduced in the early 1970s emphasized that, because of limited time, knowledge, and computational ability, we are forced to rely on heuristics that provide useful guidance but also produce characteristic biases (see Gilovich *et al.*, 2002; Kahneman *et al.*, 1982). It was, for example, proposed that the target attribute of probability is often substituted by heuristic variables, as when the probability that an instance belongs to a category is assessed by its *similarity* to the category prototype, or the probability of an event is assessed by the *ease* with which examples are brought to mind (Kahneman & Frederick, 2002). Because, in contrast to 'extensional' properties like frequency and set size, 'intensional' variables like similarity and availability do not obey probability theory people make characteristic judgment errors. For example, reliance on representativeness (similarity) allows for the over-estimation of the probability of conjunctions relative to the probability of the conjuncts, and for neglect of the base-rates relative to Bayes' theorem (Gilovich *et al.*, 2002; Kahneman *et al.*, 1982).

As with the intuitive statistician, the heuristics and biases perspective highlights performance, but here the limitations of intuitive judgment are brought to the forefront. The heuristics and biases program has been extremely influential, inspired much new research, and organized large amounts of empirical data (Gilovich *et al.*, 2002). Yet, there remains an aching tension between this view and the extensive body of data supporting the view of 'the intuitive statistician' (Peterson & Beach, 1967; Sedlmeier & Betsch, 2002).

This tension has served to inspire two new research programs in the domain of judgment and decision making. The first program is concerned with the ecological rationality of fast and frugal heuristics when applied to structures of real environments, thereby wedding the Brunswikian tradition to Herbert Simon's (1990) work on bounded rationality (see Gigerenzer *et al.*, 1999; Brighton & Gigerenzer, this volume). On this view, the rationality of judgment is best understood as 'bounded' and as emerging from an interaction between simple heuristics and properties of environments. The second research program, the naïve intuitive statistician, is the subject of the rest of this chapter.

The naïve intuitive statistician in abstract

The three assumptions that define the '*naïve intuitive statistician*' (Fiedler & Juslin, 2006b) integrate several aspects of these previous two research programs: Firstly, people have a remarkable ability to store frequencies and their judgments are accurate expressions of these frequencies (see Estes, 1976; Gigerenzer & Murray, 1987; Peterson & Beach, 1967; Zacks & Hasher, 2002, for reviews). The working assumption is that the processes operating on the proximal information provide accurate description of the samples, and often in terms of extensional properties (relative or natural frequencies), and, as such, do not involve heuristic processing based on intensional properties like similarity or ease of retrieval.

Secondly, people are naïve with respect to the external sampling biases in the information from the environment and more sophisticated sampling constraints (Einhorn & Hogarth, 1978; Fiedler, 2000). In essence, people tend spontaneously to 'assume' that the samples they encounter are representative of the relevant populations. Thirdly, people are naïve with respect to the sophisticated statistical properties of statistical estimators, such as whether an estimator as such is biased or unbiased. They thus tend spontaneously to 'assume' that the properties of samples can be used directly to describe the populations. Although the naivety with regard to biased input and biased estimators are conceptually distinct the process is the same; the direct use of sample properties as proxies for population properties.

The metaphor of the naïve intuitive statistician highlights both the cognitive mechanisms and the organism–environment relations that support the judgments, tracing biases not primarily or exclusively to the cognitive mechanisms that describe the samples, but to biases in the input and the naivety with which samples are used to describe the populations (Fiedler & Juslin, 2006a). On this view, the cognitive algorithms are not inherently irrational, but knowledge of more sophisticated properties of samples are regarded as hard-earned and fairly recent cultural achievements (Gigerenzer *et al.*, 1989; Hacking, 1975).

The relationship between the research programs is summarized in Fig. 11.1. The problem involves three components, the *environment*, the *sample* of information available to the judge, and the *judgment* that derives from this sample (Fiedler, 2000). These components, in turn, highlight two interrelationships, the degree to which the sample is a veridical description of the environment and the degree to which the judgment is a veridical description of the sample. When biased judgment occurs in real environments or with task contents that involve general knowledge acquired outside of the laboratory, both of these interrelations are 'unknowns' in the equation. The heuristics and biases program accounts for biases in terms of heuristic description of the samples (Fig. 11.1B), but rarely is this locus of the bias actually validated empirically (although there are exceptions e.g., Schwarz & Wänke, 2002).

Benefiting from the research inspired by the intuitive statistician (Fig. 11.1A) in the 60s that, in effect, ascertained one of the 'unknowns' by demonstrating that judgments can fairly be accurate descriptions of experimentally controlled samples, the naïve intuitive statistician emphasizes deviations between sample and population properties as the cause of biased judgments (Fig. 11.1C). This view is inherently more consistent both with the results supporting the intuitive statistician and the many demonstrations of judgment biases. In the following we illustrate how the naïve intuitive statistician complements the other perspectives by considering how it can illuminate a number of key phenomena in the literature.

The naïve intuitive statistician at work: a few examples

The literature contains an increasing number of examples of phenomena that may ultimately be better addressed in terms of the metaphor of the naïve intuitive statistician than the original frameworks that often emphasize heuristic processing or motivational biases. In the following we provide a few selective examples of such phenomena. The reader is referred to Fiedler (2000) and Fiedler and Juslin (2006a) for more extensive treatments.

Judgment and decision making. Many traditional 'availability biases' are better explained by accurate description of biased samples, rather than by the reliance on heuristics that are inherently incompatible with normative principles. One traditional illustration of the availability heuristic, for example, refers to peoples' perceptions of risk. Because violent deaths are more frequently reported in media they are claimed to

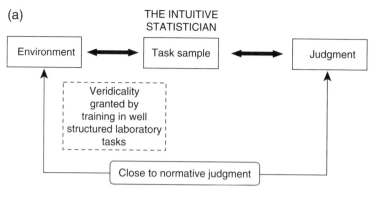

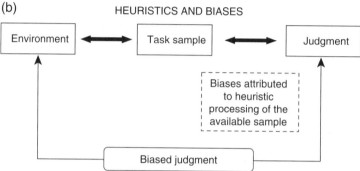

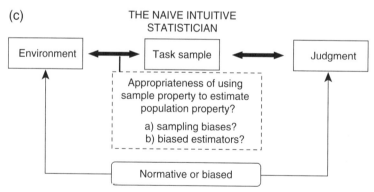

Fig. 11.1. Schematic summary of three research programs on intuitive judgment. Research guided by the perspective of the intuitive statistician (Panel A) has often found judgments that are in approximate agreement with normative models, presumably because of the concentration on well-structured tasks in the laboratory. Research on heuristics and biases (Panel B) has emphasized biases in intuitive judgment attributing them to heuristic processing of the evidence available to the judge. The naïve intuitive statistician (Panel C) emphasizes that the judgments are accurate descriptions of the available samples and that performance depends on whether the samples available to the judge are biased or unbiased, and on whether the estimator variable affords unbiased estimation directly from the sample properties. Adapted from Juslin *et al.* (2007). By permission of the American Psychological Association.

be more 'available,' easier to retrieve, than more mundane causes of death and accordingly people overestimate the risk of a violent death (Lichtenstein *et al.*, 1978).

More detailed investigations (Hertwig *et al.*, 2005), however, suggest that it is not 'ease' of retrieval, an intensional property substituting for proportion, that explains the bias, but accurate assessment of biased samples ('availability by recall,' in the terms of Hertwig *et al.*, 2005). Even if the available evidence is correctly assessed in terms of probability (proportion), if the external media coverage (Lichtenstein *et al.*, 1978) or the processes of search or encoding in memory (Kahneman *et al.*, 1982) yield biased samples the judgment is biased. In these situations it is debatable whether the substitution of proportion with a heuristic variable is where the explanatory action lies. Similar considerations apply to several other demonstrations of availability bias, although there are also demonstrations that the subjective fluency can affect the judgments (Schwarz & Wänke, 2002).

Moreover, the naivety implied by the naïve intuitive statistician is an equally compelling account of the 'belief in the law of small numbers'—the tendency to expect small samples to be representative of their populations—as the traditional explanation in terms of the representativeness heuristic (Tversky & Kahneman, 1971). Indeed, in this case, it may remain unclear what the notion of representativeness adds over and above the assumption that people take small sample properties as direct proxies for population properties.

The observation of overconfidence in judgment may in part derive from accurate description of proximal samples, in at least two different ways. The confidence that people have in their answers to general knowledge items often appear to derive from assessment of sampling probabilities in natural environments, but overconfidence is contributed because they fail to correct for the selection strategies used when general knowledge items are created (Gigerenzer *et al.*, 1991; Juslin, 1994). Accordingly a meta-analysis suggests that the overconfidence is substantially reduced or eliminated when the general knowledge questions are randomly sampled from predefined natural environments (Juslin *et al.*, 2000). Second, confidence may reflect the experience that people have, but they may fail to correct for the effects of actions taken on the basis of the confidence judgment that constrains the feedback received (Einhorn & Hogarth, 1978). The experience of mostly hiring personnel that prove successful in their work position may foster confidence in one's ability to recruit personnel, even though it may actually be the case that the rejected applicants, the performance of which is never known, would have been equally successful at work.

Traditionally, normative and descriptive decision theories, such as, for example, prospect theory (Kahneman & Tversky, 1979) have taken the properties of the utility function, like diminishing return, as givens incorporated by the appropriate selection of function forms and parameters. *Decision by sampling theory* (Stewart *et al.*, 2006, Stewart & Simpson, this volume), by contrast, shows how ordinal comparisons and frequency counts based on retrieval of small samples *explain* properties of the value function and probability weighting assumed by prospect theory (Kahneman & Tversky, 1979), such as the concave utility function and losses looming larger than gains. Consistently with the naïve intuitive statistician, a crucial part of the explanation is the relationship between small proximal samples and the distributions of values and probabilities in real environments.

In addition to the above examples, within judgment and decision making, where familiar psychological phenomena can be given a new, often more straightforward, and illuminating treatment, a number of more recent studies verify the naivety implied by the naïve intuitive statistician in a direct manner. People, for example, accurately assess the variance in a sample but fail to understand that sample variance needs to be corrected by $n/(n-1)$ to be an unbiased estimate of population variance (Kareev *et al.*, 2002). People likewise appear to under-weigh rare events in risky decisions from experience because small samples seldom include the rare events (Hertwig *et al.*, 2004, but see Fox & Hadar, 2006, for an interpretation in terms of the *Prospect Theory* plus sampling error).

Social psychology. Likewise, many biases in social psychology may derive not primarily from biased processing per se, but from inabilities to correct for the effects of sampling strategies (see Fiedler, 2000 for a discussion). One recent and striking example is provided by Denrell (2005). Denrell showed that biases in impression formation traditionally explained by cognitive and motivational factors may often arise from accurate description of samples that are biased as a side effect of sampling strategies. Because you are inclined to terminate the contact (the sampling) with people whom you get an initial negative impression of, you are unlikely to correct an initial false negative impression. By contrast, a false positive impression encourages additional sampling that serves to correct the false impression. The net effect is a bias, even if the samples are correctly described. Denrell shows how these sampling strategies interact in interesting ways with factors of social psychological concern.

Although the examples in this section illustrate how relocating the explanatory locus from heuristic processing of proximal samples to sample-environment relations may improve our understanding of phenomena, in general these studies were not explicitly (or implicitly) inspired by the metaphor of the naïve intuitive statistician. Therefore, we end by describing a theory explicitly guided by this metaphor, the naïve sampling model, that attempts to explain some of the more perplexing results observed in studies of overconfidence.

In-depth application: the naïve sampling model

Of central interest in research on probability judgment is the degree to which the subjective probabilities are realistic or calibrated (Lichtenstein *et al.*, 1982). In particular, people are sometimes too confident in their judgments, for instance, when they are asked which of the two cities, London or Berlin, that has more inhabitants or to predict whether or not it will rain tomorrow. In these examples confidence is expressed as a *probability judgment* concerning events. Alternatively, people may express their confidence in their beliefs as an *intuitive interval* for an unknown quantity under a pre-stated probability level, such as a 90% confidence interval for the stock value of a company in the next quarter.

That the confidence judgments are too high vis-à-vis the corresponding hit-rate is referred to as *overconfidence*. Some authors argue that the overconfidence in general derives from cognitive processing biases (e.g., Griffin & Tversky, 1992; Koriat *et al.*, 1980), while others suggest that with many probability judgment tasks there is little evidence for general biases in the cognitive processing, such as confirmatory memory search, after controlling for statistical artifacts and effects of biased task selection (Gigerenzer *et al.*, 1991; Juslin *et al.*, 1997, 1999, 2000, 2003; Juslin & Persson, 2002; Klayman *et al.*, 1999).

Intuitive confidence intervals are, however, associated with extreme overconfidence bias also after controlling for artifacts and the bias is substantially larger than with probability judgment. Indeed, the typical hit rate associated with a 100% confidence interval is not 100% but often fall in the region of 40–50% (see Juslin *et al.*, 2007). Given the enormous magnitude of the effect, in novices and experts (Russo & Schoemaker, 1992) the phenomenon is not only theoretically puzzling but of profound applied concern.

The previous explanations of this finding such as the *anchoring-and-adjustment heuristic* (Tversky & Kahneman, 1974), selective memory retrieval (e.g., Soll & Klayman, 2004) or trade-off effects between the aims of being accurate and informative (e.g., Yaniv & Foster, 1997) have in general proven to be insufficient accounts of the phenomenon (see Juslin *et al.*, 2007 for a discussion). This pattern, that probability judgment and interval production generate robustly different overconfidence biases for the same judgment content, is referred to as *format dependence* (Juslin *et al.*, 1999; Juslin & Persson, 2002).

The *Naïve Sampling Model* (NSM) is a recent attempt to explain the extreme overconfidence bias with interval production and the phenomenon of format dependence (see Juslin *et al.*, 2007 for details). The processing steps of the NSM are summarized in Fig. 11.2. When a person is presented with a probe for an unknown quantity the NSM assumes that some known fact about the probe is retrieved. For example, when asked for the population of London, a person may retrieve the fact that London is a European capital (the cue). The cue defines an *objective environmental distribution* (OED) of target values of observations that satisfy the cue, in our example, the distribution of population figures of European capitals. In the person's experience a subset of the target values in the OED have been encoded in memory and this set of known target values defines the *subjective environmental distribution* (SED: e.g., the set of European cities for which the population is known). When the cue is retrieved in response to the probe, a sample of *n* observations is retrieved from the SED to form a *subjective sample distribution* (SSD). An important assumption of the NSM is that the sample size is small (3–7 similar observations) and constrained by short-term memory capacity.

The NSM assumes that the properties of the SSD are directly used to estimate the corresponding population properties. With probability judgment, the proportion of observations in the sample that satisfy the event is reported as the assessed probability. To assess the probability that London has more than 5 million inhabitants, for example, you may retrieve a sample of *n* population figures of European capitals. The proportion in this sample that has a population in excess of 5 million defines the probability judgment. To produce, say, a 90% confidence interval you may report the median in the SSD as your best guess and use limits in the SSD that cover 90% of the sample directly to estimate the 90% coverage of population figures for European capitals, which is the produced interval.

In one sense, the cognitive processes are essentially the same with both judgment formats: A sample of similar observations is retrieved from memory and directly

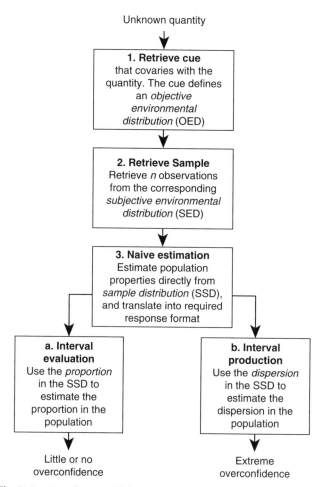

Fig. 11.2. The Naïve Sampling Model (NSM) of format dependence. Adapted from Juslin *et al.* (2007). By permission of the American Psychological Association.

expressed as required by the format, as a probability (proportion) for interval evaluation and as limits of a distribution with interval production. Despite the apparent innocence of the assumptions, the NSM implies that they entail two nontrivial origins of overconfidence.

Biased or unbiased estimators

Confidence expressed as probability judgments involves the estimation of a *proportion*. If both the probe and the SSD are randomly sampled from the OED (e.g., European capitals) the proportion in the SSD satisfying the event estimates the probability that the probe satisfies the event (London has more than 5 million inhabitants). Sample proportion P is an unbiased estimator of population proportion p. If you, for example, randomly sample n individuals from a population with a proportion of p individuals with an IQ score that exceeds, say 120, and measure this score, the average sample proportion P of individuals that exceeds an IQ of 120 is p. If people's estimates of probability is computationally equivalent to—or plainly is—a sample proportion, these judgments should show minor amounts of overconfidence.

Interval production involves estimation of a *dispersion* of plausible values based on subjective assessment of a coverage interval (Poulsen *et al.*, 1997) for a distribution of similar values in the environment (the OED) (a xx% coverage interval should include xx% of the distribution). The NSM implies that again people take the SSD as a proxy for the OED, which is used to estimate an interval that covers a certain central proportion of the OED. If, for example, the limits 1 and 6 million cover 90% of the values in the SSD, this is taken as evidence that these limits also cover 90% of the values in the OED (e.g., 90% of all the European capitals have populations between 1 and 6 millions). Even if the SED is perfectly representative of the OED, this naive and direct use of the SSD to estimate a probability distribution leads to overconfidence for two different reasons: First; sample dispersion D is an inherently biased estimator of population dispersion d (this is why the variance in a sample is corrected with $1/(1-n)$ when used to estimate population variance). If you, for example, sample individuals and measure their IQ from a population of individuals with IQ dispersion d, the average sample dispersion D is systematically smaller than d.

Second, the distribution in a small sample is on average dislocated relative to the population distribution, further decreasing the actual proportion of the OED that falls within the intervals specified by the SSD (as related to the use of the t- rather than the z-distribution for statistical inference at small n). If a 90% confidence interval for the population of London is produced by retrieving a small sample of similar cites and reporting the lower and upper limits that include 90% of these values, this will produce too tight intervals with overconfidence. Computer simulations verify that the NSM predicts the patterns of overconfidence observed in data (see Fig. 11.3 and Juslin *et al.*, 2007).

Biased or unbiased subjective environmental distributions

The second factor that determines the extent of overconfidence is the degree to which the SED is representative of the OED. One condition with a close match is random sampling where all deviations between the SED and the OED arise from random sampling error. In principle, the distribution of population figures of European capitals encoded in memory could be a random sample of the European capitals, but more often biases are expected, as when people possess more knowledge about the larger European capitals. In general (but not always) SED-biases contribute more overconfidence bias (see Juslin *et al.*, 2007).

The NSM therefore states two origins of overconfidence: First, the use of sample coverage to estimate population coverage contributes a strong bias towards overconfidence with interval production regardless of what target variable is estimated. Second, a SED that deviates from the OED contributes to an overconfidence bias with both interval production and probability judgment that is idiosyncratic to the target variable. According to the NSM, format dependence arises because with probability judgment only the (possibly zero) bias in the SED contributes to the overconfidence; with interval production both the biased estimator, sample coverage, and the bias in the SED contributes to the overconfidence.

(a)

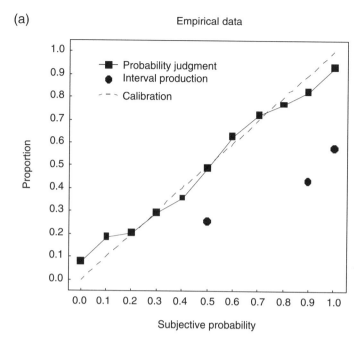

(b)

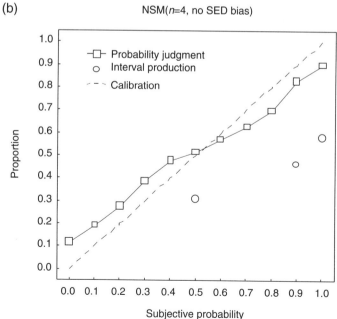

Fig. 11.3. Panel A: Empirical data for full-range probability assessment and interval production in regard to world country populations from Juslin *et al.* (2003). Panel B: The corresponding predictions by the NSM. Adapted from Juslin *et al.* (2007). By permission of the American Psychological Association.

Sample size as short-term memory capacity

It is a central notion of the NSM that humans rely on a limited sample of the environment. In principle, this limitation can be envisioned either as a capacity constraint within long-term (referred to as *n* by *LTM*) or short-term (referred to as *n* by *STM*) memory. The explicit assumption in the NSM of a short-term memory capacity limitation (*n* by *STM*) accordingly makes strong predictions about the effects of task experience and about the relationship between short-term memory capacity and overconfidence, and these predictions differ with probability judgment and interval production. Because the same independent variables produce divergent results we refer to these effects as *dissociations*.

A format-experience dissociation. With probability judgment, because sample proportion is an unbiased estimator, the overconfidence derives entirely from bias between SEDs and OEDs. Given immediate and accurate feedback domain expertise should provide ample opportunity to correct these deviations. With interval production expertise can likewise eliminate the bias from a biased SED, and thus diminish the overconfidence. However, because the sample size is architecturally constrained by short-term memory capacity, the overconfidence that derives from naïve use of sample coverage is not automatically cured by more experience. That is, with interval production overconfidence remains large despite extensive task experience, yet with probability judgment already modest task experience should afford close to zero overconfidence (*a format-experience dissociation*).

A format-short-term memory dissociation. Sample size as short-term memory capacity implies that with interval production the overconfidence should be related to both short-term memory capacity and the bias between the SED and the OED, but with probability judgment only the latter should be predictive. If additional training provides observations that are representative of the OED, the SED-bias should gradually become less important as all the participants attain SEDs that approximate the OEDs, but the relationship between short-term memory capacity and overconfidence should prevail despite extensive training.

An obvious alternative possibility is that more experience makes larger samples available to the judge. This implies either that the judge can retrieve all observations stored in long-term memory (the SED) at the time of judgment or, perhaps more plausibly, that the judge can retrieve some abstract summary representation already computed from this information. This suggests that with both formats the overconfidence should decrease with additional experience and the format dependence accordingly diminish. In addition, the degree of overconfidence exhibited by someone should not primarily be related to short-term memory capacity, but instead to the total amount of experience digested or, given the same extent of training, to the capacity to encode this experience into memory.

In the following section we review empirical data collected to test three main predictions by the NSM: First, that changing the proximal estimator variable implied by the assessment format for exactly the same events from coverage to proportion has a profound effect on the overconfidence; second, experimentally controlled OEDs in laboratory tasks directly affect the confidence intervals produced; and third, that while overconfidence with interval production is strongly related to short-term memory

capacity and not eliminated by extensive experience, the overconfidence with probability judgment is not related to short-term memory capacity but rapidly reduced by
representative outcome feedback.

Empirical evidence

Biased or unbiased estimators

A confounding in most studies of format dependence (Juslin *et al.*, 1999; Juslin &
Persson, 2002) is that they have compared formats that involve the assessment of one
fractile of the subjective probability distribution ('What is the probability that the
population of Thailand exceeds 25 million?') with production of intervals that involve
two fractiles of the subjective probability distribution. In an attempt to avoid this
confound we contrasted the interval production format with the *interval evaluation*
format ('What is the probability that the population of Thailand lies between 25 and
45 million?') where the event also involves the joint assessment of two fractiles of the
subjective probability distribution.

In Winman *et al.* (2004) the interval production and the interval evaluation formats
were compared for the same events, both within and between subjects. The participants
first produced intervals that defined events, and later the probability of these events
(intervals) was assessed. As predicted by the NSM there was significantly and substantially more overconfidence in the interval production condition than in the interval
evaluation condition, although the events were matched on an item-by-item basis. The
most remarkable demonstration was that participants were strongly susceptible to
format-dependence also for intervals they had produced *themselves* (see Experiment 1).

In Experiment 2 in Winman *et al.* (2004) the NSM was used to design a method to produce intuitive confidence intervals, but in a way that minimizes the overconfidence with
interval production. The ADaptive INterval Adjustment (ADINA) procedure proposes a
sequence of intervals, each of which changes in size in response to the probability assessment for the previous interval, with the effect that the intervals 'home in' on a target probability. As with usual interval production the end-product is an interval with a pre-stated
probability, but the procedure requires estimates of proportion rather than coverage.

Experiment 2 had three conditions; (a) a *control condition* with ordinary interval
production; (b) an *ADINA(O)-condition* where ADINA proposes intervals centered
on the participant's *Own* point estimate. Because the interval that is assessed itself
presumably is affected by the same sampling error as the SSD used for the probability[1]

---

[1] In regard to format dependence an important aspect is whether the event in the probability
judgment is already correlated with the SSD used to assess it. The event is typically uncorrelated if it is defined *a priori*, as when the assessment concerns unknown future events (Keren,
1987; Murphy & Brown, 1985) or general knowledge questions that are randomly selected
from natural environments (Gigerenzer *et al.*, 1991; Juslin, 1994; Juslin *et al.*, 2000). Another
possibility is that the event is correlated with the SSD used to make the probability assessment.
On reason for such a correlation is *SSD overlap*. If people retrieve the same or almost the
same SSD when making a point estimate a correlation arises when the event (the interval), as
in the *ADINA(O)* condition, is defined by the person's best guess.

the NSM predicts less overconfidence than in the control condition, but not zero overconfidence. (c) An *ADINA(R)-condition* where ADINA locates intervals centered on a *Random* value. Because the interval is randomly and independently placed the NSM predicts a larger decrease in overconfidence. In effect, the ADINA(R)-condition transforms the task into a standard full-range probability judgment task and the NSM therefore predicts close to zero overconfidence.

Figure 11.4A confirms the predicted pattern with extreme overconfidence bias for the control condition and close to zero overconfidence for the ADINA(R)-condition. The hit-rate is similar in all three conditions, but whereas the subjective probability assigned is too high in the control condition it is quite accurate with ADINA(R). However, these initial intervals are not yet intervals associated with the pre-specified target probability. Figure 11.4B that presents the mean subjective probability and hit rate for the final 'homed-in' intervals confirms the profound reduction in overconfidence, with extreme overconfidence for the control condition and close to zero overconfidence for the ADINA(R)-condition. In this case the subjective probability is almost the same—at the levels defined by the desired probabilities—but overconfidence is diminished by a manipulation that increases the too low hit rates in the control condition so that they approximate the stated probabilities. In sum: ADINA allows control of the overconfidence either by reducing the subjective probability to the hit rate (Fig. 11.4A), or by increasing the hit-rate to the subjective probability (Fig. 11.4B).

Biased or unbiased subjective environmental distributions

The NSM implies that people possess subjective counterparts (the SEDs) of the ecological distributions (the OEDs), and that the intuitive confidence intervals derive from retrieval operations (sampling) on these representations. In order to test this implication we conducted an experiment in a controlled laboratory task that manipulated the OEDs in order to establish that people have the cognitive capacities to generate SEDs that represent the OEDs and that when encountering an unknown object the uncertainty expressed by a confidence interval is determined by the SED (see Juslin *et al.*, in press for details).

The participants were exposed to an OED that was either U-shaped or inversely U-shaped (range = 1–1000). The U-shaped OED condition had a high frequency of values close to 1 and to 1000 and the inversely U-shaped OED condition consisted predominantly of target values close to 500. The task involved, after a training phase, estimation of the revenue of both old (encountered during training) and new (not encountered during training) fictive business companies. To directly elicit the SEDs the participants also estimated the relative frequency of observations in ten intervals evenly distributed over the OED range.

As predicted if people are able to represent the OEDs, the assessed SEDs were bimodal in the U-shaped condition and unimodal in the inversely U-shaped condition. The results also showed that both the standard deviation and the interval size (for the new items) were significantly larger in the U-shaped condition compared to the inversely U-shaped condition. Thus, when encountering unknown objects the participants appeared to rely on previously experienced distributions in expressing intuitive confidence intervals. In short, the study demonstrated that people are

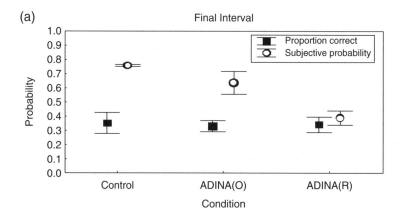

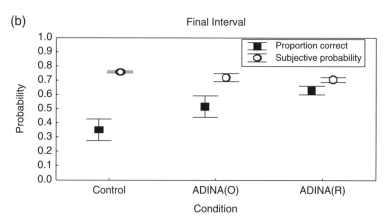

Fig. 11.4. Panel A: Mean confidence and proportion of intervals that include the population value as computed from the response to the first *a priori* interval for each of the three assessment methods (with 95% CI, *n* = 15). Panel B: Mean confidence and proportion of intervals that include the population value as computed for the final, 'homed in,' confidence intervals for each of the three assessment methods (with 95% CI, *n* − 15). Overconfidence is the difference between the mean confidence and the proportion. Adapted from Winman *et al.* (2004). By permission of the American Psychological Association.

sensitive to the OEDs with SEDs that largely mirror the OEDs, interval sizes are affected by the OED manipulation in the way predicted by NSM, and a direct measure of the SED verifies that the SED is strongly linked to the interval size.

Sample size as short-term memory capacity

Considering the *format-experience dissociation* the literature on expert judgment provides indirect support. There are several examples of experts that make well-calibrated probability judgments (e.g., Keren, 1987; Murphy & Brown, 1985), but there are few examples of well-calibrated experts with interval production (Lichtenstein *et al.*, 1982; Russo & Schoemaker, 1992), which favors the short-term memory interpretation of the sample size. For example, Russo and Schoemaker (1992) investigated experts from a large number of professions using interval production tasks tailored for the experts' fields of knowledge (such as advertising, money management, and petroleum industry). Of more than 2,000 individuals, 99% were overconfident. That experts with many years in a profession generally are highly overconfident suggests that they are unable to profit from the large number of observations in long-term memory for eliminating the overconfidence with interval production.

In the most comprehensive study to date of individual differences in cognitive abilities and their relationship to judgment and decision making, Stanovich and West (1998, 2000) reported significant positive correlations between cognitive abilities and performance on tasks from the heuristics and biases paradigm (e. g., base-rate tasks, selection tasks, hindsight bias). One exception to this pattern was *knowledge calibration*, the task addressed here. Stanovich and West (1998) used half-range probability judgment and found a low negative correlation between overconfidence and cognitive abilities. Insofar as the measures of cognitive abilities draw on short-term memory capacity the low correlations are consistent with the NSM because, in contrast to interval productions, probability judgment involves an unbiased estimator and the correlation with short-term memory capacity should be low.

In Hansson *et al.* (2006) we investigated the role of short-term memory capacity (n by STM), the total number of observations stored in long-term memory (n by LTM), and the role of several additional cognitive abilities (problem solving and episodic memory) in a laboratory learning task. Nominally the task involved estimates of the revenue of companies, but unbeknownst to the participants the distributions were from a real environment (the world country populations), which they had to learn from 'scratch' in the laboratory.

The NSM predicts that overconfidence in interval production should correlate negatively with n by STM and that overconfidence should be extreme also after extensive experience. In the probability judgment task overconfidence should not correlate with short-term memory and be reduced by outcome feedback. The alternative hypothesis, that the sample size is constrained by n by LTM, predicts that experience should eliminate overconfidence with both formats and overconfidence should correlate with n by LTM.

Experiments 1 and 2 from Hansson *et al.* (2006) varied the extent of training in conditions with immediate, complete, and accurate outcome feedback from very modest (68 trials), over intermediate (272 trials) to extensive (544 trials). Figures 11.5A and B summarize the results with interval production after 68, 272, and 544 training trials. As illustrated in Fig. 11.5A, the proportions of correctly recalled target values (and thus n by LTM) increased significantly with training, from less than 10% of all 136 target values in each training block after 68 training trials to more than 30% after 544 training trials. As predicted there is persistent extreme overconfidence with interval production even after 544 trials with feedback. This is remarkable because conditions with immediate, unambiguous, and representative feedback have

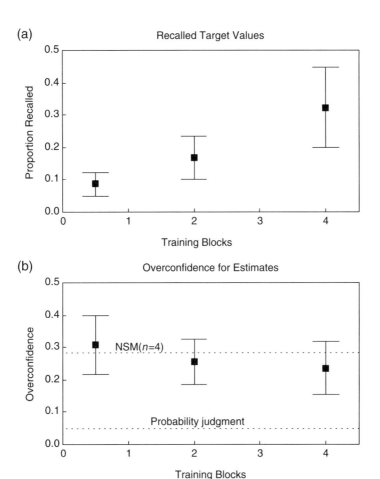

Fig. 11.5. Panel A: Proportion of correctly recalled target values as a function of the number of training blocks in a laboratory learning task. The main effect of number of training blocks (1/2 a block is 68 training trials, 2 blocks is 244 training trials, and 4 blocks is 544 training trials) is sizeable and statistically significant. Panel B: Overconfidence in interval production as a function of the number of training blocks in a laboratory learning task (1/2 a block is 68 training trials, 2 blocks is 244 training trials, and 4 blocks is 544 training trials). Overconfidence is the difference between the probability of the interval and the hit-rate of target values included by the interval. The main effect of number of training blocks is small and not statistically significant. The dotted line denoted 'NSM(n=4)' represents the prediction by NSM assuming sample size 4 and no SED bias. The lower dotted line denoted 'probability judgment' refers to the observed overconfidence in the interval evaluation task after 68 training trials.

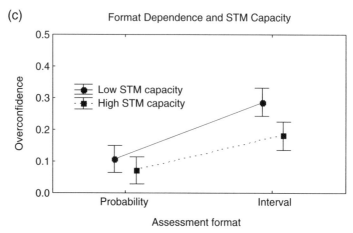

Fig. 11.5 (*Cont.*) Panel C: Overconfidence and the statistically significant interaction effect between short-term memory capacity and assessment format. Adapted from Hansson *et al.* (2006). By permission of the American Psychological Association.

traditionally been presumed to be optimal for attaining well-calibrated judgments (Keren, 1991; Lichtenstein *et al.*, 1982). Consistently with the research on experts (Russo & Schoemaker, 1992) and as predicted by the NSM, however, experience appears to have a minimal effect on the overconfidence with interval production.

In addition to *n* by LTM, as estimated by the proportion of correctly recalled target values participants were measured with a standard digit-span test to estimate *n* by STM. The results indicated that after 68 training trials no independent variable was significantly related to overconfidence, but after 272 training trials overconfidence was significantly related to *n* by STM. After 544 training trials there was even a stronger relation with *n* by STM.[2] In none of the experiments is *n* by LTM significantly related to overconfidence and nominally often the relation is of the wrong sign (larger *n* by LTM suggests more overconfidence).

In Experiment 3, a larger participant sample was additionally measured in fluid intelligence (RAPM; Raven, 1965) and episodic memory (a version of Wexler's paired-associates). The purposes of Experiment 3 were to inquire if the correlation between short-term memory capacity and overconfidence obtains also when we control for individual differences in intelligence and episodic memory capacity and to test the interaction predicted by the NSM: more overconfidence with interval production, but this difference should be especially pronounced for people with low short-term memory capacity. To test this interaction, the participants were divided into low or high short-term memory capacity based on a median split separately within each condition.

----

[2] Our interpretation was that after 68 training trials the effects of short-term memory capacity were overshadowed by large idiosyncratic differences in the variability in the small samples of target values encoded in long-term memory. This idiosyncratic difference in the variability diminishes with more training.

The interaction in Fig. 11.5C confirms the prediction by the NSM. In the interval evaluation condition (probability judgment) there is no significant difference between the participants with low and high short-term memory capacity, but in the interval production condition there is significantly more overconfidence bias for participants with low short-term memory capacity. Entering RAPM and episodic memory as covariates in the analysis had no significant effects on the correlations or the significant interaction in Fig. 11.5C.

General discussion

In this chapter we have discussed an 'ecological approach' to cognition, the naïve intuitive statistician that, in certain ways, falls half-way between rational analysis (Anderson, 1990) and the traditional approaches to ecological psychology (Brunswik, 1955; Gibson, 1979). As in rational analysis, rationality is entered as a theoretical assumption, but here it refers to the processing of the proximal sample and serves to relocate the explanatory burden to the relationship between the proximal sample and the distal variables. As with rational analysis, this assumption is tentative and may need to be relaxed by assumptions of cognitive limitations in view of empirical evidence. In regard to many phenomena heuristic processing is still likely to be a vital part of the explanation. As in traditional approaches to ecological psychology (Brunswik, 1955; Gibson, 1979), however, the rationality of the observed *behavior* is an empirical issue determined by the organism–environment relations.

The naïve intuitive statistician is a metaphor for human judgment that is especially suitable for making sense of the somewhat contradictory results from the previous research paradigms. The main idea is that much more about human judgment can be illuminated if the attention is directed, not only to the cognitive processes, but to the information that the cognitive processes act upon. Error or biases in judgment can with equal force be understood not primarily as the results of an inherently irrational (or heuristic) cognitive processing of the available samples, but by biases in the input from the environment and the naivety with which people generalize from the proximal samples they have available (Fiedler, 2000; Fiedler & Juslin, 2006a). In this chapter we have reviewed some of the mounting evidence that many phenomena in the literature may receive more straightforward and illuminating treatment from the perspective of the naïve intuitive statistician.

We illustrated the metaphor with the NSM, directly inspired by the naïve intuitive statistician, that accounts for some of the more intriguing and unresolved issues in research on confidence judgment: the extreme overconfidence with intuitive confidence intervals and the format dependence effect. According to the NSM judgments elicits retrieval of a small sample of similar observations from long-term memory. The sample size is constrained by short-term memory limiting the amount of information that is available at the time of judgment. People are *naïve*, directly taking sample properties as proxies for population properties producing contradictory results depending on the assessment format. Importantly, the NSM allows us not only to predict the overconfidence bias, but also to reduce it substantially. This illustrates that identifying the exact origin of the observed bias may be crucial for curing it.

One could raise the question if this *naivety* should be interpreted as yet another 'cognitive processing' deficit. Although the outcome in the application above is the same, overconfidence, we simultaneously demonstrated that this naivety supports rational behavior for some sample properties (e.g., proportion). The more intricate statistical knowledge required to interpret sample properties such as dispersion can be regarded as a sophisticated and recent cultural achievement (Gigerenzer *et al.*, 1989; Hacking, 1975). If we also consider, as demonstrated, that the information (sample size) available for processing is constrained by short-term memory it becomes understandable why these biases are often surprisingly resistant to additional experience. Regardless of the preferred semantics, the NSM specifies the conditions that turn 'irrational' behavior into 'rational' behavior without changing the stated goal of the behavior, thereby providing the 'how and when' of the biases.

Both the approaches of the naïve intuitive statistician and rational analyses (e.g., Anderson, 1990; Oaksford & Chater, 1998) highlight the role of environment over cognitive mechanism and both agree that the environment is of probabilistic character. The metaphor of the naïve intuitive statistician, however, actualizes at least two issues not addressed in the context of rational analysis. First, despite the acknowledgment of probabilism in the Bayesian analysis, the notion of 'sampling' is intriguingly absent in rational analysis. The organism that is rationally analyzed apparently lives in the world of probability theory (infinite populations), but real organisms live in a world of statistics (finite samples).

In fact, a striking example of this complication is provided by the discussion of the 'robustness' of cognitive algorithms and of the 'bias/variance dilemma' provided in another chapter of this volume (Brighton & Gigerenzer, this volume). With infinite sample size the crucial concern is to base the judgment on an estimator that minimizes bias (systematic error), because with infinite sample size random error converges to zero. But when a small sample is used the precision of each estimate (low variance) may be more important than a zero bias at the level of expected values. Accordingly, rational adaptation based on small samples need not suggest the same solutions as rational adaptation based on infinite sample size.

Second, it is at present unclear how to address the, sometimes striking, naivety illustrated in this chapter from the standpoint of rational analysis. From our point of view, however, the need for a rational analysis also of this behavior is not an option, but a necessity. Until we have understood the adaptive forces that maintain this naivety, we have not fully understood and explained the associated phenomena. As has been shown in this chapter and elsewhere (Fiedler, 2000; Fiedler & Juslin, 2006a; Juslin *et al.*, 2007) a lot of human behavior can be understood by combining information sampling with adaptive cognition.

References

Anderson, J. R. (1990). *The adaptive character of thought*. Hillsdale, NJ: Lawrence Erlbaum.

Brighton, H., & Gigerenzer, G. (in press). Probabilistic minds, Bayesian brains, and cognitive mechanisms: Harmony or dissonance? In M. Oaksford & N. Chater (Eds.), *Probabilistic approaches to cognition*. Oxford: Oxford University Press.

Brunswik, E. (1955). Representative design and probabilistic theory in a functional psychology. *Psychological Review*, **62**, 193–217.

Denrell, J. (2005). Why most people disapprove of me: Experience sampling in impression formation. *Psychological Review*, **112**, 951–978.

Edwards, W. (1982). Conservatism in human information processing. In D. Kahneman, P. Slovic, & A. Tversky (Eds.), *Judgment under uncertainty: Heuristics and biases* (pp. 359–369). New York: Cambridge University Press.

Einhorn, H. J., & Hogarth, R. M. (1978). Confidence in judgment: Persistence of the illusion of validity. *Psychological Review*, 85, 395–416.

Estes, W. K. (1976). The cognitive side of probability learning. *Psychological Review*, **83**, 37–64.

Fiedler, K. (2000). Beware of samples! A cognitive-ecological sampling approach to judgment biases. *Psychological Review*, **107**, 659–676.

Fiedler, K., & Juslin, P. (2006a). *Information sampling and adaptive cognition*. New York: Cambridge University Press.

Fiedler, K., & Juslin, P. (2006b). Taking the interface between mind and environment seriously. In K. Fiedler & P.Juslin (Eds.), *Information sampling and adaptive cognition*. New York: Cambridge University Press.

Fox, C. R., & Hadar, L. (2006). 'Decision from experience' = sampling error + prospect theory: Reconsidering Hertwig, Barron, Weber & Erev (2004). *Judgment and Decision Making*, **1**, 159–161.

Gibson, J. J. (1979). *The ecological approach to visual perception*. Boston: Houghton Mufflin.

Gigerenzer, G., Hoffrage, U., & Kleinbolting, H. (1991). Probabilistic mental models: A Brunswikian theory of confidence. *Psychological Review*, **98**, 506–528.

Gigerenzer, G., & Murray, D. J. (1987). *Cognition as intuitive statistics*. Hillsdale, NJ: Erlbaum.

Gigerenzer, G., Swijtink, Z., Porter, T., Daston, L., Beatty, J., & Kruger, L. (1989). *The empire of chance*. Cambridge: Cambridge University Press.

Gigerenzer, G., Todd, P. M., & the ABC Research Group (1999). *Simple heuristics that make us smart*. New York: Oxford University Press.

Gilovich, T., Griffin, D., & Kahneman, D. (2002). *Heuristics and biases: The psychology of intuitive judgment*. Cambridge: Cambridge University Press.

Griffin, D., W., & Tversky, A. (1992). The weighing of evidence and the determinants of confidence. *Cognitive psychology*, **24**, 411–435.

Hacking, I. (1975). *The emergence of probability*. London: Cambridge University Press.

Hammond, K. R. (1996). *Human judgment and social policy: Irreducibly uncertainty, inevitable error, unavoidable injustice*. New York: Oxford University Press.

Hammond, K. R., & Stewart, T. R. (Eds.). (2001). *The essential Brunswik; Beginnings, explications, applications*. Oxford: Oxford University Press.

Hansson, P., Juslin, P., & Winman, A. (2006). *The role of short term memory and task experience for overconfidence in judgment under uncertainty*. Manuscript submitted for publication.

Hasher, L., & Zacks, R. T. (1979). Automatic and effortful processes in memory. *Journal of Experimental Psychology: General*, **108**, 356–388.

Hertwig, R., Barron, G., Weber, E. U., & Erev, I. (2004). Decisions from experience and the effect of rare events in risky choice. *Psychological Science*, **15**, 534–539.

Hertwig, R., Pachur, T., & Kurzenhäuser, S. (2005). Judgments of risk frequencies: Tests of possible cognitive mechanisms. *Journal of Experimental Psychology: Learning, Memory and Cognition*, **35**, 621–642.

Juslin, P. (1994). The overconfidence phenomenon as a consequence of informal experimenter-guided selection of almanac items. *Organizational Behavior and Human Decision Processes,* **57**, 226–246.

Juslin, P., Olsson, H., & Bjorkman, M. (1997). Brunswikian and Thurstonian origins of bias in probability assessment: On the interpretation of stochastic components of judgment.

Juslin, P., & Persson, M. (2002). PROBabilities from EXemplars (PROBEX): A 'lazy' algorithm for probabilistic inference from generic knowledge. *Cognitive Science,* **26**, 563–607.

Juslin, P., Wennerholm, P., & Olsson, H. (1999). Format dependence in subjective probability calibration. *Journal of Experimental Psychology: Learning, Memory, and Cognition,* **28**, 1038–1052.

Juslin, P., Winman, A., & Hansson, P. (2007). The naïve intuitive statistician: A naïve sampling model of intuitive confidence intervals. *Psychological Review,* **114**, 678–703.

Juslin, P., Winman, A., & Olsson, H. (2000). Naive empiricism and dogmatism in confidence research: A critical examination of the hard-easy effect. *Psychological Review,* **107**, 384–396.

Juslin, P., Winman, A., & Olsson, H. (2003). Calibration, additivity, and source independence of probability judgments in general knowledge and sensory discrimination tasks. *Organizational Behavior and Human Decision Processes,* **92**, 34–51.

Kahneman, D., & Frederick, S. (2002). Representativeness revisited: Attribute substitution in intuitive judgment. In T. Gilovich, D. W. Griffin, & D. Kahneman (Eds.), *Heuristics and biases: The psychology of intuitive judgment* (pp. 49–81). New York: Cambridge University Press.

Kahneman, D., Slovic, P., & Tversky, A. (1982). *Judgment under uncertainty: Heuristics and biases.* Cambridge: Cambridge University Press.

Kahneman, D., & Tversky, A. (1979). Prospect theory: An analysis of decision under risk. *Econometrica,* **47**, 263–291.

Kareev, Y., Arnon, S., & Horwitz-Zeliger, R. (2002). On the misperception of variability. *Journal of Experimental Psychology: General,* **131**, 287–297.

Keren, G. (1987). Facing uncertainty in the game of bridge. *Organizational Behavior and Human Decision Processes,* **39**, 98–114.

Keren, G. (1991). Calibration and probability judgments. Conceptual and methodological issues. *Acta Psychologica,* **77**, 217–273.

Klayman, J., Soll, J. B., Gonzalez-Vallejo, C., & Barlas, S. (1999). Overconfidence: It depends on how, what, and whom you ask. *Organizational Behavior and Human Decision Processes,* **79**, 216–247.

Koriat, A., Lichtenstein, S., & Fischhoff, B. (1980). Reasons for confidence. *Journal of Experimental Psychology: Human Learning and Memory,* **6**, 17–118.

Lichtenstein, S., Fischhoff, B., & Phillips, L. D. (1982). Calibration of subjective probabilities: The state of the art up to 1980. In D. Kahneman, P. Slovic, & A. Tversky (Eds.), *Judgment under uncertainty: Heuristics and biases* (pp. 306–334). New York: Cambridge University Press.

Lichtenstein, S., Slovic, P., Fischhoff, B., Layman, M., & Combs, B. (1978). Judged frequency of lethal events. *Journal of Experimental Psychology: Human Learning and Memory,* **4**, 551–578.

Murphy, A. H., & Brown, B. G. (1985). A comparative evaluation of objective and subjective weather forecasts in the United States. In G. Wright (Ed.), *Behavioral decision making* (pp. 329–359). New York: Plenum Press.

Oaksford, M., & Chater, N. (1998). *Rational models of cognition.* Oxford: Oxford University Press.

Peterson, C. R., & Beach, L. R. (1967). Man as an intuitive statistician. *Psychological Bulletin, 68*, 29–46.

Poulsen, O. M., Holst, E., & Christensen, J. M. (1997). Calculation and application of coverage intervals for biological reference values. *Pure and Applied Chemistry, 69*, 1601–1611.

Raven, J. C. (1965). *Advanced progressive matrices: Sets I and II*. London: Lewis.

Runeson, S., Juslin, P., & Olsson, H. (2000). Visual perception of dynamic properties: Cue heuristics versus direct-perceptual competence. *Psychological Review, 107*, 525–555.

Russo, J. E., & Schoemaker, P. J. (1992). Managing overconfidence. *Sloan Management Review, 33*, 7–17.

Schwarz, N., & Wänke, M. (2002). Experimental and contextual heuristics in frequency judgment: Ease of recall and response scales. In P. Sedlmeier & T. Betsch (Eds.), *Etc. Frequency processing and cognition* (pp. 89–108). Oxford, UK: Oxford University Press.

Sedlmeier, P., & Betsch, T. (2002). *Etc. Frequency processing and cognition*. Oxford, UK: Oxford University Press.

Simon, H. A. (1990). Invariants of human behavior. *Annual Review of Psychology, 41*, 1–19.

Soll, J. B., & Klayman, J. (2004). Overconfidence in interval estimates. *Journal of Experimental Psychology: Learning, Memory, and Cognition, 30*, 299–314.

Stanovich, K. E., & West, R. F. (1998). Individual differences in rational thought. *Journal of Experimental Psychology: General, 127*, 161–188.

Stanovich, K. E., & West, R. F. (2000). Individual differences in reasoning: Implications for the rationality debate? *Behavioral and Brain Sciences, 23*, 645–726.

Stewart, N., & Simpson. (in press).? In Eds. M. Oaksford & N. Chater (Eds.), *Probabilistic approaches to cognition*. Oxford: Oxford University Press.

Stewart, N., Chater, N., & Brown, G. D. A. (2006). Decision by sampling. *Cognitive Psychology, 53*, 1–26.

Tversky, A., & Kahneman, D. (1971). Belief in the law of small numbers. *Psychological Bulletin, 2*, 105–110.

Tversky, A., & Kahneman, D. (1974). Judgment under uncertainty: Heuristics and biases. *Science, 185*, 1124–1131.

Winman, A., Hansson, P., & Juslin, P. (2004). Subjective probability intervals: How to cure overconfidence by interval evaluation. *Journal of Experimental Psychology: Learning, Memory, and Cognition, 30*, 1167–1175.

Yaniv, I., & Foster, D. P. (1997). Precision and accuracy of judgmental estimation. *Journal of Behavioral Decision Making, 10*, 21–32.

Zacks, R. T., & Hasher, L. (2002). Frequency processing: A twenty-five year perspective. In P. Sedlmeier & T. Betsch (Eds.), *Frequency processing and cognition* (pp. 21–36). New York: Oxford University Press.

Chapter 12

A decision-by-sampling account of decision under risk

Neil Stewart and Keith Simpson

University of Warwick, Coventry, UK

Abstract

In decision by sampling (DbS), the subjective value of an attribute value is derived from a series of binary, ordinal comparisons with a sample of attribute values from the immediate context and from long-term memory. Here, we extend DbS to account for choices between risky prospects by using the binary, ordinal comparisons to increment accumulators for each prospect. The model correctly predicts the direction of preference for all 16 prospects from the Kahneman and Tversky (1979) data set and produces a high correlation between choice proportions and model predictions.

A decision-by-sampling account of decision under risk

Most models of decision under risk are derived from or are closely related to expected utility theory, which is the standard normative model of decision under risk. Consider, for example, the first choice in Table 12.1. Prospect A offers a .33 probability of 2,500, a .66 probability of 2,400, otherwise a .01 probability of 0. Prospect B offers a 2,400 for certain. According to expected utility theory, each monetary amount should be transformed into a utility and then the prospect with the higher expected (average) utility should be preferred. The function relating money to utility is typically concave, with each unit of incremental wealth having positive but diminishing marginal utility. Prominent descriptive models derived from the expected utility framework include: subjective expected utility theory (Edwards, 1962); prospect and cumulative prospect theories (Kahneman & Tversky, 1979; Tversky & Kahneman, 1992); regret theory (Loomes & Sugden, 1982); rank-dependent utility theory (Quiggin, 1983); decision field theory (Busemeyer & Townsend, 1993); the transfer-of-attention-exchange model (Birnbaum & Chavez, 1997); and aspiration level theory (Lopes & Oden, 1999).

Rather than beginning with expected utility theory and modifying it to describe actual choice behaviour, decision by sampling (DbS, Stewart, Chater, & Brown, 2006) begins with consideration of the basic cognitive tools available and examines how decisions might be made using these tools. In the original presentation of the model,

Table 12.1. Problems from Kahneman and Tversky (1979).

Problem	N	Prospect A			Prospect B		
		Amount	Probability	Choice Share	Amount	Probability	Choice Share
1	72	2,500	.33	18%	2,400	1.00	82%
		2,400	.66				
		0	.01				
2	72	2,500	.33	83%	2,400	.34	17%
		0	.67		0	.66	
3	95	4,000	.80	20%	3,000	1.00	80%
4	95	4,000	.20	65%	3,000	.25	35%
3'	95	− 4,000	.80	92%	− 3,000	1.00	8%
4'	95	− 4,000	.20	42%	− 3,000	.25	58%
7	66	6,000	.45	14%	3,000	.90	86%
8	66	6,000	.001	73%	3,000	.002	27%
7'	66	− 6,000	.45	92%	− 3,000	.90	8%
8'	66	− 6000	.001	30%	− 3,000	.002	70%
11	70	Given 1,000 initially					
		1,000	.50	16%	500	1.00	84%
12	70	Given 2,000 initially					
		− 1,000	.50	69%	− 500	1.00	31%
13	68	6,000	.25	18%	4,000	.25	82%
					2,000	.25	
13'	64	− 6,000	.25	70%	− 4,000	.25	30%
					− 2,000	.25	
14	72	5,000	.001	72%	5	1.00	28%
14'	72	− 5,000	.001	17%	− 5	1.00	83%

Note. Amounts are in Israeli pounds.

Stewart *et al.* (2006) considered how the subjective value of an attribute value was derived on-the-fly from a comparison with a sample of other attribute values drawn from real-world distributions. In this chapter, we extend DbS to offer an account of choices involving these attribute values.

Attribute values

DbS differs from expected utility theory and the related descriptive models above in abandoning the notion of stable, internal psychoeconomic functions that transform money into utility and probability into subjective probability. Instead, the subjective value of an attribute value is constructed from a series of binary, ordinal comparisons within a set of attribute values sampled both from the immediate context of the decision and from long-term memory. For each attribute value, a frequency count is kept of the number of favourable comparisons. The proportion of favourable comparisons is given by the proportion of attribute values in the sample compared to which the the target attribute value appears more favourable. For example, within the sample of possible gains {1, 5, 12, 33, 45, 82} the subjective value of a gain of 12 is 2/5 because comparisons to 2 of the 5 other items in the set (specifically, 1 and 5) are favourable.

Comparisons are assumed to be ordinal, to a first approximation, because of the relative ease of ordinal comparisons: Choosing one thing over another is easy, but valuing one thing in terms of the other is hard. It is easy to say one prefers Option A over Option B, but much harder to say that Option A is 1.4 times better than Option B. This ordinal assumption is consistent with the relatively short time participants take to make choices between simple risky prospects (e.g., a .50 probability of 100) and the much longer time taken to provide certainty equivalents for the same risky prospects.

The sample to which an attribute value is compared comprises items from both the immediate context and from long-term memory. We refer to this sample as the *decision sample*. For example, in making the first choice in Table 12.1 the attribute values from the immediate context (0, 2,400, and 2,500 for pay off and .01, .33, .66, and 1.00 for probability) will make up part of the decision sample. But the attribute values from long-term memory are not as easily knowable. Stewart *et al.* (2006) made the assumption that the distribution of attribute values in long-term memory reflects the real-world distribution of attribute values (Anderson, 1990; Anderson & Milson, 1989; Anderson & Schooler, 1991; Chater & Brown, 1999; Oaksford & Chater, 1998; Shepard, 1987). Further, Stewart *et al.* showed that the shapes of the standard psychoeconomic functions which describe people's decisions so well (concave utility functions, inverse-S-shaped probability weighting functions, and hyperbolic temporal discounting functions) can be simply derived from the real-world distributions of gains, losses, probabilities, and delays.

As an example, Fig. 12.1 shows cumulative frequency plots for the distributions of prices for various categories of product available from www.argos.co.uk. The product categories seem less strange if you know that they were just the first four product categories advertised on the website front page on the 14th December 2006, just before Christmas. Cumulative frequencies were normalized to lie between 0 and 1. Normalized cumulative frequencies *are* the probability of a favourable comparison. For example, in Panel A, about two thirds of watches cost less than £50 so, in the context of a sample of watch prices, a target attribute value of £50 has a subjective value of two thirds. Because there are more small prices than large prices, each of the plots in Fig. 12.1 is concave. This replicates the concave shapes for supermarket foods and credits and debits from current/checking accounts found by Stewart *et al.* (2006).

The decision-by-sampling model of decision under risk

Thus far, DbS has been used to account for the shapes of the various psychoeconomic functions. In this chapter, we provide a preliminary extension of the model to account

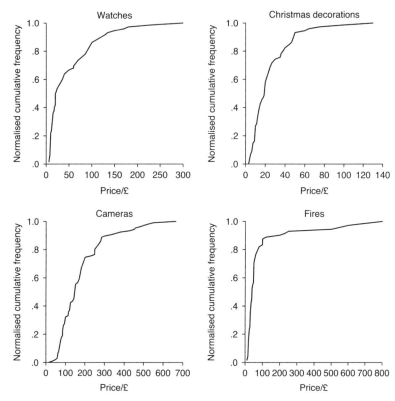

Fig. 12.1. Cumulative frequency distributions for the prices of four different categories of product available from www.argos.co.uk.

for choice behaviour in decision under risk. As before, the core assumptions are (a) binary, ordinal comparison with (b) a small sample of attribute values and (c) frequency accumulation of the number of successes.

The Kahneman and Tversky (1979) data set

As an initial test of the model, we have selected the 16 monetary prospects from Kahneman and Tversky (1979, see Table 12.1). Problems 1 and 2 are a variant of the Allais (1953) common consequence effect. Problem 2 is generated from Problem 1 by removing a .66 chance of 2,400 from both prospects. The reversal of preference between Problems 1 and 2 violates expected utility theory. Problems 3 and 4 are a variant of the Allais common ratio effect. Problem 4 is generated from Problem 3 by reducing the probability of each outcome by a constant factor. Again, the reversal of preference between Problems 3 and 4 violates expected utility theory. Problems 7 and 8 have a similar structure.

Problems 3′, 4′, 7′, and 8′ are derived from Problems 3, 4, 7, and 8, respectively by changing the signs of all of the outcomes so that gains are replaced with losses. In each case, switching from gains to losses reverses the pattern of preference. Kahneman and Tversky (1979) termed this the reflection effect. Problems 11 and 12 also follow this pattern and show the same effect. Here, however, an initial bonus of 1,000 was given before Problem 11 and 2,000 before Problem 12. Participants failed to integrate the bonus with the gains and losses in the problems. Doing so renders the two problems identical and thus the preference reversal between Problems 11 and 12 again violates expected utility theory.

Problems 13 and 13′ test the shape of the utility function. The preference for Prospect B in Problem 13 shows that the utility function is concave for gains. The preference for Prospect A in Problem 13′ shows that the utility function is convex for losses. Problems 14 and 14′ test the shape of the probability weighting function and are consistent with people overweighting small probabilities.

The model

The model is quite simple. On each time step, a *target* attribute value is selected from one prospect and a binary, ordinal comparison is made to another *comparison* attribute value selected from the decision sample. For each prospect, a frequency accumulator tallies the number of favourable binary, ordinal comparisons. The prospect with the higher tally is chosen when the difference between accumulator tallies reaches a threshold.

Target attribute selection is random

An attribute type—either payoff or probability—is randomly selected on each trial. Though the probability of selecting either payoff or probability could be a free parameter, for simplicity we have assumed that each type is equally likely to be sampled. A prospect—in the binary choice case either Prospect A or Prospect B—is also randomly selected, again with equal likelihood. Finally, a branch within the chosen prospect is randomly selected, again with equal probability for each branch. The random selection of attribute, prospect, and branch, completely identifies a particular target attribute value.

Implicit zero outcomes

Though Kahneman and Tversky (1979) did not always explicitly present the probability of a zero outcome, we do always include zero outcomes as a branch of the prospect. This is reasonable, as participants surely do consider the possibility of zero outcomes. For example, in Problem 14, when participants are offered an .001 chance of 5,000 they surely also consider the .999 chance of receiving nothing. Thus, the prospect presented to participants as '5,000 .001' has two branches: .001 chance of 5,000 and .999 chance of 0.

Comparison attribute value selection is random

A comparison attribute value is randomly selected from the decision sample. The comparison attribute value is selected from either the attribute values of the other prospect (i.e., the immediate context) or from long-term memory. Though the probability of sampling from the immediate context rather than long-term memory could be a free parameter, for simplicity, we assume each source is equally likely to be sampled. If the comparison attribute value comes from the opposite prospect, a branch is selected at random. If the comparison attribute value comes from long-term memory, then the attribute value is drawn randomly from the distribution in long-term memory.

Long-term memory attribute value distributions

Under the general assumption that long-term memory distributions reflect the structure of the real world, Stewart *et al.* (2006) used the credits and debits from people's current/checking accounts to approximate the distribution of gains and losses in memory. Here, we assume that samples from long-term memory are drawn randomly from this distribution. The exact distributions are given in Fig. 12.2. Amounts have been converted into Israeli pounds using the exchange rate of 1.00 GPB = 2.14 Israeli pounds. This conversion rate was derived from the median net family income in Israel in 1979 (Kahneman & Tversky, 1979, p. 264) and in the UK in 2003/2004 (Office of

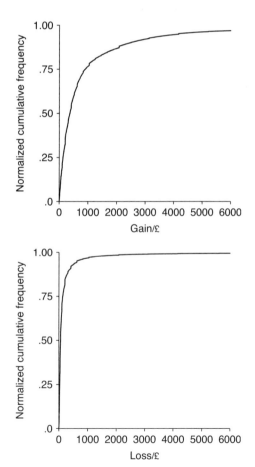

Fig. 12.2. The distribution of gains and losses in long-term memory. Modified from *Cognitive Psychology*, *53*, Stewart, Chater, and Brown, Decision by Sampling, 1–26, 2006, with permission from Elsevier.

National Statistics, 2006, p. 76). Implicit in this conversion is the assumption that the distributions of gains and losses in the UK in 2003 has the same structure as the distribution in Israel in about 1977. In the distribution, small gains are more frequent than large gains; small losses are more frequent than large losses; and small losses are more frequent than small gains.

To approximate the distribution of probabilities in memory, we used the distribution of probability phrases in the British National corpus (Stewart *et al.*, 2006). The exact cumulative frequency distribution that we used is shown in Fig. 12.3. Large and small probabilities are much more frequent than moderate probabilities.

Binary, ordinal comparison

Once a target attribute value and a comparison attribute value have been randomly selected, they are compared. If the target value is more favourable than the comparison value, then the accumulator for the target prospect is increased. For the target value to be considered favourable, it must exceed the comparison attribute by a threshold amount. For amounts, this threshold was 50. For probabilities the threshold was .1. Though more complicated schemes for imperfect ordinal comparison are possible (see Brandstätter *et al.*, 2006; Kornienko, 2004; Rubinstein, 1988), we chose this because it is simple and gives very similar results to more complex models.

Comparing probabilities

A note on comparing probabilities is required. Consider, for example, Problem 2. Prospect A has two branches: a .33 chance of 2,500 and a .67 chance of 0. Prospect B also has two branches: a .34 chance of 2,400 and a .66 chance of 0. Suppose that the probability attribute is selected, that Prospect A is selected, and that the second

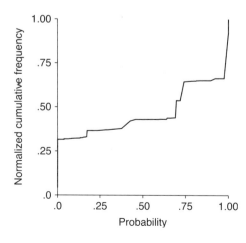

Fig. 12.3. The distribution of probabilities in long-term memory. Modified from *Cognitive Psychology*, *53*, Stewart, Chater, and Brown, Decision by Sampling, 1–26, 2006, with permission from Elsevier.

branch is selected giving a target attribute value of .67. Further, suppose that the comparison attribute value is to be selected from the immediate context (i.e., Prospect B), and that the first branch is chosen giving a comparison attribute value of .34. It is nonsensical to compare .67 with .34 and conclude that .67 is more favourable (and thus that the accumulator for prospect A should be incremented) because .67 is the probability of a 'bad thing' (i.e., a 0 outcome) whereas .34 is the probability of a 'good thing' (i.e., receiving 2,400). Instead, one should conclude that the comparison is unfavourable for Prospect A and Prospect A's accumulator should remain unincremented.

More generally we suggest that, when comparing probabilities, the valence of the associated outcome must be considered. The probability of a 'bad thing' (no matter how large) will always be less favourable than the probability of a 'good thing' (no matter how small). Our rules for discriminating between 'good things' and 'bad things' are simple (see Table 12.2). When all outcomes are gains or zero, a probability of a zero outcome (or of a small gain within threshold of zero) is bad. When all outcomes are losses or zero, a probability of a zero outcome (or of a small loss within threshold of zero) is good. This scheme can be implemented quite simply in the mathematics of the model by representing the probabilities of bad things using negative numbers.

Returning to the previous example, Problem 2 from Table 12.1 is in the domain of gains. Because the probability of .67 in Prospect A is associated with a zero outcome (a bad thing) it is given a negative valence. As a result a comparison of the .34 probability in Prospect B with the .67 probability in Prospect A results in an increment for Prospect B's accumulator. Similarly, the probability of .66 in Prospect B is given a negative valence and thus a comparison of the .33 probability in Prospect A with the .66 probability in Prospect B results in an increment for Prospect A.

Reaching a decision

The decision process is terminated when the difference in accumulator tallies reaches a predefined threshold. In the modelling here, the threshold was arbitrarily set at 4. The prospect with the accumulator with the highest tally wins. For two prospect problems, this scheme is equivalent to a random walk. Below we show that alternative decision mechanisms (e.g., absolute thresholds, fixed sampling) produce very similar results.

Model fits

For each problem, the model was run 1,000 times to generate the probability that Prospect A was chosen. Figure 12.4 shows the proportion of participants choosing

Table 12.2. The valence of a probability is determined by its associated outcome.

Choice domain		Associated outcome	
	Loss	Zero (or within threshold of zero)	Gain
Gains	-	Negative	Positive
Losses	Negative	Positive	-

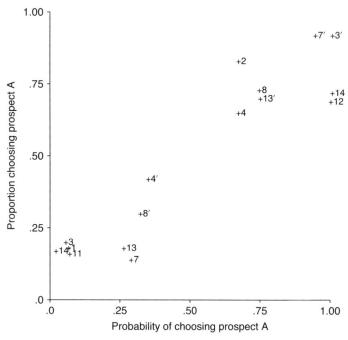

Fig. 12.4. Actual choice proportions plotted against model predictions.

Prospect A for each problem as a function of the probability of the model choosing Prospect A. Each point corresponds to a problem in Table 12.1. The correlation between empirical choice proportions and the model's predictions is good, $r^2 = .87$, $n = 16$. For each problem, the model predicts the correct pattern of preference (traditionally, models of decision under risk predict only the direction of preference for a choice). Of the 14 models tested by Brandstätter *et al.* (2006), including cumulative prospect theory (Tversky & Kahneman, 1992) and transfer of attention exchange (Birnbaum & Chavez, 1997), only the priority heuristic (Brandstätter *et al.*, 2006) matches this level of performance.

Weighting of amounts and probabilities

In the above modelling we assumed that payoffs or probabilities were equally likely to be selected. Figure 12.5A shows how the correlation between data and model predictions and also the number of predictions in the correct direction of preference varies as a function of the probability of selecting the payoff attribute over the probability attribute. Model performance is good for a wide range of weightings. However, when payoff is selected about three or more time more often than probability, performance drops. With such weighting, the model makes incorrect choices for Problems 7, 7′, 12, 13, and 13′. These problems have prospects with low probabilities associated with the larger payoffs, which appear favourable when probability is ignored.

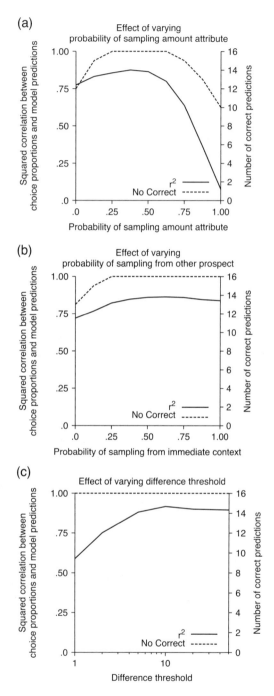

Fig. 12.5. The effect of varying model parameters.

Weighting of immediate context and long-term memory in sampling

In the above modelling we assumed comparison attribute values were equally likely to be sampled from the immediate context or from long-term memory. Figure 12.5B shows how model performance varies as a function of the probability of sampling from the immediate context vs. long-term memory. Again, model performance is robust for a wide range of parameter values, with slightly better performance when sampling is from the other prospect. However, it is worth noting that without some sampling from long-term memory prospects with the same ordinal structure would be indistinguishable.

Using uniform distributions of attribute values

To investigate the contribution that the distribution of attribute values in long-term memory had, we replaced sampling from the distributions in Figs. 12.2 and 12.3 with sampling from uniform distributions in the ranges 0–6,000 for gains, - 6,000 to 0 for losses, and 0–1 for probabilities. With uniform sampling, the model still predicted the correct direction of preference for all 16 problems, and the correlation between choice proportions and model predictions was only slightly reduced, $r^2 = .82$.

Difference threshold

Figure 12.5C shows the effect of varying the threshold for the difference in accumulator tallies required to make a decision. For a wide range of thresholds, the model always predicts the correct pattern of preference. For thresholds of more than about 5 tallies, the correlation between empirical choice proportions and model predictions is very good.

Alternative stopping rules

We tested two alternative stopping rules. First we tried an absolute threshold, with the decision finishing when either accumulator reaches a given count. Very similar results are obtained under this scheme, with r^2 varying from .79 with a threshold of 5 to .92 with higher thresholds. For all 16 problems, the model always predicted the correct pattern of preference. Second, we tried terminating the decision after a fixed number of comparisons. Again, performance was very similar, with r^2 varying from .80 with 5 comparisons up to .89 with more comparisons. For all 16 problems, the model always predicted the correct pattern of preference. Because these results are so similar to those from the original difference threshold model, we would expect more complicated schemes— such as leaky competing accumulators (Usher &McClelland, 2001), diffusion models (Ratcliff *et al.*, 1999), or ballistic accumulators (Brown & Heathcote, 2005)—to have similar success.

Discussion

In this chapter we have presented the first steps towards extending the DbS framework to predict choices between risky prospects and have accounted for the Kahneman and Tversky (1979) data set. The ability to fit this data follows from the main assumptions of the DbS framework originally presented by Stewart *et al.* (2006).

Specifically, a series of binary, ordinal comparisons are made between attribute values from the immediate context and from long-term memory. Accumulators track the favourable comparisons between each prospect, with the winning prospect selected when its tally exceeds the tally of the other prospect by some threshold. It is promising that such a simple model does well, though conclusions about the ultimate success of the DbS model will have to wait for further tests.

DbS and prospect theory

It is useful to compare the accounts of prospect theory and DbS. For example, prospect theory is able to predict the preference shift for the common consequence effect (Problems 1 and 2 in Table 12.1) because of the shape of the probability weight function. Crucially, the probability weighting function is shaped so that the value of the drop from a probability of 1.00–0.34 for 2,400 for Prospect B is subjectively larger than the drop from a probability of 0.66–0.00 for 2,400 for Prospect A even though the drops are objectively equal (Kahneman & Tversky, 1979). DbS also predicts the pattern of preference shift for Problems 1 and 2, in part for the same reason. Because of the distribution of attribute values in long-term memory, the subjective values of the probability attributes will follow the above pattern as Stewart *et al.* (2006) describe. But the decision sample also differs between the two problems, and this also contributes to the explanation of the common consequence effect. In fact, the differing decision sample is sufficient to explain the effect even when the distribution of attribute values is long-term memory is assumed to be uniform. Although the distribution of attribute values in long-term memory does not change between Problems 1 and 2, the distribution in the immediate context does. Table 12.3 shows the subjective attribute values resulting from comparisons with the immediate context for each problem. For each attribute value in the first half of the table, the second half of the

Table 12.3. Illustration of DbS predictions for Problems 1 and 2.

Problem	Prospect A Amount	Probability	Prospect B Amount	Probability
Attribute values repeated from Table 1				
1	2,500	.33	2,400	1.00
	2,400	.66		
	0	.01		
2	2,500	.33	2,400	.34
	0	.67	0	.66
Corresponding probability of favourable comparison with immediate context				
1	1	0	1/3	1
	0	0		
	0	0		
2	1	1/2	1/2	1/2
	0	0	0	0

table gives the corresponding probability that a comparison with a randomly selected attribute value from the opposite prospect will be favourable. For example, for the .33 probability of a 'good thing' in Prospect A from Problem 2 compares favourably with the .66 probability of a 'bad thing' in Prospect B but not with the .34 probability of a 'good thing'. Thus, the probability of a favourable comparison is 1/2. In Problem 1, the overall average probability of a favourable comparison for Prospect A is 1/6. The overall average probability of a favourable comparison for Prospect B is 2/3, greater than for Prospect A. In Problem 2, because the immediate context is different, this effect is reversed (3/8 for Prospect A and 1/4 for Prospect B). In summary, DbS accounts for the results because of the constant distribution of attribute values in long-term memory and because of the change in the distribution in the immediate context.

DbS as an improper linear model

One distinctive characteristic of the DbS framework is that it treats probability and payoff attribute values in the same way. All of the models derived from the expected utility framework, including prospect theory, subjective expected utility theory, rank dependent utility theory and cumulative prospect theory, TAX, regret theory, aspiration level theory, and decision field theory, use probability information to weight outcomes. Possibly the only exceptions are the priority heuristic (Brandstätter et al., 2006) and the stochastic difference model (Gonzalez-Vallejo, 2002). The motivation for treating all attribute values in the same way comes from our basic assumption that people must make the best decisions that they can with the tools that they have, and that they use the same tools whatever the attribute they are dealing with, be it price, probability, time, quality, etc. But this represents a serious departure from the consensus, for probability and amount information are essentially combined additively instead of multiplicatively as they are in the normative model. In the choice literature, there has been little in the way of direct comparison of additive and multiplicative models (in contrast to the study of pricing and attractiveness judgements). Such comparison is currently under way in our laboratory.

In fact, classifying the DbS model as purely additive is not quite accurate, because probabilities were given a valence depending upon whether the associated outcome was a good or bad thing. Given the commutativity of multiplying probabilities and outcomes, the convention of taking expectations (weighting outcomes by probabilities) is mathematically indistinguishable from weighting probabilities by outcomes. In DbS, probabilities are given unit weights or +1 or −1 depending upon the valence of their associated outcome. Dawes (1979) has demonstrated that improper linear models with unit weighting often perform as well as models with optimal weighting. Although outcomes contribute independently to the accumulation for each prospect, using outcomes to give improper weights to probabilities is important in achieving the model's fit to the data.

DbS and the priority heuristic

The DbS model presented here does have some similarity to Brandstätter et al.'s (2006) priority heuristic approach. Under the priority heuristic, participants are hypothesised to first compare prospects on the minimum payoff. If the payoffs are discriminated, the prospect with the higher minimum is selected. Otherwise, the probability of the minimum payoff is considered. Again, if the probabilities can be discriminated the prospect with the lower probability is selected. Otherwise, finally, the prospect with the higher maximum payoff is selected. In our DbS approach, similar ordinal comparisons are made, though in a random order. This suggests that the ordering in the priority heuristic might be relaxed. DbS might also be more robust in the face of pathological prospects that might be designed to break the priority heuristic.

Prospect relativity

In DbS, the attributes of one prospect are judged relative to the attributes of another prospect. Thus, the subjective value of a prospect will depend upon the other prospects that accompany it, and will vary from context to context. There is some evidence to support this assumption. Stewart et al. (2003) presented participants with two sets of prospects. Within each set, prospects varied systematically from a small probability of a large payoff to a large probability of a small payoff. One set contained prospect that were all relatively low in risk, and the other set contained prospect that were all relatively high in risk. So, for example, a participant with a preference for low-risk prospects should select a prospect in the middle of the low-risk set, but would be forced to select the lowest-risk prospect in the high-risk set. Similarly, a participant with a preference for high-risk prospects should select a prospect in the middle of the high-risk set, but would be forced to select the highest-risk prospect in the low-risk set. In fact, data suggested that participants did not have stable risk preferences. In a between-participants manipulation, the pattern of preference was the same in the two sets and did not show any indication that participants were sensitive to the overall level of risk in each set. Participants only seem to have been sensitive to the relative levels of risk within each set (see also Benartzi & Thaler, 2001; Birmbaum, 1992).

Limitations

The simple threshold strategy we use here for binary, ordinal comparisons is sufficient for the Kahneman and Tversky (1979) data, but may ultimately need to be revised when considering other data sets. To illustrate, consider two prospects matched on all attribute values. Then introduce a small, below threshold change on one attribute for one prospect. For example, consider a choice between a .3 chance of 70 and a .3 chance of 71. The simple strategy outlined here would predict indifference, because 70 and 71 differ by less than the threshold, but people would presumably have a preference for the latter.

A second example reveals a possible problem with branch coalescing. Consider a choice between 1,000 for sure and a .5 chance of 1,000 otherwise 1,100. Though the latter is clearly better and stochastically dominates the former, the DbS model presented here predicts a preference for the former. This occurs because the .5 probability of 1,000 and the .5 probability of 1,100 in the second prospect are both worse than the 1.00 chance of 1,000 in the first prospect when probabilities are compared.

This problem can be addressed by altering the valences attached to the probabilities. Because here, as there is no zero outcome in either prospect, 1,000 is the worst outcome that can occur, and probabilities of receiving 1,000 should be considered as probabilities of a 'bad thing'. With this modification, DbS predicts a strong preference for the second prospect, in line with intuition.

In highlighting these limitations we acknowledge that the use of a simple threshold in our binary, ordinal comparisons may be too simplistic. As such, it can be considered a place holder for a more complete model of comparison.

Conclusion

Originally, DbS provided an account of why the psychoeconomic functions inferred from choice behaviour take the form they do. Here we have shown that the same principles can be used to build a more complete choice model, which accounts for some of the most infamous violations of expected utility theory.

Author note

Neil Stewart, Department of Psychology University of Warwick; Keith Simpson, Department of Psychology University of Warwick.

Source code for the DbS model is available from http://www.stewart.psych.warwick.ac.uk/. We are grateful to Nick Chater and Marius Usher for their reviews.

References

Allais, M. (1953). Le comportement de l'homme rationel devant le risque, critique des postulats et axiomes de l'école américaine. *Econometrica*, **21**, 503–546.

Anderson, J. R. (1990). *The adaptive character of thought.* Hillsdale, NJ: Erlbaum.

Anderson, J. R., & Milson, R. (1989). Human memory: An adaptive perspective. *Psychological Review*, **96**, 703–719.

Anderson, J. R., & Schooler, L. J. (1991). Reflections of the environment in memory. *Psychological Science*, **2**, 396–408.

Benartzi, S., & Thaler, R. H. (2001). Naive diversification strategies in defined contribution saving plans. *The American Economic Review*, **91**, 79–98.

Birnbaum, M. H. (1992). Violations of the monotonicity and contextual effects in choice-based certainty equivalents. *Psychological Science*, **3**, 310–314.

Birnbaum, M H., & Chavez, A. (1997). Tests of theories of decision making: Violations of branch independence and distribution independence. *Organizational Behavior and Human Decision Processes*, **71**, 161–194.

Brandstätter, E., Gigerenzer, G., & Hertwig, R. (2006). The priority heuristic: Making choices without trade-offs. *Psychological Review*, **113**, 409–432.

Brown, S., & Heathcote, A. (2005). A ballistic model of choice response time. *Psychological Review*, **112**, 117–128.

Busemeyer, J. R., & Townsend, J. T. (1993). Decision field theory: A dynamic-cognitive approach to decision making in an uncertain environment. *Psychological Review*, **100**, 432–459.

Chater, N., & Brown, G. D. A. (1999). Scale-invariance as a unifying psychological principle. *Cognition*, **69**, b17–b24.

Dawes, R. M. (1979). The robust beauty of improper linear models in decision making. *American Psychologist*, **34**, 571–582.

Edwards, W. (1962). Subjective probabilities inferred from decisions. *Psychological Review*, **69**, 109–135.

Gonzalez-Vallejo, C. (2002). Making trade-offs: A probabilistic and context-sensitive model of choice behavior. *Psychological Review*, **109**, 137–154.

Kahneman, D., & Tversky, A. (1979). Prospect theory: An analysis of decision under risk. *Econometrica*, **47**, 263–291.

Kornienko, T. (2004). *A cognitive basis for cardinal utility*. Unpublished manuscript.

Loomes, G., & Sugden, R. (1982). Regret theory: An alternative theory of rational choice under uncertainty. *Economic Journal*, **92**, 805–824.

Lopes, L. L., & Oden, G. C. (1999). The role of aspiration level in risky choice: A comparison of cumulative prospect theory and SP/A Theory. *Journal of Mathematical Psychology*, **43**, 286–313.

Oaksford, M., & Chater, N. (1998). *Rationality in an uncertain world: Essays on the cognitive science of human reasoning*. Hove, England: Psychology Press/Erlbaum.

Office for National Statistics. (2006). *Social trends 2006*. http://www.statistics.gov.uk/socialtrends36/.

Quiggin, J. (1993). *Generalized expected utility theory: The rank-dependent model*. Norwell, MA: Kluwer Academic Publishers.

Ratcliff, R., Van Zandt, T., & McKoon, G. (1999). Connectionist and diffusion models of reaction time. *Psychological Review*, **106**, 261–300.

Rubinstein, A. (1988). Similarity and decision-making under risk (Is there a utility theory resolution to the Allais Paradox?) *Journal of Economic Theory*, **46**, 145–153.

Shepard, R. N. (1987). Evolution of a mesh between principles of the mind and regularities of the world. In J. Dupré (Ed.), *The latest on the best: Essays on evolution and optimality*. Cambridge, MA: MIT Press.

Stewart, N., Chater, N., & Brown, G. D. A. (2006). Decision by sampling. *Cognitive Psychology*, **53**, 1–26.

Stewart, N., Chater, N., Stott, H. P., & Reimers, S. (2003). Prospect relativity: How choice options influence decision under risk. *Journal of Experimental Psychology: General*, **132**, 23–46.

Tversky, A., & Kahneman, D. (1992). Advances in prospect theory: Cumulative representation of uncertainty. *Journal of Risk and Uncertainty*, **5**, 297–323.

Usher, M., & McClelland, J. L. (2001). The time course of perceptual choice: The leaky, competing accumulator model. *Psychological Review*, **108**, 550–592.

Chapter 13

The neurodynamics of choice, value-based decisions, and preference reversal

Marius Usher

School of Psychology, Birkbeck, University of London, London, UK

Anat Elhalal

School of Psychology, Birkbeck, University of London, London, UK

James L. McClelland

Department of Psychology, Stanford University, Palo Alto, CA, USA

A theory of choice is paramount in all the domains of cognition requiring behavioural output, from perceptual choice in simple psychophysical tasks to motivational *value*-based choice, often labelled as *preferential* choice and which is exhibited in daily decision-making. Until recently, these two classes of choice have been the subject of intensive but separate investigations, within different disciplines. Perceptual choice has been investigated mainly within the experimental psychology and neuroscience disciplines, using rigorous psychophysical methods that examine behavioural accuracy, response latencies (choice-RT), and neurophysiological data (Laming, 1968; Ratcliff & Smith, 2003; Usher & McClelland, 2001; Vickers, 1979). Preferential choice, such as when one has to choose an automobile among a set of alternatives that differ in terms of several attributes or dimensions (e.g., quality and economy) has been investigated mainly within the economics and the social science disciplines, using mainly reports of choice preference. Unlike in perceptual choice, where the dominant models are *process* models that approximate *optimality* (Bogacz *et al.*, 2007; Gold & Shadlen, 2002) based on the Sequential Probability Ratio Test (SPRT; Barnard, 1946; Wald, 1947), the literature on preferential choice has emphasised a series of major deviations from *normativity* (Huber *et al.*, 1982; Kahneman & Tversky, 1979, 2000; Knetch, 1989; Simonson, 1989; Tversky, 1972; Tversky & Kahneman, 1991). This has led to the proposal that decision-makers use a set of disparate heuristics, each addressing some other aspect of these deviations

(LeBoef & Shafir, 2005).[1] Because of this, it is difficult to compare the two types of theories and to discuss their implications for issues related to optimality and to principles of rational choice.

Two recent types of research are providing, however, the opportunity to bridge this gap. First, neurophysiological studies of value-based decisions have been carried out on behaving animals (Glimcher, 2004; Sugrue *et al.*, 2004, 2005). Second, a series of neurocomputational models of preferential choice have been developed, which address the *process* by which preferential choice is issued (Steward, this volume; Roe *et al.*, 2001; Usher & Mclelland, 2004). It is the synthesis of these two lines of work that defines the new field of *neuroeconomics,* whose central aim is to understand the principles that underlie value-based decisions and the neural mechanisms through which these principles are expressed in behaviour. A major insight of neuroeconomics is that these principles can be modelled as implementing an optimising solution to some survival/reproductive challenge in the evolutionary environment (Wikipedia).

The aim of this chapter is to review some of the neurocomputational work by contrasting the various processing assumptions and the way they account for one of the most intriguing patterns in the choice data: *contextual preference-reversal.* We start with introducing a very simple process model of choice, called the leaky competing accumulator (LCA) model (Usher & McClelland, 2001), which has been developed to account for both perceptual and preferential choice data. We will then review some of the data on preference reversal, and on framing effects, which are the main targets of the neurocomputational theories discussed later. Then we will discuss two such theories, the decision-field theory (DFT) developed by Busemeyer and colleagues (Busemeyer & Diederich, 2002, Busemeyer & Johnson, 2003; Diederich, 1997; Roe *et al.*, 2001) and an extension of the LCA. We examine some similarities and contrasts between the models that lead to a set of experimental predictions. Finally, we present experimental data aimed at testing these predictions and consider their implications for the issue of rationality in choice.

Perceptual-choice, optimality, and the LCA model

Consider a simple task that illustrates a typical example of perceptual choice. In this task, the observers (humans or animals) are presented with a cloud of moving dots on a computer screen (Britten *et al.*, 1993). On each trial, a proportion of the dots are moving coherently in one direction, while the remaining dots are moving randomly. The observer's task is to indicate the direction of prevalent motion. The time of the response is either 'up to the observer' (and is measured as a function of the stimulus property and the response accuracy) or is controlled by a response signal (and the accuracy is measured as a function of the observation time). This task presents the basic demand the observer has to accomplish for performing the task: decide which of

---

[1] One notable exception is work by Tversky and colleagues (e.g., Tversky, 1972; Tversky & Simonson, 1993), who developed a number of mathematically rigorous process models.

a number of options match best a noisy signal. As the noise varies in time, a good way to perform the task is to integrate the evidence from sensory neurons over time (this is consistent with the neural data; Schall, 2001; Shadlen & Newsome, 2001). This integration averages out the noise, allowing the accuracy of the choice to increase with time. The quality of the decision (measured in terms of accuracy per time-taken to make the response, or response-rate) depends on the response-rule and the way in which the evidence is integrated.

A variety of models have been proposed to account for rich data patterns that involve not only accuracy and mean-RTs but also RT-distributions (Smith & Ratcliff 2004). Here we will focus on one such model, the LCA (Usher & McClelland, 2001), which is framed at a neural level and yet is simple enough so that it can be mathematically analysed and its parameters can be manipulated so as to optimise performance. As the main aim of this chapter is to understand value-based decisions, we will only present a brief summary here, but see Bogacz et al. (2007) for a detailed and rigorous account.

The model assumes that for each choice option there is a response unit that accumulates evidence in favour of this option. Figure 13.1 illustrates the model, for the case of binary choice. The accumulation of the evidence (or activation) is subject to temporal decay (or leak) and the various response units compete via lateral (and mutual) inhibition. The decay and the lateral inhibition (k and w) are the important parameters that affect the network's choice pattern and performance. In addition each unit's activation is truncated at zero, reflecting the biological constraint that activations correspond to neuronal firing rates, which cannot be negative. This is also reflected in the use of the threshold-linear output function, $f(x)$. Mathematically this can be formulated and simulated as:

$$dy_i = \left(-ky_i - w\sum_{\substack{j=1 \\ j \neq i}}^{N} f(y_j) + I_i \right) dt + c_i dW_i$$

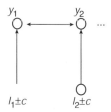

Fig. 13.1. LCA model for binary choice. The variables y_1 and y_2 accumulate noisy evidence (I_1, I_2). The units compete due to lateral inhibition (w). To generalize for n-choice, one adds units, which compete with each other by lateral (all to all) inhibition (Usher & McClelland, 2001).

where the final term (dW) corresponds to the differential of a (stochastic) Wiener process (Gaussian noise of amplitude c). Finally, the response is issued when the first of the accumulators reaches a common response criterion. This criterion is assumed to be under the control of the observer, reflecting speed-accuracy tradeoffs.

The model's choice pattern depends essentially on the relative values of the decay and the inhibition parameters. When decay exceeds inhibition the model exhibits recency (it favours information that arrives late in time), but when inhibition exceeds decay, it exhibits primacy. Neither of these results produces the highest accuracy possible. However, when decay and inhibition are balanced (decay = inhibition) the network performs optimally. Indeed, in this case the model's behaviour mimics the optimal Sequential Probability Ratio Test (SPRT). This means that among all possible procedures for solving this choice problem, it minimizes the average decision time (DT) for a given error rate (ER).

One advantage of this neural model over other (more abstract) models such as the random-walk, is that it is easy to generalise to choice among more than two alternatives. In this case, all the units representing the alternative choices race towards a common response criterion, while they all simultaneously inhibit each other. This mutual inhibition allows the network choice to depend on relative evidence, without the need for a complex readout mechanism that would depend on computing the difference between the activations of the most active unit and the next most active. Moreover, as discussed in detail in Bogacz *et al.* (2007), the threshold-nonlinearity (the truncation of negative activations at zero) is critical in maintaining this advantage when the input favours only a small subset of a larger ensemble of options. The reason for this is that with the threshold-nonlinearity, the activation of all the non-relevant units is maintained at zero, rather than becoming negative and sending uninformative (positive) input into the relevant competing units (see Bogacz *et al.*, 2007). This feature is important in our application of the LCA model to value-based choice.

Value-based decisions, preference-reversal, and reference effects

Although we assume that both perceptual and value/motivational decisions involve a common selection mechanism, the basis on which this selection operates differs. The aim of this section is to review the underlying principles of value-based decisions, focusing on a series of puzzling patterns of preference reversal in multi-attribute choice (see Stewart & Simpson, this volume, for a discussion of risky choice), which raise challenges for an optimal or normative theory of choice.

Unlike in perceptual choice, the preferential choice cannot be settled on the basis of perceptual information alone. Rather, each alternative needs to be evaluated in relation to its potential consequences and its match to internal motivations. Often, this is a complex process, where the preferences for the various alternatives are being constructed as part of the decision process itself (Slovic, 1995). In some situations, where the consequences are obvious or explicitly described, the process can be simplified. Consider, for example, a choice between three flats, which vary on their properties as described on a number of dimensions (number of rooms, price, distance from work, etc).

The immediate challenge facing a choice in such situations is the need to convert between the different currencies, associated with the various dimensions. The concept of *value* is central to preferential choice, as a way to provide such a universal internal currency. Assuming the existence of a value function, associated with each dimension, a simple normative rule of decision-making, the *expected-additive-value*, seems to result. Accordingly, one should add the values that an alternative has on each dimension and compute expectation values when the consequences of the alternatives are probabilistic. Such a rule is then bound to generate a fixed and stable preference order for the various alternatives. Behavioural research in decision-making indicates, however, that humans and animals violate expected-value prescriptions and change their preferences between a set of options depending on the way the options are described and on a set of contextual factors.

First, the preference between alternatives depends and may reverse depending on a reference, which corresponds either to the present state of the decision-maker, or to an *expected* state, which is subject to manipulation. Consider, for example the following situation (Fig. 13.2a). When offered a choice between two job alternatives *A* and *B*, described on two dimensions (e.g., distance from home and salary) to replace an hypothetical job that is being terminated—the *reference*—(R_A or R_B) participants prefer the option that is more similar to the reference (Tversky & Kahneman, 1991).

Second, it has been shown that the preference between two options can be reversed by the introduction of a third option, even when this option is not being chosen. Three such situations have been widely discussed in the decision-making literature, resulting in the *similarity*, the *attraction*, and the *compromise* effects (Tversky, 1972; Simonson, 1989; Huber *et al.*, 1982). To illustrate these effects consider a set of options, *A*, *B*, *C*, and *S*, which are characterized by two attributes (or dimensions) and which are located on a decision-maker indifference curve: the person is of equal preference on a choice between any two of these options (Fig. 13.2b). The *similarity* effect is the finding that the preference between *A* and *B* can be modified in the favour of *B* by the introduction of a new option, *S*, similar to *A* in the choice set. The *attraction* effect

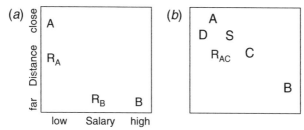

Fig. 13.2. Configurations of alternatives in the attribute space. In each panel the two axes denote two attributes (sample attributes' labels are given in panel a). Capital letters denote the positions of the alternatives in the attribute space, while letters Ri denote the reference points. (a) Reference effect in multi-attribute decision-making (after Tversky & Kahneman, 1991). (b) Contextual preference reversal: similarity, attraction and the compromise effects. Alternatives A, B, C, S lie on the indifference line.

corresponds to the finding that, when a new option similar to *A*, *D*, and dominated by it (*D* is worse than *A* on both dimensions) is introduced into the choice set, the choice preference is modified in favour of *A* (the similar option; note that while the similarity effects favours the dissimilar option, the attraction effect favours the similar one). Finally, the *compromise* effect corresponds to the finding that, when a new option such as *B* is introduced into the choice set of two options *A* and *C*, the choice is now biased in favour of the intermediate one, *C*, the compromise.

Third, a large number of studies indicate that human (and animal) observers exhibit *loss-aversion*. A typical illustration of loss-aversion was shown in the following study (Knetch, 1989). Three groups of participants are offered a choice between two objects of roughly equal value (a mug and a chocolate bar), labelled here as A and B. One group is first offered the A-object and then the option to exchange it for the B-object. The second group is offered the B-object followed by the option to exchange it for A. The control group is simply offered a choice between the two objects. The results reported by Knetch (1989) are striking. Whereas the control participants chose the two objects in roughly equal fractions (56% vs. 44%), 90% of the participants in either of the groups that were first offered one of the objects prefer to keep it rather than exchange it for the other one (see also Samuelson & Zeckhauser, 1988). This effect is directly explained by Tversky and Kahneman by appealing to an asymmetric value-function, which is steeper in the domains of losses than in that of gains. Because losses are weighted more than gains, participants who evaluate their choices with the already-owned object serving as the reference point decline the exchange. [For the control participants the values may be computed either relative to the neutral reference (Tversky & Kahneman, 1991), or each option can be used as a reference for the other options (Tversky & Simonson, 1993); in both cases, there is no reference bias, consistent with the nearly equal choice fractions in this case.]

Computational models of preferential choice and of reversal effects

Recent work on neurocomputational models on preferential choice (Busemeyer & Diederich, 2002; Busemeyer & Johnson, 2003; Roe *et al.*, 2001; Stewart & Simpson, this volume; Usher & McClelland, 2004) may seem at odds with the emphasis on heuristics of choice that is the most common approach of the field.[2] We believe, however, that the two approaches are complementary (and we will discuss this further in the Discussion section), as best suggested by the pioneering research of Amos Tversky, who in addition to his work on heuristics, was one of the first to develop formal mathematical models for preferential choice. Two of his models are the *elimination by aspects* (*EBA*; Tversky, 1972), which accounts for the similarity effect, and the

---

[2] For example, our request for funding was rejected by the ESRC because one reviewer has forcefully and eloquently argued that neurocomputational models are inherently opaque and the better way to understand decision-making is via the use of heuristics.

context-dependent-advantage model, which accounts for the attraction and for the compromise effects (Tversky & Simonson, 1993).

Interestingly, however, the properties responsible for accounting for these effects have not been combined within a single model. Moreover, as observed by Roe *et al.* (2001), the context-dependent-advantage model cannot explain the preference reversals in similarity effect situations. The first unified account of all three reversal effects was proposed by Roe *et al.* (2001), using the DFT approach. More recently, Usher & McClelland (2004) have proposed a neurocomputational account of the same findings, using the LCA framework extended to include some assumptions regarding nonlinearities in value functions and reference effects introduced by Tversky and colleagues. Our approach is, in fact, a direct combination of principles used by Tversky in his previous models, within a neurocomputational framework. Another computational model, closely related to the LCA, has been proposed by Stewart (this volume).

The DFT and LCA models

Both theories are implemented as connectionist models, in which the decision-maker integrates (with decay) a momentary *preference* towards a response criterion, for each choice-alternative. These theories built upon earlier work by Tversky (1972), in assuming that the decision-makers undergo a stochastic process of switching attention between dimensions or attributes. We start with a brief formulation of the DFT model and its account of preference reversal.

The model can be viewed as a *linear* neural network with four layers (Fig. 13.3). The first layer corresponds to the input attribute values, which feed via weights into units at level 2 that correspond to the two choice alternatives. An attentional mechanism stochastically selects between the attribute units (D1 and D2), so that only one attribute (determined randomly) provides input to level 2 at each time step. Level 3 computes valences for each by subtracting the average level 2 activation of the two other alternatives from its own level 2 activation. As the attention switches between the attributes, the valences vacillate from positive to negative values. Level 4 is the choice layer, which performs a leaky integration of the varying preference-input from level 3. Competition between the options occurs at level 4, mediated by bi-directional inhibitory connections with strengths that are assumed to be distance dependent: the strengths of the inhibitory connections among units in the fourth layer decrease as the distance between them, in the attribute space shown in Fig. 13.2b, increases.

The LCA model is illustrated in Fig. 13.4. It shares many principles with its DFT counterpart but also differs on some. In the DFT the strength of the lateral inhibition is similarity-dependent (stronger for similar alternatives), while in the LCA it is similarity-independent. Furthermore, the DFT is a linear model, where excitation by negated inhibition is allowed, while the LCA incorporates important non-linearities. First, the lateral inhibition is subject to a threshold at 0, so that negative activations do not produce excitation of other alternatives. Second, the LCA incorporates a convex and asymmetric utility-value function (Kahneman & Tversky, 2000).

Like the DFT model, LCA assumes a sequential and stochastic scan of the dimensions. Also like the DFT, the LCA assumes that the inputs to the choice units are (3rd layer in

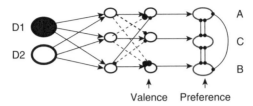

Fig. 13.3. The DFT model for reversal in multi-attribute choice (after Roe *et al.*, 2001). Solid arrows correspond to excitation and the open ones to inhibition. Option C has a stronger inhibition (double arrows) to options A and B due to the fact that the latter are more similar with C than with each other (see Fig. 13.2). At each moment the attention is focussed on one of the two attributes or dimensions.

Fig. 13.4) obtained via a pre-processing stage. In the case of the LCA, however, this involves the computation of relative differences between each option and each of the other options. Specifically, when faced with three alternative choices, participants evaluate the options in relation to each other in terms of gains or losses. Accordingly, the inputs, I, to the leaking accumulators are governed by:

$$I_1 = V(d_{12}) + V(d_{13}) + I_0; \quad I_2 = V(d_{21}) + V(d_{23}) + I_0; \quad I_3 = V(d_{31}) + V(d_{32}) + I_0.$$

where d_{ij} is the differential (advantage or disadvantage) of option i relative to option j, computed on the dimension currently attended; V is the nonlinear advantage function, and I_0 is a positive constant that can be seen as promoting the available alternatives into the choice set. The nonlinear advantage function is chosen (Tversky & Kahneman, 1991) to provide diminishing returns for high gains or losses, and aversion for losses relative to the corresponding gains.[3]

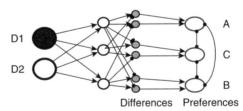

Figure 13.4. LCA model for a choice between three options characterised by two dimensions, D1 and D2. The solid arrows correspond to excitation and the open ones to inhibition. At every time step, an attentional system stochastically selects the activated dimension (D1 in this illustration). The input-item units in the second layer represent each alternative according to its weights on both of the dimensions and project into difference-input units in the 3rd layer. This layer converts the differences via an asymmetric nonlinear value function before transmitting them to choice units in the fourth layer.

---

[3] In Usher & McClelland (2004) the value function was chosen as: $v(x) = z(x)$ for $x > 0$ and $v(x) = -(z(|x|) + [z(|x|)]^2)$ for $x < 0$, where $z(x) = \log(1+x)$.

These models account for the similarity effect in the same way, and in a way that is similar to Tversky's and Kahneman's Elimination by Aspects (EBA) account: the preferences for the similar alternatives tend to rise as a result of scanning the dimension that supports them, and to fall together when attention is switched to the nonsupporting dimension. As shown in Fig. 13.5, the preferences for the similar alternatives are correlated in time and are anticorrelated with the preference of the dissimilar alternative; correlated alternatives tend to be active (or inactive) together. When they are active together, they have the opportunity to be chosen but they split these opportunities between them. On the other hand, the remaining, anti-correlated alternative is active out of phase with the other two alternatives and does not split its choice opportunities.

The two models offer different accounts of the attraction and compromise effects. While DFT relies on distant-dependent inhibition that decreases with the distance between the alternatives to produce these effects, LCA relies on *loss-aversion* (Tversky & Kahneman, 1991). According to the DFT, the attraction effect is explained as a contrast type effect: the similar options A and D have a strong inhibitory coupling because of the distance-dependent inhibition but this leads to a paradoxical boosting of the support for A because the dominated option D takes on a negative activation, which boosts the activation of A because the negative activation of D times the negative connection weight produces as positive input to A.

In LCA, both the attraction and the compromise effect are explained as a result of an asymmetric value function between gains and losses, according to which losses are weighted more than gains (and this weight asymmetry increases with the magnitude of the loss), consistent with loss-aversion. The LCA accounts for the compromise effect because the compromise has only a small disadvantage relative to either extreme, while the extremes have one small disadvantage (relative to the compromise) and one large disadvantage (relative to each other extreme). Similarly, the attraction effect is obtained because the dissimilar option, B, has two large disadvantages (relative to A and D), while A has only one large disadvantage (relative to B).

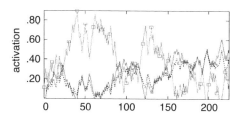

Fig. 13.5. Correlated activation of similar choice options (A, S lines with no symbols) in the LCA model. The dissimilar option, B (line with symbols) has times when it dominates the preference (reproduced from Usher & McClelland, 2004).

Discussion of computational models and further predictions

Both of the models described in the previous section can account for the three contextual reversal effects, promising thus to provide a unified explanation of multi-attribute preferential choice. The models also share many properties (the switch of attention between dimensions, the leaky integration of the valences or advantages, and the lateral inhibition between the choice units). There are, however, a few basic differences in the process by which the reversal effects arise. We focus the discussion on these core differences before turning to a set of predictions.

Non-linearity and value functions

Whereas the DFT is a linear model, there are two types of nonlinearities in the LCA model. The first one is the biological constraint that activation cannot turn negative (unlike valences in DFT) and thus there is no 'excitation by negated-inhibition'. In Usher and McClelland (2004) we have argued that this is an important biological constraint and Busemeyer and colleagues have responded by suggesting possible biological implementations of their scheme (Busemeyer *et al.*, 2005). Here we focus on a set of functional considerations.

In Section 'Perceptual-choice, optimality, and the LCA model' we reviewed the application of the LCA to perceptual choice, showing that its flexible generalisation to multiple choice (allowing it to maintain high performance at large-n) relies to a large extent on the zero-threshold nonlinearity, which makes the units that receive little support drop out of the choice process. In a linear system with many options, as is likely to be the case in daily decision-making, the many options that receive little support will become negatively activated and will send noninformative input into the relevant choice units, reducing the choice quality. This problem is likely to be exacerbated if unavailable options are assumed to compete during the choice process, as the DFT needs to assume to account for reference effects (see below).

The second type of nonlinearity assumed in the LCA but not in DFT involves the nature of the value or utility function. Whereas the DFT has a linear value function, and choice patterns such as loss-aversion are thought to be emergent (or derivative) from the model's behaviour, in the version of the LCA we used, the value-function is explicit. To illustrate this distinction, let us examine how the two approaches can account for one of the cornerstones of preferential choice: the framing effects (see Fig. 13.2a). In the LCA we are following Tversky in assuming that when the choice offers an explicit reference (a present job that is being terminated) the available options are evaluated relative to that reference. Because of the logarithmic nonlinearity of the value function, the observers will prefer A from reference Ra, but will prefer B from reference Rb.[4] To explain the reference effect, protagonists of the DFT

---

[4] This is the case even without assuming that the value function for losses is steeper than that for gains (see Bogacz *et al.*, 2007, section 5 for details). Assuming a steeper value function for losses will further amplify the effect.

have proposed that the unavailable reference option takes part in the choice process, but is not chosen because it has a low value on a third dimension: the *availability*; this makes the reference Ra, somehow similar to the dominated option D (in Fig. 13.2b) and the reference reversal effect is then explained as a contrast effect, similar to the explanation of the attraction effect. Note, however, that by assuming that unavailable options compete for choice, one has to bring in every choice act a potential large set of unattractive options. As explained above, this is likely (in a linear model) to result in a reduction of the choice quality.

In addition to this consideration, we believe that there is independent evidence in favour of nonlinearities in the value function. Consider the task facing the decision-maker in choice options such as those illustrated in Fig. 13.2. To do this one has to represent the magnitudes that correspond to the various alternatives. Since magnitude evaluation is thought to involve a logarithmic representation and is subject to Weber's law,[5] it is plausible that it also affects the value functions. This idea is not new. In fact it dates back to Daniel Bernoulli (1738/1954), who proposed a logarithmic type of nonlinearity in the value function in response to the so-called St. Petersburg paradox, almost two centuries ago.[6] Bernoulli's assumption—that internal utility is logarithmically related to objective value—offers a solution to this paradox and has been included in the dominant theory of risky choice, the prospect theory (Tversky & Kahneman, 1979). Moreover, a logarithmic function, such as $\log(1+x)$ starts linearly and then is subject to diminishing returns, which is a good approximation to neuronal input–output response function of neurons at low to intermediate firing rates (Usher & Niebur, 1996).[7]

In our recent paper (Bogacz *et al.*, 2007) we have explored the consequences of using such a logarithmic value function without the assumption of the asymmetry between gains and losses (the value for negative x, is then defined as $-\log(1 - x)$). We show there that this logarithmic assumption alone can suffice for accounting for some of the reversal effects, such as the reference effect and some aspects of the attraction and the compromise effect. We elaborate here on the latter.

---

[5] The Weber law states that to be able to discriminate between two magnitudes (e.g. weights), x and $x+dx$, the just-noticeable-difference, dx, is proportional to x itself.

[6] This paradox was first noticed by the casino operators of St. Petersburg (see for example Glimcher, 2004, pp. 188–192 for detailed descriptions of the paradox and of Bernoulli's solution). Here is a brief description. Consider the option of entering a game, where you are allowed to repeatedly toss a fair coin until 'head' comes. If the 'head' comes in the first toss you receive £2. If the 'head' comes in the second toss, you receive £4, if in the third toss, £8, and so on (with each new toss needed to obtain a 'head' the value is doubled). The question is what is the price that a person should be willing to pay for playing this game. The puzzle is that although the expected value of the game is infinite (E = $\Sigma_{i=1},\ldots, 1/2^i \, 2^i = \Sigma_{i=1},\ldots, 1 = $), as the casino operators in St. Petersburg discovered, most people are not willing to pay more than £4 for playing the game and very few more than £25 (Hacking, 1980). Most people show *risk-aversion*.

[7] While neuronal firing rates saturate, it is possible that a logarithmic dependency exists on a wide range of gains and losses, with an adaptive baseline and range (Tobler *et al.*, 2005).

The nature of the compromise effect

There are a few issues to examine in understanding why people prefer compromise options. The first explanation, originally offered by Simonson (1989) is that this is the result of a conscious justification strategy: people choose the compromise because they have an easy way to justify it to themselves and to others. Note, however, that existence of such a heuristic does not imply that there are no *additional* factors that contribute to the effect. In the following we explore a number of potential contributing factors (on top of the justification heuristics) that emerge from neurocomputational models. The first (non-justificatory) factor, we examine, involves to the way in which nonlinear utilities are combined across two or more dimensions. Assuming a logarithmic value function, $v(x) = \log(1 + x)$, one can see that when summing across two dimensions, one obtains: $U(x_1,x_2) = u(x_1) + u(x_2) = \log[1 + (x_1 + x_2) + x_1x_2]$. Figure 13.6 illustrates a contour plot of this 2D utility function.

One can observe that equal preference curves are curved in the x_1–x_2 continuum: the compromise (0.5,0.5) has a higher utility than the (1,0) or (0,1) options. While this cannot (on its own) account for the compromise effect, which requires a change in the shares of the *same* two options when a third option in introduced, it still leads to an interesting prediction. Decision-makers are likely to prefer a middle-range option (0.5, 0.5) to an extreme range one (1-x, x) for $0 < x < 0.5$, in binary choice, and the preference difference should increase the smaller x is (extreme options are less attractive than middle-range options even in the absence of context). Data supporting this prediction is presented in the following section.

Contextual contributions can further add to this tendency to choose options in the middle of the range. Two possibilities arise from the DFT and the LCA models. According to the DFT, the preference for the compromise is due to the dynamically correlated activations (the choice preferences). According to the DFT the preferences of the two extreme options are correlated with each other but not with the compromise (because of the stronger inhibition between more similar options) and thus, they split their wins, making the compromise option stand out and receive a larger share of choices (Roe *et al.*, 2001).

The process that is responsible for the effect in the LCA model is not *correlational*, but rather due (as Tversky suggested) to the nature of the nonlinearity and framing in value evaluations. Consider first, the simple logarithmic nonlinearity described above (without the asymmetry for losses) and note that the value of options defined in a

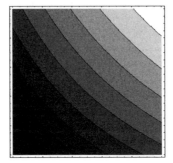

Fig. 13.6. 2D logarithmic value-function,
$U(x_1,x_2) = u(x_1)+u(x_2)$
$= \log[1 + (x_1+x_2) + x_1x_2]$

2D parametric space depends on a reference (see below). If this reference changes with the choice set, a reversal effect arises. Consider, for example, a trinary choice between options: $A = (1,0)$, $B=(0.5,0.5)$, and $C = (0,1)$ and another binary choice between options $A = (1,0)$, $B = (0.5,0.5)$. If we assume that decision makers use the minimum value on both dimensions as reference (i.e., $(0,0)$ in the trinary choice and (0.5) in the binary choice), we obtain that decision-makers will be indifferent between A and B in binary choice, but they will prefer B (the compromise) in trinary choice (see, Bogacz *et al.*, 2007). Second, the existence of an asymmetric value function, which is steeper in the domain of losses, provides another explanation, without the need to assume that the reference changes from the binary to the trinary set. In this case, all we need to assume is (following Tversky & Simonson, 1993) that decision-makers use each option as a reference to each other option (i.e., they evaluate differences rather than the options themselves). As shown in the previous section, this leads to a compromise effect because the extremes (but not the compromise) have large disadvantages that are penalised by the loss-aversive value-function.

In the following, we present some preliminary data that are aimed at testing these predictions. The first experiment examines binary and trinary preferences among options defined over two attributes with tradeoffs, by comparing a middle option (both attribute values in middle of the range) with an extreme one (one of the attributes at the high-end and the other one at the low-end). The second experiment, examines the correlational hypothesis. This is done by announcing, immediately after the decision-maker has chosen an extreme option, that this option is now unavailable and a speeded choice between the remaining two options has to be made.

Preliminary experimental investigations of the compromise effect

Experiment 1—A parametric study of the value of 2D trade-off options

The experiment was conducted on choice between options defined over two dimensions with values that create a tradeoff (Fig. 13.7). The aim was to compare the likelihood of choosing an alternative with attribute values in the middle of the range, relative to alternatives with extreme values, as a function of the distance between the extremes in the attribute space (small vs. large separation). Two groups of participants were tested. The first group were tested on trinary choice (Experiment 1A) and the second group on binary choice (Experiment 1B).

Method

Participants. Seventy-eight subjects participated in the trinary study (Experiment 1A) and 28 in the binary choice (Experiment 1B).

Design

The experiment was within-subjects with two levels: small separation (B,C,D) or (B,C) versus large separation (A,C,E), or (A,C) as illustrated in Fig. 13.7. The dependent variable was the probability of choosing the compromise and the extreme options.

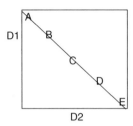

Fig. 13.7. Choice options in Experiment 1. The letters represent the alternatives on the two dimensions D1 and D2. For example, A is lowest on D2 and highest on D1. C represents the compromise and is in the middle range of both dimensions.

Materials

Experiment 1A. Each decision-problem consisted of three alternatives that differed on two dimensions. The values for extreme choices were symmetric relative to the compromise. For instance, car A is high on riding quality, but low on reliability, whereas car E is the opposite. Ten different decision problems were designed and for each problem a small separation (B,C,D) and a large separation (A,C,E) were created (materials are available online at www.bbk.ac.uk/psyc/staff/academic/musher/documents/DMproblems.pdf). These two conditions were counterbalanced so that one group of subjects were presented with the a first half of the problems in the (B,C,D) condition and the other half in the (A,C,E) condition, while the other half received the reversed pairing. The actual order of presentation of the problems was randomised.

Experiment 1B. The same materials were used, except that the 10 trinary choice problems were used to create 20 problems, which included the middle option and only one of the extremes. Each participant was presented with 10 choice problems (only one from each domain, such as laptops (below). Five of the problems involved a small separation and five of them involved a large separation. The allocation of problems to conditions was counterbalanced (four sets of problems were presented to four groups of participants).

Procedure

Experiment 1A. Participants were presented with a booklet of 10 pages, each containing one problem. They were instructed to imagine having to make a choice among three available options, which are identical on all the other properties except of the two described, and to make a selection that reflects their preference. One example is: *'Imagine you want to buy a laptop. You have a selection of three laptops, which have the same characteristics except for weight and screen size. If you had to choose one laptop out of the three, which laptop would you select?'*

	Laptop I	Laptop II	Laptop III
Weight (kg)	2.7	1.9	3.5
Screen size (")	14	13	15

Experiment 1B. The procedure was identical to experiment 1A, except for the fact that the participants were emailed the choice problems in a Word-attachment and they sent it back with their marked responses.

Results

The fraction of choices for the compromise and the extreme options are shown in Fig. 13.8 (trinary choice: left panel and binary choice right panel), for the small and the large separation conditions. [In trinary choice (left panel) the extreme conditions were averaged, thus the normalisation is: 2P(extreme) + P(compromise) =1].

The choice probabilities in trinary choice (Experiment 1A) were analysed using a 2 (extreme vs. compromise) by 2 (small vs. large separation) within subjects ANOVA. This yielded a significant main effects of compromise, $F(1,77) = 69.84$, $p < 0.001$, and of degree of separation, $F(1,77) = 42.066$, $p < 0.001$, and a highly significant interaction of compromise vs. degree of separation, $F(1,77)=42.066$, $p < 0.001$. This indicates that the compromise options receive a higher share than the extreme options and that this effect is larger at high separation (by 21%). Interestingly, a similar pattern is found in the binary choice (Experiment 1B), where participants chose the option (C) (in the middle of the value range) more than the extreme option (B, C, A or E), and this effect increases at large separations (A, E).

This suggests that the main factor that contributes to the participants' preference of the compromise option is the fact that this option is within the middle of the preference range, which has a higher 2D-value (Fig. 13.6). It is possible that a further contextual effect contributes to the compromise effect in trinary choice.[8] As the present experiments were between-participants (and there were some differences in procedure), further experiments are required to evaluate accurately the magnitude of these contributions and their dependence on the distance between the extremes. Although this experiment does not distinguish between the LCA/DFT accounts of the compromise

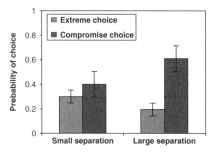 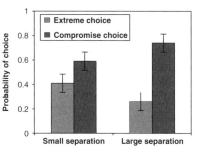

Fig. 13.8. Proportion of choices in trinary (Experiment 1A; left panel) and in binary choice (Experiment 1B; right panel). Error bars are SEM.

---

[8] This can be computed as $P_3(C)/[P_3(C) + P_3(A)] - P_2(C)/[P_2(C) + P_2(A)]$, where P3 and P2 are the trinary and binary choice probabilities.

effect, it suggests that the nonlinearity of the value function is an important contributor of the decision-makers' preference of middle-range options.

Is the compromise a dynamic correlation effect?

If the compromise effect is caused, as predicted by the DFT, by the fact that the preferences of the extremes are correlated in time, it should be possible, in principle, to detect a signature of this correlation. One way to investigate this is by presenting participants with the three-choice compromise option, and in some of the cases, following the participant's choice, announce that the option chosen is unavailable but a speeded choice is possible (under deadline) for one of the other two options. The idea is that, if the participant chose one of the extremes in her 1st choice, and if the preferences of the two extremes are correlated, then at the moment of the response, there should be a high likelihood that the preference of the other extreme is also high (relative to the compromise, which is not correlated). Thus one may predict that the participant will choose the 2nd extreme in her 2nd choice, following her 1st choice of the other extreme option. One caveat to this prediction is that, following the announcement of the unavailability of her preferred choice, the participant will restart the choice from scratch, in which case the advantage of the correlated alternative becomes immaterial. Such restart, however, is expected to lead to longer choice latencies, leading to a 2nd prediction: the choice latencies of the 2nd response should be faster when the other extreme is chosen than when the compromise is chosen (as in the latter case a restart is more likely). The LCA model makes the opposite prediction. Here the extreme options are anti-correlated (due to the scan of aspects), which together with the fact that the compromise receives more activation (due to the nonlinear value function) leads to a strong preference the compromise when a second choice is offered after the first choice (of an extreme option) is announced as unavailable.

Method

Participants. One hundred and forty-three participants volunteered to take part in this experiment (60% females; age-range 20–61 with a mean of 37).

Materials

The material consisted of 30 choice problems with three alternatives that varied on two dimensions, of a similar type to those shown in Table 13.1. Out of these problems, 25 were of the compromise form. Of those, 14 had a 2nd choice required after announcing the unavailability of the 1st chosen option. (The other 11 did not involve unavailable options so as not to create a strategy that prepares the two preferred options in advance.) A table that includes those 25 problems is available on: www.bbk.ac.uk/psyc/staff/academic/musher/documents/DMproblems.pdf

Procedure

The experiment was run on the web, using the 'express' psychology experiments package (Yule & Cooper 2003), which recorded the responses and the latencies.

The participants were instructed to imagine the situations described, as real choice situations they encounter in daily life and to indicate their preference. They were also instructed that sometimes (as in real life) an option they chose may be unavailable and that in such a case they will be able to make a 2nd choice (it was emphasized that this 2nd choice should be fast).

Results

The fraction of choices in favour of the compromise and extreme options (out of 14) in the 1st choice made is shown in Fig. 13.9 (left panel).

One can see (left panel) that, consistent with the data from Experiment 1, the participants chose the compromise option more than they chose the extreme options ($t(142) = 7.185, p < 0.001$). The fraction of choices made after a first choice, which was an extreme option announced to be unavailable is shown in the right panel. One can see that in such a situation the participants chose more than 90% the compromise option ($t(142) = 35.354, p < 0.001$).

Finally, we examine the response latencies of these 2nd choices and compare the latency of choosing the compromise over the extreme. As shown in Fig. 13.9 (right), the probability of choosing the extreme is less than 10% (only 58 participants out of the 143 made such choices, so we could only compare reaction time data for them). Although most of the responses were faster than 7 sec, indicating the participants followed the instructions of making a speeded response (this time includes the reading of the un-availability), there are also some slow RTs, that are as long as 30 sec. Eliminating such outliers (10 out of about 2000 in the whole data set), one finds that the average choice is significantly faster in the compromise 2nd choice (4.3 sec), than in the extreme 2nd choice (6.3 sec), $t(57) = 4.092, p < 0.001$. The full RT density-distributions (collapsed over all the participants) for the compromise (blue) and the extreme 2nd choices is shown in Fig. 13.10 (left). One can observe that extreme choices are slower in their mode and have a longer tail. This is consistent with RT-data from individual participants (right panel), which show slower responses for extreme (green) than to compromise (red) 2nd choices.

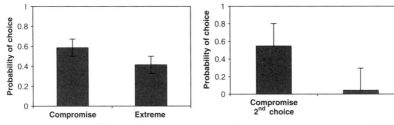

Fig. 13.9. The probability to choose the compromise and the extreme options in the first choice opportunity (left), and to choose compromise/extreme in the second choice.

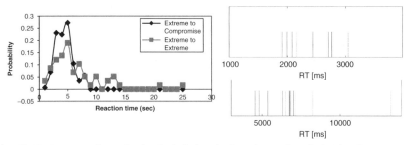

Fig. 13.10. Response latencies for 2nd choices in Experiment 2. Left: RT density-distribution of all responses of 58 participants; Right: RTs of two participants.

This result does not support the correlational hypothesis of the compromise effect, however, one cannot totally rule out such an account, because one can explain the preference for the compromise in the 2nd choice, within the DFT (J. Busemeyer, personal communication), by assuming that once an option becomes unavailable it acts as a dominated decoy and enhances the likelihood to chose the compromise (which is more similar with it), as in the attraction effect. Further studies, which contrast the magnitude of the compromise effect in situations where the extremes are available or unavailable, could help to test this proposal.

General discussion

In this chapter, we have examined how the LCA model, which was originally developed to account for perceptual choice, can be extended to preferential choice between alternatives that vary on several dimensions or attributes (see Stewart & Simpson, this volume, for a model of risky choice that treats probability and value as independent dimensions, and makes decisions on the basis of integrated comparisons). The LCA is a neurocomputational model, from a similar family with the DFT. As such, they share a similar approach, and vary on a number of important but secondary mechanisms. In the previous sections we discussed the differences between the LCA and the DFT accounts to preference reversal and we suggested possible ways to examine them.[9] Here we highlight their common approach by contrast with heuristic approaches (LeBoef & Shafir, 2005; Todd & Gigerenzer, 2000; Gigerenzer 2006) and we briefly address some implications to the debate on *rationality* in human choice.

Neucomputational models vs. heuristics

It is customary to understand choice heuristics as algorithms that are not optimal, but which can produce fast and reasonable choices for given situations (Gigerenzer, 2000, 2006). Understood in this minimal way, neurocomputational models such as DFT and

---

9 The LCA is more similar in its approach with the decision-by-sample model (Stewart, this volume), but they vary on their assumptions about the order of attentional switches (between attributes in the LCA) and between alternatives first, in the decision-by-sample).

LCA are heuristics, as they indeed *can* produce reasonable and fast choices. There is, nevertheless, a feeling that something distinguishes these models from typical heuristics. We believe that the main contrast between the two resides in the nature of the algorithm. While the typical heuristics involve rules that can be *verbally* formulated in a *propositional* format and which have a *sequential* nature, the neurocomputational algorithms are mathematical rather than propositional and they involve some degree of parallel (rather than sequential) processing. This stems from the distinction between parallel distributed processes (PDP) and symbolic ones, which has been discussed in detail in other domains of cognition (McClelland *et al.*, 1986; Rumelhart *et al.*, 1986). In the light of this distinction, a number of considerations need to be addressed [see further discussion in the BBS replies to Todd and Gigerenzer (2000), in particular: Chater, 2000; Cooper, 2000; Oaksford, 2000; Shanks & Lagnado, 2000].

The LCA approach relies on some elements of prospect theory, in particular the form of the value function and loss-aversion. In their recent heuristic proposal to preferential choice under risk, the *priority* heuristic, Brandstatter *et al.* (2006) argue against the various variants of the prospect theory on several grounds. First, they maintain that all *weighing* models based on Bernoulli type corrections of the EV principle (such as prospect theory) are overly complex, as they rely on all the information available and require both summations and multiplications. Second, they suggest that heuristics, but not the prospect theory, provides a process model of preference. Third, they argue that such heuristics are ecologically rational and that, therefore, the so-called 'violations of rationality' are a misleading outcome of our over-reliance on unrealistic EV-type rationality norms. While we are sympathetic to the rational-ecological approach, we believe that the use of mathematically defined value functions (a la Bernoulli) within neurocomputational process models can achieve more than the use of disparate verbal heuristics, on all the three grounds.

Consider simplicity considerations first. On the one hand, while weighing models are complex from a symbolic perspective (where one actually multiplies and adds values) they are not so within a PDP one, as there is nothing more straightforward than computing weighted averages that implement EV (see Figs. 13.3 and 13.4)[10] and as logarithmic nonlinearities come for free (they are assumed anyway within basic psychophysical principles of magnitude evaluations, such as Weber's law). On the other hand, there is complexity hidden in the symbolic form of some heuristics, which require fundamentally different computations for different problems within the same domain. As an example, the priority heuristic (a lexicographic type heuristic) requires different computations for choices between options that differ in EV (thus some computation of EV needs to be done anyway) and for gains vs. losses.[11] Similarly, one can

---

[10] In fact we face the inverse puzzle: what are the processes that limit a straightforward EV computation.

[11] The rationale stated for the priority heuristic is that the first concern is the lowest possible outcome (i.e., the lowest gain). By this principle, the first concern in the domains of losses should be the highest possible loss, rather than the lowest one as the heuristics assumes to account for loss-aversion. In terms of complexity this assumption is not simpler than prospect's theory asymmetry of value functions for gains and losses.

explain the preference reversal effects in 2D attribute choice with verbal heuristics of the type: in a compromise choice, choose the middle option, but in a similarity situation choose the different (extreme) option. As there is a continuity of choice options over the 2D attribute space, one has to decide when to switch from one version of the heuristic to the other; this seems thus to require a meta-model to decide on the heuristic to use. We believe that a neurocomputational approach that employs continuous functions has a better prospect of obtaining a unified account of preference. Moreover, in some conditions, such a model may be *approximately* described by a verbal heuristic. For example, the LCA has some properties in common with the EBA heuristic (the shift of attention from attribute to attribute) and one of its neural precursors (Usher & Zakay, 1993) was shown to extrapolate among a large number of heuristics in multi-attribute choice.

Second, the neural models are in essence process models, which make dynamic predictions (Usher & McClelland, 2004). While such models can obtain fast and reasonable choices like the verbal heuristics, they can also do something that, paradoxically, heuristics don't do but people (unfortunately) do: vacillate and procrastinate in their decision! For example, unlike lexicographic type heuristics, models such as LCA and DFT vacillate in their preferences. One interesting possibility is that neurocomputational models, of the type discussed here, are at the interface between purely conscious (rule based and capacity limited) lexicographic type of decision-making and intuitive/gut-feeling type of choices, which are not subject to the capacity limitations of conscious thought and are able to weigh large number of attributes in parallel (Dijksterhuis & Nordgren, 2006). Finally, we examine a few considerations on optimality and rationality principles.

Optimality and rationality

The domain of multi-attribute preference does not possess an external criterion for the value (or quality) of choice. Nevertheless, some of its ingredients, the leaky integration, the logarithmic value function, and the loss-aversion, can be interpreted in relation to adaptive principles.

In Section 'Perceptual-choice, optimality, and the LCA model', we summarised analysis that indicates optimal performance in choice under stationary conditions, when leak and inhibition are perfectly balanced. Our own experiments in perceptual choice (Usher & McClelland, 2001) and those by Hertwig *et al.* (2004) in feedback-driven value decisions, indicate that some participants show a *recency* bias (leak dominance) that results in suboptimality. One interesting possibility is that this suboptimality is the cost one needs to pay for enabling agents to maintain sensitivity to changes in their environment (Daw *et al.*, 2006)—a type of the exploitation/exploration tradeoff. Consider next the 2D value function (Fig. 13.6), which results in preference for middle-of-the-range options. This value function involves a combination of linear and multiplicative terms. The inclusion of a multiplicative term in the utility optimization is supported by a survival rationale: to survive animals need to ensure the joined (rather than separate) possession of essential resources (like food and water). In addition, the higher slope of the value function for losses (relative to gains) can be justified by the 'asymmetry between pleasure and pain' (Tversky & Kahneman, 1991). This, in turn, could be an adaptive outcome of the fact that preventing losses is more critical for survival than getting gains (a single large loss can be critical; attaining large gains is not).

As task optimality is environment-dependent, an important insight is that rational strategies of choice require the flexibility to modify the choice parameters in response to the environment and demands (under some situations inhibition dominance or linear value function are advantageous). Such flexibility, however, may be subject to limitations. Unlike Gigerenzer and colleagues (but like Tversky and Kahaneman, 2000; Kahaneman, 2003), we think that contextual reversal effects of the type discussed here demonstrate a limitation of rationality in choice preference. After all, intransitive preferences and contextual reversals can be used to manipulate agents' choice and even transform them into money pumps; even if we evolved within a different environment, it is *rational* to do well in the present one. The notion of rationality, requiring flexible responses to the present environment/tasks, should not be diluted to a fixed repertoire of strategies adaptive to past environments and tasks. The power of choice models is to account for the sources of the adaptive powers of decision-makers and their limitations, and equally important to quantify the degree of these limitations[12] and find ways to eliminate them. A recent suggestion that requires further investigation is that one can overcome limitations in the ability to integrate across dimensions by relying on intuitive[13]/implicit decion-making (Dijksterhuis, *et al*, 2006).

Acknowledgments

Thanks are due to Claudia Sitz and Yvonne Lukaszewicz for running participants in Experiments 1–2, and to David Lagnado for a critical reading.

References

Barnard, G. (1946). Sequential tests in industrial statistics. *Journal of Royal Statistical Society Supplement*, **8**, 1–26.296

Bernoulli, D. (1738/1954). Exposition of a new theory on the measurement of risk. *Ekonometrica*, **22**, 23–36.

Bogacz, R., Usher, M., Zhang, J., & McClelland J. L. (2007). Extending a biologically inspired model of choice: Multi-alternatives, nonlinearity and value-based multidimensional choice. *Philosophical Transactions of the Royal Society, B* (in press).

Brandstätter, E., Gigerenzer, G., & Hertwig, R. (2006). The priority heuristic: Making choices without trade-offs. *Psychological Review*, **113**, 409–432.

Britten, K. H., Shadlen, M. N., Newsome, W. T., & Movshon, J. A. (1993). Responses of neurons in macaque MT to stochastic motion signals. *Visual Neuroscience*, **10**(6), 1157–1169.

---

[12] In this regard, lexicographic type models are the worse off. Fortunately, only a minority of human participants exhibit intransitive preferences as predicted by such models (Tversky, 1969).

[13] But see Slovic *et al.* (2004), for an insightful discussion of the limitations and dangers of intuitive/affective preferential choice.

Busemeyer, J. R., & Johnson, J. G. (2003). Computational models of decision making. In D. Koehler & N. Harvey (Eds.), *Handbook of judgment and decision making.* Blackwell Publishing Co (To appear).

Busemeyer, J. R., & Diederich, A. (2002). Survey of decision field theory. *Mathematical Social Sciences,* **43,** 345–370.

Busemeyer, J. R., Townsend, J. T., Diederich, A., & Barkan, R. (2005). Contrast effects or loss aversion? Comment on Usher and McClelland (2004). *Psychological Review,* **111,** 757–769.

Chater, N. (2000). How smart can simple heuristics be? *Behavioural and Brain Sciences,* **23,** 745–746.

Cooper, R. (2000). Simple heuristics could make us smart; but which heuristic do we apply when? *Behavioural and Brain Sciences,* **23,** 746–747.

Daw, N. D., O'Doherty, J. P., Dayan, P., Seymour, B., & Dolan, R. J. (2006). Cortical substrates for exploratory decisions in Humans. *Nature,* **441,** 876–879.

Diederich, A. (1997). Dynamic stochastic models for decision making under time constraints. *Journal of Mathematical Psychology,* **41,** 260–274.

Dijksterhuis, A., Bos, M. W., Nordgren, L. F., & Baaren, R. B. (2006). On making the right choice: The deliberation without-attention effect. *Science,* **311,** 1005–1007.

Dijksterhuis, A., & Nordgren, L. F. (2006). A theory of unconscious thought. *Perspectives on Psychological Science,* **1,** 95–109.

Gigerenzer, G. (2006). Bounded and rational. In R. J. Stainton (Ed.), *Contemporary debates in cognitive science* (pp. 115–133). Oxford, UK: Blackwell.

Glimcher, P. W. (2004). *Decisions, uncertainty, and the brain: The science of neuroeconomics.* Cambridge, MA: MIT Press.

Gold, J. I., & Shadlen, M. N. (2002). Banburismus and the brain: Decoding the relationship between sensory stimuli, decisions, and reward. *Neuron,* **36**(2), 299–308.

Hacking, I. (1980). Strange expectations. *Philosophy of Science,* **47,** 562–567.

Hertwig, R., Barron, G., Weber, E. U., & Erev, I. (2004). Decisions from experience and the effect of rare events in risky choice. *Psychological Science,* **15,** 534–539.

Huber, J., Payne, J. W., & Puto, C. (1982). Adding asymmetrically dominated alternatives: Violations of regularity and the similarity hypothesis. *Journal of Consumer Research,* **9,** 90–98.

Kahneman, D. (2003). Maps of bounded rationality: Psychology for behavioral economics. *The American Economic Review,* **93,** 1449–1475.

Kahneman, D., & Tversky, A. (1979). Prospect theory: An analysis of decision making under risk. *Econometrica,* **XLVII,** 263–291.

Kahneman, D., & Tversky, A. (Eds.). (2000). *Choices, values and frames.* Cambridge: Cambridge University Press.

Knetch, J. L. (1989). The endowment effect and evidence of nonreversible indifference curves. *American Economic Review,* **79,** 1277–1284.

Laming, D. R. J. (1968). *Information theory of choice reaction time.* New York: Wiley.

LeBoef, R., & Shafir, E. B. (2005). Decision-making. In K. J. Holyoak & R. G. Morisson (Eds.), *Cambridge handbook of thinking and reasoning.* Cambridge: Cambridge University Press.

McClelland, J. L., Rumelhart, D. L., & the PDP Research Group. (1986). *Parallel distributed processing: Explorations in the microstructure of cognition* (Vol. 2). Cambridge, MA: MIT Press.

Oaksford, M. (2000). Speed, frugality and the empirical basis of take-the-best. *Behavioural and Brain Sciences,* **23,** 760–761.

Roe, R. M., Busemeyer, J. R., & Townsend, J. T. (2001). Multi-alternative decision field theory: A dynamic connectionist model of decision-making. *Psychological Review*, **108**, 370–392.

Rumelhart, D. L., McClelland, J. L., & the PDP Research Group. (1986). *Parallel distributed processing: Explorations in the microstructure of cognition* (Vol. 1). Cambridge, MA: MIT Press.

Samuelson, W., & Zeckhauser, R. (1988). Status quo bias in decision making. *Journal of Risk and Uncertainty*, **1**, 7–59.

Schall, J. D. (2001). Neural basis of deciding, choosing and acting. *Nature Reviews. Neuroscience*, **2**(1), 33–42.

Shadlen, M. N., & Newsome, W. T. (2001). Neural basis of a perceptual decision in the parietal cortex (area LIP) of the rhesus monkey. *Journal of Neurophysiology*, **86**(4), 1916–1936.

Shanks, D. R., & Lagnado, D. (2000). Sub-optimal reasons for rejecting optimality. *Behavioural and Brain Sciences*, **23**, 761–762.

Simonson, I. (1989). Choice based on reasons: The case of attraction and compromise effects. *Journal of Consumer Research*, **16**, 158–174.

Slovic, P. (1995). The construction of preference. *American Psychologist*, **50**, 364–371.

Slovic, P., Finucane, M. L., Peters, E., & MacGregor, D. G. (2004). Risk as analysis and risk as feelings: Some thoughts about affect, reason, risk, and rationality. *Risk Analysis*, **24**(2), 311–322.

Smith, P. L., & Ratcliff, R. (2004). Psychology and neurobiology of simple decisions, *Trends in Neurosciences*, **27**(3), 161–168.

Sugrue, L. P., Corrado, G. S., & Newsome, W. T. (2004). Matching behavior and the representation of value in the parietal cortex. *Science,* **304**(5678), 1782–1787.

Sugrue, L. P., Corrado, G. S., & Newsome, W. T. (2005). Choosing the greater of two goods: neural currencies for valuation and decision making. *Nature Review and Neuroscience,* **6**(5), 363–375.

Tobler, P. N., Fiorillo, C. D., & Schultz, W. (2005). Adaptive coding of reward value by dopamine neurons. *Science*, **307**(5715), 1642–1645.

Todd, P. M., & Gigerenzer, G. (2000). Precis of *Simple heuristics that make us smart. Behavioral and Brain Sciences*, **23**, 727–780.

Tversky, A. (1972). Elimination by aspects: A theory of choice. *Psychological Review* **79**, 281–299.

Tversky, A., & Kahneman, D. (1979). Prospect theory: An analysis of decision under risk. *Econometrica*, **47**, 263–292.

Tversky, A., & Kahneman, D. (1991). Loss aversion in riskless choice: A reference-dependent model. *The Quarterly Journal of Econometrics*, **106**, 1039–1061.

Tversky, A., & Simonson, I. (1993). Context-dependent preferences. *Management Science*, **39**, 1179–1189.

Usher, M., & McClelland, J. L. (2001). The time course of perceptual choice: The leaky, competing accumulator model. *Psychological Review*, **108**(3), 550–592.

Usher, M., & McClelland, J. L. (2004). Loss aversion and inhibition in dynamical models of multialternative choice. *Psychological Review*, **111**, 759–769.

Usher, M., & Niebur, N. (1996). Modeling the temporal dynamics of it neurons in visual search: A mechanism for top-down selective attention. *Journal of Cognitive Neuroscience*, **8**, 311–327.

Usher, M., & Zakay, D. (1993). A neural network model for attribute based decisions processes. *Cognitive Science*, **17**, 349–396.

Yule, P., & Cooper, R. P. (2003): Express: A web-based technology to support human and computational experimentation. *Behavior Research Methods, Instruments, & Computers,* **35**, 605–613.

Vickers, D. (1979). *Decision processes in perception.* New York: Academic Press.

Wald, A. (1947). *Sequential analysis.* New York: Wiley.

Part 4

Categorization and Memory

Chapter 14

Categorization as nonparametric Bayesian density estimation

Thomas L. Griffiths
University of California, Berkeley, CA, USA

Adam N. Sanborn
Indiana University, Bloomington, IN, USA

Kevin R. Canini
University of California, Berkeley, CA, USA

Daniel J. Navarro
University of Adelaide, Adelaide, SA, Australia,

Rational models of cognition aim to explain the structure of human thought and behavior as an optimal solution to the computational problems that are posed by our environment (Anderson, 1990; Chater & Oaksford, 1999; Marr, 1982; Oaksford & Chater, 1998). Rational models have been developed for several aspects of cognition, including memory (Anderson, 1990; Shiffrin & Steyvers, 1997), reasoning (Oaksford & Chater, 1994), generalization (Shepard, 1987; Tenenbaum & Griffiths, 2001), and causal induction (Anderson, 1990; Griffiths & Tenenbaum, 2005). By examining the computational problems that underlie our cognitive capacities, it is often possible to gain a deeper understanding of the assumptions behind successful models of human cognition, and to discover new classes of models that might otherwise have been overlooked.

In this chapter, we pursue a rational analysis of *category learning*: inferring the structure of categories from a set of stimuli labeled as belonging to those categories. The knowledge acquired through this process can ultimately be used to make decisions about how to categorize new stimuli. Several rational analyses of category learning have been proposed (Anderson, 1990; Nosofsky, 1998; Ashby & Alfonso-Reese, 1995). These analyses essentially agree on the nature of the computational problem involved, casting category learning as a problem of *density estimation*: determining the probability distributions associated with different category labels. Viewing category learning in this way helps to clarify the assumptions behind the two main classes of psychological models: exemplar models and prototype models. Exemplar models assume that a category is represented by a set of stored exemplars, and categorizing new stimuli involves comparing these stimuli to the set of exemplars in each category (e.g., Medin & Schaffer, 1978; Nosofsky, 1986). Prototype models assume that a category is associated with a single prototype and categorization involves comparing new stimuli to these prototypes (e.g., Reed, 1972). These approaches to category learning correspond to different strategies for density estimation used in statistics, being nonparametric and parametric density estimation respectively (Ashby & Alfonso-Reese, 1995).

Despite providing insight into the assumptions behind models of categorization, existing rational analyses of category learning leave a number of questions open. One particularly important question is whether rational learners should use an exemplar or prototype representation. The greater flexibility of nonparametric density estimation has motivated the claim that exemplar models are to be preferred as rational models of category learning (Nosofsky, 1998). However, nonparametric and parametric methods have different advantages and disadvantages: the greater flexibility of nonparametric methods comes at the cost of requiring more data to estimate a distribution. The choice of representation scheme should ultimately be determined by the stimuli presented to the learner, and existing rational analyses do not indicate how this decision should be made (although see Briscoe & Feldman, 2006). This question is complicated by the fact that prototype and exemplar models are not the only options. A number of models have recently explored possibilities between these extremes, representing categories using clusters of several exemplars (Anderson, 1990; Kruschke, 1990; Love et al., 2004; Rosseel, 2002; Vanpaemel et al., 2005). The range of representations possible in these models emphasizes the significance of being able to identify an appropriate category representation from the stimuli themselves: with many representational options available, it is even more important to be able to say which option a learner should choose.

Anderson's (1990; 1991) rational analysis of categorization presents a partial solution to this question, automatically selecting the number of clusters to be used in representing a set of objects, but has its own limitations. Anderson's approach uses a flexible representation in which new clusters are added as required. When a new stimulus is observed, it can either be assigned to one of the pre-existing clusters, or to a new cluster of its own. As a result, the representation becomes more complex as new data are observed, with the number of clusters growing as needed to accommodate the rich structures that emerge as we learn more about our environment. Accordingly, a crucial aspect of the model is the method by which stimuli are assigned to clusters. Anderson (1990; 1991) proposed an algorithm in which stimuli are sequentially assigned to clusters, and assignments of stimuli are fixed once they are made. However, this algorithm does not provide any asymptotic guarantees for the quality of the resulting assignments, and is extremely sensitive to the order in which stimuli are observed, a property which is not intrinsic to the underlying statistical model.

In this chapter, we identify connections between existing rational models of categorization and work on density estimation in nonparametric Bayesian statistics.

These connections have two consequences. First, we present two new algorithms that can be used in evaluating the predictions of Anderson's (1990; 1991) rational model of categorization. These two algorithms both asymptotically approximate the Bayesian posterior distribution over assignments of objects to clusters, and help to separate the predictions that arise from the underlying statistical model from those that are due to the inference algorithm. These algorithms also provide a source of hypotheses about the processes by which people could solve the challenging problem of performing probabilistic inference. Second, we develop a unifying model of categorization, of which existing rational models are special cases. This model goes beyond previous unifying models of category learning (e.g., Rosseel, 2002; Vanpaemel *et al.*, 2005) by providing a rational solution to the question of which representation should be chosen, and when the representation should change, based purely on the information provided by the stimuli themselves.

Identifying the connection between models of human category learning and nonparametric Bayesian density estimation extends the scope of the rational analysis of category learning. It also provides a different perspective on human category learning. Rather than suggesting that people use one form of representation or another, our approach indicates how it might be possible (and, in fact, desirable) for people to switch between representations based upon the structure of the stimuli they observe. This basic idea is similar to that underlying recent process models of category learning, such as SUSTAIN (Love *et al.*, 2004). Our contribution is a rational account of when a given representation is justified by the data given a set of assumptions about the processes by which those data are produced, providing a way to explore the assumptions that underlie human category learning. We illustrate this approach by modeling data from Smith and Minda (1998), in which people seem to shift from using a prototype representation early in training to using an exemplar representation late in training, showing that such a shift can be understood as a rational statistical inference.

The plan of the chapter is as follows. The next section summarizes exemplar and prototype models, and the idea of interpolating between the two. We then discuss existing rational models of categorization, before going on to highlight the connection between the rational model proposed by Anderson (1990, 1991) and the Dirichlet process mixture model (Antoniak, 1974; Ferguson, 1983; Neal, 1998), a statistical model that is commonly used in nonparametric Bayesian statistics. This allows us to identify two new algorithms for use with Anderson's model, which we describe and evaluate, and to use generalizations of this statistical model as the basis for a more complete account of human categorization. We summarize the ideas behind the hierarchical Dirichlet process (Teh *et al.*, 2004), and use it as the foundation for a unifying rational model of categorization. Finally, we show that this model can capture the shift from prototypes to exemplars in the data of Smith and Minda (1998).

Similarity-based models of categorization

While early work assumed that people use explicit classification rules in order to assign stimuli to categories (e.g., Bruner *et al.*, 1956), most categorization models developed in the last 30 years have assumed that categories are defined by a kind of 'family resemblance' (Rosch, 1978). The two most influential approaches have been prototype models and exemplar models, which both assume that people assign stimuli to categories based on similarity, formalized in the following manner. Given a set of N-1 stimuli with features $\mathbf{x}_{N-1}= (x_1, x_2,...,x_{N-1})$ and category labels $\mathbf{y}_{N-1}= (y_1,y_2,...,y_{N-1})$, the probability that stimulus N with features x_N is assigned to category j is given by

$$P(y_N = j \mid x_N, \mathbf{x}_{N-1}, \mathbf{y}_{N-1}) = \frac{\eta_{N,j}\beta_j}{\sum_y \eta_{N,y}\beta_y} \tag{1}$$

where $\eta_{N,y}$ is the similarity of the stimulus x_N to category y and β_y is the response bias for category y. Thus, the decision is a function of the various category similarities, and involves a straightforward application of the standard choice rule (Luce, 1959). The key difference between the models is in how $\eta_{N,j}$, the similarity of a stimulus to a category, is computed.

Exemplars and prototypes

In an exemplar model (e.g., Medin & Schaffer, 1978; Nosofsky, 1986), all of the instances of that category are stored. The similarity of stimulus N to category j is calculated by summing the similarity of the stimulus to all these stored instances. That is,

$$\eta_{N,j} = \sum_{i|y_i=j} s_{N,i} \tag{2}$$

where $s_{N,i}$ is a symmetric measure of the similarity between the two stimuli x_N and x_i. The similarity measure is typically defined as a decaying exponential function of the distance between the two stimuli, following Shepard (1987). An example of the overall similarity function is shown in the rightmost panel of Figure 14.1. In contrast, prototype models (e.g., Reed, 1972), represent a category j in terms of a single prototypical instance. In this formulation, the similarity of stimulus N to category j is defined to be,

$$\eta_{N,j} = s_{N,p_j} \tag{3}$$

where p_j is the prototypical instance of the category and s_{N,p_j} is a measure of the similarity between stimulus N and the prototype p_j. One common way of defining the prototype is as the centroid of all instances of the category in some psychological space, i.e.,

$$p_j = \frac{1}{N_j} \sum_{i|y_i=j} x_i \tag{4}$$

where N_j is the number of instances of the category (i.e., the number of stimuli for which $y_i=j$). The panel on the left of Figure 14.1 illustrates the kind of category similarity functions employed by a prototype model.

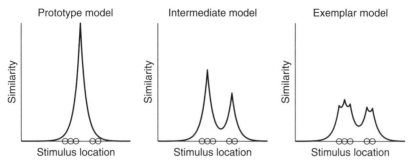

Fig. 14.1. Category similarity functions for a simple one-dimensional category. The panel on the left shows the similarity function for a prototype model, with a single prototype summarizing the structure of the category. The panel on the right shows the similarity function for an exemplar model, with the overall similarity resulting from summing a set of similarity functions centered on each exemplar. The similarity function shown in the middle panel comes from an intermediate model that groups the three stimuli on the left and the two stimuli on the right.

Broader classes of representation

Although exemplars and prototypes have dominated the modern literature, a number of authors (e.g., Kruschke, 1990; Love *et al.*, 2004; Vanpaemel *et al.*, 2005) have proposed more general classes of category representation that interpolate between prototype and exemplar models. For example, Vanpaemel *et al.* (2005) formalized a set of interpolating models by partitioning instances of each category into clusters, where the number of clusters K_j ranges from 1 to N_j. Then each cluster is represented by a prototype, and the similarity of stimulus N to category j is defined to be,

$$\eta_{N,j} = \sum_{k=1}^{K_j} s_{N,p_{j,k}} \tag{5}$$

where $p_{j,k}$ is the prototype of cluster k in category j. This is equivalent to the prototype model when $K_j=1$, and the exemplar model when $K_j=N_j$. Thus, this generalized model, the Varying Abstraction Model (VAM), is more flexible than both the exemplar and prototype models (as illustrated by the middle panel of Figure 14.1), although it raises the problem of estimating which clustering people use in any particular categorization task (for details, see Vanpaemel *et al.*, 2005).

The idea of representing a category using a set of clusters is reasonably intuitive, since explicitly labeled categories are not the only level at which homogeneity can be found in the world (Rosch, 1978). For example, while no two chairs are exactly the same, many chairs are of similar types, differing only in superficial properties like color. By clustering the instances of these similar types of chairs and storing a single prototype, we can avoid having to remember a large number of redundant instances. A similar property holds for natural categories, where, for example, species of animals might be composed of subspecies. This underlying structure supports a finer-grained representation than a single prototype, while not requiring the comprehensiveness of a full exemplar model.

Rational accounts of categorization

The models discussed in the previous section all explain categorization behavior in terms of cognitive processes, in particular similarity and choice. An alternative approach is to seek an explanation based on the form of the computational problem that underlies categorization. Following the methodology outlined by Anderson (1990), rational models of categorization explain human behavior as an adaptive solution to a computational problem posed by the environment, rather than focusing on the cognitive processes involved. Existing analyses tend to agree that the basic problem is one of *prediction*—identifying the category label or some other unobserved property of an object using its observed properties (Anderson, 1990; Ashby & Alfonso-Reese, 1995; Rosseel, 2002). This prediction problem has a natural interpretation as a form of Bayesian inference. In a standard classification task, for instance, Bayes' rule allows us to compute the probability that object N belongs to category j given the features and category labels of N-1 objects:

$$P\left(y_N = j \mid x_N, \mathbf{x}_{N-1}, \mathbf{y}_{N-1}\right) =$$

$$\frac{P\left(x_N \mid y_N = j, \mathbf{x}_{N-1}, \mathbf{y}_{N-1}\right)}{\sum_y P\left(x_N \mid y_N = y, \mathbf{x}_{N-1}, \mathbf{y}_{N-1}\right)} \times \frac{P\left(y_N = j \mid \mathbf{y}_{N-1}\right)}{P\left(y_N = y \mid \mathbf{y}_{N-1}\right)} \tag{6}$$

where we assume that the prior probability of an object coming from a particular category is independent of the features of the previous objects. In this expression, the posterior probability of category j is related to both the probability of sampling an object with features x_N from that category, and the prior probability of choosing that category. Category learning, then, becomes a matter of determining these probabilities— a problem known as *density estimation*. Since different rational models vary in how they approach this problem, we provide a brief overview of the various accounts.

The rational basis of exemplar and prototype models

Ashby and Alfonso-Reese (1995) observed that both prototype and exemplar models can be recast as rational solutions to the problem of categorization, highlighting the connection between the Bayesian solution presented in Equation 6 and the choice probabilities in the exemplar and prototype models (i.e., Equation 1). Specifically, the category similarity $\eta_{N,j}$ can be identified with the probability of generating an item, $P(x_N|y_N=j,\mathbf{x}_{N-1},\mathbf{y}_{N-1})$, while the category bias β_j corresponds naturally to the prior probability of category j, $P(y_N=j|\mathbf{y}_{N-1})$. The difference between exemplar and prototype models is thus the different ways of estimating $P(x_N|y_N=j,\mathbf{x}_{N-1},\mathbf{y}_{N-1})$. The definition of $\eta_{N,j}$ used in an exemplar model (Equation 2) corresponds to estimating $P(x_N|y_n=j,\mathbf{x}_{N-1},\mathbf{y}_{N-1})$ as the sum of a set of functions (known as 'kernels') centered on the x_i already labeled as belonging to category j, with

$$P\left(x_N \mid y_N = j, \mathbf{x}_{N-1}, \mathbf{y}_{N-1}\right) \propto \sum_{i|y_i=j} f\left(x_N, x_i\right) \tag{7}$$

where $f(x,x_i)$ is a probability distribution centered on x_i.[1] This method is widely used for approximating distributions in statistics, being a simple form of nonparametric density estimation called kernel density estimation (e.g., Silverman, 1986). In contrast, the definition of $\eta_{N,j}$ used in a prototype model (Equation 3) corresponds to estimating $P(x_N|y_n=j,\mathbf{x}_{N-1},\mathbf{y}_{N-1})$ by assuming that each category distribution comes from an underlying parametric family and then finding the parameters that best characterize the instances labeled as belonging to that category. The prototype is specified by these parameters, with the centroid being an appropriate estimate for distributions whose parameters characterize their mean. Again, this is a common method for estimating a probability distribution, known as parametric density estimation, in which the distribution is assumed to be of a known form but with unknown parameters (e.g., Rice, 1995).

The mixture model of categorization

Casting exemplar and prototype models as different schemes for density estimation suggests that a similar interpretation might be found for interpolating models. Rosseel (2002) proposed one such model—the Mixture Model of Categorization (MMC)—assuming that $P(x_N|y_N=j,\mathbf{x}_{N-1},\mathbf{y}_{N-1})$ is a mixture distribution. Specifically, each object x_i comes from a cluster z_i, and each cluster is associated with a probability distribution over the features of the objects generated from that cluster. When evaluating the probability of a new object x_N, it is necessary to sum over all of the clusters from which that object might have been drawn. Accordingly,

$$P\left(x_N \mid y_N = j, \mathbf{x}_{N-1}, \mathbf{y}_{N-1}\right) =$$

$$\sum_{k=1}^{K_j} P\left(x_N \mid z_N = k, \mathbf{x}_{N-1}, \mathbf{z}_{N-1}\right) \times P\left(z_N = k \mid \mathbf{z}_{N-1}, y_N = j, \mathbf{y}_{N-1}\right) \quad (8)$$

where K_j is the total number of clusters for category j, $P(x_N|z_N=k,\mathbf{x}_{N-1},\mathbf{z}_{N-1})$ is the probability of x_N under cluster k, and $P(z_N=k|\mathbf{z}_{N-1},y_N=j,\mathbf{y}_{N-1})$ is the probability of generating a new object from cluster k in category j. The clusters can either be shared between categories, or be specific to a single category (in which case $P(z_N=k|\mathbf{z}_{N-1},y_N=j,\mathbf{y}_{N-1})$ is 0 for all clusters not belonging to category j). This model reduces to kernel density estimation when each object has its own cluster and the clusters are equally weighted, and parametric density estimation when each category is represented by a single cluster. By a similar argument to that used for the exemplar model above, we can connect Equation 8 with the definition of $\eta_{N,j}$ in the VAM (Equation 5), providing a rational justification for this method of interpolating between exemplars and prototypes.[2]

....

[1] The constant of proportionality is determined by $\int f(x,x_i)dx$, being $\dfrac{1}{N_j}$ if $\int f(x,x_i)dx=1$ for all i, and is absorbed into β_j to produce direct equivalence to Equation 2.

[2] Note, however, that the MMC is more general than the VAM, since the VAM does not allow clusters to be shared across categories.

Anderson's rational model of categorization

The MMC elegantly defines a rational model between exemplars and prototypes, but does not determine how many clusters are appropriate for representing each category, based on the available data. Anderson (1990) introduced the Rational Model of Categorization (RMC), which presents a partial solution to this problem. The RMC differs from the other models discussed in this section by treating category labels like features. Thus, the RMC specifies a joint distribution on features and category labels, rather than assuming that the distribution on category labels is estimated separately and then combined with a distribution on features for each category. As in the MMC, this distribution is a mixture, with

$$P(\mathbf{x}_N, \mathbf{y}_N) = \sum_{\mathbf{z}_N} P(\mathbf{x}_N, \mathbf{y}_N \mid \mathbf{z}_N) P(\mathbf{z}_N) \tag{9}$$

where $P(\mathbf{z}_N)$ is a distribution over clusterings of the N objects. The key difference from the MMC is that the RMC provides an explicit prior distribution over possible partitions. Importantly, this distribution allows the number of clusters to be unbounded, with

$$P(\mathbf{z}_N) = \frac{(1-c)^K c^{N-K}}{\prod_{i=0}^{N-1}[(1-c)+ci]} \prod_{k=1}^{K} (M_k - 1) \tag{10}$$

where c is a parameter called the *coupling probability*, and M_k is the number of objects assigned to cluster k. This is the distribution that results from sequentially assigning objects to clusters with probability

$$P(z_i = k \mid \mathbf{z}_{i-1}) = \begin{cases} \dfrac{cM_k}{(1-c)+c(i-1)} & \text{if } M_k > 0 (i.e., k \text{ is old}) \\[4mm] \dfrac{(1-c)}{(1-c)+c(i-1)} & \text{if } M_k = 0 (i.e., k \text{ is new}) \end{cases} \tag{11}$$

where the counts M_k are accumulated over $\mathbf{z}_{i-1}$. Thus, each object can be assigned to an existing cluster with probability proportional to the number of objects already assigned to that cluster, or to a new cluster with probability determined by c.

Despite having been defined in terms of the joint distribution of $\mathbf{x}_N$ and $\mathbf{y}_N$, the assumption that features and category labels are independent given the cluster assignments makes it possible to write $P(x_N|y_N=j,\mathbf{x}_{N-1},\mathbf{y}_{N-1})$ in the same form as Equation 8. To do so, note that the probability that the Nth observation belongs to the kth cluster is given by,

$$P(z_N = k|\mathbf{z}_{N-1}, y_N = j, \mathbf{y}_{N-1}) \propto P(y_N = j|z_N = k, \mathbf{z}_{N-1}, \mathbf{y}_{N-1}) P(z_N = k|\mathbf{z}_{N-1}) \tag{12}$$

where we take into account the fact that this observation belongs to category y_N. The second term on the right hand side is given by Equation 11. This defines a distribution over the same K clusters regardless of j, but the value of K depends on the number of clusters in z_{N-1}. Substituting this expression into Equation 8 provides the relevant mixture model for the RMC. In general, the probabilities in Equation 12 will never be precisely zero, so all clusters contribute to all categories. The RMC can therefore be viewed as a form of the mixture model in which all clusters are shared between categories but the number of clusters is inferred from the data. However, the two models are not directly equivalent because the RMC assumes that both features and category labels are generated from the clusters. This assumption induces a dependency between labels and features, such that the prior over y_N depends on x_{N-1} as well as y_{N-1}, violating the (arguably sensible) independence assumption made by the other models and embodied in Equation 6.

The RMC comes close to specifying a unifying rational model of categorization, capturing many of the ideas embodied in other models and allowing the representation to be inferred from the data. It can also be shown to mimic the behavior of other models of categorization under certain conditions (Nosofsky, 1991). However, the model is still significantly limited. First, the RMC assumes a single set of clusters for all categories, an assumption that is inconsistent with many models that interpolate between prototypes and exemplars (e.g., Vanpaemel *et al.*, 2005). Second, the idea that category labels should be treated like other features has odd implications, such as the dependency between features and category labels mentioned above. Third, as we will discuss shortly, the approximate algorithm used for assigning objects to clusters in the RMC has serious drawbacks. In order to address these issues, we now discuss the connections between the RMC and nonparametric Bayesian statistics.

Nonparametric Bayes and categorization

One of the most interesting properties of the RMC is that it has a direct connection to nonparametric Bayesian statistics (Neal, 1998). The rationale for using nonparametric methods is that real data are not generally sampled from some neat, finite-dimensional family of distributions, so it is best to avoid this assumption at the outset. From a Bayesian perspective, the nonparametric approach requires us to use priors that include as broad a range of densities of possible, thereby allowing us to infer very complex densities if they are warranted by data. The most commonly used method for placing broad priors over probability distributions is the *Dirichlet process* (DP; Ferguson, 1973). The distributions indexed by the Dirichlet process can be expressed as countably infinite mixtures of point masses (Sethuraman, 1994), making them ideally suited to act as priors in infinite mixture models (Escobar & West, 1995; Rasmussen, 2000). When used in this fashion, the resulting model is referred to as a *Dirichlet process mixture model* (DPMM; Antoniak, 1974; Ferguson, 1983; Neal, 1998).

Although a complete description of the Dirichlet process is beyond the scope of this chapter (for more details, see Navarro *et al.*, 2006), what matters for our purposes is that the Dirichlet process implies a distribution over partitions: any two observations in the sample that were generated from the same mixture component may be treated as members of the same cluster, allowing us to specify priors over an unbounded number of clusters. In the case where N observations have been made, the prior probability that a Dirichlet process will partition those observations into the clusters z_N is

$$P(z_N) = \frac{\alpha^K}{\prod\limits_{i=0}^{N-1}[\alpha + i]} \prod\limits_{K=1}^{K}(M_K - 1)! \tag{13}$$

where α is the dispersion parameter of the Dirichlet process. This distribution over partitions can be produced by a simple sequential stochastic process (Blackwell & MacQueen, 1973), known as the Chinese restaurant process (Aldous, 1985; Pitman, 2002). If observations are assigned to clusters one after another and the probability that observation i+1 is assigned to cluster k is

$$P(z_i = k \mid z_{i-1}) = \begin{cases} \dfrac{M_K}{i-1+\alpha} & \text{if } M_k > 0 \; (i.e., k \text{ is old}) \\[3mm] \dfrac{\alpha}{i-1+\alpha} & \text{if } M_k = 0 \; (i.e., k \text{ is new}) \end{cases} \tag{14}$$

we obtain Equation 13 for the probability of the resulting partition. This distribution has a number of nice properties, with one of the most important being *exchangeability*: the prior probability of a partition is unaffected by the order in which the observations are received (Aldous, 1985). To make some of these ideas more concrete, Figure 14.2 presents a visual depiction of the relationship between the partitioning implied by the DP, the distribution over parameters that is sampled from the DP, and the mixture distribution over stimuli that results in the DPMM.

It should be apparent from our description of the DPMM that it is similar in spirit to the probabilistic model underlying the RMC. In fact, the two are directly equivalent, a point that was first made in the statistics literature by Neal (1998). If we let α=(1-c)/c, Equations 10 and 13 are equivalent, as are Equations 11 and 14. Thus the prior over cluster assignments used in the RMC is exactly the same as that used in the DPMM. Anderson (1990, 1991) thus independently discovered one of the most celebrated models in nonparametric Bayesian statistics, deriving this distribution from first principles. This connection provides us with the opportunity to draw on work related to the DPMM in statistics to develop new rational models of categorization. In the remainder of the chapter, we use this approach to explore two new algorithms for approximate Bayesian inference in the RMC and a way to significantly extend the scope of the model.

Approximate inference algorithms

When considering richer representations than prototypes and exemplars it is necessary to have a method for learning the appropriate representation from data. Using Equation 9 to make predictions about category labels and features requires summing over all possible partitions z_N. This sum becomes intractable for large N,

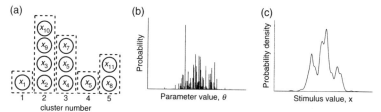

Fig. 14.2. The relationship between (a) the clustering implied by the DP, (b) the distribution over parameters that is sampled from the DP, and (c) the mixture distribution over stimuli that results in the DPMM. The clustering assignments in (a) were produced by drawing sequentially from the stochastic process defined in Equation 14, and each cluster is associated with a parameter value θ. After an arbitrarily large number of cluster assignments have been made, we can estimate the probability of each cluster, and hence of the corresponding parameter value. The resulting probability distribution is shown in (b). If each value of θ is treated as the mean of a simple normal distribution (with fixed variance) over the value of some continuous stimulus dimension, then the resulting mixture distribution drawn from the DPMM is the one illustrated in (c). While the applications considered in this chapter use stimuli that have discrete features, not a single continuous dimension, the notion of a mixture distribution is more intuitive in the continuous setting.

since the number of partitions grows rapidly with the number of stimuli.[3] Consequently, an approximate inference algorithm is needed. The RMC does provide an algorithm, but it has some significant drawbacks. In this section, we first discuss the algorithm that Anderson (1990; 1991) originally proposed for the RMC, and then use the connections with the DPMM to motivate two alternative inference algorithms, which we will compare with exact Bayesian inference and human judgments in the next section.

The existence of alternative inference algorithms for the RMC is valuable for two reasons. The first is that these algorithms provide us with a way to separate the assumptions behind the underlying statistical model—the DPMM—and the scheme used for approximate inference when evaluating the predictions of the model. This is important, because different algorithms can have properties that significantly affect the predictions of the model, such as violating the exchangeability assumption. The second is that each inference algorithm provides us with a hypothesis about how people might go about solving the challenging problem of performing the probabilistic computations involved in Bayesian inference. Rational models are useful for testing assumptions learners make about the environment, but do not generally aim to describe the psychological processes used in solving the computational problems posed by the environment. The computations involved in solving these problems are often intractable, with the overwhelming number of partitions of a set of objects being just one example of a seemingly simple problem that rapidly exceeds the

---

[3] The number of partitions of a set of N stimuli is given by the Nth Bell number, with the first ten values being 1, 2, 5, 15, 52, 203, 877, 4140, 21147, and 115975.

capacities of most computers and presumably human brains. Computer science and statistics have developed useful algorithms for approximating intractable probability distributions. Cognitive scientists can appropriate these algorithms for modeling categorization—assuming that people have rational goals and perhaps approximate the solutions using these same algorithms. Incorporating these algorithms into categorization models provides a way to convert principled rational models into practical process models, as well as tightening the link between these two levels of analysis.

The local MAP algorithm

Anderson (1990, 1991) identified two desiderata for an approximate inference algorithm: that it be incremental, assigning a stimulus to each cluster as it is seen, and that these assignments, once made, be fixed. These desiderata were based on beliefs about the nature of human category learning: that 'people need to be able to make predictions all the time not just at particular junctures after seeing many objects and much deliberation' (Anderson, 1991, p. 412), and that 'people tend to perceive objects as coming from specific categories' (Anderson, 1991, p. 411). He developed a simple inference algorithm that satisfies these desiderata. We will refer to this algorithm as the *local MAP* algorithm, as it involves assigning each stimulus to the cluster that has the highest posterior probability given the previous assignments (i.e., the maximum a posteriori or MAP cluster).

The local MAP algorithm approximates the sum in Equation 9 with just a single clustering of the N objects, z_N. This clustering is selected by assigning each object to a cluster as it is observed. The posterior probability that stimulus i was generated from cluster k given the features and labels of all stimuli, along with the cluster assignments z_{i-1} for the previous $i-1$ stimuli is given by

$$P(z_i = k|\mathbf{z}_{i-1},x_i,\mathbf{x}_{i-1},y_i,\mathbf{y}_{i-1}) \propto P(x_i|z_i = k,\mathbf{z}_{i-1},\mathbf{x}_{i-1})P(y_i|z_i = k,\mathbf{z}_{i-1},\mathbf{y}_{i-1})P(z_i = k|\mathbf{z}_{i-1}) \quad (15)$$

where $P(z_i=k|\mathbf{z}_{i-1})$ is given by Equation 14. Under the local MAP algorithm, x_i is assigned to the cluster k that maximizes Equation 15. Iterating this process results in a single partition of a set of N objects. The local MAP algorithm approximates the complete joint distribution using only this partition. In effect, it assumes that

$$P(\mathbf{x}_N,\mathbf{y}_N) \approx P(\mathbf{x}_N,\mathbf{y}_N|\mathbf{z}_N) \quad (16)$$

where z_N is produced via the procedure outlined above. The probability that a particular object receives a particular category label would likewise be computed using a single partition. Unfortunately, although this approach is fast and simple, the local MAP algorithm has some odd characteristics. In particular, the quality of the approximation is often poor, and the algorithm violates the principle of exchangeability. In fact, the local MAP algorithm is *extremely* sensitive to the order in which stimuli are observed, perhaps more than human participants are (see Sanborn et al., 2006).

Monte Carlo methods

The connection between the RMC and the DPMM suggests a solution to the shortcomings of the local MAP algorithm. In the remainder of this section, we draw on the extensive literature on approximate inference for DPMMs to offer two alternative algorithms for the RMC: Gibbs sampling and particle filtering. These algorithms are less sensitive to order and are asymptotically guaranteed to produce accurate predictions. Both are Monte Carlo methods, in which the intractable sum over partitions is approximated numerically using a collection of samples. Specifically, to compute the probability that a particular object receives a particular category label, a Monte Carlo approximation gives

$$P\big(y_N = j \mid \mathbf{x}_N, \mathbf{y}_{N-1}\big) = \sum_{\mathbf{z}_N} P\big(y_N = j \mid \mathbf{x}_N, \mathbf{y}_{N-1}, \mathbf{z}_N\big) P\big(\mathbf{z}_N \mid \mathbf{x}_N, \mathbf{y}_{N-1}\big)$$

$$\approx \frac{1}{m}\sum_{l=1}^{m} P\big(y_N = j \mid \mathbf{x}_N, \mathbf{y}_{N-1}, \mathbf{z}_N^{(l)}\big) \tag{17}$$

where $\mathbf{z}_N^{(l)}, ..., \mathbf{z}_N^{(m)}$ are m samples from $P(\mathbf{z}_N \mid \mathbf{x}_N, \mathbf{y}_{N-1})$, and the approximation becomes exact as $m \to \infty$. This is the principle behind the two algorithms we outline in this section. However, since sampling from $P(\mathbf{z}_N \mid \mathbf{x}_N, \mathbf{y}_{N-1})$ is not straightforward, the two algorithms use more sophisticated Monte Carlo methods to generate a set of samples.

Gibbs sampling

The approximate inference algorithm most commonly used with the DPMM is Gibbs sampling, a Markov chain Monte Carlo (MCMC) method (see Gilks *et al.*, 1996). This algorithm involves constructing a Markov chain that will converge to the distribution from which we want to sample, in this case the posterior distribution over partitions. The state space of the Markov chain is the set of partitions, and transitions between states are produced by sampling the cluster assignment of each stimulus from its conditional distribution, given the current assignments of all other stimuli. The algorithm thus moves from state to state by sequentially sampling each z_i from the distribution

$$P(z_i = k \mid \mathbf{z}_{-i}, x_i, \mathbf{x}_{-i}, y_i, \mathbf{y}_{-i}) \propto P(x_i \mid z_i = k, \mathbf{z}_{-i}, \mathbf{x}_{-i}) P(y_i \mid z_i = k, \mathbf{z}_{-i}, \mathbf{y}_{-i}) P(z_i = k \mid \mathbf{z}_{-i}) \tag{18}$$

where $\mathbf{z}_{-i}$ refers to all cluster assignments except for the ith.

Equation 18 is extremely similar to Equation 15, although it gives the probability of a cluster based on the all of the trials in the entire experiment except for the current trial, instead of just the previous trials. Exchangeability means that these probabilities are actually computed in exactly the same way: the order of the observations can be rearranged so that any particular observation is considered the last observation. Hence, we can use Equation 14 to compute $P(z_i \mid \mathbf{z}_{-i})$, with old clusters receiving probability in proportion to their popularity, and a new cluster being chosen with probability determined by α (or, equivalently, c). The other terms reflect the probability of the features and category label of stimulus i under the partition that results from this choice of z_i, and depend on the nature of the features.

The Gibbs sampling algorithm for the DPMM is straightforward (Neal, 1998). First, an initial assignment of stimuli to clusters is chosen. Next, we cycle through all stimuli, sampling a cluster assignment from the distribution specified by Equation 18. This step is repeated, with each iteration potentially producing a new partition of the stimuli. This process is illustrated in Figure 14.3. Since the probability of obtaining a particular partition after each iteration depends only on the partition produced on the previous iteration, this is a Markov chain. After enough iterations for the Markov chain to converge, we begin to save the partitions it produces. The partition produced on one iteration is not independent of the next, so the results of some iterations are discarded to approximate independence. The partitions generated by the Gibbs sampler can be used in the same way as samples $z_N^{(l)}$ in Equation 17.

The Gibbs sampler differs from the local MAP algorithm in two ways. First, it involves sequentially revisiting the cluster assignments of all objects many times, while the local MAP algorithm assigns each object to a cluster exactly once. Second, the cluster assignment is sampled from the posterior distribution instead of always going to the cluster with the highest posterior probability. As a consequence, different partitions are produced on different iterations, and approximate probabilities can be computed using a collection of partitions rather than just one. As with all Monte Carlo approximations, the quality of the approximation increases as the number of partitions in that collection increases.

The Gibbs sampler provides an effective means of constructing the approximation in Equation 17, and thus of making accurate predictions about the unobserved features of stimuli. However, it does not satisfy the desiderata Anderson (1990, 1991) used to motivate his algorithm. In particular, it is not an incremental algorithm: it assumes that all data are available at the time of inference. Depending on the experimental task, this assumption may be inappropriate. The Gibbs sampler is an excellent algorithm to model experiments where people are shown the full set of stimuli simultaneously. However, when the stimuli are shown sequentially, it needs to be run again

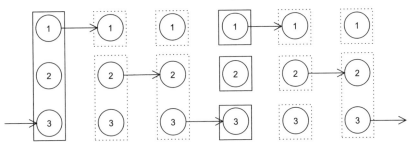

Fig. 14.3. Example of Gibbs sampling with three objects (circles, differentiated by numbers). A partition of the objects is expressed using boxes, where all objects within a box belong to the same element of the partition. At any point in time, a single partition is maintained. Stochastic transitions between partitions are produced by sequentially sampling the element of the partition to which each object is assigned from its conditional distribution given the data and all other assignments. The partition produced by a full iteration of sampling (i.e. reassignment of all three objects) is shown by the solid boxes, with the intermediate steps being illustrated by dotted boxes. After many iterations, the probability of producing a particular partition corresponds to the posterior probability of that partition given the observed data (features and category labels).

each time new data are added, making it inefficient when predictions need to be made on each trial. In such situations, we need to use a different algorithm.

Particle filtering

Particle filtering is a sequential Monte Carlo technique that can be used to provide a discrete approximation to a posterior distribution that can be updated with new data (Doucet et al., 2001). Each 'particle' is a partition $z_i^{(l)}$ of the stimuli from the first i trials. Unlike the local MAP algorithm, in which the posterior distribution is approximated with a single partition, the particle filter uses m partitions. Summing over these particles gives us an approximation to the posterior distribution over partitions

$$P\left(\mathbf{z}_i \mid \mathbf{x}_i, \mathbf{y}_i\right) \approx \frac{1}{m}\sum_{l-1}^{m}\delta\left(\mathbf{z}_i, \mathbf{z}_i^{(l)}\right) \tag{19}$$

where $\delta(z, z')$ is 1 when $z = z'$, and 0 otherwise. If Equation 19 is used as an approximation to the posterior distribution over partitions z_i after the first i trials, then we can approximate the distribution of z_{i+1} given the observations x_i, y_i in the following manner:

$$P\left(\mathbf{z}_{i+1} \mid \mathbf{x}_i, \mathbf{y}_i\right) = \sum_{\mathbf{z}_i} P\left(\mathbf{z}_{i+1} \mid \mathbf{z}_i\right) P\left(\mathbf{z}_i \mid \mathbf{x}_i, \mathbf{y}_i\right)$$

$$\approx \sum_{\mathbf{z}_i} P\left(\mathbf{z}_{i+1} \mid \mathbf{z}_i\right)\frac{1}{m}\sum_{l=1}^{m}\delta\left(\mathbf{z}_i, \mathbf{z}_i^{(l)}\right)$$

$$= \frac{1}{m}\sum_{l=1}^{m}P\left(\mathbf{z}_{i+1} \mid \mathbf{z}_i^{(l)}\right) \tag{20}$$

where $P(z_{i+1}|z_i)$ is given by Equation 14, since the only difference between z_{i+1} and z_i is the assignment of z_{i+1}. We can then incorporate the information conveyed by the features and label of stimulus $i+1$, arriving at the approximate posterior probability

$$P(\mathbf{z}_{i+1}|\mathbf{x}_{i+1}, \mathbf{y}_{i+1}) \propto P(x_{i+1}|\mathbf{z}_{i+1}, \mathbf{x}_i)P(y_{i+1}|\mathbf{z}_{i+1}, \mathbf{y}_i)P(\mathbf{z}_{i+1}|\mathbf{x}_i, \mathbf{y}_i)$$

$$\approx \frac{1}{m}\sum_{l=1}^{m}P\left(x_{i+1} \mid \mathbf{z}_{i+1}, \mathbf{x}_i\right)P\left(y_{i+1} \mid \mathbf{z}_{i+1}, \mathbf{y}_i\right)P\left(\mathbf{z}_{i+1} \mid \mathbf{z}_i^{(l)}\right) \tag{21}$$

The result is a discrete distribution over all the previous particle assignments and all possible assignments for the current stimulus. Drawing m samples from this distribution provides us with our new set of particles, as illustrated in Figure 14.4.

The particle filter for the RMC is initialized with the first stimulus assigned to the first cluster for all m particles. On each following trial, the distribution in Equation 21 is calculated, based on the particles sampled in the last trial. On any trial, these particles provide an approximation to the posterior distribution over partitions. The stimuli are integrated into the representation incrementally, satisfying one of Anderson's desiderata. The degree to which Anderson's fixed assignment criterion is

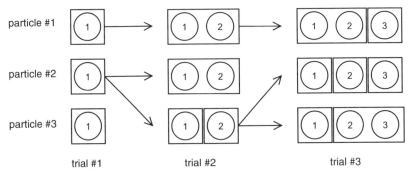

Fig. 14.4. Example of particle filtering, involving three particles and three sequentially observed objects (circles, differentiated by numbers). On any given trial, we take the sampled distribution over partitions (boxes) from previous trial, and treat it as an approximation to the full posterior over partitions for that trial (Equation 19). We then update to an approximate posterior for the current trial using Equation 21 and redraw a collection of particles. Note that since we are sampling with replacement, it is possible for particles to 'exchange histories', as is illustrated by the states of particles 2 and 3 in this figure.

satisfied depends on the number of particles. The assignments in the particles themselves are fixed: once a stimulus has been assigned to a cluster in a particle, it cannot be reassigned. However, the probability of a previous assignment across particles can change when a new stimulus is introduced. When a new set of particles is sampled, the number of particles that carry a particular assignment of a stimulus to a cluster is likely to change. For large m, the assignments will not appear fixed. However, when $m=1$, previous assignments cannot be changed, and Anderson's criterion is unambiguously satisfied. In fact, the single-particle particle filter is very similar to the local MAP algorithm: each assignment of a stimulus becomes fixed on the trial the stimulus is introduced. The key difference from the local MAP algorithm is that each stimulus is stochastically assigned a cluster by sampling from the posterior distribution, rather than being deterministically assigned to the cluster with highest posterior probability.

Comparing the algorithms to data

In this section we use data from Medin and Schaffer's (1978) Experiment 1 to compare how effective the algorithms are in approximating the full Bayesian solution, and how closely they match human performance. In order to do so, we need to specify a measure of the probability of a set of features given a particular partition. The RMC assumes that the features (and category label) of a stimulus are independent once the cluster it belongs to is known. Using this idea, we can write the probability of the features of a stimulus as

$$P\left(x_N \mid z_N = k, \mathbf{x}_{N-1}, \mathbf{z}_{N-1}\right) = \prod_d P\left(x_{N,d} \mid z_N = k, \mathbf{x}_{N-1}, \mathbf{z}_{N-1}\right)$$

where $x_{N,d}$ is the value of the dth feature of object N. In this section, we collapse the distinction between category labels and features, treating category labels simply as a special kind of discrete feature. Anderson (1991) presents the likelihood for both discrete and continuous features, but we need only consider binary features for our applications. Given the cluster, the value on each feature is assumed to have a Bernoulli distribution. Integrating out the parameter of this distribution with respect to a Beta (β_0, β_1) prior, we obtain

$$P\left(x_{N,d} = v \mid z_N = k, \mathbf{x}_{N-1}, \mathbf{z}_{N-1}\right) = \frac{B_v + \beta_v}{B. + \beta_0 + \beta_1} \tag{22}$$

where B_v is the number of stimuli with value v on the dth feature that z_N identifies as belonging to the same cluster as x_N B denotes the number of other stimuli in the same cluster. We use $\beta_0 = \beta_1 = 1$ in all simulations.

Medin and Schaffer's (1978) experiment used six training items, each consisting of five binary features (including the category label, listed last): 11111, 10101, 01011, 00000, 01000, and 10110. In an experiment with only six training examples, the exact posterior probabilities can be computed, as can the partition with the highest posterior probability (the global MAP solution). The algorithms were trained on the six examples, and the category label of a set of test stimuli (shown in Fig. 14.1) was then predicted. Three coupling probabilities were compared: $c=0.25$, $c=0.45$, and $c=0.75$. The local MAP algorithm was run on all 720 possible orders of the training stimuli. The Gibbs sampler was run for 1,100 iterations on a single training order. The first 100 iterations were discarded and only every 10th iteration was kept for a total of 100 samples. The particle filter was run with 100 particles on a single training order. Linear correlations with the human confidence ratings reported by Medin and Schaffer (1978) were computed for all algorithms.

The results shown in the top row of Figure 14.5 show that the coupling parameter does not have a large effect on the exact solution, the particle filter, or the Gibbs sampler. Moreover, the particle filter and Gibbs sampler provide good approximations to the full posterior solution.[4] In contrast, the local MAP algorithm depends heavily on the value of the coupling parameter. Furthermore, the global MAP solution, which the local MAP algorithm attempts to discover, is not a very good approximation to the full posterior, and provides a worse fit to the human data than the local MAP solution.

The fits to the human data for the two Monte Carlo algorithms are not particularly good when shown one instance of each stimulus (i.e. one block of training), but improve when they are trained on ten blocks of the six stimuli, as shown in the lower

Table 14.1. Test stimuli ordered by category 1 subject ratings from Medin & Schaffer (1978)

1111	0101	1010	1101	0111	0001	1110	1000	0010	1011	0100	0000

[4] Though not shown, a particle filter with fewer particles produced correlations to human data that were similar to those produced with 100 particles.

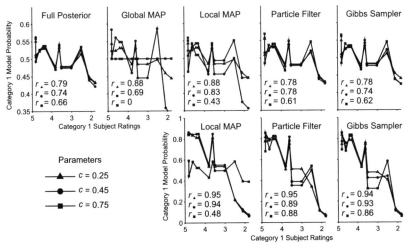

Fig. 14.5. Probability of choosing category 1 for the stimuli from the first experiment of Medin and Schaffer (1978). The test stimuli (listed in order of human preference in the legend) are along the horizontal axis. In the first row only the first six trials are presented, while in the second row ten blocks of six trials each are presented. The three lines in each panel correspond to three different coupling parameters: $c=0.25$, 0.45, or 0.75. Correlations between the human data and the simulation data are displayed on each plot for each value of the coupling parameter.

panels of Figure 14.5. This is more relevant for the different algorithms to human data, as participants in the experiment received ten blocks of training data. The full posterior is not tractable for sixty trials, but we can still compare the three approximation algorithms. Again, all of the predictions across algorithms and values of the coupling parameter are similar except for the local MAP algorithm with a high coupling parameter. Overall, the local MAP algorithm does not predict the human data any better than the other algorithms, and is in fact substantially worse for some values of the coupling parameter.

Unifying rational models using hierarchical Dirichlet processes

In the previous sections, interpreting the RMC as a DPMM allowed us to propose approximate inference algorithms that improve the fit to empirical data and better approximate the ideal Bayesian solution to the categorization problem as well as a source of hypotheses about processes by which people could perform the underlying computations. In this section we extend the approach, showing how Bayesian non-parametric models can unify all of the rational models discussed so far, subsuming prototypes, exemplars, the MMC, and RMC into a single model that learns the most appropriate representational structure. The tool that we will use to do this is the *hierarchical Dirichlet process* (HDP).

The HDP, introduced by Teh *et al.* (2004), is a straightforward generalization of the basic Dirichlet process. Observations are divided into groups, and each group is modeled using a Dirichlet process (with parameter α). A new observation is first compared to all of the clusters in its group, with the prior probability of each cluster determined by Equation 14. If the observation is to be assigned to a new cluster, the new cluster is drawn from a second Dirichlet process that compares the stimulus to all of the clusters that have been created across groups. This higher-level Dirichlet process is governed by parameter γ, analogous to α, and the prior probability of each cluster is proportional to the number of times that cluster has been selected by any group, instead of the number of observations in each cluster. The new observation is only assigned to a completely new cluster if both Dirichlet processes select a new cluster. In this manner, stimuli in different categories can end up belonging to the same mixture component, simply by being drawn from the same partition in the higher level. An illustration of this is shown in Figure 14.6.

The HDP provides a way to model probability distributions across groups of observations. Each distribution is a mixture of an unbounded number of clusters, but the clusters can be shared between groups. Shared clusters allow the model to leverage examples from across categories to better estimate cluster parameters. A priori expectations about the number of clusters in a group and the extent to which clusters are shared between groups are determined by the parameters α and γ. When α is small, each group will have few clusters, but when α is large, the number of clusters will

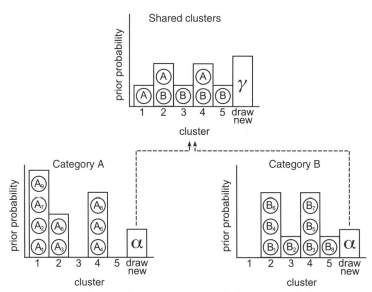

Fig. 14.6. Illustration of the HDP prior. The prior probability for each cluster at the lower level is based on the number of category examples in that cluster. If a cluster is selected from the higher level, the prior probability of clusters is based on the number of categories by which they have been selected. Completely new clusters can only be created at the higher level.

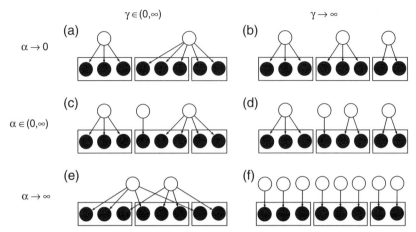

Fig. 14.7. Structural assumptions underlying different parameterizations of the HDP$_{\alpha,\gamma}$ model. The unfilled circles are clusters, the filled circles are exemplars, and the boxes indicate which exemplars belong to the same categories. Descriptions of the properties of these six models and their correspondence to existing models are given in the text.

be closer to the number of observations. When γ is small, groups are likely to share clusters, but when γ is large, the clusters in each group are likely to be unique.

We can now define a unifying rational model of categorization, based on the HDP. If we identify each category with a 'group' for which we want to estimate a distribution, the HDP becomes a model of category learning, subsuming all previous rational models through different settings of α and γ. Figure 14.7 identifies six models we can obtain by considering limiting values of α and γ.[5] We will refer to the different models using the notation HDP$_{\alpha,\gamma}$ where α and γ take on values corresponding to the values of the two parameters of the model (with + denoting a value in the interval $(0,\infty)$).Three of the models shown in Figure 14.7 are exactly isomorphic to existing models.[6] HDP$_{\infty,\infty}$ is an exemplar model, with one cluster per object and no sharing of clusters. HDP$_{0,\infty}$, is a prototype model, with one cluster per category and no sharing of clusters. HDP$_{\infty,+}$ is the RMC, provided that category labels are treated as features. In HDP$_{\infty,+}$, every object has its own cluster, but those clusters are generated from the higher-level Dirichlet process. Consequently, group membership is ignored and the model reduces to a Dirichlet process.

....

[5] The case of $\gamma \to 0$ is omitted, since it simply corresponds to a model in which all observations belong to the same cluster across both categories, for all values of α.

[6] In stating these equivalence results, we focus just on the kind of representation acquired by the model. In order to produce the same predictions for new observations, we need to assume that different values of the α and γ parameters are used in acquiring a representation and applying it. Specifically, we need to assume that $\alpha \to 0$ in HDP when making categorization decisions, guaranteeing that the new object is compared to old exemplars. A similar assumption was made by Nosofsky (1991) in showing equivalence between the RMC and exemplar models.

Figure 14.7 also includes some models that have not previously been explored in the literature on categorization. $HDP_{0,+}$ makes the same basic assumptions as the prototype model, with a single cluster per category, but makes it possible for different categories to share the same prototype—something that might be appropriate in an environment where the same category can have different labels. However, the most interesting models are $HDP_{+,+}$ and $HDP_{+,\infty}$. These models are essentially the MMC, with clusters shared between categories or unique to different categories respectively, but the number of clusters in each category can differ and can be learned from the data. Consequently, these models make it possible to answer the question of whether a particular category is best represented using prototypes, exemplars, or something in between, simply based on the objects belonging to that category. In the remainder of the chapter, we show that one of these models—$HDP_{+,\infty}$—can capture the shift that occurs from prototypes to a more exemplar-based representation in a recent categorization experiment.

Modeling the prototype-to-exemplar transition

Smith and Minda (1998) argued that people seem to produce responses that are more consistent with a prototype model early in learning, later shifting to exemplar-based representations. The models discussed in the previous section potentially provide a rational explanation for this effect: the prior specified in Equation 13 prefers fewer clusters and is unlikely to be overwhelmed by small amounts of data to the contrary, but as the number of stimuli consistent with multiple clusters increases, the representation should shift. These results thus provide an opportunity to compare the HDP to human data.

We focused on the non-linearly separable structure explored in Experiment 2 of Smith and Minda (1998). In this experiment, 16 participants were presented with six-letter nonsense words labeled as belonging to different categories. Each letter could take one of two values, producing the binary feature representation shown in Table 14.2. Each category contains one prototypical stimulus (000000 or 111111), five stimuli with five features in common with the prototype, and one stimulus with only one feature in common with the prototype, which we will refer to as an 'exception'. No linear function of the features can correctly classify every stimulus, meaning that a prototype model cannot distinguish between the categories exactly. Participants were presented with a random permutation of the 14 stimuli and asked to identify each as belonging to either Category A or Category B, receiving feedback after each stimulus. This block of 14 stimuli was repeated 40 times for each participant, and the responses were aggregated into 10 segments of 4 blocks each. The results are shown in

Table 14.2. Categories A and B from Smith and Minda (1998)

Category	Stimuli
A	000000, 100000, 010000, 001000, 000010, 000001, 111101
B	111111, 011111, 101111, 110111, 111011, 111110, 000100

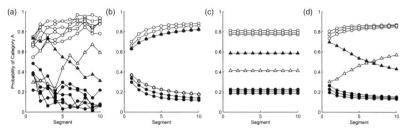

Fig. 14.8. Human data and model predictions. (a) Results of Smith and Minda (1998, Experiment 2). (b) Prototype model, HDP$_{,0}$. (c) Exemplar model, HDP$_{,}$. (d) HDP$_{+,}$. For all panels, white plot markers are stimuli in Category A, and black are in Category B. Triangular markers correspond to the exceptions to the prototype structure (111101 and 000100 respectively).

Figure 14.8 (a). The exceptions were initially identified as belonging to the wrong category, with performance improving later in training.

We tested three models: the exemplar model HDP$_{\infty,\infty}$, the prototype model HDP$_{0,\infty}$, and HDP$_{+,\infty}$. All three models were exposed to the same training stimuli as the human participants and used to categorize each stimulus after each segment of 4 blocks. The cluster structures for the prototype and exemplar models are fixed, so the probability of each category is straightforward to compute. However, since HDP$_{+,\infty}$ allows arbitrary clusterings, the possible clusterings need to be summed over when computing the probabilities used in categorization (as in Equation 17). We approximated this sum by sampling from the posterior distribution on clusterings using the MCMC algorithm described by Teh *et al.* (2004), which is a variant on the Gibbs sampling algorithm for the DPMM introduced above. Each set of predictions is based on an MCMC simulation with a burn-in of 1000 steps, followed by 100 samples separated by 10 steps each. The parameter α, equivalent to the coupling probability c, was also estimated by sampling.

As in Smith and Minda's original modeling of this data, a guessing parameter was incorporated to allow for the possibility that participants were randomly responding for some proportion of the stimuli. In practice, rational models—which have perfect memory for the stimuli and access to their features—can outperform human learners, so introducing a guessing parameter to handicap the models is a necessary part of comparing them to human data. If a model originally assigned probability $P(y_N=j)$ to categorizing a stimulus to some category, and the guessing parameter for the participant in question was ϕ, this probability would be updated to $(1-\phi)P(y_N = j) + \phi 0.5$. The guessing parameter was allowed to vary between 0 and 1 across individual participants, but was fixed per participant across every instance of every stimulus. Furthermore, the values of β_0 and β_1 in Equation 22 were fit to each participant, with the restriction that $\beta_0 = \beta_1$. Intuitively, this captures variation in the tendency to create new clusters, since the stronger bias towards feature probabilities near 0.5 resulting from high values of β_0 and β_1 makes it less likely that a new cluster will provide a better match to the particular features of a given object.

The predictions of the three models are shown in Figure 14.8. As might be expected, the prototype model does poorly in predicting the categories of the exceptions, while the exemplar model is more capable of handling these stimuli. We thus replicated the results of Smith and Minda (1998), finding that the prototype model fit better early in training, and the exemplar model better later in training. More interestingly, we also found that $HDP_{+,\infty}$ provided an equivalent or better account of human performance than the other two models after the first four segments. In particular, only this model captured the shift in the treatment of the exceptions over training. This shift occurred because the number of clusters in the HDP changes around the fourth segment: categories are initially represented with one cluster, but then become two clusters, one for the stimuli close to the prototype and one for the exception. These results are described in greater detail in Griffiths, Canini, Sanborn, and Navarro (2007).

The HDP model produces the shift from performance similar to a prototype model to performance similar to an exemplar model because this shift is justified by the data. The underlying structure—five stimuli that form a natural cluster and one exception in each category—supports a representation with more than a single cluster, and once evidence for this being the true structure accumulates, through the provision of enough instances of these stimuli, this is the structure favored by the posterior distribution. The model is able to capture similar predictions for other experiments reported by Smith and Minda (1998), as well as other standard datasets (e.g., Nosofsky *et al.*, 1994), but perhaps its greatest strength is in being able to explain how learning about one category can inform learning about another. In the general case, the HDP model allows clusters to be shared between categories, suggesting that we might be able to understand the great ease with which adults learn new categories of familiar objects (or new words) in terms of having acquired an accurate understanding of the clusters from which these categories could be composed through their previous experiences in category learning.

Conclusion

One of the most valuable aspects of rational models of cognition is their ability to establish connections across different fields. Here, we were able to exploit the correspondence between Anderson's (1990) Rational Model of Categorization and the Dirichlet process to draw on recent work in nonparametric Bayesian statistics. Using this correspondence, we identified more accurate approximation algorithms for use with Anderson's model and to define a more general rational model, based on the hierarchical Dirichlet process. The algorithms provide a source of hypotheses as to how people can solve the difficult problem of performing Bayesian inference, and the new model subsumes previous rational analyses of human category learning, indicating how learners should select the number of clusters to represent a category. The result is a picture of human categorization in which people do not use a fixed representation of categories across all contexts, but instead select a representation whose complexity is warranted by the available data, using simple and efficient approximation algorithms to perform these computations.

While our focus in this paper has been on applying ideas from statistics to cognitive science, the connection between human category learning and methods used in nonparametric Bayesian density estimation also has the potential to lead to new kinds of models that might be useful in statistics. The ways in which people use different sources of data in forming categories, combine category learning with language learning, and exploit structured knowledge as well as statistical information when categorizing objects all provide challenging computational problems that are beyond the scope of existing statistical models. Understanding how people solve these problems is likely to require thinking about categorization in terms that are more sophisticated than the schemes for density estimation summarized in this chapter, although we anticipate that similar issues of determining the complexity of the underlying representations are likely to arise, and that solutions to these problems can be found in the methods of nonparametric Bayesian statistics.

Author note

TLG was supported by a Junior Faculty Research Grant from the University of California, Berkeley, and grant number FA9550-07-1-0351 from the Air Force Office of Scientific Research. ANS was supported by a NSF Graduate Research Fellowship. DJN was supported by an Australian Research Fellowship (ARC grant DP-0773794). We thank Nancy Briggs for helpful comments, and J. Paul Minda for providing data.

References

Aldous, D. (1985). Exchangeability and related topics. In *École d'ètè de probabilitès de Saint-Flour, XIII—1983* (pp. 1–198). Berlin: Springer.

Anderson, J. R. (1990). *The adaptive character of thought*. Hillsdale, NJ: Erlbaum.

Anderson, J. R. (1991). The adaptive nature of human categorization. *Psychological Review*, **98**(3), 409–429.

Antoniak, C. (1974). Mixtures of Dirichlet processes with applications to Bayesian nonparametric problems. *The Annals of Statistics*, **2**, 1152–1174.

Ashby, F. G., & Alfonso-Reese, L. A. (1995). Categorization as probability density estimation. *Journal of Mathematical Psychology*, **39**, 216–233.

Blackwell, D., & MacQueen, J. (1973). Ferguson distributions via Polya urn schemes. *The Annals of Statistics*, **1**, 353–355.

Briscoe, E., & Feldman, J. (2006). Conceptual complexity and the bias-variance tradeoff. In *Proceedings of the 28th Annual Conference of the Cognitive Science Society*. Mahwah, NJ: Erlbaum.

Bruner, J. S., Goodnow, J. J., & Austin, G. A. (1956). *A study of thinking*. New York, NY: Wiley.

Chater, N., & Oaksford, M. (1999). Ten years of the rational analysis of cognition. *Trends in Cognitive Science*, **3**, 57–65.

Doucet, A., Freitas, N. de, & Gordon, N. (2001). *Sequential Monte Carlo methods in practice*. New York: Springer.

Escobar, M. D., & West, M. (1995). Bayesian density estimation and inference using mixtures. *Journal of the American Statistical Association*, **90**, 577–588.

Ferguson, T. (1973). A Bayesian analysis of some nonparametric problems. *The Annals of Statistics*, **1**, 209–230.

Ferguson, T. S. (1983). Bayesian density estimation by mixtures of normal distributions. In M. Rizvi, J. Rustagi, & D. Siegmund (Eds.), *Recent advances in statistics* (pp. 287–302). New York: Academic Press.

Gilks, W., Richardson, S., & Spiegelhalter, D. J. (Eds.). (1996). *Markov chain Monte Carlo in practice*. Suffolk, UK: Chapman and Hall.

Griffiths, T. L., Canini, K. R., Sanborn, A. N., & Navarro, D. J. (2007) Unifying rational models of categorization via the hierarchical Dirichlet process. *Proceedings of the Twenty-Ninth Annual Conference of the Cognitive Science Society*. Mahwah, NJ: Erlbaum.

Griffiths, T. L., & Tenenbaum, J. B. (2005). Structure and strength in causal induction. *Cognitive Psychology*, **51**, 354–384.

Kruschke, J. K. (1990). *A connectionist model of category learning*. Unpublished doctoral dissertation, University of California, Berkeley, Berkeley, CA.

Love, B. C., Medin, D. L., & Gureckis, T. M. (2004). SUSTAIN: A network model of category learning. *Psychological Review*, **111**, 309–332.

Luce, R. D. (1959). *Individual choice behavior*. New York: John Wiley.

Marr, D. (1982). *Vision*. San Francisco, CA: W. H. Freeman.

Medin, D. L., & Schaffer, M. M. (1978). Context theory of classification learning. *Psychological Review*, **85**, 207–238.

Navarro, D. J., Griffiths, T. L., Steyvers, M., & Lee, M. D. (2006). Modeling individual differences using Dirichlet processes. *Journal of Mathematical Psychology*, **50**, 101–122.

Neal, R. M. (1998). *Markov chain sampling methods for Dirichlet process mixture models* (Tech. Rep. No. 9815). Department of Statistics, University of Toronto.

Nosofsky, R. M. (1986). Attention, similarity, and the identification-categorization relationship. *Journal of Experimental Psychology: General*, **115**, 39–57.

Nosofsky, R. M. (1991). Relation between the rational model and the context model of categorization. *Psychological Science*, **2**, 416–421.

Nosofsky, R. M. (1998). Optimal performance and exemplar models of classification. In M. Oaksford & N. Chater (Eds.), *Rational models of cognition* (pp. 218–247). Oxford: Oxford University Press.

Nosofsky, R. M., Gluck, M., Palmeri, T. J., McKinley, S. C., & Glauthier, P. (1994). Comparing models of rule-based classification learning: A replication and extension of Shepard, Hovland, and Jenkins (1961). *Memory & Cognition*, **22**, 352–369.

Oaksford, M., & Chater, N. (1994). A rational analysis of the selection task as optimal data selection. *Psychological Review*, **101**, 608–631.

Oaksford, M., & Chater, N. (Eds.). (1998). *Rational models of cognition*. Oxford: Oxford University Press.

Pitman, J. (2002). *Combinatorial stochastic processes*. (Notes for Saint Flour Summer School)

Rasmussen, C. (2000). The infinite Gaussian mixture model. In *Advances in Neural Information Processing Systems* **12**. Cambridge, MA: MIT Press.

Reed, S. K. (1972). Pattern recognition and categorization. *Cognitive Psychology*, **3**, 393–407.

Rice, J. A. (1995). *Mathematical statistics and data analysis* (2nd ed.). Belmont, CA: Duxbury.

Rosch, E. (1978). Principles of categorization. In E. Rosch & B. Lloyd (Eds.), *Cognition and categorization* (pp. 27–48). Hillsdale, New Jersey: Erlbaum.

Rosseel, Y. (2002). Mixture models of categorization. *Journal of Mathematical Psychology*, **46**, 178–210.

Sanborn, A. N., Griffiths, T. L., & Navarro, D. J. (2006). A more rational model of categorization. In *Proceedings of the 28th Annual Conference of the Cognitive Science Society*. Mahwah, NJ: Erlbaum.

Sethuraman, J. (1994). A constructive definition of Dirichlet priors. *Statistica Sinica*, **4**, 639–650.

Shepard, R. N. (1987). Towards a universal law of generalization for psychological science. *Science*, **237**, 1317–1323.

Shiffrin, R. M., & Steyvers, M. (1997). A model for recognition memory: REM: Retrieving Effectively from Memory. *Psychonomic Bulletin & Review*, **4**, 145–166.

Silverman, B. W. (1986). *Density estimation*. London: Chapman and Hall.

Smith, J. D., & Minda, J. P. (1998). Prototypes in the mist: The early epochs of category learning. *Journal of Experimental Psychology: Learning, Memory, and Cognition*, **24**, 1411–1436.

Teh, Y., Jordan, M., Beal, M., & Blei, D. (2004). Hierarchical Dirichlet processes. In *Advances in Neural Information Processing Systems 17*. Cambridge, MA: MIT Press.

Tenenbaum, J. B., & Griffiths, T. L. (2001). Generalization, similarity, and Bayesian inference. *Behavioral and Brain Sciences*, **24**, 629–641.

Vanpaemel, W., Storms, G., & Ons, B. (2005). A varying abstraction model for categorization. In *Proceedings of the 27th Annual Conference of the Cognitive Science Society*. Mahwah, NJ: Erlbaum.

Chapter 15

Rational analysis as a link between human memory and information retrieval

Mark Steyvers
University of California, Irvine, CA, USA
Thomas L. Griffiths
University of California, Berkeley, CA, USA

Rational analysis as a link between human memory and information retrieval

Rational analysis has been successful in explaining a variety of different aspects of human cognition (Anderson, 1990; Chater & Oaksford, 1999; Marr, 1982; Oaksford & Chater, 1998). The explanations provided by rational analysis have two properties: they emphasize the connection between behavior and the structure of the environment, and they focus on the abstract computational problems being solved. These properties provide the opportunity to recognize connections between human cognition and other systems that solve the same computational problems, with the potential both to provide new insights into human cognition and to allow us to develop better systems for solving those problems. In particular, we should expect to find a correspondence between human cognition and systems that are successful at solving the same computational problems in a similar environment. In this chapter, we argue that such a correspondence exists between human memory and internet search, and show that this correspondence leads to both better models of human cognition, and better methods for searching the web.

Anderson (1990) and Anderson and Schooler (1991, 2000) have shown that many findings in the memory literature related to recognition and recall of lists of words can be understood by considering the computational problem of assessing the relevance of an item in memory to environmental cues. They showed a close correspondence between memory retrieval for lists of words and statistical patterns of occurrence of words in large databases of text. Similarly, other computational models for memory (Shiffrin & Steyvers, 1997), association (Griffiths *et al.*, 2007), reasoning (Oaksford & Chater, 1994), prediction (Griffiths & Tenenbaum, 2006) and causal induction (Anderson, 1990; Griffiths & Tenenbaum, 2005; Steyvers *et al.*, 2003) have shown how our cognitive system is remarkably well adapted to our environment.

Anderson's (1990) analysis of memory also showed for the first time that there are fundamental connections between research on memory and information retrieval systems. Because information retrieval systems and human memory often address similar computational problems, insights gained from information retrieval systems can be helpful in understanding human memory. For example, one component of Anderson's first rational memory model involved calculating the predictive probability that items will re-occur given their historical pattern of occurrences. The solution to this problem was based on information retrieval models developed for library and file systems (Burrell, 1980; Salton & McGill, 1983). Just as it is useful to know the probability that a book will be needed in order to make it available in short-term or off-site storage, it is useful to know whether a fact is likely to be needed in the future when storing it in memory.

Modern information retrieval research provides new tools for modeling the environment in which human memory operates, and new systems to which human memory can be compared. An important innovation has been the introduction of *statistical language models* to capture the statistics of the regularities that occur in natural language (e.g., Croft & Lafferty, 2003; Ponte & Croft, 1998). The goal of language modeling is to exploit these regularities in developing effective systems to assess the relevance of documents to queries. Probabilistic topic models (e.g., Blei *et al.*, 2003; Griffiths & Steyvers, 2004; Griffiths *et al.*, 2007; Hoffman, 1999; Steyvers & Griffiths, 2006; Steyvers *et al.*, 2006) are a class of statistical language models that automatically infer a set of topics from a large collection of documents. These models allow each document to be expressed as a mixture of topics, approximating the semantic themes present in those documents. Such topic models can improve information retrieval by matching queries to documents at a semantic level (Blei *et al.*, 2003; Chemudugunta *et al.*, 2007; Hoffman, 1999). Another important problem in information retrieval is dealing with the enormous volume of data available on the world wide web. For any query, there might be a very large number of relevant web pages and the task of modern search engines is to design effective algorithms for ranking the importance of webpages. A major innovation has been the PageRank algorithm, which is part of the Google search engine (Brin & Page, 1998). This algorithm ranks web pages by computing their relative importance from the links between pages.

In this chapter, we use these innovations in information retrieval as a way to explore the connections between research on human memory and information retrieval systems. We show how PageRank can be used to predict performance in a fluency task, where participants name the first word that comes to mind in response to a letter cue. We also give an example of how cognitive research can help information retrieval research by formalizing theories of knowledge and memory organization that have been proposed by cognitive psychologists. We show how a memory model that distinguishes between the representation of gist and verbatim information can not only explain some findings in the memory literature but also helps in formulating new language models to support accurate information retrieval.

A probabilistic approach to information retrieval

Search engines and human memory are both solutions to challenging retrieval problems. For a search engine, the retrieval problem is finding the set of documents that are most relevant to a user query. In human memory, the retrieval problem can be construed in terms of assessing the relevance of items stored in the mind to a memory probe (either internally generated or based on environmental cues). The common structure of these problems suggests a simple analogy between human memory and computer-based information retrieval: items stored in memory are analogous to documents available in a database of text (such as the world-wide web) and the memory probe is analogous to a user query. In this section, we explore how retrieval problems of this kind can be solved using statistical inference, following Anderson (1990).

Using notation appropriate to information retrieval, the problem is to assess $P(d_i|q)$, the probability that a document d_i is relevant given a query q. The query can be a (new) set of words produced by a user or it can be an existing document from the collection. In the latter case, the task is to find documents similar to the given document. In the context of memory retrieval, the term q corresponds to the memory probe and $P(d_i|q)$ is the conditional probability that item d_i in memory is relevant to the memory probe. Let us assume that there are D documents in the database and the goal is to retrieve some set of the most relevant documents as assessed by $P(d_i|q)$. This probability can be computed using Bayes' rule, with

$$P(d_i|q) \propto P(q|d_i)P(d_i) \tag{1}$$

where $P(d_i)$ gives the prior probability that an item will be relevant (before any query or cue is issued), and $P(q|d_i)$ is the probability of observing the query if we assume that item d_i was the item that was needed, also known as the 'likelihood.'

The prior probability, $P(d_i)$, can be used to capture the idea that not all items are equally important, with some items being more likely to be the target of retrieval. In search engines, this prior probability is often computed from the link structure between documents. For example, the PageRank algorithm assumes that if a document is linked to by many other important documents, then it is likely to be important. The importance of a document, also known as its PageRank, can be conceptualized as the prior probability of a document being relevant to any particular query. We will return to this idea in the next section when discussing the PageRank algorithm and its application to memory retrieval. In the rational memory model (Anderson, 1990; Anderson & Schooler, 1991, 2000), the prior probability of an item in memory being important was computed from its historical usage pattern, under the assumption that if items were recently accessed, they are likely to be accessed again. Anderson showed that this 'history' factor can explain the effects of spacing and repetition of items on retention.

The likelihood, $P(q|d_i)$, reflects how well a particular document matches a search query or cue. In the context of information retrieval, this can be evaluated using a *generative model* that specifies how the words in the query can be generated from a statistical language model that is derived separately for each document d_i. For example, probabilistic topic models (Blei *et al.* 2003; Griffiths & Steyvers, 2004; Griffiths *et al.*, 2007;

Hoffman, 1999; Steyvers & Griffiths, 2006; Steyvers *et al.*, 2006) assume that each document can be described by a mixture of topics where the topics are derived from an analysis of word occurrences in a large database of text—relevant documents have topic distributions that are likely to have generated the set of words associated with the query. We will return to this idea in a later section. In the rational memory model (Anderson, 1990; Anderson & Schooler, 1991, 2000), this likelihood term was referred to as the 'context' factor, where the context represented the information available at test to probe memory. This factor was evaluated using a simple generative model for the properties of items stored in memory.

Equation (1) forms part of a simple schema for solving retrieval problems: compute the posterior probability that each item is relevant, combining its prior probability of being relevant with a likelihood reflecting its relationship to the query or cue, and then return the items with highest posterior probability. This schema can be used to solve the retrieval problems faced both by internet search engines and by human memory, suggesting that it may be possible to find parallels between the two. We explore this possibility in the next two sections, focusing on the role of the prior in the first, and then turning to the likelihood in the second.

Google and the mind: predicting fluency with PageRank

Many search engines produce a response to a query in two stages, first identifying the set of webpages that contain the words in the query, and then ordering those pages according to the pre-computed output of a ranking algorithm. These two stages can be mapped onto the two parts of the right hand side of (1). The first stage corresponds to an assumption that the likelihood, $P(q|d_i)$, has some constant value for any page containing the query and is zero otherwise. This guarantees that only pages containing the query will have non-zero posterior probabilities, and means that the posterior probability of each page containing the query is directly proportional to its prior probability. The second stage, ordering the pages, thus reveals the prior probability assigned to each page: if the solution to the retrieval problem is to return the pages with highest posterior probability, and the posterior probability of the candidate pages is proportional to their prior probability, then a ranking algorithm implicitly assigns a prior probability to each page.

The correspondence between ranking algorithms and priors means that the prior probability that a webpage will be relevant to a user plays a central role in internet search. This raises a simple question: how should such prior probabilities be computed? While the details of the ranking algorithms used by commercial search engines are proprietary, the basic principles behind the PageRank algorithm used in the Google search engine have been published (Brin & Page, 1998). The algorithm makes use of two key ideas: first, that links between webpages provide information about their importance (and hence their probability of being the webpage that a user might seek), and second, that the relationship between importance and linking is recursive.

In addition to carrying information about different topics, webpages contain sets of links connecting them to other pages, as shown in Fig. 15.1(a). Given an ordered set of n pages, we can summarize the links between them with a $n \times n$ matrix L, where L_{ij}

(a) World wide web   (b) Semantic network

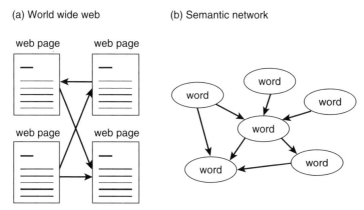

Fig. 15.1. (a) A set of webpages form a directed graph, where the nodes are pages and the edges are links. (b) Words in a semantic network also form a directed graph where the edges represent associative connections between words.

indicates that a link exists from webpage j to webpage i (the adjacency matrix of the underlying graph). This matrix provides a way to define the importance of a webpage. If we assume that links are chosen in such a way that higher importance pages receive more links, then the number of links that a webpage receives (in graph-theoretic terms, its 'in-degree') could be used as a simple index of its importance. Using the n-dimensional vector $\mathbf{p}$ to summarize the importance of our n webpages, this is the assumption that $p_i = \sum_{j=1..n} L_{ij}$.

PageRank goes beyond this simple measure of the importance of a webpage by observing that a link from a highly important webpage should be a better indicator of importance than a link from a webpage with little importance. Under such a view, a highly important webpage is a webpage that receives many links from other highly important webpages. We might thus imagine importance as flowing along the links of the graph shown in Fig. 15.1(a). If we assume that each webpage distributes its importance uniformly over its outgoing links, then we can express the proportion of the importance of each webpage traveling along each link using a matrix $\mathbf{M}$, where $M_{ij} = L_{ij} / \sum_{k=1..n} L_{kj}$. The idea that highly important webpages receive links from highly important webpages implies a recursive definition of importance, and the notion of importance being divided uniformly over outgoing links gives the equation

$$\mathbf{p} = \mathbf{Mp} \qquad (2)$$

which identifies $\mathbf{p}$ as the eigenvector of the matrix $\mathbf{M}$ with the greatest eigenvalue. The PageRank algorithm computes the importance of webpages by finding a vector $\mathbf{p}$ that satisfies this equation (ignoring a slight modification to take into account the possibility that a sequence of webpages forms a closed loop).

While the recursive definition of PageRank makes clear its assumptions about how linking affects importance, some intuitions about the factors influencing the PageRank of a page can be gained by considering an alternative route to the same formal result

(Brin & Page, 1998). We can define a random walk on the world wide web by assuming that a user starts at a randomly chosen web page, and then keeps clicking on links chosen uniformly at random from the set of links on the page reached after every click. This random walk is a Markov chain, and standard results in the mathematical theory of Markov chains indicate that, in the long run, the probability that this user lands on a particular webpage will be proportional to its PageRank.

Applying PageRank to semantic networks

The idea that that the pieces of information that are the targets of retrieval are connected to one another is not exclusive to web pages—it also appears in cognitive psychology. In an associative semantic network, such as that shown in Fig. 15.1(b), a set of words or concepts are represented as nodes connected by edges that indicate pairwise associations (e.g., Collins & Loftus, 1975). If we take this to be the representation of the knowledge on which retrieval processes operate, human memory and search engines thus address a similar computational problem: identifying the items relevant to a query from a large network of interconnected pieces of information. The empirical success of the Google search engine indicates that PageRank constitutes an effective solution to this problem. This raises the tantalizing possibility that the link structure of semantic networks might provide a guide to the relative importance of pieces of information, or, equivalently, an estimate of the prior probability with which a particular word or concept might be needed. In particular, it suggests that by computing the PageRank of the nodes in a semantic network, we might be able to predict the prominence of the corresponding words and concepts in memory.

In order to explore the possibility of a correspondence between PageRank and human memory, we constructed a task that was designed to closely parallel the formal structure of internet search (Griffiths *et al.* in press). Specifically, we wanted a task in which people had to produce items from memory that matched some query, with the hope that in doing so their responses would reflect the prior probability assigned to each item being needed. To this end, we showed participants a letter of the alphabet (the query) and asked them to say the first word that came into their head that begins with that letter (the relevant items). In the literature on human memory, such a task is used to measure fluency—the ease with which people retrieve different facts from memory, which can useful to diagnose neuropsychological and psychiatric disorders (e.g., Lezak, 1995). Each subject in the experiment gave fluency responses for 21 letters of the alphabet (excluding low frequency letters). The results were pooled across fifty subjects and responses that were given by only a single subject were excluded. Table 1 shows a sample of responses given for the letter 'd.'

Our goal was to determine whether people's responses could be predicted by PageRank computed from a semantic network constructed from word association norms collected by Nelson *et al.* (1998). These norms were collected by asking participants to name the first word that came into their head when presented with a cue in the form of another word. The norms list the associates that people produced for 5,018 words, and were collected in such a way that each word named at least twice as an associate also appears as a cue. From these norms, we constructed a directed graph in which each word was represented as a node, and an edge was introduced from each word to its associates. We then applied the PageRank algorithm to this graph.

In order to evaluate the performance of PageRank, we used several alternative predictors as controls. In one control, we compared the performance of PageRank to more conventional frequency-based measures, based on the Kucera–Francis (KF) word frequency (Kucera & Francis, 1967). Word frequency is widely used as a proxy for fluency in word recognition studies (e.g., Balota & Spieler, 1999; Plaut, *et al.*, 1996; Seidenberg & McClelland, 1989; see also Adelman *et al.*, 2006) and to set the prior probability of items in rational models of memory (Anderson, 1990). Another control was a semantic network measure that was not based on a recursive definition of importance: the in-degree of each node in the semantic network. This is the frequency with which the word was named as a response in the word association norms. The in-degree of nodes in an associative semantic network has previously been used as a predictor in a number of episodic memory studies (McEvoy *et al.*, 1999; Nelson *et al.*, 2005). In-degree differs from PageRank only in the assumption that all incoming links should be given equal weight when evaluating the importance of an item, rather than being assigned weights based on the importance of the items from which they originate.

For each letter of the alphabet, we identified all words contained in the norms that began with that letter, and then ordered the words by each of the three predictors, assigning a rank of 1 to the highest-scoring word and increasing rank as the predictor decreased. A sample of the rankings for the letter 'd' produced by PageRank, KF frequency, and in-degree is shown in Table 15.1. To compare performance of these three

Table 15.1. Most frequent responses in the fluency task for the letter 'd' and the rankings given by PageRank, In-degree, and KF frequency.

Human responses		PageRank		In-degree		KF Frequency	
DOG	(19)	DOG	(19)	DOG	(19)	DO	(2)
DAD	(16)	DARK	(3)	DEATH	(1)	DOWN	(4)
DOOR	(5)	DRINK	(1)	DRINK	(1)	DAY	(2)
DOWN	(4)	DOWN	(4)	DIRTY	(0)	DEVELOPMENT	(0)
DARK	(3)	DEATH	(1)	DARK	(3)	DONE	(1)
DUMB	(3)	DOOR	(5)	DOWN	(4)	DIFFERENT	(0)
DAY	(2)	DAY	(2)	DIRT	(0)	DOOR	(5)
DEVIL	(2)	DIRTY	(0)	DEAD	(0)	DEATH	(1)
DINOSAUR	(2)	DIRTY	(0)	DANCE	(0)	DEPARTMENT	(0)
DO	(2)	DEAD	(0)	DANGER	(1)	DARK	(3)

Note: The numbers between parentheses are frequencies in human responses. All responses are restricted to the words in the word association norms by Nelson *et al.* (1998).

predictors, we compared the median ranks. The median rank assigned by PageRank was 13, as compared to 17 for in-degree and 43 for word frequency, reflecting a statistically significant improvement in predictive performance for PageRank over the controls.

The results of this experiment indicate that PageRank, computed from a semantic network, is a good predictor of human responses in a fluency task. These results suggest that the PageRank of a word could be used in the place of more conventional frequency-based measures when designing or modeling memory experiments, and support our argument that the shared problem faced by human memory and internet search engines might result in similar solutions. One way to explain the advantage of PageRank might be to return to the idea of random walks on a graph. As mentioned above, a random internet surfer will select webpages with probabilities proportional to their PageRank. For semantic networks, the PageRank of a word is proportional to the probability of selecting that word if participants started at a random word in the semantic network and proceeded to search their memories by following associative links until they found a word that matched the query (see Griffiths *et al.*, in press, for details).

The fluency task focused on one important component in retrieval, the prominence of different words in human memory, as should be reflected in the prior $P(d_i)$. By using a letter matching task, for which the word response can either be true or false, we purposefully minimized the influence of the $P(q|d_i)$ likelihood term in (1). However, in more typical retrieval tasks, queries can relate in many ways to items stored in memory. In addition to the *form-based* matching that was emphasized in the letter-matching task, many retrieval tasks require *content-based* matching where the query and items in memory are matched at a conceptual level. In the next section, we consider the computational problem of assessing $P(q|d_i)$ using both form-based and content-based matching strategies.

Topic models to extract verbatim and gist information

In both memory and information retrieval research, one of the main problems is to specify how relevant information can be retrieved in the context of a user query or environmental cues. Memory researchers have proposed that the memory system assesses relevance at two levels of generality: verbatim and gist (Brainerd *et al.*, 1999; Brainerd *et al.*, 2002; Mandler, 1980). The gist-level representation is based on a high-level semantic abstraction of the item to be stored, whether it is a sentence, conversation or document. This gist level information can be used to disambiguate words or retrieve semantically relevant concepts during reading (Ericsson & Kintsch, 1995; Kintsch, 1988; Potter, 1993). At the verbatim level, information is stored and retrieved relatively closely to the raw physical form in which it was received and might include the specific choice of words and physical characteristics related to font and voice information. While it is probably an oversimplification to propose that the memory system utilizes only two levels of abstraction to encode and retrieve information, the distinction between gist and verbatim information has been useful to understand, at least at a conceptual level, a variety of findings in memory and language research. However, these models leave open the question of exactly how verbatim and gist level information is encoded in memory.

In information retrieval, the relevance of a query to documents can be assessed using a variety of techniques that focus on different levels of abstraction of the information contained in the document and query. The simplest keyword matching strategies do not attempt any abstraction and focus on the exact word matches between documents and queries. A widely used keyword-matching retrieval technique is based is on the term-frequency, inverse-document-frequency (TF-IDF) method (Salton & McGill, 1983). The relevance of a document is related to the number of exact word matches and inversely weighted by the number of times the query terms appear in documents across the database. One problem of this technique is that it can be overly specific. It can give low relevance scores to documents that contain words semantically related to the query. To improve the generalization in retrieval, dimensionality-reduction techniques have been developed to extract a lower-dimensional description for documents that utilizes the statistical regularities of words in natural language. This has led to techniques such as Latent Semantic Indexing (LSI; Deerwester *et al.*, 1990; Landauer & Dumais, 1997), and probabilistic analogues such as Probabilistic Latent Semantic Indexing (PLSI; Hoffman, 1999) and Latent Dirichlet Allocation (LDA; Blei *et al.*, 2003; Griffiths & Steyvers, 2004). The idea is that queries and documents can be matched in the lower-dimensional space, which often leads to higher-level semantic matches. However, in come cases these dimensionality-reduction techniques lead to *over-generalization*. Because the matching of query and document takes place entirely in the lower-dimensional 'semantic' space, all details about the individual words in query and documents are lost in this comparison. It is possible, however, that some of the individual words in the query or document were essential to assess relevance.

The difficult issue of deciding on an appropriate level of generalization to assess relevance forms an important parallel between problems studied by memory and information retrieval researchers. In the context of human memory, should information in memory be relevant only when it exactly matches the environmental cues (using verbatim information) or should the retrieval process allow some generalization in the retrieval process (using gist)? Similarly, in information retrieval, should the relevance of documents to queries be assessed more on the level of exact matches (e.g., keyword matching strategies) or should there be some attempt to extract a more general representation of documents and queries to allow for conceptual level matches?

In this section, we consider the computational problem of balancing the trade-off between specificity and generality. We will start with a description of probabilistic topic models that focus on extracting only gist-based descriptions for each document using low-dimensional semantic representations. We then introduce an extension of these models, the dual-route topic model that augments these gist-based representations with document specific representations based on specific keyword occurrences in documents. We illustrate how this model can be used to explain several findings in the memory literature such as false memory and semantic isolation effects. We will also show how this model leads to improved performance in information retrieval.

Topic models

Topic models such as PLSI and LDA are based upon the idea that documents are mixtures of topics, where a topic is a probability distribution over words. A topic model is a *generative model* for documents: it specifies a simple probabilistic procedure by which documents can be generated. In a standard topic model, to make a new document, one chooses a distribution over topics. Then, for each word in that document, one chooses a topic at random according to this distribution, and draws a word from that topic. To introduce notation, we will write $P(z|d)$ for the multinomial distribution over topics given document d, and $P(w|z = t)$ for the multinomial distribution over words w given a specific topic t. In a standard topic model, the distribution of words in document d can be decomposed as a finite mixture over T topics as follows:

$$P(w \mid d) = \sum_{t=1}^{T} P(w \mid z = t)P(z = t \mid d) \tag{3}$$

In this model, the $P(w|z = t)$ term indicates which words are important for topic t and $P(z = t|d)$ gives the importance of a particular topic in document d, which can be used as a representation of the content or gist of that document. In the LDA model, these multinomial distributions have associated priors, chosen to be Dirichlet distributions. The hyperparameters of the Dirichlet distributions indicate which kinds of multinomial distributions are likely, and control the degree of smoothing of the word counts in topics and topic counts in documents.

Given the observed words in a set of documents in a large corpus, we would like to know what set of topics is most likely to have generated the data. This involves inferring the probability distribution over words associated with each topic, $P(w|z)$, and the distribution over topics for each document, $P(z|d)$. Several statistical inference techniques have been developed to infer these distributions from large text corpora. The simulations discussed in this chapter utilized an efficient Gibbs sampling technique based on Markov chain Monte Carlo (Griffiths & Steyvers, 2004). We will not discuss the details of this procedure but we refer the interested reader to an introductory treatment by Steyvers and Griffiths (2006).

As an example of the topics that can be extracted with the topic model, we applied the topic model with $T = 1,500$ topics to the TASA corpus, a collection of over 37,000 text passages from educational materials (e.g., language & arts, social studies, health, sciences) collected by Touchstone Applied Science Associates (see Landauer *et al.*, 1998). Several topic-word distributions $P(w|z = t)$ are illustrated in Fig. 15.2. The figure shows the nine words that have the highest probability under each topic. The particular topics shown in the figure relate to various themes in agriculture and biology.

In the standard topic model, each document is described by a distribution over topics which represent the gist of a document but information about particular words is lost. For example, suppose we need to encode the following list (i.e., document) of words: PEAS, CARROTS, BEANS, SPINACH, LETTUCE, TOMATOES, CORN, CABBAGE, and SQUASH. If we encode this list as a distribution over 1,500 topics, only a few topics would receive high probability. For example, one possible distribution for this list

Topic 32	Topic 41	Topic 543	Topic 816	Topic 1321	Topic 1253
VEGETABLES	TOOLS	FARMERS	MEAT	NUTRIENTS	PLANTS
FRUITS	TOOL	CROPS	BEEF	ENERGY	PLANT
POTATOES	CUTTING	FARMING	EAT	FATS	LEAVES
FRUIT	HAND	FARMS	COOKED	VITAMINS	SEEDS
POTATO	CUT	FARM	PORK	CARBOHYDRATES	SOIL
TOMATOES	DRILL	LAND	MEAL	FOOD	ROOTS
FRESH	CHISEL	CROP	SAUCE	VITAMIN	FLOWERS
ORANGES	CARPENTER	AGRICULTURE	BREAD	MINERALS	WATER
ORANGE	METAL	GROW	COOKING	NEED	FOOD

Fig. 15.2. Example topic distributions extracted from the TASA corpus using a topic model with 1,500 topics. For each topic, the nine most likely words are shown in order of probability.

would be to give probability 0.77, 0.17, and 0.06 to topics 32, 543, and 1,253, respectively, and zero probability to all other topics. This encoding would capture the idea that the list of words contained semantic themes related to *vegetables* and *farming*. However, this encoding would not allow accurate reconstruction of the specific words that were presented. If we use (3) to reconstruct the list with these topic weights, words that were not presented on the list, such as VEGETABLES and POTATO might receive relatively higher probability. While it is a desirable feature of the model to generalize beyond the specific words on a list, what is needed is a model-based encoding that tempers this generalization with a representation for the specific words present on the list.

Dual route topic models

We developed the *dual-route topic model* to capture both the specific and general aspects of documents. This model is an extension of the LDA model that allows words in documents to be modeled as either originating from general topics, or from a distribution over words that is specific for that document. We will refer to this distribution as the *special word* distribution. An important assumption in the model is that each word originates from a single route only, but there can be uncertainty about the route allocation. Each word token in a document has an associated random variable x, taking value $x = 0$ if the word w is generated via the topic route, and value $x = 1$ if the word is generated as a special-word route. The variable x acts as a switch. If $x = 0$, the standard topic mechanism is used to generate the word: a topic is sampled from the topic distribution associated with the document and a word is sampled from the topic. On the other hand, if $x = 1$, words are sampled from the special-word distribution specific to the document. We model this as multinomial with a symmetric Dirichlet prior. The switch variable x is sampled from a document-specific Bernoulli variable λ with a symmetric Beta prior. The random variable λ determines the proportion of words associated with the special word and topic route within a document. The model specifies the following probability distribution over words in a document:

$$P(w \mid d) = P(x = 0 \mid d)\sum_{t=1}^{T} P(w \mid z = t)P(z = t \mid d) + P(x = 1 \mid d)P'(w \mid d) \quad (4)$$

where $P'(w|d)$ is the special word distribution associated with document d. Note that the model explains word occurrences as a mixture of two routes, the topic model route weighted by $P(x = 0|d)$ and the special word route weighted by $P(x = 1|d)$. If $P(x = 1|d) = 0$, the model is identical to the LDA model in (3). On the other hand, if $P(x = 1|d) = 1$, the model is identical to a unigram word model. By mixing these two components, the model allows a flexible balance between modeling general and specific aspects of documents. The latent variables in the model include the terms $P(z|d)$ and $P(w|z)$ associated with the topic model and new terms $P(x|d)$ and $P'(w|d)$. As with standard topic models, Gibbs sampling can be used to infer these distributions (see Chemudugunta et al., 2007, for details).

Explaining semantic isolation effects

The distinction between verbatim and gist level information can be useful to understand a number of findings in the memory literature, such as the semantic isolation effect. This effect is related to the classic finding by Von Restorff (1933) that information that stands out from the context is better remembered. Von Restorff effects can be based on physical or semantic characteristics, by presenting a word on a list in a unique color or font or drawing a word from a novel semantic category. Semantic isolation effects occur when words that semantically stand out from the list are better remembered.

Early explanations of the isolation effect focused on the role of attention (Jenkins, 1948) and surprise (Green, 1956). In this account, the unexpected isolated word leads to an increase in attention which enhances the encoding of the item. However, studies have shown that the isolate is not (always) rehearsed or attended more (e.g. Dunlosky et al., 2000). Also, this account cannot explain the continued presence of isolate effects even when the isolate is presented as the first word in the list. In this case, no expectations about the list contents can have been built up yet when processing the first item. An alternative account focuses on the role of memory organization with the idea that the isolate is encoded in qualitatively different ways compared to the background items (Bruce & Gaines, 1976; Fabiani & Donchin, 1995). The dual route memory model allows a computational account for the semantic isolation consistent with this proposal. In the model, the memory system utilizes qualitatively different encoding resources to encode isolate and background items. The topic route stores the gist of the list and the special-words route stores specific words such as the isolate word.

To illustrate the dual-route topic approach, we applied the model to experimental data gathered by Hunt and Lamb (2001). They compared recall performance for two lists of words, illustrated in Fig. 15.3(a). The outlier lists consisted of nine words from one category (e.g., *vegetables*) and one target word (e.g., HAMMER) from another category, whereas the control list embedded the target word in a background context that is semantically consistent. As shown in Fig. 15.3(b), Hunt and Lamb found that recall for the target word is much higher in the isolate condition, illustrating the semantic isolation effect. The finding that the target item is recalled about as well as the background items in the control list shows that this isolation effect needs to be explained by the difference in context, and not by particular item characteristics (e.g., orthography or word frequency).

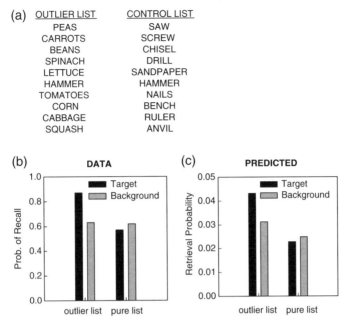

Fig. 15.3. (a) Two example lists used in semantic isolation experiments by Hunt and Lamb (2001). The outlier list has one target word (HAMMER), which is semantically isolated from the background. The control list uses the same target word in a semantically congruous background. (b) Data from Experiment 1 of Hunt and Lamb (2001) showing the semantic isolation effect (c). The predictions of the dual-route topic model.

We encoded the outlier and control lists with the dual-route topic model. To simplify the simulations, we used the same 1,500 topics illustrated in Fig. 15.2 that were derived by the standard topic model. We therefore inferred the special word distribution and topic and route weights for this list while holding fixed the 1,500 topics. We also made one change to the model. Instead of using a Dirichlet prior for the multinomial of the special-word distribution that has a single hyperparameter for all words, we used a prior with hyperparameter values that were higher for words that are present on the list than for words that were absent (0.001 and 0.0001, respectively). This change forces the model to put more a priori weight on the words that are part of the study list.

Fig. 15.4 shows the model encoding for the isolate list shown in Fig. 15.3(a). The most likely topic is the vegetable topic, with smaller probability going toward the farming and tools topics, reflecting the distribution of semantic themes in the list. The special word distribution gives relatively high probability to the word HAMMER. This happens because the model encodes words either through the topic or special word route and the probability of assigning a word to a route depends on how well each route can explain the occurrence of that word in the context of other list words.

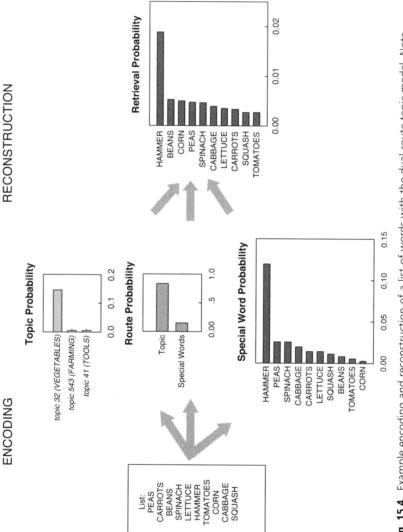

Fig. 15.4. Example encoding and reconstruction of a list of words with the dual-route topic model. Note that the topic distribution is truncated and only shows the top 3 topics. Similarly, the special-word and retrieval distributions only show the top 9 nine words from a vocabulary of 26,000+ words.

Because most of the vegetable-related words can be explained by the topic route, these words will receive lower probability from the special-word route. On the other hand, the word HAMMER, which is semantically isolated from the vegetable words cannot be explained well by the topic route, which makes it more likely to be associated with the special-word route. To simulate recall, (4) can be applied to calculate the posterior predictive probability over the whole vocabulary (26,000+ words) using the model encoding. We will refer to this as the retrieval distribution. The retrieval distribution shown in Figure 4 shows an advantage for the isolate word. This occurs because the special-word distribution concentrates probability on the isolate word, which is preserved in the reconstruction using both routes (the topic route distributes probability over all words semantically related to the list, leading to a more diffuse distribution). Figure 15.3(c) shows the model predictions for the experiment by Hunt and Lamb (2001), which exhibits the same qualitative pattern as the experimental data. Note that the retrieval probability can only be compared qualitatively to the observed recall probability. In order to fully simulate recall, we would have to implement a sampling process with a stopping rule to simulate how human participants typically produce only a subset of words from the list. For reasons of simplicity, we chose not to implement such a sampling process.

Explaining false memory effects

The dual-route topic model can also be used to explain false memory effects (Deese, 1959; McEvoy et al., 1999; Roediger et al., 2001). In a typical experiment that elicits the false memory effect, participants study a list of words that are associatively related to one word, the lure word, that is not presented on the list. At test, participants are instructed to recall only the words from the study list, but falsely recall the lure word with high probability (in some cases the lure word is recalled more often than list words). Results of this kind have led to the development of dual-route memory models where the verbatim level information supports accurate recall whereas the gist level information that is activated by the semantic organization of the list supports the intrusion of the lure word (Brainerd et al., 1999; Brainerd et al., 2002). These models were designed to measure the relative contribution of gist and verbatim information in memory but do not provide a computational account for how the gist and verbatim information is encoded in memory.

To explain how the dual-route topic model accounts for the false memory effect, we applied the model to a recall experiment by Robinson and Roediger (1997). In this experiment, each study list contains a number of words that are associatively related to the lure word, which itself is not presented on the study list. The remaining words were random filler words that did not have any obvious associative structure. In the experiment, the number of associatively related words were varied while keeping the total number of study words constant. Figure 15.5(a) shows some example lists that contain 3, 6, and 9 associates of the word ANGER which itself is not present on the list. Figure 15.5(b) shows the observed recall probabilities for the studied items and the lure word as a function of the number of associates on the list. With an increase in the number of associates, the results show an increase in false recall of the lure word

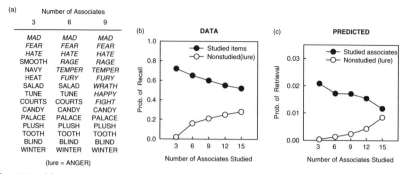

Fig. 15.5. (a) Example study lists varying the number of words associated to the lure ANGER which is not presented on the list. (b) Data from Robinson and Roediger (1997), Experiment 2, showing the observed recall probabilities for studied items and the lure item as a function of the number of associates on the list. (c) Predictions from the dual-route topic model.

and a decrease in veridical recall. We applied the dual-route topic model to this experimental setup and simulated word lists similar to those used by Robinson and Roediger (1997). Figure 15.5(c) shows that model predicts retrieval probabilities that are qualitatively similar to the observed recall probabilities. As the number of associates increases, the model will put increasingly more weight on the topic route, because the topic route can better explain the associative structure when more associates are present. By putting more weight on the topic route, this leads to an increase in generalization beyond the list words, which is associated with an increase in false recall. Similarly, with an increasing weight on the topic route, there is a corresponding decrease in weight for the special-word route. This route is needed to reconstruct the specific words present on a list and as the weight on this route decreases, there is a decrease in veridical recall. Therefore, the model explains these findings in a qualitative fashion by underlying change in the balance between gist and verbatim level information. One advantage of this model over other dual route memory models (e.g., Brainerd *et al.*, 1999; Brainerd *et al.*, 2002) is that the model explains performance at the level of individual words and specifies a representation for gist and verbatim information.

Application to information retrieval

The dual-route topic model can be applied to documents to probabilistically decompose words into contextually unique and gist related words. Such as decomposition can be useful for information retrieval because it allows queries to be matched to documents at two levels of generality: specific information captured by the special-word route and content related information captured by the topic model. To illustrate how the model operates on documents, we applied the model with $T = 100$ topics to a set of 1281 abstracts from *Psychological Review*, and separately to a set of 3,104 articles from the *New York Times*. Figure 15.6 shows fragments of two example documents

Psychological Review abstract	New York Times article
alcove attention learning covering map is a connectionist model of category learning that incorporates an exemplar based represen- tation d . l . medin and m . m . schaffer 1978 r . m . nosofsky 1986 with error driven learning m . a . gluck and g . h . bower 1988 d . e . rumelhart *et al* 1986 . alcove selectively attends to relevant stimulus dimensions is sensitive to correlated dimensions can account for a form of base rate neglect does not suffer catastrophic forgetting and can exhibit 3 stage u shaped learning of high frequency exceptions to rules whereas such effects are not easily accounted for by models using other combinations of repre- sentation and learning method.	south korea took a big step today toward opening up its state run power generation industry to foreign investors the state owned korea electric power corporation or kepco the only company in the nation involved in power generation said it would spin off six independent companies in november the company s first concrete move toward privatization in its 38 year history later this month the government will offer the six companies for sale to both foreign and domestic buyers kepco will allot 42 power generation facilities either currently in oper- ation or under construction to five hydro and thermoelectric power companies lee hyung chul director of restructuring at the utility said nuclear power plants will be separated into a

Fig. 15.6. Finding contextually unique words in two example documents. The back- ground shading indicates the probability that a word is assigned to the special-word route.

that were encoded with the dual-route topic model. The background color of words indicates the probability of assigning words to the special words topic—darker colors are associated with higher probability that a word was assigned to the special topic. The words with gray foreground colors were treated as stopwords and were not included in the analysis. The model generally treats contextually unique words as special words. This includes names of people (e.g., NOSOFSKY, SCHAFFER in the psych review abstract) and low frequency words (e.g., THERMOELECTRIC in the New York Times article).

Chemudugunta, Smyth and Steyvers (2007) reported some initial information retrieval results of the dual-route topic model. They applied the model to a several sets of articles from the TREC corpus, which was developed by the information retrieval community to compare and test methods. For each candidate document, they calculated how likely the query q was when 'generated' from the distributions associated with topics and special words. Under the assumption that the query words are generated independently, the query likelihood can be calculated by:

$$P(q \mid d) = \prod_{w \in q}\left[P(x = 0 \mid d)\sum_{t=1}^{T} P(w \mid z = t)P(z = t \mid d) + P(x = 1 \mid d)P'(w \mid d)\right]$$

(5)

where the product is over all words that are part of the query. The retrieval performance of the model can be assessed by comparing the query likelihoods to human relevance judgments that are part of the TREC database. Chemudugunta *et al.* (2007) showed that the dual-route topic model significantly outperforms a variety of information retrieval methods such as LSI and LDA which focus on content-based matching and TF-IDF which focuses on keyword matching.

The results of this test indicate that the dual-route topic model does not suffer from the weakness of techniques such as LSI and LDA, which are not able to match specific words in queries and therefore might be prone to over-generalization. Similarly, the model does not suffer from the limitations of the TF-IDF approach in terms of its ability to generalize. The results thus suggest that the best information retrieval results can be obtained by a combination of content-based and keyword-based matching techniques, paralleling contemporary accounts of the structure of human memory.

Discussion

In a rational analysis of cognition, the cognitive system is analyzed in terms of the computational demands that arise from the interaction with our environment (Anderson, 1990; Chater & Oaksford, 1999; Marr, 1982; Oaksford & Chater, 1998). We proposed that both human memory and internet search faces similar computational demands. Both systems attempt to retrieve the most relevant items from a large information repository in response to external cues or queries. This suggests not only that there are many useful analogies between human memory and internet search but also that computational approaches developed in one field potentially lead to novel insights in the other.

For example, we have shown how the PageRank algorithm, developed for the Google search engines to rank webpages, can be useful in understanding human retrieval from semantic memory. We showed how PageRank can be used to measure the prominence of words in a semantic network by analyzing the associative link structure between words. The PageRank measure outperforms other measures for prominence such as word frequency in predicting performance in a simple fluency task. We also showed how research in memory that distinguishes between verbatim and gist information can lead to new computational approaches for encoding and retrieval that are not only useful to explain phenomena such as isolation and false memory effects related to human memory, but can also lead to new information retrieval methods. The central idea in these methods is striking the right balance between content-based (i.e., gist) and form-based (i.e. verbatim) matching approaches when comparing the query to candidate documents.

There are exciting new possibilities for cognitive research in language and memory to influence the design of search engines. If the user formulates a query to a search engine, this query is likely to be influenced by a complex combination of memory and language processes. The user is unlikely to remember all the details of a particular document that needs to be retrieved and therefore cognitive theories of memory organization, encoding, retention and retrieval become relevant. Similarly, the content that is indexed by search engines is often produced by human activity that can be described and explained from a cognitive perspective. While it should not be surprising that there are many cognitive aspects to information retrieval (e.g., Spink & Cole, 2005), often such cognitive aspects are stated quite informally based on intuitive notions of user behavior. For example, in the original paper that motivated the Google search engine, Brin and Page (1998, p. 108) mentioned that the PageRank algorithm was specifically designed as a measure of importance because it 'corresponds well with people's subjective ideas of importance'. Cognitive research can help to formalize and empirically validate intuitive notions of user behavior and the representation and usage of information in memory. Therefore, the connection between cognitive and information retrieval research can work in both directions.

References

Adelman, J. S., Brown, G. D. A., & Quesada, J. (2006). Contextual diversity, not word frequency, determines word-naming and lexical decision times. *Psychological Science, 17*, 814–823.

Anderson, J. R. (1990). *The adaptive character of thought.* Hillsdale, NJ: Erlbaum.

Anderson, J. R., & Schooler, L. J. (1991). Reflections of the environment in memory. *Psychological Science, 2*, 396–408.

Anderson, J. R., & Schooler, L. J. (2000). The adaptive nature of memory. In E. Tulving & F. I. M. Craik (Eds.) *Handbook of memory* (pp. 557—570). New York: Oxford University Press.

Balota, D. A., & Spieler, D. H. (1999). Word frequency, repetition, and lexicality effects in word recognition tasks: Beyond measures of central tendency. *Journal of Experimental Psychology: General, 128*, 32–55.

Blei, D. M., Ng, A. Y., and Jordan, M. I. (2003). Latent Dirichlet Allocation. *Journal of Machine Learning Research, 3*, 993-1022.

Brainerd, C. J., Reyna, V. F., & Mojardin, A. H. (1999). Conjoint recognition. *Psychological Review, 106*, 160–179.

Brainerd, C. J., Wright, R., & Reyna, V. F. (2002). Dual-retrieval processes in free and associative recall. *Journal of Memory and Language, 46*, 120–152.

Brin, S., & Page, L. (1998). The anatomy of a large-scale hypertextual Web search engine. *Computer Networks and ISDN Systems, 30*, 107–117.

Bruce, D., & Gaines, M. T. (1976). Tests of an organizational hypothesis of isolation effects in free recall. *Journal of Verbal Learning and Verbal Behavior, 15*, 59–72.

Burrell, Q.L. (1980). A simple stochastic model for library loans. *Journal of Documentation, 36*, 115–132.

Chater, N., & Oaksford, M. (1999). Ten years of the rational analysis of cognition. *Trends in Cognitive Science, 3*, 57–65.

Chemudugunta, C., Smyth, P., & Steyvers, M. (2007). Modeling General and Specific Aspects of Documents with a Probabilistic Topic Model. In: *Advances in Neural Information Processing Systems*, 19.

Collins, A. M., & Loftus, E. F. (1975). A spreading activation theory of semantic processing. *Psychological Review, 82*, 407–428.

Croft, W. B., & Lafferty, J. (Eds.) (2003). *Language modeling for information retrieval.* Kluwer Academic Publishers.

Deerwester, S., Dumais, S. T., Furnas, G. W., Landauer, T. K., and Harshman, R. (1990) Indexing by latent semantic analysis. *Journal of the American Society for Information Science, 41(6)*, 391–407.

Deese, J. (1959). On the prediction of occurrence of particular verbal intrusions in immediate recall. *Journal of Experimental Psychology, 58*, 17–22.

Dunlosky, J., Hunt, R. R., & Clark, A. (2000). Is perceptual salience needed in explanations of the isolation effect? *Journal of Experimental Psychology: Learning, Memory, and Cognition, 26(3)*, 649–657.

Fabiani, M., & Donchin, E. (1995). Encoding processes and memory organization: A model of the von Restorff effect. *Journal of Experimental Psychology: Learning, Memory, and Cognition, 21,* 224–240.

Ericsson, K. A., & Kintsch, W. (1995). Long-term working memory. *Psychological Review, 102,* 211–245.

Green, R. T. (1956). Surprise as a factor in the von Restorff effect. *Journal of Experimental Psychology, 52,* 340–344.

Griffiths, T. L., and Steyvers, M. (2004). Finding scientific topics. *Proceedings of the National Academy of Science, 101,* 5228–5235.

Griffiths, T. L., Steyvers, M., & Firl, A (in press). Google and the mind: predicting fluency with PageRank. *Psychological Science.*

Griffiths, T. L., Steyvers, M., & Tenenbaum, J. B. (2007). Topics in semantic association. *Psychological Review, 114,* 211–244.

Griffiths, T. L., & Tenenbaum, J. B. (2005). Structure and strength in causal induction. *Cognitive Psychology, 51,* 354–384.

Griffiths, T. L., & Tenenbaum, J. B. (2006). Optimal predictions in everyday cognition. Psychological Science, 17, 767—773.

Hofmann, T. (1999) Probabilistic latent semantic indexing. In *Proc. 22nd Intl. Conf. Res. Dev. Inf. Retriev.* (SIGIR'99) (pp. 50–57). ACM.

Hunt, R. R., & Lamb, C. A. (2001). What causes the isolation effect? *Journal of Experimental Psychology: Learning, Memory, and Cognition, 27*(6), 1359–1366.

Jenkins, W. O., & Postman, L. (1948). Isolation and spread of effect in serial learning. *American Journal of Psychology, 61,* 214–221.

Kintsch, W. (1988). The role of knowledge in discourse comprehension: A construction-integration model. *Psychological Review, 95,* 163–182.

Kucera, H., & Francis, W. N. (1967). *Computational analysis of present-day American English.* Providence, RI: Brown University Press.

Lezak, M. D. (1995). *Neurological assessment* (3rd ed.). New York: Oxford University Press.

Landauer, T. K., & Dumais, S. T. (1997). A solution to Plato's problem: the Latent Semantic Analysis theory of acquisition, induction, and representation of knowledge. *Psychological Review, 104,* 211–240.

Landauer, T. K., Foltz, P. W., & Laham, D. (1998). Introduction to latent semantic analysis. *Discourse Processes, 25,* 259–284.

Mandler, G. (1980). Recognizing: The judgment of previous occurrence. *Psychological Review, 87,* 252–271.

McEvoy, C. L., Nelson, D. L., & Komatsu, T. (1999). What's the connection between true and false memories: The different roles of inter-item associations in recall and recognition. *Journal of Experimental Psychology: Learning, Memory and Cognition, 25,* 1177–1194.

Marr, D. (1982). *Vision.* San Francisco, CA: W. H. Freeman.

Nelson, D. L., Dyrdal, G., & Goodmon, L. (2005). What is preexisting strength? predicting free association probabilities, similarity ratings, and cued recall probabilities. *Psychonomic Bulletin & Review, 12,* 711–719.

Nelson, D. L., McEvoy, C. L., & Schreiber, T. A. (1998). The university of south Florida word association, rhyme, and word fragment norms. (http://www.usf.edu/FreeAssociation/).

Oaksford, M., & Chater, N. (1994). A rational analysis of the selection task as optimal data selection. *Psychological Review, 101,* 608–631.

Oaksford, M., & Chater, N. (Eds.). (1998). *Rational models of cognition.* Oxford: Oxford University Press.

Plaut, D., McClelland, J. L., Seidenberg, M. S., & Patterson, K. (1996). Understanding normal and impaired word reading: Computational principles in quasi-regular domains. *Psychological Review, 103*, 56–115.

Ponte, J. M. & Croft, W. B. (1998). A language modeling approach to information retrieval. In *Proceedings of ACM-SIGIR*, 275–281.

Potter, M. C. (1993). Very short term conceptual memory. *Memory & Cognition, 21*, 156–161.

Robinson, K. J., & Roediger, H. L. (1997). Associative processes in false recall and false recognition. *Psychological Science, 8*(3), 231–237.

Roediger, H. L., Watson, J. M., McDermott, K. B., & Gallo, D. A. (2001). Factors that determine false recall: A multiple regression analysis. *Psychonomic Bulletin and Review, 8*, 385–407.

Salton, G., & McGill, M. J. (1983). *Introduction to modern information retrieval.* New York: MacGraw-Hill.

Shiffrin, R. M., & Steyvers, M. (1997). A model for recognition memory: REM: Retrieving Effectively from Memory. *Psychonomic Bulletin & Review, 4*, 145–166.

Seidenberg, S. M., & McClelland, J. L. (1989). A distributed, developmental model of word recognition and naming. *Psychological Review, 96*, 523–568.

Spink, A., & Cole, C. (Eds.) (2005) *New Directions in Cognitive Information Retrieval.* Springer.

Steyvers, M., Griffiths, T.L. (2006). Probabilistic topic models. In T. Landauer, D McNamara, S. Dennis, and W. Kintsch (Eds.), *Latent Semantic Analysis: A Road to Meaning.* Mahwah, NJ: Erlbaum.

Steyvers, M., Griffiths, T.L., & Dennis, S. (2006). Probabilistic inference in human semantic memory. *Trends in Cognitive Sciences, 10*(7), 327–334.

Steyvers, M., Tenenbaum, J., Wagenmakers, E.J., & Blum, B. (2003). Inferring causal networks from observations and interventions. *Cognitive Science, 27*, 453-489.

von Restorff, H. (1933). Uber die Wirkung von Bereichsbildungen im Spurenfeld [the effects of field formation in the trace field], *Psychologische Forschung, 18*, 299–342.

Chapter 16

Causality in time: explaining away the future and the past

David E. Huber

University of California, San Diego, CA, USA

Abstract

This chapter is presented in three sections corresponding to three models that incorporate Bayesian explaining away between different sources. The first section considers primes and targets as potential sources without reference to time. The original ROUSE model is reformulated as a generative model, arriving at the original equations but with slightly different dependence assumptions. The second section considers a model in which past time steps explain away future times steps, thereby producing perceptual sensitivity to the onset of new objects (i.e., new events). The resultant dynamics are related to the dynamics of neural habituation in several important ways. The third section considers a model in which future time steps explain away past time steps, thereby producing sensitivity to the offset of old objects (i.e., old events). By cascading layers, a working memory system is developed that represents the temporal rank ordering of objects regardless of their specific durations (i.e., scale free sequential information).

In recent years, Bayesian models of cognition have effectively explained a wide variety of cognitive behaviors ranging from visual perception (Yuille & Kersten, 2006) and eye movements (Najemnik & Geisler, 2005) to episodic memory (Dennis & Humphreys, 2001; Glanzer & Adams, 1990; McClelland & Chappell, 1998; Shiffrin & Steyvers, 1997) and implicit memory (Colagrosso *et al.*, 2004; Mozer *et al.*, 2002; Schooler *et al.*, 2001) to semantic memory (Steyvers *et al.*, 2006) and syntax (Dennis, 2005; Griffiths *et al.*, 2004). This approach brings together recent advances in computer science and engineering related to graph theory and probability theory (Pearl, 1988) in combination with the Rational Analysis of Anderson (1987; Schooler & Anderson, 1997). The Rational Analysis supposes that cognition is a problem of optimizing processes to reflect the environment that we live in. In other words, people are adapted to their environment, and this optimization problem is best understood with Bayesian statistics.

Despite the success of these Bayesian models, they say little about neural processing (although see Pouget *et al.*, 2003). In line with David Marr's three levels for theorizing about cognition (Marr, 1982), the Bayesian approach could be placed at the abstract *computational* level, rather than the lower levels of *algorithm* or *implementation*. However, as seen in this chapter, in some cases there is a more or less direct correspondence between the level of neural implementation and the level of abstract computation. The particular example under consideration examines dynamic neural processing and the ubiquitous observation of neural habituation. The claim is made that neural habituation is the brain's trick for implementing Bayesian inference for sequences of events in time.

In this chapter: (i) the notion of explaining away is introduced within a static Bayesian model; (ii) the static model is augmented by explicitly representing time in a causal graph such that previous perceptions explain subsequent perceptions (a model of new events); and (iii) the same model is considered under the assumption that temporal causality is reversed such that subsequent perceptions explain previous perceptions (a model of old events). In light of these results, inference over time may specify the dynamics of perception (explaining the near future) and short-term memory (explaining the recent past).

Responding optimally with unknown sources of evidence (ROUSE)

Before presenting the full causal model that explains the 'why' of neural habituation, several background pieces are needed. First, immediate priming data are reviewed as explained by the ROUSE model, which includes the notion that primes serve as an explanation for subsequent targets (i.e., explaining away is the central contribution of the model). Second, 'generative' Bayesian models are introduced, in which the same causal structure that produces observations also guides inference. Third, the inferential process of 'explaining away' (otherwise known as discounting) is introduced, which arises from a particular kind of causal structure. Finally, the ROUSE model is reformulated as a truly generative model and the original equations are re-derived starting with a causal graph under the assumption that entire distributions of objects serve as causes. This first section is solely concerned with static models (i.e., time is not explicitly represented), but the data and model serve as the basis for incorporating time in the second and third sections.

Explaining away and priming

There are many methods for examining the immediate effect of one word on another when we read. Such 'priming' effects usually produce facilitation when a prime word and a subsequent target word are related, with this facilitation resulting in faster responding for lexical decision or naming tasks or more accurate responding with threshold identification tasks. This is called priming because the first word 'primes the pump' for the second word. Such tasks have established a large number of prime-target relationships that produce facilitation, including but not limited to orthographic (Evett & Humphreys, 1981; Meyer *et al.*, 1974; Peressotti & Grainger, 1999), phonemic (Goldinger, 1998; Lukatela *et al.*, 2002; Lukatela *et al.*, 1998), associative-semantic (McKoon & Ratcliff, 1992; Mcnamara, 1992; McNamara, 1994; Meyer & Schvaneveldt, 1971; Perea & Gotor, 1997), and syntactic (Ferreira, 2003) similarity, to name just a few.

In our research, we sought to understand the nature of priming itself rather than asking what primes what. Therefore, we modified the task of threshold identification so that we could examine the costs and benefits associated with priming (Huber *et al.*, 2002; Huber *et al.*, 2001; Huber *et al.*, 2002; Weidemann *et al.*, 2005). As seen in Fig. 16.1, participants attempted to identify target words flashed at the perceptual threshold, with this threshold set separately for each participant. Rather than naming the flashed target, accuracy was measured by means of a forced-choice between a target and a foil. Immediately before the flash of the target word, one or two primes were presented, which were on average non-diagnostic (i.e., primes were just as likely to

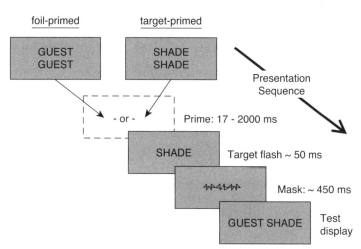

Fig. 16.1. Sequence of events for the priming data shown in Fig. 16.2. Primes were presented for 17, 50, 150, 400, or 2,000 ms. Target flash durations were determined separately for each participant to place performance at 75% on average (perceptual threshold). Mask durations were set such that the total time between target flash onset and test display onset was 500 ms. Trial-by-trial feedback was provided to minimize strategic responding.

indicate the wrong answer as the correct answer). Furthermore, participants were instructed that there was no effective strategy in relation to explicit use of the primes and trial-by-trial accuracy feedback reinforced this assertion. These procedures were implemented in order to assess the implicit inference process in the priming of perceptual evidence while reducing strategic responding.

Use of forced-choice testing allowed conditions that primed the correct answer (target-primed) but also other conditions that primed the incorrect answer (foil-primed). Not shown in the figure are still other conditions that primed neither choice word (neither-primed) or conditions that primed both choice words equally (both-primed). The example in Fig. 16.1 and the data of Fig. 16.2 tested repetition priming, which is found to sometimes produce facilitation but other times produce priming deficits (Bavelier *et al.*, 1994; Evett & Humphreys, 1981; Hochhaus & Johnston, 1996; Huber *et al.*, 2001). As seen in Fig. 16.2, which was reported by Huber (in press), brief prime durations resulted in a 'preference' for whichever word was primed. This helped performance in the target-primed condition but harmed performance in the foil-primed condition (the neither-primed baseline condition lay between these conditions for all prime durations shown in Fig. 16.2). However, for prime durations of 400 ms or longer, this preference reversed its direction, and the preference against choosing primed words lowered performance for the target-primed condition but raised performance when the foil was primed.

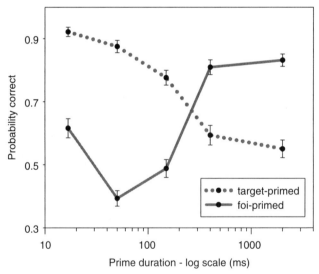

Fig. 16.2. Accuracy for the experiment shown in Fig. 1 (Huber, in press). As prime duration increased, there was initially a preference to choose primed words, resulting in better performance when the target was primed and worse performance when the foil was primed. For longer prime durations this preference changed to a preference against choosing primed words. This experiment also included the neither-primed condition, which appeared roughly halfway between the target-primed and foil-primed conditions at all prime durations.

Complicating things further, the both-primed conditions, not shown in Fig. 16.2, always revealed deficits as compared to the neither-primed baseline conditions (Huber *et al.*, 2002a; Huber *et al.*, 2001; Huber *et al.*, 2002b; Weidemann *et al.*, 2005). In order to make sense of these results and other results with orthographic and semantic priming, Huber *et al.* (2001) proposed a Bayesian model that included the offsetting forces of source confusion (unknown sources of evidence) and discounting (responding optimally). Source confusion assumes that people are confused about what was presented when and where, tending to mistake the prime for the target. Discounting is enacted at the level of individual features during the decision process in relation to the choice words and it assumes that features known to have been primed should be assigned a lower level of evidence.

Beyond producing accurate fits to data such that the degree of source confusion and the degree of discounting can be quantified (e.g., similar to use of signal detection theory to quantify sensitivity and bias), ROUSE also proved remarkably effective in producing a priori predictions. For instance, the Bayesian discounting based on observed features predicts that even extreme discounting will fail to eliminate or reverse the direction of priming in some situations. Critically, even fully discounted features provide a measure of positive evidence, and, therefore, discounting efficacy relies upon a relative deficit. In other words, discounting only works if it serves to lower the evidence provided by features that would otherwise strongly indicate the target. Huber *et al.* (2002a) analyzed the mathematics of ROUSE, revealing that discounting efficacy relies on (1) a sufficient number of features participating in the decision; (2) sufficient presentation of the target; and (3) sufficient similarity between primes and primed alternatives. By separately increasing similarity between the choice words (e.g., choice between LIED and DIED, decreasing target duration (including a condition where no target was flashed), and decreasing similarity between primes (the number of letters in common), each of these predictions was empirically confirmed; these manipulations changed a condition that produced negative priming into one that produced positive priming.

Despite this success, the original ROUSE model was not truly generative because it did not use a causal structure to specify the joint probability distribution. Instead, it was assumed that in general choice words were independent and that features were independent, with these assumptions made in order to simplify the math rather than as the result of a particular causal structure. In what follows, I reformulate ROUSE as generative model by means of a plausible causal structure. In this reformulation, the original equations follow naturally from this structure, which stipulates instead that words are mutually exclusive and that features are only conditionally independent. These causal assumptions lend greater plausibility and wider applicability to ROUSE, releasing the original model from overly constraining assumptions of independence.

Generative models of cognition

Some Bayesian models can be termed 'generative', meaning that they define a causal structure that is used both for production and for inference. Examples of generative model are commonly found in the study of language where the same causal structure produces text and is used to understand the text produced by others (Dennis, 2005;

Griffiths *et al.*, 2004; Steyvers & Griffiths, 2005; Steyvers *et al.*, 2006). Figure 16.3 provides a more mundane example of a generative model that highlights the phenomenon of explaining away.

According to Fig. 16.3, there are two causes of the observation that a light is out: Either the electricity is out or the bulb is broken. It is important that the connection between these causes and the observation is drawn with an arrow that points in a particular direction. These arrows indicate the direction of causation and the pattern of causal links across the entire graph specifies whether causes and effects are dependent or independent (Castillo *et al.*, 1997). The part of the figure to the left is the real world producing observations from this causal structure. Inside the observers head, cognition assumes this causal structure and the goal is to infer states of the world based upon limited observations (e.g., the light is out, but the cause is unknown).

In Fig. 16.3, the two causes converge on a common effect, which defines a situation in which 'explaining away' can occur. In the absence of any observations regarding the light (i.e., if it is not known whether the light is on or off), the two causes are truly unrelated and independent; the status of the electricity has nothing to do with whether the filament in the light bulb is intact. However, once the common effect is observed, this introduces dependence between the causes. For instance, imagine that you are in a room with single light bulb that suddenly goes out, leaving you in the dark. The first thing you might do is attempt to turn on the stereo. But why would you do this and what does the stereo have to do with the light bulb? The answer is that you're establishing the status of one of the two possible causes. If the stereo works, then you know that the electricity is not out and at that point you are essentially certain that the light bulb needs to be replaced. One can write the equation, p(bulb broken | light out, electricity on), which has value 1.0. However, what is the corresponding value of p(bulb broken | light out, electricity off)? This second expression is close to 0,

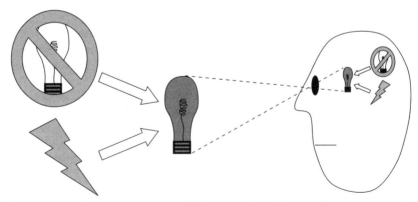

Fig. 16.3. Example of a generative model that includes real causes (electricity out and broken bulb) and an observation (loss of light). Electricity out and broken bulb are usually independent but become dependent once the loss of light is observed. Given the loss of light, if one cause is known to exist, then the probability of the other cause is less (explained away).

and equal to the prior probability that the bulb is broken in general. In other words, this second expression is the probability of a coincidence such that the bulb happened to be break at the same time that the power went out. This is explaining away; if the electricity out provides an explanation of the light out, then the probability that the bulb is broken is much less. This defines a dependency between otherwise independent causes—the probability of bulb broken depends on the status of the electricity, but this is true only when observing that the light is out.

Reformulating ROUSE as a generative model

As seen in Fig. 16.4 and Table 16.1, ROUSE assumes three possible causal sources for the observed features in the word identification task (these features could be thought of as letters, but our results suggest higher level semantic features also play a role in

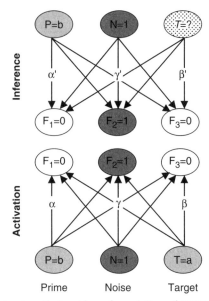

Fig. 16.4. The causal structure that guides reformulation of ROUSE as a generative model. The Prime and Target nodes are distributions over all possible words. The features are binary, taking on value 0 or 1, depending on whether they have been activated by any of the three sources. The probability of feature activation conditional on only the Prime, only the Target, or only Noise, is equal to α, β, or γ respectively. For the Prime and Target these conditional probabilities only apply to features contained within a particular word whereas Noise always applies. The task of inference is to determine the Target distribution given the observed feature states and the observed Prime. This inference is achieved with estimated conditional probabilities, α', β', and γ'. When α is underestimated there is too little explaining away from the prime and when α is overestimated there is too much explaining away from the prime. Dark gray indicates active features and white indicates inactive features. Light gray is used to indicate that the particular prime word within the discrete Prime distribution is known.

Table 16.1 Conditional probabilities for combinations of sources

Possible sources	Inactive/Mismatch	Active/Match
Noise	$(1-\gamma)$	$1-(1-\gamma)$
Prime or noise	$(1-\alpha)(1-\gamma)$	$1-(1-\alpha)(1-\gamma)$
Target or noise	$(1-\beta)(1-\gamma)$	$1-(1-\beta)(1-\gamma)$
Target or prime or noise	$(1-\beta)(1-\alpha)(1-\gamma)$	$1-(1-\beta)(1-\alpha)(1-\gamma)$

forced-choice threshold identification). All features exist in one of two observed states: Either features are observed to be active, or they are observed to be inactive. The generative process defined by this causal structure stochastically produces patterns of active/inactive features according to the probabilities found in Table 16.1. The appropriate equation depends on which sources could produce a particular feature based upon the 'true' prime and target presented on a particular trial (noise matches all features). After stochastically producing a pattern of active/inactive features, the model next performs inference based on the observed states of feature activation. In this reformulation of ROUSE, the causal structure in Fig. 16.4 is used to derive this inference.

The original ROUSE model assumed that each word was a binary distribution, similar to the features. Therefore, features were divided into those that matched the target choice alternative versus those that matched the foil choice alternative under the assumption that the choice words were independent. However, this reformulation employs probability distributions over all possible words rather than a binary word representation. Thus, the prime is a distribution over all words for the status of the word that was presented first (the prime) and the target is a distribution over all words for the status of the word that was presented second (the target). The key calculation is inference for the target distribution under the assumption that the prime is a known word (i.e., one word in the prime distribution is set to probability 1.0 and the rest set to 0.0). Although the distribution for the second word is referred to as the 'target distribution', it is important to keep in mind that this distribution contains probabilities both for the particular target word as well as the particular foil word that subsequently appear in the force-choice test display. Furthermore, because this is a distribution over all possible words, the entire pattern of feature activation over all possible features is considered, rather than just the features that pertain to the choice alternatives. Features that do not match either choice word may play an important role in other paradigms, such as naming, in which case all responses need to be considered. However, in light of the particular choices that appear at the end of a forced-choice trial, the large number of features that do not match either choice alternative provide a constant term that applies equally to both choices. Thus, for this particular situation, only features that match the target or match the foil matter in forced-choice testing.

The conditional probabilities that determine the generation of feature activation (α for primes, β for targets, and γ for noise) are not necessarily the same conditional probabilities used for inference. In other words, one set of parameters generates feature activation (source confusion), but a slightly inaccurate set of parameters might be used to determine accuracy from the observed pattern of activation (discounting). In this manner discounting is often incommensurate with source confusion, resulting in positive or negative priming. These potentially misestimated probabilities correspond to the prime symbols in the upper portion of Fig. 16.4. Active features that are a common effect of both a particular prime and a particular target are features that are explained away (discounted). Such features do not provide strong evidence in favor of the target considering that these features may have arisen from the prime rather than the target. If the estimate of prime activation, α', is set too low, then there is too little explaining away, resulting in a preference for primed words, but if the estimate is set too high, then there is too much explaining away, resulting in a preference against primed words.

$$p(T,P,N,F_1,F_2,F_3,...) = p(T)p(P)p(N)\prod_i p(F_i \mid T,P,N) \tag{1}$$

To infer the target distribution (i.e., calculate the posterior distribution of potential target words based on the observed pattern of active/inactive features), the causal structure seen in Fig. 16.4 is used to simplify the joint probability distribution through the implied independence relationships. For this causal structure, the target distribution, the target distribution, and the noise sources are independent of each other in the absence of knowing the status of the features. Therefore, in writing out the joint probability distribution (1), these three probabilities, $p(T)$, $p(P)$, and $p(N)$ are extracted first in order to simply the expression; because the features are not observed at this point in the factorization, there is no need to write these causes as conditional probabilities. Furthermore, with these causes now specified, the features become independent of each other. Therefore, the factorization is completed in (1) through the product over all possible features, i, conditioned on the prime, target, and noise distributions.

$$p(T = a \mid P,N,F_1,F_2,F_3,...) = \frac{p(T = a,P,N,F_1,F_2,F_3,...)}{p(P,N,F_1,F_2,F_3,...)} \tag{2}$$

Equation 2 is the probability that the target is a particular word (T=a) conditioned on the prime, noise, and all observed features. By convention, use of italics indicates that a variable may take on any possible value whereas use of non-italics indicates that a variable is set to a specific value. Equation 2 is definitional and true regardless of the causal structure. Inclusion of the causal constraints from (1) yields (3).

$$p(T = a \mid P,N,F_1,F_3,F_3,...) = \frac{p(P)p(N)}{p(P,N,F_1,F_2,F_3,...)}$$
$$x\, p(T = a)\prod_i p(F_i \mid T = a,P,N) \tag{3}$$

The original ROUSE model was formulated for forced-choice performance but (3) (and more simply Equation 4) can be applied to many situations, such as lexical decision, speeded naming, or threshold identification with naming as the response. Performance in these tasks is a function of the probability that the target is the correct answer, p(T=a), as compared to all other possible answers contained in the target distribution. The ratio to the right of the equals sign in (3) combines terms that are the same across the entire target distribution, and, thus, this ratio does not change across different conditions of interest in most situations (i.e., provided that all primes, features, and noise sources are equally likely in the various experimental conditions, this ratio is constant). For convenience, this term is dropped and replaced with a proportional relationship, yielding (4).

$$p\big(T = a \mid P,N,F_1,F_2,F_3,...\big) \propto p\big(T = a\big)\prod_i p\big(F_i \mid T = a,P,N\big) \qquad (4)$$

Equation 5 can be converted into a relationship of equality by calculating this expression for all possible target words followed by normalization against the sum of the calculations. The term, p(T=a), is the prior probability that a particular word is the target. This term is typically the same across all conditions. However, comparisons between different classes of objects (for instance high versus low frequency words) may affect these priors. In addition, task specific manipulations may serve to make some classes of objects more likely (e.g., an experiment that only uses nouns as targets), which would likewise affect these priors. The final term in (4) is the probability of observing features in their known active/inactive states given a particular target and the known values of the prime and noise; it is this last term that enacts explaining away.

For the particular task of forced choice testing, the situation is further simplified by taking (3) as calculated for the correct target word (T=a) and dividing it by Equation 3 as calculated for the incorrect foil (T=b), yielding the likelihood of choosing the correct answer, seen in (5).

$$\frac{p\big(T = a \mid P,N,F_1,F_2,F_3,...\big)}{p\big(T = b \mid P,N,F_1,F_2,F_3,...\big)} = \frac{p\big(T = a\big)}{p\big(T = b\big)} \prod_i \frac{p\big(F_i \mid T = a,P,N\big)}{p\big(F_i \mid T = b,P,N\big)} \qquad (5)$$

In order to implement ROUSE using (5) (or more generally Equation 4), specific probabilities need to be entered for observed feature activation conditioned on the observed sources. The equations in Table 16.1 not only generate patterns of active/inactive features, but these same equations are used to fill in appropriate values for the probability of particular features existing in the observed active/inactive state given the particular target word under consideration (a or b) and the known prime word. The only difference is that estimated probabilities are used in the equations of Table 16.1 instead of the 'true' probabilities. Thus, simulation with ROUSE consists of a generative pass, which stochastically determines the particular feature observations, followed by inference to determine accuracy for that trial (however, see Huber, 2006, for a method of implementing ROUSE without stochastic feature generation).

To see how these equations are used, consider the particular feature T___, the particular prime TRIP, and the particular target TOWN. This feature matches both prime and target (and all features match noise), and, thus, the probability that this feature will be active is found in the lower right-hand entry of Table 16.1. If indeed this feature is activated, this same conditional probability is also used to infer the probability for the particular possible target words TRIP in the target distribution of (4), although in this case estimated values are used for the parameters.

Generative ROUSE model conclusions

Equation 5 is the same equation appearing in the original ROUSE model, and it specifies that forced-choice accuracy is the ratio of priors for the two choice words multiplied by the likelihood ratios that come from each of the features. Critically, derivation of (5) in this reformulation did not assume that choice words were independent, such as was assumed in the original ROUSE model. Instead, (5) was derived by assuming that the choice words are mutually exclusive because they are both part of the same discrete probability distribution for the second word presented in the sequence (i.e., the target distribution). Also, derivation of (5) did not assume that the features are in general independent, such as was assumed in the original ROUSE model. Instead, (5) was derived by assuming that the feature are in general dependent but that the features become independent when conditioned on the three sources. Because this reformulation is a generative model, these new assumptions were drawn directly from the causal structure shown Fig. 16.4. In developing this reformulation, (4) was derived, which is generally applicable to any identification paradigm such as speeded naming, lexical decision, or threshold identification without forced choice testing. This provides an avenue for extension of ROUSE to these other identification paradigms.

Explaining away the future (what's new)

Despite the success of ROUSE in explaining a number of non-intuitive results related to similarity and to the efficacy of discounting (Huber *et al.*, 2002a), this static version of the model does not explain why brief prime durations result in too little explaining away while long duration primes result in too much explaining away. Instead, application of ROUSE requires a different set of parameters for each prime duration (i.e., fitting the data seen in Fig. 16.3 would require 5 α values and 5 α' values). A better solution would be that these effects emerge naturally from a single set of parameters in a model that explicitly includes timing. Therefore, Huber and O'Reilly (2003) developed an alternative account based on the dynamics of neural habituation. Their model naturally captured the data of Fig. 16.3 because brief primes result in lingering activation that blends with the target whereas long duration primes habituate and actually lessen the response to a repeated target. In this section, the neural habituation model is briefly summarized and it is demonstrated that a Bayesian model that explicitly incorporates time produces similar behaviors.

Neural habituation

The brain includes many mechanisms that produce habituation in the presence of an ongoing stimulus. One way to quantify the joint action of these mechanisms is to drive a sending neuron (pre-synaptic membrane potential) while recording from a receiving neuron (post-synaptic membrane potential). This is precisely what Tsodyks and Markram did (1997), observing that the synapse appears to lose resources as a function of recent activity, thereby temporarily lowering the efficacy of the connection between the two cells. Abbott *et al.* (1997) developed a mathematical model of this habituation and Huber and O'Reilly (2003) derived a 'rate-coded' version of the model that does not require simulation of spiking neurons.

In the dynamic neural network of Huber and O'Reilly (2003), every simulated neuron within a 3 layer network activates (pre-synaptic membrane potential, v) according to (6), in which *netin* refers to the summed excitatory input, L is a constant leak current, I is the strength of inhibition, and o refers to the post-synaptic effect of the sending cell.

$$\frac{\Delta y}{S} = (1-v)netin - v(L + Io) \tag{6}$$

Equation 6 specifies how the pre-synaptic membrane potential changes at every millisecond. Each layer of the model incorporates all-to-all inhibition (however, (6) and the right-hand panel of Fig. 16.5 only include self inhibition) and the simulated cells of each layer integrate information at a layer-specific rate, S.

$$\frac{\Delta a}{S} = [R(1 - a)] - Do \tag{7}$$

Equation 6 is similar to a large number of other neural network models but the new element is a second time dependent variable, a, which captures the depletion, D, and recovery, R, of synaptic resources in the face of ongoing synaptic output, o. Because D is greater than R, the synapse quickly loses its resources and requires some time to recover. Equation 7 presents the updating of this synaptic 'amplitude'. In order to

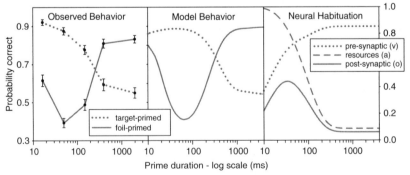

Fig. 16.5. Results with the 3-layer dynamic neural network of Huber and O'Reilly (2003), which included neural habituation. The right-hand panel illustrates neural habituation using parameters for the bottom visual feature layer as dictated by (6–8). The simulated cell was driven with *netin*=1.0 and the other parameters were: S=0.054, D=0.324, R=0.022, I=0.3, θ=0.15, and L=0.15.

produce output, o, the pre-synaptic cell needs to spike, which happens with probability $v - \theta$ (i.e., there is a threshold for activity), and the post-synaptic amplitude of each spike is a, resulting in (8).

$$o = (v - \Theta)a \tag{8}$$

The three panels of Fig. 16.5 show (1) observed behavior; (2) predicted behavior of the 3-layer dynamic neural network with habituation (the decision rule was to choose the word that reached its highest level of output first); and (3) an example of neural habituation for a simulated cell from the bottom visual feature layer of the model using (6–8). Additional details are reported by Huber and O'Reilly (2003), but hopefully this is sufficient to give a qualitative sense of the model. As seen in Fig. 16.5, there is a close correspondence in the initial build up and then elimination of the preference for repeated words as a function of prime duration and the build up and then habituation in the post-synaptic effect of visual features in the presence of ongoing input. Because the visual features project to orthographic features, this imparts lingering orthographic activation from the prime that reaches a peak but then habituates for longer primes. This lingering activation boosts a repeated target, but, with sufficient habituation, the lingering activation is reduced and, furthermore, the orthographic response becomes sluggish due to depletion of resources.

A cascaded hidden Markov model for new events

In order to extend the ROUSE model by explicitly including inferences over time, a temporal causal structure is needed. Hidden Markov Models (HMMs) provide a mechanism to represent time in a causal model because time is implemented as a continually unfolding chain of steps, with each step causally related to the prior time step. HMMs successfully capture sequential processing and have been applied to long-term priming (Colagrosso *et al.*, 2004; Mozer *et al.*, 2002) and other phenomena. Perhaps their most well known use is in the realm of phonology and their application in speech recognition software (Jaffe *et al.*, 1964; Mari *et al.*, 1997; Ostendorf *et al.*, 1996; Seward, 2004). The bottom half of Fig. 16.6 (not including the event layer) portrays the classic form of an HMM, with links pointing forward in time and other links pointing from objects towards observations. For the remainder of this chapter, the more neutral term of 'objects' is used rather than 'words' because the models are broadly applicable to a wide variety of stimuli and paradigms. A standard HMM is a generative model because real objects in the world cause observations and inference is performed on these observations to determine which objects were likely to have produced them (i.e., perception as an inferential problem).

It is often useful to breakdown the problem of inference over time into different layers of abstraction, such as with a generative grammar model of sentence processing (Crocker & Brants, 2000), or a perceptual layer followed by a response layer (Mozer *et al.*, 2002). These models are referred to as 'cascaded HMMs' and are typically implemented by performing inference in the lowest layer based on observations and then performing inference in the next layer based on the results of the lower layer, etc. In other words, these models are implemented by severing the dependence relationships between levels of the inferential cascade. This is done because including dependence

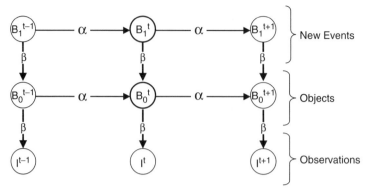

Fig. 16.6. A cascaded hidden Markov model that includes a layer for inferring objects based on observations and a second layer for inferring new events based on objects. Each vertical column represents a different time step. Because of the converging causal arrows in the object layer, an object from the last time step can explain away a new event. Therefore, event perception is mainly sensitive to the change of objects (i.e., object onset). All nodes represent discrete distributions over all possible objects and all nodes include noise as a possible source, with probability γ (not shown).

relationships between layers is computationally difficult, but, as presented next, inclusion of these dependencies naturally includes explaining away over time, thus producing behaviors that are similar to the neural dynamics of habituation.

In the notation applicable to Fig. 16.6, specific points in time are indicated by the superscript on variables and a particular layer in the HMM is indicated by the subscript. In light of the working memory model presented in the next section, nodes are referred to with variable B, indicating Buffer. Dependencies in time (i.e., horizontal connections) correspond to conditional probabilities with parameter α and dependencies in detection (i.e., vertical connections) correspond to conditional probabilities with parameter β. In this manner, the static version of ROUSE is related to this dynamic version in terms of the explaining away from prior time steps (corresponding to the prime with parameter α) versus explaining away from new events, such as the second word in the sequence (corresponding to the target with parameter β). As with the static version of ROUSE, every node also includes noise as a potential source of activation with probability γ (not shown in Fig. 16.6). Unlike the static version, this version does not include features and, instead, all nodes are entire distributions over all possible objects. This was largely for reasons of simplification, and the object node at each time step could be replaced with all possible feature nodes at each time step, thereby maintaining the ability of the model to represent similarity through proportions of shared features.

The model seen in Fig. 6 includes an additional layer, 'new events', which is not typically included in an HMM. However, this is still in keeping with a generative model framework if it is assumed that events are the underlying cause of new objects. Thus, while things tend to persist over time with a previous object causing its ongoing presence at the next point in time (the α links), new events are the reason that objects change (the β links). Although the new event layer is the same distribution over objects as appears at the object layer, its interpretation is that of the event of a new object—thus, the new event layer is inherently transient. However, inclusion of α links in the event layer allows that events are not entirely discrete in time such that events linger for awhile (e.g., an ongoing event). This latter assumption is critical in explaining why neural habituation is not instantaneous. Traditional HMMs do not include explaining away and have no converging arrows. However, by including a second layer with dependencies between layers, this model is considered a factorial HMM (Ghahramani & Jordan, 1997) because the distribution at B_0 depends both on the previous time step and on the second layer at that point in time. In this manner, previous time steps explain away ongoing objects and the inference at the new event layer becomes mainly sensitive to the onset of new objects.

Unlike the static version of ROUSE, exact inference in this model is intractable considering that every time step depends on every other time step and every time step contains a factorial connection (Ghahramani & Jordan, 1997). Instead, approximate inference is achieved by means of Gibbs sampling (Albert & Chib, 1993). In the Gibbs sampling algorithm, the entire chain is initially randomly sampled according to the priors (e.g., every node at every time step is randomly set to a particular object as drawn from the uniform discrete distribution). Then, the entire chain is repeatedly stepped through in permuted order. With each step, one node is chosen, the posterior probability distribution at that node is calculated based on the current values of the other nodes (i.e., local inference), and, finally, a new particular value for the chosen node is sampled from the newly calculated local posterior distribution. After an initial 'burn-in' period (set to 1,000 iterations in the reported results), the model sufficiently departs from the initial priors to allow collection of 'counts' that are used to determine the posterior distribution over the entire chain of time steps. Counts are the number of times that each object is sampled for every node and every time step. For the reported simulations, 100,000 counts were collected. Between collection of each count, the chain was stepped through 4 times in permuted order to provide relative independence between counts. The value of 4 was determined by examining the asymptotically low value for the correlation between one count and a subsequent count.

Gibbs sampling turns an intractable global inference problem into a relatively easy local inference problem. With this method, the causal graph need only provide the joint probability distribution for a local area as dependent upon just one node of the causal chain over time. Because the other values of the other nodes are known through stochastic sampling, this 'severs' the dependence relationships from propagating down the entire chain. The observations, I, are specified for a particular simulation (e.g., this is perceptual input) and so only two equations are needed to perform local inference. As before, these are derived from the causal structure (Fig. 16.6 in this case). The first of these equations (9) is the probability that a node in the object layer, B_0^t, takes on the value j, conditional on the other nodes.

$$p(B_0^t = j) \propto p(B_0^t = j \mid B_1^{t-1}, B_1^t) \, p(B_0^{t+1} \mid B_0^t = j, B_1^{t+1}) \, p(I^t \mid B_0^t = j) \qquad (9)$$

As in the static version of ROUSE, there is no need to express this as an equality relationship and the posterior distribution is turned into a true distribution by dividing

(9) by the sum of (9) as calculated for all values of the object j. The first term two terms in (9) to the right of the proportional symbol include explaining away based on the prior time step and event perception (i.e., both an α link and a β link, with noise γ always as a source). The third term only includes a β link between the object node and an observation. In calculating the local posterior distribution for a particular object node, the equations of Table 16.1 are used for the terms of (9) as dictated by the existence of a possible α source or a β source and whether the nodes match or mismatch in object value.

$$p(B_1^t = j) \ \propto \ p(B_1^t = j \mid B_1^{t-1}) \, p(B_1^{t+1} \mid B_1^t = j) \, p(B_0^t \mid B_0^{t-1}, B_1^t = j) \qquad (10)$$

Equation 10 is the local posterior probability distribution of an event node. This equation consists of two α only links and one explaining away term with α and β. In theory, the causal chain continues endlessly into the future and endlessly into the past. However, simulations are over a prescribed number of time steps. Equations 9 and 10 are modified slightly for the first and last time steps because there is no known value for the time step prior to the first or the time step after the last time step. Instead, it is assumed that these time steps beyond the boundaries are set to uniform priors.

The neural habituation model of Huber and O'Reilly (2003) not only produces realistic habituation functions with ongoing stimulation, but it also produces behaviors at the offset of a stimulus that correspond to the finding that some cells linger in their response while others exhibit a rebound effect and fall below baseline firing rates with the offset of the preferred stimulus (Duysens et al., 1985). Lingering responses are seen for a simulated cell that has a 0 baseline firing rate (the low baseline panel of Fig. 16.7) and are due to gradual leaking of membrane potential. In contrast, a rebound effect is seen for a simulated cell that is driven above zero even in the absence of the preferred stimulus (the high baseline panel of Fig. 16.7). For both the high and low baseline situations there is a lingering depletion of synaptic resources past removal of the preferred input. However, synaptic depression is not the same as post-synaptic inhibition, and can only produce a relative deficit. Therefore, the slower process of recover only produces the apparent rebound in the non-zero baseline situation, serving to keep post-synaptic depolarization below the ultimate baseline level until synaptic resources are fully recovered.

As seen in Fig. 16.7, not only is the cascaded new event HMM capable of producing something analogous to neural habituation, but it also produces offset behaviors similar to simulated cells with low or high baseline firing rates. In these simulations, the cascaded HMM was shown 3 different objects in succession with each object observed for 10 time steps. Unlike the static version of ROUSE, this was not done by generating stochastic patterns of activation. Instead, the goal here was to examine the temporal properties of the inference process and so an idealized sequence of observations was presented to the model. Thus, while this model is capable of generating observations, this aspect of the model is not currently utilized. The figure shows the probabilities at the object and event layers appropriate to the second object (the first and third objects are presented to place the model in an appropriate 'baseline' state before and after the second object). At the time of the onset of the second object, the object layer reaches its peak probability for that object, and, thus, the event probability reaches its peak

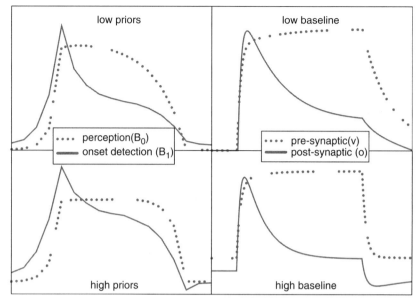

Fig. 16.7. Comparison between the forward directed cascaded HMM seen in Fig. 16.6 and the neural habituation model of Huber and O'Reilly (2003). Neural habituation was simulated with the same parameters as Fig. 16.5 for a 500 ms presentation with *netin* set at 1. Low baseline corresponded to *netin* at 0 all other times and high baseline corresponded to *netin* at 0.3 all other times. For the cascaded HMM, α and β were both set to 1.0 in order to produce strong explaining away from prior time steps as well as strong sensitivity to new observations. 5 possible values existed for every node in the high prior simulation and γ was set at 0.2. 100 possible values existed for every node in the low prior simulation and γ was set at 0.02.

value as well. However, subsequent time steps are progressively explained away by prior time steps within the object layer and so the event probability is progressively lowered (but it retains some probability due to the inclusion of α links within the event layer).

With offset of an observation, the probabilities return to baseline levels. However, the path that the probabilities take in reaching baseline is a function of how many other potential objects exist (high versus low priors) as well as the strength of the α links. Based on the forward directed α links, the time step just prior to offset stipulate that the object probabilities should continue unabated. However, because a new observation overrides object perception, this forward prediction is not born out. Therefore, the event layer has even a greater reason to expect anything but the previous object (i.e., a rebound due to excessive explaining away). Conversely, the α links within the event layer work against this effect and tend to produce maintenance of the previous event. When there are few alternative possibilities (5 total possible objects for high priors), the rebound effective is large enough to overcome a maintenance, but when there are many alternative possibilities (100 total possible objects for low priors), the rebound effect is negligible and the model produces some degree of persistence.

Forwards causation model conclusions

Having developed a cascaded HMM with event detection, the goal is not necessarily to promote its widespread use in modeling experimental results, particular in light of the difficult nature of inference. Instead, this serves as an existence proof, demonstrating the similar dynamic properties in both the Bayesian model and the dynamics of neural habituation. If the cascaded HMM is treated as an ideal observer model under the assumed causal structure, then neural habituation can be viewed as a useful mechanism for calculating approximate inference over time. Thus, neural habituation is not merely an artifact or some sort of capacity limitation, but, instead, neural habituation is a trick that has evolved to solve the difficult problem of deciding whether a particular observation is something new within the ongoing stream of observations (i.e., event detection), or, whether the observation should instead be considered a lingering response to something that was previously identified. In relating the causal graph to neural processing, it is suggested that neural habituation is the natural result of a perceptual system that is constantly trying to predict the future and determine what's new.

Explaining away the past (what's old)

This section considers the same cascaded HMM from Section 'Explaining away the future (what's new)' with the assumption that the causal time links are reversed in their direction, pointing towards the past rather than the future. This is done, not in the service of any particular behavioral result, but, rather, simply as an exploration of the computational properties under this assumption. The claim is not that causation is literally flowing backward (although note that the equations of Physics are symmetric in time). Instead, the question is whether inference based on backwards causation may be useful. The model in Section 'Explaining away the future (what's new)' assumed forwards causation and produced behaviors that were predictive of the near future, which is likely to be useful in many situations in which a response is required when the environment changes. In contrast, a model with backwards causation 'postdicts' the past, which could be useful when events from the recent past are no longer at hand, but perhaps important for sequential processing. As seen below, this inferential process can be used to build a working memory system that keeps track of recent events in the order in which they occurred (see Miyake & Shah, 1999 for different views on working memory).

Working memory buffers are created by cascading one layer into the next within this backwards causation model. Analogous to event detection in Section 'Explaining away the future (what's new)', this produces the most recent past event in the layer above object perception, the event before that in the next layer, and so on. Thus, the model keeps track of the last N objects in the order in which they arrived. This representation may be desirable for sequential learning because it is 'scale free' over time, keeping track of the rank order relationship of the last N objects regardless of how quickly or slowly they occurred.

Higher-order dependencies in a hidden Markov model

Figure 16.8, not including the dashed links, is a classic HMM with forward directed links from the last time step. For reasons of computational complexity, applications of HMM's typically only include these first-order dependencies (i.e., what follows what). However, some applications of HMM's find that higher-order dependencies produce more accurate identification based on the expanded temporal context (Mari *et al.*, 1997). Inclusion of the dashed links in Figure 16.8 is an example of a third-order HMM. Beyond reasons of computational complexity, one advantage of first-order HMM's is that first-order relationships are scale free and are preserved regardless of the rate at which a sequence is presented. However, higher-order sequential information is important in many situations and the model presented next provides an alternative method for including higher-order links that depends on the sequence of objects, rather than the timing of objects.

A cascaded hidden Markov model for old events

Figure 16.9 gives an example of the backwards causation model with one layer for object perception and three additional layers for past events (working memory buffers). The model can be built with any number of layers although each additional layer adds complexity and becomes progressively imprecise in representing past objects. The reported simulations used 4 total layers but the dashed links in the figure were not implemented. The dashed links are included in the figure to portray the analogue of higher-order links from past objects in the sequence. Even though these dashed links appear within the same time step, they are effectively links from the past, similar to the dashed links in Fig. 16.8. However, unlike Fig. 16.8, these links constitute a scale-free higher-order dependence because the representations in the buffers are largely independent of the rate at which objects are presented.

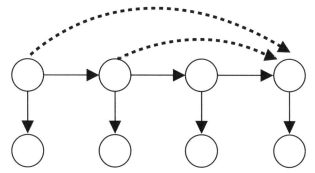

Fig. 16.8. A traditional HMM with first-order dependencies is shown for the solid links. Inclusion of the dashed links creates a third-order HMM in which the next time step is predicted based upon the factorial combination of the previous three time steps.

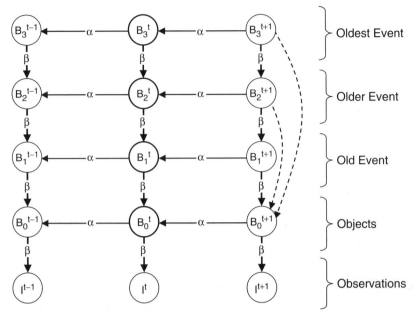

Fig. 16.9. A cascaded hidden Markov model that includes backwards causation. This produces a model that is sensitive to order of past events. Therefore, these layers implement working memory buffers that represent the sequence of objects regardless of the rate of the sequence. The dashed links represent higher-order terms from past events and are analogous to the dashed lines in Fig. 16.8, except that these apply to past events rather than past time steps.

As with the forwards causation model, approximate inference in this backwards causation model is implemented with Gibbs sampling and the necessary equations are the joint probability distributions for a node at each layer, with all other nodes existing with known values. In general, the local posterior probability distribution for some layer n, where n is neither the object layer 0 nor the top buffer N, is calculated according to (11), which includes three different explaining away terms with both α and β links (as before, noise is always a source with probability γ). Equations 12 and 13 modify this expression for the object layer B_0, and the top buffer B_N, respectively.

$$p(B_n^t = j) \propto p(B_n^t = j \mid B_n^{t+1}, B_{n+1}^t) \, p(B_n^{t-1} \mid B_n^t = j, B_{n+1}^{t-1}) \, p(B_{n-1}^t \mid B_{n-1}^{t+1}, B_n^t = j) \quad (11)$$

$$p(B_0^t = j) \propto p(B_0^t = j \mid B_0^{t+1}, B_1^t) \, p(B_0^{t-1} \mid B_0^t = j, B_1^{t-1}) \, p(I^t \mid B_0^t = j) \quad (12)$$

$$p(B_N^t = j) \propto p(B_N^t = j \mid B_N^{t+1}) \, p(B_N^{t-1} \mid B_N^t = j) \, p(B_{N-1}^t \mid B_{N-1}^{t+1}, B_N^t = j) \quad (13)$$

The two simulations reported in Fig. 16.10 were designed to demonstrate the buffering capacities and scale-free nature of this backwards causation model. The parameters for the forward causation model were set to produce abrupt event detection through explaining away ($\alpha=1$ and $\beta=1$), such that the last time step fully explains a persistent object, but an event also fully explains a new object. In contrast, the backwards causation model is used to build a working memory system and must attempt to satisfy the contradictory goals of maintaining objects while also allowing that new objects enter the buffering system. This was achieved by setting maintenance to a decent but not excessive level (α=0.7) and by setting detection to a sizable but nonetheless smaller value (β=0.3).

For both simulations there were 100 possible objects and the sequence provided to the observation nodes consisted of the same 3 objects cycling in the same order. These three objects correspond to the solid, dashed, or dotted probability lines, respectively. The simulation reported in (a) changed objects every 10 times steps whereas the simulation in (b) changed objects every 5 time steps. This is analogous to use an HMM for speech recognition with higher-order dependencies as applied to talkers who differ in rate of speech by as much as a factor of two. The vertical bars in each simulation demonstrate that both simulations are able to faithfully represent the order of the last 3 objects (assuming that the object with the highest probability is selected); in both simulations the object layer B_0 represents the current object, the first working memory buffer B_1 represents the most recent object, and the second working memory buffer B_2 represented the object before that. The third working memory buffer is not shown in Fig. 16.10 for reasons of simplicity, but, also, because the last buffer often

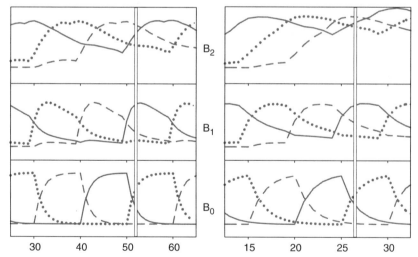

Fig. 16.10. Results from simulating the backwards causation model seen in Fig. 16.9 with a repeating sequence of three objects. Simulation in the left graph presented a new object every 10 time steps while simulation in the right graph presented a new object every 5 time steps. The solid, dashed, and dotted lines are the probabilities of the three presented objects. The vertical bars in each simulation highlight a point in time to demonstrate that both simulations represent with highest probability the current object in B_0, the most recent object in B_1, and the object before than in B_2, despite the fact that one sequence was twice as fast. All nodes consisted of distributions over 100 possible objects. The other parameters were $\gamma=1 \times 10^{-10}$, α=0.7, and β=0.3.

fails to faithfully represent previous objects because it does not have a layer above to explain away its representation from objects even further in the past. Figure 16.10 was accomplished with N=3 (4 layers). Additional simulations with N set to higher values revealed that the model can continue to buffer past objects, but that with each additional layer the model becomes progressively inaccurate and the probabilities become closer and closer to uniform priors. Presumably this is because even very small amounts of noise result in temporal uncertainty ad the noise is propagated across multiple inferential steps.

Backwards causation model conclusions

The forwards causation model in the previous section, which proved useful for detecting new events, is likewise useful as a model of past events and maintenance of previous objects when the direction of the causality in time is reversed. Furthermore, cascading one event layer into the next produced a buffering system such that the cascade keeps track of previous objects in the order they were presented. This could be viewed as a scale-free rank order working memory system that encodes sequences in a similar manner regardless of the rate that they occur. Implementation of causal links from higher layers directly onto current object perception (i.e., the dashed links in Fig. 16.9) could be used to establish sequential learning that applies to similar sequences even if the sequences do not occur at the same rate.

The reported simulations were implemented with identity transition matrices. In other words, α and β links consisted of α or β for the conditional probability values along the diagonal for each object as a function of every other object, and the off diagonal elements were all set to zero. This was done because the simulations were an exploration of dynamic properties rather than an analysis of perceptual competence or sequential learning. Future applications of the model could include these off diagonal elements so that previous objects predict different subsequent objects, perhaps as learned from large corpora of follows and precedes data (Dennis, 2005; Griffiths *et al.*, 2004), or perhaps as specified by associative norms (Nelson *et al.*, 1994). The same off diagonal elements may play a role in working memory too, providing an explanation as to why known sub-sequences enable apparent increases in capacity through chunking (Baddeley, 1994).

The forwards causation model for event perception used parameters to promote abrupt onsets. In contrast, the parameters for the past events model of working memory were set to allow some degree of maintenance as well as sensitivity to new offsets of objects. The setting of maintenance (α) and change detection (β) is tricky in several respects. If change detection is too high, then presentation of a new observation immediately propagates through the entire cascade of buffers. Conversely, if maintenance is set too high, then it is difficult to swap objects between buffer states. What appears to work is that both parameters are set to sizable levels with maintenance greater than change detection. In addition, noise needs to be set as low as possible.

In theory the backwards causation model is also a generative model, although, like the forwards causation model, it was not used for its ability to produce sequences of observations. Nevertheless, conditional probabilities (the parameters α and β) that produce desirable inferential characteristics are perhaps interpretable in light of environmental statistics; presumably the ratio of α to β is something like the frequency for maintenance of objects as compared to the frequency for events (object change). Recently we performed a series of experiments that manipulated the statistics of repetition frequency within different blocks of trials in threshold word identification (Weidemann *et al.*, in press). In using the static version of ROUSE to explain the results, we found that the most sensible account assumed the system adopts different estimates of source confusion (i.e., different α' levels) to handle repetition frequency. Furthermore, the empirical evidence suggested that these adaptations to the local statistics were rapid as revealed by the lack of differences between the first block of trials with a new frequency and a subsequent block that contained the same frequency of repetitions. Despite this rapid adaptation, discounting behavior was also sensitive to the global statistics of the entire experiment and with each change in the local statistics, behavioral changes in discounting were attenuated. Therefore, we modeled the current estimate of source confusion as a mixture of the current statistical regularities combined with the previous statistical regularities. This suggests that learning appropriate parameters for detection and maintenance is multifaceted, involving both short-term and long-term statistical regularities.

Conclusions

Section 'Responding Optimally with Unknown Sources of Evidence (ROUSE)' of this chapter set the stage by presenting an overview of generative models based on causal graphs, with the reformulation of the ROUSE model providing a specific example. Sections 'Explaining away the future (what's new)' and 'Explaining away the past (what's old)' were an exploration of this same explaining away model as applied to time steps rather than temporally unspecified primes and targets. In Section 'Explaining away the future (what's new)', it was demonstrated that explaining away from past time steps produces a model that is sensitive to the onset of new objects (i.e., new events) and that these inferential dynamics are similar to the dynamics of neural habituation both in terms of the lessening of a response in light of an ongoing observation, but, also in terms of the offset behavior with either a lingering response or a rebound response. In Section 'Explaining away the past (what's old)' it was demonstrated that explaining away from future time steps produces a model that is sensitive to the offset of old objects (i.e., past events) and that this can be used to produce a scale-free working memory system that buffers objects in rank order, regardless of the timing of the objects. Results from the forwards and backwards causation models suggest that these two types of temporal inference may serve as fundamental building blocks for perception (predicting the future) and working memory (postdicting the past).

Author note

David E. Huber, Department of Psychology, University of California, San Diego. This research was supported by NIMH Grant MH063993-04. Correspondence concerning this article should be addressed to David E. Huber, Department of Psychology,

University of California, San Diego, 9500 Gilman Drive, La Jolla, CA 92093-0109. E-mail may be sent to dhuber@psy.uscd.edu.

References

Abbott, L. F., Varela, J. A., Sen, K., & Nelson, S. B. (1997). Synaptic depression and cortical gain control. *Science, 275*(5297), 220–224.

Albert, J. H., & Chib, S. (1993). Bayes inference Via Gibbs sampling of autoregressive time-series subject to Markov mean and variance shifts. *Journal of Business & Economic Statistics, 11*(1), 1–15.

Anderson, J. R. (1987). A rational analysis of human-memory. *Bulletin of the Psychonomic Society, 25*(5), 342–342.

Baddeley, A. (1994). The magical number 7—still magic after all these years. *Psychological Review, 101*(2), 353–356.

Bavelier, D., Prasada, S., & Segui, J. (1994). Repetition blindness between words: nature of the orthographic and phonological representations involved. *Journal of Experimental Psychology: Learning, Memory, & Cognition, 20*, 1437–1455.

Castillo, E., Gutierrez, J. M., & Hadi, A. S. (1997). *Expert systems and probabilistic network models.* New York: Springer-Verlag.

Colagrosso, M. D., Mozer, M. C., & Huber, D. E. (2004). Mechanisms of skill refinement: A model of long-term repetition priming. In *Proceedings of the 25th Annual Conference of the Cognitive Science Society.* (pp. 687–692). Hillsdale, NJ: Erlbaum Associates.

Crocker, M. W., & Brants, T. (2000). Wide-coverage probabilistic sentence processing. *Journal of Psycholinguistic Research, 29*(6), 647–669.

Dennis, S. (2005). A memory-based theory of verbal cognition. *Cognitive Science, 29*(2), 145–193.

Dennis, S., & Humphreys, M. S. (2001). A context noise model of episodic word recognition. *Psychological Review, 108*(2), 452–478.

Duysens, J., Orban, G. A., Cremieux, J., & Maes, H. (1985). Visual cortical correlates of visible persistence. *Vision Res, 25*(2), 171–178.

Evett, L. J., & Humphreys, G. W. (1981). The use of abstract graphemic information in lexical access. *Quarterly Journal of Experimental Psychology: Human Experimental Psychology, 33A*(4), 325–350.

Ferreira, V. S. (2003). The persistence of optional complementizer production: Why saying 'that' is not saying 'that' at all. *Journal of Memory and Language, 48*(2), 379–398.

Ghahramani, Z., & Jordan, M. I. (1997). Factorial hidden Markov models. *Machine Learning, 29*(2–3), 245–273.

Glanzer, M., & Adams, J. K. (1990). The mirror effect in recognition memory—data and theory. *Journal of Experimental Psychology-Learning Memory and Cognition, 16*(1), 5–16.

Goldinger, S. D. (1998). Signal detection comparisons of phonemic and phonetic priming: The flexible-bias problem. *Perception & Psychophysics, 60*(6), 952–965.

Griffiths, T., Steyvers, M., Blei, D. M., & Tenenbaum, J. B. (2004). Integrating topics and syntax. In L. K. Saul (Ed.), *Advances in neural information processing systems* (Vol. 17, pp. 537–544): MIT Press.

Hochhaus, L., & Johnston, J. C. (1996). Perceptual repetition blindness effects. *Journal of Experimental Psychology-Human Perception and Performance, 22*(2), 355–366.

Huber, D. E. (2006). Computer simulations of the ROUSE model: An analytic method and a generally applicable techniques for producing parameter confidence intervals. *Behavior Research Methods, 38*, 557–568.

Huber, D. E. (in press). Immediate Priming and Cognitive Aftereffects. *Journal of Experimental Psychology: General*.

Huber, D. E., & O'Reilly, R. C. (2003). Persistence and accommodation in short-term priming and other perceptual paradigms: Temporal segregation through synaptic depression. *Cognitive Science, 27*(3), 403–430.

Huber, D. E., Shiffrin, R. M., Lyle, K. B., & Quach, R. (2002a). Mechanisms of source confusion and discounting in short-term priming 2: effects of prime similarity and target duration. *Journal of Experimental Psychology: Learning, Memory, & Cognition, 28*(6), 1120–1136.

Huber, D. E., Shiffrin, R. M., Lyle, K. B., & Ruys, K. I. (2001). Perception and preference in short-term word priming. *Psychological Review, 108*(1), 149–182.

Huber, D. E., Shiffrin, R. M., Quach, R., & Lyle, K. B. (2002b). Mechanisms of source confusion and discounting in short-term priming: 1. Effects of prime duration and prime recognition. *Memory & Cognition, 30*(5), 745–757.

Jaffe, J., Cassotta, L., & Feldstein, S. (1964). Markovian model of time patterns of speech. *Science, 144*(362), 884–886.

Lukatela, G., Eaton, T., Lee, C. H., Carello, C., & Turvey, M. T. (2002). Equal homophonic priming with words and pseudohomophones. *Journal of Experimental Psychology-Human Perception and Performance, 28*(1), 3–21.

Lukatela, G., Frost, S. J., & Turvey, M. T. (1998). Phonological priming by masked nonword primes in the lexical decision task. *Journal of Memory and Language, 39*(4), 666–683.

Mari, J. F., Haton, J. P., & Kriouile, A. (1997). Automatic word recognition based on second-order hidden Markov models. *IEEE Transactions on Speech and Audio Processing, 5*(1), 22–25.

Marr, D. (1982). *Vision: a computational investigation into the human representation and processing of visual information*. San Francisco: W.H. Freeman.

McClelland, J. L., & Chappell, M. (1998). Familiarity breeds differentiation: A subjective-likelihood approach to the effects of experience in recognition memory. *Psychological Review, 105*(4), 724–760.

McKoon, G., & Ratcliff, R. (1992). Spreading activation versus compound cue accounts of priming: mediated priming revisited. *Journal of Experimental Psychology: Learning, Memory, & Cognition, 18*(6), 1155–1172.

Mcnamara, T. P. (1992). Theories of priming.1. Associative distance and lag. *Journal of Experimental Psychology-Learning Memory and Cognition, 18*(6), 1173–1190.

McNamara, T. P. (1994). Theories of priming: II. Types of primes. *Journal of Experimental Psychology: Learning, Memory, & Cognition, 20*(3), 507–520.

Meyer, D. E., & Schvaneveldt, R. W. (1971). Facilitation in recognizing pairs of words: evidence of a dependence between retrieval operations. *Journal of Experimental Psychology, 90*(2), 227–234.

Meyer, D. E., Schvaneveldt, R. W., & Ruddy, M. G. (1974). Functions of Graphemic and Phonemic Codes in Visual Word-Recognition. *Memory & Cognition, 2*(2), 309–321.

Miyake, A., & Shah, P. (1999). *Models of working memory: Mechanisms of active maintenance and executive control*. Cambridge; New York: Cambridge University Press.

Mozer, M. C., Colagrosso, M. D., & Huber, D. E. (2002). A rational analysis of cognitive control in a speeded discrimination task. In T. G. Dietterich, S. Becker, & Z. Ghahramani (Eds.), *Advances in Neural Information Processing Systems* 14 (pp. 51–57). Cambridge, MA.

Najemnik, J., & Geisler, W. S. (2005). Optimal eye movement strategies in visual search. *Nature, 434*(7031), 387–391.

Nelson, D. L., McEvoy, C. L., & Schreiber, T. A. (1994). *The University of South Florida word association, rhyme and word fragment norms.*Unpublished manuscript.

Ostendorf, M., Digalakis, V. V., & Kimball, O. A. (1996). From HMM's to segment models: A unified view of stochastic modeling for speech recognition. *IEEE Transactions on Speech and Audio Processing, 4*(5), 360–378.

Pearl, J. (1988). *Probabilistic reasoning in intelligent systems: Networks of plausible inference.* San Mateo, Calif.: Morgan Kaufmann Publishers.

Perea, M., & Gotor, A. (1997). Associative and semantic priming effects occur at very short stimulus-onset asynchronies in lexical decision and naming. *Cognition, 62*(2), 223–240.

Peressotti, F., & Grainger, J. (1999). The role of letter identity and letter position in orthographic priming. *Perception & Psychophysics, 61*(4), 691–706.

Pouget, A., Dayan, P., & Zemel, R. S. (2003). Inference and computation with population codes. *Annual Review of Neuroscience, 26*, 381–410.

Schooler, L. J., & Anderson, J. R. (1997). The role of process in the rational analysis of memory. *Cognitive Psychology, 32*(3), 219–250.

Schooler, L. J., Shiffrin, R. M., & Raaijmakers, J. G. W. (2001). A Bayesian model for implicit effects in perceptual identification. *Psychological Review, 108*(1), 257–272.

Seward, A. (2004). A fast HMM match algorithm for very large vocabulary speech recognition. *Speech Communication, 42*(2), 191–206.

Shiffrin, R. M., & Steyvers, M. (1997). A model for recognition memory: REM—retrieving effectively from memory. *Psychonomic Bulletin & Review, 4*, 145–166.

Steyvers, M., & Griffiths, T. (2005). The topics model for semantic representation. *Journal of Mathematical Psychology, 49*(1), 92–93.

Steyvers, M., Griffiths, T. L., & Dennis, S. (2006). Probabilistic inference in human semantic memory. *Trends in Cognitive Sciences, 10*(7), 327–334.

Tsodyks, M. V., & Markram, H. (1997). The neural code between neocortical pyramidal neurons depends on neurotransmitter release probability. *Proceedings of the National Academy of Science of the United States of America, 94*(2), 719–723.

Weidemann, C. T., Huber, D. E., & Shiffrin, R. M. (2005). Spatiotemporal confusion and compensation in visual word perception. *Journal of Experimental Psychology: Human Perception and Performance, 31*, 40–61.

Weidemann, C. T., Huber, D. E., & Shiffrin, R. M. (in press). Prime diagnosticity in short-term repetition priming: Is primed evidence discounted even when it reliably indicates the correct answer? *Journal of Experimental Psychology: Learning, Memory, & Cognition.*

Yuille, A., & Kersten, D. (2006). Vision as Bayesian inference: analysis by synthesis? *Trends in Cognitive Sciences, 10*(7), 301–308.

Chapter 17

Compositionality in rational analysis: grammar-based induction for concept learning

Noah D. Goodman

Massachusetts Institute of Technology, Cambridge, MA, USA

Joshua B. Tenenbaum

Massachusetts Institute of Technology, Cambridge, MA, USA

Thomas L. Griffiths

University of California, Berkeley, CA, USA

Jacob Feldman

Rutgers University, New Brunswick, NJ, USA

Rational analysis attempts to explain aspects of human cognition as an adaptive response to the environment (Marr, 1982; Anderson, 1990; Chater *et al.*, 2006). The dominant approach to rational analysis today takes an ecologically reasonable specification of a problem facing an organism, given in statistical terms, then seeks an optimal solution, usually using Bayesian methods. This approach has proven very successful in cognitive science; it has predicted perceptual phenomena (Geisler & Kersten, 2002; Feldman, 2001), illuminated puzzling effects in reasoning (Chater & Oaksford, 1999; Griffiths & Tenenbaum, 2006), and, especially, explained how human learning can succeed despite sparse input and endemic uncertainty (Tenenbaum, 1999; Tenenbaum & Griffiths, 2001). However, there were earlier notions of the 'rational' analysis of cognition that emphasized very different ideas. One of the central ideas behind logical and computational approaches, which previously dominated notions of rationality, is that meaning can be captured in the structure of representations, but that compositional semantics are needed for these representations to provide a coherent account of thought. In this chapter we attempt to reconcile the modern approach to rational analysis with some aspects of this older, logico-computational approach. We do this via a model—offered as an extended example—of human concept learning. In the current chapter we are primarily concerned with formal aspects of this approach; in other work (Goodman *et al.*, in press) we more carefully study a variant of this model as a psychological model of human concept learning.

Explaining human cognition was one of the original motivations for the development of formal logic. George Boole, the father of digital logic, developed his symbolic language in order to explicate the rational laws underlying thought: his principal work, *An Investigation of the Laws of Thought* (Boole, 1854), was written to 'investigate the fundamental laws of those operations of the mind by which reasoning is performed,' and arrived at 'some probable intimations concerning the nature and constitution of the human mind' (p. 1). Much of mathematical logic since Boole can be regarded as an attempt to capture the coherence of thought in a formal system. This is particularly apparent in the work, by Frege (1892), Tarski (1956) and others, on model-theoretic semantics for logic, which aimed to create formal systems both flexible and systematic enough to capture the complexities of mathematical thought. A central component in this program is *compositionality*. Consider Frege's Principle[1]: each syntactic operation of a formal language should have a corresponding semantic operation. This principle requires *syntactic* compositionality, that meaningful terms in a formal system are built up by combination operations, as well as *compatibility* between the syntax and semantics of the system.

When Turing, Church, and others suggested that formal systems could be manipulated by mechanical computers it was natural (at least in hindsight) to suggest that cognition operates in a similar way: meaning is manipulated in the mind by computation[2]. Viewing the mind as a formal computational system in this way suggests that compositionality should also be found in the mind; that is, that mental representations may be combined into new representations, and the meaning of mental representations may be decomposed in terms of the meaning of their components. Two important virtues for a theory of thought result (Fodor, 1975): productivity—the number of representations is unbounded because they may be boundlessly combined—and systematicity—the combination of two representations is meaningful to one who can understand each separately.

Despite its importance to the computational theory of mind, compositionality has seldom been captured by modern rational analyses. Yet there are a number of reasons to desire a compositional rational analysis. For instance, productivity of mental representations would provide an explanation of the otherwise puzzling ability of human thought to adapt to novel situations populated by new concepts—even those far beyond the ecological pressures of our evolutionary milieu (such as radiator repairs and the use of fiberglass bottom powerboats).

We will show in this chapter that Bayesian statistical methods can be fruitfully combined with compositional representational systems by developing such a model in the

---

[1] Compositionality has had many incarnations, probably beginning with Frege, though this modern statement of the principle was only latent in Frege (1892). In cognitive science compositionality was best expounded by Fodor (1975). Rather than endorsing an existing view, the purpose of this chapter is to provide a notion of compositionality suited to the Bayesian modeling paradigm.

[2] If computation is understood as *effective* computation we needn't consider finer details: the Church-Turing thesis holds that all reasonable notions of effective computation are equivalent (partial recursive functions, Turing machines, Church's lambda calculus, etc.).

well-studied setting of concept learning. This addresses a long running tension in the literature on human concepts: similarity-based statistical learning models have provided a good understanding of how simple concepts can be learned (Medin & Schaffer, 1978; Anderson, 1991; Kruschke, 1992; Tenenbaum & Griffiths, 2001; Love *et al.*, 2004), but these models did not seek to capture the rich structure surely needed for human cognition (Murphy & Medin, 1985; Osherson & Smith, 1981). In contrast, the representations we consider inherit the virtues of compositionality—systematicity and productivity—and are integrated into a Bayesian statistical learning framework. We hope this will signpost a road toward a deeper understanding of cognition in general: one in which mental representations are a systematically meaningful and infinitely flexible response to the environment.

In the next section we flesh out specific ideas of how compositionality may be interpreted in the context of Bayesian learning. In the remainder of the chapter we focus on concept learning, first deriving a model in the setting of feature-based concepts, which fits human data quite well, then extending to a relational setting for role-governed concepts.

Bayesian learning and grammar-based induction

Learning is an important area of application for rational analysis, and much recent work has shown that inductive learning can often be described with Bayesian techniques. The ingredients of this approach are: a description of the data space from which input is drawn, a space of hypotheses, a prior probability function over this hypothesis space, and a likelihood function relating each hypothesis to the data. The prior probability, $P(h)$, describes the belief in hypothesis h before any data is seen, and hence captures prior knowledge. The likelihood, $P(d|h)$, describes what data one would expect to observe if hypothesis h were correct. Inductive learning can then be described very simply: we wish to find the appropriate degree of belief in each hypothesis given some observed data, that is, the posterior probability $P(h|d)$. Bayes' theorem tells us how to compute this probability,

$$P(h|d) \propto P(h)P(d|h), \tag{1}$$

identifying the posterior probability as proportional to the product of the prior and the likelihood.

We introduce syntactic compositionality into this setting by building the hypothesis space from a few primitive elements using a set of combination operations. In particular, we will generate the hypothesis space from a (formal) grammar: the productions of the grammar are the syntactic combination rules, the terminal symbols the primitive elements, and the hypothesis space is all the well-formed sentences in the language of this grammar. For instance, if we used the simple grammar with terminal symbols a and b, a single non terminal symbol A, and two productions $A \rightarrow aA$ and $A \rightarrow b$, we would have the hypothesis space $\{b, ab, aab, aaab, \ldots\}$.

This provides syntactic structure to the hypothesis space, but is not by itself enough: compositionality also requires compatibility between the syntax and semantics. How can this be realized in the Bayesian setting? If 'we understand a proposition when we know what happens if it is true' (Wittgenstein, 1921, Proposition 4.024), then the likelihood function captures the semantics of each hypothesis. Frege's principle then suggests that each syntactic operation should have a parallel semantic operation, such that the likelihood may be evaluated by applying the semantic operations appropriate to the syntactic structure of a hypothesis[3]. In particular, each production of the grammar should have a corresponding semantic operation, and the likelihood of a hypothesis is given by composition of the semantic operations corresponding to the productions in a grammatical derivation of that hypothesis.

Returning to the example above, let us say that our data space consists of two possible worlds—'heads' and 'tails.' Say that we wish the meaning of hypothesis aab to be 'flip two fair coins and choose the 'heads' world if they both come up heads' (and similarly for other hypotheses). To capture this we first associate to the terminal symbol a the number $s(a) = 0.5$ (the probability that a fair coin comes up heads), and to b the number $s(b) = 1$ (if we flip no coins, we'll make a 'heads' world by default). To combine these primitive elements, assign to the production $A \rightarrow aA$ the semantic operation which associates $s(a) \cdot s(A)$ to the left-hand side (where $s(a)$ and $s(A)$ are the semantic values associated to the symbols of the right-hand side). Now consider the hypothesis aab, which has derivation $A \rightarrow aA \rightarrow aaA \rightarrow aab$. By compatibility the likelihood for this hypothesis must be $P(\text{'heads'} \mid aab) = 0.5 \cdot 0.5 \cdot 1 = 0.25$. Each other hypothesis is similarly assigned its likelihood—a distribution on the two possible worlds 'heads' and 'tails.' In general the semantic information needn't be a likelihood at each stage of a derivation, only at the end, and the semantic operations can be more subtle combinations than simple multiplication.

We call this approach *grammar-based induction*. Similar grammar-based models have long been used in computational linguistics (Chater & Manning, 2006), and have recently been used in computer vision (Yuille & Kersten, 2006). Grammars, of various kinds and used in various ways, have also provided structure to the hypothesis spaces in a few recent Bayesian models in high-level cognition (Tenenbaum *et al.*, 2007; Tenenbaum *et al.*, 2006).

Grammar-based induction for concept learning

In this section we will develop a grammar-based induction model of concept learning for the 'classical' case of concepts which identify kinds of objects based on their features. The primary use of such concepts is to discriminate objects within the kind from those without (which allows an organism to make such subtle, but useful, discriminations as 'friend-or-foe'). This use naturally suggests that the representation of such a concept encodes its recognition function: a rule, which associates to each object a truth value ('is/isn't'), relying on feature values. We adopt this view for now, and so we wish to establish a grammatically generated hypothesis space of rules, together with compatible prior probability and likelihood functions, the latter relating rules to observed objects through their features.

---

[3] It is reasonable that the prior also be required to satisfy some compatibility condition. We remain agnostic about what this condition should be: it is an important question that should be taken up with examples in hand.

We will assume for simplicity that we are in a *fully observed* world **W** consisting of a set of objects **E** and the feature values $f_1(x),\ldots,f_N(x)$ of each object $x \in$ **E**. (In the models developed below we could use standard Bayesian techniques to relax this assumption, by marginalizing over unobserved features, or an unknown number of objects (Milch & Russell, 2006).) We consider a single labeled concept, with label $\ell(x) \in \{1,0\}$ indicating whether x is a positive or negative example of the concept. The labels can be unobserved for some of the objects—we describe below how to predict the unobserved labels given the observed ones.

Let us say that we've specified a grammar $\mathcal{G}$—which gives rise to a hypothesis space of rules $\mathcal{H}_\mathcal{G}$—a prior probability $P(F)$ for $F \in \mathcal{H}_\mathcal{G}$, and a likelihood function $P(\mathbf{W},\ell(\mathbf{E})|F)$. We may phrase the learning problem in Bayesian terms: what degree of belief should be assigned to each rule F given the observed world and labels? That is, what is the probability $P(F|\mathbf{W},\ell(\mathbf{E}))$? As in Eq. (1), this quantity may be expressed:

$$P(F|\mathbf{W},\ell(\mathbf{E})) \propto P(F)P(\mathbf{W},\ell(\mathbf{E})|F) \tag{2}$$

We next provide details of one useful grammar, along with an informal interpretation of the rules generated by this grammar and the process by which they are generated. We then give a more formal semantics to this language by deriving a compatible likelihood, based on the standard truth-functional semantics of first-order logic together with a simple noise process. Finally we introduce a simple prior over this language that captures a complexity bias—syntactically simpler rules are *a priori* more likely.

Logical representation for rules

We represent rules in a concept language, which is a fragment of first-order logic. This will allow us to leverage the standard, compositional, semantics of mathematical logic in defining a likelihood, which is compatible with the grammar. The fragment we will use is intended to express definitions of concepts as sets of implicational regularities amongst their features (Feldman, 2006). For instance, imagine that we want to capture the concept 'strawberry' which is 'a fruit that is red if it is ripe.' This set of regularities might be written $(T \Rightarrow \text{fruit}(x)) \wedge (\text{ripe}(x) \Rightarrow \text{red}(x))$, and the definition of the concept 'strawberry' in terms of these regularities as $\forall x$ strawberry $(x) \Leftrightarrow ((T \Rightarrow \text{fruit}(x)) \wedge (\text{ripe}(x)) \Rightarrow \text{red}(x)))$.

The full set of formulae we consider, which forms the hypothesis space $\mathcal{H}_\mathcal{G}$, will be generated by the context-free 'implication normal form' (INF) grammar, Fig. 17.1. This grammar encodes some structural prior knowledge about concepts: labels are very special features (Love, 2002), which apply to an object exactly when the definition is satisfied, and implications among feature values are central parts of the definition. The importance of implicational regularities in human concept learning has been proposed by Feldman (2006), and is suggested by theories which emphasize causal regularities in category formation (Ahn *et al.*, 2000; Sloman *et al.*, 1998; Rehder, 1999). We have chosen to use the INF grammar because of this close relation to causality. Indeed, each implicational regularity can be directly interpreted as a causal regularity; for instance, the formula ripe $(x) \Rightarrow \text{red}(x)$ can be interpreted as 'being ripe *causes* being red.' We consider the causal interpretation, and its semantics, in Appendix A.

$$
\begin{array}{llll}
(1) & S \rightarrow \forall x \, \ell(x) \Rightarrow I & \text{'Definition of } \ell \text{'} \\
(2) & I \rightarrow (C \Rightarrow P) \wedge I & \text{'Implication term'} \\
(3) & I \rightarrow T & \\
(4) & C \rightarrow (P \wedge C) & \text{'Conjunction term'} \\
(5) & C \rightarrow T & \\
(6) & P \rightarrow F_1 & \text{'Predicate term'} \\
& \vdots & \\
& P \rightarrow F_N & \\
(7) & F_1 \rightarrow f_1(V) = 1 & \text{'Feature value'} \\
(8) & F_1 \rightarrow f_1(V) = 0 & \\
& \vdots & \\
& F_N \rightarrow f_N(V) = 1 & \\
& F_N \rightarrow f_N(V) = 0 & \\
(9) & V \rightarrow x & \text{'Object variable'}
\end{array}
$$

Fig. 17.1 Production rules of the INF Grammar. S is the start symbol, and I, C, P, F_i, V the other non-terminals. There are N productions each of the forms (6), (7), and (8). In the right column are informal translations of the meaning of each non-terminal symbol.

Let us illustrate with an example the process of generating a hypothesis formula from the INF grammar. Recall that productions of a context-free grammar provide re-write rules, licensing replacement of the left-hand-side non-terminal symbol with the string of symbols on the right-hand-side. We begin with the start symbol S, which becomes by production (1) the 'definition' $\forall x \, \ell(x) \Leftrightarrow I$. The non-terminal symbol I is destined to become a set of implication terms: say that we expand I by applying production (2) twice (which introduces two implications), then production (3) (which 'ties off' the sequence). This leads to a conjunction of implication terms; we now have the rule:

$$\forall x \, \ell(x) \Leftrightarrow ((C \Rightarrow P) \wedge (C \Rightarrow P) \wedge T)$$

We are not done: C is non-terminal, so each C-term will be expanded into a distinct substring (and similarly for the other non-terminals). Each non-terminal symbol C leads, by productions (4) and (5),[4] to a conjunction of predicate terms:

$$\forall x \, \ell(x) \Leftrightarrow ((P \wedge P \Rightarrow P) \wedge (P \Rightarrow P))$$

Using productions (6) and (7) each predicate term becomes a feature predicate F_i, for one of the N features, and using production (8) each feature predicate becomes an assertion that the ith feature has a particular value[5] (i.e., $f_i(V) = 1$, etc.):

$$\forall x \, \ell(x) \Leftrightarrow$$
$$((f_1(V) = 1) \wedge (f_3(V) = 0) \Rightarrow (f_2(V) = 1))$$
$$\wedge((f_1(V) = 0) \Rightarrow (f_4(V) = 1))$$

---

[4] The terminal symbol T stands for logical True—it is used to conveniently terminate a string of conjunctions, and can be ignored. We now drop them for clarity.

[5] For brevity we consider only two-valued features: $f_i(x) \in \{0,1\}$, though the extension to multiple-valued features is straightforward.

Finally, there is only one object variable (the object whose label is being considered) so the remaining non-terminal, V denoting a variable, becomes x:

$$\forall x \, \ell(x) \Leftrightarrow$$
$$((f_1(x) = 1) \wedge (f_3(x) = 0) \Rightarrow (f_2(x) = 1))$$
$$\wedge((f_1(x) = 0) \Rightarrow (f_4(x) = 1))$$

Informally, we have generated a definition for l consisting of two implicational regularities relating the four features of the object—the label holds when: f_2 is one if f_1 is one and f_3 is zero, and, f_4 is one if f_1 is zero. To make this interpretation precise, and useful for inductive learning, we must specify a likelihood function relating these formulae to the observed world.

Before going on, let us mention a few alternatives to the INF grammar. The association of definitions with entries in a dictionary suggests a different format for the defining properties: dictionary definitions typically have several entries, each giving an alternative definition, and each entry lists necessary features. From this we might extract a disjunctive normal form, or disjunction of conjunctions, in which the conjunctive blocks are like the alternative meanings in a dictionary entry. In Fig. 17.2(a) we indicate what such a DNF grammar might look like (see also Goodman *et al.*, in press). Another possibility, inspired by the representation learned by the RULEX model (Nosofsky *et al.*, 1994), represents concepts by a conjunctive rule plus a set of exceptions, as in Fig. 17.2(b). Finally, it is possible that context-free grammars are not the best formalism in which to describe a concept language: graph-grammars and categorial grammars, for instance, have attractive properties.

Likelihood: compositional semantics and outliers

Recall that we wish the likelihood function to be compatible with the grammar in the sense that each production rule has a corresponding 'semantic operation.' These semantic operations associate some information to the non-terminal symbol on the left-hand side of the production given information for each symbol of the right-hand side.

(a)	(b)
$S \to \forall x \, \ell(x) \Leftrightarrow (D)$	$S \to \forall x \, \ell(x) \Leftrightarrow ((C) \wedge E)$
$D \to (C) \vee D$	$E \to \neg(C) \vee E$
$D \to T$	$E \to T$
$C \to P \wedge C$	$C \to P \wedge C$
$C \to T$	$C \to T$
$P \to F_i$	$P \to F_i$
$F_i \to f_i(V) = 1$	$F_i \to f_i(V) = 1$
$F_i \to f_i(V) = 0$	$F_i \to f_i(V) = 0$
$V \to x$	$V \to x$

Fig. 17.2 (a) A dictionary-like DNF Grammar. (b) A rule-plus-exceptions grammar inspired by Nosofsky *et al.* (1994).

For instance the semantic operation for $F_1 \rightarrow f_1(V) = 1$ might associate to F_1 the Boolean value *True* if feature one of the object associated to V has value 1. The information associated to F_1 might then contribute to information assigned to P from the production $P \rightarrow F_1$. In this way the semantic operations allow information to 'filter up' through a series of productions.

Each hypothesis in the concept language has a grammatical derivation, which describes its syntactic structure: a sequence of productions that generates this formula from the start symbol S. The semantic information assigned to most symbols can be of any sort, but we require the start symbol S to be associated with a probability value. Thus, if we use the semantic operations one-by-one beginning at the end of the derivation for a particular hypothesis, F, we will arrive at a probability—this defines the likelihood $P(\mathbf{W}, \ell(\mathbf{E})|F)$. (Note that compositionality thus guarantees that we will have an efficient dynamic programming algorithm to evaluate the likelihood function.)

Since the INF grammar generates formulae of predicate logic, we may borrow most of the standard semantic operations from the model-theoretic semantics of mathematical logic (Enderton, 1972). Table 17.1 lists the semantic operation for each production of the INF grammar: each production which introduces a boolean operator has its conventional meaning, we diverge from standard practice only when evaluating the quantifier over labeled objects. Using these semantic rules we can evaluate the

Table 17.1 The semantic type of each non-terminal symbol of the INF grammar (Fig. 17.1), and the semantic operation associated to each production

Symbol	Semantic Type	Production	Semantic Operation
S	p	$S \rightarrow \forall x \, \ell(x) \Leftrightarrow I$	Universal quantifier with outliers (see text).
I	$e \rightarrow t$	$I \rightarrow (C \Rightarrow P) \wedge I$	For a given object, True if: the I-term is True, and, P-term is True if the C-term is True.
		$I \rightarrow T$	Always True.
C	$e \rightarrow t$	$C \rightarrow P \wedge C$	For a given object, True if both the P-term and C-term are True.
		$C \rightarrow T$	Always True.
P	$e \rightarrow t$	$P \rightarrow F_i$	True when the F_i term is True.
F_i	$e \rightarrow t$	$F_i \rightarrow f_i(V) = \text{val}$	True if the value of feature i for the object identified by the V-term is val.
V	e	$V \rightarrow x$	A variable which ranges over the objects $\mathbf{E}$.

Note: each semantic operation associates the indicated information with the symbol on the left-hand-side of the production, given information from each symbol on the right-hand-side. The semantic type indicates the type of information assigned to each symbol by these semantic rules: p a probability, t a truth value, e an object, and $e \rightarrow t$ a function from objects to truth values.

'definition' part of the formula to associate a function $D(x)$, from objects to truth values, to the set of implicational regularities. We are left (informally) with the formula $\forall x \, \ell(x) \Leftrightarrow D(x)$. To assign a probability to the S-term we could simply interpret the usual truth-value $\wedge_{x \in E} \ell(x) \Leftrightarrow D(x)$ as a probability (that is, probability zero if the definition holds when the label doesn't). However, we wish to be more lenient by allowing exceptions in the universal quantifier—this provides flexibility to deal with the uncertainty of the actual world.

To allow concepts which explain only some of the observed labels, we assume that there is a probability e^{-b} that any given object is an outlier—that is, an unexplainable observation which should be excluded from induction. Any object which is not an outlier must satisfy the 'definition' $\ell(x) \Leftrightarrow D(x)$. (Thus we give a probabilistic interpretation to the quantifier: its argument holds over a limited scope $S \subseteq \mathbf{E}$, with the subset chosen stochastically.) The likelihood becomes:

$$P\big(\mathbf{W}, \ell(\mathbf{E}) \big| F\big) \propto \sum_{S \subseteq \mathbf{E}} (1 - e^{-b})^{|S|} (e^{-b})^{|\mathbf{E}| - |S|} \bigwedge_{x \in S} \ell(x) \Leftrightarrow D(x)$$

$$= \sum_{S \subseteq \{x \in \mathbf{E} | \ell(x) \Leftrightarrow D(x)\}} (1 - e^{-b})^{|S|} (e^{-b})^{|\mathbf{E}| - |S|}$$

$$= e^{-b|\{x \in \mathbf{E} | \neg(\ell(x) \Leftrightarrow D(x))\}|}. \tag{3}$$

The constant of proportionality is independent of F, so can be ignored for the moment, and the last step follows from the Binomial Theorem. If labels are observed for only a subset $\mathbf{Obs} \subseteq \mathbf{E}$ of the objects, we must adjust this likelihood by marginalizing out the unobserved labels. We make the *weak sampling* assumption (Tenenbaum & Griffiths, 2001), that objects to be labeled are chosen at random. This leads to a marginalized likelihood proportional to (3): $P\big(\mathbf{W}, \ell(\mathbf{Obs}) \big| F\big) \propto P\big(\mathbf{W}, \ell(\mathbf{E}) \big| F\big)$. In Appendix B we give the details of marginalization for both weak and strong sampling assumptions, and consider learning from positive examples.

A syntactic prior

By supplementing the context-free grammar with probabilities for the productions we get a prior over the formulae of the language: each production choice in a grammatical derivation is assigned a probability, and the probability of the derivation is the product of the probabilities for these choices (the is the standard definition of a *probabilistic* context-free grammar used in computational linguistics (Chater & Manning, 2006)). The probability of a given derivation is:

$$P\big(T \big| \mathcal{G}, \tau\big) = \prod_{s \in T} \tau(s), \tag{4}$$

where $s \in T$ are the productions of the derivation T, and $\tau(s)$ their probability. The set of production probabilities, τ, must sum to one for each non-terminal symbol. Since the INF grammar is a unique production grammar—there is a single derivation, up to order, for each well-formed formula—the probability of a formula is given by (4). We will write F for both the formula and its derivation, hence (4) gives the prior probability for formulae. (In general, the probability of a formula is the sum of the probabilities of its derivations.) Note that this prior captures a syntactic simplicity bias: smaller formulae have shorter derivations, thus higher prior probability.

Since have no a priori reason to prefer one set of values for τ to another, we assume a uniform prior over the possible values of τ (i.e., we apply the principle of indifference (Jaynes, 2003)). The probability becomes:

$$
\begin{aligned}
P(T|\mathcal{G}) &= \int P(\tau) \prod_{s \in F} \tau(s) d\tau \\
&= \int \prod_{s \in F} \tau(s) d\tau \\
&= \prod_{Y \in N} \beta(|\{Y \in F\}| + 1),
\end{aligned}
\tag{5}
$$

where $\beta(\vec{v})$ is the multinomial beta function (i.e., the normalizing constant of the Dirichlet distribution with vector of parameters $\vec{v}$, see Gelman *et al.*, (1995)), and $|\{Y \in F\}|$ is the vector of counts of the productions for nonterminal symbol Y in the derivation of F.

The RR$_{\text{INF}}$ model

Collecting the above considerations, the posterior probability is:

$$
P(F|\mathbf{W}, \ell(\mathbf{Obs}))
$$

$$
\propto \left(\prod_{Y \in N} \beta(|\{Y \in F\}| + 1) \right) e^{-b|\{x \in \mathbf{Obs} | \neg(\ell(x) \Leftrightarrow D(x))\}|}.
\tag{6}
$$

This posterior distribution captures a trade-off between explanatory completeness and conceptual parsimony. On the one hand, though some examples may be ignored as outliers, concepts which explain more of the observed labels are preferred by having a higher likelihood. On the other hand, simpler (i.e., syntactically shorter) formulae are preferred by the prior.

Equation (6) captures ideal learning. To predict empirical results we require an auxiliary hypothesis describing the judgments made by groups of learners when asked to label objects. We assume that the group average of the predicted label for an object e is the expected value of $\ell(e)$ under the posterior distribution, that is:

$$
P(\ell(e)|\mathbf{W}, \ell(\mathbf{Obs})) = \sum_{F \in \mathcal{H}_{\text{INF}}} P(\ell(e)|F) P(F|\mathbf{W}, \ell(\mathbf{Obs})).
\tag{7}
$$

Where $P(\ell(e)|F)$ will be 1 if $\ell(e)$ is the label of e required by F (this exists uniquely for hypotheses in our language, since they provide a 'definition' of the label), and zero otherwise. This *probability matching* assumption is implicit in much of the literature on rational analysis. We will refer to this model, the posterior (6) and the auxiliary assumption (7), as the *Rational Rules* model of concept learning based on the INF grammar, or RR$_{\text{INF}}$.

We can also use (6) to predict the relative weights of formulae with various properties. For instance, the Boolean complexity of a formula (Feldman, 2000), cplx(F), is the number of feature predicates in the formula. (E.g., $T \Rightarrow (f_1(x) = 1)$ has complexity 1, while $(f_2(x) = 0) \Rightarrow (f_1(x) = 1)$ has complexity 2.) The weight of formulae with complexity C is the total probability under the posterior of such formulae:

$$\sum_{F \text{ st. cplx}(F)=C} P\big(F\big|\mathbf{W}, \ell(\mathbf{Obs})\big). \tag{8}$$

Similarly, the weight of a feature in formula F is the number of times this feature is used divided by the complexity of F, and the total feature weight is the posterior expectation of this weight—roughly, the expected importance of this feature.

Comparison with human concept learning

The RR_{INF} model provides a simple description of concept learning: from labeled examples one forms a posterior probability distribution over the hypotheses expressible in a concept language of implicational regularities. How well does this capture actual human concept learning? We compare the predicted generalization rates to human data from two influential experiments.

The second experiment of Medin and Schaffer (1978) is a common first test of the ability of a model to predict human generalizations on novel stimuli. This experiment used the category structure shown in Table 17.2 (we consider the human data from the Nosofsky *et al.* (1994) replication of this experiment, which counter-balanced physical feature assignments): participants were trained on labeled positive examples A1 ... A5, and labeled negative examples[6] B1 ... B4, the objects T1 ... T7 were unlabeled transfer stimuli.

As shown in Table 17.2 the best fit of the model[7] to human data is quite good: $R^2 = 0.97$. Other models of concept learning are also able to fit this data well: for instance $R^2 = 0.98$ for RULEX, a process model of rule learning (Nosofsky *et al.*, 1994), and $R^2 = 0.96$ for the context model of Medin and Schaffer (1978). It is worth noting, however, that the RR_{INF} model has only a single parameter (the outlier parameter b), while each of these models has at least four parameters.

We may gain some intuition for the RR_{INF} model by examining how it learns this concept. In Fig. 17.3(a) we have plotted the posterior complexity distribution after learning, and we see that the model relies mostly on single-feature rules. In Fig. 17.3(b) we have plotted the posterior feature weights, which show greater use of the first and third features than the others. Together these tell us that the RR_{INF} model focuses primarily on single feature rules using the first and third features (i.e., $\forall x\ \ell(x) \Leftrightarrow (T \Rightarrow (f_1(x) = 0))$ and $\forall x\ \ell(x) \Leftrightarrow (T \Rightarrow (f_3(x) = 0)))$ with much smaller contributions from other formulae.

----

[6] Participants in this study and the next were actually trained on a pair of mutually exclusive concepts A and B. For simplicity, we account for this by averaging the results of the RR_{INF} model where A is the category and B the complement with vice versa. More subtle treatments are possible.

[7] We have optimized very roughly over the parameter b, taking the best fit from $b = 1, ..., 8$. Model predictions were approximated by Monte Carlo simulation.

Table 17.2 The category structure of Medin & Schaffer (1978), with the human data of Nosofsky *et al.* (1994), and the predictions of the Rational Rules model at b = 1

Object	Feature Values	Human	RR$_{INF}$
A1	0001	0.77	0.82
A2	0101	0.78	0.81
A3	0100	0.83	0.92
A4	0010	0.64	0.61
A5	1000	0.61	0.61
B1	0011	0.39	0.47
B2	1001	0.41	0.47
B3	1110	0.21	0.22
B4	1111	0.15	0.08
T1	0110	0.56	0.57
T2	0111	0.41	0.44
T3	0000	0.82	0.94
T4	1101	0.40	0.44
T5	1010	0.32	0.29
T6	1100	0.53	0.57
T7	1011	0.20	0.14

The object T3 = 0000, which never occurs in the training set, is the prototype of category A in the sense that most of the examples of category A are similar to this object (differ in only one feature) while most of the examples of category B are dissimilar. This prototype is enhanced relative to the other transfer stimuli: T3 is, by far, the most likely transfer object to be classified as category A by human learners. The Rational Rules model predicts this prototype enhancement effect (Posner & Keele, 1968) because the dominant formulae $\forall x \; \ell(x) \Leftrightarrow (T \Rightarrow (f_1(x) = 0))$ and $\forall x \; \ell(x) \Leftrightarrow (T \Rightarrow (f_3(x) = 0))$ agree on the categorization of T3 while they disagree on many other stimuli. Thus, together with many lower probability formulae, these hypotheses enhance the probability that T3 is in category A, relative to other training stimuli.

A similar effect can be seen for the prototype of category B, the object B4 = 1111, which *is* in the training set. Though presented equally often as the other training examples it is judged to be in category B far more often in the test phase. This enhancement, or greater degree of typicality, is often taken as a useful proxy for category centrality (Mervis & Rosch, 1981). The Rational Rules model predicts the typicality effect in a similar way.

Another important phenomenon in human concept learning is the tendency, called selective attention, to consider as few features as possible to achieve acceptable classification accuracy. We've seen a simple case of this already predicted by the RR$_{INF}$

model: single feature concepts were preferred to more complex concepts
(Fig. 17.3(a)). However selective attention is particularly interesting in light of the
implied tradeoff between performance and number of features attended. Medin,
Altom, Edelson, and Freko (1982) demonstrated this balance by studying the category
structure shown in Table 17.3. This structure affords two strategies: each of the first
two features are individually diagnostic of category membership, but not perfectly
so, while the correlation between the third and fourth features is perfectly diagnostic.
It was found that human learners relied on the more accurate, but more complicated,

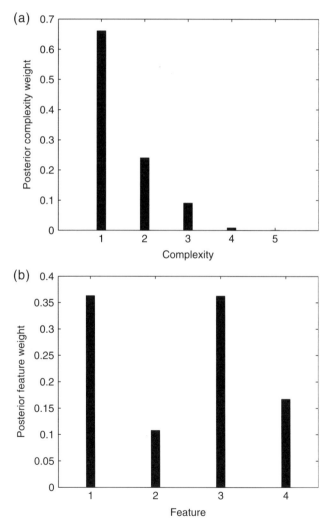

Fig. 17.3 (a) Posterior complexity distribution (portion of posterior weight placed on formula with a given number of feature literals) for the category structure of Medin &
Schaffer (1978), see Table 2. (b) Posterior feature weights.

Table 17.3 The category structure of Medin *et al.* (1982), with initial and final block mean human classification responses of McKinley and Nosofsky (1993), and the predictions of the RR_{INF} model at parameter values $b = 3$ and $b = 6$

Object	Feature Values	Human, initial block	Human, final block	RR_{INF}, $b = 3$	RR_{INF}, $b = 6$
A1	1111	0.64	0.96	0.96	1
A2	0111	0.64	0.93	0.59	0.99
A3	1100	0.66	1	0.96	1
A4	1000	0.55	0.96	0.60	0.99
B1	1010	0.57	0.02	0.41	0.01
B2	0010	0.43	0	0.04	0
B3	0101	0.46	0.05	0.41	0
B4	0001	0.34	0	0.04	0
T1	0000	0.46	0.66	0.14	0.64
T2	0011	0.41	0.64	0.14	0.63
T3	0100	0.52	0.64	0.51	0.64
T4	1011	0.5	0.66	0.51	0.64
T5	1110	0.73	0.36	0.86	0.36
T6	1101	0.59	0.36	0.86	0.36
T7	0110	0.39	0.27	0.49	0.36
T8	1001	0.46	0.3	0.5	0.36

correlated features. McKinley and Nosofsky (1993) replicated this result, studying both early and late learning by eliciting transfer judgments after both initial and final training blocks. They found that human subjects relied primarily on the individually diagnostic dimensions in the initial stage of learning, and confirmed reliance on the correlated features later in learning. (Similar results have been discussed by Smith and Minda (1998).) Our RR_{INF} model explains most of the variance in human judgments in the final stage of learning, $R^2 = 0.99$ when $b = 6$, and a respectable amount early in learning: $R^2 = 0.70$ when $b = 3$. These fits don't depend on precise value of the parameter; see Fig. 17.4 for fits at several values. We have plotted the posterior complexity weights of the model for several values of parameter b in Fig. 17.5(a), and the feature weights in Fig. 17.5(b). When b is small the model relies on simple formulae along features 1 and 2, much as human learners do early in learning. The model switches, as b becomes larger, to rely on more complex, but more accurate, formulae, such as the perfectly predictive rule $\forall x\, \ell(x) \Leftrightarrow ((f_3(x) = 1) \Rightarrow (f_4(x) = 1)) \wedge ((f_4(x) = 1) \Rightarrow (f_3(x) = 1))$.

These results suggest that grammar-based induction is a viable approach to the rational analysis of human concept learning. Elsewhere (Goodman *et al.*, in press) we further investigate the ability of the Rational Rules model (based on the DNF grammar of Fig. 17.2(a)) to predict human generalization performance and consider in detail the relationship between the full posterior distribution and individual learners.

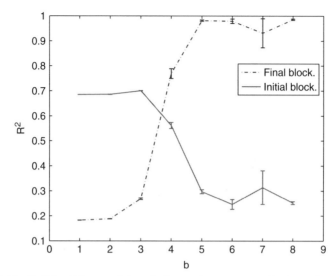

Fig. 17.4 The fit (R^2) of RR_{INF} model predictions to human generalizations of McKinley & Nosofsky (1993) (see Table 3), both early and late in learning, for several different values of the parameter b. (Error bars represent standard error over five runs of the Metropolis algorithm used to approximate model predictions.)

Role-governed concepts

So far we have focussed on a concept language which can describe regularities among the features of an object. Is this feature-oriented model sufficient? Consider the following anecdote: A colleague's young daughter had been learning to eat with a fork. At about this time she was introduced to modeling clay, and discovered one of its fun properties: when you press clay to a piece of paper, the paper lifts with the clay. Upon seeing this she proclaimed 'fork!' It is unlikely that in extending the concept 'fork' to a lump of modeling clay she was finding common features with the spiky metal or plastic forks she had seen. However, it is clear that there is a commonality between the clay and those utensils: when pressed to an object, they cause the object to move with them. That is, they share a common *role* (in fact, a causal role—see Appendix A).

This anecdote reminds us that an object has important properties beyond its features—in particular, it has relationships with other objects. It also suggests that the defining property of some concepts may be that of filling a particular role in a relational regularity. Indeed, it is easy to think of such *role-governed* concepts: a key is something which opens a door, a predator is an animal which eats other animals, a mother is a female who has a child, a doctor is a person that heals illnesses, a poison is a substance that causes illness when ingested by an organism, and so forth. The critical commonality between these concepts is that describing them requires reference to a

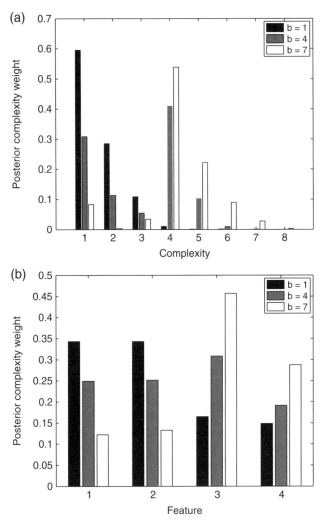

Fig. 17.5 (a) Posterior complexity distribution on the category structure of Medin *et al.* (1982), see Table 3, for three values of the outlier parameter (b) Posterior feature weights.

second object or entity; the contrast with simple feature-based concepts will become more clear in the formal representations below. The importance of relational roles in concept formation has been discussed recently by several authors. Markman and Stilwell (2001) introduced the term role-governed category and argued for the importance of this idea. Gentner and colleagues (Gentner & Kurtz, 2005; Asmuth & Gentner, 2005) have extensively considered relational information, and have found differences in the processing of feature-based and role-based categories. Goldstone, Medin, and Gentner (1991) and Jones and Love (2006) have shown that role information effects the perceived similarity of categories.

It is not difficult to imagine why role-governed concepts might be important. To begin, role-governed concepts are quite common. In an informal survey of high frequency words from the British National Corpus, Asmuth and Gentner (2005) found that half of the nouns had role-governed meaning. It seems that roles are also more salient than features, when they are available: children extend labels on the basis of functional role (Kemler-Nelson, 1995) or causal role (Gopnik & Sobel, 2000) in preference to perceptual features. For instance, in the study of Gopnik and Sobel (2000) children saw several blocks called 'blickets' in the novel role of causing a box (the 'blicket detector') to light when they were placed upon it. Children extended the term 'blicket' to other blocks which lit the box, in preference to blocks with similar colors or shapes. However, despite this salience, children initially form feature-based meanings for many categories, such as 'uncle' as a friendly man with a pipe, and only later learn the role-governed meaning (Keil & Batterman, 1984).

We have demonstrated above that grammar-based induction, using a concept language that expresses feature-based definitions, can predict effects found in concept learning that are often thought to be incompatible with definitions. It is interesting that many authors are more willing to consider role-governed concepts as definitional (Markman & Stilwell, 2001) or rule-like (Gentner & Kurtz, 2005), than they are for feature-based concepts. Perhaps then a concept language, like that developed above, may be especially useful for discussing role-governed concepts.

Representing roles

Just as one of the prime virtues of compositionality in cognition is the ability to explain the productivity of thought, a virtue of grammar-based induction in cognitive modeling is a kind of 'productivity of modeling': we can easily extend grammar-based models to incorporate new representational abilities. The hypothesis space is extended by adding additional symbols and production rules (with corresponding semantic operations). This extended hypothesis space is not a simple union of two sets of hypotheses, but a *systematic* mixture in which a wide variety of mixed representations exist. What's more, the inductive machinery is automatically adapted to this extended hypothesis space—providing a model of learning in the extended language. This extension incorporates the same principles of learning that were captured in the simpler model. Thus, if we have a model that predicts selective attention, for instance, in a very simple model of concepts, we will have a generalized form of selective attention in models extended to capture richer conceptual representation.

How can we extend the feature-based concept language, generated by the INF grammar, to capture relational roles? Consider the role-governed concept 'key,' which is an object that opens a lock. We clearly must introduce relation primitives, such as 'opens,' by a set of terminal symbols $r_1, \ldots, r_M$. With these symbols we intend to express 'x opens y' by, for instance, $r_1(x, y)$; to do so we will need additional variables (such as y) to fill the other roles of the relation. With relation symbols and additional variables, and appropriate production rules, we could generate formulae like: $\forall x \, \ell(x) \Leftrightarrow (r_1(x, y) = 1)$, but this isn't quite complete—*which* objects should y refer to? We need a quantifier to bind the additional variable. For instance, if there is *some* lock which the object must open, we might write $\forall x \, \ell(x) \Leftrightarrow (\exists y \, r_1(x, y) = 1)$.

In Fig. 17.6 we have extended the INF grammar to simple role-governed concepts. The generative process is much as it was before. From the start symbol, S, we get $\forall x\, \ell(x) \Leftrightarrow (Qy\, I)$. The new quantifier symbol Q is replaced with either a universal or existential quantifier. The implication terms are generated as before, with two exceptions. First, each predicate term P can lead to a feature or a relation. Second, there are now two choices, x and y, for each variable term V. We choose new semantic operators, for the new productions, which give the conventional interpretations.[8]

Let us consider the concepts which can be described in this extended language. The concept 'key' might be expressed: $\forall x\, \text{Key}\,(x) \Leftrightarrow (\exists y\,(T \Rightarrow \text{Opens}(x,y)))$. There is a closely related concept, 'skeleton key,' which opens *any lock*: $\forall x\, \text{Key}\,(x) \Leftrightarrow (\forall y\,(T \Rightarrow \text{Opens}\,(x,y)))$.[9] Indeed, this formal language highlights the fact that any role-governed concept has a *quantification type*, $\forall$ or $\exists$, and each concept has a twin with the other type.

Though we have been speaking of role-governed and feature-based as though they were strictly different types of concept, most concepts which can be expressed in this language mix concepts and features. Take, for instance $\forall x\, \text{shallow}\,(x) \Leftrightarrow \forall y\,(\text{likes}(x,y) \Rightarrow \text{beautiful}(y))$, which may be translated 'a shallow person is someone who only likes another if they are beautiful.' It has been pointed out before that concepts may be best understood as lying along a feature–relation continuum (Gentner & Kurtz, 2005; Goldstone *et al.*, 2003). Nonetheless, there is a useful distinction between concepts which can be expressed without referring to an additional entity (formally, without an additional quantifier) and those which cannot.

$$S \to \forall x\, \ell(x) \Leftrightarrow (Qy\, I)$$
$$Q \to \forall$$
$$Q \to \exists$$
$$I \to (C \Rightarrow P) \wedge I$$
$$I \to T$$
$$C \to P \wedge C$$
$$C \to T$$
$$P \to F_i$$
$$P \to R_j$$
$$Fi \to f_i(V) = 1$$
$$Fi \to f_i(V) = 0$$
$$Ri \to r_j(V,V) = 1$$
$$Rj \to r_j(V,V) = 0$$
$$V \to x$$
$$V \to y$$

Fig. 17.6 The INF Grammar extended to role-governed concepts. (Indices $i \in \{1,...N\}$ and $j \in \{1...M\}$, so there are M relation symbols R_i etc.)

---

[8] That is, '$Rj \to r_j(x, y) = \text{val}$' evaluates the jth relation, '$Q \to \forall$' associates the standard universal quantifier to Q (and, *mutatis mutandis*, for '$Q \to \exists$'), and V is assigned independent variables over E for x and y. It would be more complicated, but perhaps useful, to allow outliers to the additional quantifier, as we did for the quantifier over labeled objects. This would, for instance, allow skeleton keys which only open *most* locks.

[9] We name relations and features in this discussion for clarity.

(Though note the concept 'narcissist,' a person who loves himself, which involves a relation but no additional entity.)

Learning roles

The posterior for the feature-based RR_{INF} model can be immediately extended to the new hypothesis space:

$$P(F|\mathbf{W},\ell(\mathbf{Obs})) \propto$$
$$\left(\prod_{Y \in N} \beta(|\{Y \in F\}|) + 1\right) e^{-b|\{x \in \mathbf{Obs}|\neg(\ell(x) \Leftrightarrow (Qy\, D(x,y)))\}|}, \qquad (9)$$

where $D(x, y)$ is the set of implicational regularities, now amongst features and relations, and $Qy\, D(x, y)$ is evaluated with the appropriate quantifier. We now have a model of role-governed concept learning. Defining this model was made relatively easy by the properties of compositionality, but the value of such a model should not be underestimated: to the best of our knowledge this is the first model that has been suggested to describe human learning of role-governed concepts. (There have, however, been a number of Bayesian models that learn other interesting conceptual structure from relational information, for instance Kemp *et al.* (2006).)

The extended RR_{INF} model is, unsurprisingly, able to learn the correct role-governed concept given a sufficient number observed labels (this limit-convergence is a standard property of Bayesian models). It is more interesting to examine the learning behavior in the case of an ill-defined role-governed concept. Just as a concept may have a number of characteristic features that rarely line up in the real world, there may be a collection of characteristic roles which contribute to the meaning of a role-governed concept. (This collection is much like Lakoff's idealized cognitive models (Lakoff, 1987); the 'entries' here are simpler yet more rigorously specified.) For instance, let us say that we see someone who is loved by all called a 'good leader', and also someone who is respected by all called a 'good leader'. It is reasonable to think of these as two contributing roles, in which case we should expect that someone who is both loved and respected by all is an especially good 'good leader'. Let us see whether we get such a generalized prototype effect from the RR_{INF} model.

Starting with our 'good leader' example we construct a simple ill-defined role-governed concept, analogous to the concept of Medin and Schaffer (1978) considered above. In Table 17.4 we have given a category structure, for eight objects with one feature and two relations, that has no feature-based regularities and no simple role-based regularities. There are, however, several imperfect role-based regularities which apply to one or the other of the examples. Transfer object T4 is the prototype of category A in the sense that it fills all of these roles, though it is not a prototype by the obvious distance measure.[10]

----

[10] Prototypes are often treated as objects with smaller bit-distance (Hamming distance between feature vectors) to examples of the category than to its complement. If we extend this naively to bit-distance between both feature and relation vectors we find that the distance between A1 and T4 is larger than that between B1 and T4, so T4 is not a prototype of category A.

Table 17.4 An ill-defined role-governed category. The objects A1 and A2 are positive examples, B1 and B2 are negative examples, and T1–T4 are unlabeled transfer objects. It may be convenient to think of r_1 as 'loved-by' and r_2 as 'respected-by,' and the concept label as 'good leader'

Object	f_1	r_1:	A1	A2	B1	B2	T1	T2	T3	T4	r_2:	A1	A2	B1	B2	T1	T2	T3	T4
A1	0		1	1	1	1	1	1	1	1		0	1	0	0	0	0	1	0
A2	1		1	1	1	1	0	0	1	0		1	1	1	1	1	1	1	1
B1	0		0	1	1	1	0	1	0	1		1	0	1	1	0	1	1	1
B2	1		1	0	0	1	1	0	1	1		0	0	0	1	0	1	0	1
T1	0		0	0	0	1	1	0	0	0		0	0	1	0	1	0	1	0
T2	0		0	1	1	0	1	0	1	0		0	0	1	0	1	0	1	1
T3	1		1	1	1	1	1	1	1	1		1	1	1	1	1	0	1	1
T4	1		1	1	1	1	1	1	1	1		1	1	1	1	1	1	1	1

Table 17.5 shows formulae found by the extended RR_{INF} model, together with their posterior weight. The highest weight contributors are the two imperfect role-based regularities ('someone who is loved by all' and 'someone who is respected by all'), each correctly predicting 75% of labels. After these in weight comes a perfectly predictive, but more complex, role-governed formula ('someone who is respected by all those who don't love her'). Finally, there are a number of simple feature-based formulae, none of which predicts more than 50% of labels. The predicted generalization rates for each object (i.e., the posterior probability of labeling the object as an example of category A) are shown in Table 17.6. There is one particularly striking feature: transfer object T4 is enhanced, relative to both the other transfer objects and the examples of category A. Thus, the extended RR_{INF} model exhibits a generalized prototype enhancement effect. This is a natural generalization of the well-known effect for feature-based concepts, but it is not a direct extension of similarity-based notions of prototype. The emergence of useful, and non-trivial, generalizations of known learning effects is a consequence of compositionality.

We can also explore the dynamics of learning for role-governed concepts. We would particularly like to know if the reliance on features relative to that on relations is expected to change over time. To investigate this we generated a world **W** at random,[11] and assigned labels in accordance with the role-governed concept $\forall x\, \ell(x) \Leftrightarrow (\exists y\, r_1(x,y) = 1)$. As a measure of feature and relation weights we use the posterior expectation of the number of features or relations used in a formula; by averaging over many random worlds we get a qualitative prediction for typical learning. In Fig. 17.7 we have plotted these feature and relation weights against the number of observed labels. We see a clear feature-to-relation transition: early in learning features are of primary importance, as observations accumulate relations become more important, and eventually the correct role-governed concept is learned.

Table 17.5 The six highest posterior weight formulae from the extended RR_{INF} model applied to the world of Table 4

Weight	Formula
0.178	$\forall x\, \ell(x) \Leftrightarrow (\forall y(T \Rightarrow (r_2(x,y) = 1)))$
0.178	$\forall x\, \ell(x) \Leftrightarrow (\forall y(T \Rightarrow (r_1(x,y) = 1)))$
0.049	$\forall x\, \ell(x) \Leftrightarrow (\forall y(((r_2(x,y) = 0) \wedge T) \Rightarrow (r_2(x,y) - 1)))$
0.016	$\forall x\, \ell(x) \Leftrightarrow (\forall y(T \Rightarrow (f_1(x) = 1)))$
0.016	$\forall x\, \ell(x) \Leftrightarrow (\exists y(T \Rightarrow (f_1(y) = 1)))$
0.016	$\forall x\, \ell(x) \Leftrightarrow (\exists y(T \Rightarrow (f_1(y) = 1)))$

[11] Each random world had 15 objects, 5 features, and 2 relations. The binary features were generated at random with probability 0.5, the binary relations had probability 0.05 (providing sparse matrices).

Table 17.6 Generalization rates predicted by the extended RR_{INF} model for the category of Table 4

Object:	A1	A2	B1	B2	T1	T2	T3	T4
Rate:	56%	59%	25%	23%	25%	26%	56%	81%

Recall children's shift for words like 'uncle,' from a feature-based interpretation to a role-based one. The qualitative feature-to-relation transition predicted by the extended RR_{INF} model suggests that this shift may in fact be the result of rational belief updating rather than limited resources or a domain general shift (e.g., from concrete to abstract understanding).

Discussion

The previous sections may be thought of as an extended example illustrating our view on what compositionality should mean in Bayesian rational analysis. The key features of our grammar-based induction approach to concept learning are the use of a concept language and a likelihood function compatible with the grammar of this language—the concept language lays the foundation for the virtues of compositionality, while compatibility gives the theory its semantic teeth. The RR_{INF} model is a case study of this approach.

We compared the feature-based version of the RR_{INF} model to human data from two concept learning experiments, and found extremely good fits, comparable to the

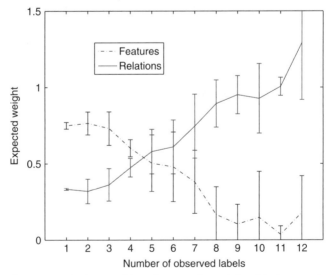

Fig. 17.7 A feature-to-relation transition: the posterior weight of features and relations versus number of labels observed. Labels are consistent with the role-governed concept $\forall x \ell(x) \Leftrightarrow (\exists y\, r_1(x, y) = 1)$. Error bars are standard deviation over 10 randomly generated worlds.

best existing models. This is particularly encouraging because the RR_{INF} model has only one free parameter—far fewer than other models. The RR_{INF} model has similarities with several well established models of concept learning. Like the RULEX model of Nosofsky *et al.* (1994), the RR_{INF} model learns a mixture of rule-like representations. However, while RR_{INF} is a computational-level rational model, the RULEX model is a process-level model. Thus the RR_{INF} model complements other efforts by providing a missing level of explanation to the rule-based approach to concept learning. RR_{INF} shares with other rational analyses of concept learning, such as Anderson's rational model (Anderson, 1990), its underlying Bayesian inductive principles—but existing rational models learn similarity-based representations that lack compositionality. One of the primary objections to similarity-based theories of concepts has been the lack of compositionality, which makes it difficult to to express rich relationships between concepts (Murphy & Medin, 1985) or to usefully combine concepts (Osherson & Smith, 1981). The grammar-based induction approach is well suited to address these concerns while still providing precise, and testable, computational models.

We leveraged compositionality to extend the RR_{INF} model to role-governed concepts by adding additional primitives to the concept language (relations and an additional quantified variable), expanding the set of productions to make use of these primitives, and specifying semantic operations for the new productions. Because the inductive semantics of RR_{INF} is compositional, the new pieces integrate naturally with the old, and the learning model continues to 'makes sense' in the extended setting. This extension provides usefully expressive representations, and several interesting learning effects were noted, but future work is needed to empirically test and refine this form of the model.

The representations used in the RR_{INF} model were derived from mathematical logic. We drew not only on the syntax of logic, but also, in order to build a compatible likelihood, on the model-theoretic semantics of logic. These model-theoretic methods have already been used in several branches of cognitive science. In the psychology of reasoning, for instance, mental-model theory (Johnson-Laird, 1983) was inspired by model-theoretic notions of deductive truth. A bit farther afield, formal semantics, beginning with Montague (1973), has elaborated a detailed mathematical logic of natural language semantics. This *intensional* logic is also founded on mathematical model theory, though on the more modern notion of possible worlds. Formal semantics has developed a unique array of rich, and mathematically rigorous, representations relevant to cognition. These representations go far beyond the first-order logic used here, and are sure to be of interest as grammar-based induction is extended.

We have emphasized the notion of a concept language in which hypotheses are represented. This concept language, of course, is meant to be an internal mental language, which may not be verbalizable or even consciously accessible. Philosophical theories of mind based on an internal mental language ('mentalese') have a considerable history, via the language of thought hypothesis (Fodor, 1975). A key argument for these theories is that a language of thought might be sufficiently expressive for cognition because it inherits the virtues of compositionality; but an unresolved puzzle is what form the compositional semantics might take, in order to usefully connect mentalese to observations of the world. Our efforts in this chapter offer one solution: the language of thought can find its semantics in compositional prescriptions for induction—in particular, in likelihood and prior functions compatible with the syntax of mentalese. A moral can also be drawn in the other direction: the hypothesis spaces of Bayesian cognitive modeling, to the extent that they describe actual mental representations, can be seen as portions of the language of thought.

References

Ahn, W.-K., Kim, N., Lassaline, M. E., & Dennis, M. J. (2000). Casual status as a determinant of feature centrality. *Cognitive Psychology, 41*, 361–416.

Anderson, J. R. (1990). T*he adaptive character of thought.* Hillsdale, NJ: Erlbaum.

Anderson, J. R. (1991). The adaptive nature of human categorization. *Psychological Review, 98*(3), 409–429.

Asmuth, J., & Gentner, D. (2005). Context sensitivity of relational nouns. In *Proceedings of the twenty-seventh annual meeting of the cognitive science society* (pp. 163–168).

Boole, G. (1854). *An investigation of the laws of thought: On which are founded the mathematical theories of logic and probabilities.* Walton and Maberly.

Chater, N., & Manning, C. D. (2006). Probabilistic models of language processing and acquisition. *TRENDS in Cognitive Sciences, 10*, 335–344.

Chater, N., & Oaksford, M. (1999). Ten years of the rational analysis of cognition. *Trends in Cognitive Science, 3*(2), 57–65.

Chater, N., Tenenbaum, J. B., & Yuille, A. (2006, July). Probabilistic models of cognition: Conceptual foundations. *Trends in Cognitive Sciences, 10*(7), 287–291.

Enderton, H. B. (1972). *A mathematical introduction to logic.* New York: Academic Press.

Feldman, J. (2000). Minimization of Boolean complexity in human concept learning. *Nature, 407*, 630–633.

Feldman, J. (2001). Bayesian contour integration. *Perception & Psychophysics, 63*(7), 1171–1182.

Feldman, J. (2006). An algebra of human concept learning. *Journal of Mathematical Psychology, 50*, 339–368.

Fodor, J. A. (1975). *The language of thought.* Cambridge, MA: Harvard University Press

Frege, G. (1892). Uber Sinn und Bedeutung. *Zeitschrift fur Philosophie und philosophische Kritik, 100*, 25–50.

Geisler, W. W., & Kersten, D. (2002). Illusions, perception and Bayes. *Nature Neuroscience, 5*(6), 508–510.

Gelman, A., Carlin, J. B., Stern, H. S., & Rubin, D. B. (1995). *Bayesian data analysis.* New York: Chapman & Hall.

Gentner, D., & Kurtz, K. (2005). Categorization inside and outside the lab. In W. K. Ahn, R. L. Goldstone, B. C. Love, A. B. Markman, & P. W. Wolff (Eds.), (pp. 151–175). APA.

Goldstone, R. L., Medin, D. L., & Gentner, D. (1991). Relational similarity and the nonindependance of features in similarity judgments. *Cognitive Psychology, 23*, 222–262.

Goldstone, R. L., Steyvers, M., & Rogosky, B. J. (2003). Conceptual interrelatedness and caricatures. *Memory and Cognition, 31*, 169–180.

Goodman, N. D., Tenenbaum, J. B., Feldman, J., & Griffiths, T. L. (still in press). A rational analysis of rule-based concept learning. *Cognitive Science.*

Gopnik, A., Glymour, C., Sobel, D. M., Schulz, L. E., Kushnir, T., & Danks, D. (2004, Jan). A theory of causal learning in children: causal maps and Bayes nets. *Psychological Review, 111*(1), 3–32.

Gopnik, A., & Sobel, D. (2000). Detecting blickets: How young children use information about novel causal powers in categorization and induction. *Child Development, 17*(5), 1205–1222.

Griffiths, T. L., & Tenenbaum, J. B. (2006). Optimal predictions in everyday cognition. *Psychological Science, 17*(9), 767–773.

Halpern, J. Y., & Pearl, J. (2001). Causes and explanations: A structural-model approach. part i: Causes. In *Proceedings of the seventeenth conference on uncertainty in artificial intelligence.*

Jaynes, E. T. (2003). *Probability theory: The logic of science.* Cambridge: Cambridge University Press.

Johnson-Laird, P. N. (1983). *Mental models: Towards a cognitive science of language, inference, and consciousness.* Cambridge, MA: Harvard University Press.

Jones, M., & Love, B. C. (2006). Beyond common features: The role of roles in determining similarity. *Cognitive Psychology.*

Keil, F. C., & Batterman, N. (1984). A characteristic-to-defining shift in the development of word meaning. *Journal of Verbal Learning and Verbal Behavior, 23*, 221–236.

Kemler-Nelson, D. G. (1995). Principle-based inferences in young children's categorization: Revisiting the impact of function on the naming of artifacts. *Cognitive Development, 10*, 347–380.

Kemp, C., Tenenbaum, J. B., Griffiths, T. L., Yamada, T., & Ueda, N. (2006). Learning systems of concepts with an infinite relational model. In *Proceedings of the twenty-first national conference on artificial intelligence (aaai-06).*

Kruschke, J. K. (1992, Jan). ALCOVE: An exemplar-based connectionist model of category learning. *Psychological Review, 99*(1), 22–44.

Lagnado, D. A., & Sloman, S. (2002). Learning causal structure. In *Proceedings of the Twenty-Fourth Annual Meeting of the Cognitive Science Society.* Erlbaum.

Lakoff, G. (1987). *Women, fire, and dangerous things: What categories reveal about the mind.* Chicago: University of Chicago Press.

Love, B. C. (2002). Comparing supervised and unsupervised category learning. *Psychonomic Bulletin & Review, 9*(4), 829–835.

Love, B. C., Gureckis, T. M., & Medin, D. L. (2004). SUSTAIN: A network model of category learning. *Psychological Review, 111*(2), 309–332.

Markman, A. B., & Stilwell, C. H. (2001). Role-governed categories. *Journal of Experimental and Theoretical Artificial Intelligence, 13*(4), 329–358.

Marr, D. (1982). *Vision.* Freeman Publishers.

McKinley, S. C., & Nosofsky, R. M. (1993). *Attention learning in models of classification.* ((Cited in Nosofsky, Palmeri, and McKinley, 1994))

Medin, D. L., Altom, M. W., Edelson, S. M., & Freko, D. (1982). Correlated symptoms and simulated medical classification. *Journal of Experimental Psychology: Learning, Memory, and Cognition, 8*, 37–50.

Medin, D. L., & Schaffer, M. M. (1978). Context theory of classification learning. *Psychological Review, 85*, 207–238.

Mervis, C. B., & Rosch, E. H. (1981). Categorization of natural objects. *Annual Review of Psychology, 32*, 89–115.

Milch, B., & Russell, S. (2006). General-purpose mcmc inference over relational structures. In *Proc. 22nd conference on uncertainty in artificial intelligence (uai)* (pp. 349–358).

Montague, R. (1973). The proper treatment of quantification in ordinary English. In J. Hintikka, J. M. E. Moravcsik, & P. Suppes (Eds.), *Approaches to natural language* (pp. 221–242). Dordrecht: D. Reidel.

Muggleton, S. (1997). Learning from positive data. In *Selected papers from the 6th international workshop on inductive logic programming* (p. 358–376). Springer-Verlag.

Murphy, G. L., & Medin, D. L. (1985). The role of theories in conceptual coherence. *Psychol Rev, 92*(3), 289–316.

Nosofsky, R. M., Palmeri, T. J., & McKinley, S. C. (1994). Rule-plus-exception model of classification learning. *Psychological Review, 101*(1), 53–79.

Osherson, D. N., & Smith, E. E. (1981, Feb). On the adequacy of prototype theory as a theory of concepts. *Cognition, 9*(1), 35–58.

Pearl, J. (2000). *Causality: models, reasoning, and inference.* Cambridge University Press.

Posner, M. I., & Keele, S. W. (1968). On the genesis of abstract ideas. *Journal of Experimental Psychology, 77*(3), 353–363.

Rehder, B. (1999). A causal-model theory of categorization. In M. Hahn & S. C. Stones (Eds.), *21st annual conference of the cognitive science society* (pp. 595–600). Vancouver.

Sloman, S. A., Love, B. C., & Ahn, W. kyoung. (1998). Feature Centrality and Conceptual Coherence. *Cognitive Science, 22*, 189–228.

Smith, J. D., & Minda, J. P. (1998). Prototypes in the mist: The early epochs of category learning. *Journal of Experimental Psychology: Learning, Memory, and Cognition, 24*, 1411–1436.

Steyvers, M., Tenenbaum, J. B., Wagenmakers, E. J., & Blum, B. (2003). Inferring causal networks from observations and interventions. *Cognitive Science, 27*, 453–489.

Tarski, A. (1956). The Concept of Truth in Formalized Languages. *Logic, Semantics, Metamathematics*, 152–278. (Originally 'Der Wahrheitsbegriff in den formalisierten Sprachen', 1935.)

Tenenbaum, J. B. (1999). *A Bayesian framework for concept learning.* Unpublished doctoral dissertation, Massachussets Institute of Technology, Cambridge, MA.

Tenenbaum, J. B., & Griffiths, T. L. (2001). Generalization, similarity, and Bayesian inference. *Behavioral and Brain Sciences, 24*, 629–641.

Tenenbaum, J. B., Griffiths, T. L., & Kemp, C. (2006). Theory-based bayesian models of inductive learning and reasoning. *Trends in Cognitive Sciences, 10*, 309–318.

Tenenbaum, J. B., Griffiths, T. L., & Niyogi, S. (2007). Intuitive theories as grammars for causal inference. In A. Gopnik & L. Schulz (Eds.), *Causal learning: Psychology, philosophy, and computation.* Oxford: Oxford University Press.

Wittgenstein, L. (1921). *Tractatus logico philosophicus (routledge classics).* Routledge.

Woodward, J. (2003). *Making things happen: a theory of causal explanation.* New York: Oxford University Press.

Xu, F., & Tenenbaum, J. B. (2007). Word learning as bayesian inference. *Psychological Review.*

Yuille, A., & Kersten, D. (2006). Vision as bayesian inference: analysis by synthesis? *Trends in Cognitive Sciences, 10*, 301–308.

Appendix A

Causal regularities

The INF grammar, which we have used to generate the concept language of the RR_{INF} model, represents the defining properties of a concept as a set of implicational regularities. As we indicated in the main text, it is intuitive to interpret these implications as causal relations. For instance the regularity $Ripe(x) \Rightarrow Red(x)$ for the concept 'strawberry,' might be interpreted as meaning that, if x is a strawberry, then x being ripe *causes* x to be red. This interpretation becomes especially interesting for the extension of RR_{INF} to role-governed concepts. Take the example of a 'poison'; a poison is a substance that, when inside an organism, causes injury. We might write this as:

$$\forall x \; poison(x) \Leftrightarrow (\forall y \; in(x,y) \wedge organism(y) \Rightarrow injured(y)).$$

To see why the causal interpretation is important, consider the case of Socrates, who drank hemlock and died. If Socrates had been cured in the nick of time, should we conclude that hemlock is not a poison? This is the conclusion we must draw if we interpret the '$\Rightarrow$' as material implication. From the causal interpretation, however, hemlock may still be a poison: by intervening on the injury of socrates we supersede the causal regularity that would otherwise hold (Pearl, 2000). Indeed, interpreted causally this definition of 'poison' is useful for crafting many interventions—e.g., if we'd like to injure someone, we may introduce a poison into them—and answering counterfactuals—e.g., if Socrates had been a rock, the poison hemlock would not have injured him.

Causal knowledge tells you how to make things happen—this is the thesis that has recently been argued in philosophy (Woodward, 2003) and cognitive science (Pearl, 2000; Gopnik *et al.*, 2004; Lagnado & Sloman, 2002; Steyvers *et al.*, 2003). Thus, if we have a causal feature-based definition of a concept A, we know how to make things happen to the properties of an A, by manipulating other properties of that A (e.g., we know to make a strawberry red by ripening it). If we have a causal role-governed definition of concept A, we know how to make things happen to an A using another object, or vice versa (e.g., we can open a lock by using its key). (Notice that it is a very small step from here to the notion of using an object as a tool.) Formally, a regularity is causal if we know how to evaluate it under all possible sets of interventions.

We can formally extend the compositional semantics of the RR_{INF} model to this causal interpretation by specifying the likelihood function under intervention. We follow the *structural equation* approach of Halpern and Pearl (2001), with some embellishments to maintain compatibility of the likelihood with the grammar. Say that the intervention condition $\mathcal{I}$ is the set of interventions performed: each intervention is on one feature-object pair or relation-object-object triple. Let $\mathbf{W}_{\mathcal{I}}$ and $\ell(\mathbf{E})_{\mathcal{I}}$ be the observed features and labels under this intervention condition. We first extend the semantic information associated with the evaluation of a feature or relation: $f_i(x)$ – val is now associated to a function from objects to a pair of truth values. The second truth value, the *intervention value*, indicates whether an intervention has been performed at this feature-object pair (i.e., whether the pair f_i, x is in $\mathcal{I}$). The same extension holds, *mutatis mutandis*, for relations. Next we alter the semantic operation associated to the (production which introduces an) implication $C \Rightarrow P$: when the intervention value of the P-term is True, the implication is evaluated as True (i.e., it is ignored), otherwise it is evaluated as usual. The remaining semantic operations are unchanged. Putting these together we may evaluate the extended likelihood $P\left(\mathbf{W}_{\mathcal{I}}, \ell(\mathbf{E})_{\mathcal{I}} \middle| F, \mathcal{T}\right)$ under a given intervention condition.

This extension is conceptually simple—ignore any implicational regularities on whose implicand an intervention is performed—the slight subtlety comes from the need to maintain compatibility between the likelihood and grammar. We achieved this by extending the semantic information given a *specific* intervention condition, and adjusting the semantic operations. Another, more general, option would be to extend the semantic types to include interventions as an argument (e.g. $e \rightarrow t$ would becomes $(e, i) \rightarrow t$). This is similar to the possible worlds technique used in intensional logic (Montague, 1973).

Appendix B

Sampling assumptions

In the main text we derived an expression for the likelihood of a world with observed labels for all objects:

$$P\big(\mathbf{W}, \ell(\mathbf{E})|F\big) \propto e^{-bO_\ell(\mathbf{E})}. \tag{10}$$

Where $O_\ell(\mathbf{E}) = \big|\{x \in \mathbf{E} | \neg(\ell(x) \Leftrightarrow D(x))\}\big|$ is the number of labeled examples which don't satisfy the 'definition' part of F. If labels are observed for only a subset $\mathbf{Obs} \subseteq \mathbf{E}$ of the objects, then we must marginalize over the unobserved labels (we write $\overline{\mathbf{Obs}} = \mathbf{E} \setminus \mathbf{Obs}$ for the set of objects with unobserved labels):

$$
\begin{aligned}
P\big(\mathbf{W}, &\ell(\mathbf{Obs}), \overline{\mathbf{Obs}}|F\big) \\
&= \sum_{\ell(\overline{\mathbf{Obs}})} P\big(\mathbf{W}, \ell(\mathbf{E}), \overline{\mathbf{Obs}}|F\big) \\
&= \sum_{\ell(\overline{\mathbf{Obs}})} P\big(\overline{\mathbf{Obs}}|F, \mathbf{W}, \ell(\mathbf{E})\big) P\big(\mathbf{W}, \ell(\mathbf{E})|F\big) \\
&\propto \sum_{\ell(\overline{\mathbf{Obs}})} P\big(\overline{\mathbf{Obs}}|F, \mathbf{W}, \ell(\mathbf{E})\big) e^{-bO_\ell(\mathbf{E})} \\
&= e^{-bO_\ell(\mathbf{Obs})} \sum_{\ell(\overline{\mathbf{Obs}})} P\big(\overline{\mathbf{Obs}}|F, \mathbf{W}, \ell(\mathbf{E})\big) e^{-bO_\ell(\overline{\mathbf{Obs}})}
\end{aligned} \tag{11}
$$

Now we will need to make a *sampling assumption* (Tenenbaum & Griffiths, 2001) about how the objects with observed labels were chosen from among all the objects. Two standard choices are *weak sampling*, that $\mathbf{Obs}$ are chosen at random, and *strong sampling*, that $\mathbf{Obs}$ are chosen explicitly to be positive (or negative) examples of the concept.

Weak sampling

If $\mathbf{Obs}$ is chosen independent of $F, \mathbf{W}, \ell(\mathbf{E})$, for instance if it is chosen at random from among all objects, then:

$$
\begin{aligned}
P\big(\mathbf{W}, \ell(\mathbf{Obs}), \overline{\mathbf{Obs}}|F\big) &\propto e^{-bO_\ell(\mathbf{Obs})} \overset{\sigma}{-} \sum_{\ell(\overline{\mathbf{Obs}})} e^{-bO_\ell(\overline{\mathbf{Obs}})} \\
&= e^{-bO_\ell(\mathbf{Obs})} \sum_{i=0}^{|\overline{\mathbf{Obs}}|} \binom{|\overline{\mathbf{Obs}}|}{i} e^{-bi} \\
&\propto e^{-bO_\ell(\mathbf{Obs})}
\end{aligned} \tag{12}
$$

Where we have used the fact that $\ell(x) \Leftrightarrow D(x)$ is true for exactly one of the two values of $\ell(x)$, and the sum is then independent of F.

Weak sampling is a reasonable assumption when there are both positive and negative examples, and no external reason to assume that examples are chosen to be exemplary. We have used this weak sampling likelihood for the examples in the main text, since it is both reasonable and simple in those settings.

Strong sampling

If, on the other hand, only positive examples are observed (Tenenbaum, 1999), or in certain pedagogical situations (Xu & Tenenbaum, 2007), it is more reasonable to make a strong sampling assumption: positive (and negative) examples are chosen from among those objects which satisfy (respectively, don't satisfy) the concept at hand. For simplicity let us assume that we have only positive examples, that is $\ell(x) = 1$ for all $x \in \mathbf{Obs}$. We will assume that $\mathbf{Obs}$ is chosen at random from among objects which satisfy the concept, thus:

$$P\big(x \in \mathbf{Obs}\big|F, \mathbf{W}, \ell(\mathbf{E})\big) \propto \frac{1}{\big|\{y \in \mathbf{E}\big|\ell(y) = 1\}\big|}. \tag{13}$$

(Note that we have allowed repeated samples, for simplicity.) From this we can derive an expression for the likelihood:

$$P\big(\mathbf{W}, \ell(\mathbf{Obs}), \mathbf{Obs}\big|F\big)$$

$$\propto e^{-bO_\ell(\mathbf{Obs})} \sum_{\ell(\mathbf{Obs})} \Bigg(\prod_{x \in \mathbf{Obs}} P\big(x \in \mathbf{Obs}\big|F, \mathbf{W}, \ell(\mathbf{E})\big) \Bigg) e^{-bO_\ell(\overline{\mathbf{Obs}})}$$

$$= e^{-bO_\ell(\mathbf{Obs})} \sum_{\ell(\mathbf{Obs})} \Bigg(\prod_{x \in \mathbf{Obs}} \frac{1}{\big|\{y \in \mathbf{E}\big|\ell(y) = 1\}\big|} \Bigg) e^{-bO_\ell(\overline{\mathbf{Obs}})}$$

$$e^{-bO_\ell(\mathbf{Obs})} \sum_{\ell(\mathbf{Obs})} \frac{e^{-bO_\ell(\overline{\mathbf{Obs}})}}{\big|\{y \in \mathbf{E}\big|\ell(y) = 1\}\big|^{|\mathbf{Obs}|}} \tag{14}$$

Learning from positive examples

Using the strong-sampling-based likelihood, (14), we may describe learning from only positive examples. Importantly, the denominator in (14) causes the smallest concept consistent with the labeled examples to be the most likely (this is the *size principle* of Tenenbaum (1999)); this leads the learner to select the most restrictive (hence informative) concept even when the evidence is equally consistent with broader concepts. This learning situation has been studied extensively in the context of feature-based categories (Tenenbaum, 1999; Xu & Tenenbaum, 2007; Muggleton, 1997), but it is particularly interesting in the setting of role-governed concepts. Indeed, note that any set of positive examples that is compatible with a universally quantified regularity is also compatible with an existential regularity (but not vice versa: the existential form is less restrictive than the universal form). For instance, if we see several 'poisons' injure several different people, should we infer that 'poison' is governed by a universal or existential quantifier (i.e., that there is *someone* who every poison injures, or that a poison injures *anyone*)? Under the weak sampling likelihood we must wait until these are distinguished by negative evidence (e.g., a non-poison which injures a few people), but with the strong sampling likelihood the more restrictive hypothesis—the universal regularity—is favored, all other things being equal.

Part 5

Learning about Contingency and Causality

Chapter 18

Through the looking glass: a dynamic lens model approach to multiple cue probability learning

Maarten Speekenbrink and David R. Shanks

University College London, London, UK

Despite what the somewhat technical name might suggest, multiple cue probability learning (MCPL) problems are commonly encountered in daily life. For instance, we may have to judge whether it will rain from cues such as temperature, humidity, and the time of year. Or, we may have to judge whether someone is telling the truth from cues such as pitch of voice, level of eye contact, and rate of eye blinks. While informative, these cues are not perfect predictors. How do we learn to solve such problems? How do we learn which cues are relevant, and to what extent? How do we integrate the available information into a judgement?

Applying a rational analysis (Anderson, 1990; Oaksford & Chater, 1998), we would answer these questions by specifying a rational model, and then compare individuals' judgements to the model-predicted judgements. Insofar as observed behaviour matches the predicted behaviour, we would conclude that people learn these tasks as rational agents. Here, we take a slightly different approach. We still use rational models, but rather than comparing predicted behaviour to actual behaviour (a comparison in what we might call observation space), we make the comparison in parameter space.

To be a little less obscure, let's take an agent who must repeatedly predict share price from past share price. A rational agent would make predictions which are optimal given an observed pattern of past share price. The question is whether a real (human) agent makes predictions as the rational agent would. Assume current share price Y_t is related to past share price Y_{t-1} as $Y_t = \beta Y_{t-1}$, where β is an unknown constant. In order to make accurate predictions, the agent must infer the value of β from repeated observations of share price. A rational agent, with optimal estimates w_t, will make predictions $\hat{y}_t = w_t Y_{t-1}$. Since the relation is rather simple, and the agent is rational, the inferences w_t (and hence predictions $\hat{y}_t$) will be accurate quite quickly. Enter the real (rational?) agent, making predictions R_t. Rather than assuming these predictions follow from rational estimates w_t, we assume they are based on $R_t = u_t Y_{t-1}$, where u_t is a coefficient not necessarily equal to w_t. Thus, we assume the same *structural* model for rational and actual predictions, but allow for different parameters u_t and w_t. By comparing u_t to w_t, we can see how the real agent's learning compares to the rational agent's learning. Moreover, we can compare both u_t and w_t to the true value β, to see how well the rational and real agent adapt to the environment.

The values of u_t can be estimated in different ways. A common approach is to assume that the real agent learns in a similar way to the rational model; for instance, by changing u_t according to the error of predictions. To match the values of u_t to the real agent's predictions, the changes are allowed to be of a sub-optimal magnitude. The fitted learning model is then used to derive the values of u_t. This procedure is reasonable if the agent learns according to the model. However, as the estimates of u_t are constrained by the learning model, they will be biased if the agent learns in a different way. An alternative approach is to make minimal assumptions regarding the process by which u_t changes (i.e., not assuming the change is related to the error of prediction), and estimate u_t directly from the predictions and cues (e.g., Kelley & Friedman, 2002; Lagnado *et al.*, 2006). The resulting 'unconstrained' estimates will not be biased towards the learning model, and hence provide more information regarding its validity.

The lens model

Our analysis owes much to Brunswik's (1955) lens model. The lens model has its origins in perception, and was proposed to describe how organisms perceive a distal (unobservable) criterion, through proximal (observable) cues. Hammond *et al.* (1966) formulated the lens model in statistical terms, and proposed it as a general framework for judgement analysis. Since then, the lens model has been a standard tool in the study of multiple cue probability learning (Cooksey, 1996). Figure 18.1 depicts a simple version of the lens model. The left-hand side of the lens represents the environment, consisting of the cues and the criterion. How well an individual can perceive, judge, or predict the criterion (we will use the generic term 'respond' from now on), depends on the relation between the cues and the criterion. Adopting the standard terminology, we will refer to these relations as *cue validity*. The right-hand side of the lens represents the response system, consisting of the cues and the responses. The relations between the cues and the responses reflect how an individual actually uses the cues in forming a response. These relations are referred to as *cue utilization*. How well an individual performs in a multiple cue task depends on the relation between the criterion and the responses; central to the lens model is that this relation can be ascertained by comparing cue validity and utilization.

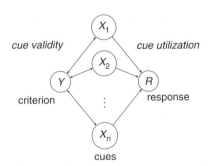

Fig. 18.1 The lens model.

Usually, the parameters of the lens model are estimated by multiple regression analysis. For instance, estimates of cue validity are obtained as the regression coefficients of a model which relates the criterion to the cues. Similarly, by regressing the responses onto the cues, we can obtain estimates of cue utilization. In its original form, the lens model is static, and provides constant cue validity and utilization weights for a period in time (e.g., the duration of the task). As such, these estimates are valid under the assumption that the environment and the response system are stationary. However, in a typical MCPL task, the environment is unknown to the agent, who must infer its structure as the task progresses. As such, even if the environment is stationary, the response system (which relies on these inferences) will be non-stationary. Of course, we could apply the lens model after an extensive period of training, such that learning will have converged to a particular representation of the environment. However, we are interested in the learning process itself, in how an agent learns to adapt his/her predictions to the structure of the environment. To study this process, we must deal with non-stationarity.

Previously, 'rolling regression' has been proposed as a method to estimate the changes in cue utilization (Kelley & Friedman, 2002; Lagnado *et al.*, 2006). In rolling regression, the regression model is repeatedly fitted to a moving window of trials. For a window of size W, cue validity and utilization at trial t are estimated from regression models applied to observations from trials $t-W+1$ to t. While this method is a straightforward extension of usual lens model analysis, it has certain drawbacks. For one, utilization and validity can only be estimated from trial W onwards. Since the window size may have to be large to get reliable estimates, this will be problematic if we are interested in the early stages of learning. And although the window size allows manipulation of something akin to memory limits, the type of memory represented is not very plausible. More particularly, each observation within the window affects estimates to a similar extent, but observations outside the window have no effect. A more gradual form of memory loss seems more appropriate. Finally, as a method of tracking slowly changing weights, rolling regression is not optimal in a statistical sense. In this chapter, we will propose an alternative method, which has clear advantages over rolling regression.

Overview

In the remainder of this chapter, we will first describe a generalized lens model, which is still static, but incorporates situations in which linear regression is unsuitable. We then extend this framework into a dynamic lens model, which is suitable for non-stationary environments and response systems. Of particular interest in the context of rational analysis is that we can replace part of the model with a rational learning model. This allows a comparison between the structure of the environment, optimal inference, and actual inference as evident from the responses made. Finally, we will illustrate the methods by re-analysing data from an earlier MCPL study (Lagnado *et al.*, 2006).

A framework for MCPL

In multiple cue probability learning tasks, the objective is to make a prediction R of the value of a criterion variable Y, on the basis of a number of cues X_j. The relation between criterion and cues $\mathbf{X} = (X_1, \ldots, X_n)^\mathsf{T}$ is probabilistic, and each cue pattern is associated with a probability distribution over the possible values of Y,

$$P(Y|\mathbf{x}) = P(Y, \mathbf{X} = \mathbf{x}) / P(\mathbf{X} = \mathbf{x}). \tag{1}$$

This conditional probability distribution is initially unknown, and has to be inferred from repeated observations of training pairs $(y, \mathbf{x})$ drawn from the environmental distribution $P(Y, \mathbf{X})$.

Generalized linear model

We consider environments which fit in the framework of generalized linear models (McCullagh & Nelder, 1983, see also Dobson, 2002). That is, we assume the conditional distribution $P(Y|\mathbf{X})$ to be a member of the exponential family, and the existence of a function g and parameters $\boldsymbol{\beta} = (\beta_1, \ldots, \beta_m)^\mathsf{T}$ such that

$$g(\mu_x) = \mathbf{z}^\mathsf{T}\boldsymbol{\beta}, \tag{2}$$

where T denotes the (matrix) transpose. The link function g linearizes the relation between the criterion and the *effective cue pattern* $\mathbf{z}$, which is a vector of dimension m. If Y is Normally distributed, a good choice is the identity function $g(\mu_x) = \mu_x$. When the distribution of Y is binomial, a logit function $g(\mu_x) = \log(\mu_x/(1-\mu_x))$ is often used. The effective cue pattern $\mathbf{z}$ is related to the actual cue pattern $\mathbf{x}$ (a vector of dimension n) as

$$\mathbf{z} = h(\mathbf{x}). \tag{3}$$

Often, h will be the identity function, so that the effective cue pattern is the original cue pattern. This corresponds to the assumption that the cues affect the criterion independently. If this assumption does not hold, the effective cue vector can be extended to include interaction between the cues. In this case, the dimension of $\mathbf{z}$ will differ from the dimension of $\mathbf{x}$. When the cues are categorical variables, function h will map the cue patterns to corresponding patterns of dummy variables. Finally, function h can also represent the mapping of cue patterns to their representation in some psychological space.

The lens model fits neatly into our framework. We assume that $P(Y|\mathbf{X})$ and $P(R|\mathbf{X})$ are of the same form (e.g., both normal or both binomial), with expectations $E(Y|\mathbf{x}) = E(Y|\mathbf{z}) = \mu_z$ and $E(R|\mathbf{x}) = E(R|\mathbf{z}) = \rho_z$, that g and h are identical for both the environment and response system,

$$g(\mu_z) = \mathbf{z}^\mathsf{T}\mathbf{v}, \tag{4}$$

and

$$g(\rho_z) = \mathbf{z}^\mathsf{T}\mathbf{u}. \tag{5}$$

Here, $\mathbf{v}$ represents cue validity, and $\mathbf{u}$ cue utilization. For our purposes, it is crucial that h, and as a result the effective cue vector $\mathbf{z}$, is identical in both models. Without this equivalence, cue validity and utilization are not directly comparable.

Since the dimension of **v** is usually smaller than the number of possible cue patterns, learning is simplified. Rather than having to infer the conditional distribution (or expected value) of the criterion for each cue pattern **x** directly, the agent infers the value of **v**, and determines the conditional distribution from these. Estimates of **v** will be more reliable than direct estimates of $P(Y|\mathbf{x})$ or $E(Y|\mathbf{x})$, and also require less storage in memory than a direct representations of these.

Optimal responses

Associated with the response and the criterion is a loss function $L(R,Y)$, and the objective for the agent is to give responses $R = r_x^*$ to cue patterns **x** which minimize the expected loss

$$r_x^* = \arg\min_r E(L(r,Y) \mid \mathbf{x}). \tag{6}$$

For real-valued criterion and predictions, a squared loss function

$$L(r,y) = (r - y)^2 \tag{7}$$

is often used, and the optimal prediction is the expected value

$$r_x^* = E(Y \mid \mathbf{x}) \equiv \mu_x . \tag{8}$$

In terms of cue validity, this can be rewritten as

$$r_x^* = g^{-1}\left(\mathbf{z}^\mathsf{T}\mathbf{v}\right), \tag{9}$$

where g^{-1} denotes the inverse of the link function g. For nominal criterion and responses in the same set, a $0-1$ loss function

$$L(r,y) = \begin{cases} 0 & \text{if } r = y \\ 1 & \text{if } r \neq y \end{cases}, \tag{10}$$

is usually appropriate, and the optimal prediction is

$$r_x^* = \arg\max_y P(Y = y \mid \mathbf{x}). \tag{11}$$

When the criterion $Y = \{0,1\}$ is dichotomous, this can be rewritten in terms of cue validity as

$$r_x^* = \begin{cases} 0 & \text{if } \mathbf{z}^\mathsf{T}\mathbf{v} < 0 \\ 1 & \text{otherwise} \end{cases}. \tag{12}$$

Dynamic lens model

As noted earlier, standard lens model analysis is static, by which we means that validity and utilization are assumed to be constant over trials t. In standard MCPL tasks presented in laboratory studies, the environment is often stationary, so that this assumption will hold for cue validity. However, as a result of learning, cue utilization will change with t. To study learning, we need to take a dynamic viewpoint in which we explicitly focus on trial-by-trial changes in cue utilization.

In dynamic lens model analysis, both cue validity and utilization are allowed to vary over time. A graphical representation of the structure of the dynamic lens model is given in Fig. 18.2. To account for the changes in cue validity and utilization, we need a (stochastic) model for the change process. In most MCPL experiments, the environment is under control of the experimenter, and the dynamics of cue validity will be known. Determining the dynamic process of cue utilization will be more challenging. While there are many possibilities, the assumption of a simple random walk will suffice in most cases. That is, we assume

$$\mathbf{u}_t = \mathbf{u}_{t-1} + \mathbf{e}_t, \tag{13}$$

with $\mathbf{e}_t \sim N(\mathbf{0}, \Sigma_u)$, i.e., following a zero-mean multivariate normal distribution with covariance matrix Σ_u. The model for the responses resulting from the combination of (5) and (13) is known as a dynamic generalized linear model (West & Harrison, 1997). When the process for environmental change is also unknown, a similar model can be used for cue validity.

Estimation of $\mathbf{u}_t$ from all observations R_t, $\mathbf{x}_t$, $t = 1,\dots,T$, where T denotes the total number of trials, is known as smoothing. When Σ_u is known and the conditional distribution $P(R_t|\mathbf{x}_t, \mathbf{u}_t)$ is Normal with known variance, optimal estimates can be derived analytically, and the solution is known as the Kalman smoother (e.g., Durbin & Koopman, 2001; West & Harrison, 1997). When R_t is not normally distributed, analytical solution are usually unavailable, and approximate methods must be used. In the application described later, we will use a Monte Carlo Markov Chain (MCMC) procedure for this purpose.

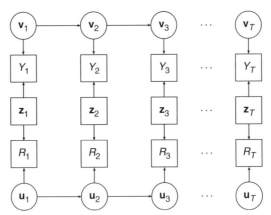

Fig. 18.2 The dynamic lens model. Observed variables are depicted in squares, while unobserved (latent) variables are depicted in circles. The criterion Y_t is dependent on the effective cue vector $\mathbf{z}_t$ and cue validity $\mathbf{v}_t$. The response R_t depends on the effective cue vector and cue utilization $\mathbf{u}_t$. Cue validity $\mathbf{v}_t$ depends on previous cue validity $\mathbf{v}_{t-1}$, and utilization $\mathbf{u}_t$ on previous utilization $\mathbf{u}_{t-1}$.

Incorporating rational models

In the dynamic lens model, trial-by-trial variation in utilization is assumed to be independent of (variation in) cue validity. While this assumption may be false if an agent makes accurate inferences of cue validity, the assumption reflects the wish to 'let the data speak for itself'. If validity and utilization are indeed related, this should be evident from the (estimated) validity and utilization weights. As such, the dynamic lens model allows one to analyse learning without making explicit assumptions regarding how this learning proceeds. Of course, rational models do make such assumptions, which is part of their strength. To incorporate rational learning models, we need to extend the response part of the dynamical lens model.

A graphical representation of the extended model is given in Fig. 18.3. The model now consists of three related sub-models, one for the environment, one for learning, and one for the responses. The model of the environment, consisting of the criterion, cues and cue validity, is identical to the one in Fig. 18.2. The learning model consists of the criterion, effective cue pattern, and inference. Here, the agent infers validity $\mathbf{v}_t$ from training pairs $(y_t, \mathbf{z}_t)$. We will denote the inference of $\mathbf{v}_t$ as $\mathbf{w}_t$. As before, the response model consists of the responses, effective cue patterns, and cue utilization. In this context, utilization is referred to as predicted utilization $\hat{\mathbf{u}}_t$, to distinguish it from the utilization in Fig. 18.2. Predicted utilization does not depend on previous utilization, but on the current inferred cue validity $\mathbf{w}_t$, and changes in $\hat{\mathbf{u}}_t$ are taken to depend completely on changes in $\mathbf{w}_t$.

The models in Figs. 18.2 and 18.3 can be made equivalent by removing the links from $\mathbf{z}_{t-1}$ and Y_{t-1} to $\mathbf{w}_t$, and assuming identity of $\mathbf{w}_t$ and $\hat{\mathbf{u}}_t$. However, learning

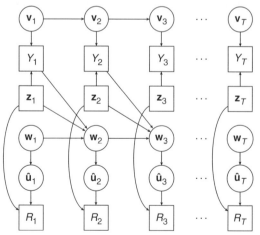

Fig. 18.3 A general model of learning and prediction in MCPL. The criterion Y_t depends on the effective cue vector $\mathbf{z}_t$ and cue validity $\mathbf{v}_t$. Inferred cue validity $\mathbf{w}_{t+1}$ depends on the previous inference $\mathbf{w}_t$, effective cue vector $\mathbf{z}_t$, and criterion Y_t. Predicted cue utilization $\hat{\mathbf{u}}_t$ depends on the inferred cue validity $\mathbf{w}_t$. The prediction Rt depends on predicted cue utilization $\hat{\mathbf{u}}_t$ and effective cue vector $\mathbf{z}_t$.

models which incorporate these links are of main interest here. We will describe such models in the next section.

Learning in the weather prediction task

Up to now, the models have been described in general terms. We will now apply them to an MCPL task which has received much attention over recent decades, especially in the field of neuroscience. In the so-called weather prediction task (Knowlton *et al.*, 1994), the objective is to predict the state of the weather (sunny or rainy) on the basis of four 'Tarot cards' (cards with geometrical patterns). On each trial t, one to three cards are presented, and the agent is asked whether the weather will be sunny or rainy. Each cue pattern is associated with the state of the weather with a different probability. These probabilities are given in Table 18.1. The environment is constructed so that each card is associated with the outcome with a different probability. For example, the probability of rainy weather is 0.2 over all the trials on which card 1 is present, 0.4 for trials on which card 2 is present, 0.6 for trials on which card 3 is present, and 0.8 for trials on which card 4 is present. Thus, two cards are predictive of rain, one strongly (card 4), one weakly (card 3), and two cards are predictive of sun, one strongly (card 1), one weakly (card 2). A more detailed description of the weather prediction task can be found in Lagnado *et al.* (2006).

Table 18.1 Learning environment in the weather prediction task. P(sun|pattern) denotes the actual conditional probability of sunny weather, while m_z is the predicted probability (see text).

Pattern	Cards present	z	Total	P(pattern)	P(sun|pattern)	m_z
A	4	0001	19	0.095	0.895	0.891
B	3	0010	9	0.045	0.778	0.641
C	3,4	0011	26	0.130	0.923	0.936
D	2	0100	9	0.045	0.222	0.359
E	2,4	0101	12	0.060	0.833	0.821
F	2,3	0110	6	0.030	0.500	0.500
G	2,3,4	0111	19	0.095	0.895	0.891
H	1	1000	19	0.095	0.105	0.109
I	1,4	1001	6	0.030	0.500	0.500
J	1,3	1010	12	0.060	0.167	0.179
K	1,3,4	1011	9	0.045	0.556	0.641
L	1,2	1100	26	0.130	0.077	0.064
M	1,2,4	1101	9	0.045	0.444	0.359
N	1,2,3	1110	19	0.095	0.105	0.109
Total			200	1.00		

Environment

The environment consists of the criterion Y_t and the cue patterns x_t. The model of the environment consists of the criterion, effective cue patterns z_t, and cue validity weights v_t. The environment is stationary, so that cue validity is independent of trial t, and $v_t = v_{t+1} = v$, for all t. The criterion is dichotomous, and $P(Y_t = y|x_t)$ is constant and a Bernouilli distribution,

$$P(Y = y \mid x) = \mu_x^y (1 - \mu_x)^{1-y}, \tag{14}$$

where we use the scoring of $y = 1$ for rainy, and $y = 0$ for sunny weather. Since the cues are categorical variables, with g being the logit-function, there will exist a function h and vector v such that (4) will hold.[1] The resulting model can be recognized as a logistic regression model. For simplicity, we will let z be a binary vector of dimension 4, in which the elements are binary dummy variables for the main effects of the four cues. In other words, the outcome is assumed to be a function of the additive combination of the individual cue validities. The resulting values for z can be found in Table 18.1, and the associated cue validities are $v = (-2.10, -0.58, 0.58, 2.10)^\mathsf{T}$.

We should note that the model is not entirely correct, and the predicted values $m_z = g^{-1}(z^\mathsf{T}v)$ only approximate μ_x. In the correct model, z also contains dummy variables for all cue interactions, resulting in a vector of dimension 14 rather than 4. For practical purposes, the resulting 10 additional parameters were deemed unnecessary (and possibly detrimental, as the increase in parameters will decrease the reliability of their estimates, and result in generally poorer inferences in a limited data set). As can be seen in Table 18.1, the approximation with z is generally quite close, but fails somewhat for the relatively rare patterns B, D, K, and M. This is due to the fact that the model assumes $P(Y|\text{pattern B}) = P(Y|\text{pattern K})$ and $P(Y|\text{pattern D}) = P(Y|\text{pattern M})$, while in reality, they are different (e.g., the effect of card 2 is stronger in the presence of cards 1 and 4 than in their absence). Finally, as the deviations from the predictions m_z are not drastic, and there is much evidence to suggest that simple additive rules of cue integration are a default strategy (Cooksey, 1996; Einhorn et al., 1979; Hastie & Dawes, 2001), we expect z to be adequate to model the responses.

Learning process

The objective for the agent is to infer cue validity v, and then base responses on these inferences. There are many ways in which cue validity can be inferred. As depicted in Fig. 18.3, a restriction we place is that observations of the cues and criterion affect inferences only once. In other words, we assume an on-line learning process, such that learning consists of updating inference w_t on the basis of y_t and z_t. We will describe two learning strategies in more detail, a Bayesian and an associative procedure.

---

[1] In general, for a binary cue vector x, h can be a function which maps x to a set of 2^n dummy variables (n is the dimension of x), representing an intercept, the main effects, and all possible (two-way, three-way, etc.) interactions between the cues. The resulting saturated model has the same number of validity parameters as possible cue patterns and can fit any set of conditional probability distributions $P(Y|x)$ for these possible patterns x perfectly.

Bayesian learning

On-line learning has a natural representation in Bayesian terms. In Bayesian learning, a learner represents the uncertainty regarding $\mathbf{v}$ as a probability distribution over $\mathbf{v}$. After each trial t, this probability distribution is updated by incorporating the new evidence presented on that trial. Letting $P_t(\mathbf{v})$ denote the prior probability distribution, the posterior distribution after trial t is the product of the prior distribution $P_t(\mathbf{v})$ and the likelihood $P(y_t|\mathbf{v},\mathbf{z}_t)$ of $\mathbf{v}$ for observations y_t and $\mathbf{z}_t$, i.e.,

$$P_{t+1}(\mathbf{v}) = P(y_t|\mathbf{v},\mathbf{z}_t)P_t(\mathbf{v})/K, \tag{15}$$

where the proportionality constant $K = \int P(y_t|\mathbf{v},\mathbf{z}_t)P_t(\mathbf{v})d\mathbf{v}$ ensures that $P_{t+1}(\mathbf{v})$ is a probability distribution. The likelihood is given in (14). If the agent has to give a point estimate $\mathbf{w}_{t+1}$ of $\mathbf{v}$, (s)he may give the posterior expectation of $\mathbf{v}$, or the maximum a posteriori (MAP) value of $\mathbf{v}$. When we represent an agent's learning state in terms of inference $\mathbf{w}_t$, we choose the first option.

Associative learning

In associative learning, a learner adapts associations between cues and criterion on the basis of observations. The Rescorla–Wagner model (Rescorla & Wagner, 1972) is a long-time favourite for associative learning, and is equivalent to a single-layer feed-forward network, where the weights are adapted according to the LMS (or delta) rule (Gluck & Bower, 1988). We use a somewhat different representation than Gluck and Bower (1988) with a logistic rather than linear activation function. This has the advantage that the model provides direct estimates of the (conditional) probability of the criterion, rather than having to transform the activation later to derive these probabilities. The associative model learns by a gradient descent on the cross-entropy error (Bishop, 1995), resulting in the following rule for trial-by-trial updates of inferred cue validity:

$$\mathbf{w}_{t+1} = \mathbf{w}_t + \eta_t(y_t - m_{t,z})\mathbf{z}_t, \tag{16}$$

in which η_t stands for the *learning rate*, and $m_{t,z}$ is the current inference of the expected value of the criterion

$$m_{t,z} = g^{-1}(\mathbf{z}_t^\mathsf{T}\mathbf{w}_t), \tag{17}$$

with g^{-1} denoting the inverse of the (logit) link function. Note that if an identity link function were used, (16) would be identical to the weight updates of Gluck and Bower (1988). The effect of the logit link function is that the absolute weights can grow without bound, while the predictions $m_{t,z}$ are still on the same scale as the criterion Y_t.

Under certain conditions,[2] it can be shown that repeated application of (16) will result in inferences $\mathbf{w}_t$ which converge to $\mathbf{v}$ as $t \to \infty$ (Robbins & Monro, 1951). A simple scheme obeying these conditions is $\eta_t = \eta/t$. Another option, which does not guarantee convergence, is a constant learning rate $\eta_t = \eta$, for which (16) becomes the LMS rule (Gluck & Bower, 1988). With such a constant learning rate, $\mathbf{w}_t$ will fluctuate

---

[2] These conditions are (1) $\lim_{t\to\infty}\eta_t = 0$, (2) $\sum_{t=1}^{\infty}\eta_t = \infty$, and (3) $\sum_{t=1}^{\infty}\eta_t^2 < \infty$.

around $\mathbf{v}$ as $t \rightarrow \infty$, with variance roughly proportional to η. Although inference with a constant learning rate is not consistent in the statistical sense (the variance of estimations does not approach 0 as $t \rightarrow \infty$), it is preferable over a decreasing learning rate when the environment is non-stationary (i.e., when $\mathbf{v}_t$ changes with t).

Response process

Having inferred the cue validity weights, the agent must form a prediction. Under squared loss, the (subjectively) optimal prediction would be $r^*_{t,z} = m_{t,z}$, as in (8). However, since the agent must predict the state of the weather, and not the probability of a state of the weather, this optimal response is not an allowed prediction. For responses $R_t \in \{0,1\}$ in the same set as the criterion, squared loss is identical to 0–1 loss, and the optimal prediction is as in (11), which can be restated as

$$r^*_{t,z} = \begin{cases} 0 & \text{if } m_{t,z} < .5 \quad (\text{or equivalently } \mathbf{z}^\mathsf{T}\mathbf{v} < 0) \\ 1 & \text{otherwise} \end{cases}. \tag{18}$$

Since the optimal prediction is a deterministic function of $\mathbf{z}_t$ and $\mathbf{w}_t$, the distribution $P(R_t|\mathbf{z}_t)$ for an optimally responding agent is degenerate (all probability mass is on a single point). This is somewhat problematic for our model; therefore, we let the variability of predictions approach 0, rather than being 0 exactly. More precisely, we assume that responses are made by a variant of Luce's (1959) choice rule

$$P(R_t = 1 \mid z_t) = \frac{m^\lambda_{t,z}}{m^\lambda_{t,z} + (1 - m_{t,z})^\lambda}, \tag{19}$$

in which parameter λ determines the *consistency* of responses. The effect of this parameter is depicted in Fig. 18.4. For a rational agent, $\lambda \rightarrow \infty$, so that the relation between $m_{t,z}$ (the inferred probability of the criterion) and the probability of the response approaches a step function. The distribution $P(R_t|\mathbf{z}_t)$ is still a Bernouilli distribution, with parameter $\rho_{t,z} = g^{-1}(\mathbf{z}_t^\mathsf{T}\hat{\mathbf{u}}_t)$. Finally, it is easy to prove (e.g., Speekenbrink *et al.*, 2007) that the assumed response function results in a linear relation between inferred validity and predicted utilization

$$\hat{\mathbf{u}}_t = \lambda \mathbf{w}_t. \tag{20}$$

For a rational agent, absolute utilization weights are thus infinitely larger than the absolute inferred validity weights. We will assume a similar response rule for actual individuals, but with λ possibly not approaching infinity.

Application

Lagnado *et al.* (2006, Experiment 1) collected data from 16 healthy human subjects on the weather prediction task, and used rolling regression analysis to estimate rational inference and cue utilization. Here, we will re-analyse their data using the dynamic lens and rational models.

Are Bayesian and associative learning rational?

The two learning models have different properties. Here, we will address how they compare, assuming a maximizing response strategy. To derive inferences $\mathbf{w}_t$ from

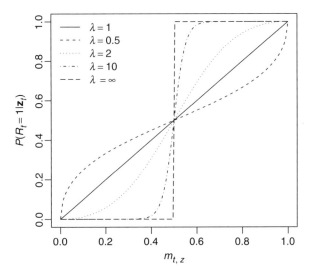

Fig. 18.4 Effect of response consistency λ on the relation between $m_{t,z}$ the (inferred) expected value of the criterion, and $P(R_t = 1 \mid \mathbf{z}_t)$, the probability of response.

Bayesian learning, we discretisized the parameter space (i.e., the domain of $\mathbf{v}$) as a multidimensional grid with 7^4 equally spaced points, and then applied exact Bayesian inference on this grid.[3] A uniform prior $P_1(\mathbf{v})$ was used. Such a uniform prior is optimal when no prior information about $\mathbf{v}$ is present, and results in rapid convergence of $\mathbf{w}$ to $\mathbf{v}$. For the rational version of the associative model with decreasing learning rate, we used a learning rate of $\eta_t = 5.66/t$, where the constant (5.66) was derived as 1 over the largest eigenvalue of the expected Hessian matrix, evaluated at the optimal parameter vector. This is an optimal learning rate for the environment (e.g., LeCun et al., 1998). For the associative model with constant learning rate, we used a value of $\eta_t = 0.32$ (this value resulted in the best predictions in a simulation study with 500 randomly generated WP tasks of 200 trials each). For both associative models, the weights $\mathbf{w}_1$ were initialized to 0.

We used the three learning models to form inferences $\mathbf{w}_t$ in 1000 simulated weather prediction tasks of 200 trials each. These inferences were then used to form responses by a maximizing strategy, as in (18). We then compared the expected performance of the rational agents between the different models. For each set of trials, expected performance is computed as

$$\frac{1}{T}\sum_{t=1}^{T}(r_t P(Y = 1 \mid \mathbf{x}_t) + (1 - r_t)[1 - P(Y = 1 \mid \mathbf{x}_t)]. \tag{21}$$

The maximum performance in the weather prediction task is 0.83, which is only obtained by giving the optimal response on each trial. The mean expected performance was 0.81 $(SD = 0.01)$ for the Bayesian model, 0.80 $(SD = 0.02)$ for the associative model with decreasing learning rate, and 0.81 $(SD = 0.01)$ for the associative model

---

[3] We used grid points $-3, -2, -1, 0, 1, 2$ and 3 for each cue.

with constant learning rate. These values are all rather close to the maximum performance, and while the difference between the models is not large, a repeated measures ANOVA shows it is significant, $F(2,1998) = 326.56$, $p < .001$. Paired-sample t-tests show that the Bayesian model performs significantly better than the associative model with decreasing or constant learning rate, $t(999) = 21.65$, $p < .001$, and $t(999) = 21.37$, $p < .001$, respectively, while the associative model with constant learning rate performed better than the one with decreasing learning rate, $t(999) = 13.16$, $p < .001$. A maximizing Bayesian thus outperformed a maximizing associative learner in this environment. It is somewhat surprising that the constant learning rate outperformed the decreasing learning rate in the associative model. This is due to the fact that, in a few cases, relatively improbable cue-criterion pairs at the start of the task pushed the model to a suboptimal solution. Due to the decreasing learning rate, it then takes relatively long to move to the optimal solution. Thus, although convergence to the optimal solution is guaranteed, and the optimal learning rate should result in an optimal rate of convergence, actual convergence can be very slow due to 'adverse' initial observations. Other schemes, in which the learning rate only decreases after an initial period of constant learning, can help avoid such problems.

Model fitting

Out of the three learning strategies, Bayesian learning was best. Here, we will compare the different strategies in how well they describe participants' learning. We fitted several versions of each model to the data.

For the Bayesian learning model, we fitted versions with different prior distributions on the weights **v**. All prior distributions were multivariate Normal, $\mathbf{v} \sim N(0, \Sigma)$, with the covariance Σ a diagonal matrix with elements σ. The first model ($B.0$) was identical to the rational Bayesian model used earlier, and had a uniform prior over **v**, i.e. $\sigma \to \infty$. In the second model, $B.\sigma$, we estimated the prior standard deviation σ as a single free parameter. In the third model, $B.\sigma_i$, σ was estimated separately for each individual. In all these models, we fixed the response scaling parameter to $\lambda = 1$. We thus assumed a probability matching strategy, rather than a maximizing strategy. Probability matching is often found in research with real subjects (Shanks *et al.*, 2002), so this is likely to describe participants' responses better than a pure maximizing strategy. Moreover, the models are more distinguishable under probability matching. However, we also fitted variants of each model in which the response scaling parameter λ_i was estimated as a free parameter for each individual. These models are referred to as before, but with a λ_i added (e.g., $B.0$ becomes $B.0.\lambda_i$, $B.\sigma$ becomes $B.\sigma.\lambda_i$, etc.). As before, the Bayesian models were estimated by discretisizing the parameter space. The parameters σ and λ were estimated by maximum likelihood.[4]

We also fitted several versions of the associative learning model. As mentioned earlier, we used a version with a decreasing learning rate, referred to as A, and one with a constant learning rate, referred to as Ac. We fitted the rational versions described earlier, with learning rate $\eta_t = 5.66/t$ for model $A.0$ and $\eta_t = .32$ for model $Ac.0$. We also

---

[4] We maximized the likelihood of responses R_{it} following from a Bayesian agent i learning about criterion Y_{it} and responding according to the response process in (19).

fitted models, $A.\eta$ and $Ac.\eta$, in which a single learning rate parameter was estimated as a free parameter, as well as models $A.\eta_i$ and $Ac.\eta_i$, in which the learning rate was estimated freely for each individual. In all these models, we assumed probability matching, but we also fitted versions in which the consistency parameter λ_i was estimated for each participant. As before, parameters η and λ were estimated by maximum likelihood.

The results of the model fitting are given in Table 18.2. This table contains the values of the McFadden pseudo-R^2 (e.g., Dobson, 2002) and the Bayesian Information Criterion (BIC, Schwarz, 1978). The pseudo-R^2 represents the proportional improvement in the log-likelihood of the fitted model over a minimal model, and values between 0.20 and 0.40 are usually taken to indicate good fit. The pseudo-R^2 does not take the number of estimated parameters into account. Since the versions of the models differ in this respect, the BIC provides a better criterion for comparison. The pseudo-R^2 of all models is in the acceptable range. However, the associative model with decreasing learning rate is clearly outperformed by the other two models. When we compare the Bayesian learning models with the BIC, we see that $B.\sigma.\lambda_i$ fitted best. The estimated parameter $\sigma = 0.77$ indicates that individuals learned slower than a Bayesian learner with a uniform prior. The mean response consistency λ_i was 1.41, with a standard deviation of 0.65. For the associative model with decreasing learning rate, the best fitting model was $A.\eta.\lambda_i$. The estimated parameter $\eta = 3.41$ indicates slower learning than the optimal value (5.66). The mean of λ_i was 1.07, with a standard deviation of 0.47. For the associative model with a constant learning rate, the best fitting model was $Ac.0.\lambda_i$. Hence, there was no strong evidence that participants' learned at a different rate than optimal (indeed, the estimated learning rate in model $Ac.\eta.\lambda_i$ was $\eta = 0.28$, which is only slightly below the optimal $\eta = 0.32$). The mean of λ_i was 1.39, with a standard deviation of 0.70.

Overall, model $Ac.0.\lambda_i$ fitted the data best. This corroborates an earlier finding in an experiment with amnesic and control groups (Speekenbrink et al., 2008), where the associative model with a constant learning rate also fitted best (although there, we did not include a Bayesian model with estimated prior variance). The model fits are not informative as to the reason for this better fit. Since inference $\mathbf{w}_t$ converges to $\mathbf{v}$ for both the Bayesian model and associative model with decreasing learning rate, but not the associative model with a constant learning rate, the better fit of the latter could be due to this difference. To get more insight into the reasons for relative misfit, we compare the predicted cue utilization to the unconstrained estimates of cue utilization.

Cue utilization

The dynamic generalized linear model was used to estimate the utilization weights. The parameters $\mathbf{u}_t$ in this model were estimated by MCMC analysis, using the WinBUGS software (Spiegelhalter et al., 2003).[5]

---

[5] As a prior distribution for each cue utilization weight u_j, we used an (independent) zero-mean Normal distribution with a variance of 1. As a prior distribution for Σ, the covariance matrix of $\mathbf{e}_t$, we used an inverse Wishart distribution with 16 degrees of freedom and covariance matrix $\mathbf{V} = \text{diag}(1, 1, 1, 1)$. For all estimations, we ran three parallel Markov chains, with a burn-in period of 4000 and a further 20,000 draws for the actual estimation.

Table 18.2 Model fits: pseudo-R^2 and Bayesian Information Criterion (BIC). Best fitting models are signalled in bold.

#par	Model	pseudo-R^2	BIC	Model	pseudo-R^2	BIC	Model	pseudo-R^2	BIC
0	$B.0$	0.321	3010.51	$A.0$	0.222	3452.49	$Ac.0$	0.341	2922.98
16	$B.0.\lambda_i$	0.360	2967.14	$A.0.\lambda_i$	0.291	3273.68	$Ac.0.\lambda_i$	0.387	**2846.08**
1	$B.\sigma$	0.332	2971.92	$A.\eta$	0.261	3286.06	$Ac.\eta$	0.343	2921.72
17	$B.\sigma.\lambda_i$	0.374	**2913.68**	$A.\eta.\lambda_i$	0.295	**3262.25**	$Ac.\eta.\lambda_i$	0.388	2852.85
16	$B.\sigma_i$	0.354	2992.42	$A.\eta_i$	0.290	3275.89	$Ac.\eta_i$	0.370	2925.38
32	$B.\sigma_i.\lambda_i$	0.383	2995.35	$A.\eta_i.\lambda_i$	0.314	3300.86	$Ac.\eta_i.\lambda_i$	0.397	2933.39

The estimated cue utilization profiles are depicted in Fig. 18.5. As can be seen, most individuals adapted their utilization rather quickly to the environment. Moreover, the weights diverge in the expected direction, and weights for strongly predictive cards (1 and 4) are more extreme than those for weakly predictive cards (2 and 3). When we compare the cue utilization weights to the cue validity weights (-2.10, -0.58, 0.58, and 2.10 for the four cues respectively), we see that for most participants, utilization weights are more extreme than cue validity, reflecting a tendency towards a maximizing strategy.

To gain some more insight into the validity of the different learning models, we can compare the estimated cue utilization weights to those predicted by the learning models. In Fig. 18.6, we have done so for the best (1), closest to average (10) and worst performing (7) individuals. For the best and average individuals, the utilization profiles predicted by best fitting models $B.\sigma.\lambda_i$ and $Ac.0.\lambda_i$ are quite close to each other, and reasonably close to the estimated utilization. The profiles predicted by $A.\eta.\lambda_i$ are

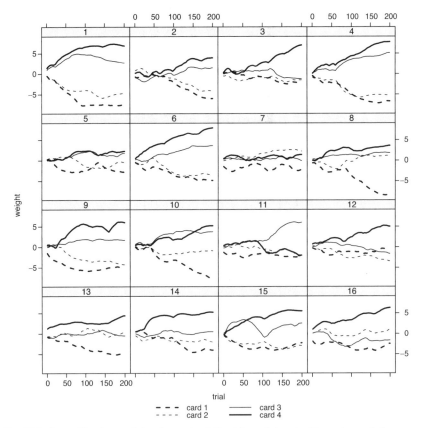

Fig. 18.5 Cue utilization weights for each of the 16 participants. Strongly predictive cards (1 and 4) have thick lines, weakly predictive cards (2 and 3) thin lines. Cards predictive of sun (1 and 2) have solid lines, cards predictive of rain (3 and 4) have broken lines.

further removed. For the worst performing individual, all predicted profiles are very close to each other. This is mainly due to the low consistency parameter λ_i, which was estimated around 0.5 in all three models. This individual hardly appeared to use cards 3 and 4, and, while predictive of rain, used card 2 as predictive of sun (cue validity is negative, but utilization positive).

In Fig. 18.7, we averaged the estimated and predicted utilization profiles over participants. We also included the average rational inference $\bar{w}_t$, as derived from models $B.0$, $A.0$ and $Ac.0$. Comparing the estimated utilization to the rational inference, we see that at the end of the task, utilization weights were more extreme than rational inference, again indicating a tendency towards maximizing (i.e., consistency $\lambda > 1$).

Interestingly, the model-predicted utilization was closer to the rationally inferred validity than to estimated utilization. While the consistency parameter allows predicted utilization to be more extreme than the inferred validity, and hence closer to the estimated utilization weights, on average, the estimated consistency parameter failed to match the two. As such, the models predict responses to be more variable

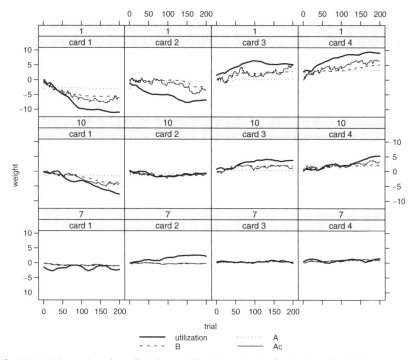

Fig. 18.6 Estimated and predicted cue utilization weights for the best (top), closest to average (middle) and worst (bottom) performing participants. Participants' performance was computed by (21). Predicted utilization weights were derived from the best fitting Bayesian model (B), best fitting associative model with decreasing learning rate (A) and best fitting associative model with constant learning rate (Ac) (in the main text, these are referred to as $B.\sigma.\lambda_i$, $A.\eta.\lambda_i$, and $Ac.0.\lambda_i$ respectively).

than estimated. There are a number of possible reasons for this. First, we should note that due to the logit link function, differences on the higher ends of the scale affect the probability of responses less than differences nearer the middle of the scale (i.e., nearer 0). For example, the difference between $u = 1$ and $u = 2$ corresponds to a difference in probability of 0.15, while a difference between $u = 8$ and $u = 7$ corresponds to a difference in probability of 5.76×10^{-4}. As such, matching observed to predicted utilization at the start of the task is more important than matching them at the end of the task. That said, an interesting possibility is that consistency was not constant, as assumed, but increased over time. Comparison of the individual estimated and predicted utilization showed that, in most cases, they matched quite well in the first part of the task, but that later in the task, estimated utilization started to diverge from the predicted utilization. In those cases, the observed responses indicated a pure maximizing strategy.[6] At the start of the task, this pure maximizing was clearly not evident. Such possible changes in consistency deserve further attention, although their identification will probably require strong constraints on the change process.

Comparing predicted utilization to rationally inferred validity, we see that the shapes of the lines match more closely for the associative model with constant learning rate than for the other models. While rational inference by the Bayesian model and associative model with decreasing learning rate show quick convergence, rational inference from the associative model with constant learning rate is more 'linear' like the shape of the estimated utilization curves. By decreasing the prior variance in the Bayesian model, learning becomes slower (and more 'linear'). Although the associative model with constant learning rate fitted participants' responses best, the difference with the best fitting Bayesian model was not large. This is also evident from Fig. 18.7, which shows that the predicted utilization from both models is rather similar. As such, the apparent gradual learning could be due to participants being conservative Bayesian learners, or associative learners geared towards a non-stationary environment. At present, there is little to distinguish between these two accounts. However, environments encountered by participants outside the laboratory will often be (slowly) changing. Hence, if learning is geared towards non-stationary environments, this can be given a rational explanation.

Conclusion

In this chapter, we introduced the dynamic lens model and a general framework to study learning in multiple cue probability learning tasks. As in the original lens model, the objective is to compare cue utilization to rational utilization and the structure of the environment. By allowing utilization and validity to change over time,

---

[6] While a pure maximizing strategy corresponds to infinite utilization weights, the estimated utilization weights are evidently not infinite. However, an absolute utilization weight of 11 (e.g., participant 1, cue 1, Fig. 18.5), is practically infinite, as the predicted probability of a suboptimal response to card 1 is approximately only 1 in 100,000. The random-walk assumption, which predicts relatively smooth trial-by-trial changes in utilization, keeps the estimated utilization within bounds.

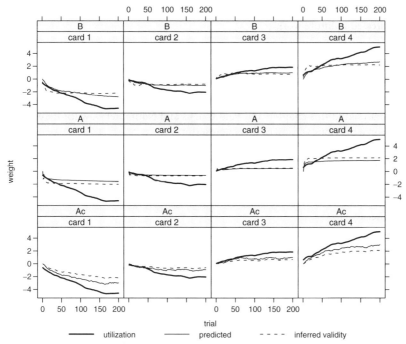

Fig. 18.7 Mean estimated cue utilization weights (utilization), mean predicted cue utilization weights (predicted), and rationally inferred cue validity weights (inferred validity), for the Bayesian model (B), associative model with decreasing learning rate (A) and constant learning rate (Ac).

the dynamic lens model offers a fine-grained overview of the learning process, allowing for a precise comparison of observed and ideal learning dynamics.

Applying the methods to the weather prediction task, we showed that participants learned to predict the criterion rather well. This learning was best described by an associative learning model with a constant learning rate, and participants appeared to learn at an optimal rate for the task. Furthermore, the average response consistency showed participants responded in a better way than probability matching. However, using the dynamic lens model to obtain relatively unconstrained estimates of cue utilization, we saw that participants' responses were more indicative of a maximizing strategy than predicted from the learning models. As such, the response part of these models failed to match predicted and estimated utilization. A possible reason for this discrepancy is that participants became more consistent as the task progressed. The discrepancy was only evident from a comparison between the unconstrained estimates of utilization and those predicted from the rational learning models. This illustrates the advantages of combining the dynamic lens model and rational analysis.

The sorts of interesting question our framework raises are: what happens in a changing environment, how many cues can individuals learn about, how do results from tasks with a discrete criterion, such as the weather prediction task, generalize to tasks with a continuous criterion, such as forecasting share price? These questions will be addressed in future work.

Acknowledgements

This research was supported by the ESRC Centre for Economic Learning and Social Evolution (ELSE). The authors would like to thank David Lagnado for providing the data analysed in this chapter, and Paul Cairns and Nathaniel Daw for helpful comments on a previous version of this manuscript.

References

Anderson, J. R. (1990). *The adaptive character of thought*. Hillsdale, NJ: Lawrence Erlbaum.

Bishop, C. M. (1995). *Neural networks for pattern recognition*. Oxford, UK: Oxford University Press.

Brunswik, E. (1955). Representative design and probabilistic theory in a functional psychology. *Psychological Review*, **62**, 193–217.

Cooksey, R. W. (1996). *Judgment analysis*. San Diego: Academic Press.

Dobson, A. J. (2002). *An introduction to generalized linear models* (2nd ed.). Boca Raton: Chapman & Hall.

Durbin, J., & Koopman, S. J. (2001). *Time series analysis by state space methods*. Oxford: Oxford University Press.

Einhorn, H. J., Kleinmuntz, D. N., & Kleinmuntz, B. (1979). Linear regression and process-tracing models of judgment. *Psychological Review*, **86**, 465–485.

Gluck, M. A., & Bower, G. H. (1988). From conditioning to category learning: An adaptive network model. *Journal of Experimental Psychology: General*, **117**, 227–247.

Hammond, K. R., Wilkins, M. M., & Todd, F. J. (1966). A research paradigm for the study of interpersonal learning. *Psychological Bulletin*, **65**, 221–232.

Hastie, R., & Dawes, R. M. (2001). *Rational choice in an uncertain world*. Thousand Oaks: Sage.

Kelley, H., & Friedman, D. (2002). Learning to forecast price. *Economic Inquiry*, **40**, 556–573.

Knowlton, B. J., Squire, L. R., & Gluck, M. A. (1994). Probabilistic classification learning in amnesia. *Learning & Memory*, **1**, 106–120.

Lagnado, D. A., Newell, B. R., Kahan, S., & Shanks, D. R. (2006). Insight and strategy in multiple cue learning. *Journal of Experimental Psychology: General*, **135**, 162–183.

LeCun, Y., Bottou, L., Orr, G. B., & Miller, K. R. (1998). Efficient backprop. In G. B. Orr & K. R. Miller (Eds.), *Neural networks: Tricks of the trade* (pp. 9–50). Berlin: Springer-Verlag.

Luce, D. R. (1959). *Individual choice behavior*. New York: Wiley.

McCullagh, P., & Nelder, J. A. (1983). *Generalized linear models*. London: Chapman & Hall.

Oaksford, M., & Chater, N. (Eds.). (1998). *Rational models of cognition*. Oxford: Oxford University Press.

Rescorla, R. A., & Wagner, A. R. (1972). A theory of Pavlovian conditioning: Variations in the effectiveness of reinforcement and nonreinforcement. In A. H. Black & W. F. Prokasy (Eds.), *Classical conditioning II: Current research and theory* (pp. 64–99). New York: Appleton-Century-Cross.

Robbins, H., & Monro, S. (1951). A stochastic approximation method. *Annals of Mathematical Statistics*, **22**, 400–407.

Schwarz, G. (1978). Estimating the dimension of a model. *Annals of Statistics*, **6**, 461–464.

Shanks, D. R., Tunney, R. J., & McCarthy, J. D. (2002). A re-examination of probability matching and rational choice. *Journal of Behavioral Decision Making*, **15**, 233–250.

Speekenbrink, M., Channon, S., & Shanks, D. R. (2008). Learning strategies in amnesia. *Neuroscience and Biobehavioral Reviews*.

Spiegelhalter, D., Thomas, A., Best, N., & Lunn, D. (2003, January). *WinBUGS version 1.4 user manual*. Cambridge. (Available from http://www.mrc-bsu.cam.ac.uk/bugs)

West, M., & Harrison, J. (1997). *Bayesian forecasting and dynamic models* (2nd ed.). New York: Springer.

Chapter 19

Semi-rational models of conditioning: the case of trial order

Nathaniel D. Daw
New York University, NY, USA

Aaron C. Courville
Université de Montréal,
Montreal, QC, Canada

Peter Dayan
University College London, London, UK

Introduction

Bayesian treatments of animal conditioning start from a generative model that specifies precisely a set of assumptions about the structure of the learning task. Optimal rules for learning are direct mathematical consequences of these assumptions. In terms of Marr's (1982) levels of analyses, the main task at the computational level would therefore seem to be to understand and characterize the set of assumptions from the observed behavior. However, a major problem with such Marrian analyses is that most Bayesian models for learning are presumptively untenable due to their radically intractable computational demands.

This tension between what the observer *should* and what she *can* do relates to Marr's (1982) distinction between the computational and algorithmic levels, Chomsky's (1965) distinction between performance and competence, and Simon's (1957) notion of bounded rationality. As all these examples suggest, we need not simply abandon normative considerations in favor of unconstrained, cheap and cheerful heuristics. Indeed, the evolutionary argument often taken to justify a normative approach (that organisms behaving rationally will enjoy higher fitness) in fact suggests that, in light of computational costs, evolution should favor those who can best and most efficiently *approximate* rational computations.

In short, some irrational models are more rational than others, and it is these that we suggest should be found to model behavior and its neural substrates best. Here, in search of such models, we look to the burgeoning and theoretically sophisticated field studying approximations to exact Bayesian inference.

The major difficulty facing such analyses is distinguishing which characteristics of observed behavior relate to the underlying assumptions, and which to approximations employed in bringing them to bear. This is particularly challenging since we do not know very much about how expensive computation is in the brain, and therefore the potential tradeoff between costs and competence. As with all model selection questions, the short answer to the question of assumption versus approximation is, of course, that we cannot tell for sure.

In fact, that assumption and approximation are difficult to distinguish is a particularly acute problem for theorists attempting to study normative considerations in isolation, which motivates our attempt to study both together. In practice, we may hope that credible candidates for both assumptions and approximations have different and rather specific qualitative fingerprints. In this chapter, we explore these ideas in the context of models of Pavlovian conditioning and prediction experiments in animals and humans. In particular, we address the recent trenchant discussion of Kruschke (2006), who argued against pure Bayesian learning models in favor of a particular heuristic treatment based on the effects of trial ordering in tasks such as backward blocking (Lovibond *et al.*, 2003; Shanks, 1985; Wasserman and Berglan, 1998) and highlighting (Kruschke, 2003, 2006; Medin and Bettger, 1991). His 'locally Bayesian' model, while drawing on Bayesian methods, neither corresponds to exact inference nor is motivated or justified as an approximation to the ideal.

While we agree with Kruschke that features of the data suggest something short of ideal reasoning in the statistical models we consider, we differ in the substance of the alternative modeling frameworks that we employ. On our analysis, at the computational level, effects of the ordering of trials bring up the issue of assumptions about how task contingencies change. The qualitative fingerprint here is *recency*—for most credible such models, recent trials will provide more information about the present state of affairs than distant trials. We show that some trial order effects emerge from optimal inference. For others, notably highlighting, which appears to be inconsistent with recency, we consider the effects of inferential approximation. We show how *primacy* effects, as seen in highlighting, qualitatively characterize a number of simplified inference schemes.

We start by describing the Kalman filter model of conditioning (Dayan *et al.*, 2000), which arises as the exact inference process associated with an analytically tractable, but highly simplified, Bayesian model of change. We show that this model leads to certain trial order effects, including those associated with backward blocking; we then consider inferential approximations in this framework and their implications for trial ordering in highlighting. We conclude with a discussion of how approximations might be explicitly traded off by reasoning about their accuracy.

Learning as filtering

The generative model

Consider a prediction problem in which, on trial t, the subject observes a possibly multidimensional stimulus $\mathbf{x}_t$ and must predict an outcome r_t. In a classical conditioning experiment, $\mathbf{x}$ might be a binary vector reporting which of a set of stimuli such as tones and lights were present and r some continuously distributed amount of food subsequently delivered. We denote possible stimuli as A, B, C and write a unit

amount of food as R. In this case, the animal's prediction about r is of course measured implicitly, e.g. through salivation. In a human experiment using, for instance,
a medical cover story, $\mathbf{x}$ might report a set of foods (e.g. $\mathbf{x}=AC$), with r being a binary
variable reporting whether a patient developed an allergic reaction from eating them
(e.g. $r = R$ or 0).

We briefly review a familiar statistical approach to such a problem (e.g. Dayan and
Long, 1998; Griffiths and Yuille, this volume). This begins by assuming a space of
hypotheses about how the data ($\mathcal{D}$, a *sequence* of $\mathbf{x}{\rightarrow}r$ pairs) were generated. Such
hypotheses often take the form of a parameterized stochastic data generation process,
which assigns probability $P(\mathcal{D} \mid \theta)$ to each possible data set $\mathcal{D}$ as a function of the
(initially unknown or uncertain) parameter settings θ. Then, conditional on having
observed some data (and on any prior beliefs about θ), one can use Bayes' rule to
draw *inferences* about the posterior likelihood of the hypotheses (here, parameter set-
tings), $P(\theta \mid \mathcal{D})$. Finally, to choose how to act on a new trial T, with stimuli $\mathbf{x}_T$, the
subject can calculate the predictive distribution over r_T using the posterior-weighted
average over the outcomes given the stimuli and each hypothesis:

$$P(r_T \mid \mathbf{x}_T, \mathcal{D}) = \int d\theta P(r_T \mid \mathbf{x}_T, \theta) P(\theta \mid \mathcal{D}) \tag{1}$$

The interpretive power of the approach rests on its normative, statistical foundation.
Indeed, the whole procedure is optimal inference based on just the generative model
and priors, which collectively describe what is known (or at least assumed) about how
the data are generated.

The generative models of conditioning based on these principles typically split into
two pieces. First, they assume that included in θ is one or more sets of values $\mathbf{w}_t$ that
govern a distribution $P(r_t \mid \mathbf{x}_t, \mathbf{w}_t)$ over the output on trial t given the stimuli. Second,
they assume something about the probabilistic relationship between the parameters
$\mathbf{w}_t$ and $\mathbf{w}_{t+1}$ associated with successive trials. The job of the subject, on this view, is to
estimate the posterior distribution $P(\mathbf{w} \mid \mathcal{D})$ from past outcomes so as to predict
future outcomes. We discuss the two pieces of the models in turn.

Parameterized output distribution

One standard assumption is that the outcome r_t on trial t is drawn from a Gaussian
distribution:

$$P(r_t \mid \mathbf{x}_t, \mathbf{w}_t, \sigma_o) = N\left(\sum_j' w_{tj} \cdot x_{tj}, \sigma_o^2\right) \tag{2}$$

Here, the weights $\mathbf{w}_t$ specify the mean outcomes w_{tj} expected in the presence of each
stimulus j individually, and σ_o is the level of noise corrupting each trial. We typically
assume that σ_o is known, although it is formally (though not necessarily computationally) easy to infer it too from the data.

There are various points to make about this formulation. First, note that Equation 2
characterizes the outcome r_t conditional on the input $\mathbf{x}_t$, rather than modeling the
probability of both variables jointly. In this sense it is not a full generative model for
the data $\mathcal{D}$ (which consist of both stimuli and outcomes). However, it suffices for the

present purposes of asking how subjects perform the task of predicting an r_t given an $\mathbf{x}_t$. We have elsewhere considered full joint models (Courville *et al.*, 2003, 2004, 2006).

Second, in Equation 2, the mean of the net prediction is assumed to be a *sum* of the predictions w_{tj} associated with all those stimuli x_{tj} present on trial t. This is ecologically natural in some contexts, and is deeply linked to the Rescorla–Wagner (1972) model's celebrated account of cue combination phenomena such as blocking and conditioned inhibition. However, there are other possibilities in which the stimuli are treated as *competing* predictors (rather than cooperating ones: Jacobs *et al.*, 1991a,b). For instance, one alternative formulation is that of an additive mixture of Gaussians, which uses an extra vector of parameters $\pi_t \in \theta$ to capture the competition:

$$P(r_t \mid \mathbf{x}_t, \mathbf{w}_t, \sigma_o, \pi_t) \propto \sum_j \pi_{tj} x_{tj} \mathcal{N}(w_{tj}, \sigma_o) + (1 - \pi_t \cdot \mathbf{x}_t) \mathcal{N}(w_{t0}, \sigma_o) \qquad (3)$$

Here, on each trial, a single stimulus j is chosen from those present with probability π_{tj} (or a background stimulus with the remaining probability) and its weight alone provides the mean for the whole reward. This is known to relate to a family of models of animal conditioning due to Mackintosh (1975; see Dayan & Long, 1998; Kruschke, 2001), and formalizes in a normative manner the notion in those models of cue-specific attentional weighting, with different stimuli having different degrees of influence over the predictions.

Finally, the Gaussian form of the output model in Equation 2 is only appropriate in rather special circumstances (such as Daw *et al.*, 2006). For instance, if r_t is binary rather than continuous, as in many human experiments, it cannot be true. The obvious alternative (a stochastic relationship controlled by a sigmoid, as in logistic regression) poses rather harder inferential problems. The common general use of the Gaussian illustrates the fact that one main route to well-found approximation is via exact inference in a model that is known to be only partially correct.

Trial ordering and change

Equation 2 and its variants capture the characteristics of a single trial, t. However, the data $\mathcal{D}$ for which the subject must account are an ordered series of such trials. The simplest way to extend the model to the series is to assume that the observations are all independent and identically distributed (IID), with $\mathbf{w}_t = \mathbf{w}, \forall t$, and:

$$P(\mathcal{D} \mid \mathbf{w}, \sigma_o) = P(r_1, ..., r_T \mid \mathbf{x}_1, ..., \mathbf{x}_T, \mathbf{w}, \sigma_o) = \prod_{t=1}^{T} P(r_t \mid \mathbf{x}_t, \mathbf{w}, \sigma_o) \qquad (4)$$

Since the product in Equation 4 is invariant to changes in the order of the trials t, *exact* inference in this model precludes any effect of trial ordering. Kruschke (2006) focuses his critique on exactly this issue.

However, the assumption that trials are IID is a poor match to a typically nonstationary world (Kakade and Dayan, 2002). Instead, most conditioning tasks (and also the real-world foraging or inference scenarios they stylize) involve some sort of change in the contingencies of interest (in this case, the coupling between stimuli $\mathbf{x}$ and outcomes r, parameterized by $\mathbf{w}$). If the world changes, an ideal observer *would not* treat the trials as either unconditionally independent or having identical distributions, but instead, different outcome parameters $\mathbf{w}_t$ may obtain on each trial, making:

$$P(\mathcal{D} \mid \mathbf{w}, \sigma_o) = P(r_1, ..., r_T \mid \mathbf{x}_1, ..., \mathbf{x}_T, \mathbf{w}, \sigma_o) = \prod_{t=1}^{T} P(r_t \mid \mathbf{x}_t, \mathbf{w}_t, \sigma_o) \quad (5)$$

Nonstationarity turns the problem facing the subject from one of inferring a single $\mathbf{w}$ to one of *tracking* a changing $\mathbf{w}_t$ in order to predict subsequent outcomes. To complete the generative model, we need to describe the change: how the $\mathbf{w}_t$ that applies on trial t relates to those from previous trials. A convenient assumption is first-order, independent Gaussian diffusion:

$$P(\mathbf{w}_{t+1} \mid \mathbf{w}_t, \sigma_d) = \mathcal{N}(\mathbf{w}_t, \sigma_d^2 \mathbf{I}) \quad (6)$$

As for the observation variance σ_o^2, we will assume the diffusion variance σ_d^2 is known.

Together, Equations 2, 5, and 6 define a generative model for which exact Bayesian inference can tractably be accomplished using the Kalman (1960) filter algorithm, described below. It should be immediately apparent that the assumption that $\mathbf{w}_t$ is changing gives rise to trial ordering effects in inference. The intuition is that the parameter was more likely to have been similar on recent trials than on those further in the past, so recent experience should weigh more heavily in inferring its present value. That is, the model exhibits a recency bias. But note that this bias arises automatically from normative inference given a particular (presumptively accurate) description of how the world works.

Here again, the Gaussian assumption on weight change may accurately reflect the experimental circumstances, or may be an approximation of convenience. In particular, contingencies often change more abruptly (as between experimental blocks). One way to formalize this possibility (Yu and Dayan, 2003, 2005) is to assume that in addition to smooth Gaussian diffusion, the weights are occasionally subject to a larger shock. However, the resulting model presents substantial inferential challenges.

The Kalman filter

Consider the generative model of Equations 2, 5, and 6. As is well known, if prior beliefs about the weights $P(\mathbf{w}_0)$ take a Gaussian form, $\mathcal{N}(\hat{\mathbf{w}}_0, \Sigma_0)$, then the posterior distribution having observed data for trials up to $t - 1$, $P(\mathbf{w}_t \mid \mathbf{x}_1...\mathbf{x}_{t-1}, r_1...r_{t-1})$ will also be Gaussian, $\mathcal{N}(\hat{\mathbf{w}}_t, \Sigma_t)$. That is, it consists of a belief $\hat{\mathbf{w}}_t$ about the mean of the weights and a covariance matrix Σ_t encoding the uncertainty around that mean. Because of the Gaussian assumptions, these quantities can tractably be updated trial by trial according to Bayes theorem, which here takes the form (Kalman, 1960):

$$\hat{\mathbf{w}}_{t+1} = \hat{\mathbf{w}}_t + \kappa_t (r_t - \hat{\mathbf{w}}_t \cdot \mathbf{x}_t) \quad (7)$$

$$\Sigma_{t+1} = \Sigma_t - \kappa_t \mathbf{x}_t \Sigma_t + \sigma_d^2 \mathbf{I} \tag{8}$$

with *Kalman gain* vector $\kappa_t = \Sigma_t \mathbf{x}_t^T / (\mathbf{x}_t \Sigma_t \mathbf{x}_t^T + \sigma_o^2)$. Note that the update rule for the mean takes the form of the Rescorla–Wagner (1972) (delta) rule, except with each stimulus having its own individual learning rate given by the appropriate entry in the Kalman gain vector.

The Kalman filter of Equations 7 and 8 is straightforward to implement, since the sufficient statistics for all the observations up to trial t are contained in the fixed-dimensional quantities $\hat{\mathbf{w}}_t$ and Σ_t. Indeed, this is why the assumptions underlying the Kalman filter have been made as approximations in cases in which they are known not to hold.

This completes the normative treatment of learning in a non-stationary environment. In the next section, we apply it to critical examples in which trial order has a significant effect on behavior; in the subsequent section, we consider approximation schemes employing inexact inference methods, and consider the sorts of normative trial order effects they capture, and the non-normative ones they introduce.

Backward blocking and highlighting

We illustrate the effects of trial ordering in the Kalman filter model using two key order sensitive paradigms identified by Kruschke (2006), backward blocking (e.g. Lovibond *et al.*, 2003; Shanks, 1985; Wasserman and Berglan, 1998) and highlighting (Kruschke, 2003, 2006; Medin and Bettger, 1991). In particular, we consider the effect of a priori nonstationarity in the Kalman filter ($\sigma_d^2 > 0$) compared, as a baseline, against the same model with $\sigma_d^2 = 0$, which is equivalent to the IID assumption of Equation 4 and is therefore trial ordering invariant.

Backward blocking

Table 19.1 details an experiment in which stimuli A and B are paired with reinforcement over a number of trials (we write this as $AB \rightarrow R$), and responding to B alone is then tested. Famously, predictions of R given B probes are attenuated (*blocked*) when the $AB \rightarrow R$ training is preceded by a set of $A \rightarrow R$ trials, in which A alone is paired with reinforcement (Kamin, 1969). One intuition for this *forward blocking* effect is that if reinforcement is explicable on the basis of A alone, then the $AB \rightarrow R$ trials do not provide evidence that B is also associated with reinforcement. This particular intuition is agnostic between accounts in which stimuli cooperate or compete to predict the outcome.

Table 19.1. Experimental paradigms

	Phase 1	Phase 2	Test	Result
Forward blocking	$A \rightarrow R$	$AB \rightarrow R$	B?	R attenuated
Backward blocking	$AB \rightarrow R$	$A \rightarrow R$	B?	R less attenuated
Highlighting	$AB \rightarrow R \times 3n$,	$AB \rightarrow R \times 1n$,	A?	R
	$AC \rightarrow S \times 1n$	$AC \rightarrow S \times 3n$	BC?	S

The next line of the table shows the experimental course of *backward* blocking (Shanks, 1985), in which the order of these sets of trials is reversed: $AB{\rightarrow}R$ trials are followed by $A{\rightarrow}R$ trials and then by a test on B alone. Backward blocking is said to occur if responding to B is attenuated by the $A{\rightarrow}R$ post-training. The intuition remains the same—the $A{\rightarrow}R$ trials indicate that B was not responsible for reinforcement on the $AB{\rightarrow}R$ trials. However, what makes backward blocking interesting is that this lack of responsibility is only evident *retrospectively*, at a point that B is no longer provided.

Backward blocking is an example of 'retrospective revaluation,' in which subsequent experience (with A) changes the interpretation of prior experience (with B). As we will discuss, the mere existence of retrospective revaluation strongly constrains what sort of inferential approximations are viable, because particular information must be stored about the initial experience to allow it to be reevaluated later. Critically, backward blocking tends to be weaker (that is, responding to B less attenuated) than forward blocking (e.g. Lovibond *et al.*, 2003). Since forward and backward blocking just involve a rearrangement of the same trials, this asymmetry is a noteworthy demonstration of sensitivity to trial order (Kruschke, 2006), and thus refutation of the IID model.

The simulation results in figure 19.1a confirm that forward and backward blocking are equally strong under the IID Kalman filter model. It may not, however, be obvious *how* the rule accomplishes retrospective revaluation (Kakade and Dayan, 2001). Figure 19.1b illustrates the posterior distribution over w_A and w_B following $AB{\rightarrow}R$ training in backward blocking. The key point is that they are anticorrelated, since together they should add up to about R (1, in the simulations). Thus, if w_A is greater than $R/2$, then w_B must be less than $R/2$, and vice-versa. Subsequent $A{\rightarrow}R$ training indicates that w_A is indeed high and w_B must therefore be low, producing the effect. In terms of the Kalman filter learning rule, then, the key to backward blocking is the off-diagonal term in the covariance matrix Σ, which encodes the anticorrelation between w_A and w_B, and creates a *negative* Kalman gain κ_{tB} for stimulus B during the $A{\rightarrow}R$ trials in which B is not present (Kakade and Dayan, 2001).

Figure 19.1c shows the same experiments on the non-IID Kalman filter. Here, consistent with experiments, backward blocking is weaker than forward blocking. This happens because of the recency effect induced by the weight diffusion of Equation 6—in particular (as illustrated in Figure 19.1d), the presumption that w_A and w_B are independently jittered between trials implies that they become less strongly anticorrelated with time. This suppresses retrospective revaluation. Forward blocking is not similarly impaired because the presumptive jitter on w_A is mean-preserving and does not therefore attenuate the belief (from $A{\rightarrow}R$ trials) that A is responsible for subsequent reinforcement on $AB{\rightarrow}R$ trials, in which $r_t - \hat{\mathbf{w}}_t \cdot \mathbf{x}_t = 0$.

Highlighting

The phenomenon of highlighting, which involves the base rates of outcomes, is rather more challenging for the Kalman filter (Kruschke, 2006). In this paradigm (see Table 19.1), three stimuli A,B,C are associated with two outcomes R and S according to $AB{\rightarrow}R$ and $AC{\rightarrow}S$. However, although equal numbers of both trial types are delivered, they are presented unevenly across the course of training, with

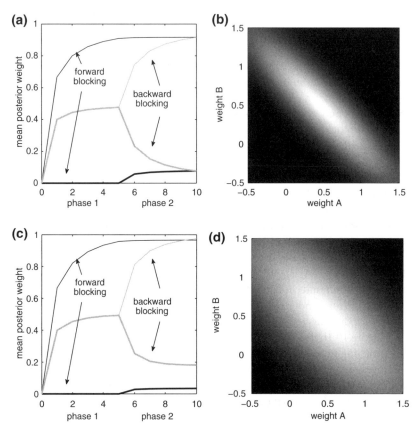

Fig. 19.1. Simulations of forward and backward blocking using the Kalman filter model. a: Estimated mean weights $\hat{w}_A$ (upper thin lines) and $\hat{w}_B$ (lower thick lines) as a function of training in the IID Kalman filter ($\sigma_d^2 = 0$; $\sigma_o^2 = 0.5$); the endpoints for forward and backward blocking are the same. b: Joint posterior distribution over w_A and w_B at start of phase 2 of backward blocking; the two weights are anticorrelated. c & d: Same as a & b, but using the non-IID Kalman filter ($\sigma_d^2 = 0.1$); backward blocking is attenuated.

$AB \rightarrow R$ predominating early (e.g. by a factor of three), and $AC \rightarrow S$ late (by the same factor).

The results show a mixture of what appear to be recency and primacy effects. In particular, tested on A after training, subjects predict R (the more common outcome in the first block); but tested on the novel combination BC, subjects predict S (the more common outcome in the second block of trials). Note that in the balanced form of the task presented here (Medin and Bettger, 1991; Kruschke, 2006) overall, B (and indeed A) is paired with R exactly as many times as C with S, so any asymmetry in the predictions must result from trial ordering.

These equalities imply that the IID model does not exhibit highlighting, a fact confirmed by the simulations in Figure 19.2a. To make the point in an extreme way, we

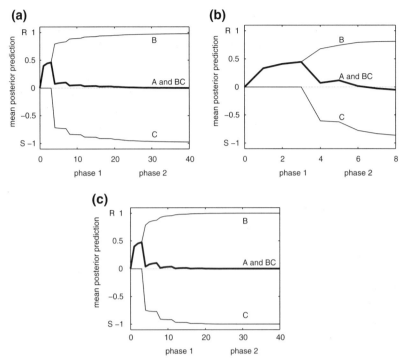

Fig. 19.2. Simulations of highlighting using the Kalman filter model. Development of mean estimates for test stimuli ($\hat{w}_A$ and $\hat{w}_B + \hat{w}_C$) illustrated as thick line (both are the same, see main text); $\hat{w}_B$ and $\hat{w}_C$ illustrated individually with thin lines. a: IID Kalman filter ($\sigma_d^2 = 0$; $\sigma_o^2 = 0.5$); b: the non-IID Kalman filter ($\sigma_d^2 = 0.1$) shown with few trials and $\sigma_o^2 = 1.0$ to demonstrate pre-asymptotic behavior. c: Aymptotic behavior of the non-IID Kalman filter with many trials ($\sigma_d^2 = 0.1$; $\sigma_o^2 = 0.5$).

assumed that $R = 1$ and $S = -R = -1$, so the two outcomes are in direct competition.[i] What may be less immediately obvious is that the non-IID model also fails to show highlighting (Figure 19.2b). This can be seen in two ways; first the recency bias implies that both A and BC slightly favor S, the outcome predominantly received in the second block. Second, it is straightforward to verify that it will always be true that $\hat{w}_A = \hat{w}_B + \hat{w}_C$, for all parameters and after any sequence of the two trial types. Thus the model can never capture the pattern of results from highlighting, in which A and BC finish with opposite associations.

Further, given sufficient trials, even the non-IID Kalman filter will actually conclude that $\hat{w}_A = 0$, and use only $\hat{w}_B$ and $\hat{w}_C$ to predict R and S respectively—with all

---

[i] This assumption may be more or less appropriate to particular empirical settings, depending for instance on whether the cover story and response requirements frame the outcomes as mutually exclusive. In any case, our models and arguments extend to the case with two nonexclusive outcomes.

predictions balanced even though the base rates are locally skewed (Figure 19.2c). It is intuitive that the Kalman filter should be asymptotically insensitive to the base rates of stimuli, since it is attempting only to estimate the probability of R *conditional* on the stimuli having occurred, i.e. regardless of their base rate. The mechanism by which this occurs is again dependent on retrospective revaluation: initially, the Kalman filter attributes the predominance of S trials in the second block to both A and C (Figure 19.2b); given more experience, and through the medium of the anticorrelation in the posterior between w_A and both w_B and w_C, it revalues A as wholly unpredictive and attributes all S to C (Figure 19.2b).

Summary

We have so far examined how trial ordering effects arise naturally in a simple Bayesian model. Because they follow from assumptions about change, these generally involve some sort of recency effect, though this can be manifest in a fairly task-dependent manner.

Backward blocking is a straightforward consequence of the generative model underlying the non-IID Kalman filter. The pattern of results from highlighting is not: Quite uncharacteristic for inference in a changing environment, the latter seem to involve in part a primacy effect for $A{\rightarrow}R$.

One noteworthy aspect of these investigations is the importance of retrospective revaluation to both experiments. Backward blocking, of course, is itself a retrospective revaluation phenomenon; however, that it is weaker than forward blocking indicates that the revaluation is less than perfect. Similarly, one feature of highlighting is the failure retrospectively to determine that stimulus A is unpredictive, after it had been initially preferentially paired with R. This is particularly clear in a version of highlighting discussed by Kruschke (2003, 2006), which starts just like backward blocking with a block of only $AB{\rightarrow}R$ trials. Retrospective revaluation is closely tied to Bayesian reasoning, in that it typically seems to involve reasoning about the whole distribution of possible explanations (as in Figure 19.1d), rather than just a particular estimate (as in the Rescorla–Wagner model, which fails to produce such effects).

As we discussed in the introduction, there are at least three strategies to follow in the face of the failure of this simple model to account for highlighting. The first is to downplay the emphasis on principled reasoning and seek a heuristic explanation (Kruschke, 2006). The second is to consider it as a failure of the generative model and to seek a more sophisticated generative model that perhaps better captures subjects' beliefs about the task contingencies. While there are doubtless exotic beliefs about change processes and cue-combination rules that would together give rise to highlighting, we have not so far discovered a completely convincing candidate. Instead, we would suggest that the Kalman filter's behavior is characteristic of inference in a changing environment more generally. As we have seen, trial order sensitivities in Bayesian reasoning ultimately arise from the a priori belief that trials are not identically distributed. A reasonable general assumption is that trials nearer in time are more similar to one another than to those farther away—predicting, all else equal, a recency bias. Together with the fact that failures of retrospective revaluation are characteristic of a number of well-founded inferential approximation strategies, as we discuss below, this observation motivates the third approach: to consider that the phenomenon actually arises from a failure of the brain to implement correct inference.

Approximate inference

In the face of generative models that are much more complicated and less tractable than that in Equations 2, 5, and 6, statisticians and computer scientists have developed a menagerie of approximate methods. Such approximations are attractive as psychological models because they offer plausible mechanistic accounts while maintaining the chief advantage of Bayesian approaches: *viz* a clear grounding in normative principles of reasoning.

Tools for inferential approximation may crudely be split into two categories, though these are often employed together. Monte Carlo techniques such as particle filtering (e.g. Doucet *et al.*, 2000) approximate statistical computations by averaging over random samples. While these methods may be relevant to psychological modeling, the hallmarks of their usage would mainly be evident in patterns of variability over trials or subjects, which is not the focus of the present work. We will focus instead on deterministic simplifications of difficult mathematical forms (e.g. Jordan *et al.*, 1999), such as the usage of lower bounds or maximum likelihood approximations. One critical feature of these approximations is that they often involve steps that have the consequence of discarding relevant information about past trials. This can introduce trial order dependencies, and particularly effects similar to primacy. In this section, we will demonstrate some simple examples of this.

Assumed density filtering

The Kalman filter (Equations 7, 8) updates its beliefs recursively: the new belief distribution is a function only of the previous distribution and the new observation. In many cases, we may wish to maintain this convenient, recursive form, but simplify the posterior distribution after each update to enable efficient approximate computation of subsequent updates. Such methods are broadly known as *assumed density* filters (see Minka, 2001, who also discusses issues of trial ordering). Typically, the posterior distribution is chosen to have a simple functional form (e.g. Gaussian, with a diagonal covariance matrix), and to have its parameters chosen to minimize a measure (usually the so-called Kullback–Liebler divergence) of the discrepancy between it and the best guess at the true posterior. Because of this minimization step, this approximation is sometimes called *variational* (Jordan *et al.*, 1999).

Clearly such an approximation introduces error. Most critical for us is that these errors can be manifest as trial ordering effects. In the Kalman filter update, the previous belief distribution can stand in for all previous observations because the posterior distribution is a *sufficient statistic* for the previous observations. The recursively computed posterior equals the posterior conditioned on all the data, and so for instance the IID filter (the Kalman filter with $\sigma_d = 0$) can correctly arrive at the same answer no matter in what order trials are presented. In backward blocking, for instance, $\hat{w}_B$ is retrospectively revalued on $A \rightarrow R$ trials without explicitly backtracking or reconsidering the previous $AB \rightarrow R$ observations: the posterior covariance Σ summarizes the relevant relationship between the variables. A simplified form of the posterior will not, in general, be a sufficient statistic; how past trials impact the posterior may then depend on the order they arrived in, even in cases (e.g. the IID filter) for which the exact solution is order-invariant. This can disrupt retrospective revaluation, since the ability to reinterpret past experience depends on its being adequately represented in the posterior.

Simulations

Perhaps the most common assumed density is one in which the full posterior factorizes. Here, this implies assuming the joint distribution over the weights is separable into the product of a distribution over each weight individually. For the Kalman filter, this amounts to approximating the full Kalman filter covariance matrix Σ by just its diagonal entries,[ii] thus maintaining uncertainty about each weight but neglecting information about their covariance relationships with one another.

Since we have already identified the covariance terms as responsible for backward blocking we may conclude immediately (and simulations, not illustrated, verify) that this simplification eliminates backward blocking while retaining forward blocking.

A subtler trial order dependence also arises in the form of a robust highlighting effect (Figure 19.3a). This traces to three interlinked features of the model. First, much like attentional variables in associative accounts of highlighting (Kruschke, 2003), in the Kalman filter, the uncertainties about the weights (the diagonal elements of the covariance matrix) control the rate of learning about those weights (Dayan and Long; Kakade and Dayan, 2002). More uncertain weights get a larger gain κ and a bigger update from Equation 7; when stimuli are observed, the uncertainties about them (and subsequent learning rates) decline, whereas when stimuli are unobserved, their uncertainties increase. This means (Figure 19.3b) that on $AC \rightarrow S$ trials in the first block, C (which is rarely observed) learns more rapidly than A (which is commonly observed). Conversely, A is likely to be paired with R the first few times it is seen, when its learning rate is highest. Second, the weights of presented stimuli must interact additively to produce the outcome (Equation 2). A's association with R will therefore reduce B's association with it (since the two weights must additively share the prediction on $AB \rightarrow R$ trials), whereas C's association with S will be correspondingly enhanced by additionally having to cancel out A's opposing prediction of R. Finally, since the covariance is not represented, A is never retrospectively revalued as a nonpredictor—its initial association with R instead persists indefinitely as a primacy effect. There is a continuum of possible values $\hat{w}_A$, $\hat{w}_B$ and $\hat{w}_C$ that together add up to explain exactly the results of both trial types (specifically $\hat{w}_B = 1 - \hat{w}_A$ and $\hat{w}_C = -1 - \hat{w}_A$ for any $\hat{w}_A$); lacking revaluation, this model sticks with the first one it finds.

Note also that the venerable Rescorla–Wagner model results from one further simplification over this one: the assumption that the learning rates are simply constant (if perhaps stimulus-dependent), i.e. that the uncertainties are never updated. This is motivated by the fact that, under special circumstances, for instance, if each stimulus

---

[ii] This minimizes the KL-divergence from the full covariance Gaussian among the class of all diagonal distributions.

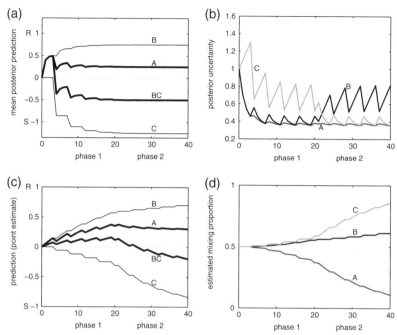

Fig. 19.3. Simulations of highlighting in approximate Bayesian reasoning. (a) Highlighting in the Kalman filter with diagonalized assumed covariance ($\sigma_d^2 = 0.1$; $\sigma_o^2 = 0.5$) . (b) Posterior uncertainty about each weight as a function of training; w_C is more uncertain in first phase, highlighting it. (c) Highlighting in the additive Gaussian mixture model using EM ($\eta = 0.1$; illustrated are the point estimates of the three individual weights and, for compound BC, the net outcome expectation weighted by mixing proportions). (d) Development of estimates of mixing proportions with training; C is highlighted.

is presented on every trial, the Kalman filter ultimately evolves to a fixed asymptotic learning rate (the value at which information from each observation exactly balances out diffusion in the prior). However, from the perspective of highlighting, this is a simplification too far, since without dynamic learning rates C's learning about S is not boosted relative to A. Similar to the full Kalman filter, no highlighting effect is seen: the local base rates predominate. The lack of covariance information also prevents it from exhibiting backward blocking.

Maximum likelihood and expectation maximization

Similar phenomena can be seen, for similar reasons, in other approximation schemes. We exemplify this generality using a representative member of another class of inexact but statistically grounded approaches, namely those that attempt to determine just a maximum likelihood point-estimate of the relevant variables (here the means $\hat{\mathbf{w}}$) rather than a full posterior distribution over them. Often, these methods learn using some sort of hill climbing or gradient approach, and, of course, it is not possible to employ Bayes' theorem directly without representing some form of a distribution.

As for assumed density filters (and for the Rescorla–Wagner model, which can also be interpreted as a maximum-likelihood gradient climber), the failure to maintain an adequate posterior distribution curtails or abolishes retrospective revaluation.

Another example is a particular learning algorithm for the competitive mixture of Gaussians model of Equation 3. We develop this in some detail as it is the canonical example of a particularly relevant learning algorithm and is related to a number of important behavioral models (Kruschke, 2001; Mackintosh, 1975), though it does have some empirical shortcomings related to its assumptions about cue combination (Dayan and Long, 1998). Recall that, according to this generative model, one stimulus out of those presented will be chosen and the outcome will then be determined solely based on the chosen stimulus' weight. Learning about the weight from the outcome then depends on unobserved information: which stimulus was chosen. *Expectation-maximization* methods (Dempster *et al.*, 1977; Griffiths and Yuille, this volume) address this problem by repeatedly alternating two steps: estimating the hidden information based on the current beliefs about the weights ('E step'), then updating the weights assuming this estimate to be true ('M step'). This process can be understood to perform coordinate ascent on a particular error function, and is guaranteed to reduce (or at least not increase) the error at each step (Neal and Hinton, 1998).

An online form of EM is appropriate for learning in the generative model of Equation 3. Assume for simplicity that the weights do not change, i.e., that Equation 4 obtains. At each trial, the E step determines the probability that the outcome was produced by each stimulus (or the background stimulus 0), which involves a Bayesian inversion of the generative model:

$$q_{tj} \propto x_{tj}\hat{\pi}_{tj} \exp(-(r_t - \hat{\omega}_{tj})^2/\sigma_0^2)$$

Here, the background mixing proportion $\hat{\pi}_{t0} = \max(1 - \hat{\pi}_t \cdot \mathbf{x}_t, 0)$ and the constant of proportionality in $\mathbf{q}_t$ arrange for appropriate normalization. The model then learns a new point estimate of the weights $\hat{\mathbf{w}}$ and the mixing proportions $\hat{\boldsymbol{\pi}}$ using what is known as a partial M step, with the predictions associated with each stimulus changing according to their own prediction error, but by an amount that depends on the responsibilities accorded to each during the E step:

$$\hat{w}_{t+1,j} = \hat{w}_{tj} + \eta q_{tj}(r_t - \hat{w}_{tj}) \tag{9}$$

$$\hat{\pi}_{t+1,j} = \hat{\pi}_{tj} + \eta x_{tj}(q_{tj} - \hat{\pi}_{tj}) \tag{10}$$

Here, η is a learning rate parameter, which, as for the Rescorla–Wagner rule, by being fixed, can be seen as a severe form of approximation to the case of continual change in the world.

Simulations

Like most other more or less local hill climbing methods, the fact that the M-step in this algorithm is based on the previous, particular, parameter settings (through the medium of the E-step) implies that there are trial order effects akin to primacy. As Figure 19.3c illustrates, these include highlighting, which arises here because the responsibilities (and the estimated mixing proportions $\hat{\pi}$ that determine and are determined by them) take on an attentional role similar to the uncertainties in the diagonalized Kalman filter account. In particular, A and B share responsibility q (Figure 19.3d) for the preponderance of R in the first block. This reduces the extent to which $\hat{w}_B$ learns about R (since the effective learning rate is ηq_B), and the extent to which B contributes to the aggregate prediction during the BC probe (since B's contribution to the expectation is proportional to $\hat{\pi}_B$). Meanwhile, by the second block of trials, the model has learned that A has little responsibility (because $\hat{\pi}_A$ is low), giving a comparative boost to learning about $\hat{w}_C$ during the now-frequent S trials. Less learning about $\hat{w}_A$ due to its lower responsibility also means its association with R persists as a primacy effect. These biases follow from the way the evolving beliefs about the stimuli participate in the approximate learning rule through the determination of responsibilities—recall that we derived the model using the IID assumption and that *optimal* inference is, therefore, trial order independent.

Note that unlike the diagonal Kalman filter example of Figure 19.3a, the highlighting effect here doesn't arise until the second block of trials. This means that this EM model doesn't explain the 'inverse base rate effect,' (Medin and Edelson, 1988) which is the highlighting effect shown even using only the first block when R predominates. One reason for this, in turn, is the key competitive feature of this rule, that the predictions made by each stimulus do not interact additively in the generative rule (Equation 3). Because of this, while stimuli may share *responsibility* for the outcome, the net prediction doesn't otherwise enter into the learning rule of Equation 9, which still seeks to make each stimulus account for the whole outcome on its own. In highlighting, this means A's association with R cannot directly boost C's association with S during the first phase. The same feature also causes problems for this model (and its associative cousins) explaining other phenomena such as overshadowing and inhibitory conditioning, and ultimately favors alternatives to Equation 3 in which cues cooperate to produce the net observation (Dayan and Long, 1998; Hinton, 1999; Jacobs *et al.*, 1991a).

Despite this failure, the competitive model does exhibit forward blocking, albeit through a responsibility-sharing mechanism (Mackintosh, 1975) rather than a weight-sharing mechanism like Rescorla–Wagner (simulations not illustrated). More concretely, stimulus A claims responsibility for R on $AB{\rightarrow}R$ trials, due to already predicting it. This retards learning about B, as in blocking. However, given that it is based only on a point-estimate, it retains no covariance information, and so, like Rescorla–Wagner, cannot account for backward blocking.

Summary

We have shown how two rather different sorts of inferential approximation schemes, in the context of two different generative models for conditioning, both disrupt retrospective revaluation—abolishing backward blocking and producing a highlighting effect. Exact Bayesian reasoning is characterized by simultaneously maintaining the correct likelihood for every possible hypothesis. This is what enables retrospectively revisiting previously disfavored hypotheses when new data arrive, but it is also the main source of computational complexity in Bayesian reasoning and the target for simplification schemes. In short, primacy effects—the failure retrospectively to discount an initially favored hypothesis—are closely linked to inferential approximation.

We have used extreme approximations to expose this point as clearly as possible. While the experiments discussed here both suggest that retrospective revaluation is attenuated, that effects like backward blocking exist at all rules out such extreme approaches. In the following section, we consider gentler approximations.

Blended and mixed approximations

So far, neither the Bayesian nor the approximately Bayesian models actually exhibits the combination of recency and primacy evident in backward blocking and highlighting. In fact, this is not hard to achieve, as there are various models that naturally lie between the extremes discussed in the sections on exact and approximate inference. The cost is one additional parameter. In this section, we provide two examples, based on different ideas associated with approximating the Kalman filter.

Reduced-rank approximations

In the section 'Assumed density filtering,' p. 437, we considered the simplest possible assumed density version of the Kalman filter, in which the posterior fully factorized, having a diagonal covariance matrix (Figure 19.3a). This method fails to exhibit backwards blocking, since it cannot represent the necessary anticorrelation between the predictions of the two CSs that arises during the first set of learning trials.

A less severe approximation to the posterior is to use a reduced-rank covariance matrix. We use one that attempts to stay close to the *inverse* covariance matrix, which (roughly speaking) characterizes certainty. An approximation of this sort allows the subject to carry less information between trials (because of the reduction in rank), and can also enable simplification of the matrix calculations for the subsequent update to the Kalman filter (Treebushny and Madsen, 2005).

More precisely, we approximate the inverse posterior covariance after one trial, $(\Sigma_t - \kappa_t \mathbf{x}_t \Sigma_t)^{-1}$, by retaining only those n basis vectors from its singular value decomposition that have the highest singular values, thereby minimizing the Frobenius norm of the difference. On the next trial we reconstruct the covariance as the pseudo-inverse of the rank-n matrix plus the uncertainty contributed by the intervening drift, $\sigma_d^2 \mathbf{I}$.

Figure 19.4a,b shows the consequence of using a rank-2 approximation ($n = 2$) to the covariance matrix. This results in highlighting without further disrupting backward blocking, which, in any case, only requires a two-dimensional posterior. A general prediction of this sort of resource bottleneck approach is that the effects of approximation should become more pronounced—e.g. retrospective revaluation more attenuated—for problems involving higher dimensional and more intricately structured posteriors.

Mixing filters

A different possibility is to mix the exact and diagonally approximated Kalman filters more directly. Here the idea is that there may be mixing at the behavioral level of distinct

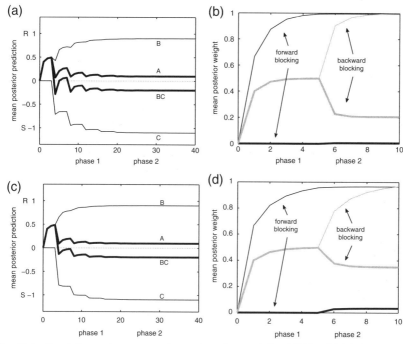

Fig. 19.4. Simulations of two approximate Bayesian models exhibiting highlighting and backwards blocking. (a,b) Reduced-rank covariance Kalman filter $(\sigma_d^2 = 0.1; \sigma_o^2 = 0.5; n = 2)$. (c,d) Blended full/diagonal covariance Kalman filter $(\sigma_d^2 = 0.1; \sigma_o^2 = 0.1)$.

underlying psychological and/or neural processes, one corresponding to each model. In some circumstances—for instance, when the diagonal elements of the covariance matrix are anyway small—the additional accuracy to be gained by maintaining the full covariance matrix may not justify the additional energetic costs relative to the particularly simple diagonal version. Such considerations suggest that the brain could adaptively trade off whether to employ approximation based on a sort of meta-rational cost-benefit analysis. In this case, blending would appear in results via the average over trials or subjects. A slightly different version of this idea would suggest that subjects actually compute both forms simultaneously, but then reconcile the answers, making an adaptive decision how much to trust each, much as in other cases of Bayesian evidence reconciliation (Daw *et al.*, 2005). The 'exact' computation might not always be the most accurate, if in biological tissue the extra computations incur additional computational noise; it might therefore be worthwhile to expend *extra* resources also computing a less noisy approximation.

Figure 19.2c,d shows simulations of a model which performs mixing by multiplying the off-diagonal elements of the covariance Σ by 0.7 at each step. This restricts the efficacy of retrospective revaluation without totally preventing it, allowing both backward blocking, which is curtailed relative to forward blocking, and highlighting.

Discussion

Summary

In this chapter, we have focused on the intricacies of inference in Bayesian models of conditioning. We used theory and simulations to show how particular classes of effects in learning (e.g. backward blocking) can arise from optimal inference in the light of a simple generative model of a task, and others (e.g. highlighting) from more or less extreme, but still recognizable approximations to optimal inference. This work on sensitivity to trial order is clearly only in its infancy, and the data to decide between and refine the various different models are rather sparse. However, just as we try to differentiate subjects' assumptions in exact Bayesian modeling, we hope in the future to adjudicate more definitively between different approximation methods by identifying tasks that better expose their fingerprints. Here, we have focused on trial order, but many similar issues arise in other areas of conditioning, such as stimulus competition.

Locally Bayesian learning

One spur to study trial order was the recent article by Kruschke (2006). He pointed out the apparent contradiction between the recency in backward blocking and the primacy in highlighting, and noted the implications of the IID assumption for both phenomena. Kruschke framed these findings by contrasting classic associative learning models (which explain highlighting via ideas about stimulus attention) with a particular IID Bayesian model (which explains retrospective revaluation). Rather than addressing the IID assumption (which, of course, Bayesian models need not make), he proposed a 'locally Bayesian' model blending features of both of these approaches. This model consists of interconnected modules that are Bayesian-inspired in that each updates a local belief distribution using Bayes' rule, but heuristic in that the 'observations' to which Bayes' rule is applied are not observed data but instead synthetic quantities constructed using an ad-hoc message-passing scheme. Although the individual modules treat their synthetic data as IID, trial ordering effects emerge from their interactions. The theoretical status of the heuristic, for instance as a particular form of approximation to a well-found statistical procedure, is left unclear.

We have attempted to address the issues central to highlighting and backwards blocking in unambiguously Bayesian terms. We develop a similar contrast between exact and approximate approaches, but rather than seeing statistical and associative learning as contradictory and requiring reconciliation, we have stressed their connection under a broader Bayesian umbrella. The approximate Kalman filters discussed in the previous section retain a precise flavor of the optimal solutions, while offering parameterized routes to account for the qualitative characteristics of both backwards blocking and highlighting.

It is also possible to extend this broader Bayesian analysis to the mixture model from the section on expectation maximization, p. 439, and hence nearer to Kruschke's (2006) locally Bayesian scheme. The mixture model fails to exhibit retrospective revaluation since it propagates only a point, maximum likelihood, estimate of the posterior distribution over the weights. This could be rectified by adopting a so-called *ensemble learning* approach (Hinton and van Camp, 1993; Waterhouse *et al.*, 1996), in which a full (approximate) distribution over the learned parameters is maintained and propagated, rather than just a point estimate. In ensemble learning, this distribution is improved by iterative ascent (analogous to E and M steps) rather than direct application of Bayes' rule.

One online version of such a rule could take the form of inferring the unobserved responsibilities, and then conditioning on them as though they were observed data (see also the mixture update of Dearden *et al.* 1998). Since it conducts inference using synthetic in place of observed quantities, this rule would have the flavor of Kruschke's locally Bayesian scheme, and indeed would be a route to find statistically justifiable principles for his model. However, this line of reasoning suggests one key modification to his model, that the unobserved quantities should be estimated optimally from the statistical model using an E step, obviating the need for a target propagation scheme.

Bayes, Damn Bayes, and approximations

At its core, the Bayesian program in psychology is about understanding subjects' behavior in terms of principles of rational inference. This approach extends directly beyond ideal computation in the relatively small set of tractably computable models into approximate reasoning in richer models. Of course, we cannot interrogate evolution to find out whether some observable facet of conditioning arises as exact inference in a model that is a sophisticated adaptation to a characteristic of the learning environment that we have not been clever enough to figure out, or as an inevitable approximation to inference in what is likely to be a simpler model. Nevertheless, admitting well found approximations does not infinitely enlarge the family of candidate models, and Occam's razor may continue to guide.

Waldmann *et al.* (2007; this volume) pose another version of our dilemma. They agree with Churchland (1986) that the top-down spirit of Marrian modeling is always violated in practice, with practitioners taking peeks at algorithmic (psychological) and even implementational (neural) results before building their abstract, computational accounts. However, unlike the approach that we have tried to follow, their solution is to posit the notion of a minimal rational model that more explicitly elevates algorithmic issues into the computational level.

We see two critical dangers in the Waldmann 'minimal rationality' programme, one associated with each of the two words. One danger Marr himself might have worried about, namely the fact that minimality is in the eye of the beholder (or at least the instruction set), and that our lack of a justifiable account of the costs of neural processing makes any notion of minimality risk vacuity. The second danger is that by blending normative considerations with incommensurate pragmatic ones, minimal rationality risks being a contradiction in terms. We agree with Waldmann and colleagues' criticism that rational theorists have sometimes been a bit glib relating theories of competence to performance, but we see the solution in taking this distinction more seriously rather than making it murky. Since computational and algorithmic levels involve fundamentally different questions (e.g. why versus how), we suggest preserving the innocence of the computational account, and focusing on approximations at the algorithmic level.

Finally, as we saw in 'Mixing filters', p. 442, one important facet of approximate methods is that it is frequently appropriate to maintain multiple different approximations, each of which is appropriate in particular circumstances, and to switch between or blend their outputs. To the extent that different approximations lead to different behavior, it will be possible to diagnose and understand them and the tradeoffs that they (locally) optimize. Our understanding of the blending and switching process is less advanced.

In the present setting, the idea goes back at least to Konorski (1967) that Pavlovian learning can employ both a stimulus-stimulus pathway (which is more cognitive in this respect and echoes our full Kalman filter's representation of interstimulus covariance) and a simpler stimulus-reward one (perhaps related to our diagonalized Kalman filter); such processes also appear to be neurally distinguishable (Balleine and Killcross, 2006). In fact, there is evidence for similar behavioral dissociations coming from attempts to demonstrate retrospective revaluation in rats (Miller and Matute, 1996). When training is conducted directly in terms of stimulus-reinforcer pairings, no retrospective revaluation is generally seen (as with our diagonalized covariance Kalman filter), but revaluation does succeed in the more obviously cognitive case in which the paradigms are conducted entirely in terms of pairings between affectively neutral stimuli, one of which (standing in for the reinforcer) is finally associated with reinforcement before the test phase.

Parallel to this in the context of instrumental conditioning is an analogous division between an elaborate, cognitive, (and likely computationally noisy) 'goal-directed' pathway, and a simpler (but statistically inefficient) 'habitual' one (Dickinson and Balleine, 2002). In this setting, the idea of normatively trading off approximate value-inference approaches characteristic of the systems has been formalized in terms of their respective uncertainties, and explains a wealth of data about what circumstances favor the dominance of goal-directed or habitual processes (Daw et al., 2005). It would be interesting to explore similar estimates of uncertainty in the mixed Kalman filters and thereby gain normative traction on the mixing.

References

Balleine, B. W., & Killcross, S. (2006). Parallel incentive processing: An integrated view of amygdala function. *Trends in Neurosciences*, **29**, 272–279

Chomsky, N. (1965) *Aspects of the Theory of Syntax*. MIT Press.

Churchland, P. S. (1986). *Neurophilosophy: Toward a unified science of the mind-brain*. Cambridge, MA: MIT Press

Courville, A. C., Daw, N. D., Gordon, G. J., & D. S. Touretzky (2003). Model uncertainty in classical conditioning. In *Advances in Neural Information Processing Systems* (Vol. 16). Cambridge, MA: MIT Press.

Courville, A. C., Daw, N. D., & Touretzky, D. S. (2004). Similarity and discrimination in classical conditioning: A latent variable account. In *Advances in Neural Information Processing Systems* (Vol. 17). Cambridge, MA: MIT Press.

Courville, A. C., Daw, N. D., & Touretzky, D. S. (2006). Bayesian theories of conditioning in a changing world. *Trends in Cognitive Sciences*, **10**, 294–300.

Daw, N. D., Niv, Y., & Dayan, P. (2005). Uncertainty-based competition between prefrontal and dorsolateral striatal systems for behavioral control. *Nature Neuroscience*, **8**, 1704–1711.

Daw, N. D., O'Doherty, J. P., Seymour, B., Dayan, P., & Dolan, R. J. (2006). Cortical substrates for exploratory decisions in humans. *Nature*, **441**, 876–879.

Dayan, P., & Long, T. (1998). Statistical models of conditioning. *Advances in Neural Information Processing Systems*, **10**, 117–123.

Dayan, P., Kakade, S., & Montague P. R. (2000). Learning and selective attention. *Nature Neuroscience*, **3**, 1218–1223.

Dearden, R., Friedman N., & Russell S. J. (1998). Bayesian Q-learning. In *Proceedings of the 15th National Conference on Artificial Intelligence (AAAI)*, 761–768.

Dempster A. P., Laird N. M., & Rubin D. B. (1977). Maximum likelihood from incomplete data via the EM algorithm. *Journal of the Royal Statistical Society B*, **39**, 1–38.

Dickinson, A., & Balleine, B. (2002). The role of learning in motivation. In C. R. Gallistel (Ed.), *Stevens' handbook of experimental psychology Vol. 3: Learning, Motivation and Emotion* (3rd ed., pp. 497–533). New York: Wiley.

Doucet, A., Godsill, S., & Andrieu, C. (2000). On sequential Monte Carlo sampling methods for Bayesian filtering. *Statistics and Computing*, **10**, 197–208.

Griffiths, T. L., & Yuille, A. (2007). Technical introduction: A primer on probabilistic inference. 2007. (this volume).

Hinton, G. (1999). Products of experts. In *Proceedings of the Ninth International Conference on Artificial Neural Networks (ICANN99)*, pp. 1–6.

Hinton, G., & van Camp, D. (1993). Keeping neural networks simple by minimizing the description length of the weights. In *Proceedings of the Sixth Annual ACM Conference on Computational Learning Theory*, pp. 5–13.

Jacobs, R. A., Jordan, M. I., & Barto, A. G. (1991a). Task decomposition through competition in a modular connectionist architecture: The what and where vision tasks. *Cognitive Science*, **15**, 219–250.

Jacobs, R. A., Jordan, M. I., Nowlan, S. J., & Hinton, G. E. (1991b). Adaptive mixtures of local experts. *Neural Computation*, **3**, 79–87.

Jordan, M. I., Ghahramani, Z., Jaakkola, T. S., & Saul, L. K. (1999). An introduction to variational methods for graphical models. *Machine Learning*, **37**, 183–233.

Kakade, S., & Dayan, P. (2001). Explaining away in weight space. In *Advances in Neural Information Processing Systems* (Vol. 13). Cambridge, MA: MIT Press.

Kakade, S., & Dayan, P. (2002). Acquisition and extinction in autoshaping. *Psychological Review*, **109**, 533–544.

Kalman, R. E. (1960). A new approach to linear filtering and prediction problems. *Transactions of the ASME–Journal of Basic Engineering*, **82**, 35–45.

Kamin, L. J. (1969). Predictability, surprise, attention, and conditioning. In B. A. Campbell & R. M. Church (Eds.), *Punishment and aversive behavior* (pp. 242–259). New York: Appleton-Century-Crofts.

Konorski, J. (1967) *Integrative activity of the brain*. University of Chicago Press: Chicago.

Kruschke, J. K. (2001). Toward a unified model of attention in associative learning. *Journal of Mathematical Psychology*, **45**, 812–863.

Kruschke, J. K. (2006). Locally Bayesian learning with applications to retrospective revaluation and highlighting. *Psychological Review*, **113**, 677–699.

Kruschke, J. K. (2003). Attention in learning. *Current Directions in Psychological Science*, **5**, 171–175.

Lovibond, P. F., Been, S.-L., Mitchell, C. J., Bouton, M. E., & Frohardt, R. (2003). Forward and backward blocking of causal judgment is enhanced by additivity of effect magnitude. *Memory and Cognition*, **31**, 133–142.

Mackintosh, N. J. (1975). A theory of attention: Variations in the associability of stimuli with reinforcement. *Psychological Review*, **82**, 532–552.

Marr, D. (1982). *Vision: A computational approach*. San Francisco, CA: Freeman and Co.

Medin, D. L., & Bettger, J. G. (1991). Sensitivity to changes in base-rate information. *American Journal of Psychology*, **40**, 175–188.

Medin, D. L., & Edelson, S. M. (1988). Problem structure and the use of base-rate information from experience. *Journal of Experimental Psychology: General*, **117**, 68–85.

Miller, R. R., & Matute, H. (1996). Biological significance in forward and backward blocking: Resolution of a discrepancy between animal conditioning and human causal judgment. *Journal of Experimental Psychology: General*, **125**, 370–386.

Minka, T. (2001). *A family of algorithms for approximate Bayesian inference*. PhD thesis, Massachusetts Institute of Technology.

Neal, R. M., & Hinton, G. E. (1998). A view of the EM algorithm that justifies incremental, sparse and other variants. In M. I. Jordan (Ed.), *Learning in graphical models* (pp. 355–368). Kluwer Academic Publishers.

Rescorla, R. A., & Wagner, A. R. (1972). A theory of Pavlovian conditioning: The effectiveness of reinforcement and non-reinforcement. In A. H. Black & W. F. Prokasy (Eds.), *Classical conditioning, 2: Current research and theory* (pp. 64–69). New York: Appleton Century-Crofts.

Shanks, D. R. (1985). Forward and backward blocking in human contingency judgement. *Quarterly Journal of Experimental Psychology*, **37B**, 1–21.

Simon, H. (1957). A behavioral model of rational choice. In *Models of man, social and rational: Mathematical essays on rational human behavior in a social setting*. Wiley, New York.

Treebushny, D., & Madsen, H. (2005). On the construction of a reduced rank square-root Kalman filter for efficient uncertainty propagation. *Future Generation Computer Systems*, **21**, 1047–1055.

Waldmann, M. R., Cheng, P. W., Hagmayer, Y., & Blaisdell, A. P. (2007). Causal learning in rats and humans: A minimal rational model (this volume).

Wasserman, E. A., & Berglan, L. R. (1998). Backward blocking and recovery from overshadowing in human causal judgment: The role of within-compound associations. *Quarterly Journal of Experimental Psychology*, **51B**, 121–138.

Waterhouse, S., MacKay, D., & Robinson, T. (1996). Bayesian methods for mixtures of experts. *Advances in Neural Information Processing Systems*, **8**, 351–357.

Yu, A. J., & Dayan, P. (2003). Expected and unexpected uncertainty: ACh and NE in the neocortex. In *Advances in Neural Information Processing Systems* (Vol. 15). Cambridge, MA: MIT Press.

Yu, A. J., & Dayan, P. (2005). Uncertainty, neuromodulation, and attention. *Neuron*, **46**, 681–692.

Chapter 20

Causal learning in rats and humans: a minimal rational model

Michael R. Waldmann,
University of Göttingen, Göttingen, Germany

Patricia W. Cheng,
University of California, Los Angeles, USA

York Hagmayer, and
University of Göttingen, Göttingen, Germany

Aaron P. Blaisdell
University of California, Los Angeles, CA, USA

Introduction

People's ability to predict future events, to explain past events, and to choose appropriate actions to achieve goals belongs to the most central cognitive competencies. How is knowledge about regularities in the world learned, stored, and accessed? An intuitively plausible theory that has been developed in philosophy for many centuries assumes that *causality* is the 'cement of the universe' (Mackie, 1974), which underlies the orderly relations between observable events. According to this view some event types, causes, have the capacity or power to generate their effects. To be a successful agent we need to have causal representations that mirror the causal texture of the world.

The philosopher David Hume questioned this view in his seminal writings (Hume, 1748/1977). He analyzed situations in which we learn about causal relations, and did not detect any empirical input that might correspond to evidence for causal powers. What he found instead was repeated sequence of a pair of spatio-temporally contiguous events, but nothing beyond. Therefore he concluded that causality is a cognitive illusion triggered by associations. Hume did not question that we believe in causal powers, he merely argued that there is nothing in our experiential input that directly corresponds to causal powers.

The psychology of learning has adopted Hume's view by focusing on his analysis of the experiential input. According to many learning theories, causal predictions are driven by associative relations that have been learned on the basis of observed covariations between events (e.g., Allan, 1993; Shanks & Dickinson, 1987). Similar to Pavlov's dog, which has learned to predict food when it hears a tone (i.e., classical conditioning), or to a rat's learning that a lever press produces food (i.e., instrumental conditioning), we learn about predictive relations in our world. There is no need for the concept of causality in this view. Thus, following the epistemology of logical positivism the concept of causality was dropped altogether and replaced by predictive relations exhibited in covariational patterns between observable events.

What do we gain by having causal representations beyond what we already can do with predictive relations gleaned from learning data? Developing earlier work on causal inference (e.g., Goodman, 1983; Kant, 1781/1965; Skyrms, 2000), philosophers and psychologists have analyzed this question in great depth in the past decades and have pointed to several crucial differences (see Pearl, 1988, 2000; Spirtes et al., 1993; Woodward, 2003): (1) If we had no causal knowledge we could not represent the difference between causal and spurious statistical relations, such as the relation between barometers and the weather. Barometers covary with the weather as does smoking with heart disease. However, the first relation is spurious due to a common cause, atmospheric pressure, whereas the second describes a direct causal relation. Hence, if we mechanically change the reading of the barometer, the weather will not be affected, whereas giving up smoking will decrease the likelihood of heart disease. This distinction is crucial for planning actions (see Woodward, 2003). We can generate events by intervening in their causes, whereas interventions in spurious correlates are ineffective. (2) Another important aspect of causality is its inherent directionality. Causes generate effects but not vice versa. For example, the thrusting position of a fist on a pillow causes the indentation in the pillow, rather than vice versa. In contrast, covariations are undirected and therefore do not allow us to make informed inferences about the outcomes of interventions. (3) A final example of the advantages of causal representations is their parsimony when multiple events are involved. For example, learning predictive relations between six events requires us to encode 15 pairwise covariations. Only some of the necessary information may have been made available to learners, however. In contrast, causal models allow us to form more parsimonious representations and make informed guesses about covariations we may never have observed. For example, if we know that one event is the common cause of the other five, we can infer all 15 covariations from knowledge of the causal strength between the cause and each of its five effects (see Pearl, 1988, 2000; Spirtes et al., 1993).

Following Hume, learning theory has focused on the covariations inherent in the learning input, and has neglected how covariations give rise to causal representations. The basic claim was that knowledge about causal relations is nothing more than knowledge of covariations. However, there is another route that can be traced back to Kant's (1781/1965) view of causality. Hume, who did not deny the possibility of hidden causal powers, was indeed right when he pointed to covariations as the primary experiential input suggesting the existence of causal relations. However, his empiricist epistemology was mistaken. As many philosophers of science have revealed, apart from concepts referring to observable events, our theories also contain theoretical concepts that are only indirectly tied to the observable data (see Glymour, 1980; Quine, 1960; Sneed, 1971). Thus, it is possible to grant that we only have covariational data to support causal hypotheses, while retaining the view that we go beyond the information given and use covariations along with background assumptions to induce genuinely *causal* relations.

Cheng (1997) was the first to take this path in psychology. She has developed a theory (power PC theory), which formalizes how we can infer unobservable causal powers from covariations (see also Buehner & Cheng, 2005). According to this view, we enter the learning process with abstract assumptions about causes generating or preventing effects in the potential presence of hidden causal events. These assumptions combined with learning input allow learners to induce the causal power of events.

Causal-model theory (Waldmann & Holyoak, 1992) whose focus is on more complex causal models similarly has stated that people interpret covariations in light of prior assumptions about causal structures. A consequence of this view, supported in numerous empirical studies, is that identical learning input may lead to different causal representations depending on the characteristics of prior assumptions (see Waldmann *et al.*, 2006, for an overview).

Most recently, causal Bayes net theory has been proposed as a psychological theory of causal cognitions (Gopnik *et al.*, 2004; Sloman, 2005). Whereas power PC and causal-model theory were developed as psychological theories, causal Bayes net theory was originally developed by philosophers, computer scientists, and statisticians as a rational tool for causal discovery in empirical sciences (see Pearl, 1988; Spirtes *et al.*, 1993). Thus, primarily this approach aimed at developing a complex, normative theory of causal induction, and only secondarily claimed to be a psychological theory of everyday learning.

Given that the majority of learning theories have asserted that causal learning can be reduced to forming associations, one of the main goals in the empirical studies of power PC and causal-model theory was to test these theories against the predictions of associative theories (see Cheng, 1997; Buehner & Cheng, 2005; Waldmann, 1996; Waldmann *et al.*, 2006, for overviews). For example, Buehner *et al.* (2003) tested a novel pattern of an influence of the base rate of the effect on judgments of causal strength predicted by the power PC theory and no other theories. They showed that when a question measuring estimated causal strength is unambiguous, the results supported the key prediction of power PC theory that people use estimates of causal power to assess causal strength (see also Wu & Cheng, 1999; Liljeholm & Cheng, 2007). Waldmann and colleagues have shown that people are sensitive to causal directionality in learning (e.g., Waldmann, 2000, 2001) and to the difference between causal and spurious relations (Waldmann & Hagmayer, 2005). All these findings are inconsistent with the predictions of associative learning theories.

With the advent of causal Bayes net theory there is a major new competitor for power PC and causal-model theory, which often makes similar predictions as these theories. In fact, some have argued that previously developed theories such as power PC theory can be modeled as a special case of causal Bayes nets (see Glymour, 2001). We therefore think it is time to take a closer look at discriminating between different computational theories of causal reasoning.

Developing and testing rational models: the dominant view

Thus far, all theories of causal cognitions are developed at the computational level, which, according to Marr's (1982) famous distinction, is concerned with the goals and constraints rather than the algorithms of computations. Moreover, all theories share the view that a rational analysis of what an organism should compute should be the starting point of a successful theory in this field.

Anderson's (1990) book on rational models has been one of the main influences of the current collection. In the first chapters of this book he proposed a methodological strategy for developing rational models, which will provide the starting point of our discussion (see also Chater & Oaksford, 2004). Anderson (1990) motivates rational modeling by pointing to the problems of empirically identifying theories at the implementation level. In psychology we use observable inputs and outputs to induce unobservable mechanisms. Theoretically all mechanism hypotheses are equivalent that generate the same input-output function. This, according to Anderson (1990), leaves us with the problem of the unidentifiability of psychological theories at the mechanism level. Whenever such theories compute identical input–output functions a decision between them is impossible.

An alternative strategy, according to Anderson (1990), is to abandon the search for mechanisms and focus on rational modeling. He postulates six steps in developing a rational model: (1) We need to analyze the goals of the cognitive system, and (2) develop a formal model of the environment to which the system is adapted. (3) Psychology only enters in the form of *minimal* assumptions about computational limitations. These assumptions should be minimal, according to Anderson, to guarantee that the analysis is powerful in the sense that the predictions mainly flow from an analysis of the goals of the cognitive system and the environment and do not depend on assumptions about (unidentifiable) mechanisms. Then (4) a rational model is developed that derives the optimal behavioral function given the stated constraints of the environment and the organism. (5) Finally, these predictions can be compared with the results of empirical behavioral studies. (6) If the predictions are off, the process iterates by going back and revising previous analyses.

This view has been very popular in causal reasoning research, especially in the Bayesian camp. For example, Steyvers *et al.* (2003) defend the priority of rational analysis over theories of psychological implementation. They argue that their model attempts to explain people's behavior 'in terms of approximations to rational statistical inference, but this account does not require that people actually carry out these computations in their conscious thinking, or even in some unconscious but explicit format.' (p. 485). After this statement they acknowledge that simple heuristics might also account for their findings. Similarly, Gopnik *et al.* (2004) pursued the goal to show that the inferences of preschoolers were consistent with the normative predictions of causal Bayes nets, while ignoring that simpler and less powerful causal approaches can account for many of the presented findings.

Thus, there is a tendency of some researchers in this field to focus on the global fit between a single rational model and observed behavior. Alternative theories are either neglected or reinterpreted as possible implementations of the rational account. In our view, it is time to reconsider the relation between rational models and empirical evidence, and revisit the research strategy Anderson (1990) has proposed.

The indeterminacy of rational models

The underdetermination of psychological theories by the data has been one of the driving forces behind Anderson's (1990) rational analysis approach. However, in our view this argument is not restricted to theories at the mechanism level. The underdetermination problem is a general issue for empirical sciences regardless of whether they study the mind or environmental processes (Quine, 1960). In most areas, multiple theories compete, and it is far from clear whether a unique theory will emerge as a winner. Let us revisit some of Anderson's methodological steps in light of this problem in the area of causal reasoning, and show that there is theory competition at each step:

Step 1 requires an analysis of the goals of the cognitive system. It can easily be seen that in causal reasoning research the goal specifications have been highly dependent on the theory that is endorsed by the researcher. An associationist will see the ability to predict events as the primary goal of cognitive systems; somebody who sees causal forces and mechanisms as the basis of causality will instead choose the understanding of causal systems as primary; finally, a causal Bayes net researcher might focus on the goal of representing interventions and observations within a unified causal representation. Of course, all these approaches might be partially correct. But these examples show that there is theory dependence already at the level of the postulation of goals.

Step 2 focuses on the analysis of the environment. Again research on causality provides an excellent example for the theory-ladenness of environmental theories. Causal Bayes net theory is a recent example of a theory whose primary goal was to provide a framework for describing and discovering causal relations in the environment (Pearl, 2000; Spirtes et al., 1993). However, apart from causal Bayes nets there is a wealth of alternative theories of causality which are in part inconsistent with each other but still claim to provide a proper representation of causal relations in the world (see Cartwright, 1989, 2004; Dowe, 2000; Shafer, 1996).

Step 4, the development of a rational model, is clearly dependent on the model of the environment, and is therefore subject to the same constraints. Causal Bayes net theory is a good example of this dependence as it has simultaneously been proposed as a psychological theory (Gopnik et al., 2004) and as a theory of scientific discovery of causal models in the environment (Spirtes et al., 1993). However, other psychological theories of causality were similarly influenced by normative models. Associative accounts such as the probabilistic contrast model (Cheng & Novick, 1992) have predecessors in philosophy (Suppes, 1970; Salmon, 1980) as have psychological theories (Ahn et al., 1995; Shultz, 1982) focusing on causal mechanisms (Dowe, 2000; Salmon, 1984).

The main goal of the present section is to show that it is premature to expect that a careful analysis of the goals of the cognitive system and the environment will generate a unique rational model. The recent debate on the proper rational model for logical or probabilistic reasoning is a good example of how different assumptions may lead to competing theories (see Oaksford & Chater, 2007). We have argued that the steps postulated by Anderson (1990) are tightly constrained by each other. Goals, environment and cognitive systems need to be modeled as a whole in which all components influence each other, and jointly should be confronted with empirical data. A rational model for the aplysia will surely look different from one for humans. Consequently, we have to be concerned with the possibility of multiple competing rational models that need to be tested and evaluated.

Minimal rational models as a methodological heuristic

We will defend the position that it is useful to consider whether there are alternative rational theories which are less computationally demanding while still fully account-ing for the data (see also Daw *et al.*, this volume, for a different but similarly motivated approach). This methodological heuristic we will call *minimality* require-ment. Given the indeterminacy at all levels, it is clear that rational models, just like models at other levels, need to be empirically tested. Due to the potential tradeoffs between goals, environment, (innate and acquired) learning biases and information processing limitations, different rational models can be developed and will therefore compete. How can competing rational models be tested? We will discuss some general principles:

(1) The more psychological evidence we consider, the higher the likelihood that we will be able to empirically distinguish between theories. For example, causal Bayes net theory (Gopnik *et al.*, 2004) requires sensitivity to conditional dependence and independence information, whereas alternative theories do not. Showing that people can or cannot pick up conditional dependency information might there-fore be relevant for distinguishing between theories. Of course, answering the question of what computations organisms can accomplish is not always easy. For example, many psychologists believed that we cannot, explicitly or implicitly, compute multiple regression weights until a theory, the Rescorla–Wagner model (1972), was developed which shows how such weights can be computed with fairly easy computational routines.

(2) A minimal model allows us to understand better which conclusions are war-ranted by the evidence and which not. Moreover, they give us a better under-standing of what aspects of theories are actually empirically supported, and which are in need of further research. Minimality is a particularly useful heuristic when theories that are hierarchically related compete with each other. For exam-ple, power PC theory can be modeled as a special case of causal Bayes nets (see Glymour, 2001). However, this does not mean that all the evidence for power PC theory immediately is inherited by causal Bayes net theory, because this more complex theory may exaggerate the computational capacities of organisms.

(3) Empirical tests of rational models proposed in the literature often blur the dis-tinction between rational models of scientific discovery and of a rational model of the mind. Causal Bayes net theory is an extreme example, as virtually the same model has been postulated for both areas. However, due to different information processing constraints of computers versus humans, a rational model in Artificial Intelligence will certainly be different from one developed in psychology. The dis-tinction between the normative and the psychological is particularly important when it comes to the question of how heuristics or psychological theories relate to rational models. Often it is argued that rational models let us understand what

heuristics try to compute. This is certainly useful as long as it is clear that the rational model merely provides a normative analysis of the situation to which an organism adapts rather than a computational model of the mind. For example, the Bayesian inversion formula can be seen as a tool to compute normative responses in a diagnostic judgment task. But that does not mean that the availability heuristic (Tversky & Kahnman, 1973) should be regarded as an implementation of the normative formula. Heuristics and rational models may lead to similar judgments in a wide range of cases; nevertheless they compute different functions. The goal of minimal rational modeling is to discover the function people are actually computing (see also Danks, this volume). Then it might be informative to compare the predictions of minimal rational models with normative rational models.

Causal learning as a test case

Research on causal learning represents an ideal test case for the question of how rational models should be evaluated. In the past decade several theories have been proposed that compete as rational accounts of causal learning. Since it is not possible to discuss all theories, we will focus on three approaches and discuss them on the basis of recent evidence from our laboratories:

(1) *Associative Theories.* Standard associative accounts of causal learning (e.g., Rescorla-Wagner, 1972) will serve as a base-line for our discussion. To demonstrate that human or nonhuman animals are indeed using *causal* representations, it is necessary to show that the obtained experimental effects cannot be explained with a simpler associative account such as merely predictive learning. According to associative theories events are represented as *cues* and *outcomes* rather than causes and effects (see also Waldmann, 1996; Waldmann *et al.*, 2006). Cues are events that serve as triggers for outcome representations regardless of whether they represent causes or effects. Thus, associative theories are insensitive to causal directionality. Moreover, it is assumed that learning is sensitive to observational covariations rather than causal power (see Cheng, 1997). Thus, there is no distinction between covariations based on spurious (e.g., barometer-weather) as opposed to causal relations (atmospheric pressure-barometer). Finally, covariation knowledge may be acquired between different observable events (i.e., classical conditioning) or between acts and outcomes (i.e., instrumental learning).

(2) *Causal Bayes Nets.* Currently different variants of causal Bayes nets are being developed, which compete with each other (see Gopnik & Schulz, 2007, for an overview). We are going to focus on the version proposed by Gopnik *et al.* (2004). In this framework causal models are represented as directed acyclic graphs, which contain nodes connected by causal arrows. 'Acyclic' means that the graph does not contain loops. It is assumed that the graphs satisfy the Markov condition which states that for any variable X in a set of variables S not containing direct or indirect effects of X, X is jointly independent of all variables in S conditional on any set of values of the set of variables that are direct causes of X. An effect of X is a variable that is connected with a single arrow or a path of arrows pointing from X to it.

Figure 20.1 shows an example of three basic causal models. Model A (left) represents a common-cause model in which a common cause (e.g., atmospheric pressure) both causes effect_1 (e.g., barometer) and effect_2 (e.g., weather). The two direct causal links imply covariations between the common cause and either effect. Moreover, the Markov condition implies that the two effects should be spuriously correlated but become independent conditional on the states of their common cause. Model B (middle) represents a causal chain, which has similar implications. The initial cause should covary with effect_1 and effect_2, which is caused by effect_1. Due to the Markov condition, the cause and effect_2 should become independent conditional on effect_1. Finally, Model C (left) represents a common-effect model. In the absence of further external common causes of the two causes 1 and 2, these causes should covary with their joint effect but be mutually marginally independent. However, the causes should become dependent conditional on their common effect.

An important claim of Gopnik *et al.* (2004) is that people should be capable of inducing causal structure from conditional dependence and independence information. Again the Markov assumption along with additional assumptions (e.g., faithfulness) is central for this achievement. Gopnik *et al.* (2004) discuss two Bayesian induction strategies. According to *constraint-based learning* people should analyze triples of events (such as in Fig. 20.1) within causal models and select between causal models on the basis of conditional dependence and independence information. Sometimes this will yield several (Markov equivalent) alternatives. Additional cues (e.g., temporal order information) may help to further restrict the set of possibilities. An alternative to this bottom-up approach are *Bayesian algorithms*, which assign prior probabilities to possible causal models, which are updated by the application of Bayes' theorem given the actual data. Both methods rely on conditional dependence and independence information implied by the Markov condition.

Apart from allowing us to predict events, causal models can also be used to plan actions. Unlike associative theories, causal models are capable of representing the relation between inferences based on observations of events and inferences based on interventions in these events (see also Hagmayer *et al.*, 2007). For example, the common-cause model depicted in Fig. 20.1A implies that the observation of effect_1 (e.g., barometer) allows for inferring the state of effect_2 (weather) based

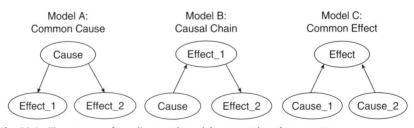

Fig. 20.1. Three types of acyclic causal models connecting three events.

on the diagnostic link between effect_1 (atmospheric pressure) and its cause, and the predictive link between the cause and effect_2. However, manipulating the reading of the barometer by tampering with it should not affect effect_2. Causal Bayes nets allow for modeling this difference by modifying the structure of the graph (Pearl, 2000; Spirtes *et al.*, 1993; Woodward, 2003). Deterministic manipulations of effect nodes render the state of these nodes independent of its causes, as long as some plausible boundary conditions apply (e.g., independence of the instrumental action with the relevant events of the causal models). This can be modeled by removing the arrow between the cause and the manipulated event, which Pearl (2000) vividly called graph surgery (see Fig. 20.2).

The possibility of representing both observational and interventional inferences within a single causal model is one key feature of causal Bayes nets that render them causal. The fact that interventions often imply modifications of causal models turns interventions into an additional powerful tool to induce causal structure. Learning can capitalize from both observational and interventional information and combine these two components during learning (see Gopnik *et al.*, 2004).

(3) *Single-effect Learning Model.* Given our interest in minimal rational models it is useful to test the simplest possible theory of causal learning as an alternative account. Buehner and Cheng (2005) have proposed that organisms primarily focus on evaluating single causal relations during learning. The individual links are integrated into a causal model or causal map (Gopnik *et al.*, 2004; Waldmann & Holyoak, 1992). Should several causal relations contain overlapping events it is possible to make inferences across complex causal networks by chaining the links. The focus on evaluating a single causal relation does not imply that causes of the same effect *e* that are not currently evaluated are ignored; accounting for *e* due to causes other than the candidate *c* is an essential part of inferences about the

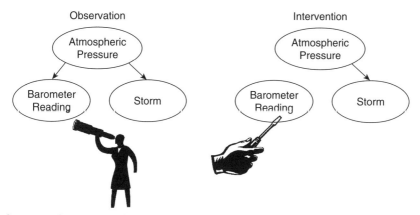

Fig. 20.2. Observing an effect (left) versus intervening in an effect (right) of a common cause: While an observation of an effect allows inferring the presence of its cause, an intervention in the same variable renders this variable independent of its cause. See text for details.

relation between c and e. Thus, the common-effect structure (e.g., Fig. 20.1C) is the basic unit in which learning occurs, as has been assumed by previous psychological learning theories (e.g., Cheng, 1997; Griffiths & Tenenbaum, 2005; Rescorla & Wagner, 1972). A single-effect learning strategy may be an effective default strategy because, in contrast to the typical wealth of data mined by Bayes nets algorithms, information available to humans and other species regarding relevant causal variables may often be very limited. The information available may be further impoverished by the reasoner's memory and attention constraints. The present chapter will review and explain how, under causal-power assumptions (Cheng, 1997), (1) complex causal models (Waldmann & Holyoak, 1992) are constructed via single-effect learning, and (2) making predictive and diagnostic link-by-link inferences based on the models account for observational and interventional inferences within complex causal networks.

Review of causal model construction via single-effect causal learning

Cheng's (1997) power PC theory provides an account of the learning of the strength of the primary unit of causality—a causal relation between a single candidate cause and a single effect. Whereas associative theories merely encode observable covariations, causal relations do not primarily refer to observable statistics but unobservable theoretical entities. To estimate the causal strength of these unobserved causal relations several assumptions need to be made. The power PC theory partitions all causes of effect e into the candidate cause in question, c, and a, a composite of all observed and unobserved causes of e. The unobservable probability with which c *produces* e is termed *generative* power, represented by q_c. The generative power of the composite a is analogously labeled q_a. On the condition that c and a influence e independently, it follows that

$$P(e|c) = q_c + P(a|c) \cdot q_a - q_c \cdot P(a|c) \cdot q_a \qquad (1), \text{ and}$$

$$P(e|\sim c) = P(a|\sim c) \cdot q_a \qquad (2).$$

Equation (1) implies that effect e is either caused by c, by the composite a, or by both, assuming that c and a produce e independently. The difference between $P(e|c)$ and $P(e|\sim c)$ is called ΔP, which is a frequently used measure of covariation in learning research. Thus, from Equation 2, it follows that

$$\Delta P = q_c + P(a|c) \cdot q_a - q_c \cdot P(a|c) \cdot q_a - P(a|\sim c) \cdot q_a \qquad (3).$$

Equation (3) shows why covariations do not directly reflect causality. There are four unknowns in the equation. The lack of a unique solution for q_c, the desired unknown, corresponds to the intuitive uncertainty regarding q_c in this situation: if we observe the presence of a candidate cause c and its effect e, we do not know whether e was actually caused by c, by a, or by both. If c and a are perfectly correlated, we may observe a perfect covariation between c and e, and yet c may not be a cause of e because the confounding variable a may be the actual cause. The learner therefore restricts causal inference to situations in which c and a occur independently; that is, there is *no confounding*. In that special case, (3) reduces to (4):

$$q_c = \Delta P / (1 - P(e|\sim c)) \tag{4}$$

The above analysis holds for situations in which $\Delta P \geq 0$. A similar derivation can be made for situations in which $\Delta P \leq 0$, and one evaluates the *preventive* causal power of c.

The 'no confounding' prerequisite that follows from Equations 3 and 4 explains why interventions have special status as a method for inducing causal power. Interventions typically are assumed to occur independently of the other causes of the target event. This prerequisite also explains why when an intervention is believed to be confounded (e.g., placebo effect; see Buehner & Cheng, 2005; Cheng, 1997), it is not different from any other confounded observation; in this case interventions do not have any special status. Note that to satisfy the 'no confounding' assumption, one does not need to know the identities of other causes or observe their states; one only needs to know that these causes, whatever they may be, occur independently of the candidate cause (e.g., consider the case of random assignment to a treatment and a no-treatment group). Confounding may of course be due to observed alternative causes as well. Research on confounding by observed causes has shown that people are aware of the confounding and therefore tend to create independence by holding the alternative cause constant, preferably in its absent value (see, for example, Waldmann & Hagmayer, 2001; Spellman, 1996).

Thus, while the focus is on the learning of a single causal relation, the possibility of the effect due to other causes is acknowledged. (Information about multiple candidate variables is of course required when one evaluates a conjunctive candidate cause, one that involves a combination of variables.) The single-effect learning theory explains why causal learning can proceed even when one has explicit knowledge of the states of only two variables, the candidate cause and the target effect. The work on causal Bayes nets, in which 'no confounding' is not a general prerequisite for causal learning, have not considered the role of this prerequisite in the case of link-by-link single-effect learning, arguably the most common type of biological learning.

In summary, the basic unit of causal analysis is a common-effect network with an observable candidate cause, alternative hidden or observable causes, and a single effect. These three event types allow organisms to go beyond covariational information and estimate theoretical causal entities.

Causal directionality

A key feature of causal relations is their inherent causal directionality. Causes generate effects but not vice versa. Correct assessments of causal power require the distinction between causes (c, a) and effect (e). However, it is a well-known fact that causal directionality cannot be recovered from covariation information between two events alone. For example, a flagpole standing on a beach covaries with its shadow on the sand as does the shadow with the flagpole, but the flagpole causes the shadow rather than vice versa. Covariations are symmetric whereas causal power is directed.

Learners' sensitivity to causal directionality has been one of the main research areas of causal-model theory (see Waldmann, 1996; Waldmann *et al.*, 2006, for overviews). According to this theory people use non-statistical *cues* to infer causal directionality (see Lagnado *et al.*, 2007). These cues, although fallible, provide the basis for hypotheses regarding the distinction between causes and effects. What cues are typically used?

Interventions are arguably the best cue to causal directionality. Manipulating a variable turns it into a potential cause, and the change of subsequent events into potential effects. Interventions are particularly useful if they are not confounded (i.e., independent), which may not always be the case, as mentioned earlier. Interventions, particularly unconfounded ones, are not always available. *Temporal order* is another potent cue. Typically cause information temporally precedes effect information. However, the phenomenal representational capacities of humans allow for a decoupling between temporal and causal order. For example, a physician may see information about symptoms prior to the results of tests reflecting their causes, but still form a correct causal model. Research on causal-model theory has shown that humans are indeed capable of focusing on causal order and disregarding temporal cues in such situations (e.g., Waldmann & Holyoak, 1992; Waldmann *et al.*, 1995; Waldmann, 2000, 2001). *Coherence* with prior knowledge is a further potent cue to causal directionality (see also Lien & Cheng, 2000). For example, we know that electrical switches are typical causes even when we do not know what a particular switch causes in a learning situation. Prior knowledge may finally be invoked through *communication*. Instructions may teach us about causal hypotheses.

Diagnostic causal inference under causal-power assumptions

Cheng (1997) and Novick and Cheng (2004) focused in their analysis on *predictive* inferences from cause to effect. Causal relations may also be accessed in the opposite *diagnostic* direction from effect to cause. Research on causal-model theory has shown that people are capable of diagnostic inferences in trial-by-trial learning situations (see Reips & Waldmann, 2008; Waldmann *et al.*, 2006). The same causal-power assumptions underlying predictive inferences apply to diagnostic inferences. These assumptions are defaults (see Cheng, 2000, for an analysis of various relaxations of these assumptions); the first two are empirical, and may be revised in light of evidence:

(1) C and alternative causes of E influence E independently,

(2) causes in the composite background A could produce E but not prevent it,

(3) causal powers are independent of the occurrence of the causes, and

(4) E does not occur unless it is caused.

Below we illustrate how these assumptions can be applied to explain a variety of related diagnostic inferences. Consider, for example, diagnostic inferences regarding a causal structure with two causes of a common effect E: C→E ← D. How would explanation by causal powers account for the simplest diagnostic inference—the intuition that having knowledge that E has occurred, compared to the absence of such knowledge, would lead to the inference that each of the causes is more likely to have?

Similarly, how would this approach explain the intuition that given knowledge that E has occurred, the target cause C is less likely to have occurred if one now knows that an alternative cause D has occurred, compared to when one does not have such knowledge (the 'explaining away' or discounting phenomena)?

A basic case of single-effect diagnostic inference and some special variations

Here we show a causal-power explanation of an intuitive diagnostic inference from the occurrence of E to the occurrence of target cause C, namely, the intuition that the probability of C occurring given that E has occurred, $P(c|e)$, is higher than the unconditional probability of C occurring, $P(c)$. In our derivations below, c represents the event that C has occurred, and likewise for d and e with respect to cause D and effect E.

Let q_C be the generative power of C to produce E,

q_D be the generative power of D to produce E,

$e_{C\text{-}only}$ be the event that E is produced by C alone (i.e., not also by D), and

e_D be the event that E is produced by D, whether or not it is also produced by C.

By definition of conditional probability,

$$P(c \mid e) = \frac{P(c,e)}{P(e)} \tag{5}$$

Event e can be decomposed into e_D and $e_{C\text{-}only}$, two mutually exclusive events. Making use of this decomposition of e, and of causal-power assumptions, to put the right-hand-side of Equation 1 into causal power terms, one obtains:

$$\frac{P(c,e)}{P(e)} = \frac{P(d) \cdot q_D \cdot P(c) + \left[1 - P(d) \cdot q_D\right] \cdot P(c) \cdot q_C}{P(d) \cdot q_D + \left[1 - P(d) \cdot q_D\right] \cdot P(c) \cdot q_C} \tag{6}$$

The numerator shows the probabilities of the two conjunctive events – (1) C occurring and E caused by D, and (2) C occurring and E caused by C alone. The components of each conjunctive event occur independently of each other. From (5) and (6), it follows that:

$$P(c \mid e) = P(c) \cdot \frac{P(d) \cdot q_D + \left[1 - P(d) \cdot q_D\right] \cdot q_C}{P(d) \cdot q_D + P(c) \cdot \left[1 - P(d) \cdot q_D\right] \cdot q_C} \tag{7}$$

From (7) it is easy to see the relation between $P(c)$ and $P(c|e)$. In the trivial case in which $P(c) = 1$, $P(c|e)$ of course also equals 1.

When C does not always occur

But in the more interesting case, if $P(c) < 1$, Equation 7 implies that

$$P(c|e) > P(c), \tag{8}$$

thus explaining the basic diagnostic intuition that knowing that a particular effect has occurred increases the probability that its causes have occurred. As can be seen from (7), this inequality holds regardless of the magnitude of q_D, as long as $p(d) \neq 1$; for example, in the trivial case in which C is the only cause of E (i.e., when $q_{-D} = 0$), (7) implies that given that E has occurred, the probability of C occurring is increased to 1. (See section on 'Intervening versus Observing' regarding the special case in which both $p(d)$ and q_D equal 1.)

Combining link-by-link inferences

The capacity to access causal relations in the predictive and diagnostic direction allows us to make inferences consecutively across causal networks by going from one link to the other. For example, the basic diagnostic inference just shown can be applied to the common-cause model (Fig. 20.1A) to infer the state of effect_2 from the state of effect_1 (treating effect_1 as the common effect E in the basic learning unit): First, diagnostically infer that the cause must have occurred when effect_1 is observed (i.e., P(c|effect_1)=1; this is the single-cause special case in (7) in which P(d)=0 or $q_{c \to effect\_1} = 0$); that is, there is no causal influence from D to effect_1. Second, infer the state of effect_2 from the presence of the cause just inferred (i.e., P(c|effect_1) · $q_{c \to effect\_2}$, where $q_{c \to effect\_2}$ is the causal power of c to produce effect_2). Note that Equation 7 would similarly apply for the more general other case in which P(d)>0 and $q_{c \to effect\_1} > 0$; that is, there is a causal influence from D to effect_1. In the case in which D is a background cause that is constantly present, P(d)=1. Similar consecutive inferential steps can be derived for the chain model; for example, with respect to the causal chain C→effect_1→effect_2 (Fig. 20.1B), P(*effect_2*|*c*) = $q_{c \to effect\_1}$ · $q_{effect\_1 \to effect\_2}$. More generally, for diagnostic reasoning Equation 7 applies, and for predictive reasoning the causal powers of the relations in question apply.

It is important to note that combining these steps builds on individual links rather than any quantitatively coherent causal model representation. Note that in our derivations we did not use the Markov constraint in any of our inferential steps. Thus, it is not necessary to assume that learners use the Markov constraint in their inferences. Inferential behavior consistent with the Markov condition is in these cases a side effect of chaining the inferences, it is not an explicit part of the postulated graphical representation. For example, for the common-cause structure (Fig. 20.1A), a reasoner may or may not take the additional step of inferring the independence between effect_1 and effect_2 conditional on the common cause. If that step is not taken, say, during the initial learning of the structure when attention is focused on the learning of individual links, then a violation of that independence relation (as implied by the Markov condition when applied to the structure) will go unnoticed. Thus, more generally, although under conditions in which typical attention and memory constraints are bypassed, model construction via link-by-link causal inference will be consistent with the Markov condition, in typical situations conforming to the Markov condition for inferences regarding relationships between indirectly linked variables will depend greatly on attentional and memory factors.

Common-effect models (Fig. 20.1C) provide another interesting test case because normatively it is not permissible to chain the predictive link between cause_1 and effect, and then proceed in the diagnostic direction from the effect to cause_2 while disregarding the first link. Chaining these two inferences would erroneously predict a correlation between the two variables that are not directly linked, violating the Markov assumption as applied to Fig. 20.1C. Doing so would mean that all three models in Fig. 20.1 make the same predictions regarding the indirectly linked variables (the two effects of the common-cause model, the two causes of the common-effect model, and the cause and effect_2 in the causal chain model). However, whereas effects make each cause individually more likely, diagnosing a target cause when an alternative cause is present should make the target cause less likely than when the state of the alternative cause is unknown (i.e., explaining away). Correct inferences within a common-effect model need to consider all three event types defining causal relations: (1) target cause, (2) target effect, and (3) alternative observable and unobservable causes.

Explaining away

To explain 'explaining away' in causal-power terms, let us return to Equation 7 (assuming $P(c) < 1$). One can see that as $P(d)$ increases, $P(c|e)$ decreases, as does the difference between $P(c|e)$ and $P(c)$ (although, as just explained, $P(c|e)$ is still greater than $P(c)$ because $P(c) < 1$). In the special extreme case in which $P(d) = 1$, the left-hand-side of (7) becomes $P(c|e,d)$, and $P(c|e)$ is at its minimum (assuming unchanged causal powers). That is, the probability of C given that both E and D have occurred is less than the probability of C given E when the state of D is unknown. More generally, (7) implies that knowing that one of the two causes of an effect has occurred, relative to not knowing that, reduces the probability that the other cause has occurred (the case of discounting or explaining away):

$$P(c|e,d) < P(c|e) \qquad (9)$$

We assume that people are capable of making the above inferences when their attention is brought to the relevant variables. An interesting test case for our model, however, concerns cases in which participants consecutively access the two links of a common-effect model, in the order cause_1, effect, and cause_2. People's focus on single links may mislead them into making a simple diagnostic inference from the effect to cause_2 while disregarding the previously accessed link from cause_ 1 to its effect (see below for empirical evidence). They make the mistake of inferring P(effect| cause_1) followed by P(cause_2| effect), instead of making a one-step inference regarding P(cause_2 | effect, cause_1) as just shown (see (9)).

Intervening versus observing

A final important question refers to the distinction between intervening and observing within the single-effect learning model. Observing an effect provides diagnostic evidence for its cause, whereas intervening on the effect does not. We have already elaborated on how observational diagnostic inferences should be handled. A simple model of interventional inferences would just add a causal link from the intervening agent to the manipulated variable, thus creating a new common effect structure in which the agent is a new cause (see Fig. 20.3) (see also Dawid, 2002). Let alternative cause D in this case be the added intervening agent (see Fig. 20.3). The inferences following hypothetical interventions then follow from (7), which implies explaining away when multiple causes compete for predicting a specific effect (see also Morris & Larrick, 1995). Consider the simple case in which the target cause C and the intervening agent D are the only causes of E. The analysis generalizes to more complex cases involving multiple causes of E in addition to the intervening agent.

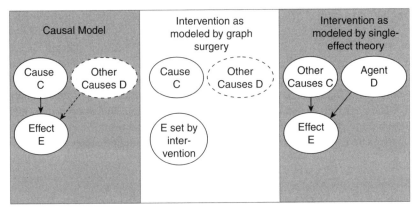

Fig. 20.3. Modeling intervention in an effect according to causal Bayes net theory and the single-effect learning theory. See text for details.

The above diagnostic inference regarding an intervention is the special case of (7) in which the intervention is always successful in producing the target effect, namely, $P(d) \cdot q_D = 1$. In that case, according to (7),

$$P(c|e) = P(c) \tag{10}.$$

That is, knowing that E has occurred does not affect the probability of C. The difference shown in our analysis between the result indicated in (10) and that in (8) explains the distinction between inferences based on intervening to obtain an effect versus merely observing the effect.

Note that when the intervention is viewed as deterministic and independent of the other cause, this analysis yields the same results as graph surgery, without removing the causal link between the usual cause and the target effect. In this special case, the manipulated effect and its usual cause become independent, which means that this cause occurs at its base rate probability.

Probabilistic Interventions

Beyond this special case the present analysis also allows for predicting the outcomes of hypothetical interventions that only probabilistically alter their target variable, or that are confounded with other events in the causal model. For example, as explained earlier, (7) shows that when the intervention is only probabilistically successful (i.e., $q_D < 1$), one can in fact infer from knowing that E has occurred (whether or not E was caused by D, the intervening variable) that the probability of C is increased relative to not knowing that E has occurred (i.e., $P(c|e) > P(c)$, Equation 8). That is, there should be no graph surgery. Thus, the classical diagnostic analysis has the advantage of greater generality.

Empirical case study 1: causal learning in rats

Although in the past decades there has been a debate about whether human causal learning can be reduced to associative learning processes or not (see Cheng, 1997; Shanks &

Dickinson, 1987; Waldmann *et al.*, 2006; special issue of Learning & Behavior, 2005, Volume 33(2)), until recently most researchers have agreed that nonhuman animals are incapable of causal reasoning. Although many of these psychologists believed that even infants have the capacity for causal representations, they drew a line between human and nonhuman animals, turning causal reasoning into a uniquely human capacity similar to language. For example, Povinelli argued about chimpanzees that 'their folk physics does not suffer (as Hume would have it) from an ascription of causal concepts to events which consistently co-vary with each other' (Povinelli, 2000, p. 299; see also Tomasello & Call, 1997, for a similar argument). Gopnik and Schulz (2004, p. 375) claimed: 'The animals seem able to associate the bell ringing with food, and if they are given an opportunity to act on the bell and that action leads to food, they can replicate that action. Moreover, there may be some transfer from operant to classical conditioning. However, the animals do not seem to go directly from learning novel conditional independencies to designing a correct novel intervention.'

Blaisdell *et al.* (2006) tested whether rats are capable of causal learning and reasoning. Their goal was to show that rats distinguish between causal and spurious relations, and are capable of deriving predictions for novel actions after purely observational learning. Their experiments were modeled after a previous study on humans (Waldmann & Hagmayer, 2005). In this study participants were provided with instructions suggesting a common-cause or a causal chain model and were given data to learn about the base rates of events and about the causal strength of the causal links. In the test phase, participants were given questions regarding hypothetical observations and hypothetical interventions. For example, in one experiment they learned about a common-cause model (see Fig. 20.1A), and then were asked in what state effect_2 would be given that effect_1 was observed (observation question). The corresponding intervention question asked participants about effect_2 when effect_1 was manipulated by an external intervention. The responses showed that participants were sensitive to the distinction between observing and intervening consistent with the assumption that they had formed a causal representation of a common-cause or causal chain model. They also proved sensitive to the size of the causal strength parameters and the base rates.

In Blaisdell *et al.*'s study (2006) rats also went first through a purely observational learning phase. In their Experiment 1, rats observed three types of trials, a light followed by a tone, the light followed by food, or a click occurring simultaneously with food. These three trial types were separately presented several times during a week (see Fig. 20.4). The idea was to present rats with the individual links of a common-cause model with temporal cues suggesting the roles of potential causes and effects. We chose to separately present the link information to avoid that rats would form a model in which the two effects are directly causally instead of spuriously linked. This learning procedure was motivated by research on second-order conditioning. Yin, Barnet, and Miller (1994) have shown that with few trials rats that separately learn about two links of a chain tend to associate the first event with the last event although these two events never co-occurred. In second-order conditioning they are in fact negatively correlated. Only with many trials do rats notice the negative (inhibitory) relation. Following these findings we chose trial numbers that favored the integration of the separate links into a model in which all events are positively associated.

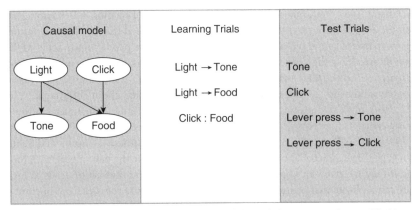

Fig. 20.4. Causal model presened to rats in Blaisdell *et al.* (2006, Experiment 1)(left). Each causal link was presented separately (→ signifies temporal order,: signifies simultaneous presentation)(middle). Test trials presented either the alternative effect of the cause of food (tone), the second cause of food (click), or these two events as a causal outcome of lever presses (click and tone were counterbalanced)(right). Rats' expectations of the presence of food were assessed by measuring their search behavior (nose poking). See text for further details.

This prediction was supported in the subsequent test phase in which rats were presented with the tone as a cue (observation test). The results showed that the tone apparently led them to believe that food was present, which was measured by the time they searched for food in a niche (i.e., nose poking). This behavior is consistent with the view that the rats accessed a common-cause model to infer from one effect (tone) to the other (food)(see Fig. 20.5). The crucial test involved a novel intervention. In this part of the test phase, a lever the rats had never seen before was introduced into the cage. (Actually there were also levers during the observation tests but pressing the levers there did not cause an event.) Whenever the rats curiously pressed the lever, the tone was presented (intervention test). Now, although tone and food had been associated by the rats in the learning phase as indicated in the observational test phase, they were less inclined to search for food after the lever presses (see Fig. 20.5). Blaisdell *et al.* (2006) viewed this behavior as evidence for the rats having formed a common-cause model in which, consistent with the Markov condition, a spurious positive correlation is implied by the two generative causal links emanating from the common cause. Whereas in the observation test rats apparently reasoned from one effect through the common cause to the second effect, they seemed to be aware of the fact that during the intervention test they and not necessarily the light were the cause of the tone. This is consistent with the view that the rats assumed that light and tone are independent during the intervention.

One could argue that the rats may have been distracted by the lever presses and therefore may have been reluctant to search for food. This possibility is ruled out by further test conditions in which the rats either observed the click or pressed the lever, which generated the click signal (see Fig. 20.4). In this condition rats expected food regardless of whether they heard the click or pressed the lever generating the click

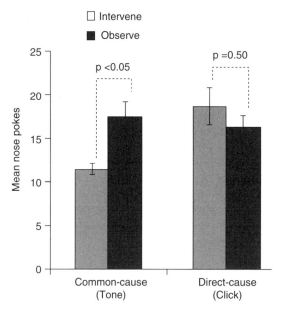

Fig. 20.5. Results of Blaisdell *et al.* (2006, Experiment 1, reproduced with permission). Rats either observed tone and intervened in click, or observed click and intervened in tone (tone and click were counterbalanced).

(see Fig. 20.5). This pattern is again consistent with the assumption that rats had formed causal knowledge. Regardless of whether a direct cause is observed or generated by an intervention the effect should occur. As an additional test, Blaisdell *et al.* (2006) presented in a second experiment a causal chain in which, again using a second-order conditioning procedure (sensory preconditioning), the tone preceded light which in turn preceded food. Consistent with a causal analysis the rats expected food regardless of whether they observed the tone or generated it with the lever. This shows again with a second-order conditioning task that the rats were not generally reluctant to expect food after a novel intervention. We will now revisit the results of Blaisdell *et al.* (2006) discussing them in greater detail in the context of the three models.

Associative theory

Although previous research on second-order conditioning has focused on chain-like structures and not common-cause models, the findings are consistent with second-order conditioning in both experiments. However, why second-order conditioning occurs is not entirely clear, especially because it seems to be dependent on trial number (Yin *et al.*, 1994). According to associative theories, rats should associate light with tone, and light with food. If this is represented in the typical one-layer network with one cue (light) and two independent outcomes (tone, food), two positive associative weights should be formed for either link. Without any further learning these outcomes would indeed be correlated, which is consistent with the findings in the observational test phase. However, this prediction only holds if it is assumed that the inhibitory relation between the two outcomes tone and food is not encoded, at least with few trials. Thus, according to the associative view, rats might associate tone with food through second-order conditioning when the additional assumption is made that no associations between outcomes will be learned. However, the associative view breaks down when the intervention test is considered. It cannot explain why, given that rats associate tone with food, they nonetheless did not expect food when their actions caused the tones.

It is important to note that acquisition-based theories (e.g., Rescorla & Wagner, 1972) do not predict that lever presses compete with light as an explanation of tones because the light-tone trials and the lever press-tone trials were separately presented, thus preventing cue competition.[1] Another possible argument might be that the intervention test is in fact a novel instrumental conditioning task. Thus, rats may not expect food in Experiment 1 because the instrumental action is novel so that they had not formed any associations between lever presses, tone and food. However, this explanation is contradicted by the direct cause (click) condition and by the causal chain experiment (Experiment 2). In these conditions, interventions and observations led to equal amounts of search for food. In sum, the results by Blaisdell *et al.* (2006) are inconsistent with current associative theory.

Causal Bayes nets

Causal Bayes net theory (Gopnik *et al.*, 2004) can be applied to both the learning phases and the testing phases of Blaisdell *et al.*'s (2006) experiments. It is obvious that a bottom-up constraint-based learning algorithm is incapable of explaining the results of the learning phase, even when temporal order cues are used that aid the induction process. The temporal order of events suggests that light is a potential cause of tone and of food. However, the learning patterns are inconsistent with a common-cause or causal chain model in which the Markov condition holds. For example, in Experiment 1 rats observe the patterns light-tone-absence of food ($P(t.l.\sim f)$) or light-food-absence of tone ($P(l.f.\sim t)$), along with additional click-food trials. According to the Markov condition, $P(t|l.f)$ should be equal to $P(t|l.\sim f)$. But the first probability is zero, the second probability is one, which clearly violates the Markov condition. The same problem arises for the causal chain condition (Experiment 2) in which tone is negatively correlated with food.

An alternative to constraint-based learning might be a Bayesian algorithm which assigns prior probabilities to all possible models. It might be possible to develop a model, which makes use of temporal order cues (i.e., light is the potential cause) and assigns very high prior probabilities to common-cause and causal chain models that honor the Markov condition. This model might also predict Yin *et al.*'s (1994) finding that the negative correlation in the chain structure only becomes salient after many trials. However, this model is computationally very demanding. Bayesian algorithms typically require many learning trials to converge, more than are usually presented in experiments with humans and nonhuman animals (see Tenenbaum & Griffiths, 2003). Moreover, it is post hoc: The strong assumption needs to be made that rats represent

---

[1] Matute and Pineño (1998) and Escobar, Matute, and Miller (2001) found evidence that cues that had been paired separately to a common outcome can compete, but in recent studies we (Leising, Wong, Stahlman, Waldmann, & Blaisdell, in press) have demonstrated that even this associative mechanism cannot account for the effects reported by Blaisdell *et al.* (2006).

simple causal models as priors that are strong enough to override the violation of the Markov condition for those models (e.g., the common-cause model in Figure 1A rather than one with added inhibitory links between the two effects). Thus far, there is no independent evidence for this claim.

The results of the test phase are indeed consistent with the assumption that rats formed and accessed a Bayesian common-cause or causal chain network in Experiments 1 and 2 (Blaisdell *et al.*, 2006). However, the causal Bayes net account suffers from the problem that it is unclear how these models were induced from the learning data. Thus, there is a gap between learning and testing that currently cannot easily be filled by causal Bayes net theory.

Single-effect learning model

According to this theory simultaneously considering complex patterns of events involving multiple effects is too demanding for rats (and possibly also often for humans). Instead we assume that rats focus their attention on single effects, as mentioned earlier. According to this model, in the learning phase rats should either focus on the light-tone, or the light-food relation. (There is also the click-food link which we will ignore in this section.) According to the model temporal cues are used to distinguish potential causes (e.g., light) from potential effects (tone, food). When the light cue is present, rats may learn to expect both tone and food. However, the focus on single effects will lead the rats to update with respect to one effect at a time. Hence, once tone or food is present, they should focus on learning the link that leads to the present effect, and ignore the second link.

This model therefore explains how rats learn about two separate links that happen to share a common element without assuming that they use information about how the indirectly linked elements are related to each other. More specifically, it need not be assumed that the rats make the Markov assumption and represent the three events as part of a Bayesian common-cause model.

How does the single-effect learning model explain the behavior in the test phase? During the observation tests rats hear tones as cues. The tones lead them to diagnostically infer the light. Then they proceed in the predictive direction from light to food. The link-by-link inferences according to this model explain why the rats expect food although in the learning phase tone and food are negatively correlated. Since the links overlap in the light event, rats are capable of making an inference across the network. It is important to note that there is no need to assume that rats represent a coherent common-cause model obeying the Markov assumption. Inferences consistent with the Markov condition are a side effect of chaining separately represented links in the common-cause and the chain models; the Markov condition is neither part of the representation of available information nor of the computational steps involved in the inference processes.

One curious finding is that in the test phase rats infer food from a tone cue although light—the common cause—is absent. This creates an inconsistency between (1) the inference steps going from tone to light and then to food, and (2) the observed information. One possible explanation might be that in the test phase the rats focus on the target cue but do not check whether the state of other events outside their attentional focus is consistent with their predictive steps. This may be particularly plausible to rats in Experiment 1 because the effect of lever presses—the tones— should occur *after* their usual cause, the light, so that the absence of the light might not be salient.[2] Both the learning and the test phases show that rats do not seem to treat absent events outside their attentional focus as informative (see below for further elaborations).

The second test condition involves interventions. According to the single-effect learning model interventions are represented as external causes. In Blaisdell *et al.*'s (2006) experiments this means that the lever presses should be represented as an additional cause of tones, which turns the tones into a common effect of light and lever presses. In the test phase lever presses deterministically cause tones. Although lever presses cause tones only in the absence of light, a plausible assumption is that human and nonhuman animals tend to view their arbitrary interventions as independent of alternative causes. This should lead to a discounting of the cause (light) and hence to a lowering of the expectation of food.

Under the condition that lever presses are viewed as deterministic and independent causes, it is possible to infer the probability of light. We have already shown that in this special case there should be complete explaining away of the tone by the lever press, with light to be expected to occur at its base rate (see (10)). Again the inference is modeled as a chaining of individual links. First, as explained by comparing Equation 10 with Equation 8, the presence of the tone after an intervention, relative to merely observing the tone, should lead to a lowered expectation of light; second, the expectation of light in turn should lead to a lowered expectation of food. This prediction is equivalent to the assumption of graph surgery in a causal Bayes model but it neither requires the assumption that the common cause renders its effects conditionally independent (i.e., Markov condition) nor the deletions of preexisting causal relations. Traditional explaining away will generate the same prediction as graph surgery, and additionally has the advantage of being the more general account (e.g., probabilistic interventions; conditional or confounded interventions) (see also Dawid, 2002).

The single-effect learning model in its present version predicts inferences conforming to a common-cause model with positively correlated effects regardless of whether the effects were positively or negatively correlated in the learning phase, if the relation between the two effects is unnoticed. The positive correlation is generated as a consequence of sequential access to individual causal links, rather than being directly acquired during the learning phase. If increasing the number of trials increases the chance that the relation between the two effects is noticed, however, this model would also be consistent with Yin *et al.*'s (1994) finding that with many trials rats become aware of the negative correlation of the indirectly related events. The assumption that the Markov condition is merely a consequence of link-by-link inference under propitious

---

[2] This assumption is actually less plausible in the chain condition of Experiment 2 in which light follows tone. Interestingly, Blaisdell *et al.* (2006) needed to hide the light behind a salient cover to obtain second-order conditioning. Hiding the light makes its absence ambiguous, it could be absent but it could also be merely invisible.

circumstances rather than a constraint in inference explains why support for the role of that condition can vary from situation to situation. Once the salient individual causal relations are learned, rats may become capable of attending to less salient relations. According to this view, learning is dependent. At the beginning of the learning phase all attention needs to be devoted to picking up single cause-effect contingencies. Once learning is stabilized, this may free attention limitations.

In summary, the single-effect learning model provides the most parsimonious account of the three theories of Blaisdell *et al.*'s (2006) results. The model implies that rats indeed learn and reason about causal relations in a sense that is inconsistent with current associative theories. Moreover, it demonstrates that computations using the Markov condition underlying causal Bayes nets are not necessary to account for the data. Furthermore, the less computationally demanding causal inferences in the single-effect model can explain what Bayes net theory fails to explain. Thus, the model is an example of a minimal rational model.

Empirical case study 2: combining causal relations

We rarely acquire knowledge about complex causal models all at once. Often we only learn about fragments of causal knowledge, which we later combine to more complex causal networks (see also Lagnado *et al.*, 2007; Waldmann, in press). For example, we may learn that we tend to get a stomach ache when we eat sushi or when we take an aspirin. We may never have taken aspirin with sushi but still will have a hunch what the effect on our stomach might be.

Hagmayer and Waldmann (2000; in preparation) have investigated the question of how people combine individually learned causal relations (see also Ahn & Dennis, 2000; Perales *et al.*, 2004). In a typical experiment participants had to learn about the causal relations between the mutation of a fictitious gene and two substances. The two relations were learned on separated trials so that no information about the covariation between the two substances was available. Although the learning input was identical, the instructions about the underlying causal model differed in the contrasted conditions. To manipulate causal models participants were either told that the mutation of the fictitious gene was the common cause of two substances, or they were told that the two substances were different causes of the mutation of the gene. The strength of the causal relations was also manipulated to test whether people are sensitive to the size of the parameters when making predictions (Fig. 20.6 only shows the results for the conditions in which strength was strong). Note that participants, like the subjects in Blaisdell *et al.*'s (2006) rat studies, learned about each causal link individually. However, participants were told that the events involved in the two causal relations were studied at two universities, which invites the inference that the second cause or effect currently not presented is not necessarily absent but simply not measured.

The main goal of the study was to test what predictions people would make about the correlation between the events that were presented in separate trials. A correlation should be expected between the two substances when they were effects of a Bayesian common-cause model that honors the Markov condition with the size of the correlation being dependent on the size of causal strength of the causal links. By contrast,

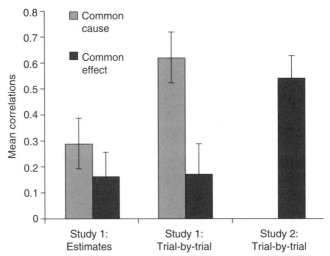

Fig. 20.6. Selected results from Hagmayer and Waldmann (2000; in prep.). In study 1, participants first made multiple trial-by-trial predictions of the two effects (common-cause model) or the two causes (common-effect model) based on the assumed presence or absence of the cause or the effect, respectively (middle). Subsequently they provided conditional frequency judgments concerning the two effects (common-cause model) or the two causes (common-effect model)(i.e., estimates, left). In the second study (right), participants were requested to predict, again across several trials, first the common effect on the basis of information about cause_1, and then to diagnose cause_2. The graph shows the mean correlations (and standard errors) that were derived from participants' conditional frequency estimates or the patterns generated in the trial-by-trial judgments.

two causes of a common effect should be independent regardless of the strength of the causal relations.

To test this knowledge, participants were given two different tasks in Study 1: In the first task, participants were given new cases along with information about whether a mutation had occurred or not. Their task was to predict on each trial whether each of the two substances was present or absent. Thus, in the common-cause condition people predicted the presence or absence of the two effects based on information about the presence or absence of the common cause, in the common-effect condition people diagnosed the presence or absence of each cause based on information about the presence or absence of the common effect. This way, participants made predictions for the two substances they had never observed together. Across multiple predictions participants generated a correlation between the two substances that could be used as an indicator of the expected implied correlations. The second task asked participants directly to estimate the conditional frequency of the second substance in a set of trials given that the first substance was either always present or always absent: These two estimates were combined to calculate the inferred correlations between the substances.

The results of this and other experiments show little sensitivity to the differences between common-cause and common-effect models in the conditional frequency estimations. Although some basic explicit knowledge cannot be ruled out (see Perales *et al.*, 2004), Hagmayer and Waldmann's (2000, in preparation) experiments show that people exhibit little awareness of the relation between the causal strength of the links and the implied spurious correlation. By contrast, the task in which participants made trial-by-trial predictions corresponded remarkably well to the predictions entailed by the contrasted causal models. Whereas a spurious correlation was predicted in the common-cause condition, the predicted correlation stayed close to zero in the common-effect condition (see Fig. 20.6).

In further experiments Hagmayer and Waldmann (in preparation) followed up on the online trial-by-trial prediction measure, which in the first experiment yielded results corresponding to Bayesian common-cause and common-effect models. As it turns out, this effect can only be found in a task in which the two substances were predicted simultaneously. In Study 2 participants again learned the individual links of a common-effect model. Now one of the tasks was to first predict the effect based on one cause, and then make inferences about the other cause. In this study people's inferences exhibited a spurious correlation between the causes of a common effect, similar to what they predicted for the effects of a common cause. We will again use these studies to evaluate the different theoretical accounts.

Associative theory

Associative theories could be used to explain why people generate a correlation between multiple outcomes of a common cue, as in the common-cause condition of the first study of Hagmayer and Waldmann (2000; in preparation). Within a one-layer network multiple outcomes of a common cue should be correlated. This theory may also explain the correlation of multiple causes of a common effect found in the second study as an instance of second-order learning. However, this model is refuted by the finding in Study 1 that, when the cue represented a common effect and the outcomes alternative causes, with identical learning input participants did not generate a correlation between the causes in their trial-by-trial predictions. This result clearly supports causal over associative learning theories. It also demonstrates people's capacity to separate the representation of causes and effects from the representation of temporally ordered cues and outcomes: Although effect information temporally preceded cause information in the common-effect condition of Study 1, participants correctly induced a common-effect model. This finding adds to the substantial number of studies that have shown that humans are capable of disentangling temporal order from causal order (see Lagnado *et al.*, 2007; Waldmann, 1996; Waldmann *et al.*, 2006, for overviews).

Causal Bayes nets

Unlike in Blaisdell *et al.*'s (2006) studies, the learning phases in these experiments do not violate the Markov condition. Learners may learn about each link separately, and make assumptions about the probable state of the third event that currently was not measured. With the aid of the instructions that suggested which events were causes and effects, it is possible to learn a common-cause and common-effect model that is consistent with the Markov condition by updating causal strength estimates within the instructed model. Causal Bayes net theory can also explain why people in Study 1 generate correlations in the common-cause condition, but not in the common-effect condition. These inferences also fall out of the assumption that people represent and access Bayesian causal models that honor the Markov condition. However, causal Bayes net theory fails to explain why people only conformed to the predictions of this theory when they made trial-by-trial online predictions but not when they made conditional frequency judgments. Causal Bayes net theory, being derived from a normative theory of theory discovery, predicts behavior conforming to their normative prescriptions regardless of the way the data are presented or the test questions are asked. Consequently, causal Bayes net theory also fails to explain why people generate a correlation between alternative causes of a common effect when asked about the two links consecutively, as in Study 2. This inference clearly violates the assumptions underlying common-effect models.

Single-effect learning theory

For the learning phase we assume that participants, like the rats in Blaisdell *et al.* (2006), update each link individually. Unlike associative theories, this theory distinguishes between causes and effects, and can therefore capture the difference between diagnostic effect-cause and predictive cause-effect learning. Information is stored in the weight and direction of individual links in a causal network. Due to its focus on individual causal effects, the theory explains why participants in the first study did not have explicit knowledge (i.e., conditional frequency estimates) about the structural implications of common-cause versus common-effect models. Moreover, this theory predicts that learners correctly generated the correlations implied by the different causal models. In the common-effect condition in Study 1, learners were presented with a common-effect model with a single effect and alternative causes. The task was to simultaneously diagnose the alternative causes on the basis of specific effect tokens, which served as cues. According to our analysis, learners should focus on individual effects and be aware of the 'discounting' of a cause by alternative observable and unobservable causes (9). Thus, learners should be reluctant to infer the presence of multiple causes, when one cause sufficiently explains the effect. In contrast, in the common-cause condition learners should generate predictions by focusing on one effect after the other. This strategy would generate correlated effects although participants may not become aware of the correlation. Interestingly, this prediction is supported by the fact that learners did not show any awareness of the effect correlation in the conditional frequency judgments although these judgments followed the online trial-by-trial generation phase in Study 1 (see Fig. 20.6).

The results of Study 2 can also be explained by the single-effect learning model. In this study participants were led to consecutively access the two causal links. Diagnosing a cause from a single effect may be ambiguous for learners. If they simply focus on the state of the effect as unconditional information and compute the likelihood of the second presented cause, the effect should provide positive diagnostic support for the cause. Only if learners consider that the effect token can be produced by cause_1 should the diagnostic inference to effect_2 be lowered. However, this inference requires considering all three events at once. In Study 1, the task highlighted the potential competition of the two causes by having learners diagnose them both at once, whereas in Study 2 the consecutive nature of the task may have led participants to access the second link while disregarding the first link, as they would do in a causal chain or common-cause situation. Thus, in sum, the single-effect learning account provides the broadest and at the same time simplest model for the data.

Note that in Hagmayer and Waldmann's (2000, in preparation) studies cover stories were used that encouraged the assumption that the currently non-observed second effect may actually be present but is just not shown. Thus, participants knew that the fact that they only see one effect at a specific learning trial does not necessarily mean that the second effect is absent. We did not present participants with a learning phase in which a common cause generates negatively correlated effects, as in Blaisdell *et al.*'s (2006) study. Consistent with our speculation on the role of attention in rats' learning, we predict that human learners, due to their greater attention span, should in fact become aware of the negative correlation between the effects of a common cause much earlier if this information is saliently presented.

Nevertheless, we expect that learning about a common cause with negatively correlated effects is actually a more difficult task than learning about standard common-cause models. Not only the single-effect learning model, but also causal Bayes net models cannot easily represent such causal structures. A typical solution, to add an inhibitory link between the effects, seems rarely plausible as a description of the underlying causal mechanisms. One example for such an atypical common-cause model would be a situation in which a beam emitting x-rays could be spatially focused on two different locations. Another example, which is suggested by Cartwright (1989), is the negative dependency that arises when one has a limited amount of money for buying meat and vegetables in a grocery store so that the first (presumably independent) decision limits the second. In both scenarios, a simple representation of the common cause as independently influencing two effects is inappropriate. A deeper re-representation is required that reflects the underlying mechanism or capacity limitations. Instead of inferring the state of the common cause from one effect, and using this state to make further inferences, different hidden properties of the cause need to be induced and used for inferences in these more complex scenarios (see Rehder & Burnett, 2005, for relevant findings). In sum, we assume that more complex structures are indeed learnable but that they require some extra effort. The initial bias of learners may still be the simpler inferences afforded by the proposed single-effect learning model.

Conclusion

Our test cases demonstrated the value of rational models while at the same time adhering to the traditional standards of empirical theory testing. Like other psychological theories, rational models can be tested against each other. We also demonstrated the usefulness of the heuristic to search for minimal rational models. Our two test cases showed that both human and nonhuman animals go beyond the information given by inferring unobservable causal processes on the basis of observable data.

Thus, Hume's view that we are restricted to observable covariations is refuted. Both causal Bayes net theory and our single-effect learning theory provide a rational account of causal learning. Both theories claim that the goal of causal learning is to adapt to the causal texture of the world, but based on different assumptions about cognitive capacities their answers are different.

The search for minimality highlights the deficits of causal Bayes net theory. The problem with this theory is that it is overly powerful. It was originally developed as a normative tool and is therefore developed to yield normative answers in all possible circumstances. Thus, it is ill-prepared to account for failures and strategy-based restrictions of human and nonhuman learning, and it overestimates the complexity of reasoning in biological systems. Causal Bayes net theory makes strong assumptions about the structure of causal network (i.e., Markov condition) that may be method-ologically useful but may not represent what people and animals actually believe (see also Cartwright, 2001, 2004). Thus far, there is little evidence that people assume the Markov condition when reasoning about causal models (see Rehder & Burnett, 2005). Although it is possible to construct a more complex Bayes net with hidden nodes that predicts violations of the Markov condition in inference patterns (e.g., Rehder & Burrett, 2005) it remains to be seen whether the structural constraints underlying these models prove plausible as accounts of reasoning and learning. Our single-effect learning theory showed that it is possible to model reasoning regarding causal models without using the Markov condition as a constraint. Depending on the task requirements, such as the way the knowledge is accessed however, the predictions may or may not conform to the Markov condition.

Although the empirical evidence we presented favored the single-effect learning model, it is too early to decide whether it will prove superior in other learning scenar-ios as well. We have already discussed the problems that arise with unusual causal structures, such as common-cause models with negatively correlated effects. Moreover, we have only discussed studies in which learners were presented with individual causal relations in the learning phase. This may have favored strategies consistent with our model. Future research will have to test the generality of this theory, for example, in learning situations in which multiple effects are presented simultaneously.

We presented two sets of studies to illustrate how rational models can be tested. Although in early stages of research there may be only a single rational model, the possible tradeoffs between different factors entering rational model construction make it likely that in more advanced stages there will be competing theories. Theories can best be evaluated when they are compared with each other. Each of the three the-ories we have selected is supported by empirical evidence, which the researchers endorsing the theories discuss in the articles presenting the theories. Fitting data to individual models is not a very convincing way to test theories (see Roberts & Pashler, 2000). Most of the time there is evidence supporting the theories, and data contra-dicting the theory can often easily be explained away as noise, performance factors, or as results which do not fall under the scope of the theories. A more promising strategy is to test specific competing theories against each other. Unlike what Anderson (1990) has proposed we believe that all the relevant psychological evidence that can be found should be brought to bear on the models. Taking into account all available psychological data reduces rather than increases the possibility of indeterminacy. Currently indeterminacy seems more like a theoretical than a practical threat anyhow. We are not aware of any cases in psychology in which theories make identical predictions in all situations. Should this case occur, then there is indeed no way to decide between the equivalent theories except on the basis of other criteria, such as simplicity. However, we are far from reaching the luxurious state of having to choose between equivalent theories.

References

Ahn, W.-K., & Dennis, M. J. (2000). Induction of causal chains. In L. R. Gleitman & A. K. Joshi (Hrsg.), *Proceedings of the Twenty-Second Annual Conference of the Cognitive Science Society*. Mawah, NJ: Erlbaum.

Ahn, W.-K., Kalish, C. W., Medin, D. L., & Gelman, S. A. (1995). The role of covariation versus mechanism information in causal attribution. *Cognition, 54*, 299–352.

Allan, L. G. (1993). Human contingency judgments: Rule-based or associative? *Psychological Bulletin, 114*, 435–448.

Anderson, J. R. (1990). *The adaptive character of thought*. Hillsdale, NJ: Lawrence Erlbaum Associates.

Blaisdell, A. P., Sawa, K., Leising, K. J., & Waldmann, M. R. (2006). Causal reasoning in rats. *Science, 311*, 1020–1022.

Buehner, M. J., & Cheng, P. W. (2005). Causal learning. In K. J. Holyoak & R. G. Morrison (Eds.), *Cambridge handbook of thinking and reasoning* (pp. 143–168). Cambridge, UK: Cambridge University Press.

Buehner, M. J., Cheng, P. W., & Clifford, D. (2003). From covariation to causation: A test of the assumption of causal power. *Journal of experimental Psychology: Learning, Memory, and Cognition, 29*, 1119–1140.

Cartwright, N. (1989). *Nature's capacities and their measurement*. Oxford: Clarendon Press.

Cartwright, N. (2001). What is wrong with Bayes nets? *The Monist, 84,* 242–264.

Cartwright, N. (2004). Causation: One word, many things. *Philosophy of Science, 71*, 805–819.

Chater, N., & Oaksford, M. (2004). Rationality, rational analysis and human reasoning. In K. Manktelow & M. C. Chung (Eds.), *Psychology of reasoning: Theoretical and historical perspectives* (pp. 43–74). Hove, Sussex: Psychology Press.

Cheng, P. W. (1997). From covariation to causation: A causal power theory. *Psychological Review, 104*, 367–405.

Cheng, P.W. (2000). Causality in the mind: Estimating contextual and conjunctive causal power. In F. Keil & R. Wilson (Eds.), *Cognition and explanation* (pp. 227–253). Cambridge: MIT Press.

Cheng, P. W., & Novick, L. R. (1992). Covariation in natural causal induction. *Psychological Review, 99*, 365–382.

Dawid, A. P. (2002). Influence diagrams for causal modelling and inference. *International Statistical Review, 70*, 161–189.

Dowe, P. (2000). *Physical causation*. Cambridge, UK: Cambridge University Press.

Escobar, M., Matute, H., & Miller, R. R. (2001). Cues trained apart compete for behavioral control in rats: Convergence with the associative interference literature. *Journal of Experimental Psychology: General, 130*, 97–115.

Glymour, C. (2001). *The mind's arrows: Bayes nets and graphical causal models in psychology*. Cambridge, MA: MIT Press.

Glymour, C. (1980). *Theory and evidence*. Princeton: Princeton University Press.

Goodman, N. *Fact, fiction, and forecast* (4th ed.). Cambridge, MA. Harvard University Press.

Gopnik, A., & Schulz, L. E. (Eds.)(2007). *Causal learning: Psychology, philosophy, and computation*. Oxford University Press.

Gopnik, A., & Schulz, L. E. (2004). Mechanisms of theory-formation in young children. *Trends in Cognitive Sciences, 8*, 371–377.

Gopnik, A., Glymour, C., Sobel, D. M., Schulz, L. E., Kushnir, T., & Danks, D. (2004). A theory of causal learning in children: Causal maps and Bayes nets. *Psychological Review, 111*, 3–32.

Griffiths, T. L., & Tenenbaum, J. B. (2005). Structure and strength in causal induction. *Cognitive Psychology, 51*, 285–386.

Hagmayer, Y., & Waldmann, M. R. (2000). Simulating causal models: The way to structural sensitivity. In L. Gleitman & A. Joshi (Eds.), *Proceedings of the Twenty-second Annual Conference of the Cognitive Science Society* (pp. 214–219). Mahwah, NJ: Erlbaum.

Hagmayer, Y., & Waldmann, M. R. (in preparation). *Integrating fragments of causal models: Theory- and simulation-based strategies*. Unpublished manuscript.

Hagmayer, Y., Sloman, S. A., Lagnado, D. A., & Waldmann, M. R (2007). Causal reasoning through intervention. In A. Gopnik & L. E. Schultz (Eds.), *Causal learning: Psychology, philosophy, and computation* (pp. 86–100). Oxford University Press.

Hume, D. (1748/1977). *An enquiry concerning human understanding*. Indianapolis: Hackett Publishing Company.

Kant, I. (1781/1965). *Critique of pure reason*. Macmillan, London.

Lagnado, D. A., Waldmann, M. A., Hagmayer, Y., & Sloman, S. A. (2007). Beyond covariation. Cues to causal structure. In A. Gopnik & L. E. Schultz (Eds.), *Causal learning: Psychology, philosophy, and computation* (pp. 154–172). Oxford University Press.

Leising, K., Wong, J., Stahlmann, W. D., Waldmann, M. R., & Blaisdell, A. P. (in press). The special status of actions in causal reasoning in rats. *Journal of Experimental Psychology: General*.

Lien, Y., & Cheng, P. W. (2000). Distinguishing genuine from spurious causes: A coherence hypothesis. *Cognitive Psychology, 40*, 87–137.

Liljeholm, M., & Cheng, P. W. (2007). When is a cause the 'same'? Coherent generalization across contexts. *Psychological Science, 18*, 1014–1021.

Mackie, J. L. (1974). *The cement of the universe. A study of causation*. Oxford: Clarendon Press.

Marr, D. (1982). *Vision*. San Francisco, CA: W. H. Freeman.

Matute, H. & Pineño, O. (1998). Stimulus competition in the absence of compound conditioning. *Animal Learning & Behavior, 26*, 3–14.

Morris, M. W., & Larrick, R. P. (1995). When one cause casts doubt on another: A normative analysis of discounting in causal attribution. *Psychological Review, 102*, 331–355.

Novick, L. R., & Cheng, P. W. (2004). Assessing interactive causal power. *Psychological Review, 111*, 455–485.

Oaksford, M., & Chater, N. (2007). *Bayesian rationality*. Oxford: Oxford University Press.

Pearl, J. (1988). *Probabilistic reasoning in intelligent systems: Networks of plausible inference*. San Mateo, CA: Morgan Kaufmann Publishers.

Pearl, J. (2000). *Causality: Models, reasoning, and inference*. Cambridge, MA: Cambridge University Press.

Perales, J. C., Catena, A., & Maldonado, A. (2004). Inferring non-observed correlations from causal scenarios: The role of causal knowledge. *Learning and Motivation, 35*, 115–135.

Povinelli, D. J. (2000). *Folk physics for apes*. Oxford, England: Oxford University Press.

Quine, W. V. O. (1960). *Word and object.* Cambridge, Mass.: MIT Press, *55* 9–22.

Rehder, B., & Burnett, R. (2005). Feature inference and the causal structure of categories. *Cognitive Psychology, 50,* 264–314.

Reips, U.-D., & Waldmann, M. R. (2008). When learning order affects sensitivity to base rates: Challenges for theories of causal learning. *Experimental Psychology, 55,* 9–22.

Rescorla, R. A., & Wagner, A. R. (1972). A theory of Pavlovian conditioning: Variations in the effectiveness of reinforcement and non-reinforcement. In A. H. Black, & W. F. Prokasy (Eds.), *Classical conditioning II. Current research and theory* (pp. 64-99) New York: Appleton-Century-Crofts.

Roberts, S., & Pashler, H. (2000). How persuasive is a good fit? A comment on theory testing. *Psychological Review, 107,* 358–367.

Salmon, W. C. (1980). Probabilistic causality. *Pacific Philosophical Quarterly, 61,* 50–74.

Salmon, W. C. (1984). *Scientific explanation and the causal structure of the world.* Princeton, NJ: Princeton University Press.

Shafer, G. (1996). *The art of causal conjecture.* Cambridge, MA: The MIT Press.

Shanks, D. R., & Dickinson, A. (1987). Associative accounts of causality judgment. In G. H. Bower (Ed.), *The psychology of learning and motivation: Advances in research and theory* (Vol. 21, pp. 229–261). New York: Academic Press.

Shultz, T. R. (1982). Rules of causal attribution. *Monographs of the Society for Research in Child Development, 47* (No.1).

Skyrms, B. (2000). *Choice & chance: An introduction to inductive logic* (4th ed.). Belmont, CA: Wadsworth/Thomson Learning.

Sloman, S. A. (2005) *Causal models: How we think about the world and its alternatives.* Oxford: Oxford University Press.

Sneed, J. D. (1971). *The logical structure of mathematical physics.* Dordrecht: Reidel.

Spellman, B. A. (1996). Acting as intuitive scientists: Contingency judgments are made while controlling for alternative potential causes. *Psychological Science, 7,* 337–342.

Spirtes, P., Glymour, C., & Scheines, P. (1993). *Causation, prediction, and search.* New York: Springer-Verlag.

Steyvers, M., Tenenbaum, J. B., Wagenmakers, E-J., & Blum, B. (2003). Inferring causal networks from observations and interventions. *Cognitive Science, 27,* 453–489.

Suppes, P. (1970). *A probabilistic theory of causality.* Amsterdam: North Holland.

Tenenbaum, J. B., & Griffiths, T. L. (2003). Theory-based causal inference. *Advances in Neural Information Processing Systems, 15,* 35–42.

Tomasello, M, & Call, J (1997). *Primate cognition.* Oxford: Oxford University Press.

Tversky, A., & Kahneman, D. (1973). Availability: A heuristic for judging frequency and. probability. *Cognitive Psychology, 5,* 207–232.

Waldmann, M. R. (1996). Knowledge-based causal induction. In D. R. Shanks, K. J. Holyoak & D. L. Medin (Eds.), *The psychology of learning and motivation, Vol. 34: Causal learning* (pp. 47–88). San Diego: Academic Press.

Waldmann, M. R. (2000). Competition among causes but not effects in predictive and diagnostic learning. *Journal of Experimental Psychology: Learning, Memory, and Cognition, 26,* 53–76.

Waldmann, M. R. (2001). Predictive versus diagnostic causal learning: Evidence from an overshadowing paradigm. *Psychological Bulletin & Review, 8,* 600–608.

Waldmann, M. R. (in press). Combining versus analyzing multiple causes: How domain assumptions and task context affect integration rules. *Cognitive Science.*

Waldmann, M. R., & Hagmayer, Y. (2001). Estimating causal strength: The role of structural knowledge and processing effort. *Cognition, 82,* 27–58.

Waldmann, M. R., & Hagmayer, Y. (2005). Seeing vs. doing: Two modes of accessing causal knowledge. *Journal of Experimental Psychology: Learning memory and Cognition, 31,* 216–227.

Waldmann, M. R., & Holyoak, K. J. (1992). Predictive and diagnostic learning within causal models: Asymmetries in cue competition. *Journal of Experimental Psychology: General, 121,* 222–236.

Waldmann, M. R., Hagmayer, Y, & Blaisdell, A. P. (2006). Beyond the information given: Causal models in learning and reasoning. *Current Directions in Psychological Science, 15,* 307–311.

Waldmann, M. R., Holyoak, K. J., & Fratianne, A. (1995). Causal models and the acquisition of category structure. *Journal of Experimental Psychology: General, 124,* 181–206.

Woodward, J. (2003). *Making things happen. A theory of causal explanation.* Oxford: Oxford University Press.

Wu, M., & Cheng, P. W. (1999). Why causation need not follow from statistical association: Boundary conditions for the evaluation of generative and preventive causal powers. *Psychological Science, 10,* 92–97.

Yin, H., Barnet R. C., & Miller R. R. (1994). Second-order conditioning and Pavlovian conditioned inhibition: Operational similarities and differences. *Journal of Experimental Psychology: Animal Behavior Processes, 20,* 419–428.

Chapter 21

The value of rational analysis: an assessment of causal reasoning and learning

Steven Sloman and Philip M. Fernbach

Brown University, Providence, RI, USA

Our goal in this chapter is a rational analysis of human causal reasoning and learning. We take a rational analysis to be an assessment of the fit between data and a certain kind of model (Danks's chapter offers a more multi-faceted view of rational analysis). In the rational analysis tradition of Anderson (1990) and Oaksford and Chater (1998; in press), the term 'rational' has come to have three different meanings that vary in normative force. The first section of this chapter will be devoted to explicating these different meanings and evaluating their usefulness. The second section will apply these interpretations to assess the rationality of causal reasoning and learning.

The value of a rational model

In the rational analysis tradition, 'rational model' and 'computational model' tend to be used synonymously (e.g., Griffiths *et al.*, in press). Danks (Chapter 3, this volume) challenges this equation. According to Marr (1982), who introduced the computational level of description, a computational model describes the goal of a computation, why it is appropriate, and the logic of the strategy by which it can be carried out. What is missing from Marr's analysis is what determines the computation. Is it determined through an analysis of the task or must the analyst first observe what computation is actually being performed before engaging in a computational analysis? This is the critical question in determining whether or not a computation is 'rational.' Here are three different senses of 'rational model':

Normative model

This sense of rational model has its origins in Savage's (1972) analysis of subjective probability, a concept whose influence in psychology is primarily due to Kahneman and Tversky (1982). A rational model in this sense is a representation of the best way to perform a task. Given some goal, a normative model dictates what is necessary to achieve that goal. For instance, in the context of causal reasoning, if a machine is broken, a normative model might dictate the most cost-effective action to fix it.

The construction of normative models is a critical theoretical activity for two reasons. First, it is necessary for evaluating how well people perform. Normative models define optimal performance (relative to some goal) and in that sense set the standard for determining the validity of human judgment. Second, a normative model is necessary for isolating cognitive processes. On the assumption that people try to perform tasks well, people will always attempt to perform according to normative dictates. Therefore, good performance is a result of both cognitive processing and the constraints imposed by a task. But there is no way to distinguish the contribution of each and thus isolate the role of cognitive processing when performance is accurate. Only errors make the distinction possible because only errors do not reflect task constraints and thus must reflect cognitive processes. However, errors are defined in contrast to a normative model, a model of correct performance. In this sense, error provides a window onto processing, and the nature of processing can only be inferred in light of a normative model. Other aspects of processing, like time course or neural locus, don't necessarily require a normative model but often benefit from one.

The brunt of a normative analysis is to show that a particular type of model describes the best way to perform a task. That's the very object of a normative analysis; to show, for instance, that a Bayesian model of a task is normative for that task. In that sense, the modeling framework used to perform this kind of rational analysis is valid by hypothesis. It is not merely assumed, used for expository purposes, or used as a source of theoretical ideas. It is the object of evaluation. This distinguishes this form of rational analysis from the type espoused by Oaksford and Chater (in press), as we discuss below.

Normative analysis in the face of resource constraints

The type of normative analysis inspired by Simon (1955; 1956) evaluates performance not only with respect to the constraints imposed by a task—how best to perform a task—but also by the constraints that come to the task with the performer (cf. Cherniak, 1986; Harman, 1995). The performer has only limited time and energy, limited working memory capacity, limited knowledge, etc. Performance can be evaluated with respect to a model that describes optimal performance given a set of a priori constraints of this kind.

As long as the constraints are a priori and not chosen to make performance look more rational after the fact, this kind of model inherits the virtues of the simpler kind of normative model (i.e., type i). It defines a reasonable notion of rationality: doing the best that one is able to in order to achieve a goal. Moreover, it defines a model that supports inferences about the nature of processing. To the extent that a person deviates from the dictates of this model, it must be due to the nature of his or her mental processes and not to the constraints under which her or she is performing. In fact, it supports stronger inferences than the first type of model because errors with respect to this type of model cannot be attributed to the cognitive constraints that the model already embodies.

The costs of this kind of model are of two kinds. First, it is more complicated than the first kind because it must represent additional constraints. Second, its validity is more tenuous because it rests on more assumptions, namely that the constraints it imposes are real.

A model of what people are computing

The third sense of rational analysis, introduced by Anderson (1990) and further developed by Oaksford and Chater (in press), involves incorporating performance data into a normative modeling framework in order to use that framework to describe what people are actually computing. Generally this involves first choosing a modeling framework (normally Bayesian analysis) and then representing people's task assumptions within that framework. This kind of analysis involves a modeling plus testing cycle: A model is constructed out of a normative framework, its fit to data is assessed, then the model is changed to accommodate deviations, again its fit is assessed, and so on until an empirically adequate model is arrived at.

The model that results from this process does not have a claim to optimality or to normativity in any other sense because it is evaluated empirically, not in terms of the goodness of the actions that can be derived from it (Danks, this volume, argues that both are necessary). Hence this modeling enterprise is essentially descriptive, not rational. Once descriptive assumptions are incorporated, if those assumptions do not themselves have normative justifications, then any model that incorporates them has no claim to rationality. If the assumptions do have normative justification, then they should have been incorporated into the initial formulation of the model, because the fact that they describe behavior adds nothing to the justification.

We consider two counterarguments to our claim. First, one might argue that a computational model derived by embedding descriptive facts into a normative framework inherits rational properties from the normative framework. Oaksford and Chater (in press) argue that such a model will lead to 'successful thought and action in the everyday world, to the extent that it approximates the optimal solution specified by rational analysis.' (p. 32). If the model does approximate the optimal solution, then we tend to agree. We do note though that approximating an optimal solution is not necessarily the best that a constrained performer can do. In principle, a model that makes systematic errors can do better than a model that approximates optimality as long as the degree of error of the first model is small relative to the closeness to optimality of the second model. More crucially, we reject the rational inheritance argument because new facts without normative justification have the potential to lead a normative model completely astray; its recommendations for action can potentially be spectacularly wrong.

To take a prominent example in the analysis of belief, one might argue against the received wisdom that people's probability judgments are non-Bayesian (Tversky & Kahneman, 1983) by softening assumptions about what a Bayesian model should compute. One might argue that in fact judgments are Bayesian, people simply use unexpected prior probabilities in their computations (Tenenbaum & Griffiths, 2001a). We set aside whether people's judgments can actually be explained this way and focus instead on whether such an account would rationalize judgments were it able to fit the data. Clearly such an account, if valid, would reveal systematicity in people's judgments and would in that sense provide a valuable descriptive model. Were such a model descriptively valid, we might even say that people are 'coherent' in the sense that some beliefs could be derived from others (given the model).

However, such beliefs—even if coherent—would not have any rational justification, even partial justification. Prior probability distributions could be constructed that would be guaranteed to render judgments that were close to useless (for instance, a prior distribution that was the complement of true prior probabilities). The fact that people are coherent does not provide a rationalization of their beliefs if they are consistently wrong. It is easy to be coherent once you give up on accuracy.

The descriptive success of such a model does indicate that, at a coarse level, people are sensitive to the variables that the normative analysis says they should be sensitive to. For example, in the probability judgment case, the empirical success of a Bayesian model with arbitrary priors suggests that people are sensitive to priors even if the specific priors that they use have no justification. More generally, the normative framework plus descriptive facts approach does offer a method of demonstrating that people are sensitive to cues that they should be sensitive to. Clearly though the approach is overkill in this regard. An experiment that simply manipulated the relevant cue and showed that people respond accordingly would allow the same inference. There is no need to quantitatively fit model to data to find this out.

We briefly consider a second prominent example of a model of this type, the Oaksford and Chater (1994) interpretation of the Wason four-card selection task in terms of optimal data selection. On one hand, we have great sympathy for the idea that the Wason task asks participants to choose the experiments that would be informative for determining the probability of a hypothesis (a conditional rule). The Wason task is not a deductive task in that it does not ask about the deductive validity of an argument. So far, the Oaksford and Chater insight strikes us as a radically new and persuasive normative model of the task (a rational analysis of the first type). On the other hand, Oaksford and Chater go beyond this rational analysis by invoking the rarity assumption. This assumption turns out to be necessary to explain many of people's selections. The assumption of rarity makes sense in some contexts (the probability of encountering a non-black thing is indeed incomparably higher than the probability of encountering a black raven). But it doesn't hold in general; specifically, it doesn't hold in the abstract Wason four-card selection task (relative to one another, neither vowels, nor consonants, nor odd or even numbers are rare). Importing the principle into the model therefore has only a descriptive motivation, not a normative one that holds in general. The resultant model loses its rational basis once this assumption is made. Assuming rarity can cause the selection of non-optimal data.

A second counterargument to our claim that the normative framework plus descriptive facts approach does not provide a rational analysis is that, sometimes, we can only discover people's goals by examining their behavior. Once we see what they have done, we can find a reason for it; i.e., we can construct a justification after the fact. This position completely obscures the normative/descriptive distinction. Some justification can indeed always be constructed after the fact but that justification has no warrant to be called normative. Maybe people's goals are not what we expected them to be, but we cannot determine their goals and evaluate their procedure for obtaining them from the same data. People are guaranteed to come out smelling of roses that way. We might be able to determine what people's goals are and how they arrive at them via a modeling process like this, but in that case our method serves merely as a heuristic for constructing descriptive theories, not a rational justification for behavior. Of course, there's nothing wrong with constructing descriptive theories. But calling them 'rational' just confuses the issue.

In sum, the normative framework plus descriptive facts approach to rational analysis is not a rational analysis at all in the sense of having any normative justification. The modeling framework used to perform this kind of analysis is not valid by hypothesis. The hypothesis in this case concerns an aggregate of normative and descriptive assumptions and thus cannot be shown valid by an analysis of the situation; performance itself must be considered. Therefore, what is learned is relative to independent empirical demonstration. Descriptive models can and have emerged from this enterprise, but any claim to rationality is circular.

Are causal reasoning and learning rational?

Reasoning

Rational reasoning

Normative models of causal reasoning have attempted to justify causal claims using counterfactual reasoning (Lewis, 1973), probability theory (Suppes, 1970), and a calculus of intervention (Pearl, 2000; Spirtes *et al.*, 1993; Woodward, 2003). Despite the divergence of views about the foundations of causal reasoning, we believe that philosophers and psychologists would mostly agree on what constitutes good causal reasoning for the types of cases that we will focus on.

When reasoning about a well-defined situation, people tend to be highly sensitive to the structure of the causal relations connecting events. An elegant demonstration of this can be found in Cummins *et al.* (1991) and Cummins (1995) who asked people to evaluate the strength of conditional arguments such as

> If I eat candy often, then I have cavities.
> I eat candy often.
> Therefore, I have cavities.

Eating candy is a cause of having cavities but it is neither sufficient (regular tooth brushing will prevent cavities) nor necessary (drinking soda pop can lead to tooth decay even in people who don't eat candy). So the causal relation invokes both disabling conditions and alternative causes. If people evaluate conditional arguments by reasoning causally—i.e., in a way that respects actual causal constraints that are generally known but not mentioned in the argument—then they will not find an argument such as this highly compelling despite the fact that it seems to conform to a valid logical schema, modus ponens. And people don't find it highly compelling. From this and a number of related arguments, Cummins and her colleagues conclude that human reasoning is more sensitive to causal content than to syntactic form. A corollary of this conclusion is that people are effective at reasoning with causal structures that involve a variety of disabling conditions and alternative causes. This explains why people are so good at understanding conditional statements despite the range of causal structures to which they can make reference (Bennett, 2003).

Another normative constraint on causal reasoning is the need to distinguish intervention and observation (Pearl, 2000; Spirtes *et al.*, 1993; Woodward, 2003). Observing an event licenses inference about that event's causes. For instance, observing Team A beat Team B provides evidence that Team A is stronger than Team B (and therefore, say, more likely to beat Team C). Intervening to produce the event blocks such diagnostic inferences. If I drug Team B in such a way that they are guaranteed to lose to Team A, then the loss no longer provides evidence that Team A is stronger than Team B because the loss has an overwhelmingly strong alternative explanation, namely my malevolent behavior. Strong interventions on an event cut the diagnostic link from the event to its normal causes, eliminating some of the inferences that would otherwise be possible. Understanding that intervention introduces temporary independence between an effect and its cause is particularly important in the context of decision making because choice is related to intervention (Meek & Glymour, 1994; Sloman & Hagmayer, 2006).

People are exquisitely sensitive to the logic of intervention. Sloman and Lagnado (2004) gave people simple and more complicated scenarios with well-specified causal structures and then asked them to make inferences about the scenarios with counterfactual conditionals. When the conditionals involved imagined interventions (e.g., if the effect had been prevented), people were much less likely to infer a change in the state of the cause than they did when the conditional involved an imagined observation (e.g., if the effect had been observed to not occur). People distinguished interventions from observations whether the relations were deterministic or probabilistic. The difference did not arise when the scenarios involved logical rather than causal relations. Waldmann and Hagmayer (2005) report supportive data in the context of reasoning and Hagmayer and Sloman (2007) find evidence for sensitivity to intervention in the context of choice. Even rats are sensitive to the logic of intervention (Waldmann & Blaisdell, this volume).

Another normative property of causal reasoning is screening-off (Pearl, 1988). Screening-off relates statistical dependence and independence between variables to structural relations among causes. The simplest case of screening-off arises in a causal chain. If A causes B and B causes C and if the value of B is fixed, then A and C are independent, $P(C|A,B) = P(C|B)$. In other words, the influence of A on C is mediated by B. Therefore, if the value of B is constant, A and C must be unrelated. Blok and Sloman (2006) tested people's sensitivity to this logic by giving people questions like the following:

a. The power strip isn't working, what's the probability that the computer isn't working?

b. The outlet and the power strip aren't working, what's the probability that the computer isn't working?

On the assumption that the relevant causal model for both of these cases is

Power flow in the outlet → Power flow in the power strip → Power flow in the computer

Screening-off would dictate that the answer to the two questions should be the same. Accordingly, Blok and Sloman found that the probability judgments did not differ significantly. Moreover, most people agreed with the causal model. Note however that when the task was changed slightly, when people had to choose the case with the higher probability for the computer functioning, they chose a. more often than b. Perhaps because of the presence of an apparently irrelevant cause, knowing the outlet didn't function made the causal argument that the computer wouldn't function seem weaker. Chaigneau *et al.* (2004) also report violations of screening-off with chain structures but their stimuli came from a different domain. They described common objects by their causal structures and then asked people to name them or to infer their function.

Systematic error in causal reasoning

Several theorists have also argued that screening-off should occur for common cause structures like the following (Pearl, 1988, 2000; Spirtes *et al.*, 1993, but see Cartwright, 2002, for counter-arguments):

Power flow in the lamp ← Power flow in the outlet ← Power flow in the computer

In this case, the claim is that fixing the power flow in the outlet renders power flow in the lamp and the computer independent. Any statistical relation between the lamp and the computer's power flow is due to their common cause, the outlet. So if power flow in the outlet is fixed, there is no remaining source of covariation between the lamp and the computer.

Blok and Sloman (2006) tested screening-off with common cause structures using questions with the general form of a. and b. above. Violations were rampant. Knowing one effect did not occur reduced the probability of the other effect even when people knew that the common cause hadn't occurred. This happened using both rating and choice tasks. Walsh and Sloman (in press) obtained parallel results using different materials and a different judgment task. Walsh and Sloman argue that the violations are due to the nature of the explanations that people generate for whatever facts are presented. Rehder and Burnett (2005) found small violations of screening-off when they asked people to make inductions about the properties of category members.

People are known to make other systematic causal reasoning errors. The simplest illustration is that people tend to believe that a cause provides more evidence for an effect than an effect does for a cause. For example, people estimated that the conditional probability that a girl has blue eyes given that her mother has blue eyes is higher than that a mother has blue eyes, given that her daughter has blue eyes (Tversky & Kahneman, 1980; Weidenfeld *et al.*, 2005). This is rational if and only if the marginal probability of the effect is greater than that of the cause. But this is implausible in the example at hand. Blok and Sloman (2006) made a parallel observation in the context of probability judgments using questions of the type illustrated above.

Another type of error that can occur is a tendency to rely too much on a single causal model thereby neglecting alternatives. This tendency has been observed during performance of a number of tasks like probability judgment (Dougherty *et al.*, 1997) and troubleshooting (Fischhoff *et al.*, 1978). Chinn and Brewer (2001) presented people with an article reporting a theory of a scientific phenomenon. The arguments in favor of the theories were either weak or strong in terms of the amount of evidence and credibility of the sources. Next, participants were shown an article from proponents of the other theory. Articles read first proved to be more convincing regardless of the strength of the argument. The common explanation for all these phenomena is that people make inferences from the causal model that they find most plausible at the moment of judgment rather than moderating their inferences by taking other reasonable causal possibilities into account.

The logic of causal intervention is also violated by some instances of self-deception. Quattrone and Tversky (1994) asked a group of students to hold their arms in very cold water for as long as they could. Half of the group was told that people can tolerate cold water for longer if they have a healthy type of heart, while the other half was told that the healthy heart causes decreased tolerance. The first group lasted longer than the second. This kind of behavior is not consistent with causal logic because changing tolerance for cold would not change the type of heart one has and all participants must have known this. In fact, the result was obtained even for those who denied that their behavior was affected by their knowledge of the hypothesis. Their claim that they were not affected by the hypothesis (p) along with the demonstrable fact that they were affected by it (not p) satisfies the usual definition of self-deception (Sackeim & Gur, 1978; Sahdra & Thagard, 2003; Talbott, 1995). Bodner and Prelec (2002) ascribe cases of self-deception to self-signaling. People violate the logic of causation in order to signal information about themselves to others and also to themselves. Quattrone and Tversky's (1984) participants aimed to signal to themselves that they possessed a good heart.

Other violations can result in tangible loss. Many people co-operate in a one-shot prisoner's dilemma game (e.g., Morris *et al.*, 1998; Shafir & Tversky, 1992). Co-operation is inconsistent with a desire to maximize the utility of causal consequences (Nozick, 1995) because whatever the opponent does, a player does better by not co-operating. In a related vein, many people choose one box when put in a Newcomb's Paradox situation even when choosing two boxes is the dominant option (i.e., it is better regardless of the state of the game). Whatever people are doing in these situations, they are not correctly determining the joint effects of their actions and the environment and choosing so as to maximize their benefits.

There are many plausible explanations why people violate causal logic in these cases. Here we focus on their justification, not their explanation. Talbott (1995) argues that even a coherent, rational agent will sometimes benefit by self-deception. Rational agents have an interest not only in obtaining favorable outcomes, but also in believing certain facts about the world whether they are true or not. For example, we all have an interest in believing that our parents love us. As long as we're not so duped that we fail to foresee some horrible event, like abuse or abandonment, we benefit by believing that we are important enough to deserve love whether or not it is true. Similarly, the belief that there is hope in our future is of value whether true or not. Talbott proves that under a set of reasonable assumptions about belief and its utility and about gathering evidence for belief, a Bayesian utility maximizer should act to maintain desirable beliefs rather than to remain unbiased, as long as the desirable beliefs do not have sufficiently bad consequences.

Mild to moderate self-deception has psychologically positive consequences (see Taylor & Brown, 1986, 1994). People have inflated views about their traits (Brown, 1986) and abilities (Campbell, 1986; Dunning *et al.*, 2004, provide a review). Those positive self-illusions elevate people's mood, their well-being, and their self-esteem

(Taylor & Brown, 1988, 1994). Moreover, self-serving signaling of capabilities strengthens people's belief in personal control (Bandura, 1977). Mild to moderate forms of self-deception can increase mental health. This helps to explain the voluminous evidence for motivated reasoning (e.g., Blanton & Gerrard, 1997; Kunda, 1990) and memory (Erdelyi, 1996). This kind of reasoning neglects causal beliefs for the sake of a desired conclusion having positive emotional consequences.

Implications for the rationality of causal reasoning

In summary, causal reasoning proves to be well described by rational principles in some respects. People also seem to understand the difference between observation and intervention. People are highly sensitive to causal structure, adjusting their inferences appropriately in the face of enabling and disabling conditions and appropriately screening-off variables when the mediating variable is fixed in a chain structure. But people also make systematic errors. They do not always screen-off when they should such as when a common cause is fixed. They are more willing to make causal inferences than diagnostic ones along the same causal path and people tend to rely too much on a single causal model. Finally, people can act in ways that violate their own causal beliefs such as in cases of self-deception, co-operation in two-player games, and certain self-serving biases in reasoning and decision making.

Our conclusion is that people indeed have the tools for effective causal reasoning, but clearly there is room for improvement. We have to remind ourselves to consider alternative possibilities and to consider with deliberation whether evidence really supports our conclusion and to what extent.

Self-deception and other acts of self-signaling are clearly errors of causal reasoning and yet they have a justification stemming from goals broader than the narrow goal of getting a particular answer correct. Indeed, we have seen that they can be justified in a Bayesian framework by considering their relative utility. But whatever process supports these acts also supports acts that have no justification. If one's goal is to maximize income, then co-operating on a single-shot Prisoner's Dilemma makes no sense nor does choosing one box in a Newcomb's Paradox (see Nozick, 1995, for explanation) once backwards-causality is ruled out (see Shafir & Tversky, 1992, for such a case). Not all acts of signaling can be justified even if some have psychological benefits.

Learning

Evidence for rationality

The debate about the rationality of inference in the context of causal learning has focused on how people learn causal relations based on contingency information. The typical experiment presents a participant with frequency data about the covariation of a putative cause (e.g., a drug) and an effect (e.g., curing a disease) either in trial-by-trial or tabular form. These data can be viewed in terms of a two-by-two table, based on the presence or absence of the cause and effect. This literature has shown that people tend to differentially weight the cells when making inferences. They pay most attention to the data in which both the cause and effect are present and the least attention to the data in which both are absent. This has been taken as evidence for the non-rationality of human contingency judgments on the assumption that all cells should have equal weight in determining whether or not there is a causal relation.

Anderson (1990) however has argued that a normative causal inference from contingency data should differentially weight the cells and should do so in precisely the way that people do. He proposes a Bayesian model of contingency learning in which the likelihood of the data under a target causal model is compared to the likelihood of the data under an alternative model. The target causal model posits some probability of the effect in the presence of the cause and some probability of the effect in the absence of the cause. The alternative model posits that the effect occurs with some base probability that is independent of the proposed cause. According to the Bayesian learning model, the amount of evidence that each of the cells provides for one or the other causal model is a function of these three probabilities and reflects how well the data in the cell distinguishes the two models. It turns out that the cause present/effect present cell is the most diagnostic as long as the probability of the effect in the absence of the cause in the target model is close to the base probability in the alternative model. To see why, consider an example: Suppose I want to determine whether eating a particular salad dressing causes me to have an upset stomach. I might assume that if the salad dressing is the culprit, most of the time that I eat it I will feel unwell. Presumably I am unlikely to have an upset stomach whether the salad dressing does make me ill but I don't eat it or if the salad dressing is not the cause of my illness. Under these conditions, eating the salad dressing and getting sick provides strong evidence for the causal model in which the salad dressing is a cause of illness because under the alternative model, such an outcome is unlikely. Conversely, not eating the salad dressing and feeling fine provides little evidence to discriminate the models. Under both models such an outcome is likely. Thus the differential cell weighting can be interpreted as evidence that people's causal inferences from contingency data are informed by a rational inference rule that gives greatest weight to data that are informative given the task. The key assumption is that the task is not one of determining the raw probability of a causal relation, but of comparing two causal models.

The developmental literature also reveals some support for a causal learning mechanism that is guided by normative principles like explaining away one cause by virtue of the presence of a second cause. Between the ages of three and four, children begin to make causal inferences that are consistent with a Bayesian prescription. Sobel *et al.* (2004) performed a series of 'blicket detector' experiments with three and four-year-olds in which children observed certain objects or combinations of objects activating a machine (the 'blicket detector') and were asked to infer whether a particular object would do so (i.e. whether it was a 'blicket'). In one condition, two objects, A and B, activated the machine together, and in a subsequent trial, A failed to activate the machine alone. Participants were asked to infer the identity of B. As A alone did not elicit the effect, participants should have inferred a causal relation between B and the detector. In a second condition, A and B again activated the detector together but this time A subsequently activated the machine alone. Because a causal relation between A and the detector provided an explanation for the effect in the first trial, participants should have discounted B as a cause. Indeed, 4-year-olds were likely to call B a 'blicket' in the first condition, but were unlikely to do so in the second. In another experiment, the degree of discounting was modulated by varying the base-rate of 'blickets', again consistent with rational norms. These findings demonstrate some rationality in causal learning in young children.

Evidence against rationality

Not all aspects of causal learning have a rational justification. Even within the contingency learning paradigm there is some counter-evidence in the way that participants respond to sample size. As the number of observations increases, differences in the probability of an effect in the presence and absence of a putative cause increase support for a causal relation because these differences are proportionally less likely to be due to chance. However, Anderson and Sheu (1997) found that participants were not sensitive to sample size when inferring causal relations from contingency data.

Moreover, when more complex causal learning tasks have been investigated, further problems arise for a rational account. In both the contingency learning and blicket detector paradigms the experimental task is relatively simple. In contingency learning, the structure of causal relations is evident. There is one putative cause and one effect and the task is to determine whether there is a causal relation from the former to the latter. Likewise, experiments in the developmental literature typically define the putative causes (e.g., actions on objects) and effects (e.g., responses by a detector). Causal relations are often deterministic and experiments consist of very few trials. Under these conditions people perform quite well. However, real world causal learning often has many potential variables and no *a priori* structure.

Some recent work has examined more complex causal learning paradigms. Lagnado and Sloman (2004) had participants observe data from a three-variable causal model and asked them to infer the causal structure responsible for generating the data. In one of the cover stories the causal structure represented a chemical process for production of a perfume and the causal variables were the presence of an acid, the presence of an ester and the ultimate creation of the perfume. On a given trial a participant might observe that the acid and ester were present and the perfume was created. On a subsequent trial he or she might observe that the acid was present, the ester was absent and the perfume was not created, and so on. Steyvers *et al.* (2003) used a similar paradigm in which the causal structure was represented by the mind-reading capabilities of aliens. In contrast to contingency learning, experiments of this type necessitate consideration of many more possible causal relations and frequency information cannot be summarized in a two-by-two table. The results of these experiments are striking in the degree of sub-optimality they reveal. Given just observation data, people rarely infer the model actually generating the data. When allowed to make interventions, performance improves, but still surprisingly few people are able to reconstruct the model that produced the data.

One of the reasons for people's difficulty may be that these experiments provide few cues to causal structure beyond covariation and there is little evidence that people are capable of tracking the statistics of the data presented during these tasks (Lagnado *et al.*, in press). The contingency learning literature shows that given access to the necessary data, some participants can make inferences in line with normative models, but in causal structure learning experiments limitations in tracking covariation online may lead participants to rely on other sources of information to make inferences.

One important cue to causal structure is temporal contiguity. Events that happen close in time are often causally related, and the direction of the relation is informed by their temporal order (effects never precede their causes). Lagnado and Sloman (2006) have shown that people easily learn causal structure from temporal cues and that temporal cues often trump covariation as a source of information for causal learning. In one experiment, participants observed virus propagation among computers in a network. On a given trial, each computer was either infected or clean, and after observing many trials the participant was asked to identify the pathway that viruses were being transmitted along. Covariation data was consistent with a particular causal structure but the temporal order was manipulated to favor a different structure. (i.e., participants were told that a virus could be transmitted from one computer to another, but show up in the second computer before the first). The only way to recover the true structure was to ignore the temporal information and use covariation. Even though participants were told that the temporal information was uninformative they still tended to make inferences consistent with it and inconsistent with the covariation data. White (2006) also found that participants tend to rely on temporal information rather than covariation when making causal inferences. Hagmayer and Waldmann (2002) and Buehner and May (2002) have shown that people can adjust their inferences to the expected time scale of events. This provides further evidence that people are highly sensitive to temporal information.

Another important source of information is background knowledge that constrains the set of plausible causal structures. For example, if my washing machine started making horrid noises I might reason that a broken part was responsible, and infer that replacing the part might fix the problem. I would be unlikely to make the same inference if my child were making horrid noises. One of the main findings of research in the scientific reasoning paradigm is that children and adults' theoretical beliefs about causal structure bias the way that new information is interpreted (Kuhn & Dean, 2004). In scientific reasoning experiments a participant is given covariation data for several putative causes and an effect and must infer the actual causes. Participants tend to rely on their beliefs about the mechanisms responsible for the causal relation rather than the covariation information when making inferences. For example, participants asked to identify the causes of the success of a children's show sometimes choose humor even if such an inference is not supported by the data.

A key difference between cues such as temporal order and background knowledge on one hand and covariation on the other is that the former are available on individual trials whereas covariation is based on integrating over multiple trials. Tracking covariation is often difficult and therefore other sources of information are used. Much of causal learning may use simplifying heuristics that are sensitive to trial-to-trial cues (Fernbach, 2006; Lagnado et al., 2007). Under many conditions, these heuristics approximate normative inferences but they can also result in systematic errors.

Fernbach (2006) offers evidence that trial-to-trial cues are used to learn causal structure. Participants observed interventions on a three-variable causal system composed of binary slider bars and had to infer the causal model generating the data. For each causal model, participants observed five interventions, and prior to each one the intervened-on slider bar was identified. Thus the intervention provided a trial-to-trial cue. The participant knew that the intervened-on slider bar moved first and that if any other slider bar moved it was a direct or indirect effect. The majority of participants' responses can be explained by a simple heuristic that asserts a direct causal relation between the intervened-on variable and any other variables that were activated during that intervention. One characteristic result was that when the generative model was a chain (e.g., slider A causes slider B and slider B cause slider C) few participants ever inferred chains. Instead they tended to infer confound models, three-link models that include links from the root variable to both of the other variables and a link from the second variable in the chain to the third (e.g., A causes B, A causes C, and B causes C). Use of a heuristic based on the interventional cue offers a simple account of this result. In the case of an A causes B causes C chain, a participant will rarely get evidence for A to B and B to C links without simultaneous evidence for an A to C link because A and B will rarely both be active in the absence of C. Participants were thus unaware that the link from the second variable to the third was unnecessary to explain the data and systematically inferred extraneous links.

Several counter-normative phenomena of human cognition may be due to the sub-optimality of simplifying heuristics used for causal learning. For instance, both animals (Skinner, 1947) and people (Ono, 1987) have been shown to infer a causal relation between unrelated events based on few or even a single observation of temporally contiguous events. This type of learning may be the source of superstitious behavior. Another example mentioned above is that people tend to be biased in interpreting evidence to accord with pre-existing beliefs about causal mechanism. Such biases may stem from the relative ease of accessing and using background knowledge as opposed to covariation data.

Implications for the rationality of causal learning

In summary, people learn causal relations in a way that is consistent with some rational principles from the age of 4 or younger. In contingency learning, people may differentially weight types of evidence in a way that allows the diagnosis of competing models. Likewise, 4-year-olds are sensitive to rational principles such as explaining away and to base rates. But even in these relatively simple tasks there is evidence of systematic bias, such as sample size neglect. When the task is more complex, people are incapable of tracking covariation and using it to make effective statistical inferences about causal relations. Thus it is unlikely that the dominant mechanism for real world causal learning is anything like a system that tracks the covariation of events and performs a statistical inference over the data. Rational models of the type proposed by Anderson (1990), Tenenbaum and Griffiths (2001b), and Gopnik *et al.* (2004) are probably not accurate as comprehensive accounts of causal learning.

Rather, causal learning is often based on heuristics sensitive to cues other than covariation such as temporal information, background knowledge, and interventions. This is similar in spirit to Anderson and Sheu's (1995) claim that 'subjects look for quantities that are easy to compute and which are causally relevant and make their judgments with respect to these' (p. 39) and Kuhn and Dean's (2004) claim that the strategies people use to solve causal inference problems vary within and across individuals depending on the nature of the task. Though these heuristics are generally effective they do lead to systematic biases.

Conclusion

A number of important models of reasoning and learning have come out of the tradition that associates itself with rational analysis (e.g., Oaksford & Chater, 1994; Steyvers et al., 2003). The models are computational in the sense that they hypothesize a functional relation that people are trying to accomplish. But the models are descriptive, not normative. The models include assumptions chosen to fit data, not only to satisfy task constraints or resource limitations, and in that sense have no claim to rationality. Rational frameworks offer a rich menu of mathematical tools that should be made use of by theorists, but if the model includes assumptions chosen to fit the data, the model no longer has a rational basis.

Some theorists argue that a framework that supports coherent reasoning has a kind of rationality even if it includes false beliefs. But reasoning logically about false statements does not lead to truth. Analogously, reasoning coherently about false beliefs is not a form of rationality. It might be rational to run away from a tiger, but running away from a bunny rabbit is not rational even if you believe the rabbit is a tiger.

We reiterate that our goal is not to damn the descriptive value of the kind of models that have been and will be developed in the rational analysis tradition. In fact, we suspect that models of reasoning and learning will always require some notion of maximizing performance to account for human flexibility and adaptiveness. This is obvious when modeling thinking in the real world. People learn (eventually) to fix their bicycles effectively. But this kind of display of everyday rationality does not entail that normative models serve as a prototype for descriptive models. It merely tells us that descriptive models require a quality control or error-reduction mechanism. Normative models may inspire hypotheses about what those mechanisms might look like, but the normative and descriptive models remain distinct entities and we should identify them that way in order to maintain coherence and clarity in our theorizing.

Our reviews of causal reasoning and learning have revealed some of the reasons that rational models have had limited descriptive power; others are reviewed by Danks (this volume). Although causal reasoning can be highly effective and demonstrates exquisite sensitivity to causal considerations, it shows some definite deficiencies. In order to solve a huge variety of complex and subtle problems, it has developed strategies that lead to systematic bias. Similarly, causal learning can pick up on a variety of trenchant cues to figure out the causal structures that relate events. Yet it fails to pick up on some of the most valuable information, like covariational data, and it often guesses using a smorgasbord of strategies. Treating people as rational may not be irrational but it is a mistake; it fails to identify some of the aspects of cognition that are uniquely human.

Acknowledgements

This work was supported by NSF Award 0518147. We thank York Hagmayer for useful discussion.

References

Anderson, J. R. (1990). *The adaptive character of thought*. Hillsdale, NJ: Lawrence Erlbaum Associates.

Anderson, J. R., & Sheu, C.-F. (1995). Causal inference as perceptual judgments. *Memory & Cognition*, **23**, 510–524.

Bennett, J. (2003). *A philosophical guide to conditionals*. Oxford University Press. Oxford, UK.

Buehner, M. J., & May, J. (2002). Knowledge mediates the timeframe of covariation assessment in human causal induction. *Thinking and Reasoning*, **8**, 269–295.

Cartwright, N. (2002). Against modularity, the causal Markov condition, and any link between the two: Comments on Hausman and Woodward. *The British Journal for the Philosophy of Science*, **53**(3), 411–453.

Chaigneau, S.E., Barsalou, L.W., & Sloman, S. (2004). Assessing the causal structure of function. *Journal of Experimental Psychology: General*, **133**, 601–625.

Cherniak, C. (1986). *Minimal rationality*. Cambridge: MIT Press.

Cummins, D.D. (1995). Naive theories and causal deduction. *Memory and Cognition*, **23**, 646–658.

Cummins, D.D., Lubart, T., Alksnis, O. and Rist, R. (1991). Conditional reasoning and causation. *Memory and Cognition*, **19**, 274–282.

Dougherty, M. R. P., Gettys, C. F., & Thomas, R. P. (1997). The role of mental simulation in judgments of likelihood. *Organizational Behavior and Human Decision Processes*, **70**, 135–148.

Fernbach, P. M. (2006), Heuristic causal learning, *First Year Project, Brown University*.

Fischhoff, B., Slovic, P., & Lichtenstein, S. (1978). Fault trees: Sensitivity of estimated failure probabilities to problem representations. *Journal of Experimental Psychology: Human Perception and Performance*, **4**, 330–344.

Gopnik, A., Glymour, C.,Sobel, D. M.,Schultz, L. E., Kushir, T., & Danks, D. (2004). A Theory of causal learning in children: Causal maps and Bayes nets. *Psychological Review*, **111**, 3–132.

Griffiths, T. L., Kemp, C., & Tenenbaum, J. B. (in press). Bayesian models of cognition. In R. Sun (ed.), *Cambridge Handbook of Computational Cognitive Modeling*. Cambridge University Press.

Hagmayer, Y., & Waldmann, M. R. (2002). How temporal assumptions influence causal judgments. *Memory & Cognition*, **30**, 1128–1137.

Harman, G. (1995). Rationality. In E. E. Smith & D. N. Osherson (Eds.), *Thinking (an invitation to cognitive science* (Vol. 3). Cambridge: MIT Press.

Kuhn, D., & Dean, Jr., D. (2004). Connecting scientific reasoning and causal inference. *Journal of Cognition and Development*, **5**(2), 261–288.

Lagnado, D. A., Waldmann, M. R., Hagmayer Y., & Sloman, S. A. (in press). Beyond covariation: Cues to causal structure. In A. Gopnik & L. Schulz (Eds.), *Causal learning: Psychology, philosophy, and computation* (pp. 154–172). Oxford: Oxford University Press.

Lagnado, D., & Sloman, S.A. (2004). The advantage of timely intervention. *Journal of Experimental Psychology: Learning, Memory, and Cognition*, **30**, 856–876.

Lagnado, D., & Sloman, S. A. (2006). Time as a guide to cause. *Journal of Experimental Psychology: Learning, Memory, and Cognition*, **32**, 451–460.

Lewis, D. (1973). *Counterfactuals.* Cambridge: Harvard University Press.

Marr, D. (1982) *Vision.* San Francisco: W.H. Freeman.

Meek, C., & Glymour, C. (1994). Conditioning and intervening. *The British Journal for the Philosophy of Science* **45**, 1001–1021.

Oaksford, M., & N. Chater (Eds.) (1998). *Rational models of cognition.* Oxford: Oxford University Press.

Oaksford, M., & N. Chater (in press). Bayesian rationality: The probabilistic approach to human reasoning. Oxford: Oxford University Press.

Ono, K. (1987). Superstitious behavior in humans. *Journal of the Experimental Analysis of Behavior*, **47**, 261–271.

Rehder, B., & Burnett, R. (2005). Feature inference and the causal structure of categories. *Cognitive Psychology*, **50**, 264–314.

Savage, L. J. (1972). *The foundations of statistics* (2nd ed.). New York: Dover.

Simon, H. A. (1955). A behavioral model of rational choice. *Quarterly Journal of Economics*, **69**, 99–118.

Simon, H. A. (1956). Rational choice and the structure of the environment. *Psychological Review*, **63**, 129–138.

Shafir, E., & Tversky, A. (1992). Thinking through uncertainty: Non-consequential reasoning and choice. *Cognitive Psychology*, **24**, 449–474.

Skinner, B. F. (1947). 'Superstition' in the pigeon. *Journal of Experimental Psychology*, **38**, 168–172.

Sobel, D. M., Tenenmaum J. B., & Gopnik, A. (2004). Children's causal inferences from indirect evidence: Backwards blocking and Bayesian reasoning in preschoolers. *Cognitive Science*, **28**, 303–333.

Steyvers, M., Tenenbaum, J., Wagenmakers, E.-J., & Blum, B. (2003). Inferring causal networks from observations and interventions. *Cognitive Science*, **27**, 453–489.

Suppes, P. (1970). *A probabilistic theory of causality.* Amsterdam: North Holland Publishing Company.

Tenenbaum J. B., & Griffiths T. L. (2001a). The rational basis of representativeness. 23rd *Annual Conference of the Cognitive Science Society*, 1036–1041.

Tenenbaum, J., & Griffiths, T. L. (2001b). Structure learning in human causal induction. *Advances in Neural Information Processing Systems* (Vol. 13). Cambridge, MA.

Tversky, A., & Kahneman, D. (1980). Causal schemas in judgment under uncertainty. In M. Fishbein (Ed.), *Progress in social psychology* (pp. 49–72). Hillsdale NJ: Erlbaum.

Walsh, C., & Sloman, S. A. (in press). Updating beliefs with causal models: Violations of screening off. In M. A. Gluck, J. R. Anderson, & S. M. Kosslyn (Eds.), *Memory and Mind: A Festschrift for Gordon H. Bower.* New Jersey: Lawrence Erlbaum Associates.

Weidenfeld, A, Oberauer, K, & Hornig, R. (2005). Causal and noncausal conditionals: an integrated model of interpretation and reasoning. *Quarterly Journal of Experimental Psychology A*, **58**(8), 1479–1513.

White, P. A. (2006). How well is causal structure inferred from cooccurrence information? *European Journal of Cognitive Psychology*, **18** (3), 454–480.

Chapter 22

The probabilistic mind: where next?

Nick Chater

University College London, London, UK

Mike Oaksford

Birkbeck College London, London, UK

The chapters in this book provide an overview of the state-of-the-art of the application of probabilistic ideas to high-level cognition. Our aim in this concluding chapter is to reflect on themes and points of difference raised in these chapters; consider relationships between this work and broader developments in the cognitive sciences; and to give some personal views concerning possible future directions for the field.

We group the themes in this section under four interconnected topics: The meaning of rational analysis; whether probability is what the brain is computing; the relation between models of 'low-high' and 'high-level' cognition; and the relation of probability to traditional concepts in cognitive science: logic and structured mental representations. The particular themes that we have drawn out provide, of course, a partial and personal perspective on the state of current research, and likely directions for future work. Readers of this book will, no doubt, draw out of range of different themes and morals; and in pursuing and developing those themes, they will help construct the next phase of research on the probabilistic analysis of the mind.

The meaning of rational analysis?

Explanation in the social and biological sciences is suffused, through-and-through, with teleology: i.e., explanation in terms of purpose (Boden, 1972; Wright, 1976). It is difficult to conceive of the explanation of any physiological process without reference to the role that this process plays in sustaining the survival and reproduction of the organism. It is equally hard to imagine explanation in economics that does not assume that, to some degree, consumers choose their behaviour (e.g., what to consume, how to deploy their labour) according to their interests. Physiological mechanisms, and economic choices, have a *point*—and attempting biological or social research without attempting to spell at what this point is might be, seems, from a practical point of view, infeasible.

We stress practical feasibility here, because it might be argued that, in theory at least, teleological discussion can be eliminated. Indeed, one perspective on the Darwinian revolution in biology is the thought that teleological explanation *can* be eliminated—that is, biological structures have the form they do because they have been selected for, rather than because they have a particular functional role. The forces of selection tend to lead, according to this viewpoint, to biological structures that are highly organized—and hence the components in such structures can often be viewed, heuristically, as having a particular form, because this form serves a particular role especially effectively. Thus, the hollow bones of a bird may be explained because these bones have the function of minimizing weight, in view of the critical importance of weight for flighted creatures; and the precise shape of the wing and structure of the feathers may be partially explained in terms of their aerodynamic properties. But, it might be argued, such functional talk is no more than talk. Perhaps there is no fact of the matter about the 'true' function of different biological structures and processes— merely a historical story concerning which anatomical and functional variants reproduced particularly well.

Yet, from a pragmatic standpoint, understanding biological or social structures seems, at minimum, extremely difficult with allowing functional descriptions, whether, in theory, they may be eliminable or not. Similarly, we suggest, the task of providing a functional account of the brain—presumably in information processing terms—is equally essential for the cognitive and brain sciences. But building such a functional account requires understanding *what* computational problems the brain is attempting to solve; and how it is attempting to do so.

Characterising these problems requires specifying, to some degree at least, the objectives of the cognitive system; the environment in which it operates; and (optionally) the representational and processing restrictions under which it operates. Rational analysis (Anderson, 1990) involves using these constraints to determine how, in principle, the problem *should* be solved—i.e., to best meet the system's objectives, in its particularly environment, and given the constraints under which it operates. Working out how the problem should be solved may proceed informally or using mathematical methods. An informal argument might be: recent information is more accessible to memory than less recent information, because recent information is more likely to be needed. Another might be: unusual occurrences are more accessible in memory, because they are more informative and/or more likely to be needed again. This type of functional argument can be made more concrete, and its predictions more specific, by estimating 'need probabilities' for new information from the structure of the environment; and may be turned into mathematical form (Anderson & Milson, 1989; Anderson & Schooler, 1991; Schooler & Anderson, 1997).

Where does probability enter into functional arguments of this type? We suggest that it enters in an innocuous and uncontroversial way (we shall turn to more controversial issues later). Specifically, given the uncertain character of the sensory, environment (and, perhaps, ineliminably uncertain features of the neural, cognitive and motoric processes over which the analysis is defined), functional arguments will typically be couched in, among other things, probabilistic language. But this is nothing unusual—and in particular makes no claims about what the cognitive system is computing (see Danks, this volume). Thus, probability theory may be a useful tool in determining the optimal memory retention function; but this does not imply that the brain is computing, and implementing, this function, any more than the bird is making aerodynamic calculations in order to optimise the shape of its wing.

Is probability what the brain is computing?

The phrase 'the probabilistic mind' (and relatedly, the probabilitistic brain, e.g., Rao *et al.*, 2002) is typically intended to claim not merely that the probability is a useful tool for studying optimality, in the context of cognitive processes. It is typically presumed to involve a much stronger claim: that the mind should be viewed as, among other things, carrying out, perhaps to some approximation, probabilistic *calculations*. Many degrees of approximation can be considered, of course. At the coarsest level, probabilistic analysis may provide purely directional predictions concerning how some aspect of cognitive performance may be manipulated. Thus, if 'conditioning' is viewed as an inference problem for finding evidence for a link between stimuli, or between stimuli and response, then situations in which that inference is made more difficult (e.g., the timing between stimuli is irregular, the correlation between stimuli is reduced, more distractor stimuli are present, and so on) will weaken the link that an animal or person makes between stimulus and response. At the other extreme, the learning system may be viewed as precisely implementing a particular Bayesian inference regime. According to this view, not only should quantitative manipulations of inferentially relevant environmental variables have quantitatively predictable effects; but there is also the possibility that the neural basis of the underlying calculations may be identified. Indeed, some neuroscientific data does appear to provide corroboration for the viability of this latter approach—e.g., single cell recordings have yielded cells that respond to 'evidence' (roughly, log-likelihood ratio) between one of two perceptual hypotheses, in a motion discrimination task (e.g., Gold & Shadlen, 2001); and imaging, and other, evidence has implicated the dopamine system as providing a representation of predicted reward (e.g., Schultz *et al.*, 1997), the detailed behaviour of which appears to distinguish elegantly between different accounts of reinforcement learning (Niv *et al.*, 2006).

The chapters in this book take a variety of stances which lie between these two extremes—and most researchers take a fairly agnostic view concerning the level of detail at which they presume probabilistic analysis should be applied. We suggest that this issue is likely not to have a blanket answer, but will need to be addressed case by case. Thus, there may be some areas of cognition where probabilistic calculations are highly optimized. Thus, for example, we might speculate that perceptuo-motor control might be achieved by a highly optimized probabilistic processing mechanism. After all, perceptuo-motor coordination is underpinned by very extensive neural machinery; and has a long evolutionary history, during which optimisation of a dedicated computational machinery might have evolved. By contrast, explicit verbal judgement, decision making and reasoning problems, which are typical tasks in the psychological laboratory, are likely to be dealt with in a much more ad hoc way by the cognitive system—it seems unlikely that these problems are solved by reference to a well optimised probabilistic reasoning system (although see Griffiths & Tenenbaum, 2006).

There may, moreover, be cognitive domains in which probability has *no* descriptive role in understanding cognitive processes. Gigerenzer (Brighton & Gigerenzer, this volume; Gigerenzer & Goldstein, 1996; Gigerenzer & Todd, 1999; Todd & Gigerenzer, in press) argues that probabilistic calculations are frequently intractable, and that the cognitive system has, instead, evolved a flexible 'toolbox' of heuristics for judgement and decision making. Gigerenzer views this perspective as developing out of Simon's (1955) concept of 'bounded rationality'—i.e., that the cognitive system uses a set of tractable heuristic methods that work 'well-enough' given the actual constraints of the environment. Thus, algorithms such as 'take-the-best' (Gigerenzer & Goldstein, 2006) which makes judgements based on a single differentiating feature between options, or the priority heuristic (Brandstätter *et al.*, 2006) which makes decisions-under-risk using a single differentiating feature, do not implement probabilistic calculations at any level of description (although see, e.g., Chater *et al.*, 2003; Oppenheimer, 2003; Birnbaum, in press, who argue that simple heuristics may not be sufficient to capture human decision making behaviour).

From the perspective of rational analysis, it is natural to want to recast bounded-rationality explanation in optimality terms—as constituting optimal, or at least good, solutions to the problem that the cognitive system faces, given its specific environment, and given the cognitive resources that it is able to deploy. Thus, rational analysis can, potentially, provide an explanation of *why* a particular heuristic is successful. Thus, even where the brain is not making probabilistic calculations, it is possible that a probabilistic rational analysis may help to explain why its heuristics have a particular form (Chater *et al.*, 2003; Martignon & Hoffrage, 1999). But this attempt to turn any problem of doing 'well-enough' into a problem of optimization given a set of computational constraints, may not always be useful. Indeed, it is typically the case that optimality calculations, subject to constraints, are usually more difficult than optimality calculations without such constraints. Hence, it may be that, in many cases at least, all that can be done is to show that a certain cognitive strategy works; providing a 'rational analysis' for why it has just the properties it does may not be feasible. Thus, recasting bounded rationality in terms of rational analysis may fail. Indeed, if the task of finding an 'optimal' or 'near optimal' cognitive solution is difficult, it is entirely possible that evolution and learning have also failed to find it—i.e., that the heuristics that the cognitive system uses may be the best it can find; but these might be very far from any 'optimal solution.'

If there are aspects of cognition which have this character—and indeed, it may be that there are many—then it may still be possible to describe the heuristics that are used—indeed, Gigerenzer's attempt to characterise the 'adaptive toolbox' aims to take just this strategy. A more pessimistic perspective, though, is that areas in which 'optimal' explanation is not viable may be areas in which cognitive science is likely to be intractable. Without the guiding principles of an understanding of what function a cognitive process or mechanism serves, the task of finding out its structure may be hopelessly intractable. For most problems, the space of optimal solutions is small; the space of heuristic approximations is spectacularly large; and hence searching in that space may ultimately be scientifically unproductive.

There is, though, a middle ground between assuming perfect (and computationally intractable) Bayesian rationality, and the applying a toolbox of heuristics. Graphical models (e.g, Pearl, 1988) and their many variants, including many types of connection network (Neal, 1996), have provided a natural machinery in which to represent probabilistic knowledge in a way that distributes knowledge across simple processing units and their interconnections, in an interpretable and computationally useable way. Methods such as Markov Chain Monte Carlo (see Griffiths and Yuille, this volume) asymptote to give solutions to potentially computationally intractable problems—and where the problems are intractable, this implies, of course, that this asymptote will not be reached. Nonetheless, it is credible that running such methods over short periods (i.e., well before asymptote) may yield usable approximations—and may do so in a natural and reliable way (so that, for example, more time will lead to more accurate responding). Thus, this type of computation may provide general purpose methods for approximate probabilistic inference. Moreover, graphical models of this type can also be trained using a range of techniques from machine learning—so that it is possible to understand, at least in principle, how approximate probabilistic inferential mechanisms can be acquired by the agent.

The idea that the brain operates by applying algorithms of this kind is, to some degree, immanent in much early work on connectionist networks (e.g., the Boltzmann machine of Ackley *et al.*, 1985); and underpins much work in theoretical neuroscience (e.g., Dayan & Abbot, 2001). Indeed, it has recently been argued (e.g., Knill & Pouget, 2004) that even very basic properties of neural spiking may subserve the representation of probability distributions—i.e., apparent neural 'noise' may have a critical role in representing uncertainty in the brain.

Low-level vs high-level cognition

For basic perceptual and motor processes, human performance is widely viewed as close to optimal, in a Bayesian, probabilistic sense. Borrowing the language of our discussion of high-level cognitive processes, the claim is that perceptual and motor performance very closely fits a probabilistic rational analysis, concerning, e.g, how different sources of information should be integrated, or how trajectories should be planned and controlled in order to minimize motor error (Ernst & Banks, 2004; Knill & Richards 1996; Körding & Wolpert, 2004; Stocker & Simoncelli, 2006; van Beers *et al.*, 1999).

How far will precise models that can be developed in these more constrained domains prove to be valuable sources of insight into the modelling of the types of higher level cognitive processes that are described in this book. That is, to what extent might it be possible to build 'upwards' from an understanding of what appear to be more elementary cognitive processes, to understand cognition more broadly?

We believe that this is likely to be a crucial question for the development of probabilistic approaches to the mind and brain. An optimistic viewpoint would be that the mechanisms of neural coding can be isolated in simple cases, and then generalized to more complex cases; a less optimistic viewpoint would be that 'optimal' performance in simple perceptuo-motor tasks may be achieved by the application of a highly flexible and intelligent perceptual processing machinery, rather than a dedicated neural hardware for elementary probabilistic calculations (e.g., Bogacz, 2007). If this latter point is correct, then the neural machinery involved in even relatively simple inferences may be elaborate. An analogy from colour may be helpful. Suppose that we start from the assumption that there are three primary colours, red, green and blue. We might suppose, therefore, that if we could understand how each of these colours is perceived, then it should be possible to understand how complex combinations of them are perceived—i.e., to understand the general case of colour vision.

This conjecture is, however, not correct: the perception of any colour, including the primary colours, is a function of the proportions of activity from each of the three cones cells, each of which is very broadly tuned in the frequency spectrum; and, for that matter, those proportions are themselves scaled, for each patch in the image, by an average across the material surrounding that patch. Indeed, perception of any colour, including the 'basic' primary colours depends also on the broader interpretation of the visual environment. If a patch is perceived as lying behind a semi-transparent film; or as lying in shadow; or reflecting a bright light source, and so on, then there will be significant implications for its perceived colour (e.g., Adelson, 2000). Moreover, these facts concerning the environmental circumstances in which a patch is embedded may, of course, themselves rely on inferences from a wide range of further pieces of sensory information. So, perceiving a 'focal' red is, on this viewpoint, no more straightforward than perceiving any other, putatively 'mixed' colour; and the perception of any colour may involve extremely complex information processing, potentially drawing on information that is, prima facie, beyond the domain of colour entirely.

Thus, the question of whether a particular information processing task is 'elementary,' is theoretically loaded. This is, perhaps, not a startling or unfamiliar conclusion—but it does have considerable relevance for the project of developing rational models of cognition. For example, it is frequently assumed, in the tradition of Hume, Pavlov and Skinner, that learning dependencies between otherwise arbitrarily connected items (e.g., a light and a shock; a lever press and food reward) constitute an elementary learning operation; and thus that the processes underlying such associations will be more elementary than those involved in, say, learning how to manipulate a complex physical object. Thus, we might presume that, if one could understand the processes by which Pavlov's dogs make elementary associations, it might subsequently be able to build upwards to understanding the processes by which a dog learns the causal properties of a stick or bone, with sufficient subtlety to be able to manipulate, carry and fetch it. Yet it is not clear that conditioning does form such a elementary learning process—in humans, it is known that putative 'conditioning' is radically influenced by background knowledge and verbal instructions in a way that suggests that putative associative links should rather be viewed as conjectures, subject to influence by arbitrarily complex and wide-ranging inferences. Moreover, in animals, influences of, for example, similarity and part-whole relations on learning suggests that mere contingency relationships are not all that is involved in determining learning performance (Rescorla, 1988).

More broadly, learning probabilistic or causal relationships, whether in humans or animals, is often studied on the assumption that the key data concern contingency relationships between potential causes and effects. Yet different literatures, e.g., on perceptual causality (e.g., Heider & Simmel, 1944; Michotte, 1963/1946; Scholl & Tremoulet, 2000) and perceptual grouping indicate that, with richer stimuli, people frequently make strong links between events, even on a single trial—based on, e.g., temporal and dynamic connections between them. This raises the question of whether contingency relationships are cognitively 'natural' basic components, or whether a much richer perceptual and inferential system is in play in discovering causal and probabilistic relationships; and this sophisticated system will struggle, as best it can, in stripped down experimental contexts, where there are merely arbitrary contingency relationships between events to work on.

As a final illustration, consider the problem of learning to categorise objects. In general, there is a close relationship between finding categories, and finding relationships between those categories. So, for example, finding grammatical categories may naturally be assumed to be intimately related to the problem of finding grammatical rules defined over those categories; and there is an equally close relationship between the problem of defining scientific concepts (mass, force, acceleration) and scientific laws (force = mass × acceleration). This type of chicken-and-egg relationship between categories and the regularities defined over them suggests that categorization is intrinsically bound up with the broader problem of constructing theories of the world (e.g., Lyon & Chater, 1990; Murphy & Medin, 1985). Yet theories of classification are frequently studied using stimuli over which no regularities are defined— because the stimuli are arbitrary (e.g., consisting of random dot patterns, simple geometric shapes, and so on). Similarly, many models of categorization (e.g., Griffiths *et al.*, this volume; Pothos & Chater, 2002) consider the problem of learning categories as primarily a matter of clumping together similar items—there is no question of learning regularities that might obtain over those items, since in the experimental context, no such regularities are defined. Again, a critical question is whether or not this type of 'simplified' case can be viewed as fundamental. For example, many authors view similarity, and clumping together similar items, as primitive relationships, that serves as the starting point for the construction of higher level regularities and categories (e.g., Goldstone, 1994; Quine, 1960). If this is right, then constructing models of these processes is both an important objective in itself, and a potentially important step towards building models of higher level cognition. Conversely, though, if categorization under 'normal conditions' is intrinsically bound up with building theories of the domain under consideration, then stripped down stimuli may engage rich, general-purpose inferential processes—but where those processes are struggling to deal with impoverished input.

Goodman *et al.* (this volume) provide an insightful investigation into how probabilistic methods may be extended to deal with some aspects of these complexities. One interpretation of this type of work is purely 'instrumentalist'—i.e., it provides a specification of how 'intelligence' operates, in certain domains, which captures and clarifies relevant intuitions, without making strong claims about underlying cognitive machinery. It may therefore be expected to provide useful insights into human intelligence, in the same way as a good chess playing programme provides insights into Grandmaster chess. Indeed, given the profundity of the general problem of probabilistic inferences with arbitrary amounts of world knowledge (the notorious 'frame problem,' e.g., McCarthy & Hayes, 1969; Pylyshyn, 1987), it is not presently clear whether probabilistic methods should be viewed as providing a general framework for understanding the nature of common-sense inference as a whole. Instead, it may be better to think of the conceptual, mathematical and computational methods of modern probability as no more than helpful tools for considering, piecemeal, specific inferential relations—and this may be a productive line of inquiry, even if no 'working model' of common-sense thought in general is possible. The persistent record of failure of general-purpose techniques for formalizing knowledge and inference in artificial intelligence (e.g., McDermott, 1987) should lead to the expectation that modern probabilistic techniques are unlikely to sweep aside all the problems of understanding commonsense intelligence.

There are, we suggest, two ways in which probabilistic models may develop. Starting from very specific cognitive domains (e.g., presumed basic learning processes; presumed 'low-level' processes in perception), it might be possible to build increasingly general, 'high-level' cognitive models. This is the direction currently being pursued in Bayesian approaches to computer vision, motor control, computational linguistics, and theories of learning and neural function (Dayan & Abbot, 2001). Conversely, starting from general observations about patterns of probabilistic inference (e.g., understanding phenomena such as explaining away, the relevance of evidential diversity, the relationship between simplicity and probability, and so on, see, e.g., Bovens & Hartmann, 2003), we may attempt to shed light on lower level psychological phenomena. This is the strategy inspired, for example, by models of causality in artificial intelligence (e.g., Pearl, 1988, 2000; Glymour, 2002); mathematical theories of inductive inference (e.g., Solomonoff, 1978), the Bayesian approach to the philosophy of science (Howson & Urbach, 1993), and Bayesian decision theory (Berger, 1985).

The chapters of this book indicate that both strategies can be highly productive—sometimes operating simultaneously. The coming decade will see how far working from basic cognition 'up' or from general normative principles 'down' prove to be useful complementary research strategies for cognitive science.

Probability, structured representation, and logic

One of the most important developments in the application of probability in artificial intelligence and cognitive science has been the increasing focus on defining probabilistic models over *structured* representations, such as graphs, trees and grammars. In computational linguistics, for example, there has been considerable progress on the problem of parsing using probabilistic constraints. Here, the goal of parsing can be treated in a fairly traditional way—as reconstructing a parse-tree for the linguistic input—such a tree is a prototypical structured representation. But the method for inferring such trees is probabilistic—grammatical rules, and other pieces of linguistic information are assigned probabilities, and the goal of the parse is to infer the most likely parse, often using Bayes' theorem. Moreover, learning grammars, can be viewed in precisely the same light; the grammar itself is a structured representation, which may, or may not, have any explicit probabilistic component (e.g., probabilities of grammar rules); but *learning* the grammar may, nonetheless, be a probabilistic task—and Bayes' theorem or closely related methods such as Minimum Description Length (MDL, Rissanen, 1987) and Minimum Message Length (MML, Wallace & Freeman, 1987) may be used for such learning. A particularly clear-cut instance of this general trend is inductive logic programming (e.g., Muggleton, 1999). Here, the representations to be learned are formulae in a logic-programming language (which can be interpreted as a fragment of traditional first-order predicate logic); and yet the process of *induction* is modelled in a Bayesian/MDL framework.

It should be clear, then, that there is no intrinsic tension between the structured representations which are much discussed and studied in traditional 'symbolic' cognitive science, and probabilistic methods. In practice, though, there has often been a difference of emphasis. Specifically, cognitive science in the symbolic tradition has focussed on representations. For example, the project of generative grammar has focussed on understanding the representation of grammatical knowledge, in a fairly abstract form. Probabilistic approaches, by contrast, often emphasize processing and learning—viewing both the real-time integration, and the acquisition, of knowledge as probabilistic reasoning problems. Given the technical challenges of applying probabilistic methods over complex structured representations, there is a natural tendency for two distinct research projects to emerge. One focuses on the representation, in all its complexity—e.g., attempting to distil the principles governing extremely subtle linguistic phenomena concerning hierarchies of phonological regularities (Smolensky & Legendre, 2006), the syntactic principles such as those governing binding or island constraints (Chomsky, 1981), or the principles involved in building a representation of semantic structure (Dowty *et al.*, 1981; Langacker, 1999). The other, focussed on learning and processing (e.g., Manning & Schütze, 1999), typically strips away representational complexity, using either simple Markov models, or context-free grammars and their many notational variants and extensions (e.g., dependency grammars or categorial grammars). Moreover, researchers concerned with processing and learning will often focus, as a matter of research strategy, on cognitive domains where such approximations may appear to be most adequate, although such claims can be much debated (e.g., Christiansen & Chater, 2001; McClelland & Patterson, 2002; Pinker & Prince, 1988; Pinker & Ullman, 2002; Seidenberg & MacDonald, 1999).

The development and application of increasingly sophisticated probabilistic techniques (Yuille & Griffiths, this volume) offers the opportunity to bring these streams of work together; and much of the work in this volume illustrates the potential of this approach. Tenenbaum and colleagues have been particularly active in applying probabilistic methods over sophisticated representations in a way directly relevant to the cognitive sciences (e.g., Griffiths *et al.*, in press; Sobel *et al.*, 2004; Steyvers *et al.*, 2003; Xu & Tenenbaum, 2007). The literature in machine learning and artificial intelligence provides many further examples, many of which are drawn on in this book.

In this regard, we believe that the probabilistic analysis of the mind should be viewed, not as a rallying call to revolution, but rather as a set of conceptual and technical tools which are complementary to conceptual tools associated more naturally with symbolic cognitive science (Newell & Simon, 1976). Hence, according to this viewpoint, the 'probabilistic mind' of this book is complementary to, rather than in competition with, the 'algebraic mind' of symbolic cognitive science (Marcus, 2001). Nonetheless, we suggest, too, that many cognitive phenomena that are traditionally treated by the symbolic approach look very different, from a probabilistic perspective. Thus, for example, combinatorially explosive problems, such as parsing and perception, may seem less daunting (although often still very daunting), when search can be pruned only to the most probable interpretations; probabilistic methods may provide a crisp, quantitative treatment of causality (see, e.g., Sloman & Fernbach, this volume; Waldmann *et al.*, this volume), which arguably has virtues over symbolic treatments; and many patterns of human reasoning, that are rejected as invalid by a logical analysis, can be understood in terms of justified probabilistic inference (e.g., Evans *et al.*, 2003; Hahn & Oaksford, this volume; Oaksford & Chater, this volume, 1998a, 2007).

At a general level, the challenge of applying probabilistic methods over structured symbolic representations, will only be fully met if there is a deeper understanding of how it is possible to integrate probability and logic. Logic is required to understand the meaning of complex propositions (and, by extension, complex mental states), concerning quantification, tense and aspect, possibility and necessity, and so on (Bach, 1989; Portner, 2005). But how are complex logical representations to be connected to probabilistic inference? Even the evidential relationship between a universal statement (All A are B) and a succession of instances (As which are also B) is very little understood, despite extensive probabilistic analysis (this is a form of the classic problem of induction, e.g., Fodor, 2003; Howson, 2003). While a general theory integrating logic and probabilistic notions appears distant, some promising work is underway. Aside from the work on probability and structured representations that we have described already, we note the tradition of inductive logic programming (e.g, Muggleton, 1999), in which inductive inference involves inferring a logical representation that can reconstruct the input, as briefly as possible. While inductive logic programming is most naturally conceived as searching for short programs (i.e., inferring the shortest program that will reconstruct the data, via a process of logical derivation—this is a specific case of minimum description length, e.g., Rissannen, 1987; Wallace & Freeman, 1987) it can also be interpreted in Bayesian terms. A more explicitly probabilistic approach is Bayesian logic programming, as developed by Russell and colleagues (e.g., Milch *et al.*, in press). We suspect that progress in these, and related, areas is likely to be a critical source of ideas for cognitive science, over the coming years.

Conclusion

Uncertainty, and the ability to deal with uncertainty, is central to perception, thought, decision making, and motor control. It is therefore perhaps inevitable that probabilistic notions provide an important set of tools both for understanding the problems that the cognitive system faces, and perhaps also characterising the computations that it carries out, in order to solve these problems. Yet, until relatively recently, the application of probability to cognitive modelling has been rather a minority activity. The chapters in this book indicate the variety and richness of the probabilistically-inspired work that is currently underway in the cognitive science of high-level cognitive processes—it represents a dramatic broadening and deepening of the work reported in a comparable collection, from a decade ago (Oaksford and Chater, 1998b). We look forward to seeing the emergence of the next generation of probabilistic models of cognition, which will be constructed both by the contributors to this book and its readers.

References

Ackley, D. H., Hinton, G. E., & Sejnowski, T. J. (1985). A learning algorithm for Boltzmann machines. *Cognitive Science*, **9**, 147–169.

Adelson, E. H. (2000). Lightness perception and lightness illusions. In M. Gazzaniga (Ed.), *The new cognitive neurosciences* (2nd ed., pp. 339–351), Cambridge, MA: MIT Press.

Anderson, J. R., & Milson, R. (1989). Human memory: An adaptive perspective. *Psychological Review*, **96**, 703–719.

Anderson, J. R., & Schooler, L. J. (1991). Reflections of the environment in memory. *Psychological Science*, **1**, 396–408.

Bach, E. (1989). *Informal lectures on formal semantics*. State University of New York Press.

Berger, J. O. (1985). *Statistical decision theory and Bayesian analysis* (2nd ed.). New York, NY: Springer.

Birnbaum, M. H. (in press). Evaluation of the priority heuristic as a descriptive model of risky decision making: Comment on Brandstätter, Gigerenzer, and Hertwig (2006). *Psychological Review*

Boden, M. A. (1972). *Purposive explanation in psychology*. Cambridge, MA: Harvard University Press.

Bogacz, R. (2007). Optimal decision-making theories: linking neurobiology with behavior. *Trends in Cognitive Sciences*, **11**, 118–125.

Bovens, L., & Hartmann, S. (2003). *Bayesian epistemology*. Oxford: Oxford University Press.

Brandstätter, E., Gigerenzer, G., & Hertwig, R. (2006). The priority heuristic: Making choices without trade-offs. *Psychological Review*, **113**, 409–431.

Chater, N., Oaksford, M., Nakisa, R., & Redington, M. (2003). Fast, frugal and rational: How rational norms explain behavior. *Organizational Behavior and Human Decision Processes*, **90**, 63–86.

Chomsky, N. (1981). *Lectures on government and binding: The Pisa lectures*. Holland: Foris Publications.

Christiansen, M. H., & Chater, N. (Eds.) (2001). *Connectionist psycholinguistics*. Westport, CT: Ablex.

Danks, D. (this volume). Rational analyses, instrumentalism, and implementations.

Dayan, P., & Abbot, L. F. (2001). *Theoretical neuroscience*. Cambridge, MA: MIT Press.

Dowty, D., Wall, R. E., & Peters, S., Jr (1981). *Introduction to Montague semantics*. Dordrecht: Reidel.

Ernst, M. O., & Banks, M. S. (2004). Humans integrate visual and haptic information in a statistically optimal fashion. *Nature*, **415**, 429–433.

Evans, J. St. B. T., Handley, S., & Over, D. (2003). Conditionals and conditional probability. *Journal of Experimental Psychology: Learning, Memory and Cognition*, **29**, 321–335.

Fodor, J. A. (2003). *Hume variations*. Oxford: Oxford University Press.

Gigerenzer, G., & Goldstein, D. G. (1996). Reasoning the fast and frugal way: Models of bounded rationality. *Psychological Review*, **103**, 650–669.

Gigerenzer, G., Todd, P. M., & the ABC Research Group (1999). *Simple heuristics that make us smart*. New York: Oxford University Press.

Glymour, C. (2002). *The Mind's Arrows: Bayes Nets and Graphical Causal Models*. Cambridge, MA: MIT Press.

Gold, J. I., & Shadlen, M. N. (2001). Neural computations that underlie decisions about sensory stimuli. *Trends in Cognitive Science*, **5**, 10–16.

Goldstone, R. L. (1994). The role of similarity in categorization: Providing a groundwork. *Cognition*, **52**, 125–157.

Goodman, N. D., Tenenbaum, J. B., Griffiths, T. L., & Feldman, J. (this volume). Compositionality in rational analysis: Grammar-based induction for concept learning.

Griffiths, T. L., Sanborn, A. N., Canini, K. R., & Navarro, D. J. (this volume). Categorization as non-parametric Bayesian density estimation.

Griffiths, T. L., Steyvers, M., and Tenenbaum, J. B. (in press). Topics in semantic representation. *Psychological Review*.

Griffiths, T. L., & Tenenbaum, J. B. (2006). Optimal predictions in everyday cognition. *Psychological Science*, **17**, 767–773.

Griffiths, T. L. and Yuille, A. (this volume). Technical introduction: A primer on probabilistic inference.

Hahn, U., & Oaksford, M. (this volume). Inference from absence in language and thought.

Heider, F., & Simmel, M. (1944) An experimental study of apparent behavior. *American Journal of Psychology*, **57**, 243–249

Howson, C. (2003). *Hume's problem. Induction and the justification of belief*. Oxford: Clarendon Press.

Knill, D. C., & Pouget, A. (2004). The Bayesian brain: The role of uncertainty in neural coding and computation. *Trends in Neuroscience*, **27**, 712–719.

Knill, D. C., & Richards, W. (1996). *Perception as Bayesian inference*. Cambridge University Press, New York.

Körding, K. P., & Wolpert, D. M. (2004). Bayesian integration in sensorimotor learning. *Nature*, **427**, 244–247.

Langacker, R. W. (1999). *Grammar and conceptualization*. Berlin/New York: Mouton de Gruyer.

Lyon, K., & Chater, N. (1990). Localist and globalist theories of concepts. In K. Gilhooly, R. Logie, M. Keane, & G. Erdos (Eds.), *Lines of thinking* (Vol 1, pp. 41–56). Chichester: Wiley.

Manning, C., & Schütze H. (1999). *Foundations of statistical natural language processing*. Cambridge, MA: MIT Press.

Marcus, G. F. (2001). *The algebraic mind: Integrating connectionism and cognitive science*. Cambridge, MA: MIT Press.

Martignon, L., & Hoffrage, U. (1999). Why does one-reason decision making work? a case study in ecological rationality. In G. Gigerenzer, P. M. Todd, & the ABC Research Group (Eds.), *Simple heuristics that make us smart* (pp. 119–140). New York, NY: Oxford University Press.

McCarthy, J., & Hayes, P. J. (1969). Some Philosophical problems from the standpoint of artificial intelligence. In D. Michie & B. Meltzer (Eds.), *Machine intelligence* (Vol. 4, pp. 463–502). Edinburgh: Edinburgh University Press.

McClelland, J. L., & Patterson, K. (2002). Rules or connections in past-tense inflections: what does the evidence rule out? *Trends in Cognitive Sciences*, **6**, 465–472.

Michotte, A. (1963) *The perception of causality*. New York, NY: Basic Books (original work published in French, 1946).

Milch, B., Marthi, B., Russell, S., Sontag, D., Ong, D. L., & Kolobov, A. (in press) BLOG: Probabilistic models with unknown objects. In L. Getoor & B. Taskar (Eds.), *Statistical relational learning*. Cambridge, MA: MIT Press.

Muggleton, S. H. (1999). Scientific knowledge discovery using Inductive Logic Programming. *Communications of the ACM*, **42**, 42–46.

Murphy, G. L., & Medin, D. L. (1985). The role of theories in conceptual coherence. *Psychological Review*, **92**, 289–316.

Neal, R. M. (1996) *Bayesian learning for neural networks*. Lecture Notes in Statistics No. 118, New York: Springer-Verlag.

Newell, A., & Simon, H. A. (1976). Computer science as empirical inquiry: Symbols and search. *Communications of the ACM*, **19**, 113–126.

Niv, Y., Daw, N. D., & Dayan, P. (2006). Choice values. *Nature Neuroscience*, **9**, 987–988.

Oaksford, M., & Chater, N. (1998a). *Rationality in an uncertain world*. Psychology Press: Hove, England.

Oaksford, M., & Chater, N. (Eds.) (1998b). *Rational models of cognition*. Oxford: Oxford University Press.

Oaksford, M., & Chater, N. (2007). *Bayesian rationality*. Oxford: Oxford University Press.

Oppenheimer, D. M. (2003). Not so Fast! (and not so Frugal!): Rethinking the Recognition Heuristic. *Cognition*, **90**, B1–B9.

Pearl, J. (1988). *Probabilistic reasoning in intelligent systems*. San Mateo, CA: Morgan Kaufmann.

Pearl, J. (2000). *Causality: Models, reasoning and inference*. Cambridge: Cambridge University Press.

Pinker, S., & Prince, A. (1988) On language and connectionism: Analysis of a parallel distributed processing model of language acquisition. *Cognition*, **28**, 73–193.

Pinker, S., & Ullman, M. (2002) The past and future of the past tense. *Trends in Cognitive Science*, **6**, 456–463.

Portner, P. (2005). *Formal semantics: An informal presentation*. Oxford: Blackwell Publishers

Pothos, E., & Chater, N. (2002). A simplicity principle in unsupervised human categorization. *Cognitive Science*, **26**, 303–343.

Pylyshyn, Z. W. (Ed.) (1987), *The Robot's dilemma: The frame problem in artificial intelligence*. Norwood, NJ: Ablex.

Quine, W. V. O. (1960). *Word and object*. Cambridge, MA: MIT Press.

Rao, R., Olshausen, B. A., & Lewicki, M. S. (Eds.) (2002). *Probabilistic models of the brain: Perception and neural function*. Cambridge, MA: MIT Press.

Rescorla, R. (1988). Pavlovian conditioning: Its not what you think it is. *American Psychologist*, **43**, 151–160.

Rissanen, J. (1987). Stochastic complexity. *Journal of the Royal Statistical Society*, **49**, 223–239.

Scholl, B. J., & Tremoulet, P. (2000). Perceptual causality and animacy. *Trends in Cognitive Sciences*, **4**, 299–309.

Schooler, L. J., & Anderson, J. R. (1997). The role of process in the rational analysis of memory. *Cognitive Psychology*, **32**, 219–250.

Schultz, W., Dayan, P., & Montague, P. R. (1997). A neural substrate of prediction and reward. *Science*, **275**, 1593-1599.

Seidenberg, M. S., & MacDonald, M. C. (1999). A probabilistic constraints approach to language acquisition and processing. *Cognitive Science*, **23**, 569–588.

Simon, H. A. (1955). A behavioral model of rational choice. *Quarterly Journal of Economics*, **69**, 99–118.

Sloman, S., & Fernbach, P. M. (this volume). The value of rational analysis: An assessment of causal reasoning and learning.

Smolensky, P., & Legendre, G. (2006). *The harmonic mind* (2 Volumes). Cambridge, MA: MIT Press.

Sobel, D., Tenenbaum, J. B., & Gopnik, A. (2004), Children's causal inferences from indirect evidence: Backwards blocking and Bayesian reasoning in preschoolers. *Cognitive Science*, **28**, 303–333.

Solomonoff, R. J. (1978). Complexity-Based Induction Systems: Comparisons and Convergence Theorems. *IEEE Transactions on Information Theory*, **24**, 422–432.

Steyvers, M., & Tenenbaum, J. B., Wagenmakers, E. J., & Blum, B. (2003). Inferring causal networks from observations and interventions. *Cognitive Science*, **27**, 453–489.

Stocker, A. A., & Simoncelli, E. P. (2006). Noise characteristics and prior expectations in human visual speed perception. *Nature Neuroscience*, **9**, 578–585.

Todd, P., Gigerenzer, G., & the ABC Research Group (in press). *Ecological rationality: Intelligence in the world*. New York: Oxford University Press.

van Beers, R. J., Sittig, A. C., & Gon, J. J. (1999). Integration of proprioceptive and visual position information: an experimentally supported model. *Journal of Neurophysiology*, **81**, 1355–1364.

Waldmann, M. R., Cheng, P. W., Hagmayer, Y., & Blaisdell, A. P. (this volume). Causal learning in rats and humans: A minimal rational model.

Wallace, C., & P. Freeman (1987). Estimation and inference by compact coding. *Journal of the Royal Statistical Society*, **49**, 240–265.

Wright, L. (1976). *Teleological explanations: An etiological analysis of goals and functions*. Berkeley, CA: University of California Press

Xu, F. & Tenenbaum, J. B. (in press). Word learning as Bayesian inference. *Psychological Review*.

Index